Indian Administration

Indian Administration

Hoshiar Singh
Pankaj Singh

Associate Acquisitions Editor: Qudsiya Ahmed
Associate Development Editor: Daniel Luiz
Assistant Production Editor: Barun Kumar Sarkar
Compositor: White Lotus Infotech Pvt. Ltd, Puducherry

ISBN: 978-81-317-6119-9

First Impression, 2011
Fifth Impression, 2021
Sixth Impression

Published by Pearson India Education Services Pvt. Ltd, CIN: U72200TN2005PTC057128.

Head Office: 15th Floor, Tower-B, World Trade Tower, Plot No. 1, Block-C, Sector 16, Noida 201 301, U.P., India.
Registered Office: 7th Floor, SDB2, ODC 7, 8 & 9, Survey No. 01 ELCOT IT/ ITES SEZ, Sholinganallur, Chennai 600119, Tamil Nadu, India.
Phone: 044-66540100,
Website: in.pearson.com, Email: companysecretary.india@pearson.com

Printed in India at Shree Maitrey Printech Pvt. Ltd., Noida

Contents

List of Tables

Preface

In ancient India, Kautilya's *Arthashastra* provides a detailed account of the administration during the reign of the Mauryan emperor Chandragupta I. At that time, according to Hindu tradition, the role of the King and his officers was service to and safeguarding of the people. The administrative principles of Kautilya are still relevant even after centuries for scholars and students in India.

During the medieval period, India was ruled by the Mughal emperors through their officers and feudatories. Rajputs and Muslims strove to plant an administration, the traces of which are still found in the district administration of the patvari, kotwal and kotwali.

The British, who came in pursuit of commercial interests during the Mughal king Shah Jahan's reign, slowly enslaved the country and built a new apparatus to unify their colony. The present well-developed public administration in India is the legacy of the British Raj.

In 1947, India became independent and framed its own constitution, opting for the British Parliamentary form of government. In a democratic system, public administration functions in the context of politics. With the adoption of a socialist welfare state as our goal, administration has become an important instrument of our economy and political development. Decentralization has created an environment where politics cannot be separated from administration. As a result, knowledge of the pattern and content of the country's administration has become essential.

The Indian Civil Service, which stabilized the British rule and efficiently managed the affairs of a big colony for about two centuries, today faces the crisis of legitimacy and viability. A major reason why the administration in this country is not responsive to the needs of the common man is the character and the composition of the bureaucracy. With the passage of time the process of administration has involved dichotomies and dilemmas—administration vs politics, ends vs means, values vs facts, government vs non-government sectors, centralization vs decentralization, merit bureaucracy vs representative democracy, and generalist vs specialist. A far more serious aspect is that corruption has crept into the bureaucracy with a vengeance and corruption has left little hope for an honest and efficient administration. The slow pace and poor efficiency at which the administration functions at most levels are responsible for corruption and related problems. This draws the attention to the problem of administrative reforms, a subject which has been comprehensively dealt with. While dealing with the subject, full use has been made of various committee reports that dealt with the problem in addition to Administrative Reforms Commission reports and several reports on administrative reforms by committees appointed by the state government. There is need to explore new models of administrative efficiency, effectiveness, responsiveness and accountability along with proper machinery of implementation to eradicate the dysfunctional aspects of administration.

Public administration in India is a part of graduate and postgraduate-level teaching in almost all universities in public administration and political sciences courses. There are institutes of public administration in various states which also need course material for this subject. Public administration in India is also required for competitive examinations for entry in the civil service and other public service careers. Therefore, a comprehensive text is required to fill this gap.

We are glad to produce this book, which provides a critical and analytical discussion on all the important aspects of public administration in India. The volume has some unique features: First, it covers all the major landmarks in the evolution of the Indian administration from Kautilya to the present times. Second, an attempt has been made to discuss panchayati raj and urban local government in detail after constitutionalization of local government in India. District planning and the District Planning Committee have also been discussed in detail. Third, it contains all the material that the student will need to sit for the competitive examinations.

We hope that this work will fulfil the needs of scholars, administrators, students and the general reader who is interested in the subject. It is based on books, journals, notes, files and government reports in the field. We are thankful to all those writers, researchers and administrators from whose writings we have benefitted. We also thank our publisher, Pearson Education (India), for publishing this book.

Hoshiar Singh
Pankaj Singh

The Evolution of Public Administration in India

Every civilized society needs a good administrative system, and administration is as old as our ancient civilization. Public administration is essential for executing government orders and functions. The history of ancient Indian governmental system begins from the Vedic times and continues till the establishment of Mughal rule. In the evolutionary process of Indian administration numerous administrative organizations rose and fell, but its speciality of village-focused administration still continues. The present administration, assert many scholars, is a developed form of organization and function of the old administrative system that we find mentioned in Vedic, Buddhist and Jain literature such as the *Dharmshastras*, *Puranas*, *Ramayana*, *Mahabharata*, *Manu Smriti*, *Sukra Niti* and *Arthashastra*.

In Vedic times the king was assisted in his functions by numerous officials. Both our epics, the *Ramayana* and the *Mahabharata* are replete with instances of administrative officers and their relevant departments. We find similar references in *Manu Smriti* and *Sukra Niti*. Kautilya's *Arthashastra* provides details of the offices of the state. During the reigns of Chandragupta and Ashoka, the administrative system was fully developed and Mauryan administrative institutions were further developed during the Gupta period. However, the present administrative system in India was developed by the British government. Historically, we may study Indian administration under the following heads:

1. Ancient Indian administration
2. Medieval period administration
3. British period administration

Ancient Indian Administration

The earliest reference to ancient Indian administration can be traced to the Indus Valley Civilization. The recent excavations at Harappa and Mohenjo Daro show that the cities had well planned roads with a good drainage system and similar types of houses. It also followed a system of weights and measurements and a common script. This shows the existence of a large kingdom in the area.

The Vedic Period

In the *Rig Veda* period, administrative units were known as *kull, gram, vesh* and nation. The Vedic king ruled with the help of popular bodies—the *samiti* and *sabha.* The word *samiti* means meeting together, i.e., an assembly. It was thought necessary that the king should attend the *samiti.* The *sabha* also acted as the national judicature. Thus, we learn from the Vedas that the national life and activities in the earliest times were expressed through popular assemblies and institutions.[1] The main duty of the king was to defend the people. Under his administration, the head of the army was called *senani* and the head of the village was *gramini.* The king was assisted by many ministers, chief of whom was known as the *purohit.*

The *Ramayana* and *Mahabharata* are two ancient epics of our country. In the *Ramayana* period the form of government was monarchical. The head of the administration was the king who looked after the welfare of the people. There were ministers and councillors to advise him. Monarchy was the form of government during the *Mahabharata* period. The king was responsible for the welfare of the people and there was a council of ministers and officers.

The Post-Vedic Period

During the period of the Buddha, numerous republics and *mahajanpadas* existed. Four big kingdoms of Magadha, Avanti, Vats and Kaushal also existed along with the republics. The actual power in the republics was in the hands of *sabhas*, which included both the elite as well as common people. The king was the head of the republic and was elected for a fixed period. He was accountable for his action to the council or *sabha.*

The *Arthashastra* of Kautilya is an important source from which a lot can be known about the values, norms and beliefs pertaining to public administration in ancient India. According to Kautilya, 'The king is the centre of the state.' All officers of the state were appointed and removed directly or indirectly by the king; they acted according to his commands and were accountable for the exercise of their assigned functions. The administration of justice was carried out in the name of the king and sometimes he himself presided over the royal court of justice. It was he who gave effect to the judgement of law courts and exercised his prerogative of granting mercy in suitable cases. Although legislation was not among the powers entrusted to the king, yet royal edicts, at least insofar as they related to administrative business, had the force of law. He was the supreme commander of the military forces of the country, and not infrequently, he personally led the army on the battlefield.[2] Kautilya places high importance to espionage and provides the method of selecting spies, their role in administration and the mode of their working in some detail. Kautilya was the prime minister of Chandragupta Maurya. For the first time, it was Chandragupta who succeeded in bringing the entire country from Afghanistan to the Bay of Bengal and from the Himalayas to beyond the Vindhya mountains under one direct authority.

In the *Arthashastra*, Kautilya mentions 18 high functionaries such as the *yuvraj* or the prince who was stated to succeed the king, the minister who was the supreme advisor, the *purohit,* who advised the king in governmental and religious matters and the *senapati* who was the head of the armed forces. These four persons were members of the council of ministers whom the king consulted on important matters. The other 14 were heads of the departments whom the king consulted on matters coming within their jurisdiction.

The empire was divided into provinces. The central executive controlled the home province, while the distant provinces were governed by governors appointed by the king. For administrative purpose the provinces were further subdivided into regions or districts for general administration, revenue collection and law and order. The regions were further sub-divided into villages and their heads were known as *gopas* who were equivalent to the present-day *patwaris* or *lekhpals*. The distant provinces were kept in touch with the central government through the inspection staff who submitted periodic reports by means of aregular correspondence system. The Mauryan kings had a well-organized municipal government. The cities were divided into wards for the sake of better administration.

Administrative Structures

The king was the most important element in administration. He exercised his executive authority through the central executive that consisted of *mantris, amatyas* and *sachivas*. The advice of the *mantris* was constantly sought and they were regarded as the most trusted advisors of the king and trustees of the public's interests. According to Kautilya's *Arthashastra,* the *amatyas* constituted a regular cadre of service from which higher officials such as chief priests, ministers and treasurers were recruited. The duties assigned to the *amatyas* included agricultural operations, fortification, territory welfare, collection of the royal dues and punishment of criminals. *Sachivas*, who may have been officials of a particular cadre, helped the king in the discharge of his duties in various spheres more as executors of orders rather than as councillors. The *mantris*, *amatyas* and *sachivas* seems to have enjoyed positions in a descending order, respectively. Others who formed part of the king's entourage included *parishadas* or assembly men who were the helpers of the king, the *arthakarins* who were executive officers in charge of state business, and were generally five in number in the cabinet, and the *dharmikas* who were the judges or the interpreters of law.[3] There were 18 other officers of the state known as *tirthas* who have been mentioned in the *Mahabharata* and the *Ramayana:* the *mantri,* or the chief councillor who used to offer secret advice to the king; *purohit*, the chief priest who advised on matters relating to succession, *yuvraj,* or the crown prince who preceded the *senapati channupati* or the commander-in-chief of the army who was ranked higher up in the arrangement and placement inside the army; *dyarapala* or the chamberlain; *antaravesika* or overseer of the harem who controlled the forces working inside the palace area; *dravya samchayakrit* or the chief steward concerned with financial administration; *kritya krityeshu chartham viniyoia-kali* or the chief executive officer who determined the transactions of public business; *pradeshta* or the chief judge for the administration of justice; *nagaradhyaksha* or the city prefect; *karyanirmanakrit* or the chief engineer; *dharmadhyaksha* or the president of the assembly; *dandapala* or the chief criminal judge; *durgapala* or the warden of the forts; *rashtrantpalaka* or the warden of the marches; and *atavipalaka* or the in-charge of forests.[4]

The state was divided into provinces, which were further subdivided into divisions and districts. In the Maurya and Gupta empires the provincial governors, who are described as *tatapadha-pargrahita*, were directly appointed by the king and usually were members of the royal family. The district governors were appointed by the provincial governor. They had combined judicial and administrative functions to perform. The district administration representing the state ensured the safety of the royal interests as well as of those specified in the grants for religious and charitable purposes.

The village (*gram*) was the smallest unit of the administration. The leader of the village, known as the headman, was the keystone of the village constitution. These villages were considered to be the hub of the administration. The village administration was run by the village council (*panchayat*). The *panchayat* was endowed with executive as well as judicial powers. The village officers had to maintain law and order and protect the life and property of the villagers.

The city formed a separate administrative unit headed by the governor (*nagarika purapala*). It had its own city council (*adhishthana dhiarana*). The city council was divided into committees. These were functional bodies and the council in its cooperative capacity managed general local affairs such as finance, sanitation, water supply, etc. Village autonomy and city autonomy were the seminal principles of ancient administration in India. Democracy did not have an exotic growth in India, and before the advent of British or Mughal rule, the stress was on self-governing institutions and cooperative life.[5] During the Gupta period, the local administrative units had an efficient set-up with official and non-official units working together in harmony and unison.[6]

MEDIEVAL ADMINISTRATION

This can be divided into three categories of administration according to the periods of different regimes such as: (*a*) Rajput period administration; (*b*) Sultanate period administration; and (*c*) Mughal period administration.

Rajput Period Administration

The main form of government during this period was monarchical and for the assistance of the king there was a council of ministers. The state was divided into smaller units, the biggest of which was *prant.* In brief,

> Rajput government was an amalgam of militarism, feudalism and divine-right monarchy. The chief aim of the rulers was acquisition of military glory rather than promotion of public weal. The rulers, therefore, evoked respect but not affection or gratitude. Civil and military appointments generally went to the *Brahmins* and the *Kshatriyas.* This made the rest of the people apathetic towards political affairs. By abstaining from interference in local administration, they helped to develop initiative, efficiency and self reliance among the local population.[7]

The Rajput rulers, instead of counteracting the danger from the north-west by presenting a united front, continued fighting among themselves and in some cases, perhaps, even welcomed an attack by the Muslims, provided it was directed against some of their rivals. Thus, within a short span of a few years, the greater part of northern India passed into the hands of the Muslims.[8]

Sultanate Period Administration

The Sultanate period (1206–1526) starts with the defeat of the Rajput king, Prithviraj Chauhan, at the hands of Muhammad of Ghor from Afghanistan or Shaahabuddin Ghori in 1192, and his provincial governor, Qutubuddin Aibek, who occupied the Delhi throne in 1206 as the Sultan. The Sultanate period lasted till the defeat of its last Afghan king, Ibrahim Lodhi, in 1526 in the first battle of Panipat at the hands of the Mughal dynasty founder, king Babar. The important rulers of the Sultanate period were Iltutmish, Balban, Alauddin Khilji and Muhammad Bin Tughlak. They included the Slave (1206–1290); Khilji (1290–1320); Tughlak (1320–1414); Saiyyad (1414–1451); and Lodhi (1451–1526) dynasties.

The Sultanate administration was basically military in nature; its rulers obeyed the principles and tenets of Islam and applied those in letter and spirit in their administration. They tried to adapt themselves as best as possible to Islamic injunctions, theology and law, and none of them divorced religion from administration and politics. The Sultanate, in a broader sense, could be described as a junior member of the Islamic commonwealth of nations.[9] The power and position of the sultan was supreme and he was vested with political, legal and military powers. He was also responsible for judicial administration. He took advice from his advisors but was not bound by it. Below the sultan was the *wazir* who was the head of the entire administration and had many other officers such as the *naib-wazir,* the accountant-general (*munshrif-i-mumalik*), the auditor-general (*mustauf-mumalik*), *nazir* (superintendent) *waqufi* (inspector), and several others to help him. Next to the *wazir* was the head of the military department and there were two civil *dewans*. One looked after religious matters, holy institutions and scholars, etc., and the other looked after correspondence. For administrative purposes the state was divided into *prants*. The head of the *prant* established various departments for administration. The *prants* were divided into *shikos*, whose head was known as *shikdar*. The *shikos* were divided into *sarkars*, *sarkars* into *parganas* and *parganas* into villages. *Pargana* was under the *shiqqadar* who had to look after executive affairs and land revenue. At the *pargana* level there were other officials such as *amil*. or the collector of revenue who dealt in central as well as provincial revenue, *diwan*, *fotahdar* or the local treasurer, *daroga* or the superintendent of accounts, *amin* or the surveyor, *kanungo, munshif, thanadar, patwari*, etc. The *diwan* in *sarkar* was the executive head of the *pargana*. City administration was run by a centralized bureaucracy, but the villages had some sort of self-rule. The defence of the country was manned by a standing army maintained by the centre, while the contribution of the *walis* and *vassals* in men and resources was equally available. Espionage and the postal system, confined to the royal mail alone, had developed considerably and wayside stations were set up. In short, this later phase of administration of the Delhi Sultanate was an experiment in administering the vast territory comprising heterogeneous elements that were communal and feudal and always posed danger to the central authority.[10]

Mughal Period Administration

The Mughal rule in the country was established by Babar, the founder of the Mughal dynasty, after he had won the historical battle of Panipat in 1526. But in December 1530, only after four years Babar died and his eldest son, Humayun, the heir apparent became the king. Humayun had to face a lot of difficulty in retaining his kingdom initially. He could recover his kingdom after continuous battle, but died soon in 1556 and was succeeded by his young son, Akbar, who ascended the Mughal throne after his victory in the second battle of Panipat in 1556. Akbar was the real founder of the Mughal dynasty. The first four Mughal emperors were good rulers and this dynasty flourished under Akbar, Jahangir, Shah Jahan and Aurangzeb. Aurangzeb died in 1707 and the Mughal empire disintegrated thereafter. The later Mughal emperors were not very powerful and finally the British East India Company emerged victorious. The last Mughal king, Bahadur Shah Zafar, was dethroned and exiled by the British in 1858.

The Mughal administrative system was a military rule by nature and was centralized by despotism. To the Muslim portion of the population, the sovereign was the head of both the religion and the state, and, therefore, he undertook socialist functions for them. But he followed a policy of minimum individualist interference towards his non-Muslim subjects, i.e., he contended himself with discharging only police duties and the collection of revenue. The socialistic activity, in its broadest sense of a modern state, was left to the community, society or caste brotherhood to follow, and the student of Indian administration had to tolerate this in silence. Thus, the aim of the government was extremely limited and materialistic, almost to the point of being sordid.[11]

The Mughal emperor was the head of the administration and had no cabinet but there were secretaries working as ministers. He used to keep his ministers and nobles at a distance and there was no sharing of authority. Moreover, he was not bound to consult his ministers on all matters. The authority of the king was beyond the checks of the ministers and *wazirs*. Thus, the Mughal rule was monarchical and the whole administration moved around him. He took pains to impart justice and provided judicial administrative machinery to administer justice.

There were different departments at the centre and the most important were as follows:

1. The exchequer and revenue were under the *wazir* or the high *diwan* (*diwan-i-ala.*)
2. The imperial household was under the *khan-i-saman* or the high steward.
3. The military pay and accounts office was under the *mir-i-batisi.*
4. Canon law: civil and criminal was under the *chief quazi.*
5. Religious endowments and charities were under the *chief sadar.*
6. Censorship of public morals was under the *muhtasib.*
7. The artillery was under the *mir-i-atish* or *darogha-i-topkhana.*
8. Information and intelligence were under the *daroga-i-dak-chauki.*

Besides these, there were other officials, namely, the *mirbahri* or the revenue secretary, *mirbarr* or the superintendent of forests, *qurbegi* or the lord standard bearer, *hakt-begi* or the superintendent of the royal stud, *mushrif* or the chief admiral and officer of harbours, *nazir-i-buyutad* or the superintendent of imperial workshops, *mustafi* or the auditor-general, *awarjah nawis* or the superintendent of daily expenditure at the court, *khwan salar* or the superintendent of royal kitchen and *mir arz* or the officer who presents petitions before the king.

The title of *wazir* meant the prime minister in the Mughal empire and his office received all revenue papers and returns and despatches from the provinces and the field armies. He also acted as the representative of the king on ceremonial occasions. He wrote letters 'by orders' in his own person though under the emperor's directions. Payment, except to the field army and the workmen of the state factories, was made through his department only. Some of the famous *wazir*s were also masters of Persian prose and they acted as secretaries in drafting royal letters to foreign rulers on behalf of their masters.[12]

At the provincial level, the upper level administration was an exact replica of the central administration. Provincial and district administrations were based on the *suba* and *sarkar* as unit, their heads being respectively called *subedar*s and *fauzdar*s who were assisted by *diwan*s and the *amalguzar*s, respectively. During the declining days of Mughal rule, the *sarkar* appeared to have been replaced by a larger administrative unit called the *chakla.* Below the *sarkar* was the *pargana,* which was headed by the *shiqqadar.* Decentralization was necessary for a big empire like that of the Mughals who had not disturbed the local set-up under *muqaddams* and *chaudharies.* Administration of the border areas was under *fauzdar*s, while that of port areas was under the *mutsaddi.* The head of the police in the metropolis was known as the *kotwal.* Judicial administration was handled with the help of the *qazi*s and *sardar*s. Revenue administration and military organization were the main pillars holding up the structure of the state. Assessment and collection of revenue were controlled from the centre and officers had to account the details for all receipts.[13]

The important and Herculean task of imperial administration was carried out largely by the officers in charge of the administrative units at the lower level. In doing so, they had indeed behind them the sanction of the imperial government and the provincial administration. But the safety of the empire and its peaceful and efficient administration, to a greater extent, depended on the ability and vigilance of the lower administrative machinery. The chief officers of the localities like those placed at the heads of province belonged to a *corps d'elite,* the *mansabdar*s. The *mansab* was a commission, which was held by the officers of the emperor. It was a hierarchical system that comprised the *mansabdar*s ranging from those commanding twenty horsemen to those commanding five thousand horsemen. Between these two there were innumerable grades and officers rose from grade to grade, both according to merit and favour. Another feature of the system was the fusion between civil and military functions.[14]

According to J. N. Sarkar, the renowned historian on the Mughal period, 'The Mughal system at one time spread over practically all the civilised and organised parts of India. Now it is dead in our times. Traces of it still survive. But the new has been built upon the old; our present has its roots in our past.'[15]

British Period Administration

The present administrative system in India was evolved during the East India Company's rule in the country. This period is divided into two parts for study purposes. First, East India Company's rule up to 1857 and second, British government rule from 1858 up to 1947. The East India Company came to India solely for business purposes, but later took over the government of the country. Finally, the company rule ended in 1858 and the government was taken over by the British Crown. These are some of the very important evolutionary steps in the administrative history of India. After the death of Aurangzeb in 1707, the Mughal empire began to disintegrate and the central administration became paralysed. The minor rulers, who earlier had accepted the suzerainty of Mughal emperors, started fighting among themselves. The East India Company took advantage of this situation and established its hold over several parts of the country. The battle of Plassey in 1757 paved the way for the real authority to come into the hands of the company.

In the year 1765, the East India Company secured the *diwani* rights of Bengal, Bihar and Orissa, but it did not change the administration of these provinces and mainly continued the administrative system of Mughals. However, the British wanted to reduce the exploitation of the people of these provinces by the *zamindars* and other intermediaries. Therefore, they established rapport with the people through their own officers and this led to the establishment in stages of the modern system of district administration. In 1772 they appointed supervisors in each big district, who were later nominated as collectors by the Viceroy Warren Hastings in 1772. The board of directors of the Company in 1786 directed the governor-general-in-council to place all the districts under collectors. These collectors were responsible for collection of land revenue, dispensation of civil justice and magisterial work, etc. This office is most significant even today. In the year 1829, divisional commissioners were appointed in Bengal to supervize the administration of a group of districts and this marked the beginning of the divisional commissioner system of administration, which is in vogue in states at present. Four years after receiving the *diwani,* whose conferment did not *ipso facto* make the company a sovereign authority in Bengal, Bihar and Orissa but led the way to the exercise of such authority. The company did not make any move in respect of organizing the government, which was now in a state of virtual collapse. But from 1769 onwards, the company started making experiments in this regard. At first, these proved to be not only ineffectual but almost disastrous. By 1786, however, the company appeared to have groped its way into the right direction. But even then further experiments had to be made to make the structure efficient and well-organized and the administration stable and strong.[16] Though the Company had control over some of the Indian provinces, the administration was unstable and feeble. The result was the enactment of various Acts by the British government.

For the purpose of study of the evolution of the Indian administrative system during this period, we shall divide it into the following two periods:

1. Administrative system before 1858
2. Administrative system after 1858 till 1947

The year 1773 was a landmark in the growth of Indian administration. Before 1773 there was no central authority in the country. The 1773 Act restricted the powers of the presidencies from making war or treaties without the sanction of the governor-general-in-council. This started the British Parliament's control over the affairs of the East India Company. The Pitt's India Act of 1784 placed Indian affairs under the direct control of the British government by establishing a board of control representing the British cabinet over the court of directors. 'The court of directors of the East India Company were required to pay due obedience (and be) governed and . . . bound by such orders as they shall from time to time, receive from the said board.' The appointment of governor-general was made by the directors with the approval of the Crown. The position of the governor-general became very difficult with the introduction of the system of dual control. This system, with some modifications, remained in operation till 1858. As a result the company's administration became not only cumbersome but also dilatory.

The company's rule ended with the enactment of the Government of India Act, 1858 and passed on to the Crown. The board of control and the court of directors were both abolished and their powers were given to the newly created office of the Secretary of State for India. His office was known as the India office, which enabled him to discharge his functions smoothly.

Portfolio System

The work of the government increased and its pressure was felt by the successive governors-general. Inordinate delay became unavoidable. This situation improved when an innovation known as portfolio system was introduced in 1859 by Lord Canning. According to this innovation a member of the council would be appointed in charge of one or more departments of the government by the governor-general and he would issue orders on behalf of the governor-general-in-council. The Act of 1861, Section 8, gave statutory recognition to this innovation. Whenever any other department was concerned, it was also consulted: the department of finance would advise on matters relating to finance and expenditure, similarly, the home department would advise for matters relating to the services of the general administration or internal politics. If the concerned department did not agree, the matter was referred to the governor-general. Reference to the governor-general was necessary for every important matter of any department as well as where it was proposed to overrule any local (provincial) government orders.

The portfolio system increased the efficiency and speed of the government work in the first place. Second, the members of the council were recognized as heads of their departments and had greater degree of initiative and responsibility in the working of the departments.

The Act of 1861 enlarged the executive council of the governor-general by adding a fifth member as the law member who was given power to conveniently transact the business. This Act tried to render the executive government very strong to be handicapped by any expansion of the legislature and restored the legislative powers of the local governments without affecting central control.[17] The Act of 1870 also empowered the governor-general to suspend such measures of resolutions of the councils, which may have the interest of British possessions in India. The Indian Council Act of 1892 enlarged the function and members of the legislative councils but did not implement it *in toto*. According to the Act, two-fifths of the additional members were to be non-officials. The Act also introduced the principle of election in an indirect manner. Although the Act did not provide for direct election, the mode of indirect election produced a result, which turned the balance of power against the landed aristocracy and placed legal practitioners in a dominant position.[18]

The Act of 1909, popularly known as the Morley–Minto Reforms, carried the above policy further. The Act increased the size of the legislative councils at all levels. They still remained deliberative bodies only. The indirect election system continued but for the first time separate representation was given to the Muslims.

Introduction of Local Self-Government

In 1688, a corporation was established in Madras. In 1726, corporations were created in Calcutta and Bombay. In the Presidency of Madras and Bombay, the ancient village system of rural self-government agency was retained and in the 19th century *panchayats* received encouragement from district authorities.

The Government of India resolution 1864 admitted the desirability of local people's capability to run the local affairs. A further step in the direction of local self-government was taken by Lord Mayo in 1870, popularly known as Mayo Resolution of 1870. As a result new municipal Acts were passed in various provinces between 1871 and 1874 to relieve the burden on imperial finances by levying local rates and cesses and also extended the elective principle. The next important step was taken during the viceroyalty of Ripon, who has been called the father of local self-government in India.

In 1882, the famous Ripon Resolution for local self-government was issued, which continued to influence the development of local government in India till 1947. The resolution declared, 'It is only primarily with a view to improvement in administration that this measure is being put forward and supported, it is desirable as an instrument of political and popular education.' The result was the enactment of a series of municipal Acts and enactments for rural areas.

The Decentralisation Commission in its report of 1909 emphasized the importance of village *panchayats* and recommended the adoption of special measures for their revival and growth. It also recommended reduction of government control over local bodies and augmenting the sources of income of these bodies; but neither the Government of India nor the provincial governments faithfully carried out Ripon's resolution.

The Montague–Chelmsford Report on Constitutional Reforms (1918) examined the system of local self-government prevalent in the country and stated that local bodies would be made autonomous and outside control would be minimal.

Administrative Reforms of 1919

The Government of India Act, 1919 introduced the bicameral system and demarcated the central and provincial subjects. The central list consisted of important subjects such as defence, foreign affairs, tariff and customs, railways, post and telegraphs, income tax, currency and coinage, all-India services. The provincial list included local self-government, public health, public works, education, water supply, irrigation, agriculture, land revenue, police, forests, justice, excise and fisheries, etc. The provincial subjects were further divided into 'resolved' and 'transferred' subjects. The 'reserved' subject was important, and was thus placed under the charge of councillors, who along with the governor were made responsible to the secretary of state and the central legislature. The administration of 'transferred' subjects was entrusted to the ministers responsible to the provincial legislative council. The distribution of executive power between the governor-general-in-council and the governor, acting on the advice of his ministers responsible to the provincial legislative council, was called dyarchy. This reform reduced the control of the secretary of state for India, over the central and provincial administration so far as the 'transferred' subjects were concerned; but as regard 'reserved' subjects there had been no change. This Act was a step to provide Indians with the opportunity to take charge of departments of provincial administration, not as nominated but as the elected leaders of legislatures. This new scheme was based on three principles. First, the central and provincial spheres were demarcated and distinguished from each other. Second, the provinces were considered to be the most suitable for experiment of self-government. Third, an attempt was made to give an effective voice to the people in the conduct of the central government.

Administrative Reforms of 1935

The Government of India Act, 1935 had two basic concepts: provincial autonomy and an all-India federation. In the structure of the home government, some changes were made. The Indian Council was dissolved and its place was taken by a set of advisors to the secretary of state for India, whose number was fixed between three and six. The secretary of state had the right to consult these advisors individually or collectively. The Act provided for the introduction of dyarchy at the centre. The system of dyarchy in the provinces was abolished. The federal executive was made partly responsible to the federal legislature. The executive councillors were put in charge of defence, external affairs, ecclesiastical affairs and tribal affairs, and were accountable to the governor-general and not the federal legislature. The governor-general could interfere in the work of the remaining subjects in the federal legislature on the ground that it affected the discharge of his special responsibilities. But this was never done as in doing so this scheme would not operate.

Under the federal set-up the subjects were divided into three lists, viz., the federal, provincial and concurrent lists. In the federal list there were 59 subjects of administration related to the centre. The provincial list had 54 subjects related to the provincial government. The concurrent list consisted of 36 subjects that were common to the central and provincial governments. These provisions of the Act could not be implemented at the central level, but were introduced at the provincial level in 1937.

In spite of the failure of the federal provisions of the Act, the Government of India continued its working under the provisions of the Act of 1919 with certain modifications till the Indian Independence Act of 1947 came into force. In Britain, the Labour Party came to power after the 1945 elections and initiated a new approach. The imprisoned Indian leaders were set free; elections were held to the central and provincial legislatures; and popular ministries were restored in the provinces. The famous Cabinet Mission Plan was published on 16 May 1946. An interim government was formed in 1946, with Jawaharlal Nehru as its vice-president. The Muslim League initially declined to join the interim government but agreed later on. Further, elections were held to the Constituent Assembly, which met in Delhi in December 1946. The Muslim League boycotted it. In March Lord Mountbatten was appointed governor-general and in June he formulated his scheme for the partition of country. On 18 July, the British Parliament passed the Indian Independence Act, 1947, and at midnight on 14/15 August 1947, India became a free nation. The new Constitution was adopted on 26th January 1950.

Legacies of the British Administration

India became independent at midnight on 14/15 August 1947 and British rule came to an end. A new Constitution was framed and adopted on 26 January 1950 and India became a republic. The pertinent question is what the new republic was and what was handed over by the British along with power. The answer of these questions can be found easily during the period the British governed the country by establishing various institutions. Though the Indians were very happy to get rid of the colonial rule but soon realized that the governmental system and administrative apparatus developed by the British were capable of meeting the needs of the country. Therefore, the same system was maintained for the administrative purposes of the country even after Independence, albeit with some changes as per the requirements around that time. The main features of the British governmental and administrative system were a parliamentary form of government, federal structure, governors in the states, secretariat system, central and state administration, civil services, district and regional administration, the procedures of work, rule of law, and local government, etc. These continued to be the main areas of the present Indian administrative system.

The federal structure of the Indian Constitution has its roots in the Government of India Act of 1935. The constitutional history of India shows that the Act of 1919 mentioned 'transferred subjects, which were entrusted to the ministers of the provinces accountable to the elected provincial legislatures and reserved subjects meant for officials under the governors. Thus, a dyarchy system was the main characteristic of the Act of 1919 that planted the seeds of division of subjects between the provinces and the centre. The Government of India Act, 1935, added three contributions to the political development in the country: first it established a fully responsible government in the provinces, second, it contained a list of division of powers between the provinces and the centre, and third, it established a federal court, which was a promise for the federation to come into existence. The Act of 1935 provided a model for the Indian Constitution of 1950 from all its 451 clauses. Thus, the type of federation we have adopted in our Constitution is a British legacy.

The parliamentary system of governance adopted by our Constitution is based on the British parliamentary system. The main characteristics of the system such as a nominal head of state, plural real executive in the form of council of ministers collectively responsible to the Parliament, independent judiciary, etc., influence and shape the structure and machinery of the administrative system to a large extent.

The third and most important legacy of the British was the creation of districts and the primacy given to the district administration. The reasons for this were historical. The East India Company came to India for trade and not to govern the country, but around that time, due to the diminishing powers of the Mughal emperors the political situation was fluid. In 1755 the company secured the *diwani* rights of Bengal, Bihar and Orissa to establish direct rapport with the masses. It created the office of collector to man the district administration through its own people. As a result later on all provinces were divided into districts that were grouped to form divisions. Each district was also divided into sub-divisions and these were further divided into *tehsils* or *talukas* to look after a number of villages. This order of administration had three significant features.[19] The first was that each unit should be headed by an official with overall responsibility: divisional commissioner; collector or district magistrate or deputy commissioner; sub-divisional officer; *tehsildar* or *mamlatdar,* in that order. To help the district officer there would be specialist officers such as district superintendent of police and executive engineer. In general district administration these officers would work under the leadership of district collector or deputy commissioner. The second feature was that there should be no rigid separation in terms of personnel between administrative and judicial functions, rather, there should be some measure of combination of the functions in the same person. The district officer was, therefore, collector, magistrate and administrator. The third was the introduction of boards of nominated and later elected non-officials at the district and lower levels from 1870 to particularly after Lord Ripon's resolution of 1882. These were called local self-government institutions. The record of these local self-government bodies was not glorious because they were not given substantial power to undermine the authority of the district collector. Meanwhile, the national movement leaders persuaded people not to be members of these powerless bodies; even then provinces passed innumerable legislations regarding these bodies. Thus, local self-government is also a legacy of the British rule. The administration was fully hierarchical starting from the commissioner, to the collector, to *tehsildar* and the village headman.

After the establishment of the system of district administration the need to supervize the district administration and central directives was felt, and this led to the establishment of various administrative institutions at the provincial and central levels. The office of the divisional commissioner was created for the supervision of district administration. The board of revenue system of administration was established in Madras Presidency. After 1857, when the British Crown took over the governance of the country from the East India Company, the provincial secretariat and the secretariat system was established as it exists at present in the states with various departments for the working of the provincial government. To implement the government policies various offices of the heads of departments and directorates further established their field organizations for implementation of government programmes. Departments such as agriculture, public works, irrigation and forests were established in all the provinces and these formed the model for the establishment of more departments in independent India. Further, the British developed and established a system of central administration in Delhi to control the provincial governments. Thus, the foundation was laid for the central administrative system in India with the central secretariat in Delhi at the top of this administrative pyramid.

The fourth major legacy of the British was the creation of the civil service system to man the administrative apparatus created by them. They created Indian Civil Service (ICS) as a superlative service to man the higher posts at the centre and the states. The Indian Police Service (IPS) was also established to man the higher posts in police. Recruitment to these services was based on competitive examination in which merit alone was the sole criterion. Other services were also established by the British to aid the ICS and IPS at the central and state levels for running the administration of the country. These services, with some modifications, continue even today as central services and state civil services. The personnel to the ICS were at first recruited only in England but after the Lee Commission Report (1924) the recruitment was 'Indianized'. The ICS civil servants were generalist and non-technical in character and were highly educated and carefully selected through a difficult competitive examination. They were expected to be adaptable, honest, devoted to duty, fully cooperative and broader in outlook rather than regional or provincial in loyalty. They started their career in the districts with a period of attachment under the guidance of an experienced officer and took charge of the district so that later they might also serve at the provincial secretariat for a period. They were also posted on deputation at the Central Secretariat but remained on the strength of their province of original allocation. After the deputation period they would return to their original province. The senior posts at the central level were reserved for the ICS but they were always filled on deputation from the provinces. Thus, the name 'all-India Civil Service' indicated a manner of recruitment and the coverage of all levels in the government by the civil servants. This did not imply transferability on an all-India basis. Rather, it was due to the officers' familiarity with the local people, language, needs and geography of the region. The ICS administrator always expressed his views frankly, talked freely, listened with attention, and was not hurt by external warnings or advice. The officer was expected to be immune from the pressures of organized commercial and industrial interests, never to delegate his responsibility to his subordinates and give preference to his work over all other interests. He was also expected to have enormous power of perception, understanding and knowledge of the attitude, reactions, and the requirements of the people.[20] With the transfer of power in 1947, the British rulers withdrew, but in the process left a well-trained, competent and experienced civil service that was able to take on the multifarious tasks of governance. They proved to be a tremendous asset to India in the aftermath of independence.[21] Even Jawaharlal Nehru and Sardar Patel, who were critical of the service during the national independence movement, realized the importance and relevance of the service when they saw the working of the civil servants. Nehru observed in 1949 that 'every thinking person knows that running a modern government requires the machinery of highly organized, efficient and loyal services.'

Sardar Patel, while defending the All-India Services in the Constituent Assembly, said that they were worth their weight in gold and had remarked that, 'I have worked with them during this difficult period . . . Remove them and I see nothing but a picture of chaos all over the country.' Thus, the utility of this service forced our national leaders to change their views about ICS. After Independence the service was renamed as Indian Administrative Services (IAS). This service was created mainly to maintain law and order and the collection of revenue, whereas people's welfare was not on their minds. Thus, the civil service structure was predominately generalist, and created by the British, had remained intact till date. But we need to give greater importance to technocrats. Although that alone is not enough because specialists do not influence IAS, on the contrary, it is the IAS who influences the specialist. When a technocrat occupies the chair of an IAS officer, his behaviour pattern falls in line with the bureaucrats. Therefore, these concepts need to be changed. Thus civil service in its present form is a British legacy with minor changes.

The fifth legacy was that they introduced the rule of law. The government should be run by law and nobody is above law. In other words, nobody in the land was immune from punishment if he did wrong, however highly placed he might be. In general, the British left a legal tradition whose aim was to guard against the abuse of power. The arbitrary use of authority was subjected to legal restraint and the state was not regarded as dominant or beyond challenge. The present judicial administrative system, the Supreme Court at the central level and high courts at state levels and district courts at district and sub-divisional levels, is based on legal foundations laid down by the British.

The sixth legacy was in the field of administrative procedures. The administrative system before Independence with the mechanism of checks and balances was created to control and strengthen the British empire. Most of the procedures followed were with the objective of checking the use of power by the lower level field administrators so that they could perform their duties as per the rules. The Police Act of 1861, the Indian Penal Code, the Official Secrets Act and Audit Rules, etc., were all framed by the British and have not been substantially changed after Independence to suit the changed conditions. The same rules, regulations and procedures continue to be followed even today after so many years. The 'steel frame' given by the British for the administration of the country is inflexible and we have not changed or adjusted it to suit our present needs.

The rule of law, territorial integrity and unity, access to modern language through English were the main benefits of British rule. But there was another side of the coin. The British took their wages for the good they did in India. They drained the country, once considered fabulously rich. The British did much for India in the last two centuries but they also took ample compensation.

NOTES

1. K. P. Jayaswal, *Hindu Polity* (Bangalore: Bangalore Printing and Pub. Co., 1943), pp. 12–18.
2. Pramathanath Banerjee, *Public Administraiton in Ancient India* (New Delhi: Uppal Publishing House, 1985), pp. 77–8.
3. B. N. Puri, *History of Indian Administration, Vol. I* (Bombay: Bhartiya Vidya Bhavan, 1968), pp. 19–20.
4. Ibid.
5. Frank Moraes, *Jawaharlal Nehru, A Biography* (New York: Macmillan Co., 1956), p. 407.
6. B. N. Puri, op. cit., p. 146.
7. A. B. Pandey, *Society and Government in Medieval India* (Allahabad: College Book Depot, 1969), pp. 1–9.
8. Dasharatha Sharma, *Lectures on Rajput History and Culture* (Delhi: Motilal Banarsidass, 1970), pp. 15–16.
9. B. N. Puri, *History of Indian Administration, Vol. II* (Bombay: Bhartiya Vidya Bhavan, 1975), p. 81.
10. Ibid., p. 173.
11. J. N. Sarkar, *Mughal Administration* (Calcutta: M. C. Sarkar and Sons Ltd., 1952), pp. 4–5.
12. Ibid., pp. 20–21.
13. B. N. Puri, op. cit., p. 242.
14. N. C. Roy, *The Civil Service in India* (Calcutta: K. L. Mukhopadhyay, 1960), p. 14.
15. J. N. Sarkar, op. cit., p. 3.
16. N. C. Roy, op. cit., p. 15.
17. B. B. Mishra, *The Administrative History of India 1834–1947: General Administration* (London: Oxford University Press, 1970), p. 32.
18. Ibid., p. 71.
19. W. H. Morris-Jones, *The Government and Politics of India*, 2nd edition (London: Hutchinson and Co. Ltd., 1967), pp. 21–22.
20. L. S. Rathore, *The British Administration in India: Its Legacy and the Agenda for the Future*, presidential address delivered at Mysore on the occasion of Indian Public Administration Association, XV Annual Conference on 5–6 August 1995, p. 5.
21. Ibid., p. 5.

2

Constitution and Administration

The Constitution of India creates three kinds of services: all-India services that are common to the Union and states to man certain 'strategic posts', central services including the defence services and state services. Under Article 312, the Constitution provides for the creation of more common services if the council of states passes a resolution supported by an absolute majority or if two-thirds of members are present and voting. In 1962, three more all-India services were created under this Article, namely, all-India Engineers Service, Indian Forest Service and Indian Medical Service, thus taking their number to five, but only Indian Forest Service remained.

The Constitution of India contains specific provision relating to the creation of civil services at both the Union and state levels. A perusal of Articles 308, 309 and 311 would provide a clear insight into the position of civil services in India. Further, Article 309 empowers both the Union and state governments to make arrangements for their respective services. In fact, this kind of arrangement existing under Article 309 regarding the creation of civil services at the Union and in the states looks somewhat contradictory in view of the federal political system. So the question arises as to what motivated the Constitution makers to provide for such an arrangement? The answer is that in this regard they were guided more by administrative, historical and sociological imperatives.

The point to be noted is that the states are not responsible in any way for the recruitment, training and allocation of cadres of the members of all-India services, yet these members occupy the most important positions in administration at all levels and carry on state administration as well. These services are recruited by the Union Public Service Commission (UPSC), a central personnel recruitment agency. In spite of the exclusion of states from having any say in the allocation of members of these services in the state cadres, they are constitutionally obliged to cooperate with the centre in this regard. Their only responsibility in regard to the members of all-India services is for giving them postings and transferring them from one place to another depending on administrative exigencies. Their recruitment as well as promotion depends on the service rules and regulations made by the centre. A peculiar situation may arise some day when states may refuse to take and give postings to all-India service personnel. What will happen in such a situation? How would the problem be solved conveniently as it had not been visualized by our Constitution makers? The states are bound by the obligations imposed on them by Articles 256 and 257. Any attempt of deliberate omission on the part of any state may be considered as disregarding the provisions of Articles 256 and 257. Moreover, the states are under a constitutional obligation to comply with or carry out any directives given by the centre. The failure on the part of the states to comply with any such directives given by the centre is liable to be considered by the centre as the failure of the constitutional machinery in the states. As a result, Article 356 can be used by the centre to impose president's rule in a state.

The state governments, without the prior permission of the Union government, cannot even initiate disciplinary action against the members of the all-India services. In the matter of creating the all-India services, the founding fathers were influenced by the country's administrative evolution and practices, and the absolute necessity of providing for and sustaining the country's administrative unity. In spite of criticism for excluding the states from the process of recruiting the members of the all-India services, the Constitution makers were more concerned with the country's administrative unity, which came to be affected adversely in the wake of the Partition of the country.

The members of the central services along with the members of the all-India services are responsible for administering the affairs of the union government. In regard to the central services whose members are responsible for carrying out the administration of the central government, the Parliament is empowered by Article 312 to take appropriate measures for the creation of these services. In regard to the state civil services, the state public service commissions are empowered to initiate measures necessary for recruiting the members of the state services. This is in consonance with the power conferred on the states under Article 309 in terms of which the members of the state services are recruited by the state public service commission and appointed by the state government. This power of the state governments is the logical corollary to the autonomy enjoyed by the states in regard to the administration of subjects under the purview of the state government exclusively, as has been enumerated in the state list.

The members of union territory (UT) services are recruited by the Union Public Service Commission and posted to the UTs concerned for manning administration. Therefore, there is no separate provision in the public service commission for the recruitment of members of UTs for their civil services. Thus, the treatment meted out to the UTs with regard to the method followed in recruiting members of their civil service may look like an act of serious discrimination. Critics say that this is against the basic principles of federalism. The answer to this question can be that since the UTs were created in some very peculiar circumstances, therefore, such an arrangement was envisaged.

The states have not been given any authority regarding the recruitment, training and allocation of cadre in the all-India services. This grievance was voiced by the states as well as by many critics; therefore, one important point that deserves to be noted in this respect is that one-third of the total number of posts of the all-India services that have been allocated to the states are to be filled by promotion of members of the state civil services. Thus, in actuality, the two-thirds of the total number of posts allocated to the states from the all-India services (IAS/IPS) consist of officials recruited directly by the UPSC and the remaining one-third consists of members of the state civil services recruited by the state public service commission. The state governments have a very crucial role to play concerning the promotion of members of the state civil services, who are from the state cadre, to fill up the vacancies in the all-India services. This power given to the state governments for the promotion of members of the state civil services to the all-India services is not of ordinary importance. An analysis of this provision makes it clear that the constituent states enjoy power and privilege without responsibility in the matter of filling up of one-third of vacancies in the all-India services to the total number of posts of the all-India services allocated to the states. This point needs to be noted by states and critics who consider the creation of the all-India services anti-federal. If the intention of the Constitution makers was to sidetrack the constituent states in an important matter such as this, there was absolutely no need for them to make this important concession to the states.

In fact an analysis of the provisions of Articles 14–16, 32, 335 and 337, and similarly the provisions of Articles 356 and 357 in particular, and the scheme of legislative, administrative and financial relations between the Union and the states shows they are of no less significance in influencing the relevant provisions concerning the civil services. Unless the relevant provisions that belong to these two categories, namely, the justifiable fundamental rights and Union–state relations as well as certain specific provisions concerning the people belonging to the Scheduled Castes/Scheduled Tribes, OBC and the Anglo-Indians are kept in view, it is not possible to understand and analyse the various aspects of civil services under the Indian Constitution in the proper perspective.

In this connection it would be of profound importance to analyse the far-reaching implications of Articles 14–16 and 32 with regard to the civil services for the reason that Article 14 secures to the people equality before the law within the territory of India and Article 15 prohibits the state from discriminating individually against the citizens on the grounds of religion, race, caste, sex or place of birth. In spite of this constitutional embargo imposed by Article 15 on the state, they are required to take steps for ensuring the promotion of the interests of women, children and citizens who come 'under the socially and educationally backward classes'. Under Article 15 this particular provision is of prime importance in connection with recruitment to the civil services. Similarly, Article 16 guarantees equal opportunity to the citizens in regard to employment under the state. In view of this constitutional requirement, the state is not allowed to discriminate unjustly against any citizen on the basis of religion, race, caste, class, descent or place of birth. This constitutional provision is indeed very noble and of a very extraordinary character, but under the same Article there is a constitutional rider (vide Clause 4), which requires that if the state opines that the citizens belonging to the backward classes were not adequately represented in the state civil services, steps ought to be taken for reserving appointments and posts in respect of such citizens. It may be stated that this particular provision under Article 16 contained the seeds of the policy of protective discrimination. This particular constitutional rider needs to be viewed from the angle of social justice that has come to acquire paramount importance in view of the highly heterogeneous and primordial character of the Indian society. Given the nature of the objective for which this provision was included in the Constitution it is difficult to dispute its character and intent. But unfortunately, the authorities concerned, while evincing interest in the goals and objectives of social justice warranted by social heterogeneity and primordialism, ought to have defined in a very categorical, realistic and pragmatic manner as to who constituted the backward classes. Sadly, this was not done. In the name of effectualizing the goals of social justice by pursuing a policy of protective discrimination various state governments have embarked upon policies necessitated by social, caste and communal considerations. This indeed has resulted in creating a great deal of unwarranted permissiveness and politics into the recruitment policy, which undoubtedly has affected the cause of administration greatly.

Article 32 provides for constitutional remedies by way of empowering the Supreme Court to issue directives, orders or admit writs such as *habeas corpus*, *quo warranto*, prohibition, *mandamus* and *certiorari*. These constitutional remedies envisaged by Article 32 are a boon to the citizens as well as public servants for safeguarding their rights in case these were encroached upon by any legislative or administrative act. A similar power conferred on the state high courts under Article 226 is of considerable importance in this respect. The provisions of Articles 20 and 21 are of profound significance from the point of view of public services. Article 20 envisages all the three basic principles of the rule of law. The observance of the principles of rule of law is of paramount importance in safeguarding not only the citizens in general, but also the members of the public services from any injustice being inflicted on them.

The various Articles (Nos 308–314) that deal with the several aspects of civil services, and particularly Articles 309 and 311, are of far-reaching significance because under Article 310 members of the civil services including those of the all-India services working under the aegis of Union government or under the state governments are assured of job security. This is very important from the viewpoint of members of the civil services. Unless they are assured of the permanency of job security till they attain superannuation age, it is not possible for any government to expect the member of civil services to function with a sense of dedication to the cause of public welfare.

Perusal of the provisions of Article 310 shows that it assured job security to the members of the civil services working both at the centre and in the states. In fact, a perusal of the most pertinent cases that were heard and decided by the Supreme Court and state high courts in respect of service matters pertaining to the members of the civil services convincingly establish the profound impact of the provisions of Article 310 on the service regulations and conduct rules made by the various governmental authorities under the Constitution of India. In this connection, it is necessary to remember that according to the constitutional, political and administrative theory contained in the provisions of Article 310, the members of the civil services in India hold office by the pleasure of the president and governor at the centre and in the states, respectively. Pursuant to Article 258, the Union government may confer on or entrust its powers and functions to the state government. In such an event, it becomes the responsibility of the state governmental authorities to accept the same and do the needful in that connection. This invariably stresses the additional role that the members of the state civil services as well as the all-India services from the state cadre have to play. In the event of any adverse action taken by the Union government under Article 258, this specific role of the members of the state civil services may provoke orthodox advocacy or championing of federalism and force the state to characterize the action as a glaring instance of the centre's efforts at eroding or endangering the autonomy of the states. It may look like this superficially but is not so in reality. This is because under the Indian constitutional and political set-up cooperative federalism constitutes a very significant aspect. Indeed, this emphasizes the importance of the interdependence of administrative relations between the Union and the states. Thus, this pertinent aspect of the Indian constitutional and political system needs to be given due consideration for analysing the role that the state civil services are called upon to play in the event of any adverse action initiated by the Union government pursuant to Article 258.

In terms of Article 258(A), the states are constitutionally empowered to entrust the exercise of any of their powers and functions on the Union government in case the same were conferred by the states concerned. This aspect also calls for some examination. A perusal of the provisions of Article 310 makes it clear that both the Union and the various constituent states are provided with their own distinct civil services. Hence, it is the responsibility of these separate and distinct civil services to perform their role under the Union and respective state governments. But the provisions of Article 258 and 258-A and the underlying implications of the same establish that just like the Union government, which is empowered to act in terms of Article 258 for the purposes specified therein, the states are also similarly authorized by Article 258-A to act in proper manner for the purpose or purposes envisaged therein. In the event of any of the state governments initiating action pursuant to the provisions of Article 258-A, it becomes the responsibility of the Union government and the various civil services working under its direction and authority to do the needful in case the states confer any powers and functions on the Union government by resorting to the provisions of Article 258-A. This kind of constitutional arrangement is warranted by the cooperative federalism that exists under the Indian constitutional and political set-up. Thus, an overview of provisions of Article 258 and Article 258-A makes it clear that there is a two-way traffic, i.e., the centre can, by acting under Article 258, ask the states to do the needful and in the same way the states also, by acting in terms of Article 258-A, request the centre to do the needful in a particular connection. In short this unique arrangement emphasizes the close inter-dependence of the Union and the states in the sphere of administration.

Constitutional Safeguards for Public Servants

Article 311 is of special importance from the point of view of civil services that exist and operate under the Indian Constitution. This Article specifically empowers the authorities concerned to take appropriate action such as removal or reduction in rank or dismissal of any civil servant from service, if the same was warranted by administrative exigencies. This power in terms of Article 311 is given both to the Union and the state governments. As long as the authorities concerned act impartially, judiciously, dispassionately and discreetly no undue harm would be caused to the member of civil services. But the scope for misusing or abusing or exceeding the authority or power conferred by this Article under Article 311 cannot be ruled out. In fact, an analysis of the provisions of Article 311 makes it clear that for the employees of the government there is not much scope under Article 311 as it exists today to approach the judiciary with a complaint about the arbitrary or unconstitutional character of action taken by the authorities concerned that have led to the removal or reduction in rank or summary dismissal of the employee concerned from government service. Article 311 in its present form hangs like the proverbial Damocles' sword over the heads of members of civil service.

Reservation and Administration

One very important aspect of the Indian Constitution in regard to public services is the scope for pursuing a policy of protective discrimination and its far-reaching effects on civil services both at the centre and in the states. The provisions of Articles 16(4) and 335 contain the seeds of the policy of protective discrimination. As long as these provisions continue to exist in the Constitution, it would not be possible for authorities concerned to dispense with the policy of protective discrimination. In this regard, the provisions of Article 335 have gone a step forward, unlike Clause 4 of Article 16, because they contain a directive to the Union and state governments and all other authorities in India to give due consideration to the claims of the members of the Scheduled Castes and Scheduled Tribes in the matter of recruitment to civil services.

The authorities concerned are required to bear in mind the necessity of ensuring that whatever action or measures under Article 335 are taken by them, due consideration should be given to efficiency. With this arrangement as it exists under Article 335, one cannot help claiming that in the matter of giving effect to the provisions of this Article, it would not at all be possible for the authorities concerned to act quickly keeping in mind the absolute necessity of ensuring efficiency in civil services. In spite of the most extraordinary and meticulous care taken by them regarding efficiency in administration, it could hardly be realized.

The supreme consideration that motivated and urged the founding fathers to include a provision like this in the body of the Constitution was to mitigate the evils of social heterogeneity and primordialism, and infuse a very strong dose of social justice and liberalism. In view of it, the question is: whether the underlying objective of Article 335 as conceived by the Constitution makers has been realized? It is no doubt undeniable that the efforts made by the authorities concerned to implement the provisions of Article 335 while recruiting members of the SC/STs to civil services have, indeed, gone a long way in protecting the interests of the long-neglected sections of the Indian society. To this extent, the objective of the Constitution makers has been realized, but the other very important aspect underlying this Article has not been realized fully. This aspect, indeed, refers to the necessity of maintaining efficiency profoundly influenced by the aspects of societal forces.

Constitutional Amendments and Administration

A couple of amendments enacted in the post-Constitution era were responsible for very considerably influencing the nature of the civil services under the Constitution. One such amendment in particular that was responsible for affecting the civil services particularly at the state level was the 33rd Amendment enacted in 1973. Although Article 371-D created by the 33rd Constitution Amendment (1973) aimed at providing a solution to the regional grievances, the remedy provided by this Article—which has resulted in zonalizing the civil services in Andhra Pradesh—has proved to be worse than the malaise. Civil services constitute the backbone of administration. Members of the civil services are required to think and act in broad terms of the state in the public interest as such.

Apart from the foregoing aspect of Article 371-D, it is important to consider an administrative innovation effected by this Article. This has brought into being a new administrative institution called the administrative tribunal. This was created for the purpose of going into and settling any matter pertaining to the members of the civil services of the state. Looking at this institution from the point of view of the objective for which it was created, it might be stated categorically that its creation has indeed resulted in lessening the burden of the state high court. The state high court as a result is no longer required to consider and dispose of any application by a civil servant voicing his grievances and seeking remedy in matters such as promotion, seniority, posting, etc.

But there is one very serious infirmity from which the administrative tribunal suffers. It is made clear by the provisions concerning the creation of this institution that whenever a judgement is rendered by the administrative tribunal concerning the state civil services that judgement should be given effect by the state government within a period of three months. Thus, if the state government decided not to implement the same within the stipulated period and communicated it to the administrative tribunal within the prescribed period, the party concerned has no alternative other than to appeal directly to the Supreme Court under the provisions of Article 32. Thus, the power given to the state government to act or not in respect of the judgement rendered by the administrative tribunal is not a very healthy sign. Because of this lacuna or infirmity, it should not be difficult for the state government to take advantage of it and act otherwise under the influence of political and partisan considerations. This unfortunate influence has resulted in bringing politics into an area where, strictly speaking, administrative considerations and procedural norms and niceties should have been preserved for promoting the ends of justice.

Article 247 and other relevant Articles (Articles 245–254) that deal with the legislative aspect of the Union–state relations are of vital significance from the point of view of civil services. This Article empowers the Parliament to enact legislation for the purpose of creating tribunals for dealing with such matters that cannot exclude civil services. For more than a quarter of a century the Parliament did not think in terms of legislating for effectualizing the purposes envisaged by Article 247. For the first time, the Parliament passed an act called the Special Tribunals Act in 1977. Notwithstanding this objective, the purposes for which the special tribunals were sought to be created were no less consequential vis-à-vis civil services. To that extent, the special tribunal enacted in terms of Article 247 will have to be investigated in all aspects in the light of such specific cases that would affect or involve civil services. Whether the provision for the creation of these special tribunals had in any way adversely affected or endangered the position of civil services is a matter that has to be enquired separately. But what is sought to be established is that the creation of the Special Tribunals Act is not incapable of affecting the civil services.

The administrative tribunals enjoy a status similar to that of the high courts from the point of view of jurisdiction. But there is a difference between administrative tribunals and state high courts. Barring the chairman and one or two other members of these tribunals, the rest are experienced administrators. No doubt the creation of these tribunals resulted in lessening the burden of state high courts and also provided the members of the state civil services a remedy with the objective of seeking redress of their grievances in regard to service matters. However, the creation of these institutions has not prevented the members of civil services from approaching the highest judicial tribunal in the country, the Supreme Court, for seeking remedy in case they felt aggrieved over the verdict of the central and state administrative tribunals.

The Constitution was put into effect on 26 January 1950 and it aimed largely at modernizing society, polity and economy. To emphasize the goals of modernization and development, the Indian Constitution provided for not only parliamentary system of responsible government based on periodical elections and universal adult franchise, but also envisaged the recreation of a new social order based on social, economic and political justice. These two fundamental aspects of the Indian Constitution would bear eloquent testimony to the ardent desire and determination of the founding fathers to create a new social order pervaded by the imperatives of justice and ensuring all-round development. What kind of role that the civil services are called upon to play is determined decisively by the very nature and philosophy of the concept of the state. From this angle, it is important to reiterate at this juncture the circumstances under which India sought to establish a social welfare state. This concept of state, which is in contradistinction to the police state of the British-ruled India of the 19th century, envisages a pivotal role for the civil services that constitute the backbone of administration. The ushering in of the new Constitution of India brought in its wake the era of development planning. Authorities at the highest level fully realized the imperative necessity of developmental planning under the aegis of the state, because state directed and operated development planning was warranted by the goals and objectives of social welfare—a key concept embodied in the Constitution. What is sought to be emphasized in this context is the distinctive role of civil services in the implementation of national development plans to bring about rapid social and economic development of the country. No development plan, however grand or impressive it may be, can ever be implemented properly, promptly and successfully unless a very competent civil service exists. What matters ultimately in the Indian context is achieving successful, satisfactory and prompt implementation of development plans as the key to public administration.

Public administration in the Indian context has become the most formidable instrument of the nation-building process. Among the several inputs that are required to effectively implement any such development plan in the Indian context, there is need for reasonably adequate financial, material and human resources as also competent, thoroughly overhauled and sufficiently lubricated administrative machinery to implement all such plans. What determines the success or failure of development plans and programmes is a system of development-oriented, goal-oriented and achievement-oriented public administration. The task of public administration depends ultimately on the character, determination, dedication and the role of the civil services that are responsible for manning the entire administrative system. Thus, it is very significant and absolutely necessary to emphasize the most distinctive role that civil services are called upon to play in the context of developmental planning in the post-Independence era. The civil services have to perform not only the traditional functions relating to the maintenance of law and order, but also obliged by the imperative necessity of the welfare state to play a very vital role in ensuring effective and prompt implementation of development plans. It is needless to emphasize that unless the civil services realize their responsibility and vital role as agents of change, it is absolutely impossible to hope for the implementation of plans, let alone the realization of their underlying goals.

Federal System and Administration

The federal system for governance of the country created by the Constitution for both the Union and the states is largely responsible for influencing civil services in one way or the other. If the influence of the federal system on civil services was confined only to the all-India services or central services, there would not have been any ground for voicing or expressing undue concern about the impact of federalism on civil services, but it has also influenced the state civil services. This has become possible because of the following factors:

(1) Constitutional obligations imposed by Articles 256 and 257 on the states
(2) Implications of Article 365
(3) Provisions of Articles 258 and 258-A
(4) Decisive influence exerted by the centre through the mechanism of development plans for the states

An analysis of these factors at some length will provide a clear picture about the extent to which it has become possible for the central government to influence the states civil services. From the point of view of the people favouring state autonomy and orthodox federalism, this kind of silent but spectacular encroachments caused by the federal centre on the state civil services would be very alarming and extraordinary. The scope for the federal centre to exert its influence on the states and through them on their respective civil services is rendered possible by the very nature of the Indian Constitution as well as the highly centralized federal system. To what extent would it be possible for the federal centre to exercise its influence on the states and their civil services would become still more clear whenever there is an emergency—both national emergency under Article 352 and local emergency under Article 356 necessitated by the collapse of the constitutional government in the states. A very dispassionate and judicious assessment of the implications of these two kinds of emergency serves to establish conclusively that it would not be a difficult task for the centre to influence the states and their civil services in the event of an emergency.

Although the Constitution of India has provided for three different types of emergencies, two of these, namely, national and state, respectively under Article 352 and Article 356, would considerably influence the role of civil services in the state. When there is a national emergency imposed under Article 352, the Union government stands empowered automatically to give directions to the state governments as to the manner of exercising their executive powers. Any such direction given by the centre to the states and observance of the same by the states would not fail to have its effect on the state civil services. Similarly, whenever there is national emergency, it becomes obligatory on the part of the state to ensure compliance with the laws passed by the Parliament as well as exercise of the executive powers of the Union government. This kind of constitutional obligation that the states carry out are potent enough to influence the role and working of the civil services in the states. Likewise, whenever an emergency is proclaimed and enforced under Article 356 this would result in dismissing the popular ministry, dissolving the state legislative assembly and authorizing the state governor to administer the state on behalf of the president. During such a period, the governor has to give effect to whatever directions are issued by the centre to the states. In such a situation, it is difficult for the civil services in the state to remain free from the kind of influence that the federal centre can exert on them.

Parliamentary Democracy and Administration

Our Constitution provides a parliamentary system of government, the characteristics of which include ministerial responsibility. The implication is that for administration and its faults, shortcomings and failures, the minister in charge of the portfolio will be held responsible. Therefore, he must always keep a strict supervision and control on the proper functioning of the administration of his ministry that depends on the quality of civil services. Administration has an obligation to the Constitution for proper governance of the country. Therefore, it should develop and practice the principle of political neutrality faithfully. The necessity of observing and sustaining this principle of neutrality was felt as more urgent for the survival of parliamentary democracy. Regarding the principle of political neutrality, a relevant question may be raised: is it possible, given the nature of Indian society, to develop the principle of political neutrality, and will it be observed by the civil services in India like its British counterpart? The crux of the problem in India is: Would it be practicable and feasible for the civil services in India to achieve success in this field? Our constitution makers, who realized the importance of civil service neutrality, did their best in ensuring the working of the civil services with a fair measure of success by creating provisions of independent public service commissions for their recruitment on open merit, competitive examination without favour and fear of government and providing job security to the members of the service. These measures were taken by the Constitution makers to enable civil services to develop and observe the doctrine of neutrality, but the efficacy of these measures in strengthening the civil services neutrality have been to a considerable extent neutralized by the impact of extra-constitutional factors such as charismatic leadership and one-party dominance. Although, at present, these factors are not there, even then the influence exerted by them could be seen in a very palpable manner.

Generalist Administration and Developmental Orientation

The very nature of government and its philosophy have undergone a metamorphosis since Independence. What kind of personnel is needed by the government for carrying on administration is determined by several factors. Among them, the nature of duties and responsibilities and functional obligations of the government constitute the most important one. No doubt, even today it is not difficult to see the importance of the generalist character of the civil services, but under the impact of science and technology as well as the ever-expanding activities and functions of the government necessitated by the acceptance of the concept of welfare state, the governmental authorities in the post-Independence era have been called upon to perform numerous types of developmental and welfare-oriented functions that call for the employment of persons possessing a variety of skills, knowledge and professional competence. This development has resulted in considerably changing the very character of public personnel.

In the post-Independence era, in view of the growing needs and requirements of the government, the public service commissions in India have been called upon to recruit a number of professionals as well in addition to the generalists. In fact, the creation of specialist cadres in the several ministries, departments and agencies of government that deal with such vital and crucial matters as iron and steel industry, extraction of mineral wealth, atomic energy and such other related matters have resulted in requiring the public service commissions to recruit engineers, doctors, technologists, scientists, etc. in considerable numbers. Thus, several specialist cadres have come into being in civil services. This indeed is a spectacular development. The presence of these qualified specialists in several new ministries, departments and agencies of the government has brought in its wake controversy concerning the specialists versus generalists. Before Independence, such controversy did not exist in the sphere of civil services. But as of late, this has come to the fore. In spite of this controversy concerning specialists versus generalists, the predominance of the latter is conspicuously maintained in the realm of civil services.

Autonomous Bodies and Administration

Although the Union and the state public service commissions constitute independent central personnel recruiting agencies with respect to the Union and state governments, several new personnel recruiting agencies have come into being during the last 40 years. This constitutes a very significant development vis-à-vis civil services in India. In fact because of their very nature and role in their respective fields, the emergence of a large number of autonomous public corporations, departmentally managed concerns, joint stock companies in the public sector and commissions-and-boards-type agencies has necessitated the creation of their own personnel agencies to recruit their respective administrative, managerial and technical personnel. Thus, one can see a plurality of personnel agencies apart from the public service commissions, but there is a fundamental difference between these and the newly emerged personnel agencies closely associated with corporations, commissions, boards, etc. The former are constitutionally created bodies with their own distinctive constitutional status and entity and the latter statutorily created bodies.

One of the fundamental characteristics of the relation between the state and individuals in a democratic set-up is the conferment of justifiable fundamental rights on citizens. Although members of the civil services are a part and parcel of the general body of the citizens, they differ in a discernible manner from the citizens in the matter of enjoyment of fundamental rights. This difference between civil service and citizens at large is clearly visible in respect of rights such as freedom of speech and expression and criticism, freedom to form associations and unions and freedom to stand for elections to legislative bodies and such other elected political institutions. Limitations imposed on the members of civil services in regard to the enjoyment of these rights were necessitated by the special position of the members of the civil services and their professional obligations and duties. By dint of their position as a part and parcel of the machinery of government and their responsibility for carrying on administration, they are not entitled to be treated on parity with other citizens in respect of enjoyment of the aforesaid freedoms or rights. If they are allowed to enjoy these rights in the same manner in which all other citizens are entitled to enjoy, it is bound to create a very complicated and unmanageable situation in the ranks of civil services that constitute the backbone of administration. Their non-involvement in politics and obligation to keep away from aligning themselves with political parties and the restraint placed on voicing their views publicly on matters relating to government and administration were defended by the social, moral, political and administrative imperatives of the doctrine of neutrality of civil services. The absolute necessity of developing, sustaining and observing this doctrine scrupulously is at the root of the limitations imposed on them in the matter of enjoying or exercising the said rights. There is a professional correlation between the limitations imposed on them and the kind of duties and responsibilities that are to be exercised by them as members of civil services.

Indian civil services are criticized for lack of integrity, morality and competence, and the rampant corruption in the realm of administration will have to be explained by analysing the impact of the forces of social heterogeneity and primordialism on administration. In spite of the tremendous impact of the societal forces on civil services in India since Independence, they have not completely collapsed or vanished from the scene. Despite the fact that they have been found mutilated and truncated, they have not failed in playing their role as the backbone of administration.

In the ultimate analysis, apart from the ideals or norms, what determines the actual working of the political and administrative system is the pervading impact of the social system, and this crucial point deserves to be kept constantly in view in any venture at analysing the role of civil services in India regarding the working of parliamentary democracy.

3

Parliamentary Democracy

Introduction

India adopted a parliamentary form of government after Independence based on the British model along with some features of the presidential system. Our Constitution followed the British model because most of the members of the Constituent Assembly were getting hands-on experience of working in the responsible government modelled on British parliamentary form. Therefore, it was but natural for them to have preference for this form of government instead of a presidential form of government, though some of the features of presidential form were incorporated into the Constitution.

Characteristics of the Parliamentary Form of Government

The main features of the British parliamentary democracy are:

1. In a parliamentary system, a clear distinction is made between the constitutional head of the state and the actual head of the government.
2. It has a plural executive, which means government is composed of a cabinet or a council of ministers.
3. It has collective and ministerial responsibility.
4. It enjoins the supremacy of Parliament.

Let us discuss to what extent these characteristics are present in our system of governance and how they affect our administration.

Constitutional or Nominal and Real Executive

The Constitution (Article 53) says that 'the Executive power of the Union shall be vested in the president and shall be exercised by him either directly or through officers subordinate to him in accordance with the Constitution'. Further, the Constitution gives power to the Parliament to confer 'by law functions on authorities other than the president'.[1] At first, this may seem like the president depends on Parliament for its powers, but in practice this is not so. The Parliament could function through laws made by it and every law needs the assent of the president before it could become law.[2] The Parliament does not share any executive power with the president. But the Constitution does not vest the executive powers in the president alone. According to Article 74(1), there shall be a council of ministers with the prime minister as its head, to aid and advise the president in the exercise of his powers. Thus, the president is the constitutional head of the Union while the prime minister is the actual head of the government, run by a Council of ministers. This is the pattern of British parliamentary system. But as far our president is concerned, there is a significant difference. This difference is that the British monarch is hereditary, while our president is elected by an electoral college consisting of the elected members of the Parliament and state legislatures. Thus, the electoral base of the president is larger than that of the prime minister. Though the president is the constitutional head, the Constitution has given him some powers in practice on the pattern of the presidential system.[3] For example, under Article 86 of the Constitution, he can send messages to either House of the Parliament; under Article 111, he gives his assent to the Bills; under Article 78(c), he can ask the prime minister to put the matter before the cabinet for consideration; under Article 78, it is the duty of the prime minister to keep the president informed about all the major decisions of the government, etc. Moreover, the president has many other discretionary powers, which show that our Constitution has made him the actual chief executive.[4] But everything depends on circumstances and the political situation at the time. Thus, in practice the constitutional head in India is the president, who enjoys more executive functions than the British monarch.

Plural Executive

In India, the actual powers of government are vested in the council of ministers with prime minister as its head. The head of the state forms the council of ministers. He appoints prime minister of a majority party leader. In case there is no majority, then he had a real choice. In a multi-party system like ours at present, the president can choose a prime minister, but he has not shown his preferences. He has invited a person who commands majority in the House with a combination of parties. He appoints ministers on the advice of the prime minister.

In the parliamentary form of government, the Council of ministers is the final decision-making authority. The ministers individually take decisions in their department as per the policy laid down by the cabinet. Ministers have a lot of discretion in taking decisions on the matters of ministries allotted to them. But this is also subject to the control of the council of ministers.

For the proper functioning of the cabinet, it has its own office called the cabinet secretariat, which provides necessary secretarial assistance to it.[5] The appointment of ministers for different ministries has resulted in setting up of separate ministries and departments to assist the prime minister in administration and the process of decision making and implementation of the decisions. Thus, the Indian executive is a plural one as per requirements of a parliamentary democracy.

Ministerial Responsibility and Collective Responsibility

A parliamentary system works on the well-accepted principle that ministers are individually and collectively responsible for all their official acts to the legislature, especially to the lower house that is the Lok Sabha in India, and remain in office as long as they retain its confidence.

Article 75(3) of the Constitution says that the council of ministers is collectively responsible to the house of the people, legally and constitutionally. The responsibility to the legislature means that so long as the policies and official conduct of the ministers command the support of the majority of the members of the legislature, they continue to hold the reigns of office and govern the country. But as soon as the majority is reduced into a minority and the ministry loses the confidence of the house of the people (Lok Sabha), it must resign from office.

The legislature can also express its displeasure by:

(i) Passing a vote of no-confidence motion or censuring individual ministers.

(ii) Defeating a cabinet-sponsored Bill or any other similar measure.

(iii) Imposing token cuts in the budgetary proposals, etc.

In all such situations, the council of ministers has to resign. Ministerial responsibility ensures cohesion and solidarity and accounts for the stability of the government. Moreover, responsibility and responsiveness go together and it is only in a parliamentary system of government that both can be secured.

The concept of ministerial responsibility incorporates three kinds of responsibilities that are as follows:

(i) The council of ministers is responsible to the legislature, but at the same time, every individual minister is also responsible to the legislature. When a minister is reprimanded by the legislature for his individual lapses, he has to resign. This happened in several cases such as with T. T. Krishnamachari, the then finance minister, who had to resign due to his criticism in Parliament over the Mundra deal. Similarly, V. K. Krishna Menon, the former defence minister, had to resign due to criticism in the house for non-preparation of the country's defence, etc.

(ii) Each minister is also responsible to the cabinet and by convention to the prime minister. If a minister disagrees with the policy and decisions of the cabinet, he has to resign. Examples include C. D. Deshmukh, John Mathai and Shyama Prasad Mukherjee. They tendered their resignation to the prime minister when they disagreed with the policies of the government and their resignations were later accepted by the president.

(iii) Article 75(2) of the Constitution says that a minister shall hold office during the pleasure of the president. Thus, each minister is technically responsible to the head of the state, i.e. the president. He exercises this power on the advice of the prime minister.

The concept of ministerial responsibility requires that first the administrators or bureaucracy should tender their advice, and once policies are framed and decisions taken by the minister, they should faithfully implement them even if they are against their advice. If the bureaucracy does not cooperate, the minister will not be able to discharge his responsibility properly to the Parliament. Second, the administrators should have freedom in giving advice to the minister for formulation of policies. Third, the administration has to implement the policy decisions of ministers belonging to the different political parties and having different political views. Both the ministers and administrators have to uphold the rule of law at any cost. The administrators, therefore, should have the characteristics of neutrality, anonymity and impartiality.

Parliamentary Sovereignty

The British parliament, which is our model, is sovereign. It has been said that 'the English Parliament can do anything under the sun except convert a man into woman and vice-versa'. The British constitutional expert A. V. Dicey's remark that 'the sovereignty of Parliament is from the legal point of view the dominant characteristic of our political institutions' has two main aspects:

(i) The Parliament can make any law on any subject. It can also amend and repeal any law, which it enacted earlier.

(ii) The laws so enacted by the Parliament determine the course of all ministerial and administrative actions. While the courts can examine the lawfulness of the executive action, they have no authority to declare any law as *ultra vires*.

In this sense, Indian Parliament is not sovereign. Our Constitution has not accepted the British doctrine of the absolute supremacy of the Parliament in matters of legislation. There are three main factors which limit the supremacy of the Parliament.

The powers of the Union Parliament are limited by the various administrative details. Dr Ambedkar said that, 'it is wiser not to trust the legislature to prescribe forms of administration. This is the justification for incorporating them (administrative details) in the Constitution'.[6] There are also some other factors which limit the supremacy of the Parliament. The Indian Constitution is a federal one. It provides a federal form of government not unitary one as in Britain. Thus the Indian Parliament has two fundamental restrictions in law making. First, it can legislate on subjects allotted to it in the Union list and it cannot normally intrude into the state list, which is meant for state legislatures. Second, it cannot in any way interfere with or infringe upon any of the fundamental rights guaranteed in Chapter III of the Constitution. The Supreme Court and the high courts act as guardians for the enforcement of the fundamental rights. If Parliament or state legislatures make a law that encroaches on the fundamental rights of the citizens, the courts can declare it unconstitutional and void. Third, the Constitution provides for distribution of powers between the Union and state governments. In case of disputes, some agency has to be an arbitrator between the two. Under our Constitution the high courts and the Supreme Court have been authorized to interpret the provision of the Constitution including those relating to division of powers. Fourth, there are some other factors which have further restricted the legislative authority of the Indian Parliament. For example, much of the legislative functions have been delegated to the executive because in the modern world, law making has become a highly complicated and technical affair. Moreover, due to shortage of time, the Parliament often lays down the broad principles of legislation and then leaves it to the executive branch to frame the formal and procedural details. Thus, the 'delegated legislation' has materially reduced the importance of the Parliament. As a matter of fact, most of the Bills are initiated on the floor of the Parliament by the cabinet, which with its majority support gets them passed in the legislature. The Parliament has almost become a registering body and it can hardly criticize for the reduced control of the legislative power of the cabinet.[7]

The Parliament has the authority to amend the Constitution. But the Supreme Court in its judgement has propounded a new doctrine of 'basic structure' and Parliament now cannot disturb it. While amending the Constitution if it violates that restriction it is considered void.

The constitution makers have given some more powers such as emergency and ordinance-making powers to the executive. Thus, the Constitution makes 'executive supremacy definite and complete'.[8] The Indian Parliament in comparison to executive is a powerless body. It can meet only if summoned by the executive; its bills become law only if the executive is pleased to give assent to it; it can deal in financial matters only if the executive permits. In short, there is nothing which the legislature can do without the executive whereas the latter can do many things and go on for a long time without the legislature. It can rule with old laws, promulgate ordinances, declare emergencies and spend money.[9] Now, finally, the Parliament has become a place for dull and fruitless debates, and an arena to show muscle power.

Parliamentary Control over Administration

The Parliament in India exercises control over public administration indirectly through the council of ministers, which has to answer questions in the Parliament. The other means of parliamentary control are short-notice questions, half-hour discussions, adjournment motions, no-confidence motions and other types of motions and resolutions. There are many occasions of general and special debates like the one on the presidential address to the Parliament, budget debates, zero-hour discussion, etc. when the ministers have to explain the position of the government to the Parliament and answer the criticism of the members.

Besides the above-mentioned indirect control, the Parliament exercises more direct control over administration through its committees such as public accounts committee, estimates committee, committee on public undertakings. In these committees the members of Parliament and state legislatures get an opportunity to closely scrutinize the activities of administrative departments of the governments and public undertakings. Usually the public servants are called to give evidence before these committees and this establishes their face-to-face contact with the administrators.

Indian Federalism: Nature and Problems

The administrative implications of federalism are that it entails sharing of administrative powers between the federation and federating units, i.e. the state governments. The fundamental principle of this system is the allocation of authority between the federal and the constituent governments.

The very first Article of the Constitution says, 'India that is Bharat, shall be a Union of states and not a federation of states.' Therefore, the most important question is the nature of Indian federalism.

The views of scholars and legal luminaries widely differ on the question. Generally, they are divided into three schools of thoughts. The first one considers it a federation with a strong centre.[10] The second considers it unitary rather than federal.[11] The third takes a middle position and describes it as a quasi-federal.[12]

To have our views clear on this issue we must know what is considered a federation, what are its characteristics or features and how far these features are present in the Indian Constitution. In a federation there should be a central government and state governments. Second, the powers and functions of both the central and the state governments should be defined by a written constitution. Third, there should be a clear-cut exclusive field for the centre and another exclusive field for the states. Fourth, the centre and the states should have power to function in their own field through their own agencies. Fifth, there should be an independent judiciary for the interpretation of the Constitution and adjudication of cases between the centre and states. According to these criteria, the Indian Constitution is federal and hence, India is a federation.

Written Constitution

The essential feature of a federation is that it should have a written constitution which defines the structure, organization and powers of the central as well as state governments so that both operate within their respective jurisdiction without interference in each other's functions. The Indian Constitution is a written document containing 395 Articles and 9 Schedules. In fact, the Indian Constitution is one of the most elaborate constitutions of the world.

Supremacy of the Constitution

In a federation, the Constitution should be supreme for the central and federating units. The Constitution is the supreme law of the land and central as well as state laws should be in conformity with it. In India the Constitution is supreme and central and state governments cannot bypass it. If it is bypassed or violated, then courts of law are there to ensure that the supremacy of the Constitution is upheld at all cost.

Rigid Constitution

Another essential feature of a federation is that it should be a rigid Constitution that cannot be changed easily. In our Constitution the provisions concerning the relations between the federal and state governments as well as the judicial organization of the country can be amended only by the joint action of the federal and state governments. These provisions along with two-thirds majority of the two houses of Parliament require approval by the majority of state assemblies.

Division of Powers

Another feature of a federation is the statutory division of powers between the units and the centre. In our Constitution, powers have been divided into three lists: the Union list, the state list and the concurrent list.

The Union list consists of 97 subjects such as defence, foreign affairs, railways, posts and telegraphs, currency and others. The state list consists of 66 subjects namely, public order, police, administration of justice, public health, education and agriculture, etc. The concurrent list contains 47 subjects like marriage and divorce, books and printing presses, trade unions, electricity, etc. The central government has exclusive power to legislate on the subjects mentioned in the Union list. The state governments have authority to legislate on the subjects of state list under normal circumstances. Both the centre and the state governments possess the right to legislate on the subjects contained in the concurrent list. But in case of clash between the central and state laws the former prevails. The residuary powers have been vested in the central government.

Independent Judiciary

For a federation an independent judiciary is essential. Our Constitution has provided the Supreme Court which is the highest court in India to act as the guardian and declare any law or order as unconstitutional or *ultra vires* if it contravenes any provision of the Constitution. The Supreme Court also ensures that the central and the state governments operate within the areas assigned to them in the Constitution.

Bicameral Legislature

A bicameral system of legislature is an essential feature of a federation. The Constitution of India provides a bicameral parliament consisting of the Lok Sabha and the Rajya Sabha. While the Lok Sabha comprises representatives directly elected by the people, the Rajya Sabha mainly consists of representatives elected by the state legislatures. However, all the states have not been given equal representation in the Rajya Sabha.

Unitary features of the Indian Constitution

In spite of the above federal features the framers of the Constitution have modified the true nature of Indian federation by incorporating certain non-federal features, which have led the critics to challenge its federal character and charge that it is merely federal in form but actually unitary in spirit. Some of the unitary features of our Constitution are given as follows.

A Strong Centre

The Constitution provides a very strong centre, a feature of unitary government. In the division of powers 97 items have been included into the Union list while the state list contains 66 items. Further, in the concurrent list that has 47 items the central government has an overriding hand and has residuary power over the whole territory. But keeping in view the conditions prevailing then in the country our framers of the Constitution were right in making the centre strong.

Single Citizenship

Usually under a federal government there is double citizenship, viz. each person is not only a citizen of the country but is also a citizen of a particular state in which he resides. The Indian Constitution on the other hand creates a single citizenship whose power vests in the Indian Parliament and the states do not possess any power in this regard. Every Indian is a citizen of India no matter in which state he resides.

Single Constitution for Union and State

Generally, under a federal system the states have their own separate Constitution from the Union. But in India we have only one Constitution for the Union as well as the states. The states have not been given any power to initiate amendments to the Constitution—a power which exclusively vests in the Indian Parliament. This has enhanced the powers and prestige of the centre at the cost of the states.

Centre Can Change the Name and Boundaries of States

In a federation, the centre has no right to change the boundaries of the states. But in India the centre has the right to change the boundaries of the states and to carve out one state from the other. This has been done in India on several occasions. Except for Uttar Pradesh the boundaries of all the states had been changed at one stage or another. In 1966 Haryana and Himachal Pradesh were carved out of Punjab state. Likewise the erstwhile Bombay state was bifurcated into two: Maharashtra and Gujarat. In 1971 Mizoram and Arunachal Pradesh were separated from Assam. When the very existence of the constituent unit is not guaranteed, it is certainly a deviation from a true federal system.

Single Unified Judiciary

Unlike other federations, India possesses a single unified judiciary with the Supreme Court at the apex. The Supreme Court only exercises supervision and control over the functioning of other courts. The writs of the Supreme Court are observed throughout the country in all spheres—civil, constitutional and criminal. The judges of high courts are also independent of the states, which do not possess any power with regard to their appointment, removal and service conditions. The judges are appointed by the president and can be removed by him only after they are impeached by the Parliament. Further there is no separate set of laws and a single civil and criminal procedure operates throughout the country. All these are clear pointers to the unitary character of the Constitution.

Unequal Representation of States in the Rajya Sabha

One of the characteristics of the federation is that the constituent units; of whatever size they may be, should have equal representation in the upper house of the federal legislature. In the USA, each state has two representatives in the Senate, and so is the case in Switzerland but not so in India. The representation in the council of states is on the basis of population and as a result states like UP and Bihar have more representation as compared to that from Haryana, Himachal Pradesh, Nagaland and Mizoram. This is not in accordance with a classical federal system.

Common All-India Services

The provision of common all-India Services such as the IAS, IPS and IFS are a pointer to the unitary character of the Indian Constitution. The members of these services are appointed by the president on the recommendation of the Union Public Service Commission and posted in key administrative positions in the states. The states have hardly any control over the members of these services.

Emergency Provisions

The existence of the emergency provisions in the Constitution also poses a serious threat to the federal character of our polity. The President of India under Articles 352, 356 and 360 can proclaim a state of emergency. During the emergency, the Parliament gets the power to legislate for the whole or any part of the country on the subjects of state list. An emergency can arise both in the political and financial fields. In the political field it implies that the administration of a state cannot be carried out in accordance with the Constitution of the country. In the financial field it implies that there is a great financial crisis, that cannot be solved by normal procedures. The effect in the political field would be that the administration of the state is taken over by the centre, which is against the spirit of federation.

In addition to all these above provisions, the centralized election machinery, the office of the comptroller and auditor general, appointment of governors by the president; financial dependence of state upon the centre, inter-state council and boards; appointment of an inquiry commission by the centre; centralized planning, power of the central government to issue directions to the state governments and reservation of state bills by the governors for president's assent are all such steps which makes the centre very powerful.

The working of the Constitution during these past 60 years shows that ours is a cooperative and bargaining federalism. In spite of the overriding powers of the centre some states particularly after 1967 have started showing force to the centre. In 1968, the West Bengal government of the United Front forced the centre to withdraw its then governor Dharam Vira. Likewise, governments of Kerala and West Bengal did not implement the Essential Services Ordinance of Government of India issued in 1968 to prevent the central government employees from going on strike. Similarly, the centre has not succeeded in resolving the inter-state water and boundary disputes. The cases of the boundary dispute between Punjab and Haryana and the issue of Chandigarh continue to exist even today. The dispute of Ravi-Beas and Sutlej waters between Haryana and Punjab, water disputes between Karnataka, Andhra Pradesh and Tamil Nadu, the height of Alamati Bandh between Andhra Pradesh and Karnataka, could not be resolved—by the Centre.

In Tamil Nadu, the Congress party was forced to bargain with the AIDMK in 1996—the Congress agreed not to field any candidate for the assembly seats in exchange of some seats in the Lok Sabha. In 1996, the regional parties played a leading role in the appointment of United Front government at the centre.

Conclusion

It is evident from the above that though the Indian Constitution outwardly possesses a federal structure in spirit it is unitary. Our Constitution makers deliberately made the centre strong due to many factors. These factors were to keep the fissiparous tendencies, which appeared on the eve of Partition, under control and ensure unity of the country, tackle serious law and order problem, solve the problem of food shortage which confronted the country at that time, the historical experience of weak central authority due to which the country was enslaved by foreigners, check the separatist tendencies shown by some of the princely states and follow the worldwide trend of other federations where the centre had grown strong in practice. Like other constitutions our Constitution is an instrument for the governance of the country. It is quite flexible for adoption to India's changing and growing needs.

NOTES

1. Article 53(3)(b), Constitution of India.
2. Article 111, Constitution of India.
3. See, for details, Chapter 4.
4. Ibid.
5. See for details, Chapter 10.
6. *Constituent Assembly Debates, Vol. VII*, p. 38.
7. Nirmalendu Bikash Rakshit, *Amrita Bazar Patrika*, Calcutta, 9 December 1986.
8. K. V. Rao, *Parliamentary Democracy of India*, 2nd edition (Calcutta: World Press, 1965), p. 121.
9. Ibid., p. 121.
10. These views were expressed by C. H. Allexandrowecz, who said, 'India is undoubtedly a federation in which the attributes sovereignty is shared between the centre and the states.' *Constitutional Development in India*, (Madras: Oxford University Press, 1957), p. 169. According to Sir Ivor Jennings, 'Indian Constitution is federal with strong centralising tendencies.' *Some Characteristics of the Indian Constitution* (London: Oxford University Press, 1953), p. 1. According to Dr B. R. Ambedkar, 'Federation means the establishment of a dual polity. The Draft Constitution is federal constitution as much as it establishes a dual polity . . . . This dual polity resembles American Constitution.' *Constituent Assembly Debates, Vol. VII*, p. 33.
11. K. M. Munshi and Justice Gajendragadkar, the former chief justice of India, think that it is more unitary than federal.
12. K. C. Wheare takes a middle position and describes the Indian Constitution as 'quasi-federal'.

Political Executive at the Union Level

In a democratic set-up, power vests in the people. The administration is the machinery which implements the policies and programmes of the government. The Constitution of India provides for a parliamentary system of government in which the formal powers are vested in the Union executive, which includes the president, the prime minister and the council of ministers. The president is a nominal head of the Union, whereas the council of ministers headed by the prime minister is the actual executive.

The President of India

The office of the President of India is the creation of the Indian Constitution. Article 52 creates the 'President of India' with all the executive powers of the Union vested in him and he has a vital role to play in the other wings of the government as well. The Constitution neither calls him the head of the state nor the head of the executive. The omission was deliberate.[1] The constitution makers wanted to create a 'great figure-head', or a nominal executive.

The constitution makers had tried to achieve this objective by creating a president's office with enormous powers and then making him subject to the 'aid and advice' of council of ministers, 'collectively responsible to the Lok Sabha'.

To know the real nature of Indian presidency will need a systematic study regarding the president's election, the terms and conditions of office, method of his removal, and powers and functions given to him. Moreover, the way he exercises his powers alone or with the advice of council of ministers is crucial to show his real position.

Article 54 of the Constitution provides that the president shall be elected by an electoral college consisting of (*a*) the elected members of both houses of Parliament and (*b*) the elected members of the legislative assemblies of the states. The election of the president shall be held in accordance with the system of proportional representation by means of single transferable vote and the voting at such election shall be by secret ballot.[2] Thus, it is an indirect election. The indirect election was favoured keeping in view the large size of electorate in a direct election, which will cause a great strain on the administrative machinery.

A direct election was considered meaningless for the election of a nominal head. Our first prime minister, Jawaharlal Nehru, said that a direct election would mean, 'a tremendous waste of energy and time'. The method of proportional representation was adopted to provide the minorities a better voice in the election of the head of the Union.

A presidential candidate has the following qualifications: He should be a citizen of India; be 35 years of age; possess qualifications prescribed for a member of the Lok Sabha; not hold any office of profit under the Government of India or the government of any state.

The term of office of the president is five years[3] and he may resign before the completion of his term. He can be removed from the office by a process of impeachment for violation of the Constitution.[4] This can to be initiated by either house of Parliament. The charges are to be framed in a form of resolution, signed at least by one-fourth of the total number of members of the house. The president has to be given a notice of 14 days in advance. The resolution is to be passed by two-thirds majority of the total members of the house and then it is to be sent to the other house for investigation and decision. If the house after investigation sustains the charge and passes the identical resolution with two-thirds majority of the total membership, the president ceases to hold office from the date such resolution is passed.

Power of the President

The President of India is vested with vast powers, namely, executive, legislative, judicial and emergency.

Executive Powers

He is called the 'President of India' but the Constitution makes him only the executive of the Union, while the governors are the heads of the states. Article 53 says that 'the executive powers of the Union shall be vested in the President and shall be exercised by him either directly or through officers subordinates to him in accordance with the Constitution.' At the same time, the Constitution creates a council of ministers to aid and advise the president, meaning thereby that he alone cannot exercise executive powers. However, after the passage of 42nd Amendment Act, reinforced by the 44th Amendment Act, the advice of the council of ministers is binding on him.

The entire administration of the Government of India is conducted in his name. He has powers to appoint and remove high dignitaries and commissions such as the prime ministers and other ministers, judges of the Supreme Court and high courts, governors, special officers for scheduled castes and tribes, the attorney-general, comptroller and auditor-general, chairman and members of Union Public Service Commission, Finance Commission, inter-state council, among others. He also appoints lieutenant-governors and chief commissioners for the Union Territories. For the removal of judges of the Supreme Court and high court, a special procedure has to be followed. President Shankar Dayal Sharma, while upholding constitutional propriety, forced the Himachal Pradesh Governor, Mrs Sheila Kaul, to resign from her post after a CBI enquiry implicated her in the housing scam case.[5]

He makes rule of business for the central government and allots the portfolios to the ministers. He has the right to keep himself informed of all decisions taken by the council of ministers through the prime minister. As per Article 78, the prime minister shall communicate to the president all administrative decisions and proposals for legislation.

He appoints ambassadors and high commissioners to represent India abroad. He receives the diplomatic representatives of other countries. All treaties and international agreements are negotiated and concluded in the name of the president but subsequently they are ratified by the Parliament. He is the supreme commander of the armed forces of the country, though the exercise of these powers is regulated by law. The president himself cannot raise and organize armed forces. In this sphere, law will take precedence and budget will be needed for army expenditure, which has to be passed by the Parliament. The movement and deployment of army is a technical matter and it will be based on the advice of military generals and staff, and lastly, field operations of the army would be decided by army generals and the executive has nothing to do with it.[6] In fact, in case of war, he takes immediate steps on the advice of his council of ministers, pending a formal declaration of war by the Parliament.

Legislative Powers

The Parliament is composed of the president and the two houses of Parliament.[7] Although he is not a member of Parliament, even then he has vast legislative powers. These powers can be divided into two parts. First are those powers that deal with the constitution of Parliament and its functions. Second are those that deal with actual law making.

The president has the right to nominate 12 members of the Rajya Sabha from among persons having special knowledge of literature, science, arts and social sciences.[8] He is empowered to nominate two Anglo-Indians to the Lok Sabha if no Anglo-Indian is elected to the house.

The president shall, from time to time, summon each house of Parliament to meet at such time and place as he thinks fit, but six months shall not intervene between its last sitting in one session and the date appointed for its first sitting in the next session and may, from time to time, prorogue the houses or either house, dissolve the house of the people.[9] Former President Sanjeeva Reddy dissolved the Lok Sabha on 22 August 1979[10] on the advice of the Prime Minister Charan Singh. Again on the advice of the former prime minister, Chandra Shekhar, the then President R. Venkatraman dissolved the Lok Sabha in 1991. He may address either house of Parliament or both the houses jointly and may send messages to either house of Parliament, and the matter required by the message shall be taken into consideration.

In the actual field of law making, all money Bills and a few other Bills such as that concerning the formation of new states or changing the boundaries of the states involving expenditure from the consolidated fund of India, imposing restriction of freedom of trade or commerce within the states require the prior permission of the president before they are introduced in Parliament. All other Bills passed by Parliament must get the president's assent[11] before they become law. The president also has the right to promulgate ordinances. In the context, it is notable that the president has the power to return a Bill for reconsideration by Parliament.[12] President Zail Singh did not give his assent to the Indian Post Office Amendment Bill and, subsequently, President R. Venkatraman also returned it back without his assent. For constitutional propriety President Dr Shankar Dayal Sharma declined to give assent to two ordinances, one of them seeking to create reservation for the Christian Dalits and the other attempting to shorten the duration of the poll process on the grounds that it was constitutionally improper on the eve of election.[13]

The president is empowered to promulgate ordinances when the Parliament is not in session to meet emergency situations. Thus, it is an emergency power to strengthen the hands of the executive. For example, on 7 January 1993, the president promulgated an ordinance for the acquisition of 69.703 acres of land in and around Ram Janam Bhoomi/Babri Masjid complex at Ayodhya.[14] Through this ordinance the central government took the possession, transfer of the right title and interest in relation to this area with immediate effect. The ordinance ceases to operate after six weeks of the session of the Parliament, meaning thereby that either Parliament should pass it to make it law or it would lapse after six weeks' time. This power of the president has been criticized on the basis that it is a serious limitation on democratic principles and should, therefore, need close examination.[15]

The conceptual aspect of 'ordinance' is that it facilitates good governance. The question arises whether any responsibility has been placed on the executive for the good governance of the country. Why should emergency legislation be required in our country while it is not required in other countries? To what extent is it likely to be misused in India?

The answer of the first question is plainly no; insofar as the second question is concerned there are reasons for emergency legislations such as those due to scientific and technological developments. Governance has become complex day by day and the executive should adapt quickly to changing conditions. Sometimes quick legislations are required to deal and effectively control anti-social elements. At other times, laws are declared *ultra vires* due to judicial reviews, therefore, quick steps are required for remedial purposes. The third question is whether it is liable to be misused? For the proper answer we have to see who uses this power—the president or the ministry. The ordinances are ratified most of the time by the legislature, therefore, it is clear that ministers cannot abuse this power. This can be misused in two ways. First, when the president wants to rule the country with a hand-picked ministry that did not enjoy the confidence of the Lok Sabha, and second, when the president wants to bypass the ministry as well as the legislature.

Article 123 facilitates the abuse of ordinance power: First, the president alone is to be 'satisfied' with the issuance of the ordinance. Second, no time limit is fixed for the duration of the ordinance; it can be re-issued and that too with retrospective effect. The only check is the 'session' of the Parliament, which can be called by the president in such a manner that both houses meet at different times so that the president could issue ordinances to rule the country. To rule the country, money is essential. Can the president raise and spend money by an ordinance? The answer is 'yes'. Our Constitution has put no bar on him. Lastly, can the president amend the Constitution by ordinance? There is no bar on it but this question will finally be decided by the Supreme Court.[16]

Financial Powers

The president has substantial financial powers. No money Bill can be introduced in the Parliament except on the recommendations of the president. He shall cause a statement of the estimated receipts and expenditure of the Government of India for the financial year to be laid before the Parliament. The contingency fund is at his disposal, and he alone can make advances out of it to meet unforeseen expenditures pending their authorization by Parliament. He appoints the Finance Commission and on its recommendation allocates to the states their share in the income tax proceeds. This includes distribution of export duty on jute to the concerned states.

Judicial Powers

Article 72 confers upon the president some powers of a judicial nature. He has the power to grant pardons, reprieves, respites or remissions of punishment, or to suspend, remit or commute the sentence of any person convicted of any offence in all cases where the punishment or sentence is by court martial and in other cases where the sentence is one of death or where the offence is committed against a law relating to a matter under the executive power of the Union. Moreover, the president is not answerable to any court of law. The terminology used here is explained as follows: (*a*) A 'pardon' rescinds both the sentence and conviction and absolves the offender from all punishments and disqualifications; (*b*) 'commutation' substitutes one form of punishment for another of a lighter nature, for example a death sentence may be commutated to rigorous imprisonment, rigorous to simple imprisonment, and so on; (*c*) 'remission' means reduction in the quantum of sentence without changing its character, namely, sentence of one year's imprisonment may be remitted to six months; (*d*) 'respite' means giving a lesser sentence instead of the prescribed one in view of some special facts such as pregnancy of a woman offender; (*e*) 'reprieve' means stay of execution of a sentence pending a petition or a proceeding for pardon or commutation.

Emergency Powers

President of India has been vested with extensive emergency powers to deal with abnormal conditions. The Constitution mentions three types of emergency:

(i) Emergency due to war or external aggression or internal disturbance or threat thereof (Article 352)

(ii) Emergency resulting from failure of the constitutional machinery in the states (Article 356)

(iii) Financial emergency (Article 360)

The president may proclaim an emergency if he is satisfied that a grave threat exists due to which the security of India or any part of it is threatened or is likely to be threatened by external aggression or internal disturbances. Such a proclamation may be made before the actual occurrence of war or external aggression or internal disturbance and may be revoked by a subsequent proclamation. This has to be laid before both houses of Parliament and shall cease to operate at the end of two months unless it has not been approved by both houses. If the proclamation is issued when the Lok Sabha has been dissolved or if it was dissolved within a period of two months and the Rajya Sabha gives its approval, then the proclamation is to be approved by the newly elected Lok Sabha within thirty days of its first sitting; otherwise, it will cease to operate. Under this clause the president declared emergency in 1962 and again in 1971 when China and Pakistan, respectively, attacked India. In 1965, when Pakistan attacked India, a fresh proclamation was not issued by the president because emergency proclamation issued in 1962 was still continuing. Likewise internal emergency was declared on 25 June 1975 in the name of grave danger to internal security. The 42nd Amendment of the Constitution (1976) empowers the president to make a proclamation in respect of the whole of India or a part of its territory as may be specified in the proclamation. The 44th Constitutional Amendment (1978) provides that the president shall not issue a proclamation unless the decision of the Union cabinet to this effect is communicated to him in writing.[17] The declaration of internal emergency without the approval of Parliament can remain in force for one month and the approval by Parliament will require absolute majority in both the houses and two-thirds majority of the members present and voting.

Consequence of the Proclamation

First as a result of emergency under these provisions the state's autonomy would be suspended and Parliament vested with unlimited powers to make laws for the whole or any part of India on the subjects of state list. The Union government can give directions to the states in the exercise of its power. The president can alter the provisions relating to distribution of revenue between the states and the Union. Second, the fundamental freedom guaranteed by Article 19 of the Constitution would be suspended in the whole country even if the emergency is declared in a part of the country or a state in the country. Third, the tenure of Lok Sabha and of legislative assemblies can be extended by Parliament for a period of one year at a time.

Emergency under Article 356 can be proclaimed if the president is satisfied with the report of a governor or otherwise on his own initiative that a situation has arisen in which the state government cannot carry on in accordance with the provisions of the Constitution. Such proclamation needs ratification by the Parliament within two months, otherwise after two months another proclamation is issued for six months that can further be extended for six months. Article 356 had been invoked more than a hundred times after 1950.

Consequences:

(i) The president can assume to himself all or any of the functions of the concerned state government and the power of the governor or any other authority in the state except the state legislature.

(ii) The powers of the state legislature shall be exercised by or under Parliament's authorization.

(iii) He may make such provisions that he thinks necessary or desirable for achieving the object of the proclamation.

(iv) The president may assume to himself any of the powers of the state government except the powers vested in a high court.

(v) He can authorize any expenditure from the consolidated fund of the state when the Lok Sabha is not in session.

Such a proclamation was first issued on 20 June 1951 in Punjab when no government could be formed after the fall of the Gopi Chand Bhargava ministry. In the beginning there were not many instances of its use but only after 1967 when the opposition parties came into power in the states and the Congress ruled at the centre. The non-Congress governments thrice at the centre also followed the Congress party in imposing president's rule on Congress-ruled states. It is alleged that this emergency power has been often abused and democracy has been throttled. The Janata Party government at the centre in 1977 imposed president's rule on 30 April 1977 on nine Congress-ruled states of Punjab, Haryana, Himachal Pradesh, Uttar Pradesh, Bihar, Rajasthan, Madhya Pradesh, Orissa and West Bengal while on 18 February 1980, non-Congress governments in nine states were dismissed by the Congress governments. It was also imposed due to demolition of Babri Masjid in Uttar Pradesh on 6 December 1992 as well as in Himachal Pradesh, Madhya Pradesh and Rajasthan on 15 December 1992. Imposition of president's rule has been described as a politically motivated step.[18] It has been alleged that president's rule was used to dislodge state governments run by parties or coalitions other than the party in power at the centre.

Financial Emergency

Article 360 deals with financial emergency. It says that if the president is satisfied that a situation has arisen whereby the financial stability or credit of India or any part of the territory thereof is threatened, he may, by a proclamation, make a declaration to that effect. Such a proclamation also will cease to operate at the end of two months unless before the end of such a period it has been approved by both the houses of Parliament.

The consequences of financial emergency would strengthen the hands of the Union executive. First, the president can issue directions for reduction of salaries and allowances of all Union and state officers including that of judges. Second, the Union executive may require all money Bills or other financial Bills after they are passed by the state legislatures to be reserved for the president's assent. Third, the president may take other measures to restore financial stability as he deems necessary and adequate. The language of Article 360 is ambiguous and not clear whether such an emergency will apply to the entire country or to some parts of the country.

Finance deserves very careful handling and any hasty measure may create economic instability and financial insecurity resulting in confusion and chaos. K. V. Rao apprehends that 'far from restoring confidence the declaration itself might lower our credit, create a panic and thus itself might bring about a financial instability. What is required in a grave economic crisis is expert analysis, cool thinking and a workable plan but not a panicky declaration'.[19]

Criticism of Emergency Powers

Regarding the emergency provisions H. V. Kamath and K. T. Shah thought that it was giving too much power to the chief executive. Kamath said 'that by this single chapter we are seeking to lay the foundation of a totalitarian state, a police state . . . a state where if there be peace, it will be peace of the grave and the void of the desert'. K. T. Shah observed that 'looking at all the provisions, it seems to me the name only of liberty or democracy will remain under the constitution'. Finally, Dr B. R. Ambedkar admitted that the provisions were liable to be misused and there was no check against abuse, but hoped that they would never be invoked.[20] The major criticisms of the emergency provisions are:

First the federal character of the Constitution will be throttled. The emergency under Article 352 permits the centre to control all matters including those in the state list. Second, emergency provisions are incompatible with the spirit of democracy. These powers may be used at any time to destroy the democratic fabric of the Constitution, i.e. declaration of internal emergency in June 1975, which derailed our democratic structure built by Nehru and Patel. Third, the fundamental rights are suspended during the emergency and courts are debarred from looking into the cases of restoration of these rights. Thus emergency makes fundamental rights meaningless. Fourth, the autonomy of states will be eroded during the period of emergency of any three types.

The justification of emergency provisions lies in the past history of India. Whenever the central authority weakened outsiders ruled the country. Therefore, the problem before the Constitution makers was not only to give a democratic constitution but to also provide a solid foundation of national unity and integrity. These emergency provisions were expected to be used in such actual situations. However, these powers can be misused to meet the political ends of the party in power. This can be checked by strong public opinion and democratic forces, which are essential for the success of any democracy.

Position of the President

The president enjoys vast powers as discussed above. However, in a parliamentary form of government the head of the state is a mere figurehead or a sort of constitutional ruler. But during the political crisis arising from the Congress party's withdrawal of support to United Front government led by H. D. Deve Gowda, the president's house, his moves and decisions became a matter of unusual public attention and interest. The prime minister, some senior cabinet ministers, top political leaders of almost all political parties made a beeline to the Rashtrapati Bhawan and tried to influence the president. This clearly revealed the importance of the president's role at the time of a constitutional or political crisis. Therefore, his role needs careful analysis.

The constitutional experts are divided into three groups on the issue of the position and actual powers of the President of India. The first group, comprising Austin C. H. Alexandrowics and M. C. Setalvad, hold the view that the president is a mere constitutional head similar to the English king or queen, while the second group holds the view that the president is not a figurehead. Alan Gledhill pointed that, 'without violating the Constitution, the president can establish an authoritarian government' and K. M. Munshi maintained that some of the president's powers were 'super ministerial'. More or less, Justice P. B. Mukherjee took a similar position in his Setalvad Memorial Lectures in 1966. He said that the president was 'an independent institution with independent authority and independent functions'. Prof. K. V. Rao thinks that the president is a 'constitutional autocrat'.[21] The third group took a middle position, as K. Santhanam and A. Appadorai argued that the president was a constitutional head of the state and acted ordinarily on the advice of the ministers and had unspecified 'reserve' powers as guardian of the Constitution to be used by him in his discretion. In view of the above it is pertinent to know the views of the makers of the Constitution.

The Constituent Assembly debates are the primary sources to know the view of Constitution framers about the position of Indian president. The makers think that he is only a 'constitutional king'. Dr Ambedkar said, 'the title of the functionary reminds one the president of the United States. But beyond identity of names there is nothing in common between the form of government prevalent in America and the form of government proposed under the draft constitution. Under the presidential system of America, the president is the head of the executive. Under the draft constitution, the president occupies the same position as the king under the English constitution.' Similar were the views of Jawaharlal Nehru, Aladi and others and they all hoped that our president will work like the English king as a nominal head of state. Nehru told the Constituent Assembly that 'we want to emphasise the ministerial character of the government' and 'that power really resides in the ministry and in the legislature and not in the president as such . . . we did not give him any real power, but we have made his position one of authority and dignity.'[22]

The Supreme Court and the President

The Supreme Court accepted the position of the president in normal circumstances. But in its landmark decision in *Shamsher Singh v. Punjab* the Court held that 'the President in India is not at all a glorified cipher. He represents the majority of the state, is at the apex, though only symbolically, and has rapport with the people and parties, being above politics. His vigilant presence makes for good government if only he uses what Badehot described as 'the right to be consulted, to warn and encourage'. In short, the president, like the king, has not merely been constitutionally romanticized, but in actuality vested with a pervasive and persuasive role.[23]

Dr Ambedkar opined that this phrase (to aid and advise) makes it obligatory on the part of the president not only to take advice on all matters, but also to act accordingly, except of course in the case of what he called the 'prerogatives'.[24] Thus, Dr Ambedkar himself conceded that the president could exercise 'prerogative functions' without the advice of the ministers.

Steps to Curb President's Power—Amendment of Article 74

The 42nd Amendment of the Constitution amended Article 74(i) in 1976, which reads as 'there shall be a council of ministers with the Prime Minister at the head to aid and advise the President who shall, in the exercise of his functions, act in accordance with such advice'. The Janata Party government through the 44th Amendment Act changed the 1976 provision and now it reads as:

> There shall be a council of ministers with the Prime Minister at the head to aid and advise the President who shall, in the exercise of his functions, act in accordance with such advice. Provided that the President may require the council of ministers to reconsider such advice, either generally or otherwise, and the President shall act in accordance with the advice tendered after such reconsideration.

For the first time, the President R. K. Narayanan asked the Union cabinet to reconsider its decision to impose president's rule in Uttar Pradesh on 23 October 1997 and the cabinet 'decided not to take further action' in the matter. Thus, president's rule could not be imposed in Uttar Pradesh according to the *Hindustan Times* of 23 October 1997.

In view of these amendments the position is that the president has to work according to the advice of the council of ministers.

Working of the Constitution

In the federal system powers are distributed amongst the three branches of the government on the one hand and the centre and states on the other. Each constituent naturally works under certain constraints.

But it is only logical that the council of ministers remains the de facto executive because it is fully accountable to the legislature, especially to the house of the people, which directly represents the electorate. The same thing cannot be said about the president due to his indirect election by the legislators. Jawaharlal Nehru, the first prime minister of India, made the position clear by emphasizing that the responsibility for any policy was entirely that of the government.

The working of the Presidency since 1950 shows that generally the president acts on the advice of his council of ministers but there are occasions when he has raised his voice. Our first president, Dr Rajendra Prasad in 1951 asserted his opposition to the proposed Hindu Code Bill. He ignored Prime Minister Jawaharlal Nehru's advice on his visit to the Somnath Temple and to the funeral of Sardar Patel. Further, in November 1960 in a speech at the law institute in the presence of Prime Minister Jawaharlal Nehru, he called for a detailed study of president–prime minister relationship saying that our president is elected by an electoral college while the British Crown is hereditary. Nehru was so annoyed with this speech that he advised the chairman of the law institute chief justice B. P. Sinha not to circulate the speech. Dr Rajendra Prasad was twice the President of India. He was also president of the Constituent Assembly and fully aware about his commitment to the Constitution. Hence, his view that the president was no more than a 'rubber stamp' or a passive spectator of the political goings-on should not be dismissed lightly. Both Prasad and Nehru were men of stature and they imbued democratic values; therefore, in the starting years of our democracy Prasad did not air his differences publicly.

Dr Radhakrishnan who succeeded Dr Prasad was a man of stature having an academic background and Indira Gandhi had to show due respect to him. Dr Zakir Husain, V. V. Giri, Fakhruddin Ali Ahmad and Giani Zail Singh were the personal choice of Mrs Gandhi hence they were called the prime minister's presidents. Dr Zakir Husain was a learned and cultured man who did not have to deal with thorny issues. V. V. Giri although was Indira Gandhi's choice but she considered one term as enough for him. Fakhruddin Ali Ahmad proved to be a weak president but his successor Neelam Sanjiva Reddy was not and he did indulge in politics. He 'cautioned' Prime Minister Morarji Desai on the appointment of V. Shankar as principal secretary. Further, he vetoed the outgoing Prime Minister Morarji Desai's proposal for a broadcast to the nation after his resignation from the post. He also warned the caretaker Charan Singh government not to take any major policy decisions.

When Giani Zail Singh was the president and Rajiv Gandhi was the prime minister, President Zail Singh took presidential powers to the farthest length and literally gave Rajiv Gandhi nightmares.[25] The prime minister started ignoring the president. He would not inform the president about matters that the Constitution required him to tell the president. He did not brief the president when he returned from his foreign trip. Giani Zail Singh decided to teach Rajiv Gandhi a lesson. He said, 'it was purely a dispute between a Prime Minister and a President and I wanted to prove it to the world that the chair of the President was higher than that of the Prime Minister'.[26] He withheld his assent to the Postal Bill and spoke of the president's right to dismiss his ministers but declared that he would not do it for dignity and propriety in the national interest.

R. Venkataraman, who succeeded Zail Singh as president and assumed office on 25 July 1987, faced difficult political situations of minority governments at the centre. He advised on his own prime ministers, V. P. Singh and Chandra Shekhar, to prove their majority in the Lok Sabha. He told V. P. Singh to hold his hand on policy matters following the withdrawal of BJP support to the government. He tried to rein in the Chandra Shekhar government when it functioned as a caretaker and did only what was his plain constitutional duty. But by and large he maintained constitutional propriety and worked smoothly with all the four prime ministers, i.e. Rajiv Gandhi, V. P. Singh, Chandra Shekhar and P. V. Narasimha Rao.

The relations between Dr Shankar Dayal Sharma and former Prime Minister Narasimha Rao were cordial except that at the end of the prime ministers term the president declined to give assent to two ordinances, one seeking for reservation for the Christian Dalits and the other to shorten the duration of the poll process on the ground that these were constitutionally improper on the eve of elections and asking for the resignation of Himachal Pradesh governor, Mrs Sheila Kaul, against the desire of the prime minister. After the 1996 poll no party secured majority in the Parliament, therefore, Dr Sharma invited BJP leader, Atal Bihari Vajpayee to form the government on the basis of past precedents relevant in the situation of being the single largest party and asked to prove its majority within 15 days, which Vajpayee failed to prove. Then he invited the United Front leader (a combination of 13 parties), H. D. Deve Gowda to form the government with the outside support of the Congress. He proved his majority and remained prime minister for 10 months and 10 days only because the Congress party withdrew its support and he lost the confidence vote in the house on 11 April 1997. Again Dr Shankar Dayal Sharma did not dissolve the Lok Sabha using his constitutional prerogative and gave opportunity to United Front leader Inder Kumar Gujral to form the government with the outside support of the Congress party. He took oath of office along with his council of ministers on 21 April 1997 and proved his majority within 24 hours on 22 April 1997. Thus, Dr Sharma's role saved the country from huge expenditure of mid-term poll.

On 25 July 1997 K. R. Narayanan became president and at that time United Front or the 'kind force' was in power with the outside support of the Congress. President Narayanan was a man of fair nature dedicated to his duties and took independent and impartial decisions in times of need. He did not accept the advice of the council of ministers to impose president's rule in Uttar Pradesh on 21 October 1997 and asked for its reconsideration. The next day the council of ministers decided that 'proceeding under Article 356 need not be undertaken'.

Although in 1998 the NDA emerged as the largest pre-poll alliance, but K. R. Narayanan took the precaution of asking whether Atal Bihari Vajpayee was 'able and willing' to form a 'stable government, which could secure the confidence of the house', forcing him to take responsibility for providing a stable government. Vajpayee had submitted documents in support of his claim and after satisfaction President Narayanan appointed Atal Bihari Vajpayee as prime minister on 15 March 1998. In September 1988, President Narayanan again returned a Union cabinet resolution seeking imposition of president's rule in Bihar and the suspension of the assembly for reconsideration. The government respected the president's views and on reconsideration did not press for imposition of president's rule.

A. P. J. Abdul Kalam became the president on 25 July 2002 as a consensus candidate from among different political parties. Kalam being a non-political man, questions were raised about what sort of president he would make. Kalam proved to be a president with difference. Kalam appointed a person of his choice rather than that suggested by government in the president's secretariat. On 22 August 2002, the president had returned the ordinance to amend the Representation of the People Act to the Union Cabinet, seeking some of the clarifications on the controversial provisions in the proposed ordinance. He conveyed the message to the political wing of the government that he would not be taken for granted. President Kalam also returned the office of Profit Bill to Parliament on 20 May 2006 for reconsideration. The Bill was meant to save several MPs from being disqualified. But when it was passed again by the Parliament without any amendment, he gave his assent on 21 June 2006 but only after he had extracted an assurance of review by a committee. He had no such right or power. The president is bound to give assent to a returned Bill re-enacted by Parliament without ado or demur.[27] Thus, Abdul Kalam, even without political background, became the people's president.

Pratibha Patil became the first woman president on 25 July 2007 with the support of some opposition parties such as the Left and the right-wing Shiv Sena. She has not shown a proactive role and is known as the establishment president.

CONCLUSIONS

The intention of the founding fathers of the Constitution as discussed in the Constituent Assembly debates and the analysis of the functioning of various presidents have revealed that prior to the passage of the 42nd and 44th Amendments the president could afford to be assertive. Both these amendments made the advice binding. But as per our Constitution, the president is one of the components of Parliament. As such all Bills passed by Parliament must get his assent and he has power to return a Bill for reconsideration by Parliament with 'such amendments as he may recommend'. Even in the executive realm, the president has (vide the 44th Amendment), the power to request the reconsideration of a decision of the council of ministers 'either generally or otherwise'. Thus, in respect of both these provisions of the Constitution, the president should clearly be acting independently or on his own and the president's liability to act according to the cabinet's advice is not total. And as such he has a 'supervisory veto' over the vast field of parliamentary legislation and executive (cabinet) decisions. A wilful president who is bent upon harassing the government may use the reconsideration provision to delay a large number of Bills and executive decisions communicated to him. All this is as per the constitutional provisions.

Some Basic Issues

However, there are certain areas in which the president has a good deal of discretion. These are appointment of the prime minister, dissolution of the Lok Sabha, dismissal of a government which has lost its majority in the house and refuses to quit office, and permission to prosecute a prime minister on charges of corruption against him, which is a recent phenomenon. The appointment of the prime minister is done especially when no party gets a clear majority after polls and the Parliament is hung. Such a situation occurred in 1979, when Prime Minister Morarji Desai resigned following a split in the Janata Party. President N. Sanjiva Reddy invited Charan Singh to form the first coalition government at the centre. Further, the president asked Charan Singh to seek a vote of confidence in the Lok Sabha within three weeks, because the government (coalition) was dependent on outside support from Indira Gandhi's Congress group, 'in the interest of establishing healthy conventions.' When Indira Gandhi withdrew support Charan Singh resigned immediately. The president dissolved the house setting aside claims from the new Janata Party leader, Jagjivan Ram. The president's office exercised this discretionary power for the first time in 30 years of Independence. But this became routine in the coalition era in 1989 and 1996 when the president used his discretion in the appointment of prime minister to form a stable government. No clear procedure and guidelines are available to deal with such situation; therefore, the president takes his own judgement to appoint the prime minister.

Another situation arises when an incumbent prime minister dies and a successor has to be chosen to take his/her place. On the first two occasions, after the death of Jawaharlal Nehru in 1964 and in 1966 at the time of Shastri's death an interim arrangement was made and the seniormost cabinet minister was appointed as prime minister. The permanent arrangement was later made by consensus and elections. But at the time of Indira Gandhi's death in 1984 President Zail Singh appointed Rajiv Gandhi as the prime minister even though he was not a minister at that time.

Dissolution of Lok Sabha

If a minority government loses control of the Lok Sabha after initial success of proving majority, a complicated situation might arise if the outgoing government recommends dissolution of the Lok Sabha

If a government that had the majority recommended dissolution, it cannot be ignored by the president, but in the case of a government that does not have such majority the president can exercise his discretion and judgement. With the prospects of a hung Parliament, this issue is extremely important. If the cabinet of a minority government recommends the dissolution of the Lok Sabha along with resignation by its prime minister, the president could without dissolving the house appoint some one else on some logical criterion, for instance, stability of the government. On two previous such occasions, the president dissolved the Lok Sabha, once when the Congress party of Indira Gandhi withdrew its support to the government of Chaudhary Charan Singh and Prime Minister Charan Singh's cabinet recommended dissolution of the house and again when the Congress party withdrew its support to the Chandra Shekhar government and his cabinet recommended the dissolution of the house. The president accepted the cabinet's advice because on both the occasions, it was felt that a stable alternative government could not be formed.

Dismissal of a Government

The president has to dismiss a government that has lost its majority in the house and refuses to quit office. His action in such situation is justifiable but he cannot dismiss a government that commands majority in the Parliament.

Charges of Corruption

Another important question that was raised recently was about serious allegations of corruption against the prime minister. Some persons in the name of public interest sought the permission of the president to prosecute the prime minister on charges of corruption. There is a provision in the IPC/CrPC that no public servant can be prosecuted without the sanction of the government. Generally, the sanction in such cases is accorded by the president on the advice of the council of ministers headed by the prime minister. The question here is who is to accord sanction for prosecution against the prime minister. Obviously, it is hoped the president has to perform this function from his own judgement. But this question still remains unanswered from the president's side. In such cases, the president may not accept the council of ministers' advice in order to avoid 'peril to democracy' that is the guiding principle in such matters. Ultimately it is the president's duty to 'preserve, protect and defend the Constitution' and in that he is bound by none other than his conscience. At the time of assumption of office the president takes an oath to protect and defend the Constitution. There may be some situations when the president has to think very seriously. Suppose he finds that the council of ministers headed by the prime minister is not acting according to the Constitution and indulging in large-scale corruption and scams such as urea scam, JMM bribery case, housing scam, *hawala* scam and animal husbandry fodder scam. What is he to do then? Some people say in such cases the president should take the nation into confidence and resign, the system must go on and people will know why the president resigned and will deal with their government to sort out things at their end at the time of the elections.

Further, Article 78 enjoins upon the prime minister the duty of keeping the president informed of all decisions of the council of ministers relating to the administration and proposals to administration. If a prime minister fails in this constitutional obligation, the president could certainly take the necessary steps to correct the situation.

It has to be admitted that the president is the symbol of the nation and enjoys considerable authority. However, the president is expected to act according to the advice of the council of ministers to strengthen the roots of democracy in India.

Vice-President

Article 63 of the Constitution provides for a vice-president. He is elected by an electoral college comprising the members of both the houses of Parliament at a joint session by secret ballot in accordance with the principle of proportional representation by means of single transferable vote. The necessary qualifications for the office of vice-president are: (i) He should be a citizen of India; (ii) he must be of 35 years of age; (iii) he should qualify for election as a member of the council of states; (iv) he should not be a member of Parliament or a state legislature; (v) he must not hold any office of profit under the Union or state government or local authority.

The vice-president holds the office for five years, but he may resign before the expiry of his term. The letter of resignation is to be addressed to the president. He is eligible to get re-elected to the same office. He is removable from his office by a resolution of the Rajya Sabha passed by a majority of all the members of Rajya Sabha and agreed to by the Lok Sabha. According to Article 67(b), he is to be served 14 days' notice before a notice of removal is served on him.

Functions

The vice-president acts as an ex-officio chairman of the Rajya Sabha and presides over its meetings. He enjoys the right of casting votes. He acts as the president in the event of the occurrence of any vacancy in the office of the president by reason of death, resignation or removal, or when the president is unable to perform his functions owing to absence, illness or any other cause, the vice-president shall discharge his functions until the date on which the president resumes his duties (Article 65 [i] and [ii]. The vice-president, while discharging his functions in the capacity of president, enjoys all powers, immunities and is entitled to receive such emoluments, allowances and privileges as are admissible to the president. The election of the president must take place within six months of the occurrence of the vacancy. Thus, the vice-president can act as the president for a period of six months only. In most cases, this office has been a stepping stone to the Presidency. For example, Dr Radhakrishnan, Dr Zakir Hussain, V. V. Giri, and Dr Shankar Dayal Sharma, were vice-presidents and subsequently became presidents. Bhairon Singh Shekawat was also vice-president but failed to become the president, though he fought elections. At present, Mohammad Hamid Ansari is our vice-president.

NOTES

1. K. V. Rao, *Parliamentary Democracy of India*, 2nd edition (Calcutta: World Press, 1965), p. 28.
2. Article 55, Constitution of India.
3. Article 65(1), Constitution of India.
4. Article 61, Constitution of India.
5. *Hindustan Times*, New Delhi, 21 April 1996.
6. K. V. Rao, *Parliamentary Democracy of India*, 2nd edition (Calcutta: World Press, 1965), p. 61.
7. Article 79, Constitution of India.
8. Article 80(3), Constitution of India.
9. Article 85, Constitution of India.
10. *Hindustan Times*, New Delhi, 23 August 1979.
11. Article 111, Constitution of India.
12. The president, Zail Singh, returned the India Post Office Amendment Bill without giving assent that among other things authorizes the government to intercept mailed articles. While doing so he offered his own suggestions. *The Times of India*, New Delhi, 16 January 1987.

13. S. Sahay, *Hindustan Times*, New Delhi, 26 April 1997.
14. *Hindustan Times*, New Delhi, 8 January 1993.
15. See for justification, Ambedkar's statement in the *Constituent Assembly Debates*, Vol. VIII, p. 213.
16. See for details, K. V. Rao, op. cit., p. 57.
17. Article 352(1), Constitution of India.
18. *Hindustan Times*, New Delhi, 16 December 1992.
19. K. V. Rao, *Parliamentary Democracy of India*, 2nd edition (Calcutta: World Press, 1965), p. 295.
20. *Constituent Assembly Debates*, Vol. IX, p. 177.
21. K. V. Rao, op. cit., p. 62.
22. *Constituent Assembly Debates*, Vol. IV, p. 734.
23. *All India Reporter*, 1974, S.C., p. 2224.
24. *Constituent Assembly Debates*, Vol. VII, p. 974.
25. S. Sahay, *Hindustan Times*, New Delhi, 23 March 1992.
26. *Hindustan Times*, New Delhi, 5 November 1992.
27. A. G. Noorani, *Hindustan Times*, New Delhi, 14 August 2007.

5

The Prime Minister

The prime minister is the head of the council of ministers. Article 74 creates the office of the prime minister as head of the council. It means the cabinet has its own head and that head is not the president but the prime minister. Thus, in India, constitutional recognition has been given to the office of the prime minister. As K. V. Rao says:

> The clear recognition of the Prime Minister's office has many advantages, 'It recognises his leadership, thus paving the way for homogeneity of the cabinet and its collective responsibility. It places the responsibility of choosing the other ministers on him, thus not only making the task of the President easy but also preventing the President ordinarily from dealing with 'each minister separately and singly', as Dr B. R. Ambedkar claimed, and above all, preventing the 'king's friends from being thrust into the cabinet'[1]....
>
> But K. T. Shah feared that 'the power which this Constitution as a Constitution seeks to confer upon the Prime Minister makes it inevitable that a degree of power will concentrate in his hands which may very likely militate against the working of an actual responsible and democratic government.'[2]

The Prime Minister

The office of the prime minister has become very important. The prime minister is the heart of the cabinet and actual executive of the country. The office has become so powerful that scholars and writers in recent years have started saying that India has neither a parliament nor a cabinet but a prime ministerial system of government. In order to examine the correctness of such an assertion, it would be pertinent to discuss the method of his appointment, the sources and the instruments of his powers and authority.

Appointment of the Prime Minister

The prime minister is appointed by the president and the other ministers shall be appointed by the president on the advice of the prime minister.[3] The question arises, how does the president appoint the prime minister?

Can he exercise any discretion in this matter? The question is ticklish and cannot be answered by a simple 'yes' or 'no'. It will depend upon the political situation and strength of various parties in the Lok Sabha. Ordinarily, the president appoints the prime minister as the leader of the majority party in the Lok Sabha after elections or whenever there is a mid-term vacancy in the office.

The president can exercise some discretion in the selection of the prime minister when no party commands a clear majority in the Lok Sabha. In such a situation, the president may request the single largest party to form the government or alternatively, he may allow a coalition to be formed. Such a situation developed after the elections in 1989 when no party got a clear majority in the Lok Sabha, the Congress party was the single largest party and the president invited the Congress to form the government but its parliamentary party leader, Rajiv Gandhi, declined the offer. The president then invited V. P. Singh to form the government, who commanded majority support in the Lok Sabha, with the outside support of Left parties and the BJP. Again when V. P. Singh's government was defeated in the no-confidence motion after 11 months due to withdrawal of support by the BJP, the president in turn asked the Congress and the BJP to form the government. On their decline, he invited Chandra Shekhar who claimed majority support, in the Lok Sabha with the support of Congress party but after only four months Chandra Shekhar resigned. The Lok Sabha was dissolved and fresh elections were held in 1991. In this election, also, no party got majority and Congress emerged as the single largest party. Therefore, its leader P. V. Narasimha Rao was invited to form the government and he completed full five years in the office using questionable methods to prove his majority in the house. In 1996, general elections were held and no party got majority. The president, Dr Shankar Dayal Sharma, invited the leader of the BJP, the single largest party, Atal Behari Vajpayee in the Lok Sabha to form the government, which lasted only for 13 days. He could not muster majority support in the Lok Sabha and resigned, but left a big question as to how to pass the presidential address to the Parliament, which was prepared by the BJP cabinet. After his resignation, the president invited the United Front leader, H. D. Deve Gowda to form the government who proved his majority in the house with the outside support of the CPM and the Congress party. After ten months, the Congress withdrew its support to Deve Gowda government and he was voted out in the house on 11 April 1997 and resigned. But again, after the change in UF leadership, Congress extended its support to UF government and its new leader, I. K. Gujral. He was sworn in as prime minister along with his council of ministers on 21 April 1997. The BJP alleged that the president should not have invited the United Front to form its government again on the ground that the UF was voted out in the house.

Our Constitution is silent about the appointment of the prime minister in such situations and experts differ on how the president should arrive at his decision. They say there are two options before the president. One is that he should invite the leader of the single largest party in the house to form the government. If he fails or declines the offer, then the leader of the next largest party and so on should be asked to form a government. The second option is that he should invite the largest group of political parties, which, in his opinion, can provide a stable government. Another course open to him is that he should send a message to the Lok Sabha under Article 86(2) of the Constitution to elect its leader. However, after the anti-defection law, its relevance is limited because parties will issue a 'whip' and members will vote according to party position in the house so as to retain their membership.

The president should invite that person who appears best able to command the support of a stable majority in the Lok Sabha. If there is no hope for any stable government then only the president in his discretion should ask country to go to the polls to select a leader who can provide a stable government.

In a situation when the majority party in the Lok Sabha is a house divided and faction-ridden, the president if he so decides can influence the appointment of the prime minister by inviting one faction leader as the prime minister who can later manage the majority in the party by offering ministerial berths.[4]

There were such occasions as when in 1964, the then president, Dr Radhakrishnan, decided to be neutral and appointed a caretaker prime minister. But in 1984, after the death of Indira Gandhi, our charismatic prime minister, the then President Giani Zail Singh appointed Rajiv Gandhi as the prime minister, without his election as the Congress legislature party leader. This was exactly what happened in England in 1923, 1957, 1963 and 1970 when Stanley Baldwin, Harold Macmillan, Sir Alec Douglas-Home, who was the Earl of Home, and Edward Heath, respectively, were appointed as prime ministers.

The prime minister has a number of functions to perform. He is the political chief executive, the administrative head, the leader of the Lok Sabha and the main dominating figure in the ruling party. The functions of the prime minister can be grouped under two categories: (i) political functions, (ii) administrative and executive functions.

The political functions of the prime minister can be divided into the following heads:

(a) Prime minister as the head of the council of ministers.
(b) Prime minister and the Parliament.
(c) Prime minister and his party.
(d) Prime minister and the people.
(e) Link between the president and the cabinet.
(f) Spokesman of the government on foreign policy.
(g) Prime minister and intelligence agencies.

The Prime Minister as the Head of the Council of Ministers

Constitutionally, the prime minister is the head of the council of ministers and in this capacity he constitutes, reconstitutes or reshuffles the ministry and allocates portfolios to other ministers. These are the prerogatives of the prime minister and almost all prime ministers exercise them in their discretion, except a coalition government prime minister like I. K. Gujral who had to retain all the ministers of his predecessor's government except one, because all the parties in the coalition wanted the previous cabinet to be retained. Although, theoretically, the prime minister had the prerogative of forming the ministry, in this matter he works under certain constraints. He must include his loyal friends, all the important leaders of the party or (parties) that had elected him (or her) and must give representation to all states, Union Territories and regions in the cabinet. He must include competent persons, youth for being trained and Rajya Sabha members in the cabinet. He can include persons in the council of ministers who are not members of Parliament but within six months, he or she should be a member of the Parliament; otherwise, they shall cease to be minister. B. S. Ramoowalia was not a member of any house of Parliament when he was included in the H. D. Deve Gowda cabinet in 1996; afterwards, he became a member of the Rajya Sabha before the six-month period.

The prime minister has power to reconstitute and reshuffle his ministry whenever he likes. Jawaharlal Nehru did whenever he liked it but Indira Gandhi and Rajiv Gandhi did it more often. As the head of the council of ministers, the prime minister distributes portfolios among the ministers as per his discretion but it depends upon the political stature and standing of prime minister in the party vis-à-vis other ministers in the cabinet. However, the council has been losing authority and prestige by the formation of 'inner cabinet', 'kitchen cabinet', 'super cabinet', etc. This is because in the process of collective decision making, some persons always acquire prominence and the ministers close to the prime minister tend to form the actual centre of power. The two other factors, dismissal of ministers by the prime minister and change of portfolios at any time, have also strengthened the position of the prime minister.

The Prime Minister and the Parliament

The prime minister is the leader of the Parliament. In consultation with the speaker of Lok Sabha, he determines the dates of meetings and programme of its session and on his advice, the president summons and prorogues the house. He decides which bills would be introduced in both houses of Parliament, what strategy would be adopted to push through a controversial bill, which member of his/her party would speak on a particular bill. He decides when the Lok Sabha is to be dissolved. On 7 December 1970, the president dissolved the house on the advice of the then prime minister, Indira Gandhi. Again in January 1977, on the advice of Prime Minister Indira Gandhi, the president dissolved the house. In August 1979, Chaudhary Charan Singh advised the president to dissolve the house and order new elections. In 1990, on the advice of Prime Minister Chandra Shekhar, the president dissolved the house and ordered fresh elections. Thus, it is an accepted principle that a prime minister has the right to seek a fresh mandate from the people at a time of his choice. This has made his position strong vis-à-vis members of Parliament. As leader of Parliament, he has to see that nothing should happen in any way which affects the dignity, prestige and authority of the chair. On this, the prime minister is generally assisted by the department of parliamentary affairs.

The Prime Minister and His Party

The prime minister's relationship with his party in the case of the Congress, except for a very short period in the initial years, is that he is considered supreme leader of the party. Jawaharlal Nehru combined both the posts of prime minister as well as party president for three years from 1951 to 1954. This has changed the psychology of Congress leaders and they look to the prime minister and not to the party president for political guidance. A crisis did arise in 1969, when the Congress working committee expelled Indira Gandhi (the then prime minister) from the primary membership of the party and directed the Congress parliamentary party to overthrow the prime minister, which it did not do. The prime minister is both morally and politically bound to give effect to the declared policies of the party. But after the 1969 split in the Congress party, the party was in the hands of Indira Gandhi and powers were centralized so that she did not face any problem from the organizational wing of the party. Most of the time, she held both the offices of party president and prime minister. So was the case during the periods of Rajiv Gandhi and P. V. Narasimha Rao. They were prime ministers as well as party presidents. The prime minister has an advantageous position vis-à-vis the party president as the former has a lot of patronage to distribute. As a party president, the prime minister distributes the party ticket to the candidates for Parliament and state legislatures to fight elections. This makes his position very strong in the party he heads.

The Prime Minister and the People

In a parliamentary democracy, the prime minister is more than a mere leader of the majority party in the legislature. Democracy has now become popular or populist democracy. The prime minister is the leader of masses. Elections are fought in his/her name and people vote for prime minister and not for the party. The modern means of transport and communication, especially the electronic media, have helped to establish a direct link with the people. This has strengthened the position of the prime minister and since no other person in the government can command these resources and opportunities, the prime minister stands supreme and unchallenged. Thus, good public relations are an important political function of the prime minister.

The Link Between the President and Cabinet

The prime minister serves as a channel of communication between the president and the cabinet of ministers. The duties of the prime minister mentioned in Article 78 are: (*a*) to communicate to the president all decisions of the council of ministers; (*b*) to furnish such information relating to the administration of the affairs of the Union and proposal for legislation as the president may call for; and (*c*) if the president so requires, to submit for the consideration of the council of ministers any matter on which a decision has been taken by a minister but which has not been considered by the council. He conveys messages of the president to his colleagues. No minister is authorized to see or communicate with the president without the permission of the prime minister. Former President Giani Zail Singh complained that Prime Minister Rajiv Gandhi did not keep the president informed of many matters that transpired between him and the cabinet. It created tensions between the two top functionaries and there were speculations of the president's impeachment by the Parliament or Rajiv Gandhi's dismissal by the president. This fact was confessed by the former president in an interview with the author of the book *Rajiv Gandhi, Many Facets*.[5] The smooth sailing of the government demands that the prime minister should always keep the president informed on matters of vital importance before taking action.

Spokesman of the Government on Foreign Policy

The prime minister is the spokesman of the country on all matters of foreign policy. His statements are, for the outside world, statements of policies of the nation. He represents the national, international and commonwealth conferences. Jawaharlal Nehru, Indira Gandhi and Rajiv Gandhi left their mark on such conferences and meets. For example, their contribution in non-aligned movement (NAM) has been appreciable. Rajiv Gandhi's role in SAARC has been praised even by other countries. Former Prime Minister I. K. Gujral's initiatives in developing good relations with neighbouring countries have been praised in the SAARC meet at Male in Maldives on 13 May 1997.[6]

The prime minister is also expected to keep a close watch and control on the economic situation of the country. The popularity of the government depends upon the economic condition of the country. Therefore, the prime minister is the chairman of Planning Commission and the National Development Council. The liberalization trend of the economy started by Rajiv Gandhi and followed by P. V. Narasimha Rao's government are good examples to prove the prominent role of the prime minister in this direction.

The Prime Minister's Control over Intelligence Agencies

The prime minister as the head of government exercises control over various intelligence agencies of the central government which proved to be a very potent source of power at the disposal of prime minister. These agencies were created by the British for the purpose of collecting information about crimes and dacoity and after the start of the nationalist movement these were used to collect political information. The British used these agencies to perpetuate their stranglehold over the country. But after Independence, these agencies not only continued but in fact became stronger. The important agencies include Intelligence Bureau (IB), Central Bureau of Investigation (CBI), and the Criminal Investigation Department (Special Branch). Within the IB, a special cell, popularly known as the Research and Analysis Wing (RAW), was created for external intelligence. The legitimate functions of these agencies were collection of information for security and wellbeing of the state, but they became instruments of ruling party headed by the prime minister. They were used to keep watch over the activities of opponents of the prime minister within his/her own party and opposition party leaders. The RAW director started reporting directly to the then Prime Minister Indira Gandhi bypassing the cabinet secretary. During the internal Emergency from 25 June 1975 to March 1977, it was given extensive power and was utilized excessively. The Shah Commission observed about the IB and CBI that 'the Intelligence Bureau of the Government of India was being used to maintain surveillance on the activities of some of the important leaders and ministers'. The report noted that the then CBI Director, D. Sen 'appears to have lent himself and his organization for purposes other than those which are strictly within the terms of the character of the CBI'. Recently, the CBI was again in focus. It was alleged that former Prime Minister Deve Gowda's government had used CBI to initiate cases against political rivals. It was complained that the CBI was being used for political purposes and the people were being 'framed' by the agency.

In addition to IB, CBI and CID (Special Branch) other revenue intelligence agencies are also at the disposal of the prime minister. These include directorate of revenue intelligence (DRI), directorate of enforcement (Revenue) and income-tax intelligence. The first looks after prevention of smuggling, the second endeavours to prevent foreign exchange racketeering and the third keeps an eye on evasion of income tax. There are two boards which earn huge revenues for the government: one is the central board of direct taxes and the other is the central board of excise and customs.

The Shah Commission, in its report submitted to the government in May 1978, noted that the above-mentioned revenue intelligence agencies were used by the rulers of the day to harass their political opponents in trade and industry. Following the Shah Commission report, the Janata Party government set up a committee in November 1978 under the chairmanship of a former finance secretary, M. R. Yardi, to examine the working of these agencies. He noted that so long as the two boards looked up to the minister for their day-to-day working, they could always be abused for political purposes. The committee recommended that any raids by the officers of these agencies should be on their initiative and not on guidance from the minister or the prime minister and further, the officers who conduct raids must ensure that the law was followed to the letter. The committee suggested protection to the officers and that their status and service conditions must be guarded against political harassment by way of transfers.[8]

Administrative and Executive Functions of the Prime Minister

The administrative and executive functions of chief executive can be summarized in Luther Gulick's famous acronym POSDCORB. It stands for planning, organizing, staffing, directing, coordinating, reporting and budgeting. To these, now, some more tasks such as policy formulation, decision making, public relations and administrative reforms may be added. The implications of these functions are examined below briefly.

Planning: Planning for development is an important function of the chief executive in developing countries. The prime minister in our country is the chairman of the Planning Commission, which formulates the national development plans. He is also the chairman of the national development council, which finally approves these plans. Thus, he plays a pivotal role in planning.

Organizing: Organizing means the establishment of the formal structure of authority through which work sub-divisions are arranged, defined and coordinated for a definite objective. Under our Constitution, the executive authority of the Union is vested in the president,[9] who has to work on the 'advice of the council of ministers' headed by the prime minister. The president makes rules for the more convenient transaction of the business of the Government of India for its allocation among ministers.[10]

The prime minister decides the number, nomenclature and jurisdiction of each minister/department. The prime minister can transfer ministers from one ministry to another and allocate work among them. He controls the agenda of the cabinet. It is he who decides when the cabinet shall meet. It is the prime minister who decides on the composition and functions of the standing and ad-hoc committees. He also decides the composition and functions of various commissions, boards and committees of enquiries, etc.

Staffing: Staffing includes the entire functions of recruiting and training of personnel to man the staff as well as maintaining favourable conditions at work. The prime minister in India makes all the important arrangements. He is free to choose his ministers whom he can appoint, promote and dismiss almost at will. He appoints with the approval of the president, governors of the states, ambassadors or diplomatic agents, judges of the Supreme Court and high courts and many other important personnel. In this respect, he is more powerful than the American president, whose nominations have to be approved by the Senate. As the leader of his party, the prime minister actually selects the chief minister and other ministers of states where his party rules. The prime minister, as the chairman of appointments committee of the cabinet, exercises a lot of power in making appointments to different posts. In brief, in Union government, no important appointment can be made without his approval.

Directing: Directing means the continuous task of making decisions and embodying them in specific and general orders and instructions and serving as the leader of the agency. The uniformity and tone of administration is set by the quality and number of directives issued by the chief executive. The prime minister or his secretariat constantly issue directives addressed to various ministers, departments, public undertakings, state governments, Union Territories, etc.

Coordinating: The most important function of any chief executive is coordination. It has been defined as 'the integration of the several parts into an orderly whole to achieve the purpose of the undertaking'.[11] According to G. R. Terry, 'Coordination is the orderly synchronization of efforts to provide the proper amount, timing and directing of execution resulting in harmonious and unified actions to a stated objective.'[12] In administration function and differences of opinion do occur frequently. All these have to be resolved to achieve the objective set by the government. Further, with the proliferation of government activities the importance of coordination has increased to avoid duplication and manage smooth working. The prime minister has to ensure inter-ministerial coordination.

Reporting: Reporting means 'keeping those to whom the executive is responsible informed of what is going on, which thus includes keeping himself and his subordinates informed through records, research and inspection'.[13] In the duties of prime minister the reporting system will involve two main aspects. First, there has to be a system of communication which facilitates flow of information from the grassroots level to the top. Second, there has to be a system by which the chief executive can report to the Parliament about the functioning of the government. This would include keeping the public and important pressure groups also informed about the functioning of the government.

In its report, the administrative reforms commission suggested that the prime minister should once a month meet the secretaries of important departments individually or in groups. The position as of today is that the prime minister meets the secretaries of the various departments from time to time and the ministers also write to him to keep him informed about the major events in their ministries.

Budgeting: Budgeting includes fiscal planning, accounting and control. The prime minister has to get the budget prepared and presented to the Parliament through finance minister. He executes budget, which means the exercise necessary for pre- and post-expenditure controls. These functions are performed through the minister of finance and through the auditor and comptroller-general.

Administrative Reforms: In addition to the POSDCORB functions discussed above, the prime minister has to keep the administrative organization and structure in good health to perform the functions assigned to it. With the development of science and technology and fast new means of communication like electronic media, the administration is required to perform many new tasks. This may require new institutional arrangements and major changes in their executive functions. The prime minister has to perform this important function to enhance the capability and capacity of administration by continuous reforms in the administrative structures.

Position of the Prime Minister

A perusal of the powers of the prime minister clearly shows that he enjoys tremendous powers and influence both in the executive and the legislative sphere. The prime minister is the key person in the government. He presides over cabinet meetings; he instructs, encourages and admonishes individual ministers. The entire structure of cabinet is built upon his person. He is the life and death of the cabinet. Thus, he 'is the keystone of the cabinet arch,' as Gladstone said. While Ramsay Muir said that 'the cabinet is the steering wheel of the ship of the state and Prime Minister is the steersman.' Ivor Jennings described him as 'The Sun round which the planets revolve.' He was also called 'first among equals', but now it is obsolete. The very fact that he is prime minister, means he is superior to others or above others. Peter G. Richards opined that the prime minister was *primus inter pares,* which was a serious underestimation of the prime minister's position. These epithets were used for the British prime minister, which may be applied in our context.

In India, prime minister is the actual executive. The personality of the prime minister determines the nature of the authority that he or she is likely to exercise. The working of the prime minister's style shows two types of trends, one is that of prime ministers like Nehru, Indira Gandhi and Rajiv Gandhi who were more than equals and they made the executive a prime ministerial government rather than a cabinet government, while others were like Lal Bahadur Shastri and Morarji Desai who were first among equals. The other prime ministers such as Chaudhary Charan Singh, V. P. Singh, Chandra Shekhar, P. V. Narasimha Rao, H. D. Deve Gowda, I. K. Gujral, Atal Bihari Vajpayee and Manmohan Singh are minority party prime ministers with the support of other parties, therefore, they cannot be more than first among equals. But in such situations the government has become really parliamentary.

Prime Minister's Secretariat/Office (PMO)

In a parliamentary democracy, the prime minister is the centre of power and responsibility. In situations of crisis decisions are left to the prime minister. He, therefore, needs institutional help and assistance to take immediate decisions. There is no disagreement for such support to the prime minister but there were differences as to the way in which institutional support is to be provided. Some were in favour of using already existing administrative machinery within ministries, while some favoured the prime minister's office to give direct assistance to the prime minister. There can be no question that every prime minister is entitled to have an office of his own manned by advisors loyal to him. This is the basic justification for the existence of the prime minister's office. This question was discussed by the ARC and its study team recommended setting up of such institutional support, which will not duplicate the work of existing ministries and will deal with only overall issues. Such an agency should be located in the cabinet secretariat rather than in the prime minister's office and quality experts alone should be appointed to man it. The existing institutional support consists of the cabinet committees, the secretaries committees, cabinet secretariat and the prime minister's office. The prime minister's secretariat/office occupies the status of a department of the Government of India under the Allocation of Business Rules, 1961 without any attached and subordinate office under it. This office is not responsible for the prime minister functioning as head of the cabinet. It is responsible for his functioning as chairman of the planning commission. It is an official link between the prime minister and his ministers, the president, governors, chief ministers and foreign representatives. On the public side, it is concerned with party matters, personal correspondence and complaints from public, etc.

Functions of the Prime Minister's Secretariat/Office

The functions of the prime minister's secretariat/office are as follows:

(i) To deal with all references that have, under the rules of business, come to the prime minister

(ii) To help the prime minister in respect of his/her overall responsibilities as head of government. It includes liaison with the Union ministries and the state governments on matters in which the prime minister may be interested

(iii) To help the prime minister in the discharge of his responsibilities as the chairman of the planning commission

(iv) To deal with the public relations side of the prime minister's office, that is, relations with the press, public, etc.

(v) To assist the prime minister in the examination of cases submitted to him for orders under prescribed rules

The prime minister's office is not responsible for his functions as the head of the cabinet, except for matters of personal correspondence between him and individual ministers. Generally, the personality of the prime minister and his view of his own role would greatly influence the nature and span of functions of his office. Its activities may be broadly divided into four parts. First is the processing of a large number of cases submitted by various ministries and cabinet secretary for information, approval and sanction, etc. These are basically routine matters, but this is what the bureaucracy enjoys doing the most as such cases provide ample opportunity for nitpicking and exercise of effective power at the personal level. In actual fact, the PMO has little to contribute in this area, as the government operates within an elaborate framework of rules and regulations, and the proper forum for their correct application is the ministry concerned and not the prime minister's office. It is in this area that the PMO carries the heaviest work load and this is where drastic reduction through decentralization is necessary.

The second function of the PMO concerns policy formulations. Most of the issues originate from ministries under the independent charge of cabinet ministers, and the basic input as also the policy frame is furnished by the administrative ministry. In more important cases the cabinet secretary and committee of secretaries provide useful insights and offer a wider perspective. But the prime minister may like to use his office as a sounding board on certain controversial matters or ask his staff officers to consult some outside experts.

The third function is that the prime minister would certainly like to use his office to review and monitor particular activities of some ministries, keep a tab on developments on certain fronts and, at times, depute his staff officers to undertake sensitive assignments, This is a wholly unstructured and grey area of the PMO's work, and its nature and content would differ a great deal from one prime minister to another.

The fourth vital sphere of PMO's activity has not been clearly recognized, defined or exploited. In the first instance the bright vision of the poll promises gets buried under mountains of routine and the cosy comforts of office. But it is imperative for a serious-minded prime minister, who aspires to go before the electorate again, to pick on a few long-term policy issues or ameliorative measures right at the start of his term and then entrust a special cell in his office continuously to monitor, review and assist the implementation in respect of each issue. This arrangement would necessarily involve greater centralization in one wing of the PMO. But it would be the right kind of centralization, i.e., enhancing the prime minister's ability to push forward major policy initiatives taken by his government.[14] Thus, the functional span of PMO is wide and very comprehensive.

The Evolution of the Prime Minister's Secretariat/Office

Before Independence, the executive council of the governor-general was given secretariat assistance by the secretary to the governor-general. The secretariat was a very small one that worked for the governor-general in his capacity as the head of the government. After Independence on 15 August 1947, our first prime minister, Pandit Jawaharlal Nehru, set up a personal secretariat known as the prime minister's secretariat. He established the prime minister's office as distinct from the prime minister. He was assisted by a special private secretary, K. Ram, during his 17 years tenure as prime minister. Nehru did a good part of his work through the foreign office, which he himself headed. This ministry acquired an out-of-proportion prestige and importance but it was never a power focus. With Nehru's departure the situation changed. Lal Bahadur Shastri lacked Nehru's charisma. As prime minister he was indeed 'first among equals'. To establish himself, and to make up for his comparative lack of familiarity with issues involving foreign policy, science and technology, he instinctively felt the need for a stronger office and appointed a full-fledged secretary level civil servant, L. K. Jha, to head his office with consequent increase in its size. Shastri's period as prime minister was a very short one.

After Shastri, Indira Gandhi became the prime minister and she developed the prime minister's secretariat as a powerful centre of authority as per the political and economic need of the time. The name of prime minister's secretariat was changed during the prime ministership of Morarji Desai, who clipped the wings of the prime minister's secretariat and named it as the prime minister's office. Subsequently, each prime minister maintained this office and according to their style of working its importance increased or decreased.

The Role of the PMO

During Nehru's period the decision-making centre was the cabinet secretariat and the cabinet secretary was the head of the administration and civil service. But Lal Bahadur Shastri appointed L. K. Jha, senior officer of the ICS cadre, as his secretary. His powerful and dynamic personality raised the status and stature of the secretariat. In his time the pattern emerged was that as the prime minister coordinates the work of the cabinet, and his secretary has become the coordinator of secretariat activity. This led to the 'decline of the cabinet secretariat activity to the role of clearing house for cabinet papers.'[15] Not only this Shastri in spite of a competent full-fledged foreign minister in Sardar Swaran Singh, appointed a high-powered committee of six secretaries to deal with foreign affairs. The membership comprised the cabinet secretary, two members from the finance ministry, the defence secretary, the foreign secretary and L. K. Jha, who was the secretary to the prime minister[16] although other secretaries in the foreign office were not included. As a result, deep resentment arose among bureaucrats and the secretary to the prime minister emerged as the influential civil servant. There were instructions to the ministers to keep the prime minister's secretariat in the picture in all matters of any importance and as prime minister's secretary Jha would generally have the last word. Therefore, he was called a 'super secretary'. Lal Bahadur's tenure was too brief for him to evolve a prime ministerial system.

The appointment of Indira Indira Gandhi as the prime minister was accompanied by significant changes in the economic and political environment. The economy was in a state of crisis, economic plans had decelerated to what was called a 'plan holiday'. The devaluation of the rupee turned out to be a major political fiasco without doing much good to the economy. The authority of the central government had considerably eroded. Her cabinet did not consist of like-minded persons. In such a situation the prime minister faced a two-fold challenge. The first was to establish her pre-eminence in the cabinet and the second to forge a coherent set of policies and develop a credible political stance. To meet these challenges the prime minister needed aides who were not her colleagues and who could give her professional assistance and advice. In these circumstances the prime minister 'needed a one-handed secretary to head her office, which would provide the necessary inputs for such a role'.[17] Indira Gandhi gradually expanded its strength and authority. L. K. Jha continued to be Indira Gandhi's secretary and he accompanied the prime minister on almost every foreign tour. The role of L. K. Jha provoked Hiren Mukherji to remark in the Lok Sabha that the prime minister, Indira Gandhi, was surrounded by 'political upstarts and slimy bureaucrats.'[18] This created quite a stir in the lobbies. This status was further raised when he was appointed a member of the atomic energy commission, a position hitherto reserved for the cabinet secretary. When Jha was appointed as the governor of Reserve Bank, P. N. Haksar succeeded him as the secretary to the prime minister. Haksar took full charge of the secretariat and made it the main focus of power. The entire intelligence set-up, judicial appointments, department of personnel, centre–state relations and several other instruments of authority were under its charge.[19] By the end of 1970, the prime minister's secretariat under P. N. Haksar had acquired all the lustre and authority of a power centre. The politicians, bureaucrats and the industrial barons courted it for favours and patronage. It made and unmade the ministers and decided about the composition of the party high command and its various components.[20] Haksar also fell from Indira Gandhi's grace when he advised her to keep a check on the activities of her son, Sanjay Gandhi. He had also earlier communicated his unhappiness over the style of working of L. N. Mishra, a minister, and for this he was exiled to the planning commission as its deputy chairman. Haksar was succeeded by P. N. Dhar, who was an academician. In the beginning he was called an advisor and later he was designated as secretary, but never got the coveted rank of a principal secretary.

After her Congress's landslide victory in the elections of 1971, Indira Gandhi expanded the authority of her secretariat. After imposition of internal emergency on 25th June 1975, the prime minister's secretariat became the centre of all authority and its writ began to be obeyed by all central ministers, departments and all other executive agencies; and the once powerful cabinet secretariat had to play second fiddle. During the Emergency the prime minister's secretariat was there but its powers and authority had been transferred to R. K. Dhawan, who liaised closely with Sanjay Gandhi. 'The prime minister's secretariat in reality was reduced to a post office to obtain orders from the new power caucus and communicate it to the concerned ministries.'[21]

In 1977, a big political change occurred, the Congress party was badly defeated at the polls and the new Janata Party government headed by Morarji Desai came to power. He was against the concentration of power in prime minister's secretariat; therefore, he greatly reduced its authority and its nomenclature was changed to the prime minister's office (PMO). He declared that he desired to reduce the all-powerful secretariat to the status of mere office of the prime minister, whose role would be to assist the prime minister in his task. Desai appointed V. Shankar, a retired ICS as his secretary, the cabinet secretary, Nirmal Mukherji, dealt directly with the prime minister on most of the issues, without going through his secretary. The prestige of the cabinet secretary was restored. The functions of ministries of home and finance which were taken away from them were assigned back to them. But the ministerial and bureaucratic habits continued to assign more importance to the prime minister's office even though the ministries and their political heads got back their dignity and elan.

Indira Gandhi's return to power as a result of the elections of 1979–1980 sanctified the role and status of Sanjay Gandhi. He was once again the power centre. P. C. Alexander was brought back from the UN to head the prime minister's office. Only its name had not changed, everything else had changed. The ministry of home was once again denuded of its powerful instruments. Though the prime minister's office got back its status quo and authority and acquired many additional people, Sanjay Gandhi exercised his authority mainly through R. K. Dhawan who was now elevated to the rank of a joint secretary and designated as private secretary to the prime minister.[22]

Rajiv Gandhi's period begins from November 1984 and he did not change what his mother had so firmly established. Only some more additions were made. R. K. Dhawan was banished and Makhanlal Fotedar stepped in. Sarla Grewal took over from P. C. Alexander as the prime minister's secretary. Rajiv Gandhi fashioned the prime minister's office into the kind of instrument that it used to interfere even in the minutest of detail, and duplicated the work of most departments of the central government. This extended even to external affairs with a joint secretary of the prime minister's office belonging to foreign service tendering independent advice. The size of the office grew enormously. Not only did all decisions get locked up there but a culture developed of even senior officers of ministries, not to mention ministers, trying to find out the 'mind' of the prime minister's office before formulating the simplest of proposals.[23] Rajiv Gandhi was keen to inject new ideas into the system and the PMO was tailor-made for this. PMO was very active on the economic front as Rajiv Gandhi wanted to liberalize the economy. The prime minister was keenly interested in technology; the PMO took a lot of innovative steps in the field of science and technology. Sarla Grewal, the PMO secretary, took interest in the implementation of various programmes of the prime minister.

After 1989 elections, V. P. Singh became the prime minister and his short term of nine months was full of social and political problems, but his PMO was a subdued one. So was the case during the four-month prime ministerial tenure of Chandra Shekhar. Neither V. P. Singh nor Chandra Shekhar allowed the PMO to be treated as the virtual parallel government as it used to be prior to them.

But when Congress came to power in 1991 under the leadership of P. V. Narasimha Rao, he appointed A. N. Verma, IAS, as his principal secretary and later Venugopal as secretary in the PMO.[24] By reasons of temperament or because he wanted to distance himself from the Rajiv style, Narasimha Rao opted initially for a greatly sobered down PMO. The Union minister of state for communications Rajesh Pilot commenting about the PMO said, 'We do not get instructions from the PMO.' In fact, Narasimha Rao's PMO has, so far, been the least obtrusive in the past two decades, points out a senior bureaucrat: 'it is a PMO of professionals instead of power brokers and fixers.'[25] But after two years, the position changed and Rao's PMO again became a very strong power centre. Mr Chavan, the home minister, had to contend with losing control over Kashmir affairs. 'The PMO under the command of Mr Amar Nath Varma continued calling shots in 'Home' reducing the minister to a silent spectator.'[26] A comment in a popular magazine provides a lucid account of the prime minister and PMO position.

Meanwhile, the PMO has made a comeback to the spotlight, although it is still a largely faceless organization. The person running it is fast acquiring the clout of a Gopi Arora or Vinod Pandey. Verma virtually ran the ministries in Rao's time, with every file being routed through him. The ever busy Verma also handled the foreign investment promotion board that had cleared proposals worth about Rs 1,700 crore. But his actual power, says a PMO official, lies in being Rao's 'ears'. In this capacity he played a crucial role for the prime minister in sounding out senior bureaucrats and important ministers for the selection process of new cabinet secretary. In his second year in power, surrounded by men who share his belief in striking but softly, Rao appears to have gained confidence and adapted to the rather tight fit of the Gandhi throne. Assertive, even to the point of becoming irritable, his earlier image as the elderly political statesman has been eroded. As one CPP executive member grumbles: 'None of our requests even for our constituency development schemes is entertained nowadays.' But then, with Congress party men long used to the language of the ever manoeuvring and ruthless ruler, Rao's more pragmatic colours may be his passport to success for a party wedded to the tradition of obsequiousness.'[27]

Further, newspaper reports depict that in the Narasimha Rao government, the principal secretary to the prime minister presided over the inter-ministerial committee, which gives the final nod to foreign investment proposals. Functionally, either the ministry of industry or the ministry of finance should fulfil this crucial role. The strong protest lodged by K. Karunakaran, the then minister of industries, found mention in *Business India* and *The Economic Times*. There have also been several other occasions when some central government ministries mildly pointed out that they had been overruled by the PMO.[28]

The prime minister's office of Deve Gowda though was a low profile one but the working of PMO remained the same as it was during his predecessor's time. The following examples support this point. First, the proposal of Union coal ministry to shift CKL headquarters from Calcutta to Ranchi (then in Bihar) had been blocked by the PMO.[29] Second, the public revelation of the then home minister, Indrajit Gupta, that he was not kept informed about some of the major decisions taken by the cabinet on behalf of his ministry, be it the appointment of the controversial Uttar Pradesh governor Romesh Bhandari or the intervention of the security agencies in courts in the criminal cases involving former prime minister, P. V. Narasimha Rao.[30] The PMO under Atal Behari Vajpayee was indeed top-heavy with Brajesh Mishra (prime minister's secretary) being a confidant of the BJP stalwart. Vajpayee had been under tremendous pressure to drop Brajesh Mishra in the wake of the Tehelka.com expose of murky defence deals. There is a re-employed secretary-level officer overseeing Jammu and Kashmir affairs along with another of the same rank serving as information advisor to the prime minister. There is also an additional secretary dealing with press and public relations, along with five joint secretaries who coordinate with other ministries and departments of the Union government. There has never been such a battery of high-profile officials doing duty in the PMO. The question on everyone's minds is that if the PMO is merely a facilitator with other ministries and departments as claimed by Brajesh Mishra, is there need for such a battery of officials even when the entire dynamics of governance has changed?

The PMO of Manmohan Singh is a low profile one. His background of an academic and an administrator made him a believer in consensus and not confrontation. In 2004 when the Congress emerged as the single largest party, Manmohan Singh became prime minister because he was chosen by Sonia Gandhi and was the candidate agreed upon by the Congress and the Left. He is not the leader of the party—Sonia Gandhi is—but he enjoys the full confidence of the leader. He is the important link among the coalition partners. Under Manmohan Singh the centre of power is at 10 Janpath, the residence of Congress president Sonia Gandhi and not the PMO. The party decides the policies, the government works as a facilitator. The party president is stronger than the prime minister. The coalition governments have reduced the authority of the prime minister. His decisions are a compromise. In the time of liberalization, privatization and globalization, his authority has weakened because the market is emerging as a stronger force than the state.

There is increasing consternation in political circles and outside the government that the hunger to centralize unhindered power in the PMO is assuming alarming proportions. It is apparent the political leadership believes in 'might is right' and precious little is being done to decentralize power. The distortion in the political system perpetrated by the late Indira Gandhi in making the PMO the unquestioned and unrivalled fountainhead of power is duly being taken forward by her successors irrespective of their party affiliations. Experts and politicians of various hues and shades rue the deleterious and sad state of affairs.[31]

The PMO is still functioning as an overlord of the ministry. Yet over the years ministers in most cases are thankful for being where they are and have chosen to accept the PMO as a super authority. Now it seems that a strong PMO is the only salvation for any Indian prime minister, but concentration of power is a danger to a democratic society.

NOTES

1. *Constituent Assembly Debates, Vol. VII*, p. 1160. In a cooperative federation like ours, this seems to be impossible and the prime minister would be happy to fulfil the desire of the president.
2. Ibid., pp. 1144–45. The working of the Constitution during these past 58 years proved that K. T. Shah's fears were genuine. The cabinet government has become a prime ministerial government.

3. Article 75(1), Constitution of India.
4. In England, there are such examples. In 1923 when Boner Law resigned as the prime minister, the Conservative Party, which had a majority in the House of Commons, was ready to support Lord Curzon as well as Stanley Baldwin. King George II exercised his discretion and appointed Stanley Baldwin the prime minister on the plea that he was the leader of the Conservative Party in the House of Commons. Again the monarch exercised his discretion when Sir Anthony Eden resigned as the prime minister in 1957 on grounds of ill health, people were expecting that A. R. Butler, who acted as prime minister during Anthony Eden's visit abroad, would be invited to form the government, but the Queen appointed Harold Macmillan as the prime minister. Again, after the resignation of Macmillan in 1963, the Queen appointed Sir Alec Douglas-Home, the Earl of Home, as the prime minister against the expectations of the public and violating a 40-year-old convention according to which the prime minister should not ordinarily belong to the House of Lords.
5. *Hindustan Times*, New Delhi, 5 November 1992.
6. *Hindustan Times*, New Delhi, 14 May 1997.
7. *Hindustan Times*, New Delhi, 13 May 1997. In the Lok Sabha, M. A. A. Fatmi (JD, MP) charged that CBI was being used for political purposes.
8. See, for details, *The Times of India*, 1 August 1979. This came to light when senior officers of CBI were transferred at the time Indira Gandhi came again to power in January 1980.
9. Article 53(1), Constitution of India.
10. Article 77(3), Constitution of India.
11. J. C. Charles, *Governmental Administration* (New York: Harper and Bros., 1951), p. 244.
12. G. R. Terry, *Principles of Management* (Illinois: Richard D. Irwin, Inc., 1956), p. 33.
13. A. Avasthi and S. R. Maheshwari, *Public Administration* (Agra: Lakshmi Narain Agarwal, 1996), pp. 81–82.
14. *The Times of India*, New Delhi, 3 January 1989.
15. Michael Brecher, *Succession in India: A Study in Decision Making* (London: Oxford University Press, 1966), p. 118.
16. *The Times of India*, New Delhi, 16 April 1965.
17. P. N. Dhar, *The Times of India*, New Delhi, 24 February 1989.
18. *The Statesman*, New Delhi, 12 August 1966.
19. I. K. Gujral, *Hindustan Times*, New Delhi, 14 August 1987.
20. Ibid.
21. Ibid.
22. Ibid.
23. K. V. Ramanathan, *The Indian Express*, New Delhi, 3 January 1990.
24. *Hindustan Times*, New Delhi, 3 February 1994.
25. *India Today*, 31 December 1991, p. 44.
26. *Hindustan Times*, New Delhi, 28 December 1996.
27. *India Today*, Delhi, 15 September 1992, p. 51.
28. S. C. Vajpeyi, *Hindustan Times*, New Delhi, 29 July 1996.
29. *Hindustan Times*, New Delhi, 23 August 1996. The PMO did not want to annoy the then West Bengal Chief Minister Jyoti Basu. It is believed that the PMO was apprehensive of losing the confidence of the CPM, which could have caused the fall of the government if the coal ministry went ahead with its proposal.
30. *Hindustan Times*, New Delhi, 28 December 1996.
31. *The Sunday Tribune*, spectrum, Chandigarh, 1 April 2001.

The Council of Ministers

The Constitution of India provides for a parliamentary system of government in which the president is a nominal constitutional head and the actual executive authority of the Union is exercised by the council of ministers. Article 74 of the Constitution provides for a council of ministers and states, 'there shall be a council of ministers with the prime minister at the head to aid and advise the president who shall, in the exercise of his functions act in accordance with such advice.' The 42nd Amendment of the Constitution in 1976 made it obligatory for the president to act on the advice of the council of ministers but through the 44th Amendment in 1978 he was empowered to refer such advice back for reconsideration. We shall discuss this topic under the heads: The composition of the council, the difference between the council of ministers and the cabinet, the functions of the council of ministers and finally certain observations on their working during these past years.

The Council of Ministers

Composition

The formation of the council of ministers starts with the appointment of the prime minister. The president appoints of the leader of majority party in the Lok Sabha as the prime minister. A Rajya Sabha member can also be appointed as the prime minister. When Indira Gandhi was appointed prime minister, she was member of Rajya Sabha and H. D. Deve Gowda and I. K. Gujral were also members of the Rajya Sabha. Other members of the council of ministers are appointed by the president on the advice of the prime minister. The prime minister has to keep in view a number of factors while forming his council of ministers, such as prominent leader of his party and various groups in the party, various regions, castes, communities and religions have to be provided adequate representation in the council of ministers. If any person included in the council of ministers is not a member of either house of the Parliament, within six months he has to secure the membership, otherwise, he ceases to be a member of the council of ministers. The council of ministers consists of the prime minister, cabinet ministers, state ministers, deputy ministers and parliamentary secretaries. The Constitution does not fix the size of the council of ministers. The prime minister decides the size of the ministry as per the political situation of the time. It has been varying from 50 to 60, but the number of cabinet ministers has not been more than 20 in any cabinet. In the cabinet of Prime Minister I. K. Gujral, who constituted his council of ministers on 21 April 1997, there were 34 ministers[1] including the prime minister. Out of them, excluding the prime minister, 16 were cabinet ministers and the remaining 17 were ministers of state, with nine of them holding independent charge. Later, on 1 April, he added six more ministers[2] of whom three were of cabinet rank and three were state ministers. Thus, the total number of council of ministers was 40 including 19 cabinet ministers and the prime minister.

The council of ministers hold the office during the pleasure of the president.[3] Does this mean that the president could dismiss a ministry whenever he so feels? The answer is 'no'; the ministry will remain in office as long as it commands majority in the Lok Sabha. If he does it, he may be said to be violating the Constitution. But it is really surprising that our Constitution does not mention the resignation of the ministers. Does it mean that ministers cannot resign and should always be dismissed or deemed to be dismissed?[4] Our Constitution should have mentioned it. But at present, such an action of dismissal would be considered 'unconstitutional' and if a minister loses the confidence of the prime minister, the latter requests for his resignation and it is granted.[5] The next question then would be, why is the power of dismissal provided in the Constitution? Dr B. R. Ambedkar thought that a minister could be dismissed on two grounds: first, when he loses the confidence of the house, and second, when he is found corrupt,[6] but both the grounds are not defensible. First, according to the Constitution, a vote of no confidence cannot be passed against an individual minister. Second, the president cannot dismiss a minister even if he is corrupt unless the prime minister wants it. In such a situation, the prime minister could demand the resignation. Can a whole ministry be dismissed, if found corrupt? Even this is doubtful because the remedy for corruption in a democracy of the British type seems to be public opinion, but not dismissal.[7] In democratic practice, we can say that the prime minister retains office as long as he enjoys majority in the house, while individual ministers remain in office so long as they have the confidence of the prime minister.[8]

Council of Ministers and Cabinet

Though the council of ministers and the cabinet are often treated as identical, the word 'cabinet' is not mentioned in our Constitution. The cabinet as an institution is the result of our following the British cabinet model; where cabinet has become a common word for council of ministers and it has been described as 'the steering wheel within the council of ministers'. The council of ministers is a much wider body consisting of about 50 to 60 ministers, as against the cabinet, which consists of 15 to 20 senior and important ministers who constitute the cabinet. The council of ministers does not meet as a body to transact government business. It is the cabinet that meets for the purpose and works on the principle of collective responsibility of its members. Generally, important portfolios are given to the members of the cabinet while the less important ministers are members of the council of ministers. In India, the council of ministers consists of three categories of ministers, viz., cabinet ministers, ministers of state and deputy ministers. In addition, there are certain parliamentary secretaries who are appointed by the prime minister.

The salary and allowances of the members of the council of ministers have not been fixed by the Constitution and have been left to the Parliament. Article 75(6) lays down that 'the salaries and allowances of ministers shall be such as Parliament so determines, shall be as specified in the second Schedule'.

The administrative reforms commission (ARC), commenting upon the organization of council of ministers, did not recommend independent charge to the ministers of state, but it favoured that some clear-cut responsibility should be assigned to them. The ARC recommended the continuance of the deputy ministers as it provided an opportunity for junior politicians to train themselves but found the level of parliamentary secretary redundant and recommended for its abolition. The government did accept a three-tier ministry, but did not agree to abolish the institution of parliamentary secretary because it also provides a good opportunity to train junior politicians.

Several observations and comments have been made about the classification of ministers in the council of ministers. First, the number of different categories of ministers and the number of ministers have been changing from time to time. Second, this three- or four-tier ministry is creating a hierarchy in the ministers. Some scholars feel that this is not conducive for free discussion and exchange of views or ideas. Third, neither the deputy ministers have by and large accepted their role as that of a learner nor the cabinet ministers have given them adequate functions to perform. The system is maintained because it facilitates and helps the prime minister to give due place to all the interests and age groups in the council of ministers.

Functions of the Cabinet

Constitutionally, all the executive authority of the Union government is vested in the president and the council of ministers is there to 'aid and advise' the president in the exercise of his functions. But in practice all these powers are exercised by the council of ministers on behalf of the president. The powers and functions of the council may be studied under the following heads.

Executive Functions

Although constitutionally, executive authority vests in the president, but in actual practice it is the council of ministers which exercises the executive authority of the Union government and by convention and tradition it is the cabinet, a inner body of the council of ministers, which in the words of Ramsay Muir steers the ship of the state. In certain circumstances, the cabinet can issue directives to state governments, and in an emergency, it can virtually control the state governments.

Policy formulation: The cabinet is a policy-formulating body. It formulates and finalizes all national, international and external policies for the approval of the parliament. Once the policy has been determined, it is for the ministry/department concerned to carry it out. The cabinet meets regularly once a week and takes decisions on all important issues and matters emerging from various ministries.

Legislative functions: The cabinet is the main link between the executive and the Parliament. In the words of Badgehot, 'it is the hyphen that joins, the buckle that fastens the executive and the legislative together'. In practice it is the cabinet which prepares legislative measures, introduces them and pilots them through the two houses of Parliament. The bills mooted by the private members of the house have a chance of reaching the statute book only if supported by the cabinet. It has, therefore, been aptly remarked that it is the cabinet which legislates with the advice and consent of Parliament and not vice versa.

Financial powers: The budget of the country, showing estimated income and expenditure for the ensuing year, is also prepared by the cabinet and presented to the Parliament for its approval. The Parliament is free to debate and discuss all items of the budget but it can hardly make any substantive change in it unless the government agrees to such a change. It may be noted that no money bill can be introduced in the Parliament without the prior consent of the president. This clearly shows that all money bills can be introduced in the Parliament by the cabinet only.

Foreign relations: In the field of foreign relations also the cabinet plays an important role. It determines the foreign policy of the country and decides what type of relations it should have with other countries of the world. All the international treaties and agreements are considered and approved by the cabinet.

Prime Minister I. K. Gujral held the portfolio of external affairs on the patterns of our first Prime Minister, Jawaharlal Nehru.

Control over major appointments: All important appointments reserved for action by the president under the Constitution, namely that of the attorney-general, members of the union public service commission, chief election commissioner and other election commission members, judges of the Supreme Court and high courts and governors of states are taken up in the cabinet before they are made public. All other important appointments are made by the appointments committee of the cabinet on its behalf.

As a coordinator: The cabinet is the main coordinator among all ministries and departments of government. If two ministries or departments fail to settle or sort out their differences the prime minister acts as the coordinator and arbitrator. The president or the prime minister may by general or special order bring any matter for decision by the cabinet, where such decision of particular problem will be taken by the cabinet. The cases of differences of opinion are resolved by the cabinet.

Extraordinary functions: These are the powers exercised in abnormal times. These powers include ordinance-issuing power of the president during the recess of the Parliament under Article 352. In practice ordinances are prepared by the cabinet, which advises the president to promulgate them. Similarly, emergency provisions of the constitution that authorizes the president to issue an emergency proclamation is an extraordinary power to curtail the liberties of citizens and states both in legislative and executive fields. In practice all authority is exercised by the cabinet during the period of emergency.

It is thus evident that the cabinet enjoys far-reaching powers both with regard to the formulation and implementation of internal as well as external policies of the country, although its actual importance depends upon the type of persons the cabinet is composed of at that time. Further, as Dr B. R. Ambedkar remarked while resigning from the Union cabinet on 11 October 1951, that 'the cabinet has become a merely recording and registering office of the decisions already arrived at by committees. They work behind an iron curtain.'

Cabinet Committees

The cabinet committee system is analogous to that of the British cabinet committees. Committees are basically a means to enhance the efficiency of any organization. The cabinet committees ordinarily wield real power of decision on less important general policy matters. The cabinet meets once a week, as already mentioned, therefore, only delicate and complex points, or such matters on which several ministers may differ, are taken up by the cabinet for discussion. With the growing complexity of the work of the government, the cabinet is finding it very difficult to cope with the pressure of work, leading to the formation of such small bodies like 'kitchen cabinet'/'inner cabinet', etc. to take decisions quickly. The effective and quick decision making has generated the device of cabinet committees, which has been found useful. We would discuss here some of the characteristics and advantages of the cabinet committee system.

In the transaction of cabinet business, committee system has been found to be helpful. Therefore, we discuss the advantages of this system as follows:

First, the cabinet committees save the time of the cabinet because the issues are discussed in these committees in detail and basic questions are brought out for the decisions of the cabinet. Thus, it makes the task of the cabinet much easier. In the British context Prof. G. W. Jones of the London School of Economics and Political Science said 'that it is the cabinet committees that have saved the cabinet system of government which would otherwise have crumbled under the pressure of the work'. According to Herbert Morrisons, 'this device enables ministers to bargain and compromise with each other and thus, reduces pressure of work upon the cabinet. Consequently, the cabinet is left free to devote itself to more important matters.'[9] Thus, the cabinet committees save its time and strengthen its working in all the way. Second, the committee system safeguards the principle of collective responsibility, an essential characteristic of the cabinet government. The cabinet includes a small number of ministers and those who are not members of the cabinet cannot participate in its meetings. Hence, they do not take part in the decision-making process but they are collectively responsible for such decisions. Such ministers can be included in the cabinet committees. The practice prevails in England for ministers who are not members of the cabinet to be invited to sit in cabinet committees. It has the advantage of bringing the ministers of state in closer association with the work of the cabinet. Thus, all ministers continue to be responsible for the government's action. Third, cabinet committees increase the effectiveness of political control over public services. In some countries like New Zealand, public servants are called upon by the committees to justify their proposals and comment on the problems brought forward by them for the consideration of the cabinet committees. This brings the public servants in a face-to-face relationship with their political masters and helps them to understand political realities while helping the ministers to have a better understanding of the administrative problems. Thus, public servants have a sense of participation in the policy and are in a better position to execute them. It eliminates the possibility of dominance of opinion of any one department. Fourth, 'they can also act as a collective check on individual ministers and on the Prime Minister too.'[10] Usually, the ministers are in charge of the separate departments and tend to run them as independent empires. It is difficult for the cabinet to keep a check on the working of the different ministries and departments. The cabinet committees meet regularly and act as a check on the individual ministers. It also controls the tendency of prime minister to act on his own. In the absence of cabinet committees, the prime minister performs the functions of the cabinet, which cannot meet very often. The cabinet committees control and examine the working of the ministries. Therefore, it is not necessary for the prime minister to intervene in the working of the different ministries individually. Finally, the cabinet committees focus supra-ministry attention on any particular section of administration, short of cabinet level consideration and the prime minister's intervention. These committees facilitate inter-departmental coordination by enabling the ministers to bargain and compromise with each other and reduce the pressure of work on the cabinet.

The Organization of Committees

The committees are of two types: (i) standing committees and (ii) ad-hoc committees.

(i) *Standing committees:* These committees are permanent in nature. They are appointed to make policy in some specific areas and their duration is indeterminate. They may be terminated by a fresh decision of the cabinet or by the prime minister.

(ii) *Ad-hoc committees:* Such committees are formed for the purpose of solving some specific problem submitted to the cabinet or to the prime minister. They are automatically dissolved as soon as their task is fulfilled.

The Evolution of Cabinet Committees in India

After Independence in 1947, there were two standing cabinet committees, the defence committee and the economic committee. The defence committee was established in 1947 to look after defence problems and consisted of five or six members. It had an adequate secretariat organization in the cabinet known as its military wing. The economic committee was created soon after and it consisted of six members. In due course of time, committees like the priority committee, the rehabilitation committee and the resource committee were created.

N. Gopalaswamy Ayyangar Committee's Report

In July 1948, the Union cabinet constituted a committee under the chairmanship of N. Gopalaswamy Ayyangar, minister without portfolio and an experienced administrator, to report on the reorganization of the machinery of the central government. He submitted his report in 1949 and, along with other matters, he focussed attention on the need for cabinet committees, their number, composition and functions. The report said, '. . . it is essential that there should be a proper division of labour, and effective delegation within the cabinet. This need is widely accepted in principle, and is also in accordance with actual development in recent years. All that is now necessary is to recognise this position and rationalise and establish on permanent basis the system of delegation which is growing up.'[11] In his report Ayyangar made a number of suggestions and advised the formation of three kinds of committees: standing committee, ad-hoc committee and sub-committee.

(a) *Standing committees:* These committees should be regarded as part of the permanent machinery of government and appropriate secretariat may be provided to them on a permanent basis. The procedure of their work may be laid down in the rules of business and maintained by appropriate machinery prescribed thereof; and the committees may be enabled to develop specialized knowledge and expertise in the areas of policy functions allotted to them.

(b) *Ad-hoc committees:* These committees may deal with the areas not covered by the standing committees for a particular problem. Unexpected problems arising out of particular situations may also be referred to these ad-hoc committees.

(c) *Sub-committees:* In addition to these above two types of cabinet committees, Ayyangar suggested the need for setting up of sub-committees, one each of the four bureaus under which ministries would be grouped under his plan.

Second, Ayyangar recommended the establishment of four permanent standing committees, namely; (a) defence committee; (b) economic committee; (c) administrative organization committee; and (d) parliamentary and legal affairs committee.

He suggested that the prime minister should be the chairman of two committees—defence and economic committees. The other two committees should be headed by other senior ministers. He further suggested that it would be better if some senior cabinet ministers without portfolio were to head these committees on the British pattern. Regarding the working of these committees, Ayyangar suggested that these committees should be entrusted with the authority to take binding decisions on matters within their jurisdiction. However, these decisions should be communicated to the cabinet, any cabinet minister could ask for the review of such decisions by the full cabinet; and in some cases the committee itself could refer its decisions to the whole cabinet for ratification.

Implementing the above recommendation, the Union government set up four standing committees in May 1950. These were the standing committees on defence, economy, parliamentary and legal affairs and administrative organization, the last being set up on an ad-hoc basis. A fifth standing committee was soon added to the list in the form of the appointments committee. The prime minister was given full authority to determine the composition of these committees. Each committee was given required secretariat assistance. The cabinet secretariat served the defence and economic committees, the department of parliamentary affairs and the law ministry provided secretarial assistance to the parliamentary and legal affairs committees and the appointments committee and the home ministry rendered necessary secretarial assistance to the administrative organization committee.

In 1957, the entire structure of cabinet committees was reorganized. The existing five standing committees were abolished, three ad-hoc committees dealing with transient matters were formed; and nine new standing committees were set up on economic affairs, heavy industry, defence, foreign affairs, rehabilitation, scientific matters, parliamentary and legal affairs, information and broadcasting, and appointments.

Observations of the Comptroller and Auditor-General

The first comptroller and auditor-general of India, Asok Chanda's observations in his note to the cabinet in 1958 on the working of the cabinet committees are worth mentioning here. First, he found wide variation in the strength of various standing cabinet committees, namely, the appointments committee had only two members while the heavy industry committee had twelve members. Second, the prime minister was the chairman of almost all the cabinet committees, thus making it difficult for the cabinet to play the role of revisionary authority. Third, the cabinet committees did not always include ministers concerned with their subject matters as members only. The trend was to appoint members on personal considerations. This rendered these committees less effective for quick decisions.

He made two alternative suggestions to improve the working of the committee system. First, a better solution according to him was 'to introduce decentralised coordination by grouping ministries with interrelated functions together and placing these groups under the central supervision of senior ministers without portfolio.' Second, as an alternative he suggested the creation of a super cabinet as an emergency measure to provide 'supreme direction', to the executive.

No attention was paid to these suggestions of Asok Chanda. However, after the Chinese invasion in 1962 an important committee namely, the 'emergency committee' was set up. It consisted of the prime minister as chairman and home, finance and defence ministers as members. In due course of time this committee became very important and powerful, and in practice became the 'inner cabinet' in all important matters: internal and external matters were referred to it. This committee 'virtually replaced the cabinet as the Supreme decision making body in the Government of India.'[12] After the death of Jawaharlal Nehru, it was this committee which suggested to the president the appointment of Gulzarilal Nanda as the prime minister. Lal Bahadur Shastri enlarged membership of the committee by including Indira Gandhi as the information and broadcasting minister and Sardar Swaran Singh as the external affairs minister. Even after the end of the emergency, the committee continued to dominate the decision-making process. It played a very important role at the time of the Rann of Kutch dispute with Pakistan in 1965. But in course of time it lost its predominant position.

Recommendations of the Administrative Reforms Commission

The administrative reforms commission in its report in September 1969 recommended about the working of the cabinet committees. Its main recommendations were as follows:

(1) Eleven standing committees should be set up, one each for defence; foreign affairs; economic affairs; parliamentary affairs and public relations; food and rural development; transport, tourism and communications; social service (including social welfare and family planning); commerce, industry and science; internal affairs (including centre–state relations); administration; and appointments.

(2) Membership of each committee should not normally exceed six and should include all ministers-in-charge of subjects covered by the committee.

(3) Every standing committee should be supported by a committee of secretaries which will consider in advance all matters to be taken up by the cabinet committee.

(4) Ad-hoc committees should be retained and should be confined to mere investigation and not decision making.

The Union government did not accept these recommendations but while reconstituting these committees during the year 1974 these were kept in view. In 1974 the number of such committees was 12. The committee on political affairs was the most important and took precedence over the remaining committees. All important matters relating to defence, foreign affairs and political matters were referred to this committee for decision.

The Janata Party came into power on 24 March 1977. The new ministry made extensive use of these committees. In fact the government had made it a practice to refer all important issues for discussion and detailed examination to a committee or a sub-committee. The involvement of all ministers in decision making had increased. In 1994, there were the following 13 cabinet committees.

1. Cabinet committee on political affairs
2. Cabinet committee on natural affairs
3. Cabinet committee on parliamentary affairs
4. Cabinet committee on appointments
5. Cabinet committee on accommodation
6. Cabinet committee on foreign investment
7. Cabinet committee on drug abuse control
8. Cabinet committee on price
9. Cabinet committee on ministry of welfare
10. Cabinet committee on economic affairs
11. Cabinet committee on trade and investment
12. Cabinet committee on expenditure
13. Cabinet committee on infrastructure

NOTES

1. 'I. K. Gujaral's Cabinet consists of all the Deve Gowda's Cabinet Ministers except Deve Gowda and one D. P. Yadav; because being a PM of minority United Front Government, with the Congress, CPM, support from outside, he has no free hand to choose his Council of Ministers.' *Hindustan Times*, New Delhi, 22 April 1997. 'A Prime Minister who cannot even choose his own Cabinet is not cooperative federation. It is the federal blackmail of India,' *India Today*, 15 May 1997, p. 31.
2. *Hindustan Times*, 2 April 1997.
3. Article 72(2), Constitution of India.
4. K. V. Rao, *Parliamentary Democracy of India*, 2nd edition (Calcutta: World Press, 1965), p. 73.
5. Ibid., p. 74.
6. *Constituent Assembly Debates, Vol. VII*, pp. 1185–86.
7. K.V. Rao, op. cit., p. 74.
8. Such examples are those of S. P. Mukherjee, C. D. Deshmukh, M. C. Chagla, V. V. Giri, T. T. Krishnamachari, Mahavir Tyagi, Ashok Mehta, Dinesh Singh, Morarji Desai, H. N. Bahuguna and Arjun Singh, among others.
9. Herbert Morrison, *Government and Parliamentary* (London: Oxford University Press, 1954), p. 17.
10. Ibid., p. 218.
11. *Report on the Reorganization of the Machinery of the Government of India* (New Delhi: Government of India, 1949), p. 23.
12. M. Brecher, *Succession in India: A Study in Decision Making* (London: Oxford University Press, 1966), p. 1021.

The Parliament

Under the Constitution of India the legislature of the Union is called Parliament. The legislative power of the Indian Union is vested in the president and the two houses, namely the house of the people (Lok Sabha) and the council of states (Rajya Sabha). The role of the president in the composition of Parliament and law-making has been discussed in Chapter 4 on the Union Executive, therefore, it will not be repeated here. In this chapter we will discuss the composition of the two houses, their powers and functions, limitations on those powers, if any, and the working of the parliamentary system.

The Lok Sabha

The Lok Sabha (house of the people) is known as the 'lower house' of Parliament and its members are elected directly by the people. Article 81 of the Constitution provides that the Lok Sabha shall consist of not more than 530 members chosen by direct election from territorial constituencies in the states and not more than 20 members to represent the Union territories. In addition, the president may nominate two persons from the Anglo-Indian community, if he is of the opinion that it is not adequately represented in the Lok Sabha. Thus the maximum strength of the house envisaged in the Constitution is 552.

The total elected strength of the Lok Sabha is distributed among the states in such a way that the ratio between the number of seats and the population of any state is, as far as possible, the same for all states. At present there are 545 members in the Lok Sabha.

The Parliament is empowered to readjust the representation of the electoral constituencies due to increase of population after each census. This process is known as delimitation. After each census, a delimitation commission is constituted under an Act of Parliament. The first three delimitation commissions were constituted in 1952, 1962 and 1972. Later, the fourth delimitation commission was constituted in 2002.

The commission determines the number of parliamentary constituencies in each state, their area, number of seats in each constituency and number of reserved seats for scheduled castes and scheduled tribes. The fourth delimitation commission was constituted after 30 years in July 2002 and it submitted its final report. Its recommendations were notified by the president on 19 February 2008 and it came into force with immediate effect.

The election to the Lok Sabha is conducted on the basis of adult franchise, which means that any man or woman who has completed 18 years of age is eligible to vote. The Constitution provides for secret ballot and a candidate who secures the highest number of votes is declared elected.

There are certain disqualifications laid down in the Constitution. Article 102 says, 'A person shall be disqualified (a) if holds any office of profit under the government of India or the government of any state; (b) if he is of unsound mind and stands so declared by a competent court; (c) if he is an undischarged insolvent; (d) if he is not a citizen of India, or has voluntarily acquired the citizenship of a foreign state; (e) if he is so disqualified by or under any law made by Parliament.'

The term of the Lok Sabha in India is five years from the date appointed for its first meeting. It can be dissolved before the expiry of its full term under certain constituencies when a proclamation of emergency is in force. The term of the Lok Sabha can be extended by Parliament for a period not exceeding one year at a time and not exceeding in any case a period of six months after the proclamation has ceased to operate.

The president is empowered to dissolve the Lok Sabha at any time; but he will do that on the advice of the prime minister and his council of ministers. The former prime minister, Indira Gandhi, advised the president to dissolve the Lok Sabha and order a mid-term poll. President V. V. Giri dissolved the Lok Sabha on 27 December 1970. Again in 1977 Indira Gandhi advised the president to dissolve the Lok Sabha. The president dissolved the Lok Sabha on 18 January 1977 and fresh elections were held. The Janata Party did not have a majority hence Charan Singh became the prime minister in 1979, although he did not face the Lok Sabha and his council of ministers recommended the dissolution of the Lok Sabha. Former President N. Sanjeeva Reddy dissolved the Lok Sabha on 22 August 1979 and mid-term polls were held. The Congress party headed by Indira Gandhi captured power in 1980. Likewise in 1991, 1997 and 1999, the house was dissolved and mid-term elections were held.

The president can prorogue both the houses or, alternately, either house. He is required to summon each house of Parliament from time to time to meet at such time as he thinks fit, but six months should not intervene between its last sitting in one session and the date appointed for its first sitting.

The Lok Sabha can also be summoned in a special session for disapproving the proclamation under Article 352, if a notice in writing signed by not less than one-tenth of the members of the Lok Sabha is given to the speaker. When such notice is given the president must summon the session within 14 days. The quorum for a meeting of either house of Parliament is one-tenth of the total number of members of the house. If at any time during a meeting of a house there was no quorum, the presiding officer's duty is to adjust the house or to suspend the meeting until there is a quorum. In December 2009, due to recurrence of this problem during question hour, the speaker suspended the question hour.

Speaker of the Lok Sabha

The Lok Sabha is presided over by the speaker who is elected by the house from among its members. The Constitution made references to the office of speaker and deputy speaker. Article 93 provides that the Lok Sabha shall choose members of the house to be respectively speaker and deputy speaker. If the office of the speaker or the deputy speaker even became vacant the house shall choose another member to be speaker and deputy speaker as the case may be. In the existing procedure this election is to be held on the very first sitting of the house. This meeting is to be presided over by a *pro tem* speaker and a convention is developing that the senior-most member of the house shall be nominated as a *pro tem* speaker. Both the speaker and deputy speaker are elected separately on motions moved and seconded by the respective party leaders. A convention has developed that a candidate sponsored by ruling party is elected unopposed to the office of the speaker and the candidate for the post of deputy speaker is generally from the opposition. Article 94 of the Constitution laid down that a member holding office as a speaker or deputy speaker shall vacate office if he ceased to be a member of the Lok Sabha, or if he resigned by writing in his hand or if he was removed from office by a resolution of the Lok Sabha passed by a majority of all members of the Lok Sabha. A resolution for the removal of the speaker could not be moved unless at least 14 days' notice is given to move the resolution. The same Article further says that the speaker will not vacate his office if the Lok Sabha is dissolved until immediately before the first meeting of the Lok Sabha after the dissolution. The speaker shall not preside over the meeting in which resolution for his removal in under consideration, through he would be present. The same provision is applicable for the deputy speaker. Such a resolution shall be effective only if passed by a majority of the house.

Powers and Functions of the Speaker

The speaker of Lok Sabha enjoys wide and extensive powers. Some of them are as follows:

1. His duty is to see that there is discussion and discipline in the house and that the business of the house is conducted in an orderly manner in accordance with wishes of the house.
2. The speaker is the only authority to decide who shall hold the floor and speak. Every member has to catch the eye of the speaker to get a chance to speak.
3. The speaker decides about the time which should be allotted to each item on the agenda.
4. The speaker decides what should appear in the proceedings. He has the right to expunge objectionable words, phrases and expressions from the proceedings.
5. He is the custodian of the rights and privileges of members of the Lok Sabha.
6. He certifies whether a particular bill is a money bill or not.
7. Whenever there is a joint meeting of both the houses of Parliament, the speaker presides over such meetings.
8. He decides all points of order raised during the course or discussion and his decision is binding.
9. The speaker decides which questions should or should not be admitted. It is he who allows half-an-hour discussion and admits adjournment motions. A vote of no-confidence against the government is also admitted by him.
10. The speaker admits all the resolutions for discussion and decides when a discussion on a bill should be adjourned.
11. He puts the motion to vote and announces the result of voting. In case there is a tie he casts his vote to decide the issue.
12. Without the speaker's permission no officer or employee of the Lok Sabha can appear as a witness in court of law.
13. No arrest or any other type of warrant can be issued by any executive authority against any member of the Lok Sabha within the house without speaker's prior permission.
14. He accepts all the resignations sent to him by members of the house.
15. It is the responsibility of the chair to protect the house from unnecessary executive instruction.
16. He can instruct the government to place a document on the table of the house.

The speaker authenticates all the bills passed in the house.

Thus, the speaker has vast powers and function. He is the channel of communication between the house and the president. In the house when speaker is on his feet, all the members are supposed to sit down and listen to him. If any member continues to stand that shall be treated as an affront to the speaker's dignity. He is not bound to give reasons for his decisions which cannot be challenged by any member.

The members of the Parliament must be able to work in a free atmosphere and have no fear of legal action or loss or damage in any way. Therefore, they have certain privileges, the two most important are that the members of Parliament have freedom of speech in the house and immunity from legal action in respect of anything said and done by them in Parliament or in any of the committees of Parliament. A third privilege is immunity from arrest and service of any legal process within the premises of Parliament, without the permission of the speaker or the chairman, as the case may be. The more important privileges and immunities of Parliament are as follows: (a) freedom from arrest, (b) power to summon persons, (c) power to punish for breach of privileges, (d) right to regulate its over internal proceedings, (e) right to exclude strangers.

The Rajya Sabha

The Rajya Sabha (council of states) is the 'upper house' of Parliament and it is also called the 'house of elders'. The justification of the second chamber was given by Gopalswamy Ayyanger. He said 'the most that we expect the second chamber to do is perhaps to hold dignified debates on important issues and to delay legislation which might be the outcome of the passions of the moment, to provide opportunity to seasoned people who may not be willing to participate in the debate with an amount of learning importance which we do not ordinary associate with the house of people.'[1]

Rajya Sabha: Its Composition

The maximum membership of the Rajya Sabha is limited to 250, out of which 238 members represent the states and the Union territories and 12 members are nominated by the president, on account of special knowledge or practical experience in respect of literature, science, art and social service.

The Rajya Sabha is indirectly elected (except nominated members) on a proportional representation basis by the state legislatures. On the basis of population, each state is allotted a certain number of seats in the Rajya Sabha. Article 79(4) says, 'The representatives of each state in the Rajya Sabha shall be elected by the elected members of the legislative assembly of the state in accordance with system of proportional representation by means of the transferable vote.'

The Rajya Sabha is not subject to dissolution. The term of its membership its six years, but one-third of its members retire on the expiration of every two years. The vacancies are filled through biennial elections, with the state assemblies forming the electoral college. The quorum for the meeting of the Rajya Sabha is one-tenth of the total number of members. All questions at any sitting of the house are decided by a majority of votes of the members present and voting.

The vice-president of India is its ex-officio chairman. The Rajya Sabha chose one of its members to be deputy chairman, and if the office of the deputy chairman became vacant, the Rajya Sabha chose another member to be its deputy chairman. He can resign his office by writing to the chairman. He may be removed by a resolution passed by a majority of all the members of the Rajya Sabha.

The Rajya Sabha also has a panel of members called 'vice-chairman' nominated by the chairman for the purpose of presiding over the Rajya Sabha in the absence of chairman and deputy chairman. The secretariat of the Rajya Sabha is headed by a secretary who discharges the same functions as the secretary of the Lok Sabha.

Power and Functions of the Rajya Sabha

In the legislative field, the Rajya Sabha enjoys an equal status with the Lok Sabha in all respects except in certain financial matters. A money bill or finance bill cannot be introduced in the Rajya Sabha. It is to be introduced in the Lok Sabha and after passing by the Lok Sabha, it has to be sent to the Rajya Sabha for its recommendations. Every money bill passed by the Lok Sabha will go to the Rajya Sabha for its consideration. Within 14 days of the receipt of the bill, if the Rajya Sabha passed it, the bill goes to the president for his assent. If the bill is amended or rejected by the Rajya Sabha, it goes back to the Lok Sabha where it is reconsidered and voted by a simple majority and sent to the president. Thus, in financial matters the Rajya Sabha's role is advisory and the Lok Sabha has the final say. There are numerous instances of rejection of financial bills by the Rajya Sabha. In August 1977, the Rajya Sabha objected to a bill but the objection was overruled by the Lok Sabha and the bill was considered to have been passed by both houses of Parliament. Likewise, in May 1978, the Rajya Sabha rejected a finance bill which proposed to impose excise duty on coal and electricity, but the Lok Sabha overruled the objection.

Another issue on which the Rajya Sabha asserted itself during the Janata Party regime was the appropriation bill for Rs 860.79 crores. It was adopted by the Lok Sabha on 21 December 1998 and was then sent to Rajya Sabha for its endorsement. It had been certified by the speaker as a money bill. The Congress (I) was in majority in Rajya Sabha which showed reluctant to cooperate with Janata government on the passing of the appropriation bill and therefore when the deputy chairman of the Rajya Sabha, Ram Niwas Mirdha, an astute and intelligent politician, saw that the opposition with the support of Congress (I) was determined to block the passage of the appropriation bill; he adjourned the Rajya Sabha *sine die* on 26 December. The bill became an Act on 5 January 1979, because the approval of the Rajya Sabha was not needed for a money bill. The Rajya Sabha, however, made its existence felt by not giving its approval, even though only formally.

Legislative Powers

The Rajya Sabha enjoys equal powers with Lok Sabha in the field of ordinary legislation. An ordinary bill or non-money bill can be introduced in the Rajya Sabha and it has to be approved by both houses of Parliament before it becomes an Act. The Lok Sabha has no powers to overrule the Rajya Sabha.

In March 1979, the opposition dominated Rajya Sabha inserted four amendments in the Special Courts Bill. The bill, which sought to provide for speedy trial of a certain category of offences, was amended to have a wider scope to cover offences committed not only during the Emergency but at any time. Another amendment was that the judges for the special courts would be appointed not by the government but by the chief justice of the high court in consultation with the chief justice of the Supreme Court. The amendments made by the Rajya Sabha were accepted by the Lok Sabha in May 1979, because otherwise the bill would have gone. The Congress (I) and AIADMK opposed this bill, but the other opposition parties including CPI, a long-time ally of Congress (I), went along with the Janata Party.

In January 1980, Congress (I) formed the government at the centre and Indira Gandhi became the prime minister. She had to face opposition in the Rajya Sabha because her party was not in majority there. The opposition parties were accusing the government of attempting to destabilize the states ruled by non-Congress (I) parties. The entire opposition, enjoying majority in the Rajya Sabha, sought to amend the president's address delivered to the newly-formed Lok Sabha. Such a thing had not happened in the history of Independent India. The amendment was moved by CPI leader Bhupesh Gupta and several other opposition leaders, who regretted, among other things, that the address did not take note of the disturbing attempts to engineer defections on a large scale in non-Congress (I) states to secure the dissolution of the assemblies there. The amendment was carried by 80 votes in favour and 75 against.

The cases of disagreement between the Rajya Sabha and Lok Sabha can be resolved in a joint session of Parliament in which each member has to vote. This gives an upper hand to the Lok Sabha because its membership is more than double of that of the Rajya Sabha. Until now there had been three joint sessions of both the houses summoned by the president. The first joint session took place in 1961 to resolve a deadlock on the Dowry Prohibition Bill, on which the two houses had finally agreed. The second joint session took place in 1978 on the Banking Service Commission (Repeal) Bill of 1977 and the Lok Sabha carried the day. The third joint session of Parliament was held on 26 March 2002 and the Anti-terrorist Bill (POTA) was passed. The Lok Sabha passed this Bill on 18 March, but the Bill was defeated in the Rajya Sabha on 21 March by a margin of 15 votes; hence the joint session was called.

Constitutional Amendments

To amend the Constitution, a bill is required to be passed by both the houses of Parliament. The Constitution (24th Amendment) bill 1970 was passed by an overwhelming majority in the Lok Sabha but was defeated in the Rajya Sabha by only a fraction of a vote, and consequently fell through. In 1989, the Rajiv Gandhi government suffered defeat in the Rajya Sabha for failing to carry through two Constitutional amendment bills, i.e. streamlining of *Panchayati Raj* and municipalities and corporations.

The electoral powers of the Rajya Sabha are the same as of the Lok Sabha. The Rajya Sabha plays an important role in the impeachment of the president. According to Article 61 the resolution of the removal of the president must be passed by each house by a majority of not less than two-thirds of the total membership of each house separately.

The powers of the Rajya Sabha are equal to that of Lok Sabha as for as the approval of emergency proclamations under Articles 352, 356 and 360 is concerned.

There are two other special provisions which confirm Rajya Sabha as the sole representative of the states under Article 249, the Rajya Sabha may by a resolution supported by not less than two-thirds of the members present and voting declare that it is necessary or expedient in the national interest that Parliament should make law with respect to any matter enumerated in the state list. Second, for the creation of new all-India services a resolution of Rajya Sabha, supported by a two-thirds majority is required. The Rajya Sabha passed such resolution on two occasions; one in 1961 for the creation of (i) the Indian services of engineers, (ii) Indian forest service and (iii) the Indian medical and health services; and the other in 1965 for the creation of the Indian agricultural service and the Indian education service.

The Role of the Rajya Sabha

The Constitution makers of the Indian Republic, while creating the second chamber of the legislature, had thought that it would (i) represent the views and interest of the states, (ii) would protect the interest of the states from the possible attack and interference by the Lok Sabha and Union government; (iii) that it would reflect the political complexion of the state legislatures, (iv) that through the system of proportional representation all shades of political opinion would be represented in Parliament, (v) that experience and elderly people, free from political prejudices and passion, would bring in their expertise in different fields, (vi) that it would act as a brake upon the Lok Sabha, which on occasions might seek to push bills through Parliament with undue haste and without adequate consideration and debate.

Now let us consider all these points by analysing the working of the Rajya Sabha. The Rajya Sabha functioning belied the hopes of the Constitution makers. The Rajya Sabha never bothered about the erosion of the power of states. Due to one-party, the Congress, rule in the state most of the time, the

Rajya Sabha could not adequately represent their interests. The average age of the members of the Rajya Sabha had not been higher than that of the Lok Sabha, therefore they had not provided maturity and wisdoms that was expected of them. The membership had been used to provide as rewards to those who could not be accommodated into seats of power and authority. The Rajya Sabha acted on bills in the similar way as the Lok Sabha and it quietly witnessed the virtual destruction of the federal structure of Indian polity, as had already been discussed while citing examples of dead lock between Lok Sabha and Rajya Sabha and their outcomes.

The Constitution of India had created two houses with a different composition and distinct functions have been assigned to them. But like a pair of blades in scissors, both have to function harmoniously together so as to ensure the success of parliamentary democracy in our country.

Powers of the Parliament

The powers of the Indian Parliament are quite vast and extensive, and are listed in various Articles of the Constitution. The Parliament is not a sovereign institution in India and if functions within the bounds of a written Constitution, which believes in the principles of division of power and judicial review. The powers of Parliament mentioned in the Constitution can be categories in four types, namely, law-making powers, financial powers, Constitution-amending powers and administrative powers.

The Constitution has classified the subjects for legislation into three lists: (i) the Union list (ii) the state list and (iii) the concurrent list. The Parliament has exclusive authority to make laws on the subjects mentioned in the Union list while on the subjects of the concurrent list, Parliament as well as the state legislatures have the power to make laws. But it is clearly mentioned in the Constitution that laws enacted by Parliament relating to the items of concurrent list shall prevail over corresponding legislation by the states except in such cases where the state legislation had been reserved for president and received his assent.

In special circumstances, the Parliament is empowered to make laws on the subjects mentioned in the state list; if the Rajya Sabha passes a resolution by special majority declares that it is necessary in the national interest to do so. During the proclamation of emergency, Parliament can make laws on any matter in the state list. In case a state government fails to carry out the work as per the provisions of the Constitution, the assembly may be suspended or dissolved by the president and Parliament make laws for the state. In addition to these three lists mentioned in the Constitution, the other item/matter not enumerated in these three lists belongs to Parliament. It is under the category of residuary powers. Parliament can even legislate if two or more state legislatures consider it desirable and pass resolution to that effect. Such legislation so passed has application only in the states which had requested it and those others which may adopt it afterwards by passing resolutions. Parliament is free to pass any law, for the whole or any part of the territory of India for implementing any treaty, agreement or convention with any other country or countries or any decision made at any international conference, association or other body.

The Constitution, Article 3, empowers Parliament to form a new state by separation of territory from any state or by uniting two or more states or part of states or by unifying any territory or part of any state; increase and decrease the area of any state; and the change the name of any state.

The Constitution empowers the Parliament to amend the Constitution. It can regulate the citizenship.

The political executive in India is the council of ministers and its head is the prime minister. The control of Parliament upon the executive is ensured by the provision in the Constitution that the government is answerable for all its acts or those of its officials to Parliament.

Parliament exercises control over the executive through questions, calling attention notice and other procedures like votes of censure, adjournment motions and numerous other procedures. It can also prevent the executive from taking a course of action by refusing to pass legislation required by the government or by its refusal to give its consent. Control is also exercised by various committees, like the Public Accounts Committee and the Committee of Public Undertakings.

Financial Powers

The Parliament controls the finances of the Union. It sanctions money to the government to enable it to run the administration. It may pass, reduce or reject the demands for grant presented to it by government but it cannot increase them. No taxes can be collected and no money can be spent without the authority of the Parliament.

Article 280(I) says that the president would appoint the Finance Commission, and the Parliament will determine the qualifications which will be requisite for appointment as a member of the Commission and the manner in which they would be selected. Article 302 laid down that Parliament can impose such restriction on one state and another or within any part of the territory of India as may be considered necessary in the public interest.

Judicial Powers

Parliament is empowered to make laws regulating the Constitution, jurisdiction and powers of the courts. Parliament has the power to decide the strength of judges in the Supreme Court. Parliament may by law extend the jurisdiction of a high court, to establish a common high court for two or more states and constitute a high court for a Union territory. A judge can be removed from office by the president, if a joint address passed by both houses of Parliament with a special majority is present to him. Under Article 262, Parliament can provide for the adjudication of any dispute or complaint with respect to the use, distribution or control of the water of, or in, any inter-state river or river valley. Parliament may by law provide for the establishment of an administrative tribunal for the union and separate administrative tribunal for each state or for two or more states.

Parliament could provide for the creation of one or more all-India services common to the Union and the states, if the Rajya Sabha declared by resolution supported by not less than two-thirds of the members present and voting that it was necessary or expedient to do so in national interest. Parliament could provide for appointment of a joint Public Service Commission for two or more states if those states agree to this and passed resolutions to that effect.

In the exercise of administrative powers, Parliament controls the council of ministers. As laid down in Article 75(3) of the Constitution, the council of ministers was collectively responsible to the Lok Sabha. This means that the council of ministers remains in office only so long as it enjoyed the confidence of the Lok Sabha. But in actual practice, the council of ministers stayed on in power so long as the political party to which it belonged was in majority.

Parliament can amend the Constitution in accordance with the procedure laid down in Article 368. The details of this procedure have already been discussed.

Prof. K. V. Rao holds the view that 'vis-à-vis the executive, our Parliament is a powerless body; in fact, it has no power of auto-action, no power of self-propulsion. It can meet only if summoned by the executive, its bills become law only if the executive is pleased to assent to; it can deal in financial matters only if the executive permits; in short, there is nothing which the Legislative can do without the executive, whereas the latter can do many things and get on for a long time without the legislature . . .' it can rule with old laws, promulgate ordinances, declare emergencies and spend money.[2]

Prof. K. V. Rao's views, though important, are not wholly true. The Indian Parliament has extensive powers and performs a variety of important functions. Parliament is our chief law-making body and in this respect its powers are legally limited due to the federal nature of the Indian republic and by the powers of the Supreme Court to declare parliamentary legislation void. It is further limited in an informal way, extra legally by the degree of control over it which the prime minister and party in power exercises. Parliament had the constituent powers and with certain limitations it can suitably amend the Constitution. But till Parliament amends the law or the constitutional provision, the law of the land will be as declared by the Supreme Court. Thus, in its own sphere, the Supreme Court is supreme.[3]

PARLIAMENTARY COMMITTEES

The Parliament is a big body and it is not a forum for the prompt disposal of the business. It desires serious examinations of various issues that come up before it from time to time and, therefore, much of its preliminary work is done by its committees. These committees are appointed or elected by the respective houses themselves or nominated by the presiding officers in consultation with the prime minister. Parliamentary committees are of two kinds—ad-hoc committees and standing committees. An ad-hoc committee is appointed for a specific purpose and when that is fulfilled it ceases to exist. The examples are the select and joint committees on bills. Such committees are appointed on other subjects as well. One such committee is the railways convention committee.[4]

Committees broadly fall into three categories. First are those which are concerned with organization and power of the houses; second are those that assist the houses in their legislative functions and third are those which deal with financial functions. In the first category, committees such as the committee of rules, privileges and absence of members and the business advisory committee; the legislative committees include select committees of either house and joint select committees of the two houses set up ad hoc for consideration of important bills. The three important committees in the third category are the Public Accounts Committee, the Estimates Committee and the Public Undertakings Committee. While the Rajya Sabha members are associated with the first and third categories of committees, the membership of the second committee is conferred on Lok Sabha members only. Ministers are barred from being members of these three committees.

The Public Accounts Committee consists of 15 members elected by the Lok Sabha and seven members of the Rajya Sabha are associated with it. A minister is not eligible for election to the committee. Since 1967, a member of opposition party is being appointed as the chairman of the committee. The committee scrutinized the appropriation accounts of the government of India and the reports of the comptroller and auditor-general of India. It ensures that public money was spent in accordance with Parliament's approval of the demands of various ministries, and draw attention to waste, extravagance, loss, nugatory expenditure or lack of financial integrity in public service. The life of the committee is one year.

The Estimates Committee consists of 30 members who are elected by Lok Sabha every year. A minister is not eligible for its membership. The life of the committee is one year. The committee examines estimates of the various ministries, departments and projects of the government of India and suggests economy, improvements in organization and efficiency or administrative reforms which can be effected in consistency with the policy underlying the estimates.

The committee on Public Undertakings examines the reports of the auditor-general. It also examines whether the public undertakings were being run efficiently and manages in accordance with sound business principles and commercial practices. The committee consists of 22 members—15 elected by the Lok Sabha and seven by the Rajya Sabha.

Other important committees of the Lok Sabha are the committee on government assurances, the committee on subordinate legislation and the committee on petitions. There are also three joint committees of the two houses. These are the committee on Office of Profit, the committee on the Welfare of Scheduled Castes and Scheduled Tribes, the committee on Salaries and Allowances of members of Parliament. The functions of these committees are self-explanatory.

There are consultative committees for different ministries, and these provide a forum for discussion between the ministers and members of Parliament on matters of policy and the working of the administrative departments.

Unless the presiding officer is the chairman himself, he nominates a chairman from among the members of a committee to conduct the meetings of the committee. Members take part in the discussion with the permission of the chairman. Decisions are taken by a majority vote. The conclusions of the committee are prepared in a report forums, which is presented to the Parliament.

The New Committee System in the Parliament

On 29 March 1993 the Lok Sabha unanimously took a decision to introduce the standing committee system into Indian Parliamentary Practice. While formally launching the formation of standing committees related to ministries at a function in the Central Hall of Parliament on 31 March 1993, the then Vice-President, K. R. Narayanan, inaugurating the new committee system, had hoped that 'This system, apart from dealing with the basic or ordinary issues, will tone up the functioning of Parliament.' The new committee system recommended by the rules committee and adopted by the Lok Sabha envisaged the formation of 17 joint standing committees. These committees are: Committee on Commerce, Committee on Home Affairs, Committee on Human Resource Development, Committee on Industry, Committee on Science and Technology, Environment and Forests, Committee on Transport and Tourism, Committee on Agriculture, Committee on Communications, Committee on Defence, Committee on Energy, Committee on External Affairs, Committee on Finance, Committee on Food, Civil Supplies and Public Distribution, Committee on Labour and Welfare, Committee on Petroleum and Chemicals, Committee on Railways, Committee on Urban and Rural Development.

Each committee consists of not more than 45 members—30 to be nominated by the speaker from amongst the members of the Lok Sabha and 15 to be nominated by the chairman of the Rajya Sabha from amongst the members of the Rajya Sabha. The term of the committee members is one year. The chairpersons of the various committees are nominated by the speaker in consultation with party leaders. The functions of these committees are as follows:

(a) Consideration of demand for grants
(b) Examination of bills referred to by the chairman, Rajya Sabha, or the speaker, Lok Sabha, as the case may be
(c) Consideration of annual reports
(d) Consideration of national basic long-term policy documents presented to the house and referred to the committee by the chairman or the speaker, as the case might be

Thus, these committees ensure a fuller examination and parliamentary scrutiny of grants and bills. At the same time, by relieving pressure on Parliament's time, they ensure fuller debate and discussion in the houses on important measures and policy issues. Looking to the utility of these committees, on 20 July 2004, the number of the standing committees was increased from 17 to 24 by a resolution of the

Lok Sabha. Now in each committee the Lok Sabha members will be 21 and from the Rajya Sabha 10 members. Out of these 24 committees, 16 will be from the Lok Sabha and the remaining eight from the Rajya Sabha.

The newly constituted departmentally related standing committee system is a path-breaking endeavour of parliamentary surveillance over administration, with the emphasis or long-term plans, policies, and the philosophies guiding the working of the Executive, these committees are proposed to be in a very privileged position to provide necessary direction, guidance and input for broad policy formulations and in achievement of the long-term national perspective by the Executive.[5]

The merits of the new committee system are that the Parliament is able to examine grants of departments along with detailed scrutiny of their performance.

Decline of the Parliament

The discussion of the powers of Parliament show that there is considerable erosion in the powers and influence of the Parliament and it is not sovereign due to the limitations laid down in the Constitution over its authority. Therefore, it is necessary to know the factors which are responsible for its decline.

These factors, broadly, are the Congress party's domination in Indian politics, strict party discipline, delegated legislation and complicity and vastness of government business, low level of parliamentarians, etc.

A virtual monopoly of one political party and unquestioned control of both houses of Parliament by the Congress party for about 40 years after Independence has systematically converted Parliament into a legislative rubber stamp. The opposition parties, of course, shouted and denounced government policies, but the government, due to sheer majority support, cared little for their point of view. There have been occasions when the opposition parties felt aggrieved over the disregard the government showed towards parliamentary procedures and power. On 8 December 1974, Jan Sangh leader Vajpayee, announcing his decision to resign from the Lok Sabha, said he had thought of taking that step because Parliament 'instead of exerting itself as the highest legislative body representing sovereignty of the Indian people has been reduced to a mere rubber stamp to serve the ends of the majority party.' He further said: 'No longer decisions are taken in Parliament on the basis of argument, logic and facts. Issues are decided irrespective of their merit on the basis of brute majority.'[6] Shouts and counter shouts and disorderly scenes became the order of the day in both houses of Parliament. Looking to the record of bills passed in the Lok Sabha it is evident that proper working and public discussion did not take place at all. Almost 105 statutes were passed by the house on the same day they were introduced. Twenty-three were introduced with one day's notice, eight with two, 12 with three and 10 with four-day's notice. The Anti-defection Amendment was passed with six days' notice, one day each by the Rajya Sabha and the Lok Sabha. The Punjab (59th) Amendment was debated the very day it was introduced. How can Parliament do justice to this volume of legislation? If legislative function was thwarted with such alacrity, Parliament was denied the power to discharge its responsibility from making the government accountable to the nation through Parliament.[7]

Second, the strict party discipline contributed to the decline of Parliament. Political parties manoeuvred and managed polities to get power. In order to do this, these parties devised policies and programmes, determined their aims and objective, contested elections, selected candidates for contesting elections from different constituencies, raised financial and physical resources to win and formed government if and when they secured the requisite majority. The contestants depend upon party for their resource and once a candidate had won he became tied down to the discipline and dictates of party bosses, therefore, he has to vote according to the directives of the party or otherwise he might lose his membership.

Third, delegated legislation has also caused the decline of Parliament. Nowadays, the work of the government has increased manifold because India is a welfare state and problems of national and international communities are so vast and varied that the Parliament could not provide the requisite amount of legislation. It is impossible for it to foresee all possibilities and feasibilities and the Parliament only lays down the general principles of law, and entrusts to ministers, the power to frame the regulations necessary for their implementation, a task which is called delegated legislation and is mainly done by the secretaries of the departments under the ministers. If Parliament attempted to provide all the details of the law itself, it would not be able to cope with the growing amount of government work. As a result of all these compulsions, the performance of Parliament declined and those of administrative departments had increased. Fourth, the standard of debates in Parliament has considerably fallen. Debates in Parliament were known for humour and sharp wit but today they have been reduced to character assassinations, abuse and insults. When 104 opposition members resigned from the Lok Sabha, prime minister, Rajiv Gandhi, speaking in the house, charged them with running away from Parliament. Not only has the standard of debates fallen, it has amounted to wasting time by shouting. In 14th Lok Sabha's total sitting meeting were 304, and out of 1732 hours of their meetings 415 hours were wasted in shouting.

Likewise, the situation in this regard in the 15th Lok Sabha is not better. In July 2009 budget session, 23 hours were wasted in shouting and in the winter session time was wasted shouting on the Liberhan Commission Report on Babri Masjid destruction and on the separation of Telengana issue.

Fifth, even in financial matters no accountability is shown. Each time an Appropriation Bill for voting on account was placed before Parliament, and crores of rupees were sanctioned. Even 2004–2005, the General Budget was passed without any discussion. Similarly, there was no discussion on 105 demands, and grants totalling Rs 3,39,299 crores were cleared. The Appropriations Bill giving statutory sanction to the grants passed and the 'charged' accounts was passed without discussion. This involves expenditure of over Rs 8 lakh crore. The expenditure of one session of Parliament per minute is 26 thousand rupees and an hour's expenditure is 10 lac and 60 thousand rupees. Thus, a lot of money is wasted without doing work in Parliament.

It is true that during Jawaharlal Nehru's time the Indian Parliament when in session was a business like forum with dignity and authority. Nehru's charisma enabled him to secure Parliament's approval for his policies. The members came well prepared and were heard with attention. Debates were outstanding and critical of the functioning of the executive even by the ruling party itself. The opposition was weak and fragmented but Nehru gave it a sense of participation. The credit for raising the status of Parliament goes to Nehru.

Sixth, the last factor which led to the decline of Parliament was the technicality and complexity of government business. Legislation on technical issues needs prior consultation with experts and the institutions concerned. A good deal of fact and background information is necessary before a bill was drafted. This is not within the easy reach of private members. Moreover, it is easy for the government to get all the information and adequate data before a bill was drafted and presented in Parliament. The result was that when introduced, the bills were pushed through rapidly, with the members hardly getting enough time to express their point of view.

All these factors show that India has a parliamentary form of government only in name. All the powers of Parliament have passed into the hands of the cabinet headed by the prime minister. The creation of the Prime Minister's Office as the parallel system of power meant that the prime minister dominated his colleagues.

Restoration of Parliamentary Supremacy

The powers of Parliament have declined and those of the prime minister and his cabinet have increased. The Supreme Court wanted to check this trend. The apex court did not like that the executive usurp what actually fell within the realm of the legislature. It declared in the *Golak Nath* case that the Parliament would not have, with effect from the date of judgement, i.e. 29 February 1967, the power to amend the third chapter of the Constitution, which deals with fundamental rights. Article 13(2) had already declared that the state, (which meant Parliament too), would not make any law that is an ordinary law which took away or abridged the rights conferred by that chapter. In the light of these limitations upon the law-making and Constitution-amending powers of Parliament, the Supreme Court set aside the laws which have been passed in contravention of these limitations. Two such cases are the Banking Companies (Acquisition and Transfer of Undertakings) Act, and the presidential order of 16 September 1970, derecognizing the former princes and rulers. The government of Indira Gandhi did not like the court's decisions, and at an appropriate time, she made parliamentary supremacy a reality.

Let us discuss the concept of parliamentary supremacy or sovereignty and its limitations. The India Parliament is given the same powers and functions as its counterpart in England but in terms and practice our Parliament is not sovereign as the English Parliament is. In English law, constitutional experts agree, the sovereignty of Parliament is a legal fact, as De Lolme has put it, the English 'Parliament can do everything under the scene but make a women a man and a man woman' meaning that its only limitation is set by nature. Dicey said that 'the sovereignty of Parliament is from legal point of view the dominant characteristic of our political institutions', is resolved by him into three portions: (i) There is no law which the Parliament cannot make, (ii) there is no law which Parliament cannot repeal or modify, and (iii) there is, under the English constitution, no distinction between laws which are fundamental or constitutional and other laws. Under this meaning of sovereignty, our Parliament is not sovereign. The laws it makes and repeals are limited by the Constitution. The powers of the Indian Parliaments are similar as shown by the various administrative details given in Part III (Fundamental Rights) and the state list in Schedule VII of the Constitution. This limitation is expressly made effective by giving power to the courts to decline the laws of the Parliament as unconstitutional. The Constitution makers had realized that fundamental rights could not be, and should not be, absolute. Many felt there might be situations in the life of the Nation whose rights could not be ensured, therefore, they themselves hedged some of those rights in certain important respects. The rulers of the country found that the limitations imposed upon fundamental rights in the Constitution are not enough, therefore, they began to amend and abridge some of them. The first constitutional amendment was made under Article 368 with the purpose of saving the Zamindari Abolition Act from judicial scrutiny. This was questioned in the Supreme Court in 1951 in *Shankari Prasad*'s case. The court gave the ruling that the Parliament had the power to amend Chapter III of the Constitution. Its argument was that the word 'law' in Article 13(2) was made in exercise of law-making power and not 'constitutional law' made in exercise of constituent power.

In 1961, the Kerala Land Reforms Act and in 1963, the Madras Land Reforms Act, which provided for a ceiling on land holdings, were declared by the Supreme Court as invalid. In order to save these Acts in 1964, the 17th Constitution Amendment Act was passed and all the 43 state Acts dealing with land reforms were put in the Ninth Schedule to the Constitution to save them from invalidation. In the *Sajjan Singh* case in 1965, the validity of these Acts was questioned. In this case, the Supreme Court was called upon to reconcile the provisions of Articles 13 and 368. The majority decision rejected the contention of the petitioner that Article 368 did not confer on Parliament the power to take away or abridge fundamental rights and held that the power conferred by that Article included taking away fundamental rights, and that the word 'law' in Article 13(2) did not include a constitutional law made in pursuance of Article 368. The Supreme Court stuck to the position it had taken in *Shankari Prasad*'s case.

The issue of Parliament's power to amend the Constitution for taking away or abridging any of the fundamental rights came up before the Supreme Court for the third time in the *Golak Nath* case. This case was decided by an 11 judge bench headed by chief justice K. Subha Rao. In a majority decision of six to five, the Supreme Court declared that as from the date of the judgement, that is 27 February 1967, Parliament would not have the power to make any law which took away or abridged the fundamental rights as enshrined in Chapter III of the Constitution. The chief justice observed that the fundamental rights of the citizens were over and above every other power under the Constitution and were 'primordial' and 'transcendental'. The Constitution permitted only such restrictions on them as the judges approved as reasonable, and not as Parliament sought to impose. The decision caused estrangement between the government and the Supreme Court.

Under the Banking Companies (Acquisition and Transfer of Undertakings) Act, fourteen top commercial banks of the country were nationalized, but on 10 February 1970, the Supreme Court, by a majority of 10 to 1, declared this Act to be invalid and unconstitutional, saying that the Act voided Article 14 relating to 'equality before law'. On 15 December 1970, the Supreme Court struck down the presidential order of 16 September 1970 derecognizing the former rulers and held that the power of the president under Article 36(22) did not extend to the withdrawal of recognition of all the rulers by 'a midnight order'. According to the majority decision, writ petitions were allowed with costs.

Prime Minister Indira Gandhi was left embarrassed and waited for an opportune time. The opportunity came soon after the mid-term poll of Parliament, which was held March 1971 and which gave her party 351 seats—a clear two-thirds majority to pass constitutional amendment. The Parliament passed the 24th Constitution Amendment Bill, which became an Act on 5 November 1971. A new clause (4) in Article 13 was inserted which provided for the prohibition that the 'state shall not make any law which takes away or abridges the rights conferred by Part III shall not apply to any amendment of the Constitution made under Article 368.' The original heading of Article 368 as 'procedure for amendment of the Constitution', was also amended as 'power of Parliament to amend the Constitution and procedure thereof'. The president was also bound to give assent to any amendment of the Constitution and after this amendment reassertion of parliamentary supremacy started.

In April 1972, the 25th Constitution Amendment Act was passed and it provided that restrictions on the power of Parliament under Article 13 would not apply to a law made to give effect to the policy of the state enumerated in Article 39, clauses (b)[8] and (c).[9] No such law 'shall be deemed to be void on the ground that it is inconsistent with or takes away or abridges any of the rights conferred by Article 14, Article 19 or Article 31'. This was a further step in rebuilding the Parliament as a sovereign body.

The 24th and 25th Constitution Amendment Acts were challenged in the Supreme Court by Keshwanand Bharti, a Kerala religious priest and ten others. This case was decided by a 13 judge bench headed by the Chief Justice on 24 April 1973. Nine of the judges reversed the decision given in the *Golak Nath* case and restored to Parliament the power of amending the Constitution including Part III of the fundamental rights. But it maintained that under Article 368 Parliament could not change the 'basic structure' or 'framework' of the Constitution.

This view of the Supreme Court was challenged by many on the ground that even the Constitution did not mention the basic 'structure' or 'framework' of the Constitution and a majority of the Supreme Courts judges could not determine this issue. The government was unhappy over the curtailment of Parliament's powers but did nothing to disturb the 'basic feature' of the Constitution.

On the advice of the then prime minister, President Fakhruddin Ali Ahmed proclaimed Internal Emergency in the country on 26 June 1975, and the government, taking advantage of this situation, pushed through Parliament several constitutional amendment bills meant for establishing parliamentary supremacy.

The then law minister introduced a more comprehensive amendment bill (the 42nd Amendment) in the Lok Sabha on 25 October 1976, which drastically amended Article 368. Two more clauses

4 and 5 were inserted in that Article. Clause 4 barred challenge of the 42th Amendment in any court on any ground; clause 5 stated that for removal of doubts, it was declared that there shall be no limitation whatsoever on the constituent power of Parliament to amend by way of addition, negation or repeal of the provisions of the Constitution under this (368) Article. This proviso unambiguously established parliamentary supremacy in India.

A former attorney-general of India, C. K. Daphtany, observed that the professed object of the 42 Constitution Amendment Act was in fact, assigned not to establish the supremacy of Parliament but the absolute authority of the executive as personified by the prime minister.

Justice Krishna Iyer of the Supreme Court said on 28 February 1999 that the doctrine of parliamentary supremacy was evoked by the rulers of the day just to enhance their own power and authority. They styled Supreme Court's power of judicial review as 'undemocratic' and charged it of having become a 'superlegislature'.

After the Emergency elections were held in March 1977, the Janata Party came to power at the centre and rectified many distortions introduced during Emergency, particularly with regard to the Parliament and the judiciary.

On 10 May 1980 the Supreme Court invalidated the change that had been made in Article 368 by the 42nd Amendment Act. Section 55 of that Act had inserted clauses 4 and 5 in Article 368 of the Constitution and the result was that Parliament was given unrestricted powers of passing any law to amend any part of the Constitution. In its ruling in the *Minerva Mills* case, the Supreme Court struck down that section as void and declared that the inclusion of that section was beyond the amending power of Parliament as it affected the 'basic features' of the Constitution. The effect of this decision was that Parliament's power to amend the Constitution was restricted to the extent that it could not alter the essential feature of the basic structure of the Constitution. The Indian Parliament is a creature of the Constitution by whose provisions it, therefore, is bound.

The decline of Parliament was halted by the era of coalition governments from the nineties and is still continuing. It revived the good old days of Parliament. The nature of parliamentary elections has changed. Now, it is more parliamentary than plebiscitary in the name of the prime minister, and an ordinary member of Parliament gets elected due to his own efforts and popularity than due to his national leader. He is dependent on the party for resources, support workers and organization. He develops his own strategy to win the election and his dependence on national leaders has substantially reduced. No party gets a majority and the mandate these days is a split one. Therefore, coalition is necessary and inevitable.

The authority of the prime minister has weakened because of the dependence on other coalition partners for majority support. The party discipline has remained not absolute, although defections are penalized as per the provisions of the Constitution, but not splits. Most of the time of the prime minister and his office is spent in management of coalition partners. Most of the time, by accepting their demands, the prime minister yields to please the parties who support him. The court has become active and assertive. They are effectively playing the role assigned to them by the Constitution. The Supreme Court is now perceived as a necessary restraint on the executive. As we have discussed in the next chapter, judicial activism has led the courts to become parallel centres of power and they are helping in governance. The system expects that courts should supplement the work of the executive.

The introduction of LPG reforms, i.e. liberalization, privatization and globalization have affected enormously. The market has become important and even superseded the state. There is a general decline of political authority. Factions and cliques have come into being and they operate and rule. Thus, the authority of the prime minister has declined and the authority of the Parliament has revived in this relative sense. Till the time coalition governments persist, Parliament's importance will increase in the coming years.

NOTES

1. *CAD, Vol. IV,* 1947, pp. 927–28.
2. K. V. Rao, *Parliamentary Democracy of India: A Critical Commentary* (Calcutta: The World Press Pvt. Ltd, 1965), p. 121.
3. Subhas C. Kashyap, *Parliament in the Indian Polity* (New Delhi: Government of India Press, 1987), pp. 31–33.
4. Subhas C. Kashyap, *Our Parliament* (New Delhi: NBT, 1992), p. 14.
5. *The Sunday Tribune,* Chandigarh, 1 October 2000.
6. Later, Vajpayee withdrew his resignation in deference to the wishes of his party's Central Parliamentary Board.
7. Rajeev Dhawan, 'What they did to Parliament', *The Indian Express,* 13 November 1989.
8. Article 39 (Clause B) says that 'the ownership and control of the material resources of the community are so distributed as best to subserve the common good.'
9. Article 39 (Clause C) mentions that 'the operation of the economic system does not result in the concentration of wealth and means of production to the common detriment.'

The Supreme Court of India

The Constitution of India provides for the establishment of a Supreme Court for the whole country in Part V, Chapter IV, under Articles 124 to 147 of the Constitution. The court came into being on 26 January 1950, the day on which the Constitution of free and independent India was promulgated. Till 10 October 1949, the Judicial Committee of the Privy Council in England was the highest court for the country. Later, the Federal Court set up under the Government of India Act, 1935, was the final court of appeal until the Supreme Court was constituted.

Article 124 of the Constitution provides that the Supreme Court shall consist of a chief justice and not more than seven judges. The Parliament was empowered to increase the number of judges by law. Due to the increase in the workload, the strength of the Supreme Court judges has been raised from time to time. In 1956, the Parliament used its power and framed the Supreme Court (Number of Judges) Act. This raised the number of judges to 10, excluding the chief justice. This Act was amended again in 1960 and the number of judges was raised to 14, including the chief justice. Its strength was further increased to 18 in 1977 during Janata Party rule. The Parliament in 1986 increased the number of judges and till date the Supreme Court consists of the chief justice and 25 other judges.

The Appointment of Judges

Article 124(2) of the Constitution provides that a judge of the Supreme Court shall be appointed by the president in consultation with such of the judges of the Supreme Court and of the high court in the states as the president may deem necessary for the purpose. In the case of appointment of a judge other than the chief justice, the Chief Justice of India must be consulted. A Supreme Court judge can hold office till the age of 65 years.

In the judiciary, a controversy has been raised regarding who should appoint or transfer judges. In 1993, a constitutional bench of nine judges of the Supreme Court decided that the Chief Justice of India (CJI) held the pre-eminent role in such matters. The judgement did not clearly mention whether the CJI could override his senior colleagues or was merely the first among equals. Former CJI, M. M. Punchhi, who retired in October 1998, held the view that the CJI has the key in such matters, which resulted in bringing appointments in the Supreme Court and high courts to a standstill and created a crisis situation.

In July 1998, the president sought court opinion on issues relating to the appointments of the Supreme Court judges and transfer of high court judges. The presidential reference sought clarification on certain doubts over the consultation process to be adopted by the CJI as stipulated in a 1993 case relating to appointment of judges and their transfer.

In October 1998, a bench of nine judges of the court headed by the CJI, S. P. Bhurucha, decided that for the appointment of judge of apex court, the CJI should consult a collegium of four senior-most judges of the court. The collegium should take the decision in consensus. Thus the judgement makes the CJI one among other judges in appointing colleagues.

President K. R. Narayanan, when appointing judges to the Supreme Court, wrote a note on a file recommending that Scheduled Caste and Scheduled Tribe candidates be duly considered for appointment as judges of the Supreme Court. This was the first time when the president had chosen to put his suggestion on record. The president's active intervention may inject political consideration in the appointments. Article 126 provided for appointment of an 'acting' chief justice by the president from among the other judges of the Supreme Court if by reason of absence or otherwise, the chief justice was unable to perform his duties. Article 127 provided for the appointment of an 'ad-hoc' judge. If at any time the quorum of the judges to hold or continue any session of the court was not available, the chief justice could, with the prior consent of the president and after consultation with the chief justice of the high court concerned, request in writing the attendance at the sittings of the court as an 'ad-hoc' judge for such period as might be necessary, of a judge of a high court duly qualified for appointment as judge of the Supreme Court.

Article 128 of the Constitution provides for the attendance of retired judges at the sitting of the Supreme Court if the chief justice so requested and the president gave prior consent. Such a judge was entitled to allowances determined by the president and exercised the jurisdiction, powers and privileges as were enjoyed by a regular judge.

Qualifications of Judges

A person shall not be qualified to be appointed a judge unless he (a) is a citizen of India, (b) had been for at least five years a judge of high court or of two or more such courts in succession, (c) had been for at least ten years an advocate of a high court or of two or more such courts in succession or (d) was in the opinion of the president a distinguished jurist.

The inclusion of the last provision was meant as wide open field of choice for the president but such a jurist hardly finds place in the collegiums' list, being an outsider to the system.

Tenure

There is no minimum age nor any fixed period of office prescribed for appointment as a judge of the Supreme Court. The appointment of a judge of the apex court may cease to be so, on the occasion of any one of the following (other than death) (a) on attaining the age of 65 years (b) on resigning his office in his own under his handwriting addressed to the president; (c) on being removed by the president upon an address to that effect being passed by a specified majority of each house of Parliament.

Removal

A judge of the Supreme Court can be removed only on the ground of proven misbehaviour or incapacity. He can be removed by an order of the president passed after an address from each house of

Parliament, supported by a majority of the total membership of not less than two-thirds of the members present and voting.

Salary of the Judges

The salary of judges is increased by law passed by the Parliament. In February 2009, the salary of the judges was increased by a law passed by Parliament. The salary of a CJI was rupees one lakh per month and other judges' salary was rupees ninety thousand per month. Each judge was also entitled to certain privileges, rights of leave of absence and pension and these are determined by parliamentary law from time to time. Each judge gets a rent-free house and certain other allowances and privileges. The salary of each judge is liable to income tax. Further, neither the privileges nor the allowances of a judge nor his rights in respect to leave of absence or pension shall be varied to his disadvantage after his appointment, except in times of financial emergency proclaimed by the president. The salaries of the judges may be reduced by a law of Parliament.

On 28 October 1972, the then chief justice, S. M. Sikri, stated that the pension of the judges should be almost equal to their salary so that they were not driven to seeking jobs and starting practice 'after retirement'. He also stated while inaugurating the fourth convention of all-India Tax Advocates Association in New Delhi 'that it is said that it is the deliberate policy of the government not to increase the pension and not to improve the conditions of service so that the judiciary may gradually lose its respect and importance'. He further added, 'Even if it is not the government's policy, it is having that effect.' The situation today is that due to the small number of judges a large number of cases are pending in the Supreme Court, high courts and lower courts. As the saying goes 'justice delayed is justice denied!' A large number of aggrieved persons who approached the higher judiciary to seek redress and justice of the wrong done to them either by the state or by private individuals found themselves involved in endless litigation, expenditure, agony and hardship. This situation undermines the people's trust in the judicial system.

Prohibition of Practice After Retirement

No person who has held office as a judge of the Supreme Court can be placed or act in any other court or before any other authority within the territory of India. But there is no constitutional bar against a retired judge being appointed as chairperson of any enquiry commission or for any specialized work by the government.

The Seat of the Supreme Court

Article 130 of the Constitution says the Supreme Court shall sit in Delhi or in such other place or places, as the Chief Justice of India may, with the approval of the president from time to time decide. This provision may some day clear the way for the establishment of Supreme Court benches at different places in the country, though it was justified by Dr B. R. Ambedkar in the Constituent Assembly by saying, 'suppose the capital of India was changed, we would have to amend the Constitution in order to allow the Supreme Court to sit at such other place as the Parliament may decide as the capital. Therefore, I think subsequent words are necessary.'

Supreme Court: A Court of Record

Article 129 of the Constitution made the Supreme Court a 'court of record'. A court of record was a court where of the acts and judicial proceedings were controlled for perpetual memory and which were not to be challenged or questioned. Once a court was made a court of record, the power to furnish for its own contempt necessarily followed from its position.

The Supreme Court made use of this power in a number of cases, the two important cases being those of R. K. Khadilkar, the minister of state in the Union Finance Ministry and E. M. S. Namboodiripad, the former chief minister of Kerala. The former case arose due to certain comments of the minister in a discussion organized at New Delhi by the '*Blitz* National Forum' to discuss the Supreme Court judgment in the bank nationalization case. He was quoted by the *Hindustan Times* as saying that such a decision did not enhance the prestige of the judiciary, that it will encourage 'naxalites' and that the judgement would be treated with 'more and more contempt by the ordinary people'. He said that the judges sat in 'ivory towers', and wished the Supreme Court took note 'of the changing situation and help to reform society for the benefit of the common man'. An MP, Krishna Rao, and Lt Col. H. R. Pasricha presented a petition before the Supreme Court and contended that the remarks by the ministers affected the dignity and prestige of the court and shook the confidence of the whole community by which the administration of justice was bound to be undermined. They prayed for contempt proceedings to be initiated against the minister. The court issued a show cause notice to Khadilkar asking why action should not be taken against him. The minister denied the main allegation and said that he was a firm believer in the independence and dignity of the court. The matter was closed.

The second case arose out of an appeal filed in the Supreme Court by E. M. S. Namboodripad against the judgment of the Kerala high court. The chief minister was reported to have stated on 9 November 1967, at a press conference in Trivandrum that judges were guided and dominated by class hatred, class interest and class prejudices. He also observed that the judiciary was weighted against workers, peasants and other sections of the working classes, and that the law and the system of judiciary essentially served the exploiting classes.

An advocate lodged a complaint before the Kerala high court that the chief minister had lowered the prestige of the judges in the eyes of the public, and, therefore, was guilty of contempt of the Court. The high court, by a 2–1 majority, held that the CM had committed contempt of the court, and imposed a fine of Rs 1,000 on him or in default, to undergo simple imprisonment for one month.

The CM filed an appeal before the Supreme Court, where V. K. Krishna Menon, a politician of good standing and an advocate of the Supreme Court, contended that the law of contempt must be read without encroaching upon the guaranteed freedom of speech and expression in Article 19(1)(a) of the Constitution and that the remarks made by the appellant should be viewed within the light of his political views. Chief Justice Hedayatulla, who delivered the judgement pointed that provisions of Article 19(1)(a) should be given due consideration and the provisions of the Article could not be overlooked. This clause mentions that while exercising the right of freedom of speech, contempt of court should not be committed. He upheld the contention, but reduced the fine to Rs 50 only. In December 1992, P. L. Lakhanpal, chairman, All India Jantantra Party (Democratic), filed an application against Union minister, Mohan Kumarmangalam, and West Bengal Chief Minister, S. S. Ray, before the Supreme Court. They were alleged to have said at Ahmedabad on 8 October 1972, that elected representations of the people and not 'a coterie of persons accidentally elevated to the post of judge should decide the guidelines of the society, and that the judges worked down upon the masses as common clay and thought that they had the wisdom to decide the good of all.' The speech was published in *Hindustan Times* and a notice was issued to its editor, B. G. Verghese, asking why action be not taken against him. Ray and Kumarmangalam issued a denial. Verghese offered apologies, and the matter was closed.

Jurisdiction and Powers of the Supreme Court

The Supreme Court of India is a most powerful and highest court in the country and stood at the apex of the Indian judiciary. The Supreme Court has original jurisdiction, appellate jurisdiction and advisory jurisdiction.

Article 131 gave the exclusive original jurisdiction to the Supreme Court over all disputes (i) between the government of India and one or more states; (ii) between the government of India and any state or states on the one side and one or more other states on the other, or (iii) between two or more states, if and insofar as the dispute involved any question of law or fact on which the existence or extent of a legal right depended. The Union of India and the states were endowed with a quasi-corporate personality and they could sue and be sued by one another. According to Article 71(1), the Supreme Court exercised original jurisdiction to decide all disputes and doubts arising out of or in connection with the election of the president or vice-president, and its decision is final. The election of V. V. Giri as the president of India was challenged by the opposition party members Abdul Ghani Dhar, Shiv Kirpal Singh and Phul Singh in November–December 1969, and after a long hearing the Supreme Court decided that the election was valid. The election of Gopal Swarup Pathak as Vice-President of India was challenged in September 1969 by H. V. Kamath, an MP, and Justice S.M. Sikri upheld the election.

The election of N. Sanjiva Reddy as the President of India was challenged by a Supreme Court advocate. The seven-judge Constitution bench of the Supreme Court headed by Chief Justice M. H. Beg dismissed the petition as not maintainable, on 16 February 1978. The court ruled that the procedure for questioning the presidential election having been laid down, the petitioner and did not come within the four corners of that procedure and, therefore, did not have *locus standi* to challenge the election.

Appellate Jurisdiction

The Supreme Court has appellate jurisdiction in certain cases from judgement of the high courts. The appellate jurisdiction of the Supreme Court can be divided into three categories: (i) cases involving interpretation of the Constitution, civil, criminal or otherwise; (ii) civil cases, irrespective of any constitutional question; and (iii) criminal cases irrespective of any constitutional question.

Article 132(1) provides that an appeal shall lie with the Supreme Court, whether in civil, criminal or other proceedings, if the high court certified that the case held a substantial question of law as to the interpretation of the Constitution. If the high court refuses to give such a certificate, the Supreme Court might, if it is satisfied that a case involved a substantial question of law as to the interpretation of the Constitution, grant special permission to appeal. If power of granting special permission to appeal had not been given to the Supreme Court, different high courts would have caused a good deal of confusion by giving varied and sometimes divergent meanings to the provisions of the Constitution.

In matters of civil cases, Article 133 of the Constitution provides that an appeal shall lie with the Supreme Court from any judgement, decree or final order in a civil proceeding of a high court if it certified that a case is fit for appeal to the Supreme Court. In July 1979, the Supreme Court decided to delete the rule of getting certificate from high court as a precondition for appeal because it caused lot of hardship, unnecessary expenses and delay in such cases. Article 134 of the Constitution states that an appeal shall lie with the Supreme Court from any judgement, final order or sentence in a criminal proceedings of a high court if the high court (i) had through an appeal reversed an order of acquittal of an accused person and sentenced him to death; (b) or had withdrawn for trial before itself any case from any court subordinate to its authority, and had in such trial, convicted the accused person and sentenced him to death; or (c) certified that the case was a fit one for appeal to the Supreme Court. Article 134(2) empowered the Parliament on 19 December 1969 to confer by law upon the Supreme Court any further powers to entertain and hear appeals from any judgement, final order or sentence in a criminal proceeding of a high court. The Lok Sabha passed a bill for the enlargement of appellate (criminal) jurisdiction. Every citizen now could appeal to the Supreme Court regardless of the period of imprisonment.

The provisions of Article 134 showed that appeals in criminal matters could lie with the Supreme Court in two ways—with a certificate of the high court and without such a certificate. The idea was that the Supreme Court is not bound to entertain an appeal holding a high court certificate. The Supreme Court expressed the view that normally the certificate under Article 134(1)(c) should be granted only when any question of law was involved, and that ordinarily the high courts should be courts of appeal for criminal courts.[1]

Supreme Court's Power to Grant Special Leave to Appeal

The Supreme Court has been vested with wide discretionary powers. Article 136 states that 'Notwithstanding anything in this chapter, the Supreme Court may, in its discretion, grant special leave to appeal from any judgment, decree, determination of sentence or order in any cause or matter passed or made by any court or tribunal in the territory of India!'[2]

This power has become a convenient tool in the hands of the court to review the decision of election, labour and industrialist tribunals. It, however, granted special leave sparingly, and only in cases where it considered necessary to do so in the interest of justice and only where special circumstances existed. In the opinion of M. V. Pylee, this discretionary power then became a convenient tool in the hands of the court to check unjust decisions and arbitrary acts of the Union and states governments by setting up the process of realizing the objective of a socialist pattern of society.

Advisory Jurisdiction

The advisory role of the Supreme Court is provided in Article 143(1). It is stated that if at any time it appears to the president that a question of law or fact had arisen or was likely to arise which was of such a nature and of such importance that it was necessary to obtain the opinion of the Supreme Court upon it, he/she might refer the question to that court for consideration, and the court might, after such hearing as it deemed fit, report to the president its opinion thereupon.

The Supreme Court is obliged to give its opinion on a reference made to it under clause (2) of Article 143. It is under no such obligation as regard reference under clause (1) of the same Article. The words 'may' in clause (1) and 'shall' in clause (2) led to such an inference. In legal terms, the opinion of the Supreme Court was only advisory and not binding upon the president, but in actual practice, its opinion on serious controversies has a great binding force and legally authoritative. Up to 1978, there were seven cases of reference of this class made by the president. The important among them were: the Kerala Education Bill 1957, the Indo-Pak agreement of 10 Sept 1958 relating to the exchange of territories (including Berubari Union). On 10 May 1963, the Supreme Court gave its opinion on the interpretation of Article 289 about the immunity of the state from Union taxation. On 30 September 1964, the advisory opinion was given on the conflict of jurisdiction between the Legislative Assembly of UP and the high court of the state.

Presidential election, 1994. In December 1978, the Court's opinion was on the constitutional validity of setting up of special courts to try Emergency offences. In 1992, the Cauvery Disputes Tribunal case was referred to the Supreme Court for its opinion. The Ayodhya temple dispute was referred to the Supreme Court for its opinion on whether a temple originally existed at the site where the Babri Masjid subsequently stood. The opinion of the court was that it was a superfluous issue and did not require to be answered. On 22 July 2004 the Union government, through a presidential reference under Article 143, sought the opinion of the Supreme Court in the matter of construction of the Sutlej–Yamuna Link Canal, based on the Punjab government's enactment of the Punjab Termination of Agreements Act 2004. The Act terminated all inter-state treaties/tribunals, which are yet to take effect.

In this four-point reference the president sought to know whether the Act is constitutionally valid and really discharges the State government from the water agreement. It affects the agreement of sharing of the waters of Ravi, Beas and Sutlej rivers among Punjab, Haryana, Rajasthan and Himachal Pradesh. The matter perhaps will finally be decided by a constitutional bench of the Supreme Court.

Writ Jurisdiction

The Supreme Court is the guardian of the fundamental rights and liberties of the citizens of India. Articles 14 to 31 of Part 111 of the Constitution list the various rights and Article 32 of the same part provided remedies for enforcement of those rights. The court can declare a law passed by any legislature as null and void if it encroaches upon the fundamental rights guaranteed to the people by the Constitution. The Supreme Court can issue directions or order of writs, including writs in the nature of 'habeas corpus', mandamus, 'prohibition', 'quo warranto' and 'certiorari', whichever might be appropriate, for the enforcement of any of the rights conferred. Any statute, rule, order or notification that is violative of fundamental rights can be struck down by the Supreme Court if and when challenged before it.

The Supreme Court has powers to regulate it own procedure. Cases involving interpretation of the Constitution and any reference under Article 143 (power of the president to consult the Supreme Court) is heard by five judges; other cases may be heard by a single judge or double or triple member of benches. All judgments are by majority vote and differing judges can give dissenting opinions. The trial is open and judgments are delivered in open courts.

The law declared by the Supreme Court is binding on all the courts in India and the decrees and order of the court are enforceable throughout the country. All appointments of officers and servants of the Supreme Court are made by the chief justice of India or such other judges or officer of the court as the CJI may direct. The conduct of service of officers and servants of the Supreme Court are prescribed by rules made by the chief justice, as they are approved by the president.

The expenses of the Supreme Court such as salaries, allowances and privileges, payable to the officers and servants of the courts are charged on the consolidated fund of India.

Independence of the Judiciary

In a democracy, an independent judiciary is a must to save the rights of an individual from the government. Therefore, we must understand what is meant by independence of the judiciary and the need for it in a democracy. In this context, independence has three meanings.[3] First, it means that the judiciary must be free from encroachment from other organs in its sphere, which is called separation of powers. Our Constitution makes the judiciary absolutely independent except in certain minor matters where the executive heads are given some powers of remission. In the second sense it means freedom of the judgements and decrees from executive and legislative interference. In this respect, our constitutional position is not very happy because the legislature does in some respects override the decisions of the judiciary by legislation[4] and the executive also has not, at least in some cases, so far behaved well.[5] There is another meaning to independence of the judiciary which is more important. It is that the decision of the judiciary should not be influenced by either the executive or the legislature; in other words, freedom from both fear and favour of the two other organs.

The important functions of the Supreme Court are to arbitrate in cases between governments enforcement of fundamental rights. In case of the former, the judiciary has to depend on the government but in case of the latter fundamental rights are intended as a guarantee against the 'tyranny of the majority'. So, in a democracy which recognizes majority rule, it is absolutely necessary that the judiciary be independent of the government.[6]

Now let us examine the ways and means of keeping judiciary independent, as provided in the Constitution of India. The Constitution has due provisions for maintaining the independence and impartiality of the Supreme Court. In this context the following provisions are incorporated in the Constitution.

1. Judges are appointed by the President of India. The president shall in this matter consult such judges of the Supreme Court and high courts as he may deem necessary.
2. To avoid political influence in the appointments of judges, high minimum qualification has been prescribed in the Constitution.
3. The Constitution has fixed a high retirement age for the judges. Once appointed, they can hold office till the age of 65 years.
4. Once appointed, judges cannot be removed except through a very difficult process. The only grounds on which such removal may take place are (a) proven misbehaviour and (b) incapacity.
5. The salaries of the judges and the administrative expenses of the Supreme Court are charged on the consolidated fund of India and are not subject to vote in the Parliament.
6. The actions and decisions of the judges in their official capacity are immune from criticism such that no notice may be imputed to them. Even the Parliament cannot discuss the conduct of a judge except when a resolution for his removal is being considered.
7. A Supreme Court judge cannot plead or act in any court of the country after his retirement. Even if a judge resigned from his office he is debarred from practicing.
8. Finally, the Supreme Court has complete control over its own establishment. The court determines the terms and conditions of its officers servants and appointment on their part are made by the chief justice.

It is to be examined how effective these provisions are in keeping our judiciary independent and free from fear of executive or legislature.

Regarding recruitment and removal of the judges, our Constitution makers tried to make the judges as independent as possible. Till 1993, the appointments were made by the government in consultation with the chief justice of India and chief justices of high courts. But in 1993, flouting the clear terms of Article 124(2) and 217 of the Constitution, the Supreme Court gave the CJI a veto on appointments to the Supreme Court. Further, in 1998 the Supreme Court prescribed a 'collegium' of the CJI and four most senior judges of the Court. The collegium system has been under stress since the opposition of the appointment of controversial Karnataka Chief Justice P. D. Dinakaran as a Supreme Court judge by prominent jurists and bar leaders on the ground of '"doubtful integrity". It can prove to be a turning point in the history of the Indian judiciary'. The demand for scrapping the 'collegium' system has not for the first time come under scrutiny. In the last three years the government returned the collegium's recommendations twice. First, was asking for reconsideration of a recommendation to promote a judge as a high court chief justice, who was already facing serious allegations of corruption: Second, was about raising a query on the denial of promotion to three senior high court chief justices to the Supreme Court. The Supreme Court and the Delhi High Court associations said that 'Some of the appointments made in the high courts and now even the selection of the controversial judge to the apex court, all shows that the collegium system is worse than the previous system of the executive selecting the judges.'[7] The former Union law minister, H. R. Bhardwaj, described the collegium system as nothing more than 'give and take'. Former speaker of the Lok Sabha, Somnath Chatterjee, said 'India is a only country in the world where judges appoint themselves.' The best example of the failure of the collegium system is the appointment of Soumitra Sen as judge of Calcutta High Court in 2006, even as he faced the allegation of having misappropriated Rs 50 lakh while serving as a court-appointed lawyer in 1993 in a dispute between two public sector companies. 'How is it that the collegium which cleared him for appointment did not even bother to check his credentials, when the entire record was available in the court itself', said senior lawyer Bhusan.

Union Law Minister M. Veerappa Moily said, 'There is no doubt that the country needs sweeping judicial reforms, but these cannot be done with a confrontational approach. We will talk to the judiciary about this.'

A former Supreme Court judge, Justice P. B. Sawant, said, 'The appointment of judges has to be above suspicion and the best way is to introduce transparency. The names of those proposed to be appointed judges should be put upon the court website and time should be given to the public in case anyone has objection to any name.' Judicial appointment is not a part-time job that members of the collegium (judges) can perform after doing their judicial work of deciding cases.

The top jurist of the country demanded immediate change[8] of the collegium system after the recommendation to promote as Supreme Court judge against whom serious charges were levelled. The former Chief Justice of India, Justice J. S. Verma said he would have withdrawn the recommendation to promote. 'Justice Dinakaran, had such an issue come up when I was the head of the judiciary.'[9] Thus there is a serious problem with the method of appointing judges to the higher judiciary. The problems can be set right only by a constitutional amendment which establishes a national judicial commission[10] (NJC) with jurisdiction over appointments, transfers, discipline and removal of judges. It must be accessible to the citizen, work transparently and be under the sanction of the law.

The NJC should be free to receive complaints and institute preliminary enquiries confidentially and formally if a prima facie case exists. In that event, the case must be referred to the Supreme Court. Appointments and transfer should come under its preview, exclusively.[11] There is not only no transparency in the process but also no system or method is followed for preparing shortlists or for choosing among eligible candidates. The whole process is totally arbitrary, which has led to political favouritism when appointments were in the hands of the executive, and nepotism when appointments have been with the judiciary.[12] Further, 'we need a full-time independent institution that can methodically, systematically and transparently go about the job of selecting judges of the higher judiciary.'[13]

There are certain provisions of the Constitution which curtail the independence of the judiciary. These are:

(a) The process of promotion as chief justice
(b) The possibility of promotion from the high court to the Supreme Court
(c) Possibility of executive favours after retirement[14]

The Constitution has given a place of honour to the chief justice at the centre as well as in the states. The post also carries a higher salary, therefore, every judge of the Supreme Court as well as of the high courts would aspire for the position. But this favour depends on party in power, and would inject politics in the appointment.[15] The other provision of appointment of an acting chief justice will be misused. An acting chief justice cannot be independent of the executive until he is confirmed.

Then there is appointment of the Supreme Court judges from the high courts. Though Article 124(3) does not restrict recruitment only to this source, the practice so far has been to recruit Supreme Court judges from high courts. Only once in 1964, S. Sikri was appointed directly from the Bar. Such appointment gives the double benefit one higher salary and tenure for another three years along with other emoluments and honour attached to it. It is the Constitution that gives a lever to the central cabinet to avoid such high court judges who have given judgements against the known views of the government.

There is nothing in the Constitution to prevent the judges from taking patronage of the executive during the tenure of office and after retirement as ministers, governors, ambassadors, chairmen of special tribunals after retirement, and other ad-hoc posts during office.[16] Thus, our Constitution has opened the way for this executive patronage, which might make the judges politically biased. In practice political parties may not try to allure the judges, but is natural that aspiring judges might try to placate political parties and their leaders. An independent and completely unbiased judiciary is essential for a democratic set up, and our Constitution has to incorporate provisions to achieve it at any cost.

The solution lies in making the judges a class by themselves once appointed. Some pertinent suggestions are:

1. Appointment of all judges by the president from a list prepared previously by a panel of judges or by a judicial commission for the recruitment of judges
2. Equal and more decent pay for all the judges of high courts and the Supreme Court, the post of chief justice going by rotation or by seniority with an allowance
3. Removal of judges as per procedure set in the Constitution
4. Equal retirement age for all judges of both the high courts and the Supreme Court, and more liberal pensions almost equal to pay
5. Complete bar on judges taking part in polities or accepting any other job either during office or after retirement except that of a judicial nature, and that too only on the approval of a committee of judges[17]

Supreme Court and Judicial Review

Our Constitution makers wanted a democracy where justice would be dispensed to all equally preserving the dignity of the individual and the unity of the nation. The Constituent Assembly members referred to the Supreme Court as the 'Guardian of the Constitution', 'a watch-dog of democracy and a champion of liberties'. To perform this role our Constitution is empowered with judicial review; and the sooner the courts assert their right, the better for the country and for the people. This means that the Supreme Court is empowered to review the acts and orders of the legislative and executive wings of the government and to declare them, when challenged by the affected person, null and void if those were not in accordance with the Constitution. In other words, judicial review is the power exercised by the courts of a country to ensure that such actions conform to the provisions of the Constitution. For this, a written Constitution is an essential requisite and the Constitution should not be easily and promptly amended by the executive in collaboration with legislature. If this is not so, then the Constitution will become a handmaid of the rulers of the day, and the Supreme Court will hardly be able to protect its provisions. Generally, the system of judicial review prevails better in a country having a federal constitution, in which the decision of legislature lies between the central government and members states and a bill of rights or some other system of fundamental limitations in law-making powers. This essentially requires a system of judicial review in a written and rigid Constitution, federation of states involving division of powers and fundamental rights. These are there in the Constitution but nowhere in the Constitution the term judicial review', has been used. This omission led some to conclude that the framers of the Constitution did not desire that the Supreme Court should exercise such extraordinary power. But such conclusion is erroneous. This power of the court is inherent in several provisions of the Constitution as in Articles 13, 32, 131–136, 143, 145, 226, 246, 251, 254 and 372.

Article 13 specifically mentions that any law which contravenes any of the provisions or part of fundamental rights shall be void. The Supreme Court and high courts are made the protector and guarantor of fundamental rights under Articles 32 and 226. Articles 251 and 254 say that in case of inconsistency between Union and state laws, the state law shall be void. Article 246(3) provides that the legislature of any state has exclusive power to make laws for any subject of the state. This means that if Parliament ever made a law on any such subject, except in times of emergency, it shall be void.

This again can be decided by the Supreme Court alone. Article 254 has shown that in case of inconsistency between laws made by Parliament and laws made by the legislatures of states on the subject of concurrent list, the laws made by the latter were void to the extent of repugnancy with the law of the former. This could be determined by none else but the Supreme Court.

The basic function of the courts is to adjudicate (Articles 131–136) in disputes between individuals, between individuals and the states and between the states and the Union, and while so adjudicating, the courts may be required to interpret the provisions of the Constitution and the laws and, the interpretation given by the Supreme Court becomes the law for all courts of the land. There is no appeal against the judgement of the Supreme Court.

Judicial Review of the Constitutional Amendments

The working of the Constitution and the Supreme Court up to 1967 shows that the Supreme Court held that the amendment acts were not ordinary laws and could not be struck down by the application of Article 13(2).[18]

But in the case of *Golak Nath v. The State of Punjab* (1967), which was heard by a special bench of 11 judges, the validity of three constitutional amendments (1st, 4th and 17th) was challenged. The Supreme Court, by a majority of 6 to 5, reversed its decision given in the case of *Shankari Prasad v. Union of India* (1951) and in *Sajjan Singh*'s case (1964), and declared that Parliament under Article 368 has no power to take away or abridge the fundamental rights mentioned in the Constitution.

The constitutional validity of 24th, 25th and 29th Amendments was challenged in the fundamental rights case of *Keshavananda Bharti v. State of Kerala*, 1973. The government of India claimed that it had the right as per law, to amend the provision of Constitution. The court held thatthe amending power of the Parliament is limited. While it can abridge any fundamental right or amend any provision of the Constitution, its amending power does not extend to damaging or destroying any of the essential features of the Constitution and its basic character. The fundamental rights are among the essential features of the Constitution, therefore, while they may be abridged, it cannot extend to the point of damage to or destruction of their core. Article 31(c) is void since it takes away invaluable fundamental rights, even those unconnected with property.

In the *Minerva Mills* case (1980), by a majority decision the Supreme Court struck down section 4 of the 42nd Amendment Act, which gave preponderance to the Directive Principles over Articles 14, 19 and 31 of Part 111 of the Constitution on the ground that Parts III and IV of the Constitution are equally important, and primacy of one over the other was not permissible as that would disturb the harmony of the Constitution.

Judicial Review of Legislative Enactments and Ordinances

The first case that came up before the Supreme Court was from Madras in 1951 in which the Preventive Detention Act 1950 was challenged as illegal. The court, by a unanimous decision, declared Section 14 of the Act invalid and thus showed its competence to declare void any parliamentary enactment repugnant to the Constitution. Between 1950 and 1980, the Parliament passed as many as 1999 Acts excluding Amendments, and out of them, the Supreme Court invalidated laws passed on 22 occasions. Justice V. S. Desh Pande's view was that judicial review of legislation in India should be merely based on Article 245(1) and not on Article 13. According to him, Article 245(1), interpreted broadly, would ensure the supremacy of the Constitution over all kinds of laws.[19]

Thus, a law confirmed with the Constitutional norms is valid. The responsibility of deciding the validity of law is invested in the judges of the Supreme Court. The judiciary can play this role well if the judges chosen are qualified, intelligent, impartial and independent. Intelligence is difficult to determine, but the

Constitution has laid down certain qualification for judges to ensure it. Therefore, everything depends upon the independence of the judiciary, which we have already discussed earlier. Our Supreme Court has by and large proved to be a great institution in protecting the Constitution from the onslaughts of the executive. Initially, the court was reluctant to declare parliamentary laws as unlawful, but now the position has changed after the judgement in *Golak Nath Bank Nationalisation* and privy purses cases in favour of private property. The then Prime Minister, Indira Gandhi, after this decision, developed a deep antipathy towards higher judiciary. Her close associates took advantage of the situation and persuaded her to clip the wings of the judiciary. As a result, supercession of senior-most judges followed when Justice A. N. Ray was appointed as the chief justice of the Supreme Court in 1973, and similarly Justice M. H. Baig in 1977 who superseded Justice H. R. Khanna. The choice of A. N. Ray and M. H. Baig was not inspired by any consideration of superior merit or judicial ability.[20]

Judicial Activities in India

The judiciary is one of the three pillars of our democratic political system, and is endowed with the responsibility of interpreting laws. It cannot be expected to have a purpose other than the betterment of governance at every level of the political system. The judges should have the capacity to respond to the needs of the present and vision to cope with the demands of the future. In recent years, the Supreme Court has brought about more far-reaching changes than the legislature and executive. Some would call it judicial creativity and imaginative judicial response to the varying needs of society while others would call it 'judicial activism' or the judiciary going beyond its brief.

The expression 'activism' means 'being active', 'activist' means one who is involved in intensified activities. The judges' decisions concern or covers various types of activities or issues, in this sense they are activists. Judicial decisions, opposed to the legislative and executive policy choices, are usually called judicial activism. An activist judge activates the legal mechanism and makes it play a vital role in the socio-economic process.

The legislature and the executive are supposed to be custodians of honest public life; but when they compromise with corruption or politicize it, the judiciary has to step in, which is what has happened at present. The first major case of judicial activism through social action litigation was the Bihar under trials' case; the second was the case of Agra Protective Home in 1980, when two professors of law wrote a letter to the editor of the *Indian Express* describing the barbaric conditions of detention in the home. It became the basis of a writ petition under Article 21. A similar petition in the Delhi Women's Home concerning a third-year law student of Delhi University and a social worker was also filed. In another case, a writ petition was filed by three journalists exposing a thriving market in which women were bought and sold. The petitioners demanded prohibition of the practice and immediate relief for the victims through compensation and rehabilitation.

During the era of coalition, governments became weak and administration became lethargic, self-centred and lost affectivity. At such a time the Supreme Court came to the rescue of the people and began to take cognizance of custodial deaths, bride-burning and rape in police stations. It ordered the police not to handcuff a man arrested purely on suspicion. It also ordered that no woman can be taken to a police station after dusk.

In 1993, the Supreme Court delivered judgments protecting the rights of innocents held in a mosque in Srinagar, defining the constitutional powers of the chief election commissioner, threatening closure of several industries if they continue to pollute the rivers and endanger the Taj Mahal and all government and semi-government bodies were brought under the purview of the Consumer Protection Act, 1994. In a historic verdict, the Supreme Court asked the then chief of army staff to pay Rs 60,000 to the widow and two children of an army officer who died due to 'gross negligence and callousness' of the authorities concerned some 16 years earlier.[21]

In the famous *hawala* case in which Jain brothers' diaries containing names of several politician became open, the case was given to the CBI for investigation. But the CBI, due to the involvement of big political personalities including former Prime Minister P. V. Narasimha Rao, adopted delaying tactics in investigation. The Supreme Court summoned the CBI chief to report on the hawala investigation on 22 February 1996. Supreme Court Justice J. S. Verma told the CBI: 'Be clear that your investigations should not be conducted in water tight compartment you can not close any case against any body.' On 1 March 1996 the Supreme Court ordered the CBI to refrain from reporting the progress of investigations in the multi-crore hawala case to higher administrative authorities, including the prime minister. The Supreme Court order produced the desired results and the CBI registered an FIR against the Jain brothers, and arrested S. K. Jain and N. K. Jain, raided their residences and recovered documents for further investigation. 'This was a case where the rule of law seemed to have gone of the rails,' said Supreme Court lawyer Rajiv Dhavan, 'Verma steered it back.' When Justice Verma was asked if it was judicial activism, he replied, 'As far as I am concerned, we are only making the executive work. We are not usurping its role.'

The high courts also followed the way of the Supreme Court. In September 1996, the Delhi high court appointed a fresh CBI team as Court officers to investigate the JMM case. The monitoring of the JMM and hawala cases became necessary due to persistent executive interference in CBI's investigations. Therefore, the Delhi high court insulated it from any kind of pressure in the JMM case.

The other examples of judicial activism are, the Supreme Court asking Delhi government to clean up the city, direction to the central government to explain why houses in prime aceas of Delhi were being unscrupulously allocated or requiring the Vohra Committee report to be placed before it when the same had not even been placed in Parliament or when the Supreme Court ordered hundreds of small-scale industrial units to vacate a certain area around Taj Mahal to save it from further environmental degradation. In Delhi, a large number of industries were either closed down or shifted out. Judgements like in Satish Sharma and Shiela Kaul cases, in which discretionary powers were grossly misused while allotting petrol pumps and government housing accommodation in the prime localities of Delhi. All this was done under the courts' extraordinary jurisdiction of public interest litigation.

The actual date when PIL was first taken up is not traceable, but in 1978, when the Supreme Court took cognizance of the letters by Charles Sobhraj and Sunil Batra from their prison complaining about the torture to which they and their fellow prisoners were subjected, the court treated these letters as writ petitions and proceeded to enquire into the condition of the prisoners and adjudicated accordingly. Kapila Hugorain, an advocate, filed a writ on behalf of 29,000 Bihar undertrials. The PIL helped the court to release many undertrial prisoners by its interim orders. Since then, the range of PIL has spread from the release of bonded labourers, child labourers, Nari Niketan, street hawkers and environmental issues.

It may be noted that in almost all the cases of PIL, direction has always been targeted to the lawlessness of the governments and its agencies.

Through the invention of PILs, people who were involved in perpetrating political corruption at the top were dragged into the court for the first time. This expansion of judicial power led to gradual delegitimization of duly elected governments that had became so bereft of moral authority that it could not vociferously question or oppose the persistent inroads of judicial action into its domain of authority. The cure therefore does not lie in the legitimizing this expanded judicial power but the removal of the causes which led to delegitimization of one structure of the political system. The judiciary has to be cautious in using its extraordinary powers and status. As Justice H. R. Khanna said, 'of all kinds of despotisms, judicial despotism is the most illogical, irrational and inexcusable and that the judiciary has made investigating agencies work against corrupt politicians but judges should not take over the country's governance for it can disrupt the constitutional balance and end in disaster.' Sometimes the executive and legislature have to avoid making an impression that they want to gag or suppress judicial dissent. Where the law is clear the judge should not take a long jump in the form of a PIL. Justice Markanday Katju of the Supreme Court of India said that 'Judges must know their limits and must not try to run the government. They must have modesty and humility, and not behave like emperor.'

Critical Assessment

Our judicial system is based on the English system and all of its defects are also found in our judiciary. The common complaints are that litigation is costly and protracted, that it is awfully delayed and that it is also altogether unsuited to our genius.[22]

The process of ascertaining justice through witnesses is cumbersome and complicated. Witnessing has become complicated like law, the witness need tutoring before cross-examination and even then due to court environment, fear lurks in the witness, several times the witness fails to speak correctly with the result that the judge's opinion becomes the truth, and justice become arbitrary and deviates from law. Second, the hierarchical system of our judiciary has also delayed justice and made it financially unbearable to the common man. Thousands of poor people are toiling in jails nowadays and many are going to the gallows while numerous others are deprived of their fundamental rights and property because justice is very costly and complicated. Delhi, where the Supreme Court is located, is very distant and the Supreme Court is far away for the poor man. The individual is helpless against the rich and government tyranny can go up to the Supreme Court. Thus, the poor man suffers from high cost of judicial process and the unaffordably high legal fee of a Supreme Court advocate for pleading his case. Thus, how many common men can afford to go to the Supreme Court to vindicate their ordinary rights.

The other points of citizen are that it is an elitist and antidemocratic institution. It places too much power even leading to death into the hands of a few men and women in black robes who protect the rich and powerful individuals in society. They are arbitrarily appointed and given security of tenure, but accountable to none for their decisions. Thus there is urgent need for judicial reforms for the common man's good in society.

NOTES

1. See, *Sunder Singh v. State of UP* AIR 1956 S.C. 411. Also see, *Nar Sing v. State of UP* AIR 1954 S.C., 257.
2. Article 136, Constitution of India.
3. K. V. Rao, *Parliamentary Democracy of India. A Critical Commentary*, 2nd edition (Calcutta: World Press, 1965), p. 247.
4. Examples of this sort are the Income Tax Amendment Ordinance of 1957, the 24th, 25th and 26th Constitutional Amendments in 1971 were designed to nullify the effects of the Supreme Courts' three judgements, in Golak Nath, bank nationalization and privy purses cases.
5. The cases of mercy granted by the government of Kerala during the communist regime of 1957–1959, Bombay governor in the famous 'Nanawati case', and recently, the case of mercy granted by the Haryana governor during 2000–2003 for releasing certain criminals from jail.
6. K. V. Rao, op. cit., p. 248.
7. *Hindustan Times*, New Delhi, 19 September 2009.

8. Recently, the names of five chief justices of high court of states were recommended by the collegiums on 27 August for promotion to the Supreme Court as judges. One of them was chief justice B. D. Dinakaran of Karnataka high court whose elevation as a judge of the Supreme Court was opposed by the top jurist of the country on the ground of allegations of land grabbing and disproportional assets. *Hindustan Times*, 30 November 2009.
9. *Hindustan Times*, 30 November 2009.
10. A. G. Novrani, 'Blind to Accountability', *Hindustan Times* (Chandigarh edition), 19 March 2003.
11. Ibid.
12. Prashant Bhushan, 'Judicial Accountability: Asset Disclosure and Beyond', Economic and Political Weekly, vol. XIV, no. 37, 12 and 16 September 2009, p. 10.
13. Ibid, p. 11.
14. K. V. Rao, op. cit., p. 249.
15. For example, A. N. Ray was appointed Chief Justice of India in 1973 superseding three senior judges, the appointment of H. M. Beg, Chief Justice of India by superceding Justice Khana, in 1977.
16. This patronage has been freely generalized. There are several such examples when ex-justice C. C. Biswas was first appointed minister of minority affairs in 1950 and then minister of law in 1952 in the central cabinet. Ex-justice Syed Faze Ali was appointed governor of Orissa in 1952. Ex-justice Chandra Shekhar Iyar was appointed as chairman of the delimitation commission in 1953, Chief Justice Chagla of Bombay as ambassador to America (1956), high commissioner in London (1961) and Union cabinet minister (1964). Chief Justice of India M. N. Venkatachalaiah was appointed chairman of national commission to review the working of the Constitution in 2000. Justice Ansuman Singh of Rajasthan High Court was appointed Governor of Rajasthan in 1998. Justice Kuldeep Singh was appointed Chairman of the Delimitation Commission in 2004. Justice Liberhan was appointed chairman of the commission to enquire into demolition of Babri Masjid.
17. K. V. Rao, op. cit., pp. 253–254.
18. *Shankari Prasad v. Union of India* AIR. 1951, SC 458. In Sajjan Singh's case (1964), the Supreme Court held the view that amendments cannot be declared void under Article 15(2).
19. V. S. Deshpande, *Judicial Review of Legislation* (Lucknow: Eastern Book Co., 1975.), p. 48.
20. Madhu Limaye, *Contemporary Indian Politics* (New Delhi): Radiant Publishers, 1987, pp. 122–23.
21. *Hindustan Times* (New Delhi) 1 April 1996.
22. K. V. Rao, op. cit., p. 256.

The Structure of Central Administration

The secretariat has evolved over a period of 200 years. The Chapter would include the evolution of the secretariat, its meaning, organization and role in the administrative system of the country.

The Constitution does not mention the word 'secretariat'. Article 77(3) of the Constitution lays down that the president shall make rules for the more convenient transaction of the business of the government of India and for the allocation among ministers of the said business. The secretariat is required to run the business of the government. The word 'secretariat' has been derived from the word 'secret', that means something held back or withdrawn from public knowledge or view, unrevealed, covert or confidential. The main function of the secretariat is to advise the minister in matters of policy and administration. The affairs of the state and particularly the dealings between the secretary and the minister are confidential in nature, therefore, the functions of the government appear to have become synonymous with secrecy. Thus, probably for this reason the term, 'secretariat', is derived from the word 'secret'.

During British rule in India, the government was the secretary's government. After Independence the actual power belongs to the council of ministers. The minister's obviously cannot work alone and needs assistance; therefore, for administrative purposes, the government of India is divided into ministries and departments which together constitute the 'central secretariat'. Thus, the term central secretariat is used to denote the sum total of the secretariat staff of all the departments/ministries.

There are attached offices, subordinate offices and other field agencies to implement the policies made by the ministers in consultation with the secretariat. The Constitution also provides a host of agencies independent of ministries/departments that report directly to the Union Parliament. Such agencies are the election commission, the union public service commission and the comptroller and auditor-general. In addition to these, there are staff agencies to advise the government in the field of planning but in practice it has become a parallel secretariat. Some ministers and departments share their functions with boards and commissions with some autonomy. Sometimes a ministry or department has its own advisory bodies to assist and advise on specific matters.

The Evolution of the Central Secretariat

In the beginning the secretariat in India was the office of the governor-general. The original role of the secretariat was described as, 'the Central Secretariat at Fort William in Bengal was designed to furnish the requisite information for the formulation of policy and to carry out the orders of the Company's Government.'[1] Further, B. B. Mishra said, 'before the year 1756 the president and the council at Fort William transacted all their business in one general department with the help of a secretary and a few assistants. On the arrival of packets from England the secretary laid them before the council for orders and instructions which when issued were conveyed for execution to the priorities concerned.'[2]

The Regulatory Act of 1773 for the first time created the 'supreme government', having controlling authority over the 'presidency government'. It consisted of a governor-general and four councillors in whom all the powers of controlling the military of India vested. This system continued throughout the British rule. Only the number of members of the council kept increasing. With the expansion of company's rule, it took a number of governmental functions and the role of the secretariat expanded along with its size.

Lord Cornwallis took some steps to organize and strengthen the secretariat. He created the office of the secretary-general in whom all powers and responsibilities concentrated. He later came to be known as chief secretary. Lord Wellesley also took a keen interest in reorganizing the secretariat, and his reforms work of the secretariat increased considerably both in bulk and responsibility. He raised the status of the secretary to government. He did this by raising their salaries and augmenting their responsibilities. The functions of the secretaries were extended to research and planning in addition to their ordinary routine business of execution.

At the end of the 18th century, the supreme government consisted of a governor-general and three councillors, and a secretariat of four departments. Each of them was under a secretary all of whom worked under the overall control of the chief secretary. After more than a hundred years, on the eve of the Montford Reforms in 1919, the government of India consisted of a governor-general and seven members. The secretariat also expanded and it had nine departments excluding the railway board and the Indian munitions board. The total strength of the secretariat was 29 to which 17 more officers of the two boards could be added. This number remained unchanged till the outbreak of the Second World War in 1939.

The Montague-Chelmsford Reforms of 1919 brought about a significant change in the system of administration. The reforms introduced division of functions between the centre and the provincial governments and over a large part of the field, the provinces became virtually autonomous. Only subjects like the army, post and telegraph and railways, were directly administered by the central government leaving the rest to the provincial governments. With the division of powers the central government came to administer many more areas directly. In consequence, the role of the secretariat began to change from a merely policy formulating, supervising and coordinating agency to that of an executive agency as well. The trend got further impetus by the introduction of provincial autonomy in 1937 and later by the outbreak of the Second World War. Almost overnight the central government was called upon to perform functions like civil defence, mobilization of men and material for war, food and civil supplies. As a result the post of officer on special duty was created in the department of home affairs to look after the civil defence work. Later a separate department of civil defence was created and the secretary of the department was also made the director-general of civil defence. A lot of expansion in the secretariat took place to look after many other areas. The strength of the governor-general's council increased from 7 to 14 and the number of secretariat departments rose to 19. The total strength of officials also increased up to 200, under the belief that the expansion was a temporary war-time phenomenon and would be restored to its old position once normalcy was restored with the end of the war. But, the post-war reconstruction programmes and later the advent of independence did not permit any reduction in the size of the secretariat. On the other hand post-independence problems and expanding social welfare functions of the new popular government further expanded the secretariat. Thus, the number of departments in the secretariat rose from 19 in 1945 to 74 in 1994; likewise, the number of attached and subordinate offices also increased from 20 in 1947 to about 100 in 1991.

Functions of the Secretariat

The functioning of the secretariat in our country has, by and large, been based on two principles. First, was the principle of separation of policy from its implementation—the administration in action so that the latter can be handed over to a separate agency, which enjoys certain freedom in the field of execution. Second, a transitory cadre of officers drawn from states' cadres, operating on the tenure system of staff, controlling a permanent staff is a prerequisite to the vitality of the administrative system as a whole. L. S. Amary, in his book, *Thoughts on the Constitution*, pointed out that in such a situation of dual functioning, it is the policy-making functions which are likely to suffer most. Routine business is always more urgent and calls for less intellectual efforts than the policy-making functions. As the human mind tends to follow the path of least resistance, routine functions get attended to while policy and planning matters are deferred. Therefore, it is only by the creation of a separate policy department that the general staff, freed from administration as a whole, is secured for thoughtful and effective planning. This system is known as split system.

Advantages of Split System

Many advantages have been claimed in favour of the Indian system of separation of functions. The important ones are, first, freedom from day-to-day problems of execution, which provides the opportunity to the policy makers to do whatever is necessary for forward planning. Second, the secretariat acts as the dispassionate advisor to the minister. It has no interest in any proposal. The proposals coming from the executive agencies are examined in an objective way from the larger point of view of the government as a whole. That is the reason why the secretary in the secretariat is the secretary not to his minister, but to the government as a whole. Third, the separation keeps the secretariat's size small. Fourth, this system also avoids over-centralization. The executive agencies have to be given reasonable amount of freedom in the implementation of the policies and in the functions given to them. If the field functions were to be administered from the secretariat it would have created lot of centralization and delay in disposal of work.

Functions

The secretariat, by and large, is a policy-making body that functions under the direction and control of the council of ministers. The secretariat works as a single unit and secretaries are secretaries to the Union government as a whole and not to any particular minister. A secretariat officer of and above the rank of an under-secretary signs on behalf of the President of India, that is the entire central government. Hence, Lord Canning, after 1858, granted each secretary the right of direct access to the viceroy and the governor-general started meeting each secretary once a week. Such meetings continued during British rule and today our prime minister is free to call any secretary for consultation. Therefore, the secretariat is called the government. In fact, the main function of the secretariat is to assist the minister in the discharge of his responsibilities under the Constitution. In brief, the secretariat performs the following functions:

(1) It assists the minister in the process of policy making.
(2) It assists in the framing of legislation, rules and regulations.

(3) It assists in the formulation of sectoral planning and programmes.
(4) It assists in budgeting and control of expenditure and in securing of administrative and financial approval to operational programmes and plans and their subsequent modifications.
(5) It assists in the interpretation of policies, coordinating and assisting other branches of government and maintaining contact with state administrations.
(6) It assists in initiating measures to develop better personnel and organizational competence both in the ministry/department and its executive agencies.
(7) It helps the minister in the discharge of his parliamentary responsibilities.

From the practical or operational point of view, the functions of the secretariat can be divided into two categories[3] mentioned as follows:

(a) It has to see that all papers quoted in the correspondence notes are forthcoming, properly arranged, paginated and have corrected marginal references.
(b) It has to verify the facts.
(c) It has to supply other relevant facts and figures available in the department.
(d) It has to point out the law and rules.
(e) It has to put up precedence and papers containing previous decisions and policies and to point out the relevant portions of the papers thus put up.
(f) It has to draw attention to the statutory or customary procedure required for the disposal of the case.
(g) In routine cases where there are established precedents it has to put up drafts for approval.
(h) It has to bring to notice at the proper time when some matter requires action or order.

The second category of functions are: (a) to examine the case and see that all matters requiring decision are brought forward; (b) to tabulate and summarize the information if necessary; (c) to prepare drafts according to final decisions.

The first category of functions can be performed automatically on any case without any specific directions while the second category of functions is to be performed on the specific direction of the senior officers. The secretariat, therefore, consists of two distinct categories of personnel namely, the officers and the staff. The main functions of the staff are to see that the connected papers with a case are presented to the senior officers in time along with necessary rules and regulations, procedures, precedents, etc. Afterwards, it becomes the responsibility of the officers to examine the pros and cons of the case and to present them before the minister for his policy decisions. All the cases need not to be placed before the minister. Officers at different levels have power to take decisions as per the scheme of delegation of powers approved by the minister of the cabinet.

In the words of Asok Chanda, 'The Central Secretariat is . . . the principal executive instrument of the Union government and is responsible for administering the central subjects, coordinating the activities of national importance and assisting in the formulation of foreign, economic and financial policies.'[4]

The central secretariat occupies an apex position. The administrative reforms commission (ARC) observed that 'the secretariat system of work has lent balance, consistency and continuity to the administration, and serves as a nucleus for the total machinery of a ministry. It has facilitated inter-ministry coordination and accountability to the Parliament at the ministerial level. As an institutionalized system, it is indispensable for the proper functioning of the government.'[5] Therefore, it is not surprising that the prestige of the secretariat has gone up so high because the superior position of the secretariat is recognized by its personnel who are given higher grades than their counterparts working in the field agencies. They are also entitled to special pay on their joining the secretariat.

Structure of the Secretariat

The central secretariat is a large and complex organization of various ministries and departments. There is no uniform terminology for describing the various segments of the administrative structure of the Union government. It is a collection of a large number of ministries and departments. The term 'ministry' came into vogue only after Independence. The secretariat has two distinct components; i.e., the officers and office. A ministry may have more than one department. Many large ministries like home, agriculture, finance, education, defence and external affairs have more than one department in their charge. So far as the department is concerned, it may be defined as an organizational unit for performing specific functions under the administrative control of a secretary to the government. In other words, a department is under the charge of a secretary whereas a ministry remains under the minister's charge, although this distinction is not always maintained. A ministry with more than one department may have more than one secretary. In such cases, one secretary who will represent the ministry is made superior to other secretaries. Such personnel are designated secretary-general or the principal secretary. Therefore, even if all the secretaries draw the same salary, they may not necessarily enjoy equal rank.

The pattern of a ministry's organization shows that the minister is the political head, who may be assisted by a minister of state and a deputy minister. The secretary is the administrative head of the bureaucracy under the minister. A ministry's organization is divided into the following segments with an officer in charge of each of them to expedite matters:

Department	Secretary/Additional/Special secretary
Wing	Joint/Additional secretary
Division	Director/Deputy secretary
Branch	Under-secretary
Section/Office	Section officer

The lowest of such units is the section in-charge or a section officer helped by a number of assistants. Besides stenographers who provide secretarial assistance to the senior officers, there are clerks, daftaries, typists and peons. It is also called the office. It deals with the work relating to the subject allotted to it. Two sections form the branch which is under the charge of an under-secretary also known as branch officer. Two branches constitute a division which is normally headed by a deputy secretary. With the increase in the volume of work of a ministry, one or more 'wings' are established, with a joint secretary in-charge of each wing. At the apex of the hierarchy is the department, which is headed by the secretary himself or in some cases by an additional special secretary.

We will discuss the staffing pattern of the secretariat under two heads—officers and the office.

Staffing of Officers

At the time of Independence in 1947 there was no central secretariat service to provide a permanent set of officers for the secretariat. The secretariat positions were manned by officers drawn from the provincial government and most of them returned back after serving in the secretariat for a fixed period of three to five years. This system is known as 'tenure system', as each officer so deputed has to serve the centre for a fixed number of years, i.e. three to five years. This system was created by Lord Curzon in 1905, who believed that, 'India may be governed from Simla or Calcutta, but is administered from the plains.' In his opinion, the district was the focal point of administration and all important work of administration was carried out at the district level. Therefore, he felt that the officers who had the experience of district work should be brought to the secretariat. He thought it was a good idea to keep the secretariat in touch with field situations. After serving for a fixed period in the secretariat the officers must go back to renew their field experience, which fades during the service period in the secretariat.

The staffing pattern of the secretariat by officers drawn from the states has been recommended by a number of committees and commissions. The Simon commission on decentralization in 1930 said, 'it is an accepted principle that efficient secretariat service, both in the provinces and at Delhi, depends upon a constant interchange of personnel between the district and the secretariat . . . experience gained with the central government or at the provincial secretariat service, in the system of Indian administration, proves an asset to provinces of districts . . . and intimate knowledge of the districts and provinces is invaluable in provincial and central secretariat. Circulation between them makes for vigour of the whole.'

The Wheeler committee of 1936 also supported the tenure system. According to the committee, 'The imposition of a limit to the occupancy of certain appointments has long been a feature of Indian administration and the posts governed by it range from that of the governor-general and members of the council to such junior ranks as those of under-secretaries.'[5] This system is inherent in the organization of all-India services which belong to both the central as well as the state governments. The members of these services have to function in the districts, state secretariat and central secretariat. The tenure system was adopted to use their services so that the central and the state governments could take advantage of the experience of these officers.

The Maxwell committee, reporting in 1937, favoured the tenure system. The committee recommended that the tenure of the officers at the central secretariat should be separated as far as possible by periods to be spent in the provinces and the districts where their touch with reality is revived. Similarly, officers with secretariat experience should become available to the field and they would know how to get the field problems solved from the secretariat.

Recently, the administrative reforms commission study team on personnel administration in its report in 1967 gave its wholehearted support to the tenure system and suggested the demolition of all barriers hindering smooth flow of personnel between the secretariat and the field. It recommended that the tenure system be rigidly enforced and 'officers must go back to the parent departments or state governments as the case may be for a substantial length of time—not less than the period spent outside the department/state before being considered for another assignment.'

The arguments in favour of the tenure system advanced by various committees and commissions can be systematically summarized as follows: First, the rotation of civil servants between the centre and the state governments exercises a wholesome and steady influence on the working of federal system of governance. Such a role has become significant due to strains and stresses in centre-state relations, particularly when different political parties came in power at the centre and the states. Second, when the central secretariat posts are manned by persons having experience of district and state administration then the national policies will be based on reality and such policies have less difficulty in the implementation in the field. Third, a long tenure at the secretariat results in loss of contact with field administration. In tenure system officers are sent back to the states, where they benefit the local administration by their central secretariat experience. Fourth, the tenure system benefits states. They got back officers possessing wide range of experience who have knowledge of the working of the central government as well as of national policies. Fifth, very long stay at the secretariat makes an officer stale but under the tenure system he gets an opportunity of working in a different atmosphere, which can bring freshness to his outlook. Sixth, a tenure system provides everyone an opportunity of working at different levels of administration. Seventh, the tenure system provides the necessary flexibility to the personnel management of the secretariat. Inefficient and incompetent persons can be removed without difficulty at the end of the tenure. Eighth, the system secures and consolidates administrative unity of the country and finally, it strengthens the independence of the Civil Service.

Arguments Against the Tenure System

The critics of this system have advanced several arguments against the tenure system. The important ones among them are: First, the work of the ministries has become specialised in nature but the tenure system does not ensure specialisation. Second, district experience is not required in many areas of activities that are being performed by the central government at present. Third, the tenure system has strengthened the office at the cost of the officer. A new officer depends too much on his office. This gives rise to many evils of office administration.

Operation of the Tenure System

This is to be noted that the tenure system did not apply to all the departments of the government of India. For example, foreign, political, Indian audit and accounts, posts and telegraphs, customs and income tax departments were known exceptions. There are many reasons which have worked against the operation of the tenure system.

(i) The functions of the government have become complex and multi-faceted. Nowadays, a number of specialized functions are performed in the secretariat and their number is increasing every day. Due to this trend, the area of tenure system is decreasing day by day.

(ii) The creation of central secretariat service was to man the junior positions up to the posts of under-secretaries and also several posts of deputy secretaries. Now they have even started occupying the posts of joint secretaries too. The personnel of this service are not transferable outside the secretariat. Thus, the creation of this service has further narrowed down the operation of tenure system.

(iii) The tenure system has been further hedged and modified to a great extent due to the creation of the finance commerce pool in 1938, the central administrative pool in 1957, the central economic pool, the industrial management pool and, later on, full-fledged services like the Indian economic service and the Indian statistical service. The finance commerce pool fulfilled the requirements of specialized needs of economic department and the central administrative pool, composed of officers from the IAS, central services and state services, meant to overcome the uncertainty in the matter of supply and quality of officers inherent in the tenure system.

(iv) Among the officers who come on deputation to the government of India, a large number do not want to go back and manage to stay there even after the completion of their tenure. Whenever the question of their reversion to their cadres arises, they put forward personal as well as administrative reasons for their stay. This practice has also limited the tenure systems.

(v) The present political system has also diluted the tenure system. The federal system with autonomous states is not suited to tenure system. The amateur ministers at both the central and state levels need the services of permanent advisors in the secretariat. Therefore, they select some officers of their choice to be nominated on deputation from their own states and later manage to keep them there for a very long period.

To sum up, the tenure system has been in operation since long, but now other influences have started working in the administrative field. Senior positions like deputy secretary and above are filled on the basis of staffing scheme, notified by the secretariat on 17th October 1957. As per this scheme, these posts are manned by officers of several following categories:

(i) Officers borrowed from state cadres of all-India services.

(ii) Officers borrowed on deputation from central services (Class I officers).

(iii) Officers of the selection grade of the central secretariat service.

(iv) Officers from the central administrative pool.

(v) State civil service officers whose names are included in the selected list for appointment to the IAS.

(vi) Other state civil service officers, in consultation with the Union public service commission (UPSC).

In practice, a large number of posts are filled by the officers of the IAS, Class I central services and the selection grade of the central secretariat service. The officers of the state civil services hardly get any chance to come to the central secretariat. Thus, the central government mostly depends on officers taken on deputation for a fixed tenure to man the senior posts in the secretariat, except in the ministry of external affairs where all the posts are manned by officers of the Indian Foreign Service, and in the railway ministry where officers of railway service man all the posts. Likewise officers of central legal service man all posts in the ministry of law and justice.

The central secretariat service is a major source of recruitment to the central secretariat posts, thus it will be pertinent to discuss this service in detail here.

Central Secretariat Service (CSS)

Even before independence in 1947, the need for secretariat service was felt, and the posts of assistant and assistant secretary/undersecretary were filled by officers drawn from the Imperial secretariat service. After Independence, a scheme of such a service was approved by the central government in 1948 and was called the central secretariat re-organisation and reinforcement scheme. It provided for a new service, called the central secretariat service (CSS) to replace the old Imperial secretariat Service. The new service was originally organized in four grades. But in 1959 as a result of the Second Pay Commission recommendation grades II and III were merged into one continuous class II grade. A new selection grade above grade I was also created that consisted of the post of deputy secretary and above. The main features of the central secretariat services are: first, the service provides staff not only for the central secretariat but also for most of the attached and subordinate offices, and all posts from the level of assistant up to under-secretaries are included in this service. Second, the new service was made a common service for all the ministries. This improved the opportunities and prospects of promotion for all the employees of the service. However, it was decided to introduce some element of decentralization in the service. The assistants and section officers are now divided into ministry-wise cadres, implying that the control over these levels now rests in the hands of the administrative ministries concerned. But, for purpose of promotion to grade I the field of choice consists of all the officers in the section officers grade in all the cadres. The control over grade I and selection posts now vests in the department of personnel. Third, the scheme visualized from the very beginning that a deputation reserve is needed in order to enable officers of the service to be appointed to the outside executive posts in attached and subordinate offices. This provision was made to widen the outlook and experience of the service and to strengthen the outside agencies. Finally, it was decided to establish a secretariat training school to provide systematic pre-entry training to new entrants in grades III and IV of this service. Such a school was established in May 1948 and has now been upgraded to the status of the Institute of Secretariat Training and Management (ISTM).

Posts in the selection grade are filled by promotion on the basis of merit from officers of grade I who have five years' service in the grade. Recruitment to the vacancies in the grade of section officers is made in a number of ways. One-sixth of the posts are filled through UPSC on the results of IAS entrance examination. The remaining vacancies and also the temporary vacancies are filled by promotions of assistants to the extent of two-third of the vacancies and through a limited departmental examination conducted by the UPSC for the remaining one-third.

For the grade of assistants, the original scheme envisaged a reservation of 75 per cent of the permanent vacancies for being filled by direct recruitment on the basis of open competitive examination conducted by the UPSC. However, to take care of the promotion opportunities of the upper division clerks, the quota of direct recruitment has so far been kept at 50 per cent instead of 75 per cent. The qualification prescribed for direct recruitment is a university degree. The remaining 50 per cent vacancies are filled by promotion of meritorious upper division clerks of the central secretariat clerical service.

Office Service

The office part of the secretariat is manned by persons drawn from the two services known as the central secretariat stenographers' service and the central clerical service.

Central Secretariat Stenographers' Service

This service was reorganized on 1st August 1969. It consists of four grades, such as selection grade, grade I, grade II and grade III. The third and fourth pay commissions in 1986 have improved their service conditions.

Central Secretariat Clerical Service (CSCS)

This service has only two grades, namely, upper division clerk (UDC) and lower division clerk (LDC). Recruitment to this service is at the level of LDC. Ninety per cent of the posts are filled through an all-India competitive examination and the remaining 10 per cent vacancies are filled up by a limited departmental examination of Class IV personnel who are matriculates and have more than five years of service. The examination for direct recruitment was also conducted by UPSC. It is now conducted by the institute of secretariat training and management under the department of personnel. The vacancies in the grade of UDC are filled by promotion from LDCs subject to the rejection of the unfit.

Criticism of the Secretariat

The need of the secretariat has not been questioned by its critics; rather they favour the secretariat to provide the necessary assistance to the minister in policy making. Its working methods in actual practice have been criticized on many grounds. The points of criticism were: First, the secretariat is a policy-making body, but has started taking a number of field functions also. This is not good for administrative efficiency. In such a situation, either the secretariat does not get time to concentrate on policy making or the power and authority of the field agencies is weakened. Second, the secretariat tends to indulge in empire building. The various ministries and departments tend to undertake functions which are unrelated to their activity and this often leads to unnecessary expenditure. Third, the secretariat has become an overgrown institution and over-staffing is clearly visible. To justify over-staffing the secretariat tends to engage in unnecessary work. Fourth, the secretariat personnel consider themselves superior to field agency personnel. Even a junior secretariat officer's behaviour with a senior field officer has not been good. They try to boss over them although their job is to provide them the necessary support by getting the policy framed for the performance of their field duties. The tenure system was devised for exchange of personnel between the secretariat and field offices for policies based on field experiences but in practice this purpose is not being served because now officers continue in secretariat for too long. Fifth, the secretariat has rules and procedures to be followed and the result is delay in decisions. The other reasons for delayed decisions are given as follows:

(a) Lack of adequate delegation to the field units
(b) Cumbersome procedures and unnecessary number of levels through which it has to pass before decision making
(c) Lack of feeling of responsibility and excessive dependence of higher officials on their subordinates
(d) Over-consultation, unnecessary meetings, interference from the top rungs, frequent transfers, etc. also cause delay

Sixth, the tendency to have best officers in the secretariat resulted in field agencies becoming starved for efficient officers. Finally, coordination has now become a real problem due to the proliferation of the departments in the secretariat. The process of consultation among different ministries/departments takes a lot of time. They act as separate empires and do not take an overall view of the problems involved.

The above points of criticism depict the realities of shortcomings in the secretariat. To overcome these weaknesses it would be desirable not to involve more than two levels below the authority involved in taking decisions. To avoid delay and cumbersome procedure sufficient powers should be delegated at the appropriate level. The ARC, in its report on the *Machinery of the Government of India*, has made some recommendation in this regard, which are given as follows:

A. (i) Non-secretariat organizations engaged primarily in planning, implementation, coordination and review of single development programmes or several allied programmes, covering a substantial area of the activities of the ministry and having a direct bearing on policy making should be integrated with the secretariat of the concerned ministry. Such amalgamation is especially significant in the case of activities of scientific and technical character and activities which call for a high degree of functional specialization.

(ii) The heads of non-secretariat organizations which are integrated with the secretariat should function as the principal advisors to the government in their respective areas and should enjoy a status appropriate to the nature of their duties and responsibilities. They may retain their present designations. It is not necessary to confer on them a formal ex-officio status.

(iii) In all other cases, the present distinction between policy-making and executive organizations may be continued. Such distinction is vital for protecting the operational autonomy of the regulatory executive agencies and such developmental executive organizations as are mostly engaged in promotional activities, provision of a service or production and supply of a commodity.

(iv) The executive functions at present performed by an administrative ministry or department which do not have a close bearing on policy-making should be transferred to an appropriate, existing secretariat agency or to a new executive organization specially created for the purpose, provided that the volume of the work justifies its creation.

(v) Policy personnel in departments and ministries dealing with scientific and technical matters or with functions of a highly specialized character should include persons having relevant specialized experience or expertise.

B. (i) In non-staff ministries, other than those with the board type of top management, there should be a set-up of three 'staff offices', namely; (a) an office of planning and policy; (b) a chief personnel office; and (c) a finance office. An administrative department with a heavy charge or with functions which have no close affinity with the work of other departments may have a separate planning and policy office.

(ii) The office of planning and policy should include the planning cell recommended in the ARC record of machinery for planning. This office should be continuously engaged in formulating long-term policies, carrying out policy studies and evolving a series of well-articulated policy statements. It should also deal with the parliamentary work of the department/ministry.

(iii) The chief personnel office in a ministry should serve as a focal point for the formulation and coordination of over all personnel policies, initiating measures for promoting personnel development and service rules of cadres administered by the ministry. It may also look after office management, O & M (organization and management) and general administration.

(iv) Each of the 'staff offices' should be manned by personnel having specialized knowledge and experience. The head of each 'staff office' should generally be of the rank of a joint secretary though in some cases he may even be a deputy secretary or an additional secretary, depending on the quantum of work.

(v) In addition to the three 'staff offices', each ministry should have a public relation office or unit.

(vi) The head of the 'substantive works' wing may deal directly with the chiefs of the three 'staff offices', as also with the secretary and minister on matters of technical or operational policy. Proposals having a bearing on long term policy should, however, be processed through the planning and policy office.

C. (i) Distribution of work between the wings of a ministry/administrative department and within the divisions of a secretariat wing should be based on considerations of rationality, manageability of charge and unity of command.

(ii) Each secretariat wing should have its separate identity and the budget should appear as a distinct unit in the budget of the ministry. Its head should enjoy adequate administrative and financial powers.

(iii) The head of the wing should have the primary responsibility for good administration within the wing, effective supervision and control of staff and maintenance of high standards of disciplined conduct.

(iv) The head of the wing should have considerable say in the formulation of the wing budget, creation of posts subject to budget provisions, spending of budget funds and appointments of personnel to the wing and their transfer. He should also have the necessary powers for effective day-to-day personnel management in the wing, e.g., powers to sponsor staff for training, grant honorarium, impose minor penalties and fill short-term leave vacancies.

D. (i) (a) There should only be two levels of consideration below the minister, namely, under-secretary/deputy secretary and joint secretary/additional secretary/secretary work should be assigned to each of these two levels on the lines of the desk officer's system. Each level should be required and empowered to dispose of a substantial amount of work on its own and should be given the necessary staff assistance. (b) The staffing pattern within a wing may be flexible to facilitate the employment of officers of various grades. (c) The duties and requirements of various jobs in the secretariat at each of the two levels should be defined clearly in detail on the basis of scientific analysis of work content.

(ii) For smooth and effective working of the proposed 'desk officer' system, the following measures will be necessary:

(a) Introduction of a functional system of the file index
(b) Maintenance of guard files or card indices which will contain all important precedents
(c) Adequate provision for 'leave' reserve
(d) Adequate stenographic and clerical help

(iii) (a) A policy advisory committee to consider all important issues of long term policy and to inject thinking inputs from different areas of specialisation into problem solving should be set up in each ministry or major administrative department. The committee should be headed by the secretary of the ministry and should include the heads of the three staff offices (of planning and policy, finance and personnel) and heads of important substantive work wings (including those of the non-secretariat organization integrated with the ministry/administrative department). As and when necessary, the head of governing bodies of important research and training institutions and boards and corporations outside the government may be co-opted as members of the policy advisory committee for such work as is of interest to them.

(b) Self-contained papers or memoranda, setting out problems, their various alternative solutions, merits and demerits of each alternative, etc., should be prepared for consideration by the committee and the decision arrived at should be duly recorded in the ministry.

Recent Developments

A new innovation known as 'desk system' has been introduced to eliminate dilatoriness in the functioning of the secretariat and equip it to cope effectively with the increasing demands. This system was introduced in November 1972 on the recommendations of the Deshmukh study team of the ARC.

Under this system the work of ministry or department at the lowest level is organized into different functional desks, each manned by an officer of appropriate rank, that is the under-secretary section officer or assistant, who handles the case with the adequate stenographic/clerical assistance. Two officers constitute a desk in the manner of one under-secretary and one section officer, or two section officers, or one section officer and one assistant. Each functionary is assisted by a stenographer and is known as desk officer, if he belongs to the rank of section officer or its equivalent. Assistants and their equivalents are known as desk attaches. There is no change in the designation of the under-secretary working on the desk. Functionally, the under-secretary will submit cases to the joint secretary, the desk officer to the deputy secretary/director and the desk attache to the under-secretary if it is not a desk, otherwise to the deputy secretary/director. Thus, the system is meant for speed and quality as the initial examination of cases is done at responsible level.

To conclude, in recent years the volume of secretariat work has increased manifold due to the planned economic development, the government's accountability to the Parliament and intensive scrutiny exercised by its standing committees. The need has been felt to maintain full and proper records of cases involving financial and other sanctions. But with the adoption of new economic policy and its trend of privatization, there has been a great change in this regard.

NOTES

1. B. B. Mishra, *The Central Administration of the East India Company (1733–1834)* (London: Manchester University Press, 1959), p. 64.
2. Ibid., p. 65.
3. Report of the ARC study team on the machinery of the government of India and procedures of work (New Delhi: Government of India Manager of Publications, 1967), p. 30.
4. Asok Chanda, *Indian Administration* (London: Allen & Unwin, 1967), pp. 139–40.
5. *Report of the Government of India Secretariat (Wheeler) Committee* (New Delhi: Government of India, 1936), p. 12.

The Cabinet Secretariat

A modern democratic welfare state depends on civil service for the execution of public policy and various laws of the state. In a parliamentary form of government political executive is responsible to the people through the Parliament. The efficiency of the cabinet depends on specialized and experienced administrators. Therefore, the cabinet secretariat has been established to provide the necessary secretarial assistance to the cabinet.

The Evolution of the Cabinet Secretariat

Before Independence, the executive council of the governor-general was responsible for all governmental functions. As the amount and complexity of business of the government increased, the work of the various departments was distributed amongst the members of the council only the more important cases being dealt with by the governor-general or the council collectively. This procedure was legalized by the Councils Act of 1861 during the time of Lord Canning, leading to the introduction of the portfolio system and the inception of the executive council of the governor-general.

The secretariat of the executive council was headed by the private secretary to the viceroy, but he did not attend the council meetings. Lord Willington first started the practice of having his private secretary by his side at these meetings. Later, this practice continued and in November 1935, the viceroy's private secretary was given the additional designation of secretary to the executive council.

The constitution of the interim government in September 1946 brought a change in the name, though little in function, of this office. The executive council's secretariat was then designated as the cabinet secretariat. It seems, however, at least in retrospect, that Independence brought a sort of change in the functions of the cabinet secretariat. It no longer remained concerned with only the passive work of circulating papers to ministers and ministries but developed into an organization for effecting coordination between the ministries.

An economic committee of the cabinet was set up in February 1949 with a view to speedily considering the proposals in the economic field. The secretariat of this committee was located in the ministry of finance till June 1950, when it was made a part of the cabinet secretariat and was designated as the economic wing. Later, to ensure better coordination and to avoid unnecessary duplication in the secretariat functions, this wing was merged with the main secretariat in October 1955.

In 1954, the organization and methods division was established and placed under the cabinet secretariat. In May 1964, the organization and methods division was transferred from the cabinet secretariat to the ministry of home affairs and is presently in the department of administrative reforms and public grievances of the ministry of personnel, public grievances and pension.

In 1957, a significant addition to the scope of the cabinet secretariat's functions took place with the constitution of a defence committee of the cabinet. A separate wing called the military wing was established in the cabinet secretariat for providing secretarial assistance to the committee. The officers for this wing are drawn from the defence services. The military wing has been transferred to the ministry of defence with effect from 1 July 1991.

In April 1961, the department of statistics was created as a part of the cabinet secretariat and was transferred to the ministry of planning in February 1973. The ministry of planning has been renamed as ministry of planning and programme implementation since July 1991.

The department of special economic coordination was set up under cabinet secretariat on 16 June 1962 and it was transferred to the then ministry of economic defence coordination on 14 November 1962. Presently, no such department exists in the government of India.

In July 1965, the intelligence wing was set up as a part of the cabinet secretariat to provide secretarial assistance to the joint intelligence committee.

The bureau of public enterprises was brought under the cabinet secretariat as a subject from the ministry of finance on 25 January 1966 and transferred to the then department of coordination under the ministry of finance on 2 June 1966. Later on the bureau of public enterprises was transferred to department of economic affairs under the ministry of finance on 13 June 1967. On 25 September 1935, the bureau of public enterprises was transferred to the then newly created department of public enterprises under the ministry of industry.

On 26 June 1970, besides the Department of cabinet affairs and the department of statistics under the cabinet secretariat, three more departments were created under it, namely (i) department of electronics, (ii) department of scientific and industrial research and (iii) department of personnel.

On 29 July 1970, the directorate-general of revenue intelligence-cum-directorate of enforcement was set up in the department of cabinet affairs under cabinet secretariat and on 1 August 1970, shifted to department of personnel.

The department of scientific and industrial research, which was created under the cabinet secretariat on 26 June 1970, became an independent department known as *Vigyan Aur Pradyogiki Vibhag* on 3 May 1971.

The department of electronics which was created under the cabinet secretariat on 26 June 1970 also became an independent department on 17 June 1971.

On 7 February 1973, the department of statistics, which was a part of cabinet secretariat since 9 April 1961, was transferred to the ministry of planning, and simultaneously the department of personnel was renamed as department of personnel and administrative reforms on 7 February 1973. On 7 April 1977, the department of personnel and administrative reforms was transferred to the ministry of home affairs from the cabinet secretariat. At present, the department of personnel and administrative reforms is a part of ministry of personnel, public grievances and pensions with the bifurcation as the department of personnel and training and department of administrative reforms and public grievances.

On 24 July 1981, a new department named department of ocean development was created under cabinet secretariat which became an independent department on 12 February 1982.

The directorate of public grievances was set up in the cabinet secretariat with effect from 25 March 1988 to entertain grievances from public after the complainants fail to get satisfactory redressal from the ministry/department concerned within a reasonable period of time. The directorate is authorized to take up grievances in respect of the ministry of railways, ministry of urban development, ministry of surface transport, ministry of civil aviation, department of posts, department of telecommunication, the banking division and the small savings division of the department of economic affairs.

The above description gives an account of frequent changes made from time to time in the administrative structure of the cabinet secretariat due to the reorganization of the executive functions of the Union government.

Organization of the Cabinet Secretariat

The cabinet secretariat is under the direct charge of the prime minister. The administrative head of the secretariat is the cabinet secretary, who is also the ex-officio chairman of the civil services board. At present the cabinet secretariat consists of three wings:

(i) The cabinet secretariat wing (main)

(ii) The intelligence wing

(iii) The security wing

(i) The cabinet secretariat wing (main), including DPG, has one cabinet secretary, three secretaries, one additional secretary, three joint secretaries, eight directors/deputy secretaries, one joint director and six under-secretaries or equivalent positions, thus totalling 23 officers.

(ii) The intelligence wing deals with matters relating to the joint intelligence committee. The joint intelligence committee consists of one chairman, four joint secretaries or equivalent position, one director (services), brigadier and equivalent rank officer, three staff officers of lieutenant colonel or equivalent rank, one joint director and the under-secretary, thus totalling 11 officers.

(iii) The security wing consists of one secretary (security) who looks after the security of VVIPs and controls the special protection group (SPG) meant for protection of the prime minister and other VIPs.

The organization chart (Figure 10.1) of the cabinet secretariat as on 19 September 1996 provides the details.

The main wing of the cabinet secretariat provides secretariat assistance to:

(i) The cabinet and its committees and the committee of the secretaries receive secretariat assistance from the civil wing of the cabinet secretariat. The secretarial assistance includes submission of cases to the cabinet and the committees, preparation and maintenance of records of the decision taken by the cabinet and its committees and initiation of follow-up action in the implementation of the decisions reached by the cabinet and its committees.

(ii) It is also responsible for providing secretarial assistance to the committees of the secretaries, meeting under the chairmanship of the cabinet secretary for considering and advising on the problems which require inter-ministerial consultation and coordination.

(iii) It is the responsibility of the main wing of the cabinet secretariat to lay down the rules of business and the allocation of the business of the government of India to the various ministries and the departments within the framework of the directives of the prime minister after these have been approved by the president.

Figure 10.1 *Cabinet Secretariat*

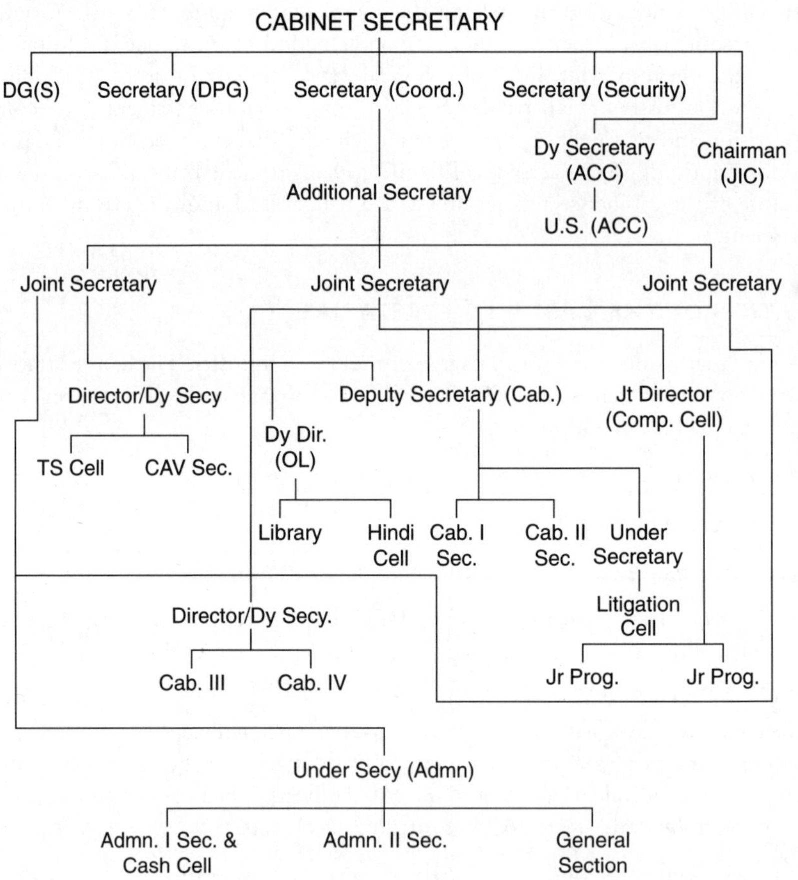

(iv) The periodical summaries and notes on the important developments of each ministry are obtained and circulated by the cabinet secretaries wing to the president, vice-president, council of ministers and other important functionaries of the government of India.

(v) Finally, it is responsible for establishing coordination and securing timely and effective action by all ministries and the departments on policy decisions which the cabinet as a whole or the prime minister have directed.

The Intelligence Wing

There is a joint intelligence committee which functions under the chairmanship of an additional secretary to the cabinet. It is the responsibility of the joint intelligence committee to collect, evaluate and present such intelligence pertaining to external threats to the national security. It also takes account of the internal factors having a bearing on national security. There is also a research and analysis wing (RAW) headed by a director. The RAW takes account of the work relating to foreign intelligence activities and of the counter intelligence abroad.

Functions of the Cabinet Secretariat

The cabinet secretariat has a very important place in the central administration. It is such a source of authority, the assistance of which enables the central government to undertake any matter of serious responsibility. The cabinet secretariat now possessing the relevant specialized field is in a position to (executive) carry out its responsibilities[1] with greater competence, initiative and efficiency. Some of the important functions of the cabinet secretariat are as follows:

1. To prepare the cabinet agenda and its minutes, to keep its records and to keep track of the progress made by administrative ministries and the department in executing the cabinet decisions
2. To know the implementing position of the decisions of the cabinet, it (cabinet, secretariat) calls for information from the various ministries and the departments which is subsequently passed on to the cabinet wherever it (cabinet) holds its meeting
3. To inform the president, vice-president and council of ministers about the major activities of the government conducted in several ministries
4. To circulate the monthly summaries and brief notes on important matters for collecting the information relating to the major activities of the government conducted in the various ministries
5. To prepare minutes of the meetings of the cabinet and its committees
6. To render its services to the committee of secretaries meeting periodically under the chairmanship of the cabinet secretary. This committee of the secretaries meets to consider and advise on problems requiring inter-ministerial consultation and coordination.
7. To lay down the rules of business and re-allocating the business of the government of India among the various ministries and the departments within the framework of directives of the prime minister, after these have been approved by the president
8. To establish coordination between the various seminars organized by the different central ministries
9. To work as the liaison agency between the state government and the central cabinet

The Role of the Cabinet Secretariat

The nomenclature of the cabinet secretariat is self-explanatory of the character of the nature of its role: It is an institution that provides the secretariat assistance to the cabinet. The role of cabinet secretariat could be explained by indicating the jurisdictional components of the cabinet.

(a) Cases pertaining to treaties, agreements and consultations with the foreign governments
(b) Cases relating to the draft legislation including of ordinances
(c) Proposals relating to the summoning of each house of Parliament by the president
(d) Those matters which the president or the prime minister might like to place before the cabinet
(e) Proposals relating to the withdrawal of court cases by the government
(f) Proposals relating to changing or modifying the already reached decisions of the cabinet

All the above-mentioned cases relate to the deliberative aspect of the cabinet and the cabinet secretariat is expected to provide necessary secretarial assistance to the cabinet in resolving these policy matters. The cabinet secretariat is basically the staff agency to the cabinet. In other words, the cabinet secretariat is the clearing house prior to the cabinet decisions.

The cabinet secretariat earlier oversaw only administrative matters. But of late, there have been deviations from this as the RAW, the SPG and secretary (security), have become part of the cabinet secretariat. A strong section is of the opinion that the cabinet secretariat should shield these additional responsibilities and be directly responsible for executive functions. Second, the creation of a separate department of personnel has resulted in an inherent conflict between the cabinet secretariat and the personnel department.

The Cabinet Secretary

He is the successor to the secretary of the viceroy's executive council in our cabinet system. Being the senior-most civil servant of the land he is the pivot of the cabinet system. During the meetings of the cabinet, he sits by the side of the prime minister to brief him on various points on the agenda. The cabinet secretary chairs the meetings of the committee of the secretaries and also presides when called on conferences of the chief secretaries. The position of cabinet secretary could be explained in between the lines of the report on reorganization of the machinery of government (1949) by N. Gopalaswami Ayyangar: 'There is a need to understand the status and functions of the cabinet secretary. The selection of this administrative officer should be on the basis of his special qualities of tact, initiative, efficiency and energy. Moreover, he should be entrusted as the head of the cabinet secretariat for securing coordination in all matters in which the cabinet as a whole or the prime minister might like to direct. He should be the administrative leader to command the respect and confidence of all ranks of civil service. So that the civil servants come to him for advice and guidance whenever there are interdepartmental difficulties. He is a sort of advisor and the conscience keeper to all the ranks of civil service in the central government administrative system.'

The cabinet secretary's office was created in India in 1950 after Independence and N. R. Pillai was the first cabinet secretary. Generally, he is the senior-most civil servant of the country, therefore, seniority should be given weightage along with merit in the selection of a cabinet secretary. Seniority alone is not an overriding factor. There have been innumerable instances in the past when the senior-most officer had been superseded while selections were carried for this post. P. K. Kaul, B. G. Deshmukh, V. C. Pande, Naresh Chandra and Zafar Saifullah were not senior-most from their respective batches. The empirical evidence thus tends to show that in India the principle established in the matter of appointment of the cabinet secretary appears to be his acceptability to the government of the day. The relevant point is that the practice of changing the cabinet secretary with change in government is wrong and harmful. It is against the sound principles of administration and should, therefore, be ended.

The administrative reforms commission had recommended that a cabinet secretary should be given a three-year tenure. Such tenure is necessary to enable him to take decisions in the right perspective and to initiate steps and measures and ensure he is there to implement them. It also enables him to withstand undue political and other pressures and take right decisions in public interest. It will also preserve and maintain the high service morale. A full tenure of three years provides stability and helps in evolving a warm working relationship between the prime minister's office and the cabinet secretary, and it also helps in the enormous amount of work that the two dozen secretaries to the various governments get done. The committee of secretaries has lost the gloss and sheen associated with it in the 1980s. Virtually a major portion of the country's administrative decisions that were thrashed out in this meeting also helped tie up loose ends and iron out the glitches among various ministries, now it is not one-fourth as effective as it was then. The reason was simple: you had a cabinet secretary who had the authority and the tenure to push his team to achieve results. The no fixed tenure posts results in a flabby and unsure bureaucracy that is now led by a captain who is changed every year. How can we expect the system to deliver in such a sorry situation.[2]

There have been 22 cabinet secretaries (up to August 1994) and the average tenure is about a year and eleven months. The last two cabinet secretaries were, therefore, only for a year each.[3]

The no fixed tenure rule generated the phenomenon of extension. Giving extension to the cabinet secretary is undesirable as it only makes his position untenable and open to all sorts of rumours and allegations. The cabinet secretary should be appointed for a fixed tenure and if this needs giving him an extension then it should be done at the time of his appointment. The prime minister should not only play favourites while appointing a new cabinet secretary. Favouritism makes the position of the cabinet secretary vulnerable and he has, of course, to pay back the favour to the prime minister and in the process he loses his moral authority over the civil service.

The Role of the Cabinet Secretary

The cabinet secretary is the head of civil service and chief advisor to the council of ministers and the prime minister, the cabinet and its committees. He coordinates the activities of various ministries and departments. He is the link between the prime minister's office and various administrative departments. He is the link between the political part of the government, i.e. the cabinet and the apolitical governmental machinery, i.e. the bureaucracy. Our first Prime Minister, Pandit Jawaharlal Nehru, decided to have a cabinet secretary, who would not be a part of the prime minister's office, deviating from British practice. In Britain there is no secretary to the prime minister, and many a time the cabinet secretary is involved in the functioning of prime minister's office.[4] Lord Mountbatten gave the sound advice to Panditji to have secretary to the prime minister different from the cabinet secretary so that the latter's position would not be politicized.

The main functions of the cabinet secretary, according to the statutory rules of business, are to provide secretariat assistance to cabinet and cabinet committees, and to formulate rules of business of the government. Its main tasks are, namely, to prepare proposals for the cabinet after consultations with concerned ministries and departments to constantly monitor and coordinate implementation of decisions taken by the cabinet and prepare papers connected with the appointments that the prime minister has to make. Some general issues taken up in the committee of secretaries and others like internal security are carefully analysed in the core group comprising the cabinet secretary, the principal secretary to the prime minister, home secretary, defence secretary, secretary RAW, director of the intelligence bureau (DIB) and chairman of the joint intelligence committee (JIC) and, on rare occasions, the secretary concerned may also be invited to the core group meetings.

The most important function of the cabinet secretary of late pertains to internal security and sifting through intelligence. It is his duty to make a coordinate assessment of a given situation or problem by absorbing the source report. If the issue is resolved in the core group, the matter is not referred to the prime minister or the cabinet.

It is for the cabinet secretary to ensure fair administration of the services. The cabinet secretary has the unenviable task of seeing that certain unhealthy linkages do not develop. He should be answerable for any decision taken, and also impart an all-India look and character to the administrative departments of various ministries. However, despite his multi-faceted role, the cabinet secretary has no say in judicial appointments.

The prime minister also gives him specific tasks from time to time, like B. G. Deshmukh a former cabinet secretary asked to set up a committee to monitor Sri Lanka situation or to take urgent action to tackle the Maldives crisis. He can also on his own initiative take certain matters he thinks necessary and urgent, like supervising steps to be taken to increase exports. Further, while taking initiative in any particular matter, he has to ensure that the concerned minister or secretary to the ministry or department does not feel that his turf is encroached upon. In very rare cases, he has to involve the prime minister's name or authority of course after getting the latter's informal clearance.

He is very close to the prime minister but he has to ensure that his politically neutral image is in no way compromised. His proximity to the prime minister also generates resentment and jealousies amongst ministers and even influential politicians. Therefore, he has to be very careful not to get involved in any controversies. As the head of the civil service he has to be impartial, not play favourites and observe the highest tradition of the civil service. He is not seen to be indifferent to the interest of non-IAS civil servants. He has to be like a father figure to the civil service and enjoy its trust fully. He is not only the principal advisor to the prime minister and the cabinet but also monitors and coordinates activities of various ministers and departments and frames new policy initiatives. The cabinet secretariat also serves as an umbrella organization for various new agencies, which for any reason cannot be located in any particular ministry or department. Even though as per tradition the cabinet secretary belongs to the ICS or IAS cadres, once he takes up the post of cabinet secretary, he does not belong to any of these services and ensures that all get due recognition and proper share of senior posts. He is the first among equals vis-à-vis his senior colleagues, but he has to justify this role by his own conduct and behaviour. He has to not only act but also has to be seen to act with fairness and impartiality.

He is the link between the political system and the civil service, mentions B. C. Deshmukh, a former cabinet secretary.[5] This political interface is a very thin line and he has literally to walk the tightrope . . . the orders of the political leadership have to be obeyed but then a mature and competent cabinet secretary has always managed to ensure that this does not damage the structure of the civil service and affect its morale. While the political system has accepted his advice. In most cases, it is unfair to expect this to happen in every case.[6] He is expected to be not only the record-keeper but often even the conscience-keeper of the cabinet. He has to be more knowledgeable than the rest in the corridors of power, in a way to be the 'king' of all trades. Mr Mirnal Mukherji, the cabinet secretary from 1977 to 1980, who had worked with three prime ministers, says, 'with Mr Morarji Desai my equation was more or less equal. With Charan Singhji I was the guide. And, well with Indiraji I was given the cold shoulder treatment.'[7] Recalling his experience, Mr V. C. Pandey says that somehow most of the unpleasant tasks end up with the cabinet secretaries. He recalls an incident when he was asked by the then foreign minister, Mr I. K. Gujral, to inform the Indian ambassador in the UK, Mr M. K. Rasgotra, to resign from his post. 'Though not very keen on the task, I had to do the dirty job.'[8]

The role of the cabinet secretary has been lucidly discussed by Khera: 'The cabinet secretary provided the eyes and ears for the prime minister to keep in touch with the process of official business in the central government. But he is in no sense the watch-dog or invigilator on behalf of the prime minister. The worst thing that could happen would be for any member of the council of ministers to feel that the cabinet secretary or for that matter any other official, is not spying on him or that the official may have the ear of the prime minister to carry tales. The cabinet secretary's is a very general staff function, not a line function in relation to the ministries. His business is to help, not to oversee.'[9] There are two other rather out of the ordinary functions performed by the cabinet secretary. 'The first is when the cabinet secretary has to act on his own authority and responsibility without the benefit of resort to the prime minister.'[10] Second, the 'cabinet secretary may also be called to serve on occasions as a sort of general official factotum, whom the prime minister deems thus to be necessary.'[11]

In brief, the cabinet secretary is usually the senior-most civil servant of the country and the official warrant of precedence gives him the first place among the civil servants. Ever since the appointment of the first incumbent to this post in 1950 the cabinet secretary invariably belonged to the cadre of the ICS till the retirement of N. K. Mukherji, the last of the cadre. After him there have been top IAS cadre officers to occupy this position. The present incumbent is K. M. Chandrasekhar. The cabinet secretary works under the direct control of the prime minister.

The institution of cabinet secretary had suffered quite a few heavy blows even before the present sordid scramble for the post could begin. Generally, three factors have been responsible for this. The first was the phenomenal rise in the power of the prime minister's principal secretary or secretary, making him, rather than the cabinet secretary, the dominant civil service figure. From the time of P. N. Haksar to the time of A. N. Verma and the present incumbent, this trend has continued 'The principal secretary of the prime minister is not the chief secretary of the government of India. His office seems to have emerged as an alternative power centre. It can lead to a number of embarrassing situations,' remarked one former cabinet secretary.[12] Second, the short tenures of cabinet secretaries during the past one decade have inevitably eroded the prestige of the post. The third and the most damaging assault on the office of cabinet secretary has been the objectionable practice under which the cabinet secretary changes every time the government changes, while in Britain a cabinet secretary serves for more than 10 years.

Administrative Reforms Commission and the Cabinet Secretariat

The administrative reforms commission was appointed by the government to study the machinery of the government of India and its procedures of work. The commission submitted its report in 1968. Some of its important recommendations relating to cabinet secretariat are as follows:

(a) Every sub-committee of the cabinet should be supported by a committee of secretaries in the cabinet secretariat to consider in advance all matters to be taken up in the cabinet sub-committee.

(b) About the role of the cabinet secretary the commission expressed its views that his role should not be limited to that of a coordinator. The cabinet secretary should also act as the principal staff advisor to the prime minister, the cabinet and the cabinet committee on important policy matters. The term of office of the cabinet secretary should be three to four years in the cabinet secretariat.

(c) The commission recommended that development of personnel should be headed by a secretary who should work under the general guidance of the cabinet secretary.

NOTES

1. S. R. Maheshwari, *Indian Administration*, 4th edition (New Delhi: Orient Longman, 1989), p. 23.
2. *Hindustan Times*, Sunday magazine, Delhi, 4 August 1996.
3. Nirmal Mukherji, 'Civil Service Chief: A Non-playing Captain', *Hindustan Times*, New Delhi, 7 August 1994, p. 13. 'Just Look at the Record Seven Cabinet Secretaries in Eight Years', 1988 T. N. Seshan; 1989 V. C. Pande; 1989 Naresh Chandra; 1992 S. Rajagopal; 1993 Zafar Saifullah; 1994 Surendra Singh and 1996 T. S. R. Subramaniam, *Hindustan Times*, Sunday magazine, New Delhi, 4 August 1996.
4. John Green Wood and David Wilson, *Public Administration in Britain Today*, 2nd edition (London: Unwin Hyman, 1989), pp. 77–83.
5. B. G. Deshmukh, 'Role of Cabinet Secretary: Post Must Not Be Politicised', *Times of India*, Delhi, 7 October 1991.
6. Ibid.
7. *Times of India*, 18 July 1993.
8. Ibid.
9. S. S. Khera, *The Central Executive* (New Delhi: Orient Longman, 1975), pp. 181–82.
10. Ibid., p. 182.
11. Ibid., p. 183.
12. *Times of India*, Delhi, 18 July 1993.

Ministries and Departments

The executive authority of the government is vested in the president. Article 53 says that 'the executive power of the Union shall be vested in the president and shall be exercised by him either directly or through officers subordinate to him in accordance with the Constitution.' Thus, all the executive functions vested in the president are carried on in two ways: (1) either directly by him or (2) through subordinate officers. But Article 53 (3) authorizes Parliament to confer 'by law functions on authorities other than the president'. Every law made by Parliament needs the assent of the president before it could become operative law. But the Constitution has created a council of ministers to 'aid and advise' the president in exercise of his executive powers. Therefore, he has to act as per the advice of the council of ministers.

During the British rule the governor-general-in-council was taking executive decisions but when the work of the government increased, portfolio system was introduced in which each member of the council was assigned a particular portfolio. All matters concerning a particular portfolio were referred to the concerned member. The matters of general policy only were referred to the council. This practice continued after Independence, the council became council of ministers/cabinet. The council of ministers, although collectively responsible to the Parliament, had individual ministers allotted to different departments for which they were individually responsible to the council of ministers as well as to the legislature. In this chapter we will discuss the allocation of work among different ministers and the manner in which the individual ministries function.

The Allocation of Business

The Constitution[1] empowered the president to make rules for the convenient transaction of the business of the government and for its allocation among ministers. The president, on the advice of the prime minister, allots ministries/departments to the ministers from time to time. The allocation of work is based on the Government of India (Allocation of Business) Rules, 1961, as amended from time to time. These rules prescribe the ministries/departments, secretariat/office in which the work of the government is carried out.

The Government of India Manual says, 'The business allotted to a ministry is normally disposed of by the minister in-charge or by an appropriate officer of the ministry under the direction of the minister.

The exercise of the responsibilities by individual ministries is, however, subject to certain conditions, such as those requiring inter-departmental consultation in matters affecting the business allotted to another minister or those requiring the submission of certain types of cases for the orders of the prime minister or the cabinet, or a committee of the cabinet. Certain classes or cases are also required to be submitted to the president before issue of orders.'

Thus, for proper working, a particular ministry is entrusted to a particular minister subject to the overall control of the prime minister and the cabinet. In the year 1947, the number of ministries was few and general ministries comprised one department with one secretary. The work of government increased due to planned economy and social welfare activities, hence, the number of departments have also increased. But to contain the size of the ministry small, it has become necessary to group a number of departments into a single ministry. As a result, many ministries have now more than one department with a secretary as the head of each department. Therefore, a minister now has more than one secretary to supervise.

Bases of Work Distribution

The distribution of work among different departments is generally made on the following basis: (a) Functional basis, i.e. functions to be performed; (b) processes involved; (c) people or clientele to be served; (d) area of operation.

The actual allocation of work, however, is not based on any single criterion. All the four bases mentioned above are used to make proper division of work among different government departments. In 1997, the executive work of the Government of India was divided into 38 ministries and 70 departments besides the cabinet secretariat, president's secretariat, prime minister's office and planning commission. The bases on which the division of work is made are given as follows:

Bases	*Ministries/Departments*
Function	Defence, education, health and family welfare
Process	Law, steel and mines
Clientele	Ministry of welfare and ministry of labour
Area	Ministry of external affairs, ministry of rural areas and employment, ministry of urban areas and employment, etc.

Detailed allocation of work is given in the end of the chapter. The allocation of work between different ministries keeps on changing from time to time. Sometimes the allocation for division of work is not based on any principle or bases but only on political or personal consideration. Independent ministries or departments are carried out for some political leaders to be accommodated as was done in the case of ministry of fertilizers and chemicals in 1993. Sometimes division of work is influenced by the considerations of weakening of some ministers. For example, when Y. B. Chawan was home minister, the CBI and IB, and department of personnel and administrative reforms were taken away from the ministry of home affairs to weaken him. Likewise, ministry of agriculture has been cut to size by taking away department of rural development, fertilizers and chemicals, etc. Thus, the division of work is not always based on rational considerations.

Working of the Ministries/Departments

A ministry may consist of one or more departments, each under the charge of a secretary. Generally a cabinet minister is in-charge of a ministry assisted by a number of ministers of state and/or deputy ministers.

Sometimes the minister of state may hold independent charge of a ministry. There are three levels seen clearly in the functioning of a ministry. These are: (i) political level, (ii) secretariat level, and (iii) executive level.

The Political Head

The minister, the state minister and the deputy minister are the political persons who are in charge of a ministry. Sometimes there may be parliamentary secretary at the bottom of political hierarchy. They occupy the position due to their political strength in the party. They are not experts or having any technical qualifications. The ministers broadly perform three types of functions. First, he initiates the broad policies which the department has to follow. He decides all the important policy questions which may come up in the functioning of the department. Second, he exercises general supervision over the implementation of the policy by the department. Third, he takes the responsibility of administration and policies of his department in the Parliament. He answers parliamentary questions relating to his department. He pilots the legislation and represents his department in the Parliament as well as before the people. Fourth, he represents his ministry in the cabinet. He has to share the collective responsibility of the cabinet to the Parliament. He has to ensure coordination of his policies with those of other ministries.

The minister of state, the deputy ministers and the parliamentary secretaries share such of the duties of the cabinet minister as assigned to them by him. Generally, they provide assistance to the cabinet minister.

The Secretariat

The political head is supported by the secretariat of the department. The function of the secretariat is to provide mature and expert advice for the formulation of policies. The secretariat is the central point of administration. The department is further sub-divided, for smooth functioning, into various units as shown below:

Department	Secretary
Wing	Additional secretary/Joint secretary
Division	Deputy secretary/Director
Branch	Under-secretary
Section	Section officer

The scheme shows that the department is sub-divided into a number of wings, each headed by additional or joint secretary. Each wing is sub-divided into divisions. The division is headed by a deputy secretary. A division is sub-divided into branches each headed by an under-secretary and a branch into sections, headed by a section officer. The functions and role of these functionaries will be discussed briefly.

Secretary—The secretary is the administrative head of the ministry or the department. He is the principal advisor to the minister on all matters of policy and administration of his ministry/department. He is fully responsible for the efficient administration of his ministry/department. He represents his ministry/department before the parliamentary committees, on public accounts, estimates committee and committee on public undertakings, etc. He keeps himself informed of the working of his department by receiving weekly summaries giving the nature of cases that have been disposed of by his subordinate officers. He can issue instructions that certain cases may be submitted directly to him. Gopalaswami Ayyangar suggested, 'A secretary should not be immersed in files and burdened with routine. It is essential that he should have time to grasp the overall picture, size up the problems facing government in the field allotted to his charge, and think and plan ahead. All these are his proper functions and must be efficiently performed. Failure to make adequate provision in this respect cannot be compensated by mere increase in the establishment under his control.'[2] The administrative reforms commission has also visualized the rule of the secretary, primarily as one of 'coordinator, policy guide, reviewer and evaluator'. Thus, the secretary is at the top of departmental authority and draws the higher salary available to a number of IAS.

Special secretary—After Independence, the original hierarchy has been disturbed by creating more than one level of authority. This undermines the solidarity, efficiency and effectiveness of hierarchical organization. The post of special secretary is a good example of such disturbance of hierarchy. Asok Chanda had pointed out, 'in 1951, a special secretary enjoying the pay, status and authority of a secretary, was appointed, for a time, to the ministry of agriculture. This was a unique post and neither the principle on which such a post was created not its relations with the permanent secretary were defined or appreciated. More recently, such a post has been revived in the ministry of external affairs to take charge of the administration of foreign service with the pay, rank and status of a secretary. The department of heavy industries in the ministry of commerce and industry has also been placed in the charge of a special secretary, but of one with the pay of a joint secretary and with an undefined status.'[3] Thus, there is no well-settled principle or rule for the appointment, rank and pay of special secretary.

Additional secretary—Originally, the office next to the secretary was the deputy secretary but in course of time new levels of special/additional/or joint secretaries were formed. In 1937 the organization and procedure committee referred to these new levels. Various committees asked to report on improvement in administration had adversely commented on the interposition of these levels, between the secretary and the deputy secretary. There is no specific unit of administration of which an additional secretary is to be in-charge. Sometimes he is given charge of a department and does the work of secretary; at other times he heads the wing and performs the work of a joint secretary. Sometimes he helps the secretary in a specified field of activity. Richard Tothenham correctly narrated the nature and role of these posts. He says, 'In my opinion there is, or should be no distinction of function, but only of pay between a joint and an additional secretary. In both cases their correct function is to relieve the secretary of a block of work and to deal directly with the member so far as that work is concerned. They should only be required in those departments . . . additional and joint secretaries should not be either cheap secretaries or expensive deputy secretaries.'[4]

The study team of the administrative reforms commission on personnel administration and the ARC itself suggested for the creation of a definite level of additional secretary. It also envisaged cases in which a wing of the ministry may be headed by an additional secretary himself instead of a joint secretary. In the larger ministries, the level of additional secretary provides considerable relief to the secretary. In practice, however, the secretary sees in him a rival to his authority and joint secretary finds in him an unnecessary interposition between themselves and the secretary.

Joint secretary—The joint secretary is generally in charge of a wing and he is vested with the maximum independence for functioning and responsibility of all business under his wing, subject to the general responsibility of the secretary for the administration of the ministry as a whole. According to A. D. Gorwala, the joint secretaries ought to in reality be what the name implies, namely, secretaries for the subject entrusted to them and joined to a more senior secretary for the convenience of administrative work. This post was created in early 1920s for three reasons. First, the increase in the functions of some departments made it difficult for one secretary to cope up with the increased work; second, it was found difficult to combine separate items of business under one secretary; and third, the emergence of two house of legislature at the centre in 1920, which necessitated the presence of senior officers in both the houses to assist the members in legislative work. The emergence of the posts of joint secretaries between the secretary and his deputy secretaries has been criticized by almost all the committees appointed by the government to suggest improvements in the administrative machiery. The Gopalaswami Ayyangar committee had called it an unsatisfactory arrangement, which causes delay and inefficiency.[5] However, in practice the joint secretaries are performing more or less the functions which the deputy secretaries used to perform earlier. Though they are in charge of the separate wing of the ministry but they function as deputies to the secretaries. They neither take any independent decisions nor do they submit files directly to the minister on the specific areas of work allotted to them.

Deputy secretary—The deputy secretary is an officer who acts on behalf of the secretary. He holds charge of a secretariat division and is responsible for the disposal of government work under his charge. He should ordinarily be able to dispose of the majority of cases coming to him on his own responsibility. Originally this officer occupied an important position but after Independence the post has been devalued and there is hardly any decision which a deputy secretary is taking on his own. He submits most of the cases to joint secretary.

Under-secretary—An under-secretary is in charge of a branch in a ministry and exercises control both in regard to the discharging of business and maintenance of discipline. The role of this officer has been detailed in the Maxwell Committee Report, 'The grade of the under secretary should ordinarily initiate action on all inward communications, immediately to the notice of the deputy secretary for any instructions which the latter might wish to give. The under secretary should dispose off minor cases on his own volition. More important files he should submit to the deputy secretary in such a form that in ordinary course the deputy secretary should be enabled to deal with the case quite briefly. Under secretaries should also attempt to reduce as far as possible the number of files to be formally submitted to the deputy secretary by taking the latter's verbal orders in appropriate cases. We consider that one of the great losses in recent years in the working of secretariat departments is the practical disappearance, due to various causes, of the summary and draft of the efficient under secretary.'[6]

Office—The secretariat consists of two types of officers; one consisting of officers who take part in the decision-making process, and the other consisting of the office which maintains and presents papers.

The functions of the office have been described in Chapter 9 on the Secretariat. The office consists of the following grades of functionaries (i) section officer, (ii) assistant, (iii) upper division clerk (UDC), (iv) lower division clerk (typist), etc.

Section Officer

The superintendents who are in charge of sections are called section officers. A section officer has to supervise the work of his staff in his section. He is responsible for handling important cases himself. He distributes the work among the staff, trains and advises them in the discharge of their duties. He coordinates the work of different functionaries in his section and ensures prompt disposal of work. He has to adopt proper methods of processing of cases, timely submission of statements and other periodical reports, proper maintenance of section diary, file registers, assistant's diaries and other necessary papers and registers. He ensures compliance of instructions for secret papers.

Assistants/Upper Division Clerks

An assistant works under the orders of the section officer and is responsible for the work assigned to him. His main functions are: First, to examine and put up suitable notes and drafts on cases quickly and submits them to the section officer after proper paging. Second, he has to maintain the assistant's diary, secure files and other registers and documents properly. Third, he has to keep papers and files in good conditions.

Some selected assistants may be authorized to submit cases directly to the branch officer. UDC generally performs similar functions to those of assistants except that they are not required to deal with important cases.

Lower division clerks—These functionaries are ordinarily given work of a routine nature such as registration of papers, maintenance of circulars and other registers, indexing, recording, preparation of arrear statements, typing, comparing and despatch, etc.

The Attached Offices

Besides the main secretariat, there are a number of attached offices at the headquarters of the Government of India. Such examples are the offices of the controller of printing, chief controller of imports and exports, agricultural marketing advisor to government of India, directorate of inspection (income tax), chief labour commissioner, etc. These will be discussed in the chapter on field agencies.

Executive Organization of the Department

The secretariat is responsible for policy-making functions of the government. Below the secretariat, there is the executive organization with a head of its own known as the head of the department. The head of the secretariat organization, i.e. secretary is not technically speaking the head of the department. He is the chief advisor to the government for the formulation of policies. Basically his duties are of a 'staff' nature rather than 'line' work. The executive organization is the 'line' machinery of the department/ministry and is also termed as a department with its own head who is officially called the head of the department. Such executive heads are designated differently in different departments. Generally he is called director or director-general, but there are also designations such as inspector-general, adviser, commissioner, etc.

Ministries/Departments of the Government

The government consists of a number of ministries/departments, number and character varying from time to time on factors such as volume of work importance attached to certain items, changes of orientation, political expediency, etc. On 15 August 1947, the number of ministries at the centre was 18.

Ministries and Departments in the Central Government in 2009

1. **Ministry of Agriculture *(Krishi Mantralaya)***
   (i) Department of Agriculture and Cooperation *(Krishi aur Sahkarita Vibhag)*
   (ii) Department of Agricultural Research and Education *(Krishi Anusandhan aur Shiksha Vibhag)*
   (iii) Department of Animal Husbandry, Dairying and fishiries *(Pashupalan, Dairy aur Matsyapalan Vibhag)*
2. **Ministry of Chemicals and Fertilizers *(Rasayan aur Urvarak Mantralaya)***
   (i) Department of Chemicals and Petro-Chemicals *(Rasayan aur Petro-Rasayan Vibhag)*
   (ii) Department of Fertilizers *(Urvarak Vibhag)*
3. **Ministry of Civil Aviation *(Nagar Vimanan Mantralaya)***
4. **Ministry of Coal *(Koyala Mantralaya)***

5. **Ministry of Commerce and Industry *(Vanijya aur Udyog Mantralaya)***
   (i) Department of Commerce *(Vanijya Vibhag)*
   (ii) Department of Industrial Policy and Promotion *(Audyogik Niti aur Samvardhan Vibhag)*
6. **Ministry of Communications and Information Technology (*Sanchar aur Soochana Praudyogiki Mantralaya*)**
   (i) Department of Telecommunications (*Doorsanchar Vibhag*)
   (ii) Department of Post (*Dak Vibhag*)
   (iii) Department of Information Technology (*Soochana Praudyogiki Vibhag*)
7. **Ministry of Consumer Affairs, Food and Public Distribution *(Upbhokta Mamle, Khadya aur Sarvajanik Vitaran Mantralaya)***
   (i) Department of Consumer Affairs *(Upbhokta Mamle Vibhag)*
   (ii) Department of Food and Public Distribution *(Khadya aur Sarvajanik Vitaran Vibhag)*
8. **Ministry of Corporate Affaire *(Korporate Karya Mantralya)***
9. **Ministry of Culture *(Sanskriti Mantralya)***
10. **Ministry of Defence *(Raksha Mantralaya)***
    (i) Department of Defence *(Raksha Vibhag)*
    (ii) Department of Defence Production and Supplies *(Raksha Utpadan aur Aapoorti Vibhag)*
    (iii) Department of Defence Research and Development *(Raksha Anusandhan aur Vikas Vibhag)*
11. **Ministry of Development of North-Eastern Region *(Uttar Poorvi Kshetra Vikas Mantralaya)***
12. **Ministry of Earth Sciences *(Bhoo Vigyan Mantralaya)***
13. **Ministry of Environment and Forests *(Paryavaran aur Van Mantralaya)***
14. **Ministry of External Affairs *(Videsh Mantralaya)***
15. **Ministry of Finance *(Vitta Mantralaya)***
    (i) Department of Economic Affairs *(Arthik Karya Vibhag)*
    (ii) Department of Expenditure *(Vyaya Vibhag)*
    (iii) Department of Revenue *(Rajaswa Vibhag)*
    (iv) Department of Disinvestment *(Vinivesh Vibhag)*
    (v) Department of Financial Services *(Vittiya Sewayen Vibhag)*
16. **Ministry of Food Processing Industries *(Khadya Prasanskaran Udyog Mantralaya)***
17. **Ministry of Health and Family Welfare *(Swasthya aur Parivar Kalyan Mantralaya)***
    (i) Department of Health and family welfare *(Swasthya aur Parivar Kalyan Mantralaya)*
    (ii) Department of Ayurveda, Yoga-Naturopathy, Unani, Siddha and Homoeopathy (AYUSH) *(Ayurveda, Yoga-Prakritik Chikitsa Paddhati, Unani, Siddha aur Homoeopathy Vibhag)*
18. **Ministry of Heavy Industries and Public Enterprises *(Bhari Udyog aur Lok Udyam Mantralaya)***
    (i) Department of Heavy Industries *(Bhari Udyog Vibhag)*
    (ii) Department of Public Enterprises *(Lok Udyam Vibhag)*
19. **Ministry of Home Affairs *(Grih Mantralaya)***
    (i) Department of Internal Security *(Antarik Suraksha Vibhag)*
    (i) Department of States *(Rajya Vibhag)*
    (iii) Department of Official Language *(Raj Bhasha Vibhag)*
    (iv) Department of Home *(Grih Vibhag)*
    (v) Department of Jammu and Kashmir Affairs *(Jammu tatha Kashmir Vibhag)*
    (vi Department of Border Management *(Seema Prabandhan Vibhag)*

20. **Ministry of Housing and Urban Poverty Alleviation *(Aawas aur Shahari Garibi Upshaman Mantralaya)***
21. **Ministry of Human Resource Development *(Manav Sansadhan Vikas Mantralaya)***
    (i) Department of School Education and Literacy *(School Shiksha aur Saksharta Vibhag)*
    (ii) Department of Higher Education *(Uchchatar Shiksha Vibhag)*
22. **Ministry of Information and Broadcasting *(Soochana aur Prasaran Mantralaya)***
23. **Ministry of Labour and Employment *(Shram aur Rozgar Mantralaya)***
24. **Ministry of Law and Justice *(Vidhi aur Nyaya Mantralaya)***
    (i) Department of Legal Affairs *(Vidhi Karya Vibhag)*
    (ii) Legislative Department *(Vidhayee Vibhag)*
    (iii) Department of Justice *(Nyaya Vibhag)*
25. **Ministry of Mines *(Khan Mantralaya)***
26. **Ministry of Minority Affairs *(Alpasankhyak Karya Mantralya)***
27. **Ministry of New and Renewable Energy *(Naveen Aur Navikarniya Oorja Mantralaya)***
28. **Ministry of Overseas Indians Affairs *(Apravasi Bharatiyon Ke Mamalon Ka Mantralya)***
29. **Ministry of Panchayati Raj *(Panchayati Raj Mantralaya)***
30. **Ministry of Parliamentary Affairs *(Sansadiya Karya Mantralaya)***
31. **Ministry of Personnel, Public Grievances and Pensions *(Karmik Lok Shikayat tatha Pension Mantralaya)***
    (i) Department of Personnel and Training *(Karmik aur Prashikshan Vibhag)*
    (ii) Department of Administrative Reforms and Public Grievances *(Prashasanik Sudhar aur Lok Shikayat Vibhag)*
    (iii) Department of Pensions and Pensioners' Welfare *(Pension aur Pension Bhogi Kalyan Vibhag)*
32. **Ministry of Petroleum and Natural Gas *(Petroleum aur Prakritik Gas Mantralaya)***
33. **Ministry of Planning *(Yojana Mantralaya)***
34. **Ministry of Power *(Oorja Mantralaya)***
35. **Ministry of Railways *(Rail Mantralaya)***
36. **Ministry of Shipping, Road Transport and Highways *(Pot Parivahan, Sarak Parivahan aur Raj Marg Mantralaya***
    (i) Department of Shipping *(Pot Parivahan Vibhag)*
    (ii) Department of Road Transport and Highways *(Sadak Parivahan Aur Raj Marg Vibhag)*
37. **Ministry of Rural Development*(Gramin Vikas Mantralaya)***
    (i) Department of Rural Development *(GraminVikasVibhag)*
    (ii) Department of Land Resources *(Bhumi Sansadhan Vibhag)*
    (iii) Department of Drinking Water Supply *(Peya Jal Poorti Vibhag)*
38. **Ministry of Science and Technology *(Vigyan aur Praudyogiki Mantralaya)***
    (i) Department of Science and Technology *(Vigyan aur Praudyogiki Vibhag)*
    (ii) Department of Scientific and Industrial Research *(Vigyan aur Audyogik Anusandhan Vibhag)*
    (iii) Department of Bio-Technology*(BiotechnologyVibhag)*
39. **Ministry of Micro, Small and Medium Enterprises *(Sukshma Laghu Aur Madhyam Udyam Mantralya)***
40. **Ministry of Social Justice and Empowerment *(Samajik Nyaya aur Adhikarita Mantralaya)***

41. **Ministry of Statistics and Programme Implementation** ***(Sankhyiki aur Karyakram Kiryanvayan Mantralaya).***
42. **Ministry of Steel** ***(Ispat Mantralaya)***
43. **Ministry of Textiles** ***(Vastra Mantralaya)***
44. **Ministry of Tourism** ***(Paryatan Mantralaya)***
45. **Ministry of Tribal Affairs** ***(Janjatiya Karya Mantralaya)***
46. **Ministry of Urban Development** ***(Shahari Vikas Mantralaya)***
47. **Ministry of Water Resources** ***(Jal Sansadhan Mantralaya)***
48. **Ministry of Woman and Child Development** ***(Mahila Aur Bal Vikas Mantralaya)***
49. **Ministry of Youth Affairs and Sports** ***(Yuva Karyakram aur Khel Mantralaya)***
50. **Department of Atomic Energy** ***(Parmanu Oorja Vibhag)***
51. **Department of Space** ***(Antariksh Vibhag)***
52. **Cabinet Secretariat** ***(Mantrimandal Sachivalaya)***
53. **President's Secretariat** ***(Rashtrapati Sachivalaya)***
54. **Prime Minister's Office** ***(Pradhan Mantri Karyalaya)***
55. **Planning Commission** ***(Yojana Ayog)*** [7]

MINISTRY OF HOME AFFAIRS

The ministry of home affairs is one of the four oldest departments set up along with the military, finance and foreign affairs by a resolution of governor-general-in-council on 29 April 1843. The home department was placed under the charge of a secretary. The department was entrusted with the functions of a heterogeneous nature such as internal law and order, political matters, civil services, police, jails, explosives factories, education, public works, public health, hospitals and municipalities, etc. With the passage of time new departments emerged and many subjects were subsequently transferred to separate departments. In the recent years functions related to personnel and administrative reforms were taken away from this ministry and were given to the department of personnel. It is considered the most important ministry in the Government of India even now.

Organization

The ministry is headed by a home minister who usually is a senior leader, and is assisted by two ministers of state. The home secretary who is a senior member of the IAS is the administrative head of the ministry. He heads many important committees and many home secretaries became cabinet secretaries and some of them have become governors of state after retirement. For example S. L. Khurana, who was the home secretary, became the governor of Tamil Nadu after his retirement, M. L. Wali became the lieutenant governor of Delhi, L. P. Singh, a former home secretary, became governor.

The secretary is assisted by additional secretaries, joint secretaries, directors, deputy directors, special assistants, under-secretaries, section officers and other staff. Presently, the ministry has four departments, namely, internal security, state, homes and official language. It also controls the allied organizations such as the intelligence bureau, the bureau of police research and development, the institute of criminology and forensic science, the national crime records bureau, the directorate of coordination (police wireless) and the Sardar Vallabhbhai Patel national police academy.

Functions

(a) *Law and order*—Although law and order is a state subject in our Constitution, yet the ministry of home affairs monitors trends and developments having a bearing on law and order including communal harmony. It also renders necessary guidance and assistance to the states and Union territories whenever required. When violent incidents cause disruption of normal life central security forces may be deployed to keep the law and order under control. To control the extremist activities of the ULFA in Assam, anti-national elements in Jammu and Kashmir and the terrorist activities in Punjab, security forces were made available to the state government. The ministry extended assistance at the time of protests against the implementation of Mandal commission's report and violent incidents due to Ram Janambhoomi–Babri Masjid issue on 6 December 1992.

(b) It administers the Indian Police Service and controls the IPS cadre. Therefore, it deals with service matters like appointments to IPS, deputation of police officers from states to the centre, their training, fixation of seniority, pay, etc. and other conditions of service. The ministry maintains paramilitary forces such as Indo-Tibetan Border Police (ITBP), the Border Security Force (BSF), the Central Industrial Security Force (CISF), CRPF, rapid action force, anti-riot force established on 7 October 1992 to control communal flare up, National Security Guards (NSG) and the Assam Rifles, etc.

(c) It conducts census after every 10 years and and is responsible for conducting peaceful elections of the Parliament and the state legislatures.

(d) It deals with the matters relating to the foreigners and citizenship.

(e) In controls the attached and allied organizations like intelligence bureau, the national police academy, the bureau of police research and development and the institute of criminology and forensic science, etc.

(f) It deals with the matters related to the jail/prison administration and reforms.

(g) The ministry works for the proper maintenance of centre–state relations and responsible for imposition of president's rule in the states.

(h) The ministry formulates programmes and schemes for relief and rehabilitation of displaced persons.

(i) The ministry has a Hindi *Salahkar Samiti*, which reviews the progress of use of Hindi as an official language in the government offices and its attached and subordinate offices.

(j) The ministry is also responsible for the administration and development of Union territories.

(k) The ministry is concerned with appointments to most of the high positions like governors, lieutenant-governors, chief commissioners, member of the inter-state commissions, etc. It issues notification of appointments and resignations of the president, vice-president, prime minister and other ministers. It is the home secretary who reads out the notifications of the appointment of the president at the oath-taking ceremony of the new president.

(l) The ministry also deals with subjects like the Padma Shree awards and Jeevan Raksha award medals, sanction of pension to the freedom fighters, grant of Indian citizenship, preparation of warrant of precedence and list of national holidays, publication of the *Gazette of India*, etc., setting up enquiry commissions, national flag, the national anthem, the national emblem, cases of nomination of members to the council of states, matters relating to grant of pardons, reprieves, suspension or commutation of a sentence of death by the president, emergency relief, creation of new state and matters connected with code of conduct of the ministers.

The Role of the Ministry of Home Affairs

The ministry commands respect for its uniqueness and senior politicians have been appointed as home ministers. Although its functions have been reduced after the creation of ministry of personnel, public grievances and pensions and ministry of welfare in 1985, but its pivotal stature in the Union cabinet still continues. Let us examine its role.

Although the ministers are allotted portfolios on the recommendation of the prime minister by the president but senior politicians next to the prime minister were given the ministry of home affairs. The experience shows that the ministry was a divided one from the very beginning because the prime minister considered strong home minister as his/her rival. Home ministers had been rendered ineffective and put on a shelf leaving the junior minister free to run the ministry as he thought best. During the Emergency, Brahamananda Reddy as home minister remained so only in name; all powers were being exercised by the minister of state, Om Mehta (nicknamed 'Home' Mehta).[8] During S. B. Chavan's period as home minister (when Rajiv Gandhi was the prime minister) his two deputies, particularly Arun Nehru, effectively ran all the affairs of the ministry. Later, when V. P. Singh was the prime minister, Mufti Mohammad Sayeed was home minister but his junior minister of state Subodh Kant Sahay handled Ayodhya matters and also charge of Punjab, Jharkhand and North-East and Kashmir was given to George Fernandes, minister of railway, at that time. Therefore, it was commented that 'at least on one count, the National Front government is no different from the previous two regimes and that is the manner in which the home ministry is run. More specifically, it is the question of who runs the ministry.'[9]

Again when Rao was the prime minister and S. B. Chavan as home minister was sidelined by his junior minister of state, Rajesh Pilot and the prime minister did not intervene in their battle. Not only this, Rajesh Pilot was being asked to attend the cabinet meetings, even when the home minister was present. This encouraged Rajesh Pilot to oppose proposals of the ministry duly approved by the cabinet minister for submission to the cabinet. The home minister keeping in view the fragile communal situation after the Ayodhya incident, had proposed to ban the 25 February 1993, mass rally of the BJP in the capital. Keeping in view the experience of Ayodhya, the BJP leadership could not be trusted to keep the rally peaceful. But in three out of four cabinet meetings in which the issue of banning the BJP rally was discussed, Rajesh Pilot opposed the proposal of the ministry. This clearly shows that prime ministers do not like home minister to be strong. In spite of all such politics the home ministry still enjoys status next to the prime minister in our country.

MINISTRY OF FINANCE

In a parliamentary democracy an effective administrative control over the receipts and expenditure of the government is very important. In India ministry of finance is made responsible for the administration of finance of the Union government. It prepares budget proposals for submissions to the cabinet and for final approval by the Parliament. Thus, it regulates the expenditure of the Union government as well as the transfer of resources to the states.

History

The time of origin of this ministry may be traced from 1810 when the Government of India created a separate department of finance. The department was not having its full time secretary till 1843. The finance secretary was responsible for conducting the entire financial operations of India. After Independence in 1947, the finance department was designated as the ministry of finance. It was having three major wings—expenditure, economic affairs and revenue. In 1949, the ministry of finance was reorganized into two departments—department of revenue and expenditure and department of economic affairs. It was further reorganized in 1958, 1964, 1966, 1967, 1969, 1970 and 1985. In 1996–1997 the ministry comprised three departments. These are the department of economic affairs, department of expenditure and department of revenue.

Organization

At present the ministry has a cabinet minister in charge who is assisted by a minister of state. The final decision regarding the number of junior ministers rests with the prime minister. The secretary is the administrative head of the ministry. Each department of the finance ministry has a secretary as its head and he is assisted by additional secretary, joint secretary, deputy secretary, director, under-secretary and other secretarial staff under him. The senior positions in the ministry are manned by the IAS but the service base of the officers in the ministry of finance is broader. In addition to the IAS, the ministry has officers from Indian audit and accounts service, the central revenue service, the central customs and excise service, the Indian railways accounts service, etc. A large number of positions at the middle level are occupied by central secretariat service personnel. The ministry at present has three departments, namely economic affairs, expenditure and revenue.

Department of Economic Affairs

The department of economic affairs is responsible for monitoring current economic trends and advising the government on all matters relating to internal and external economic management, including the working of commercial banks, term lending institutions, investment regulations, external assistance, production of currency/bank notes and coins of various denominations, postal stationery, postal stamps, etc. It is also responsible for the preparation of budgets of the Union government, the Union territories and the state government under the president's rule. This department has eight main divisions. These are as follows: economic, banking, insurance, budget, investment, external finance, currency and coinage and administration. Each division performs functions as per their nomenclatures. The department has under it two attached offices, three subordinate offices, three public undertakings, and three statutory bodies like LIC.

Department of Expenditure

The department consists of six divisions. These are as follows: plan, finance, establishment, cost accounts, organization of the controller-general of accounts, staff inspection unit and finance commission division. There is the defence accounts department under its administrative control. It has no attached or subordinate office under it.

Department of Revenue

The department of revenue under the charge of secretary (revenue) exercises administrative control in respect of matters relating to all the direct and indirect Union taxes through two statutory boards under it, viz., the central board of direct taxes and the central board of excise and customs. Each board has a chairman and six members who are ex-officio additional secretaries to Government of India. The central board of direct taxes, which controls the income-tax department, is responsible for formulation of tax administration policies. It also performs various statutory functions under the Income Tax Act 1961, the

Wealth Tax Act 1957, the Gift Tax Act, 1958 and the Expenditure Tax Act, 1987. This board functions through several attached and subordinate offices.

The central board of excise and customs formulates policy for the levy and collection of customs and control of excise duties, prevention of smuggling and administration of customs, central excise narcotics and gold control departments. The board is assisted by nine attached and subordinate offices. Organizations such as custom houses, central and excise collectorates, opium and alcohol factories and the central bureau of narcotics function under the administrative authority of the board. The other organizations under the department are as follows: the settlement commission (IT and WT); the appellate tribunal for forfeited property; the regional office of the gold control administrator, Bombay; the customs, excise and gold (control) appellate tribunal. There is also the economic intelligence bureau headed by a director general. It collects revenue intelligence and investigates economic offence and economic law enforcement.

In brief, the ministry of finance performs the main functions of policy formulation, administration of finance, raising necessary revenue, control entire government expenditure, etc.

Ministry of Personnel, Public Grievances and Pensions

The ministry was created in March 1985, after having two important functions of the home ministry, viz., public services and administrative reforms. This ministry has three departments, namely, the department of personnel and training, department of administrative reforms and public grievances and the department of pension and pensioners' welfare.

Organization

At present the ministry is headed by the prime minister who is assisted by a minister of state. The administrative head of the ministry is secretary (personnel), who is assisted by three additional secretaries. These are in charge of the administration of each of the three departments of the ministry. They have under them joint secretaries and other usual supporting staff like any other ministry and follow the tenure system. The secretary is an IAS man and other senior positions are also filled by IAS cadre. Middle level and junior posts are occupied by members of various allied services.

Functions

The ministry is the chief formulator of policy in the field of personnel management for all organizations of the Government of India. It coordinates the implementation of different aspects of the personnel management policy including administrative vigilance, reservation of services and posts for the Scheduled Castes, Scheduled Tribes and other backward classes and specified categories, joint consultation and arbitration, staff welfare, pension, administrative reforms and public grievance redressal. It looks after administrative matters relating to the administrative tribunals, UPSC, staff selection commission (SSC) IIPA, Lal Bahadur Shastri National Academy of Administration, Mussoorie, and institute of the secretariat training and management, New Delhi. Its main functions are as follows:

(i) To implement and plan the tenure system in advance, on the basis of names received from various states of such officers who would come on deputation

(ii) Cadre management

(iii) Manpower planning

(iv) Recruitment

(v) Job evaluation and position classification

(vi) Career development planning

(vii) Training and development programmes

(viii) Compensation and remuneration

(ix) Separation and terminal benefit system

(x) Conduct, discipline and public service ethics

(xi) Motivation and participation management principles and other welfare programmes

(xii) Developing personnel organization

(xiii) Administrative reforms

(xiv) O and M work

(xv) Personnel research developing guides and information and standardized procedures, etc.

The functions of the ministry are mostly related with personnel administration, a sort of 'nuts and bolts' type mostly. The vital issues of administrative accountability, ethics in administration, open administration, etc. have been ignored by the ministry, which deals with administrative reforms. It functions like a custodian of interest for government employees ignoring the feelings of citizens. The ministry, as its critics point out, has neither implemented with zeal administrative reforms to make it people-oriented nor has it succeeded in reducing citizens' grievances. Therefore, it has no vision and perspective for improving the lethargic administrative system.

NOTES

1. Article 77(3), Constitution of India.
2. *Report of the Reorganization of the Machinery of Government, 1949* (Ayyangar Report) (New Delhi: Government of India, 1957), para 14.
3. Asok Chanda, *Indian Administration* (London: Allen and Unwin, 1967), p. 147
4. R. Tottenham, *Reports on the Re-organization of Central Government, 1945 and 1946,* 2nd imprint (New Delhi: Government of India, 1955), p. 26 (two reports).
5. Ayyangar Committee Report, op. cit., p. 13
6. *Organization and Procedure (Maxwell) Committee Report* (New Delhi: Government of India, 1937), para 23.
7. *INDIA 2009,* A Reference Annual Publication Division, Ministry of Information and Broadcasting (New Delhi: Government of India, 2009), pp. 36–39.
8. *The Economic Times*, 28 April 1990.
9. *The Times of India,* New Delhi, 22 October 1990.

12

Boards, Commissions and Field Organizations

Governmental functions are operationalized by the departments manning it. However, along with departments/ministries, certain other types of organizations also exist, namely, boards and commissions. Organizations with a plural chief executive have been preferred for several kinds of governmental activities. In our country, even since 1873, executive authority was vested in the executive council of the viceroy, which after Independence in 1947 has taken a form of cabinet. Even today a board or commission plural executive has become an integral part of administrative institutions.

The question may arise as to why boards and commissions are set up over and above the departments? There has been lot of discussion about the merits of single executives or the board and commission type of plural or collegiate executive. In this chapter we will discuss first the advantages of the single chief executive system, which is the extensively used form in government organizations, and then we shall pass on to the advantages of plural executive system.

Advantages of the single chief executive system. The advantages of vesting administrative authority in an individual are many. First, in this system authority vests in a single person who can be held responsible for the results. It is he who plans the programme, executes it and applies the necessary corrections. He would be, therefore, accountable for the actions he has taken while the responsibility in a board or commission is shared between a numbers of individuals. In such a diffusion of authority nobody can be held responsible for the results of collective decision. Second, it is less expensive, while in the commission system, the meetings will be attended by a number of officials of higher level and they have to be paid their TA and DA. This causes lot of financial burden. On the other hand, in a single executive system all these expenses are not needed because such meetings are not required and files can move within the department for decisions without any expenditure. Third, in the single executive system decisions can be quickly taken. The decisions in the board or the commission take time. Sometimes the meeting is not due in near the future and sometimes differences of opinion lead to the postponement of decision. Fourth, in an individual chief executive system, he has authority to take decisions, therefore, he feels a greater sense of involvement and applies more energy and takes keen interest in its working. In a commission or board system an individual feels that he needs not apply any more effort than others, because the credit of such efforts will go to the board and not to him individually. Fifth, the line of authority is not very clear in a board or commission type of organization. This may confuse the line functionaries as to whose orders they should obey in case there is disagreement among the members. This type of problem is unknown in a single chief executive system where the line of authority is very clear.

Advantages of plural chief executive system. The board or commission system has several advantages. First, in a government department decision making is a time-consuming process. It has to pass through many levels and stages for consultation. This results in delay in decision making. In case of the plural executive the consultation process can take place across the table in a board meeting. Thus, decisions in this system take lesser time than in case of a single chief executive system. Second, an individual is more likely to succumb to pressures than a plural body like a commission or a board. Therefore, the plural system is more conducive to administrative integrity. Third, the commissions and boards are neither wholly expert committees nor purely representative bodies. A properly constituted body is a combination of both these elements to provide a balance between the specialized requirements of modern public administration and the representative character of a democratic government. Fourth, these bodies sometimes perform quasi-legislative and quasi-judicial functions in addition to their administrative functions. Such functions are better performed by a plural body than a single individual. The collective wisdom of members reduces the possibility of collusion with the clients or of individual's personal bias in judgment. Finally, the board or commission type of organization can help to relieve the central/state governments of the responsibility of control over day-to-day functioning of a service organization of the management of a business enterprise. It provides on the one hand, the necessary autonomy to the agency and on the other opportunity to the government to devise certain control mechanism to monitor the progress of the organization without undermining its autonomy.

The above discussion does not favour the establishment either of the two types of organizations. The most usual and logical form of organization appears to be the single chief system. But there are many situations in which the plural chief executive system may be found suitable. L. D. White observes that in general the burden of proof is on the advocates of boards/commissions in preference to a single executive. Even when a board or commission type of organization is preferred, the work of running the day-to-day administration or the organization is left to a single chief executive working under the overall supervision and control of the board/commission. This type of organization is very much prevalent in the private companies where the board of directors gives the necessary policy decisions, while the actual business is run by a managing director assisted by a team of executives. The board does not interfere in the day-to-day functioning of the managing director but retains control by calling for strategic information as well as by reserving some strategic decisions for itself.

According to Willoughby, the board/commission type of organization is more suitable for the following type of services. First, those services which are quasi-legislative or quasi-judicial in character such as public utility boards. They perform quasi-legislative functions inasmuch as they formulate the rules and regulations for determining the rates and conditions of providing these services. They perform quasi-judicial functions as they adjudicate upon issues that affect public and private rights as provided for in the rules. Improvement trusts and development authorities come under this category. Second, those services whose functions need the exercise of wide discretionary powers or are of a general control character as in the case of public service commissions. Third, those services where a number of varied interests are affected as in the case of arbitration or conciliation boards. Fourth, those cases which are subject to a lot of political pressures and group rivalries. In such cases various interest groups tend to sway the decisions of the government authorities in their favour through various means. In such situations the board/commission is in a better position to balance the various pulls and pressures. The tariff commission in India is an example.

To conclude, the single head is the best where the major policies and objectives of the department are well defined, where the activities are of a routine nature and where executive promptness and vigour are required to protect the vital interest of the society such as public security and law and order. The board/commission is more suitable in planning new undertakings where the questions are not well settled and constant consultations are required for deciding policies for every changing situation.

Classification of Boards and Commissions

In India there has been proliferation of new agencies after Independence to perform the new and complex functions undertaken by the government. Many boards, commissions, and corporations have been established by the Union and state governments for performing functions like examinations, providing public utility services and rendering financial assistance.

These bodies can be classified on different basis. Some of the important ones are as follows.

Classification on the Basis of Nature of Authority

On the basis of nature of authority the boards/commissions can be classified into the following three categories:

(i) Advisory boards/commissions like the small-scale industries boards.

(ii) Boards/commissions performing policy-making functions such as the planning commission.

(iii) Boards/commissions performing policy-making and executive functions, such as railway board and the atomic energy commission.

Advisory boards/commissions do not form part of the hierarchical structure of the government organization. They are usually associated with the head of the organization for the purpose of advice only. They neither share departmental responsibilities nor its policy. They only tender advice which may or may not be accepted by the head of the department. The boards/commissions which perform policy-making functions are high-powered bodies and mainly perform policy-making functions. An example is the planning commission. Some boards/commissions perform both policy making as well as its execution. The railway board is such an agency which is responsible for policy making in regard to all matters concerning Indian Railways. At the same time it is also responsible for all operational matters connected with the running of railways. Other similar boards are posts and telegraphs board, atomic energy commission, etc.

Classification on the Basis of Legal Status

On the basis of legal status, the boards/commissions can be classified into the following three categories:

(i) Boards/commissions established by the Constitution

(ii) Boards/commissions established by some special statutes

(iii) Boards/commissions established by the resolutions of the government

Constitutional Boards/Commissions

The Constitution provides for the establishment of several commissions such as:

(a) The finance commission, (b) The Union public service commission (UPSC), (c) The election commission, (d) backward class commission, (e) official languages commission.

These commissions are appointed by the president and do not come under the administrative control of any particular ministry in their day-to-day working. The members of these commissions are appointed by the president and they enjoy a security of tenure and cannot be removed from their office without following a special provision as laid down in the Constitution. Their reports are placed on the table of each house of the Parliament.

Statutory Boards/Commissions

Several boards and commissions are set up by special statutes of Parliament such as:

(i) University grants commission, (ii) railway board, (iii) central board of direct taxes, (iv) central board of excise and customs, (v) oil and natural gas commission, (vi) flood control board, (vii) atomic energy commission, etc.

These statutory boards/commissions are working under the administrative control of the ministry concerned; while some of them are ministries, namely railway board and atomic energy commission, others are also free to a large extent from regular departmental procedures. They enjoy a great deal of autonomy in their day-to-day working; but their members do not enjoy the same degree of security, independence and prestige in comparison to constitutional ones.

Boards/Commissions Set Up by Resolutions

Several boards/commissions are set up by the executive resolutions of the government, such as:

(i) Planning commission

(ii) Central social welfare board

(iii) The handicraft boards

(iv) The handloom boards

(v) The central ground water commission, etc.

These boards/commissions are created for a specific time, although the same board is attached to the concerned ministry, and are called as attached boards. Mostly, they are advisory in nature. Their members do not have any definite tenure and autonomy is limited. However, some of them are very important and high powered like the planning commission.

Classification on the Basis of Location of Board/Commission

According to the location, they may be classified into three categories as (i) boards/commissions performing the functions of the ministry and located in the ministry, (ii) boards/commissions which work as heads of the departments but outside the ministry, (iii) boards/commissions in subordinate positions.

Boards/Commissions as Ministries

These boards perform all the functions of a ministry and some of them perform executive functions also. Such boards/commissions are: (a) railway board, (b) posts and telegraph board, (c) atomic energy commission.

Such boards/commissions are constituted for organizations which deal with commercial or operating functions.

Boards as Heads of the Department

These boards function as important heads of departments under the ministries. The examples are: (a) central board of direct taxes, and (b) central board of excise and customs. These boards give directions to the field offices under them and are also responsible for their general performance. They deal with important subjects and are found very useful.

Boards in Subordinate Positions

These types of boards are a sort of departmental board. The examples are boards of education. They are concerned with laying down syllabi and courses and conduct of examinations.

Classification on the Basis of Functions

The boards/commissions can also be classified on the basis of functions they perform, these are as follows:

Developmental Boards

These boards engage in developmental activities and are categorized as development boards. These are the following:

(i) Industrial promotion board, (ii) all-India handloom board, (iii) all-India handicraft board, (iv) the export promotion council, etc.

All these bodies attempt to promote the development of some industries, agriculture and other economic activities.

Regulatory Boards

These boards generally regulate some of the activities of the people. Examples are agricultural marketing boards, which regulate the marketing activities of the agricultural production.

Mixed Boards

These boards perform both developmental as well as regulatory functions. For example, the tobacco board takes up many schemes for improving tobacco cultivation and also regulation of marketing activity of tobacco.

The boards/commissions are important forms of organizations to improve their efficiency. They can prove very useful in certain situations where rules, regulations and procedures are yet to be established.

Legally, commissions/boards are of three types. We are discussing here commissions/boards of each category. Under the first category, commissions/boards established by the Constitution, we have chosen the finance commission and the Union public service commission (UPSC); under the second category, those who have been established by the Special Statutes, we have chosen railway board and under the third category established by government resolutions we have selected the planning commission for detailed analysis.

The Railway Board

The Railway board consists of the chairman and five other members. It normally meets twice a week or can meet frequently to decide policies and other urgent cases which require the boards' consideration. The chairman convenes the meetings and presides over them. The agenda of these meetings is finalized by the chairman in consultation with other members. The secretary of the board circulates the agenda and the memorandum among the members before the meeting takes place. He submits drafts of minutes for the approval by the board. After approval of minutes by the board, necessary action is taken by the concerned officials. The minister holds the meetings of the full board whenever required to discuss and decide policy matters.

Functions

The board performs the following functions:

(a) To advise the minister on specific issues involved in policy formulation and coordination with other institutions
(b) To formulate programmes in a well-planned order to implement its policies
(c) To supervise and coordinate effectively among the various railway zones
(d) To prepare the annual budget of the railways that is placed before the Parliament by the minister of railways
(e) To determine the recruitment policy, training and service conditions of its employees and to adopt such measures as are essential to create uniformity with the other ministries and departments in matters concerning personnel management. Four railway service commissions are in operation to conduct examinations and interviews for recruitment to class III employees.
(f) To frame rules for compilation of statistical data and set procedures for assessing the works undertaken
(g) To review the trend of expenditure associated with the work performance and take necessary steps to formulate necessary regulations. All matters related to railway receipts and expenditure fall within the purview of the board.
(h) To accord sanction to those projects/works which do not fall within the purview of powers of the general manager
(i) To frame the pay and allowance structure of the railways staff in order to have uniformity
(j) To accord sanction for posts, promotions, transfers, etc. of the staff whenever these are considered necessary by the board
(k) To lay down standards of equipment and rolling stocks
(l) To formulate rules and regulations for ensuring the safety of the railways staff
(m) To bring out its annual reports showing the performance and accounts

The administrative reforms commission in its report on the railways made some recommendation for the better working of the railway board deserves special mention.

The following are some of the recommendations made by the ARC in its report on railways:

(1) The relationship of the railway board viz-à-viz the minister of railways should be patterned on the lines of the relationships as recommended in the reports on public sector undertakings as between a ministry

of overall supervision and vigilance, the larger issues involving improved efficiency of the railway system, and planning and budgeting.

(2) For efficient functioning, the railway board should be compact in size. The number excluding the chairman and the member, finance, should not exceed six.

(3) The chairman of the railway board should be selected on merit from amongst the members of the board and the members of the board should be selected on merit from amongst the general managers.

(4) The chairman and the members should have tenure of three and five years respectively. The total tenure of chairman both as chairman and member should be seven years or above.

(5) All directors of the railway board should be placed in the same pay scale.

(6) A selection committee constituted by zonal railways, and a senior officer of the board should recommend promotion of officers to the junior administrative grade.

(7) The railway board should prescribe the qualifications, training and job experience required for manning the posts, the specialization and managerial categories. The chairman and general managers should see to the establishment of a career-planning cell at the board level and zonal level, respectively.

(8) The railway board and the zonal railways should review the existing training arrangements in the light of requirements and rationalizse the training facilities where necessary.

(9) The chairman of the recruitment board may be appointed by the railway board.

(10) The director-general of the vigilance organization at the board level may work directly under the chairman of the board and report to him.

(11) The railway board should consider the closure of unremunerative railway lines where adequate modes of cheaper transport exist and where such closure will not adversely affect the public interest.

(12) The research, design and standard organization should function as an autonomous body with a governing council at the top to guide it. The chairman of the railway board should be the chairman of the governing council.

The above recommendations were fairly good and some of them have since been accepted by the government.

Field Organizations

So far we have discussed the organization of the Government of India at the Central Secretariat level. The Secretariat formulates policies and operative directions to ensure the implementation of policies while implementation of policies takes place at the field level, hence, the organization of the field office is of great importance. Generally, the field office is organized on a geographical basis in India and each ministry of the Government of India has its field offices covering a local area within a State. India is a very vast country therefore, for each department of Government of India it is not possible to deal directly with all field offices. Hence, most of the departments have state level or regional level (including more than one State) offices in an area.

The functions of the Government have become increasingly complex and multifarious. Therefore, in addition to the traditional departmental organizations a number of other forms like company, corporations, etc., have come up to perform the governmental functions. The expansion of the business activities of the government has given birth to two new forms of organizations; government companies and statutory corporations. Likewise, many registered societies have been established to handle research and training activities.

The number of executive agencies or field agencies of the government may be classified into the following categories;

(i) An attached office, for example, central public works department, directorate of plant protection quarantine and storage, etc.

(ii) A subordinate office, e.g., Sardar Patel National Police Academy, Hyderabad, inspector of explosives, Nagpur, etc.

(iii) Departmental undertakings, e.g., ordnance factories

(iv) A company registered under the Companies Act, e.g., Hindustan Steels Ltd

(v) A corporation or board set up under the Special Statute, e.g. Damodar Valley Corporation, tea board, coffee board, tobacco board, etc.

(vi) A society registered under the Societies Registration Act, e.g. Indian institute of foreign trade

We shall discuss here the field organizations of the central government which include attached offices, and subordinate offices. The other forms of organization like company, corporations, boards, etc. shall be studied separately.

Attached and Subordinate Office

The manual of office procedure defines these offices as 'where the execution of the policy of the government requires decentralization of executive direction and the establishment of field agencies, a ministry has under it subsidiary offices which are called attached and subordinate offices. Attached offices are responsible for providing executive direction required in the implementation of the policies laid down by the ministry to which they are attached. They also serve as a repository of technical information and advice to the ministry on technical aspects of questions dealt with by them. The subordinate offices function as field establishment or the agencies responsible for the detailed execution of the decisions of government. They generally function under the direction of an attached office, or in cases where the volume of executive direction involved, is not considerable, directly under the ministry.'

It is notable that there is no uniformity in the matter of executive agencies as between different ministries and departments. The ministry of external affairs has no attached office but has a couple of subordinate offices under it and it has a number of diplomatic and consular offices under it which do not fall in the category of either attached or subordinate offices. Likewise the ministry of agriculture has three departments under it. These are department of agriculture and cooperation, department of animal husbandry and dairying and department of agriculture research and education. The department of agriculture and cooperation alone has three attached offices, 39 subordinate offices, five public undertakings and five autonomous corporations under it.

Organization of Attached Offices

The organization of these offices differs from that of ministries and departments. Usually the head of such an office is a technical officer called registrar, director, director-general or chief engineer, etc. Below him there are a few technical or non-technical officers who help him in his duties. The proportion of technical and non-technical secretarial officers differs from office to office. For example, there will be a majority of technical officers in the offices of the director-general of health services and in the office of irrigation management board, while in the office of the chief controller of printing and stationery, non-technical personnel predominate. Thus, there is no common pattern of organization of attached offices. The status of heads of these offices is also not same. Some of them are headed by additional secretary or joint secretary while some others are headed by deputy secretary or director. The staff of these offices comes from the general secretariat service up to the rank of section officers.

Functions

These attached offices have a dual function. They provide technical information for the policy formulation as well as executive direction for its implementation. Therefore, they are considered field organizations because they not only issue executive directions to the subordinate offices, but are also responsible for the proper implementation of the policies. They have to coordinate the activities of the subordinate offices and keep the secretariat informed about the various problems faced in the implementation of the policies. The attached offices, thus, could be considered as the headquarters of a field organization rather than an extension of the secretariat. This is the reason that we propose to study the attached offices as field organization.

Organization of the Subordinate Offices

There is no single pattern of organizing these offices. It normally functions under an attached office. But if there is no attached office under a ministry, it directly operates under the ministry. Example of the latter type is the inspector of explosives at Nagpur. The meaning of the term subordinate offices created confusion. Even the offices of the heads of the executive departments, when not attached to the secretariat, would be termed as subordinate offices. Being field agencies concerned with implementation work, they generally have a large number of technical field staff with usual ministerial staff for administrative work. These offices are generally headed by a technical officer whose status differs from office to office depending on the nature of work. In comparison to attached offices, these offices have only limited administrative and financial powers. They have the attached offices or the ministries for obtaining sanctions even for trial matters.

Functions

The subordinate offices are concerned with the actual execution of the programmes. They are at the lower levels of administration and come in direct touch with the clientele of the programme implemented by them on behalf of the government. There is no difference of opinion about calling these subordinate offices field organizations as they are concerned with the day-to-day implementation of the programmes in the field. They are required to submit a number of periodical reports and returns to the attached office and the administrative ministry concerned to them informed of their activities. Sometimes the heads of these offices may be summoned for consultation by their superior offices. The pay scale of the personnel in these offices is generally lower as compared to those of equivalent posts in the attached offices. In fact, there is no uniformity in this matter even among the subordinate offices themselves.

This type of organization has created problems of inter-relationship between the secretariat, attached offices and subordinate offices. We propose to discuss it here.

The Relationship Between Secretariat and Executive Agencies

The secretariat is the overhead office for policy-making and legislative functions. There is tremendous pressure on the field agencies including attached and subordinate offices to show spectacular results in the implementation of the government's policies and programmes. Therefore, they should have been given necessary authority and adequate resources to deliver the goods. However, the secretariat has increased its work sphere and many executive decisions which should have been taken by the executive Heads of the Departments are usurped by the secretariat. This has created imbalance in the authority and a responsibility of the field functionaries. The result is tensions in the relations between secretariat and the field offices and the attached offices.

Complaints Against the Secretariat

The field level functionaries complain against the secretariat. Their main complaints are: First, the secretariat contributes nothing but delay to the decision making and the implementation process. Too many sanctions are required from the secretariat and each one takes a lot of time. Second, the presence of two bodies, secretariat and the attached offices leads to duplication of work. The attached office and secretariat could be merged for faster decisions. Third, the attitude of the secretariat is negative and fault finding. Most of the secretariat functionaries do not have ideas of technicalities involved in the proposals sent by the attached office. Thus, scrutiny of proposals by them results in delay, They hardly provide any additional input in comparison to supplied by the technical experts to the decision making process. Lastly, if the secretariat and attached offices are merged, the decision making would be in the hands of technical persons who alone are in a position to make a proper decision. The generalists do not understand the technical problems and their implications.

Arguments in Favour of the Secretariat

In spite of the complaints against the secretariat mentioned above, those who favour the secretariat have also argued that for proper functioning of the government, a separate secretariat is necessary. They argue that first, the minister is layman and hence needs the advice of an aide possessing the necessary detachment and objectivity and liabilities of examining the important matters in the context of the policies of the government as a whole. The secretary is the secretary to the government and not to a particular minister. Such objectivity and detachment cannot be expected from the specialist who has sent the proposal. Second, the specialist generally is very enthusiastic about his proposals. He may be obsessed with the technicalities of his discipline and perusal of his proposal by a detached person is necessary for objective and proper decision. Third, the separate secretariat is essential to ensure justice and fair play to the officers and staff working under the attached and subordinate offices. Being away from the scene, it can take an objective view concerning the staff working in the offices below them. Finally, the minister needs a staff agency to advise him on his numerous multifarious activities. This role can better be performed by the secretariat and not by an executive agency.

The Pattern of Relationship Between the Secretariat and the Field Office

In actual working of the secretariat and the field offices different kinds of relationship between the two agencies have developed in different organizations. Therefore, it would be pertinent here to discuss these emerging patterns.

The first pattern is a complete merger between the ministry and the attached offices. The examples are the railway board and the ministry of railways; posts and telegraphs board; and the ministry of communication. This pattern suits to the organizations which are dealing with operation and commercial functions. The problems arising, are of emergent nature, therefore, merger of policy making and executive functions leads to efficiency. Second, the senior officer of the ministry along with his position in the ministry is appointed head of the attached office. In this way he becomes responsible for the formulation and implementation of the policy; with the assistance of common office staff located in the ministry. The examples are: a joint secretary in the department of labour and employment is also the director-general of employment and training. Similarly, the additional secretary in the department of food is also the director-general of food.

The merit of the system is that it eliminates the distance between the secretariat and the attached office. The demerit is that it blurs the distinction between the secretariat and the head of the executive department. Therefore, it is not suitable for general application.

Third, the ministry and the executive department have separate offices but common files and single file bureau or records cell located in the organization of the executive department. The attached office submits proposals on its own files and refers the ministry along with the papers complete in all respects. After the proposal is disposed of by the ministry, the file is returned to the executive head. The single file system has been adopted by many ministries and attached offices. The example is the ministry of defence and the air force headquarters. The advantages of this system are that it avoids duplication of files, saves lot of time and decisions are taken quickly.

Fourth, in this pattern, the ministry and the executive department both have a common office, common files and a common file bureau, under the control of the executive department. The common office serves the secretariat and attached office and the clerical staff put up papers for both the sets of officers. At the secretariat level all noting is done by the officers of and above the rank of under-secretary. Such a system was in operation in the directorate-general of posts and telegraphs before the formation of the posts and telegraph board.

This pattern was recommended by the second pay commission and estimates committee of the Lok Sabha. The advantage is that in this system a proposal is examined only once; this results in quick disposal of business and saves lot of money.

Fifth, in this pattern the ministry and the executive department (attached office) have separate offices and separate files but the head of the attach office is given an ex-officio secretariat status. An example is the textile commissioner, who is the ex-officio joint secretary in the ministry of textiles. The merits of the system are that the head of the attached office brought in closer contact with the ministry's office gets more closely involved in policy making and gets certain powers to take decisions on some matters. The system serves lot of time and makes field experience available to the secretariat in a greater measure to take decisions. The demerit of the system is that it violates the principle of separation of policy making and implementation on which the secretariat is based.

Sixth, in this pattern both the ministry and the executive department have distinct and separate offices and files of their own and consultation between them takes place by self-contained communications. The pattern is based on the difference between staff and line. The ministry is staff and the attached office is line. The examples are the office of the chief engineer, central public works department in relation to the ministry of works and housing, and the director-general of All India Radio in relation to the ministry of information and broadcasting.

The merits of the system are claimed as it scrutinizes the proposals in wider perspective, it controls the enthusiastic specialist by scrutinizing their proposals and provides for the division of work between the secretariat and the attached office. On the other hand, the demerits of the scheme are that it involves duplication of work being processed in two offices, proposals of the head of the department are examined by the clerical staff level in the ministry and the secretary's views are hardly detached and objective but full of political considerations.

The above patterns of organization represent the attempts at bridging the gulf between secretariat and non-secretariat organizations through devices such as giving of ex-officio secretariat status to the heads of the executive agencies ; introduction of the single file system, placement of executive agencies etc. Recently, some other measures were also taken to remove the deficiencies in the system, important among them are giving them greater autonomy by liberal delegation of authority from the secretariat to them. Frequent consultation can solve lot of problems, therefore, proposals should be formulated after consultation with each other and the most radical suggestion is the abolition of distinction between the secretariat and non-secretariat organizations.

The study team of the administrative reforms commission (ARC) commenting on the machinery of the Government of India, recommended in February 1968 for the abolition of distinction between the two.

The ARC in its report (September 1968), however, opposed the general abolition of the distinction between the secretariat and its executive agencies, even though the commission was emphatically of the opinion 'that there should be no duplication of functions between its secretariat organization and the executive agencies of a ministry or department.' The commission analysed the work of attached and subordinate offices and found that, broadly speaking, it could be divided into the following six categories.[1]

1. Regulatory and allied activities, for example, the work done by the drug controller of India, controller of patents, chief inspector of mines, etc.
2. Activities directed at promoting developmental effort, e.g., the work done by the national savings commissioner and all-India handicrafts board
3. Education and training for government employment, profession or specialities, e.g., the work done by the Lal Bahadur Shastri academy of administration, national police academy, Indian school of mines, etc.
4. Survey and research, e.g., the work done by the Archaeological Survey of India, forest research institute and college, directorate-general of commercial intelligence statistics
5. Provision of a service or production or supply of a commodity, e.g., the work done by All India Radio directorate of field publicity, Delhi milk scheme, central public works department, etc.
6. Carving out of one or more developmental programmes covering a substantial area of the activities of the ministry including planning, coordination and review and also rendering advice, e.g., the work done by the directorate-general of health services, jute commissioner, directorate-general of shipping, etc.

In the case of the first five of the above categories, the commission recommended the continuance of the present system of differentiation between the policy making and executive agencies. It recognized that for the efficient performance of their functions, complete autonomy has to be conferred on them. It was only in the case of the sixth category of organizations that the commission recommended integration with the secretariat of the concerned ministry. The commission expressed the view that an executive organization to be shifted to the secretariat should fulfil the following conditions:

1. The work of the executive organization is primarily of a developmental character and constitutes a substantial portion of the activities of the administrative department or ministry.
2. It is actively involved in planning, coordination and review of developmental programmes and advises the ministry/department on these matters.
3. Its activities relate to an area in which the policies have to be altered or modified to meet the requirements of changes in situation, that is, where continuous feedback of field experience is essential for effective policy making.

In all other conditions the merger of secretariat with the executive agencies is not desirable. The commission agreed with the distinction between the policy-making functions and the processes of policy execution.

The Relationship Between Attached and Subordinate Offices

As already mentioned, the main function of the attached office is to give executive direction for implementation of the policies decided by the ministry to which they are attached. The subordinate offices, on the other hand, are merely field agencies which carry out the directives of the attached offices and ministries concerning the implementation of the policies. In actual practice, however, we find no such clear cut distinction of functions between the two categories of offices. At best such distinction is blurred. In 1945–1946, Tottenham said, 'No one has ever been able to arrive at a really satisfactory definition of an "Attach Office".' The only justification for such a distinction seems to be to justify lower scales of pay for the ministerial staff in subordinate than in attached offices. Tottenham, therefore, recommended the abolition of distinction between the two categories of offices. The first pay commission in 1950 also found such distinction artificial and recommended its abolition. It re commended the regrouping of offices into three categories: (i) policy-making organizations, i.e., secretariat proper; (ii) the offices of the executive heads and advisory organizations; and (iii) the offices subordinate to the above two categories. The second pay commission of 1959, however, recommended a functional classification based on two criteria, first, that offices which were associated with the shaping of policy by furnishing technical data and advice and by giving executive directions to the field agencies and which were responsible for implementing the policies of the government should be designated as attached offices. Second, those offices that were mainly responsible for the execution of government policies and programmes should be called subordinate offices. The ARC examined this problem in the wider context of secretariat and non-secretariat organizations and their relationship. However, the old pattern still continues in which the subordinate offices are treated as inferior ones in spite of the importance of the field work performed by them. The attached offices have improved their conditions and brought them almost at par with the secretariat offices. The conditions of the subordinate offices, however, continue to be deplorable. Their main problems are, first, being nearer to the people they are under constant pressure to perform various functions for which they have no authority. Second, they hardly get clear cut guidelines to perform their functions from the headquarters. Third, the staff working under subordinate offices do not get pay and salary benefits equal to that of the staff performing similar functions in the attached offices and the secretariat.

The best solution of these problems would be that the offices of the secretariat and executive heads of the departments should be separated. These offices should not be called attached offices. Field organization should consist of a clear hierarchy starting from the executive heads of the department. The department could then be sub-divided into zonal and regional offices depending upon the work load. The staff working in these fields office should get the same salaries which their counterparts get in the office of the head of the department and the secretariat. The relative salary of the officers will have to be decided on the well-known principle of equal pay for equal work.

Field Organization in Operation

The pattern of field organization has been demarcated between the unitary and multiple-type by Willoughby, a public administration expert. In a unitary system, the field units of an organization remain under the supervision and control of the regional head. The regional head is responsible to the central headquarters for the functioning of his field units and holds complete charge of the field services. The staff working in these units is responsible to him. A single line of command runs from the central office to the regional head of the field units and those heading field units receive it from their immediate boss at the regional level. In this pattern the directives to the field unit are communicated through the regional head.

Under the multiple type of field organization, there is a direct communication between the central office and the field unit. The middle office does not intervene in the supervision and control of the field agencies. The field units do have their regional supervisory authorities but there is no singular authority to control the units working in the field.

In India, the business of the government is transacted through a number of administrative sub-centres created through out the country to serve the requirements of attach areas. Such field organizations are called as subordinate offices.

Unitary System

The layout under a unitary system may be explained diagramatically by showing an instance of post office department.

Under a unitary system all these units are under the regional head who is responsible to the head office for the function of his field office (regional office) and all units.

The diagram shown above reflects that the units of a regional office have been kept under the control of the regional head, who is in his responsible to the head office for the working of the regional office and its units.

Multiple System

Figure 12.2 refers to the working of the field units under multiple system.

The diagram clearly indicates the direct relationship of sections of the head post office, viz., inland mail, foreign mail, money orders, postal orders and postal savings with its respective units in the regional

Figure 12.1 *Post office department*

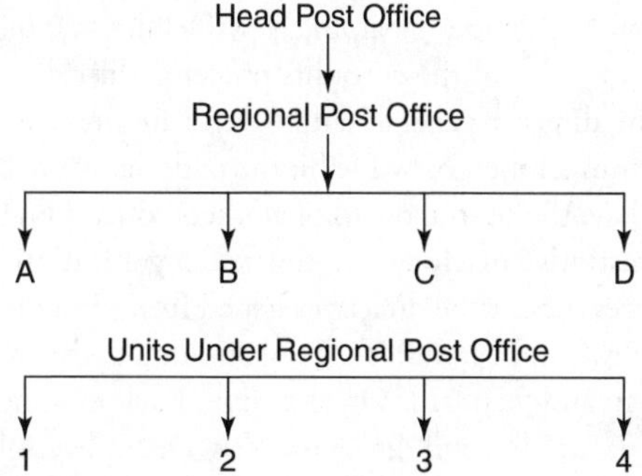

Figure 12.2 *Field units under multiple system*

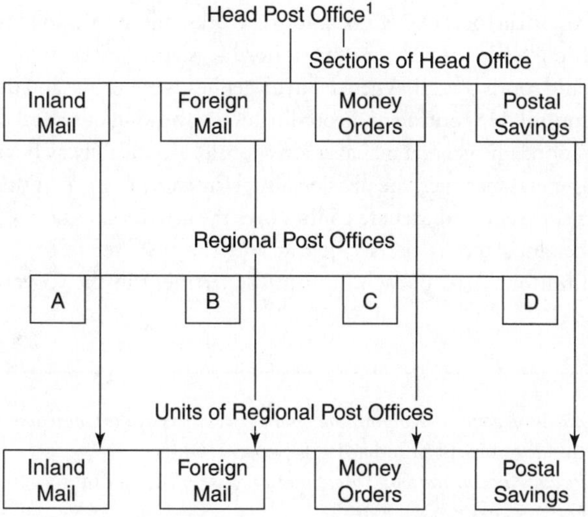

post office. There is no department that has followed or adopted the complete unitary or multiple system. For the smooth working of the department, a blend of the two systems is generally found in operation.[2]

The following two examples of organization of zonal and regional offices, ministry of labour and ministry of railways make it clear.

For example, the ministry of labour has four attached offices: (i) The director-general of employment and training is assisted by two directors who are assisted by deputy and assistant directors technical as well as non-technical staff. (ii) The chief labour commissioner is assisted by a joint labour commissioner, three deputy chief labour commissioners, three labour enforcement officers at the headquarters and thirteen regional commissioners. The field organization also consists of one deputy chief labour commissioner, and 159 labour enforcement officers. (iii) The director-general of factory advice service and labour institute is at Bombay, and three regional labour institutes at Calcutta, Kanpur and Madras. (iv) The directorate of labour bureau is headed by a director who is assisted by two offices of the bureau each at Chandigarh and Simla.

There exist 21 subordinate offices and six autonomous organizations. Some prominent subordinate offices are as follows: director-general of mines safety, Dhanbad; offices of the welfare commissioners at Bangalore, Jabalpur, Bhubaneswar, Karma, Bhilwara, Kalichedu, Panji, Allahabad and the office of the deputy welfare commissioner at Barbil, central government industrial tribunal-cum-labour court at Dhanbad (two), Bombay (two), one each at Asansol, Calcutta, Jabalpur, New Delhi, Chandigarh, and Kanpur; office of the chairman board of arbitration and office of the accounts officer audit cell at New Delhi. The autonomous organizations are the office of the director-general, employees state finance corporation, New Delhi; office of the central provident fund commissioner, New Delhi; the national council for safety in mines, Dhanbad; the national safety council, Bombay; the central board of workers education, Nagpur and the national labour institute, New Delhi. The administrative machinery in the field organization has the responsibility of administering the labour welfare activities, under the directives issued from time to time by the headquarters.

The other example is of the railway ministry: the field organization of the Indian Railways consists of two attached offices, viz, Research Design and Standards Organization, Lucknow and the office of the railway liaison officer with the director-general of supplies and disposals, New Delhi; five subordinate offices—railway rates tribunal, Madras; railway staff college, Baroda; Indian Railways institute of advanced track technology, Poona; railway service commission, Allahabad, Bombay, Calcutta and Madras and Indian Railways institute of signal engineering and telecommunication, Secunderabad. The other field organizations are the Chittaranjan Locomotive Works, Integral Coach Factory, Diesel Locomotive Works, and Metropolitan Transport projects. The entire railway functions through nine zones—northern, north-eastern, west-eastern, south-eastern, north-east frontier, central, southern and south central. A general manager heads each zone and the zonal machinery works under his administrative control. He controls and coordinates the working of several departments, functioning under the zonal administration. The general manager is responsible to the railway board. The zones are divided into divisions. Under the general manager, the divisional superintendents work in the divisions of a zone. The divisional superintendents supervise and exercise control over the activities of their respective divisions.

Thus, in India, the headquarters is the secretariat and the field refers to attached and subordinate offices, which is an organizational part of each ministry/department in the Government of India.

NOTES

1. *Report of the Administrative Reforms Commission on the Machinery of the Government of India and Its Procedure of Work* (New Delhi: Government of India, 1968), pp. 39–40.
2. C. P. Bhambhari, *Public Administration: Theory and Practice,* 12th edition (Meerut: Jaiprakash Nath & Co., 1992–1993), p. 217.

The Finance Commission

The finance commission is a quasi-judicial body and our Constitution provides a finance commission in order to advise the president in exercise of his powers under Articles 270 (2) and (3); 275; 278 (2) and 306. The president of India is required to appoint the commission from time to time. Article 280 (i) says that 'The president shall within two years from the commencement of this Constitution and thereafter at the expiration of every fifth year or at such earlier time as the president considers necessary, by order constitute a finance commission which shall consist of a chairman and four other members to be appointed by the President.'

The Appointment of Finance Commission

The finance commission is appointed by an announcement of the presidential order by the finance ministry. It comes into existence from the date of assuming charge by its chairman and the members as specified in the notification and it ceases to exist as soon as it submits its report. The average duration of the finance commission had been about sixteen months. It varied from a minimum duration of 12 months in the case of the third finance commission to more than twenty months in the case of the eighth finance commission, 30 months in the case of the ninth and 41 in the case of the tenth finance commission. An analysis of the duration of the finance commission reveals that:[1]

(a) The appointment of the finance commission was not coordinated with the presentation of the Union budget till the time of the fourth finance commission.
(b) The interval between two finance commissions has been less than five years.
(c) The duration of the finance commission has been almost stabilized.
(d) A period of nearly 16 months is just adequate for the work of the finance commission.

Composition

Under the Constitution the strength of the commission has been decided as five, including its chairman. The Parliament is free to lay down the qualifications and procedure of the appointment of the members.

In exercise of its powers the Parliament has passed the Finance Commission (Miscellaneous Provisions) Act, 1951. Accordingly, the chairman of the commission shall be selected from among the persons who have had experience in public affairs and four other members shall be selected from among persons who:

(i) are, or have been, or are qualified to be appointed as judges of a high court;

(ii) have special knowledge of the finance and accounts of the government;

(iii) have had wide experience in financial matters and in administration; or

(iv) have special knowledge of economics.

The qualifications prescribed for the members show some specialization, but the chairman's qualification is too vague. The experience in public affairs will enable the Union government to appoint political persons. Experience shows that most of the chairmen were politicians from the ruling party who did not have the requisite background and desired expertise to handle such a specialized subject. Even in regard to the wording of the qualifications for the members, the use of word 'or' in between all the four prescribed qualifications implies that all the four members may be appointed from the same field of expertise and or experience, which was not the intention of the founding fathers of the Indian Constitution. Although such an extreme situation has not arisen so far, it enables a partisan government at the centre to do it.[2] By now, we have had 13 finance commissions and, by and large, persons of stature have been appointed to serve on the commission. Our experience of the 13 finance commissions reveals that, by and large, distinguished persons have served on finance commission as chairmen and members; they are being dominated by bureaucrats in or out of service; qualifications prescribed for chairman have made it easy to appoint political leaders as chairmen for an expert body like the finance commission, the same persons have not been appointed more than once either as chairman or as members in various finance commissions except the member-secretary of the first finance commission serving on the second finance commission and one member in both the seventh and eighth finance commissions; the berth of economics have not always gone to economics and so is the case with the berth of a judicial member.

'Is it that the independence of the finance commission is not quite welcome any longer? Could a body so patently packed with 'non-men' and 'yes-men' inspire the confidence of the states?'[3]

The Finance Commission (Miscellaneous) Act, 1951, clause (3) prescribes the qualifications for the chairman and members of the commission, but it does not specify any procedure whatsoever by which they may be selected. In fact, it is interesting that the clause simply says that they 'shall be selected from among persons' who have specific type of experience. It does not say any more about the selection process.[4] Thus, it is the president who appoints the members of the finance commission. The finance commission awards vitally affect the states. Should not the states have any say in the selection of the members of the finance commission? The point here is that the president need not be bound in this matter by the advice of the Union council of ministers, who represent only the Union government's point of view, while as the head of state, the president represents the entire country, not just the Union of India. Article 74 places constraints on him in Union matters. Under Article 280 he need not be so trammelled. In this matter he should act under Article 280 and not under Article 74. One article is not subordinate to another.[5] Further, the affairs of the Union are defined in Article 246 and listed in the Seventh Schedule. The Union list has 97 items and this does not include the finance commission. In the concurrent list, there are 47 entries and item 20 on economic and social planning may be considered somewhat relevant to the question of the finance commission. This would then require consultation with the states. Thus, the case for a procedure of setting up the commission involving consultation with the states would appear to be at least desirable if not necessary.[6]

Functions of Finance Commission

The functions of the finance commission are to make recommendations to the president in respect of:

(1) The distribution of net proceeds of taxes to be shared between the Union and the states and the allocation of shares of such proceeds among the states

(2) The principles which should govern the grant-in-aid of the revenues of the states out of the consolidated fund of India

(3) Any other matter referred to the commission by the president in the interest of sound finance[7]

The specific terms of reference of each commission are drafted by the finance ministry of the central government. The president does not make an independent appraisal of the suggested terms of reference. The state governments are not consulted while deciding the terms of reference. It is suggested that the states should be consulted in matters of drafting the terms of reference.

However, there are many difficulties in working out a consensus amongst so many states with diverse situations and viewpoints. But the references are determined by the Constitution itself. Article 280(3)(a) and (b) are the references but it is only under Article 280(3)(c) that the president has some discretion. Further, it may be pointed out that mere consultation will not suffice. The Union finance ministry may circulate a draft and thus fulfil the consultation process.

Terms of Reference

In the early years, grants in lieu of export duty on jute and its products and the revenue gap grants for part B states were in the terms of reference, while the second finance commission was asked to recommend the principles of distributing the net yield from taxes levied under Article 269, such as state duty and tax on railway fares which are levied and collected by the central government but the proceeds of which should be made over to the states. Regarding the reference under any other matter, there has been no consistency. The third finance commission was not referred any additional matter, while the fourth finance commission was asked to examine the desirability of using the states' share of estate duty for the repayment of the central loans to the states; to estimate any additional burden of debt servicing expenditure that would devolve on the states; and also to examine the combined incidence of sales tax and Union excise duties on production and consumption. The fifth finance commission was asked to examine the scope for exploiting sequence sources listed under Article 269 and the state's own sources of revenue. Besides, it was asked to recommend ways and means of discouraging the states resorting to unauthorized overdrafts. The sixth finance commission was asked to examine the states' debt position vis-à-vis their non-plan capital requirements, the method of consolidating the central loans to the states and the case for a national relief fund by the contributions of the centre and states. The seventh finance commission was referred to special terms. The guidelines containing in the presidential order appointing the eighth finance commission merely repeated what the two previous finance commissions had been asked to take into consideration. A few additional questions have been referred to the commission. These concern the covering of the states' non-plan capital gap and the financing of relief expenditure. But these are the matters that the past two commissions too had dealt with in one form or the other. The only new item referred to the eighth finance commission concerns the scope for states to raise revenue from such of the Articles 268 and 269 taxes as are not levied at present.

This question was also examined by the fifth finance commission again but it is unlikely to add up to anything major if it is meant as a search for a substitute for sales tax, which the central government has committed to abolish. The ninth finance commission was asked to adopt a normative approach while assessing the receipts and expenditures on revenue account not only of the states but also of the centre, with regard to the special problems of each state and the special requirements of the central government. The commission was asked to evaluate the position of surpluses on revenue account of both the Union and the states for capital investment. The major departure in the brief given to this commission is that it was empowered to examine both plan and non-plan revenue expenditure. The first three commissions did likewise, while the fourth to eighth finance panels were confined only to non-plan account. The ninth finance commission was given directions to do its job, which was criticized by scholars who called it unconstitutional on the grounds that the finance commission is a constitutional body and the executive department (finance ministry) cannot give directive to the commission.[8] The 10th finance commission was asked to take into account the needs of the states to improve the administration and other important social services. It was also asked to review the scheme of central assistance to the states in times of natural calamities.

The terms of reference of the tenth finance commission have been drawn much more cautiously than was done for the ninth finance commission; but even then much has been said against the composition and terms of reference of the tenth finance commission. So far as the composition of the tenth finance commission is concerned, its two members including the chairman are political appointees; the others are a member of planning commission, an outside expert and a serving official, the practice of justice as a member has been discarded in its membership. The tenth finance commission was asked to keep in view the tax efforts of the states while recommending financial transfers. This is clearly partisan, because the instruction had not included the 'tax efforts' of the central government. How can the central government escape from the charge of letting down the states without making an effort to exploit the sources enumerated under Article 269 which are intended for the benefit of the states? The reduction of fiscal deficits of the states is strictly not in the hands of the finance commission; it is the job of planning commission, which decides the size of the states' plans. In such a situation, asking the tenth finance commission to formulate the fiscal deficits of the states appears to be irrelevant. Thus, it is being said that there is no novelty in the terms of reference of the tenth finance commission. These are similar to those of ninth finance commission. Several issues which were irritants in centre–state relations should have been referred to tenth finance commission.

Surveying the terms of reference of all the 13 commissions constituted so far would lead us to the following observations: First, the number of regular terms of reference has been steadily increasing. Second, the number of additional terms of reference are not increasing but also becoming a regular feature of the terms of reference of the finance commission. Third, of these additional terms of reference, the problem of states' indebtedness to the centre is being repeatedly referred to the finance commission.

Duration of the Commission

The Constitution envisages an interval of up to five years between two finance commissions. In practice, however, the commissions have been appointed earlier than the constitutionally stipulated term.[9]

Table 13.1 reveals that the maximum interval occurred between the sixth, seventh and eighth commissions. In all cases the interval is less than five years. Thus, it can be said that the central government had been respecting both the letter and spirit of the constitutional provisions.

Table 13.1 *Duration of the Finance Commission*

Finance commission	*Name of the chairman*	*Date of appointment*	*Date of submission of final report*	*Total duration*
First	K. C. Neogy	30-11-1951	30-12-1952	13 months
Second	K. Santhanam	1-6-1956	30-9-1957	13 months
Third	A. K. Chanda	15-12-1960	14-12-1961	12 months
Fourth	P. V. Rajaram	8-5-1964	12-8-1965	15 months
Fifth	Mahavir Tyagi	15-3-1967	30-6-1969	16 and a half months
Sixth	K. Brahmanand Reddy	28-7-1972	31-10-1973	14 months
Seventh	Justice J. M. Shelat	23-6-1977	28-10-1978	15 months
Eighth	Y. B. Chavan	20-6-1982	30-4-1984	21 months and 10 days
Ninth	N. K. P. Salve	17-6-1987	18-12-1989	30 months and one day
Tenth	K. C. Pant	15-6-1992	3-12-1995	41 months and 12 days
Eleventh	A. M. Khusro	1998	2000	
Twelfth	Dr C. Rang Rajan	2002	2004	
Thirteenth	Vijay Kelkar	2004	2006	

Procedure of Working

The commission starts working after its full composition and terms of reference. In the first place the commission send letters to the state governments asking them to submit estimates of their normal expenditure and amounts of revenue over the next five years. After examining the states' estimates, the commission calls the concerned state officials to Delhi for clarifications. In the second place, the commission tours all the state capitals for personally hearing the case of each state for financial assistance. Normally, the chief minister along with concerned officials, present their case before the commission. The commission also receives memoranda from individuals and associations and also studies them. At last, the commission meets in Delhi to finalize its report. The report is submitted to the president of India. On receipt of the report of the commission, the president recommends its consideration for implementation by the central cabinet. The president, under Article 281 of the Constitution is bound to 'cause every recommendation made by the finance commission together with an explanatory memorandum as to the action taken thereon to be laid before each house of the Parliament.'[10]

Like other commissions, the recommendations of the finance commission are also advisory in nature. The president is bound by the advice of the commission. But finance commission is a constitutional body, and its recommendations and explanatory memoranda regarding action taken thereon are to be placed before both the houses of the Parliament. It is thought that its recommendations will receive due consideration at the hands of the president.

Analysis of the Working of the Finance Commission

An analysis of the working of the finance commission shows that there are certain shortcomings. First, the finance commission primarily depends on the data supplied by the various states. The general nature of the states is to exaggerate their difficulties by manipulating the figures. Thus, the absence of an independent cell to collect data continuously has handicapped the working of the commission. Second, the commission's tour of the state capitals does not provide enough opportunity to make an on-the-spot study of any of the projects in progress or in operation. Only the third finance commission undertook a tour of some of the backward states to assess the adequacy of road communication before recommending special grants for that purpose. Third, all the members do not present themselves at all the hearings conducted in the state capitals because most of them are not full-time members, hence they attend to their personal work as well during these visits. This puts undue strain on the chairman and the member secretary. Fourth, most of the commissions have not found it necessary to give the details of their estimates of 'revenue gap' and 'financial need' of each state either in the report or elsewhere. Nor have they precisely stated the indices of 'backwardness' they have used and weightage given to the various factors in these indices. The failure of the finance commissions to publish such details has led the researchers to suspect that they have been trying to avoid informed criticism of their arbitrary assumptions and methods of estimation. The deliberations and findings of the commissions are thus shrouded in mystery.[11] Finally, backward and large area states such as Rajasthan and MP complain that the finance commission should take into account the large size and specific projects such as the Rajasthan canal and other needs of the states while making their recommendations for share of finances. Population only is not a sufficient criterion for such states because desert areas are not thickly populated. Such states remain disadvantageous in comparison to states that are thickly populated. They have to develop less area while they get more money.

There is a feeling that the finance commission has not been given an opportunity to do its best in matters of Union-state financial relations. The Sarkaria Commission which looked into the financial provisions of the Constitution felt that the finance commission should take upon itself the role of suggesting changes in the constitutional provisions. However, all the successive commissions have been precluded from this course of action. Although the finance commission can suggest radical changes, they are averse to suggesting large-scale changes in the federal fiscal arrangements. The finance commission has an uphill task to perform. It has to adjudicate between the conflicting claims of the Union and state governments. It has 'to satisfy the states for whom justice should appear to have been done.'[12] States generally complain that justice had not been done and a raw deal was meted out to them.

Finance Commission and Planning Commission

The proper analysis of the role and working of the finance commission requires looking into the role of the planning commission and the coexistence of these two. Both commissions work together to a common goal in their own spheres with the same tests in a spirit of non-grudging cooperation. The legal position as per Article 275(i) to grants-in-aid of revenue of the states is not confined to revenue expenditure only. It brings even the capital grants within the scope of the finance commission and there is nothing in the Constitution to prevent the finance commission to take into consideration both capital and revenue requirements of the state in the formulation of a scheme of devolution and in recommending grants under Article 265 of the Constitution. This interpretation was accepted and followed by the centre till the end of the Second Five Year Plan. In fact, the recommendations of the first two finance commissions covered both revenue and capital requirements of the states.[13] During this period, there was actually an overlap of function between finance commission and planning commission with regard to the dispensation of central grants. The planning commission began to assume responsibility for the allocation of national resources among different sectors and regions of the economy. The Constitution did not anticipate that the planning commission would perform functions similar to those of the finance commission in respect of allocation of grants.[14] The distribution between the plan and non-plan expenditure has eroded the powers of the finance commission and its role is limited to the non-plan revenue account, although there is nothing in the Constitution to place such a restriction on its functions. Plan expenditure, which is controlled by the planning commission, later becomes non-plan committed expenditure and has to be taken care of by the finance commission. Such a distinction is futile from the point of view of the broader national interest and the balanced development of the federation.[15] In spite of the resentment of the finance commission regarding the increasing importance of the planning commission due to plan and non-plan expenditure division, it continued with its work. The third finance commission, regarding the role of the finance commission, observed that 'The role of the finance commission comes to be, at best that of an agency to review the forecasts of revenue and expenditure submitted by the states and the acceptance of the revenue element of the plan as indicated by the planning commission for determining the quantum of devolution, and grants-in-aid to be made; and at worst, its function is merely to undertake an arithmetical exercise of devolution, based on accounts of assistance for each state already settled by the planning commission, to be made under different heads on the basis of certain principles to be prescribed.'

Further, the commission recommended to the central government that in future either 'enlarge the functions of the finance commission to embrace total financial assistance to be afforded to the states, whether by way of loans or devolution of revenues, to enable them to balance their normal budgets and fulfil the prescribed targets of the plan' or 'transform the planning commission into finance commission at the appropriate time.'

Out of these two alternatives, the first will be favoured because the Constitution has provision for the finance commission and not for the planning commission. The sixth finance commission accepted the planning commission 'as a major agency for chanellisation of resources for the financing of state plan.'[16] The seventh finance commission stated that 'the finance commission should leave the area of plan investments and central assistance for state plans to the planning commissions.'[17] The ninth finance commission on this issue observed that '. . . the finance commission and planning commission have independent and distinct roles to play. Neither need impinge on the other's authority or functions. . . . ' Under the scheme of Chapter I of Part XII of the Constitution, the finance commission has to decide the parameters of resources available through its judicious distribution between the centre and the states for plan and non-plan expenditures on the capital account as well as revenue account. The finance commission has to do this on the principles of justice, equity and fair play, so as to maintain fiscal equilibrium between the centre and the states as well as between one state and another. In other words, the finance commission has to maintain the fiscal balance vertically and horizontally. After the resources position of the centre and the states is determined by the finance commission, the role of the planning commission begins in determining the priorities for the planned development. Where to spend and how to spend the available resources is within the respective spheres of the centre and the states, who may with the help and guidance of the planning commission set out priorities and make the best use of the allocated funds. This is the sphere where the planning commission has an important role to play. The finance commission is not concerned with it at all.' This means the finance commission recognizes the importance of the planning commission and so long as the existing arrangement continues, the two bodies must work together rather than try to find fault with each other. The other suggestions for the better working of the finance commission are given as follows.

Suggestions for Better Working of the Finance Commission

The finance commission has a constitutional basis, therefore, we cannot think of not appointing a finance commission but have to ensure its satisfactory and efficient working.

The government of Tamil Nadu had appointed a committee[18] to inquire into the problem of centre–state relations under the chairmanship of Dr P. V. Rajamannar. In its report the committee made the following three suggestions regarding the finance commission:

(a) It should be expressly provided in the Constitution that the recommendations of the finance commission shall be binding on all the parties, the centre as well as the states.
(b) The finance commission should be a permanent body with its own secretariat.
(c) A member of the planning commission may be appointed as a member of the finance commission.

The need of the hour is that the finance commission should be given wider terms of reference in regard to financial matters, so that the demand of centre–state financial relations revision can be contained and suitably meted out.[19] Otherwise, allocation of financial resources will be a case of unity and demand of greater autonomy among the states ruled by opposition parties.

The finance commission is a statutory body to distribute the share of taxes and grants-in-aid, while planning commission is an advisory body concerned with plan grants. The main function of the finance commission is to determine the revenue gap of each state and fill it up through the devolution of taxes, duties and grants. However, the entire plan finance comes under the purview of the planning commission. The central assistance for plan project depends on the recommendations of planning commission. The finance commission cannot operate in the same field. It is, therefore, suggested that a clear demarcation of the relative scope and functions of the two commissions is desirable and the need of the hour for smooth working of both the commissions.

NOTES

1. G. Themmaiah: *A Critique of the Finance Commission* (Allahabad: Wheeler Publishing, 1981), pp. 44–45.
2. R. K. Sinha, *Fiscal Federalism in India* (New Delhi: Sterling Publishers, 1987), p. 189.
3. Eighth Finance Commission, 'Old Wine in Older Bottles', *Economic and Political Weekly*, Vol. XVII, No. 26, 26 June 1982: 1046.
4. Vinod Vyasulu, 'Finance Commission in a Federal Set-up', *Economic and Political Weekly*, 5 October 1996: 2719–20.
5. Ibid. p. 2720.
6. Ibid.
7. Article 280, Constitution of India.
8. B. P. R. Vithal and M. L. Sastry, 'Terms of Reference of Ninth Finance Commission: Some Preliminary Comments', *Economic and Political Weekly*, 25 July 1987: 1248–51.
9. G. Themmaiah, 'Some Neglected Aspects of the Finance Commission', *Indian Journal of Public Administration (IJPA)*, Vol. XX, No. 1, New Delhi, 1974: 15–31.
10. Article 281, Constitution of India.
11. M. J. K. Thavaraj, *Financial Administration of India*, 4th edition (New Delhi: Sultan Chand and Sons, 1991), p. 111.
12. J. Shiv Kumar, 'Union-State Relations', *IJPA*, New Delhi, 1970: 208.
13. M. J. K. Thavaraj, *Financial Administration of India* (New Delhi: Sultan Chand and Sons, 1994), p. 117.
14. Ibid, p. 117.
15. Report of the Third Finance Commission, New Delhi, Government of India, 1961, p. 35.
16. Report of the Sixth Finance Commission, New Delhi, Government of India, 1973, p. 5.
17. Report of the Seventh Finance Commission, New Delhi, Government of India, 1978, p. 78.
18. Report of the Centre-State Relations Inquiry Committee, Government of Tamil Nadu, 1971, p. 219.
19. The chief ministers of three non-Congress-states, Tamil Nadu, Karnataka and Andhra Pradesh and the Union territory of Pondicherry formed a council of southern states in Bangalore to review the fiscal relations between the states and the centre. *Hindustan Times*, 21 March 1983, p. 1 (city edition).

Centre–State Relations

The Constitution of India provides dual polity with a clear division of powers between Union and states, each being free to legislate within the sphere allotted to it. The Union government and states governments both draw their authority from the Constitution. The relations between the centre and states can be studied under three heads, namely, legislative, administrative and financial relations.

Legislative Relations

The Union–states relations in the legislative field have been dealt with by Articles 245 to 254 of the Constitution. It is clearly mentioned in the Constitution that the Parliament shall have exclusive jurisdiction to make laws for the whole country or any part of the territory of India so far as the subjects mentioned in the Union list are concerned. The states enjoy exclusive powers over the subjects enumerated in the state list. There is a concurrent list over which both the Union and the state government can legislate, but in the situation of clash between the laws of each other, the laws framed by the Union government will prevail. The Constitution vests the residuary powers, viz., the powers not enumerated in any of the three lists, in the central government. This shows that in this distribution of powers the Union government has an upper hand. Not only this, but under certain special circumstances the Union Parliament can make laws even on state subjects. These exceptions are:

(1) *Legislation in national interest*—Article 249 provides that if the Rajya Sabha declares a resolution by not less than two-thirds members present and voting, then it was necessary or expedient in the national interest that Parliament should make laws with respect to any matter enumerated in the state list specified in the resolution. It became lawful for Parliament to make laws for the whole or any part of the territory of India with respect to that matter during the period the resolution remained in force. Such a resolution remains in force for one year and can be further extended for one year by means of subsequent resolution.

(2) *Legislation by consent of states*—Article 252 authorizes Parliament to legislate on a subject if the legislatures of two or more states feel it desirable that for any subject mentioned in the state list. Parliament

should make a law for these or authorize to do so by passing resolutions to that effect in both the houses of their legislatures. Both the houses must approve the resolution. Thereafter, any Act passed by the Parliament shall apply to such states and to any other state by which it is adopted afterwards by passing the resolution in their houses. The Parliament has the right to amend or repeal any such Act. This Article was used in 1953 and again in 1955 when some of the state legislatures authorized Parliament to pass Estate Duty Act[1] and Prize Competition Act[2], respectively. The states of West Bengal and Bihar authorized the Parliament to legislate for the setting up of the Damodar Valley Corporation to control the Damodar river which caused floods in both the states. Similarly, Parliament enacted the Urban Land (Ceiling and Regulation) Act 1976 after eleven legislatures authorized it to enact the law under Article 252 (1) of the Constitution.

(3) *Legislation to implement international treaties*—The Parliament can make laws under Article 253 for the whole or any part of the territory of India for implementing any treaty, agreement or convention with any other country or countries or any decision made at any international conference, association or other body. K. M. Panikar considered this provision dangerous because there is no subject within the state list which may not be covered by international agreements and convention.[3] This provision has probably been made to ensure smooth implementation of the international obligations of the country.

(4) *Legislation under proclamation of emergency in a state*—Whenever an emergency is declared in the country under Article 352, the Parliament gets the power of making laws on subjects mentioned in the state list. Thus, for all practical purposes the state list is automatically converted into a concurrent list. It is important to note that in India there was Emergency between 1962 and 1968 and again between 1971 and 1977, for a total period of near about 10 years.[4] There is no such provision in other federations such as those of the USA, Canada and Australia.

(5) *Legislation due to failure of constitutional machinery in the state*—Whenever the constitutional machinery fails in the state, under Article 356 of the Constitution, president's rule is imposed, the powers of the legislature of the state become exercisable by or under the authority of the Parliament. This empowers Parliament full power to legislate on any matter included in any list with respect to the state for which a proclamation has been made under Article 356.

The provisions of Article 356 provide large scope for their political misuse and this Article has been used more than 100 times almost, in all the states on different occasions and for different reasons. This has been discussed under the emergency power of the president. The Sarkaria Commission inter alia wanted that the report of the governor on which the president is moved to action under Article 356 should be a 'speaking document' containing a precise and clear statement of all material facts and grounds. It should be given wide publicity, and president's rule in a state should be proclaimed on the basis of the report given by the governor.

(6) *Reservation of bills for the consideration of the president*—The Constitution under Article 200 provides that certain types of bills such as those which endanger the position of the high court or acquisition of or generated from inter-state river or river valley (Article 288) must be reserved by the governor for president's consideration. Some bills concerning the subjects of concurrent list under Article 254(2) may be reserved by the governor for the consideration of the president. Some of the reserved bills, after examination, were rejected by the president. These are Kerala Education Bill, 1959, M. P. Panchayat Bill, 1960; Industrial Dispute (West Bengal), Bill 1969; Kerala Land Reform (Fixation of Ceiling on Land) Second Amendment Bill, 1980. There are also examples of inordinate delay in consideration of such bills by the

president, for example, sixteen bills passed by the West Bengal assembly were pending till August 1984.[5] Likewise, a bill concerning appointment and removal of vice-chancellors passed by Haryana assembly in 1988 was returned with some suggestions after seven years. This has been criticized by the opposition parties ruling in states on the ground that the central government did not allow them to implement popular welfare measures by using this Article.

(7) *Legislative relations and the courts*—In the working of the Constitution, the question whether a particular matter falls within the ambit of one or other governments arises from time to time. Our Constitution provides that such matters have to be decided by the courts which have to make sure that no government exceeds its powers. However, the three lists of our Constitution contain over two hundred entries, although significant controversies in this area are very few. The courts have developed several judicial principles to reconcile these entries.

In India, while interpreting these three lists, Union, state and concurrent lists, the Supreme Court accepted the doctrine of 'incidental powers', which means when a legislature is given plenary power to legislate on a particular subject, there must also be implied power to make laws incidental to the exercise of such power. It is a fundamental rule of constitutional law that everything necessary to the exercise of power is included in the grant of power. Further, while interpreting the doctrine of 'incidental powers' the Supreme Court has followed the principle of 'pith and substance'.

The Doctrine of Pith and Substance

The doctrine whether a particular enactment falls under one entry or the other, is called the 'pith and substance' of such enactment and its legislative label is not taken into consideration. If the enactment substantially falls under an entry under its jurisdiction, an incidental encroachment upon another entry over which it had no competence will not invalidate the law.

The Doctrine of Harmonious Construction

This is the general principle of deciding about the validity of legislation when two different articles of the Constitution appear to point in different directions. The courts in these matters try to interpret the different provisions in such a manner as to harmonize their meanings.

Conclusion

The above discussion clearly shows that the entire scheme of the distribution of legislative powers displays a tendency towards a high degree of centralization. In spite of the Union and state list for distribution of powers between the centre and the states, the centre exercises appreciable control over their legislation.

In our constitutional distribution of legislative powers, we do have an inherent tendency for conflict between the centre and the states. Different political parties may be in office at the centre and in the states and may have their own political programmes. A party in power at state level may pass a bill within its competence to give effect to its policies of economic and political ideologies. The party in power at the centre may not approve the approach of the state and the Constitution prescribes no method to override central veto over state legislation where the centre's nod is necessary for the enactment of the state law. Second, the power of the governor to reserve a state bill for the assent of the president can also lead to tension in centre–state relations. The states ruled by the parties opposed to the party ruling at the centre may feel that the governor being an appointee of the central government may reserve a state bill for the assent of the president on political considerations rather than on merits and such controversies had arisen earlier but such issues were very few. Functionally, it is an interdependent arrangement. The constitutional provisions are flexible enough to keep pace with the developing and heterogeneous society. Therefore, the Sarkaria Commission, appointed to look into centre–state relations, has not suggested comprehensive structural changes in the fundamental scheme of the Constitution. The Commission has observed, 'the rule of federal supremacy is a technique to avoid absurdity, resolve conflicts and ensure harmony between the Unions and state laws. This principle therefore is indispensable for the successful functioning of any federal or quasi-federal constitution. It is indeed the kingpin of the federal system.[6] Draw it out, and the entire system falls to pieces.'[7]

Administrative Relations

The administrative relations between the Union and the states, as envisaged under the Constitution, serve a two-fold purpose: first, to ensure effective federal executive control of matters falling within the legislative jurisdiction of the Union Parliament and second, to minimize the possibilities of conflict between the Union and state administrative machineries. As the Union government is responsible for the government of the country, there is necessity for an effective administrative nexus between the Union and its federating units. Hence, the following provisions were incorporated in our Constitution.

The Governor as an Agent of the Centre

The Governor is appointed, transferred and dismissed by the president and holds office during his pleasure. He works as the representative of the president in the states. Raghukul Tilak, the governor of Rajasthan, and Prabhudas Patwari, the governor of Tamil Nadu were dismissed in 1980 and 1981 respectively.

The governor functions in a dual capacity as a representative of the Union government and as a Constitutional head to the state under Articles 239(2), 200 and 356 of the Constitution. He acts as a representative of the centre and performs certain important functions in this capacity. His report forms the basis of decisions about the future of the state, even leading to the imposition of president's rule under Article 356. In many cases, the governor acted as a stooge of the central government, by ousting the democratically elected governments. The end of the BJP governments in the states of Himachal Pradesh, MP and Rajasthan[8] prove this contention.

The Implementation of Central Laws

According to Article 256, the executive powers of every state shall be so exercised as to ensure compliance with laws made by Parliament and any existing laws which apply in that state and the executive power of the Union shall extend to the giving of such directions to a state as may appear to the Government of India to be necessary for that purpose. Not satisfied with the power to give directions to the states, the Constitution further calls upon every state (Article 257) not to impede or prejudice the executive power of the Union in the state. The Union government can also give direction to the state government concerning the construction and maintenance of the means of communication declared to be of national or military importance. It can also issue necessary directions to the state for the protection of the railway within the jurisdiction of the state.

The Constitution also empowers the Union executive to entrust to the officers of the state certain functions of the Union government with the consent of the government of the state. Further, Parliament might confer powers and impose duties upon the state or officers and authorities thereof in respect of a law which applied in that state and about the subject matter of which the legislature of the state had no power to make laws. The expenditure incurred by the states in discharging of these obligations has to be reimbursed by the Union government.

Article 339 (2) also extends the executive powers of the Union to the giving of directions to a state as to the drawing up and execution of schemes specified in the direction to be essential for the welfare of the scheduled tribes in the state. The president has also been empowered to give directions under Article 344(6) in regard to official languages of the Union, under Article 347 with regard to the language spoken by a section of the population of a state and under Article 350-A for providing adequate facilities for instructions in the mother tongue at the primary stage of education to children belonging to linguistic minority groups.

States to Entrust Functions to the Union

Article 258-A of the Constitution empowers the governor of the state to entrust conditionally or unconditionally certain functions with respect to which the executive power of the state extends to the officers of the Union with the consent of the Government of India.

All India Services

The framers of Indian Constitution provided all India services although separate services exist for the centre and states. Article 312 gives power to the Parliament to create more of such services when required. Recruitment to these service is made by UPSC—a central personnel agency. Their conditions of service are also regulated by the central rules and regulations and their ultimate responsibility lies with the Government of India.

These services give cohesion to the federal structure and help in achieving greater efficiency in the administration of the Union and the states. The members of these services get an opportunity of serving at the centre as well as in the states and are able to acquire national outlook as well as field knowledge at the grassroots level.

Power of Adjudication

The Parliament has been vested with power to adjudicate any dispute or complaint with respect to the use of distribution or control of the waters of or in any inter-state river or river valley. In this regard the parliament also reserves the right to exclude such disputes from the jurisdiction of the Supreme Court or other courts. The two major inter-state river disputes that have not yet been solved relate to the utilization of the waters of the Kaveri and the Yamuna. The Yamuna dispute is between Punjab and Haryana. Punjab did not allow completion of the Sutlej–Yamuna link canal to supply Haryana's share of water and this has become the cause of terrorism and militant activities in Punjab. The dispute of the Kaveri water concerned three states of Karnataka, Kerala and Tamil Nadu, mainly Karnataka and Tamil Nadu: This dispute is yet to be solved.

Article 263 provides for the prevention of inter-state disputes by empowering the president to appoint an inter-state council whenever the necessity arises. The functions of council are to enquire into and advise upon disputes which may have arisen between states; to investigate and discuss subjects in which the states or the Union have a common interest, to make recommendation for the better coordination of policy and action with respect to these subjects. In May 1990, the Government of India in pursuance of the recommendations of the Sarkaria Commission took a decision to constitute the inter-state council which comprises the prime minister as chairman, chief ministers of all states. Administrators of Union territories without legislature and six Union cabinet ministers nominated by the prime minister as members. The council is a recommendatory body and as per order of 1990, it shall meet at least thrice a year. Its meetings are held in camera and 10 members constitute the quorum. Decisions are taken by consensus and the chairman's opinion shall be final. Its first meeting was held on 10 October 1990 at New Delhi. The functions of the council include (i) investigating and discussing such subjects in which some or all the states or the Union have a common interest as may be brought before it; (ii) making recommendations upon any such subjects for the better coordination of policy and action with respect to that subject; and (iii) any other matter of general interest to the states as may be referred by the chairman. The president had exercised this power by establishing the central council of health and central council of local self government. The state Reorganisation Act of 1956 established zonal councils for advising on matters of common interest to each of the five Zones in which India had been divided, to discuss matters of common interest to the states and Union Territories comprising each Zone.

Inter-State Comity

The federal Constitution generally lays down certain rules of comity which the units take into consideration while dealing with each other. The emphasis of the Constitution is on administrative cooperation hence provision has been made for it. These include recognition of public acts, extra judicial settlements of disputes, freedom of inter-state trade, commerce and intercourse. Article 261 (i) provides that 'full-faith and credit shall be given throughout the territory of India, to public acts, records and judicial proceedings of the Union and the states.' Likewise, Article 301 specifically says that final judgements or orders delivered or passed by the civil courts in any part of India are executable in all parts of the country as per the law.

Articles 301–307 have provision for free flow of commerce and intercourse between states without any barrier. These provisions deal with both inter-state and intra-state freedom. Article 307 empowers the Parliament to establish such authority as it considers fit for enforcing the provisions of the Constitution concerning inter-state trade and commerce and entrusts on it such duties as it considers necessary.

The Constitution provides for a single judicial system, and both the Union and state governments are duty bound to give full faith and credit to public acts, records, proceedings and judicial decisions of the Supreme Court and the high courts. In the appointment of chief justice and judges of the Supreme Court as well as the high courts, the states have no say whatsoever. They are appointed by the president on the recommendations of Union government, though chief justice of India is consulted while making such appointments. The power of removal of these judges also vests in Parliament which can pass necessary resolution for their impeachment and recommend president to take necessary action. States are in no way connected with the appointment or removal of the judges of the Supreme Courts or high court.

Inquiry Commissions Against State Chief Ministers

The central government is empowered to appoint commissions of inquiry against any chief minister on the charges of corruption and malpractices. This has proved to be a good method for control over state administration. For example, such commissions were appointed against the chief minister of Punjab Sardar

Partap Singh Kairon in 1963 (Das Commission); against Karunanidhi in Tamil Nadu in 1976 (Sarkaria Commission), against Vengal Rao in Andhra Pradesh, against Devraj Urs in Karnataka, against Bansi Lal in Haryana in 1978; against Bhajan Lal in Haryana (Jaswant Singh Commission), etc. Except for one case of Kairon, the ruling party at centre did not appoint any commissions against the chief minister of their own parties.

From time to time some ad-hoc commissions were also appointed for specific matters concerning both centre and states. For example, the finance commission suggested principles for allocation of financial resources between centre and states, the states reorganization commission to demarcate boundaries of state, administrative reforms commission, to suggest ways and means to improve administration of Union as well as states, the Sarkaria Commission to review the centre–state relations, etc.

Constitutional Bodies/Institutional Arrangement for Consultation

The national development council is the important body for consultation between the central and state governments. Its organization includes all the chief ministers of the states and heads of Union territories, the Union cabinet ministers and the prime minister who is ex-officio chairman of the council. It discusses all matters affecting centre and states and provides opportunities for face to face discussions on all the problems.

Planning Commission

The planning commission, in which prime minister is the ex-officio chairman and deputy chairman and several cabinet ministers are members, is another institution to discuss and translate into administrative schemes and are included in state plans. Plan discussions with states provide a good opportunity for two-way dialogue between the centre and the states and between political wing and administrators.

Consultation Through Conferences

Apart from the above arrangements, a network of conferences has been devised for consultation between the centre and states on a wide range of subjects. These conferences take place at the political and administrative levels. The national development council, the chief minister's conference, and conference of ministers of different departments like health ministers' conference, urban and rural development ministers' conference, etc. are in existence for quite some time. The conference at the administrative level includes chief secretaries' conference, and the conference of various functional secretaries. The conference of directors general of police has become very significant due to deteriorating law and order situation in the country; similarly, the conference of vice-chancellors, engineers and various other professional level conferences.

Assessment of Constitutional Provisions

The Constitution, as discussed above, establishes supremacy of the central executive over the states in the executive field. The power of the Union to give direction and non-compliance with these directions mean a failure of constitutional machinery (Article 365) in the state. The administration of the state, on the pretext of failure of Constitution, can be taken over by the Union under Article 356. Therefore, many governments raised the demand of autonomy as they felt that the Union has been given too much control over the states to the extent of reducing the latter to a completely subordinate status. Hence, some of them have demanded the abolition or drastic revision of these provisions giving supremacy to the Union over state, particularly Articles 256, 257 and 258 of the Constitution.

The Government of India appointed the Sarkaria Commission in 1983 to review the centre–state relations. The commission submitted its report in 1988. Therefore, it is pertinent to cite the recommendations of the commission here. The commission recommends that:

(i) In a two-tier system of government with a single judiciary where the administration of Union law is largely secured through the machinery of the states, differences are bound to arise between the Union and the states in regard to the manner of implementation of Union laws and the exercise of the Union's executive powers, specially if they conflict with the exercise of the executive powers of the state. Articles 256 and 257 are essential to ensure harmonious exercise of the executive power by the Union and by the states, in keeping with the principles of Union supremacy.[9]

(ii) Before issuing directions to a state under Articles 256 and 257, the Union should explore the possibilities of settling points of conflicts by all other available means. A direction under these provisions and application of the sanction under Article 365 in the event of its non-compliance is a measure of last resort. It is required to be administered with utmost caution after all other available alternatives to resolve the deadlock or conflict had been tried and failed.[10]

(iii) According to the Sarkaria Commission, federalism is more a functional arrangement for co-operative action than a static institutional concept. Article 258 provides a tool, by the liberal use of which cooperative federalism can be substantially realised in the working of the system. The commission, therefore, recommends a more extensive and generous use of this tool, than has hitherto been made for progressive decentralization of powers to the governments of the states and/or their officers and authorities.[11]

Conclusion

The above discussion clearly shows that the states are administratively subordinate to the Union government. Therefore, regional parties like Akali Dal, DMK, AIADMK, National Conference of J&K, Telugu Desam the CPM (though a national party, it has a regional stronghold in West Bengal and Kerala) are demanding autonomy of the states. The chief ministers of opposition parties-ruled states are raising the demand of more powers to the states.

FINANCIAL RELATIONS

Generally, in a federation, along with the distribution of legislative and administrative powers, the financial resources of the country are also distributed to ensure financial independence to the units. But, the Indian Constitution does not make a clear-cut distribution of the financial resources and leaves much to be decided by the central government from time to time. Therefore, among several other federal problems, the problem of financial relationship is perhaps the most complex.[12] The Indian Constitution makes provision for the financial resources between centre and states as per their demands and necessities rather than going in for a complex separation.[13] Further, the constitutional provision of the appointment of finance commission by the president every five years is designed to solve various financial disputes between the centre and the states.[14] The Constitution divides the distribution of financial resources into two parts:

(i) Distribution of revenue between the Union and the states.

(ii) System of allocation of grants-in-aid to the states from the Union.

Scheme of Distribution of Sources of Revenue

The taxing powers of the centre and the states have been separated. The taxes which have inter-state base are levied by the centre and those with a local base by the states. The Union list contains 12 items of taxation, which fall under five categories.

(1) *Taxes exclusively assigned to the Union*—Income from certain subjects like customs and export duties, income tax, excise duties on tobacco, jute, cotton, etc., corporation tax, taxes on capital value of assets of individuals and companies; estate duty and succession duty in respect of property other than agricultural land and income from the earning departments like the railways and postal departments have been exclusively assigned to the Union government by the Constitution.

(2) *Taxes exclusively assigned to states*—Income from land revenue, stamp duty except on documents included in the Union list; succession duty and estate duty in respect of agricultural land; income tax on agricultural lands; taxes on goods and passengers carried by road or inland water; taxes on vehicles used on roads, animals, boats; taxes on the consumption or sale of electricity, toll taxes on lands and buildings; taxes on professions, trades, callings and employment; duties on alcoholic liquors for human consumption, opium, Indian hemp and other narcotic drugs; taxes on the entry of goods into the local areas, taxes on luxuries, entertainments, amusements, betting and gambling etc. has been assigned to the states.

(3) Taxes are levied by the Union but collected and appropriated by the states, viz, stamp duties on bills of exchange, cheques, promissory notes, bills of lading, letters of credit, policies of insurance and transfer of shares, etc. and excise duties on medicinal and toilet preparations, etc.

(4) Taxes are levied and collected by the Union but assigned to states. Such taxes include duties in respect of succession to property other than agricultural land; estate duty in respect of property other than agricultural land; terminal taxes on goods or passengers carried by railways, sea or air; taxes on railways freights and fares; taxes other than stamp duties on transactions in stock exchanges and futures markets; taxes on the sale or purchase of newspapers and on advertisements published therein; taxes on purchase or sale of goods other than newspapers where such sale or purchase take place in the course.

(5) Taxes are levied and collected by the Union but shared with states, viz., taxes on income other than agriculture. The basis of distribution is determined by the Parliament through a law.

Grants-in-Aid

Article 275 empowers Parliament to give financial assistance to the states in need of such assistance in the form of grants-in-aid. Grants may be broadly classified as 'plan' and 'non-plan'. Plan grants are determined by the planning commission and non-plan grants are determined by the finance commission while grants on ad-hoc basis are given by the central government to meet unforeseen situations. Grants are also given to remove interstate disparities in resources. Thus, more grants are given to backward and under-developed areas. Besides, grants-in-aid are also given in lieu of export duty on jute and jute products under Article 273 of the Constitution to jute-growing states like Assam, Bihar, Orissa and West Bengal on the basis of recommendations of the finance commission. Grants are also given for raising the administrative level of the tribal areas in Assam.

Power of Borrowing

The Union government has power for borrowing upon the security of the revenues, within or outside, subject to the limitation fixed by Parliament from time to time.[15] States have also borrowing power. States can borrow within the territory of India if they have no outstanding loan from the centre. Since in the last few years the states have heavily borrowed from the centre, therefore, the states can borrow only with the consent of the central government. The main source of borrowing of the state government is the Union government, the purpose of borrowing is generally to finance development programmes related to agriculture, industries and related matters.

Financial Emergency

During the period of financial emergency, the president can suspend the provisions of divisions of taxes between the Union and states and grants-in-aid to the states. The Union government acquires the right to issue directions to the states; reduce the salary and allowances of serving in connection with the affairs of the state including high court judges; and reserve for the consideration of the president all money bills passed by the state legislature.

Control by the Comptroller and Auditor-General of India

The comptroller and auditor-general is responsible for the maintenance of audit of Union and states accounts, is appointed by the president of India. He can direct the state governments to keep their records in a particular manner and these are bound to obey his instructions and directions.

Tension Areas in Practice

Many state governments have complained that the central assistance is not released in time. First, the release depends on audited accounts and the state governments have to depend on the central government both for the compilation and audit of their accounts. Second, the central assistance for centrally sponsored schemes is always communicated late and due to these schemes is not fully implemented or if implemented with state funds the claim of such amount is always delayed and states have to curtail their other programmes. Third, centrally sponsored schemes impose conditions and state governments are put to hardship to fulfil these conditions. Finally, even assistance announced for natural calamities takes lot of time for releasing the money due to procedural requirements.

The states have pleaded for the enlargement of states taxation powers. They feel that their resources are inelastic and the tax base is also narrow. Therefore, they demand more resources for development of the states. The broad issues are: enlargement of states own resources, pattern of devolution, states indebtedness, market borrowing and sharing of capital resources.

The Sarkaria Commission in this regard found the scheme of distribution of taxation powers basically sound, and by and large agreed with the sharing of revenues raised through taxes and resources raised by market borrowings. But the states allege that Sarkaria Commissions recommendations, by and large, favour the status quo. The overall view is that the Sarkaria Commission, taking into consideration diverse factors like devolution of more resources to the states, maintains financial discipline on Union and states had made good recommendations to solve some of the practical problems. However, the centre should be more considerate in times of natural calamities in providing assistance to the states ruled by opposition parties. A balanced, rational and practical approach by the political parties holding power at the centre and in the states can be useful for removal of grievances of opposition parties ruled states. Central institutions like the CBI should be used very carefully to fulfil the constitutional goals and not political ends but to create a congenial environment of trust and mutual dependence between centre and states.

PLANNING AND CENTRE–STATE RELATIONS

India is a developing country with vast natural resources. Therefore, it was felt that our resources should be carefully exploited to get maximum outputs. The country after Independence adopted the method of economic planning to achieve maximum developments from the available resources. In a federal country like ours the planning has to be done by the central government for the whole country by involving state governments and the people. The concept of planning and its administration has been dealt in Chapter 16. Here we are discussing mainly those aspects of planning which affect centre–state relations.

The planning commission has been created by the plan formulation of the country at the central level. Both the planning commission and national development council are the creation of a cabinet resolution and not of any central law. The national plan cannot be practical one unless it includes state plans. To prepare state plans, in most of the states, state planning boards have been set up and for the planning at the district level after 73rd and 74th constitutional amendment acts, a district planning body has been established in each district of the country.

The planning commission plays an important role in the centre–state financial relations because first, it fixes the size and priorities of the state plans. Second, it mobilizes the physical and financial resources for the state plan. Third, it reduces inter-state disparities in development. Finally, it ensures uniform rate of economic growth and social development in the states. Further, the planning commission controls the development activities of all the states. Even the legislative activities of the states mentioned in state list such as agriculture, rural development, education, minor irrigation, command area development, health and cooperation have passed into the hands of the planning commission. For example, the land reform schemes of the states were examined by the land reforms division of the planning commission. In fact, hardly there is any activity of state governments in which the planning commission is not involved. Therefore, voices were raised by the states that planning commission has become another 'super government', which had made the states subservient to the centre. The discretionary grants system on the recommendation of non-statutory body—planning commission is also opposed by the states on the grounds that it undermines their independence. The states also object to centrally sponsored scheme devices relating to the state subjects to dominate them. They demand freedom to frame schemes for their own subjects in the state list. Further, some states also feel aggrieved due to less proportion of public sector corporation investments in their states as compared to some favoured ones. They demand a rational formula for such types of investment policy framed by the planning commission. Therefore, in the end it can be concluded that the planning process has further strengthened the hold of the centre over states.

NOTES

1. On the request of nine Part A states such as Bombay, MP, Orissa, Punjab, UP and others, Parliament passed Estate Duty Act of 1953. Amal Ray, *Inter-Governmental Relations in India*, (Bombay: Himalaya Publishing House, 1974), p. 42 .
2. S. N. Jain (ed.), *The Union and the States* (Delhi: National Publishing House, 1972), p. 34.

3. Constituent Assembly Debates, Vol. V., p. 156.
4. The first proclamation of Emergency was issued on 26 October 1962 at the time of Chinese aggression and continued till it was revoked on 3 January 1971. The second time the proclamation was issued on 3 December 1971 and another proclamation was issued on 25 June 1975 due to alleged internal disturbances. Both of these were revoked on 21 March 1977.
5. *The Times of India,* New Delhi, 17 August 1984.
6. The Commission on Centre–State Relations Report, Part I (New Delhi: Government of India, 1988), p. 29.
7. Bernard Schwertz, quoted in *Ibid.*
8. *Hindustan Times,* New Delhi, 16 December 1992.
9. The Commission on Centre–State Relations Report, Part I (New Delhi: Government of India, 1988), p. 106.
10. *Ibid.,* p. 107.
11. *Ibid.,* p. 109.
12. K. Santhanam, *Union–State Relations in India* (New Delhi: Asia Publishing House, 1960), p. 29.
13. D. D. Basu, *Introduction to the Constitution of India* (New Delhi: Prentice Hall of India, 1976), p. 268.
14. M. V. Pylee, *India's Constitution* (Bombay: Asia Publishing House, 1967), p. 315.
15. Article 292, Constitution of India.

15

Union Public Service Commission

The Union Public Service Commission (UPSC) is the recruiting agency for civil services whose members control the commanding heights of the administration. The Indian Civil Service during British times was one of the finest in the world. Despite their prejudices against the ICS, the leaders of free India made it a part of the new political system and gave it the name Indian Administrative Service. Sardar Vallabh Bhai Patel realized that no democratic government could be effective without a proper, well-organized and well-disciplined civil service to carry out its will and to advise it on how to give its policies concrete and practical shape. Today, IAS officers are everywhere; in steel plants, food corporation of India, electricity boards, port trusts, radio, television, municipal corporations, registrars of cooperative societies and universities, directors of industries and commissioners of fisheries, etc. Thus, free and fair selection based on merit is essential for such an immensely important civil service. Therefore, an attempt has been made here to analyse the intention of our Constitution makers regarding the free and fair working of the UPSC in the recruitment of civil servants along with suggestions for improvement.

Historical Background

The Government of India Act, 1919 initiated the creation of the Union Public Service Commission in India. The Act was to discharge in regard to recruitment and control of the public services in India, such functions as may be assigned thereto by rules made by the secretary of state in council. 'Section 96-C of the Government of India Act, 1919 had a provision for the establishment of public service commission comprising not more than five members including its chairman. These were appointed by the secretary of state in council. The commission was given, in regard to recruitment and control of the public services, such functions as may be assigned to it by the secretary of state in council under the rules made under this section.' In 1924, the Lee Commission also recommended for the establishment of central public service commission. As a result, the public service commission was set up in India, for the first time under the provisions of this section in the year 1926. The Government of India Act, 1935 provided in Section 264 for the establishment of Federal public service commission along with public service commission for provinces. As a result of this, from 1 April 1937, the then public service commission at the centre was renamed as the federal public service commission (FPSC). In our Constitution, Article 315 also provides that 'there shall be a Union Public Service Commission (UPSC) and a Public Service Commission for each State'. Thus, on 26 January 1950, the federal public service commission became Union public service commission.

Union Public Service Commission is an agency created by the Constitution for the recruitment of the best personnel without any political and personal considerations. To what extent the UPSC has performed this duty is to be analysed. But, before evaluating the working of the UPSC we have to analyse the constitutional provisions and safeguards provided to the Commission, first, for its independent working and second, to recruit best personnel and to protect the services from political influence.

Provisions for Independent Working of the UPSC

Our Constitution makers were quite aware about the various kinds of pressures which would work at the time of selection of candidates for these coveted posts, therefore, they had taken steps for the independent working of the UPSC without external influence. These were, first, that all the members including its chairman will be appointed by the president for a fixed term of six years or until the attainment of 65 years of age, whichever is earlier. Second, the conditions of service of the members are determined by the president, but these cannot be changed to their disadvantage during their tenure. Third, a member after appointment cannot easily be removed. Article 317 provides that he can only be removed by the order of the president on the grounds of insolvency, infirmity of mind or body, or engagement in paid employment outside the office. Further, he may also be removed on the grounds of misbehaviour on specific grounds only after the Supreme Court, on a reference being made to it by the president has, on enquiry, recommended such removal. Thus, without the consent of the Supreme Court, no member can be removed. Fourth, the entire expenses of the commission including the salaries of members are charged to the consolidated fund of India; meaning thereby that the expenditure incurred on commission is not subject to the vote of Parliament. Fifth, the chairman and members of the commission are barred from taking further employment under the government except that a member can be appointed chairman of the UPSC or state public service commission provided he is below the age of 62 years. Dr Ambedkar remarked 'one way of making them independent of the executive is to deprive them of any office with which the executive might tempt them to depart from duty.' He even banned honorary posts because he further said, 'pay is not the only thing which a person obtains by reason of his post, there is such a thing as pay, pickings and pilferings.'[1]

Thus, it is very clear that the Constitution makers have tried to create an independent body for recruitment purposes but they did not succeed in making the members entirely independent of executive patronage. The ban is not against their appointment as ambassadors, vice-chancellors, governors, ministers and members of Rajya Sabha. Swaroop Singh, a former UPSC member was the governor of Gujarat and earlier was member of Rajya Sabha and A. R. Kidwai, former chairman of the UPSC was governor of Bihar and earlier also after retirement he was appointed governor. Thus, our pillars of democracy are independent of executive fears, but not of party favours.[2]

The point to which no attention was not paid by the Constitution makers is regarding the qualification of the members of the UPSC. The agency being a multipurpose body requires a combination of various types of qualities for its members. To choose the best candidates out of many, members must be capable to perform this job. The quality of administration depends upon the initial recruitment of personnel; the latter depends upon the qualifications and impartiality of the members of the UPSC. This aspect has been left to the government. The only safeguard mentioned in the Constitution in this regard is that one half members of the commission shall be persons who have 10 years' administrative experience in government jobs. About this Dr Ambedkar said, 'it is a device not to create a "paradise" for retiring officers but to provide the commission with a talent that is experienced in knowing the requirements of government.'[3] But experience shows that this provision has given place to many politically pliable and retiring administrators[4] rather than upright and honest persons.

Composition

The Constitution has not fixed the number of members of the UPSC. This is left to the president. The sanctioned strength of the commission is 10 members and a chairman. The members are appointed by the president. Here also by not fixing the number of members of the UPSC (in March 1995, the commission has a chairman and nine members), our Constitution makers have inadvertently made the executive powerful enough who could increase the number of members and appoint persons of their own choice to obey their command. The commission has its own staff for performing its functions. In 1995, the number of its staff was 2076; out of these 298 were gazetted officers and the remaining 1778 non-gazetted. Its senior staff includes one secretary, one additional secretary, one controller of examinations, one executive director (information systems), one director (examination reforms), seven joint secretaries, 14 deputy secretaries, one director (official language), one joint director (research and analysis), two joint directors (confidential), two joint directors (examination reforms), one OSD (examinations), 47 under secretaries, three managers (electronic data processing), one manager (data preparation), one manager (systems development and chief programme) and finance and budget officer, etc. The number of staff is increasing every year, which seems to be excessive and needs some check. Large-sized organizations are slow-moving organizations; therefore, the UPSC should not allow itself to become unmanageable.

Functions

The functions of the UPSC are enumerated in Article 320. These are as follows:

First, to advise the government on all matters relating to the method of recruitment and the principles to be followed in making appointment to civil services either directly or by promotion.

Second, it needs to conduct examinations for appointment to various services such as all India and central services.

Third, it needs to interview candidates for direct recruitment.

Fourth, it needs to advise the government on the suitability of candidates for promotion and transfer.

Fifth, the commission is also consulted on matters such as temporary appointments, for a period more than one year but not extending three years; and re-employment of certain retired persons.

Sixth, it needs to advise the government on all disciplinary matters affecting civil servants.

Seventh, the commission is consulted on matters relating to the regularization of appointments, claims for award of pension, reimbursement of legal expenses incurred by government servants in defending legal proceedings instituted against them while performing their official duties, claims for pension or compensation in respect of injuries sustained while on duty.

Eighth, it needs to advise the government on any other matter specifically referred to it by the President of India.

Ninth, through an Act of Parliament, more functions can be given to the Union public service commission.

Article 321 provides for conferring on the UPSC additional functions by 'an Act made by Parliament, or as the case may be, the legislature of a state may provide for the exercise of additional functions by the Union public service commission as in respect of the services of the Union or the state and also in respect of the services of any local authority or other body corporate, constituted by law or of any public institutions.' It is noteworthy that the commission cannot take up any function other than those specified in Article 320, even at the request of the Union government unless such provision has been made in the manner prescribed by Article 321.

The proviso to Article 321, however, dilutes the consultative role of the commission by authorizing the president to make regulations specifying the matters in which either generally, or in any particular class of cases or in any particular circumstances, it will not be necessary to consult the commission. This proviso has been frequently used by the Union as well as state governments. For example, the commission may not be consulted on matters relating to the reservation of posts for the backward classes, Scheduled Castes and Scheduled Tribes.

The commission is also not consulted in regard to selections for the following appointments:

(a) Membership or chairmanship of commissions or tribunals
(b) Post of highest diplomatic nature
(c) A bulk of class III and IV employees who constitute about 98 percent of central government employees are outside the purview of the commission

Thus, the jurisdiction of the commission can be reduced by taking away posts from its purview.

The public service commission has been shown as the protector of the services from the initial recruitment up to retirement of the incumbents. The functions of the commission are advisory in nature; it cannot take a decision in such matters. In the constituent assembly, this point was discussed and it was feared that if the commission is given mandatory powers then it will lead to the setting up of two governments. The prevalent view was that a 'kingdom within a kingdom' should not be created.

After a lot of discussion Dr Ambedkar told that a way had been found out by the drafting committee through a provision, that the commission will submit a 'report' of its working along with the recommendations which have not been accepted by the government to the president (Article 323[1]) who would then place it before the legislature.

Thus, a full discussion on the report by the Parliament for non-acceptance of recommendations would provide a check on the executive. These intended checks against the nepotism and favouritism of the executive are only theoretical and in practice there are many limitations. First, the Parliament, due to its busy schedule and other priorities, hardly has any time to go into the details of the 'report'. Sometimes even members do not understand the real purpose of these reports and they generally toe the government line. Second, due to strict party discipline, nothing can prevent the government from indulging in favouritism and nepotism. Third, the reports are not placed in time before the legislature due to lack of provision of time limit and thus serve no purpose at all. For example, in the year 1993 the UPSC has presented to the president its forty-first report covering the period from 1 April 1990 to 31 March 1991.

Working of the Commission

The main work of the commission is to conduct examination for the recruitment of civil servants. The examination system of the UPSC has been questioned by scholars of public administration. The examination system prior to 1979 was different. At that time candidates appeared only in the main examination. In 1975, a committee was set up under the chairmanship of D. S. Kothari to suggest the improvements in recruitment policy and selection method of the UPSC. The committee submitted its report in 1976 and recommended a preliminary screening examination for recruitment to the IAS and other central class-I services prior to main civil services examination plus an interview of 300 marks. The good points of the Kothari committee's recommendations were that it recommended a single scheme of recruitment common to the IAS, IPS and non-technical class-I central services. It means that no service is called upon to take additional examination. This was an egalitarian move and the committee welcomed it.

The main examination consists of two parts—a written examination and an interview. The written examination consists of nine papers (conventional essay type), out of many subjects each carrying 300 marks. Those who qualify the written part of the main examination are called for the interview which is conducted by the UPSC. The marks obtained in the written examination as well as in the interview are added and final merit list is prepared. Such a system of examination has been criticized on many grounds. The preliminary objective-type test to weed out candidates who are not competent enough to appear in the main examination may sound good but due to this the examination has become one of the longest recruitment test in the world, being spread over two stages and takes a whole year in finalizing the list of candidates. The 'preliminary examination' in June followed by the main examination which is divided into a written test in November and an interview in March up to May the next year. Thus, a candidate sitting for the competitive examination has to study for more than a year.

The importance of civil service examination is immense but it is unable to ensure that the best persons are selected from different regions and backgrounds. The candidates appearing in this examination have to choose two optional subjects out of about 47 widely divergent subjects, namely, animal husbandly and veterinary science, agriculture, electrical engineering, physics, chemistry, mathematics, commerce and accountancy, literature, law, history, philosophy, public administration, political science, sociology, geography and geology, etc. It is not feasible to compare the performance of a candidate in agriculture or mathematics or physics with that of another candidate who has opted for social sciences subjects such as sociology, public administration or history. Since the optional subjects account for two-thirds of the marks of the written test, one should be very serious about their relevance in judging the competitive merit of the candidates. The multiplicity of the subjects allowed by the UPSC has led to the confusion and arbitrariness in evaluation of the merit of the examinees.

A more appropriate method would be to offer a common syllabus. It should be very general in character, to test the intelligence of candidates and should not be biased in favour of any one discipline. Only in this way can comparison of scores make sense. At present some subjects such as natural science subjects, engineering and mathematics are more scoring because these are more factual and objective. On the other hand there are disciplines such as social sciences and literature which are rather abstract and subjective in character and their examiners generally do not award very high marks even for very good performance. What is more, the subjective element inherent in them ensures that the same performance can fetch high or low scores according to the whims of the examiners who happen to evaluate the answer books. Thus, the candidates offering the former group of subjects have an edge over those who have opted for the latter.

Pointing out the weaknesses of the written examination, Gorwala, in his report on public administration, said, 'there are also often complaints about the low standard of some of the papers set for optional subjects, and it is felt that candidates taking those subject have unfair advantage. This is inevitable from time to time, but in order to give as equal chance as possible, that part of the examination which is common to all candidates must form a larger proportion of the whole than at present enabling relative merit to be more properly judged.'[5] Paul H. Appleby also said that 'the criteria by which personnel are selected by the public service commission are not up to date and the examining and appraising techniques are far from modern. Selection tends to be of one type of person, which naturally perpetuates its own type. Selection is too much in terms of academic records and appraisals by experienced academic examiners, too little in terms of many other considerations as are highly important in public administration . . . too little attention in selection is given to any but the most subjective and incident attention to capacity for growth.'[6]

The questions in the main examination are of subjective nature. If not properly set, they are likely to introduce a large degree of arbitrariness and even an expert would not be able to know what to include and what to exclude in his answer. Thus, the answer has to be sketchy and arbitrary; therefore, rational evaluation will be a casualty. So it would be convenient for both the examiner and the examinees if the question clearly spelt out what is to be explained, discussed, analysed and elaborated.

Further, a simple graduation is the precondition to sit in the examination, but in actual practice much more is expected of the candidates. The course and questions are of MA standard and a few universities in metropolitan cities have this type of courses. Most of the universities located at district headquarters or below follow older and different course content. The students of these universities are at a loss and they do not know which books to read for the competitive examination for civil services. Thus, all graduates have been given equal chance to appear in the examination, but in practice a great deal of inequality is introduced in favour of post-graduates and that too of a few metropolitan universities.

Another weakness in the way of correct evaluation is that while civil service examination course contents tally with that of metropolitan advanced universities, the examiners are drawn from universities all over the country, and sometimes even retired ones are called for evaluation. The examiners of these regional universities and retired ones have no opportunity to study in-depth and such teachers are poor examiners. Only very senior and competent professors should be associated with evaluation work.

The heavy course content is also expensive if the candidate does not have the benefit of using a good university library. The books are costly nowadays and are available only in big cities. The heavy courses are not helpful in understanding the complexities of administration. Therefore, this type of knowledge leads to wastage of money and energy on the part of the candidates and the examining body. The syllabus should be prepared in such a way that it could judge the candidates' linguistic ability, mathematical aptitude, some knowledge of science and technology, logical thinking and expression, comprehension and a general awareness about the culture, politics and economy of the country. This is the only requirement for administrative competence.

The defects have also been pointed out in the oral interview. First, it is subjective and impressionistic, and it has to be admitted that there is considerable scope for the elements of chance and performance depends on the personnel of the interview board; the difference in the nature of questions put to different candidates. Thus, it is an unreliable method of judging candidates. Second, sometimes many candidates, in the atmosphere of worry and fear, become nervous and cannot express themselves well. Thus, 10 or 15 minutes' interview is not a test of the knowledge of a person. Third defect of the interview is that the members of the board are generally convent educated and they do not like the accent and pronunciation of the rural background students who have taken their education in ordinary government schools. Thus, good students suffer for no fault of theirs. A. D. Gorwala suggested replacement of interview by psychological tests. He pointed out: 'the importance of psychological test must be realized and they must gradually replace the viva voce. A 15-minute conversation with laymen, although possessing wide experience of the public service commission, can be no substitute for an expert psychological examination designed to give a scientific insight into the candidates' mental and emotional make-up. The holding of such tests will, of course, cost more but if thereby the services get better material, and there is no reason to suppose that they will not, the extra money will have been well spent.'[7] In India, this method has not yet been adopted except for selection of officers in defence forces.

Such examination system has made the present IAS elitist in character. The present system of recruitment for these services is heavily loaded in favour of middle class boys with urban background. Nearly 84 per cent of men and women in IAS come from the urban areas. The number of the rural entrants has been decreasing since 1948, the year when their number was 30.3 per cent. At one stage, it was as low as 2.8 per cent.[8] Several probationers during the period of their training at Mussoorie have complained that accent rather than content and real worth matter in IAS recruitment.[9] The research studies conducted by several scholars namely R. K. Trivedi and D. N. Rao,[10] V. Subramanian,[11] C. P. Bhambri[12] and the author[13] reveal that the sons and daughters of agriculturists are the least represented in these services and sons of higher civil servants dominated the scene; followed by the sons of university professors, doctors and lawyers. These facts reveal that these services are fast developing into hereditary services. Practically, the doors of top government services are closed for the sons of farmers and the rural poor, who are 77 per cent of the population, mostly living in rural areas. This situation needs to be rectified and our bureaucracy should be representative of various classes and communities in Indian society.

The UPSC also suffers from mismanagement of its examination system. In the past few years, preliminary examination papers were leaked to the students. People have alleged the involvements of UPSC staff in such leakage of papers who conduct examination. In the year 1991, the whole examination was cancelled due to leakage[14] of one of the question papers. In the year 1992 too a paper was leaked at the Allahabad centre for which CBI conducted enquiry and the controller of examinations of UPPSC was arrested as per press reports. Therefore, strict control and supervision is required to prevent such incidents.

Lastly, in recent years, the advice of the UPSC is being overruled by the central government.[15] It has been noticed that during the period between 1950 and 1985, in 35 years, the commission's advice was not accepted 57 times, but between 1985 and 1990 in a period of five years its advice has been overruled 92 times, a monumental increase, while in the first 35 years the annual average of cases where the UPSC was overruled came to merely 1.6 per cent or three cases in two years. In the subsequent five years, the annual average shot up dramatically to 18.4 per cent of cases. Not only this, surprisingly, in several cases the government did not give the reasons for the rejection of the commission's advice. As far as possible the recommendations of the UPSC should be accepted and if in any urgent situation government find it difficult to accept the advice, then reasons should be given in writing for non-acceptance to keep people's faith in UPSC.

Evaluation of the Working of the UPSC

The evaluation of the working of the UPSC is essential because it will prove to what extent the UPSC has achieved its objectives of free and fair selection of outstanding and meritorious candidates. The public service commissions in India are the creation of the Constitution and not of the legislature as in Britain and the USA. In India, public service commissions, in the centre as well as the states are neither subordinate to the legislature nor to the executive. But both Union and state governments, particularly the latter, have shown a tendency to bypass the commissions or reduce their usefulness. The methods generally used are:

(a) *Removal of posts from the purview of the commission.* Although in theory recruitment work to all kinds of civil posts is to be done by the commission, the Constitution has provision to exclude certain posts or categories of posts from the purview of the commission by the executive. In 1958, the president had made regulations called Union Public Service Commission (Exemption from Consultation) Regulations which have been amended from time to time. Under these regulations most of the class III and IV appointments have been taken out of the purview of the commission to lessen the burden of work but some higher appointments of important posts have also been excluded to undermine the importance of the commission.

(b) *Temporary appointments.* Temporary appointments by the government are made without consulting the commission, in the name of urgent appointments but in actual practice the government has not always followed the spirit of the rules and regulations in this respect. The annual reports of the UPSC are full of instances of governments making temporary or officiating appointments, in the beginning for less than a year and later continue them for many years and then seeking *ex post facto* concurrence of the commission. This practice violates the spirit of appointment on the basis of merit.

(c) *Delay in appointments.* The commission is criticized on the ground that it takes too much time in recruitment. In some cases the time taken is more than a year. Second, appointment orders are also issued very late by the government and such delays cause lots of other problems such as during the period in case the candidate might have joined some other job, the posts are re-advertized. Such delay also causes hardship to a temporary appointee if later on he is replaced by a candidate selected by the commission.

(d) *Deteriorating quality of the members of the commission.* The ARC study team on centre–state relationship in its report (1967) observed on the quality of the members of the UPSC that 'The need for independence and competence in members of the public service commissions is to be accepted as axiomatic and does not have to be stressed. It was realized by the makers of the Constitution and given forceful expression in the debates of the constituent assembly. Safeguards were consequently provided with a view to ensuring the independent and efficient functioning of the commissions. These safeguards have, however, proved inadequate, much more so than in the case of high courts. In many states the public service commissions have deteriorated both in the competence and independence. They have consequently not proved to be successful guardians of standards that they are meant to be and have too often succumbed to unhealthy influence, mostly from the state governments concerned. Usually surreptitious, the existence of such influences has on occasions been demonstrated in courts of law revealing not merely the amenability of the commissions concerned, but a measure of incompetence as well.[16]

Some other complaints of the commission are concerning the tailor-made advertizements favouring some candidates; abolition of posts and their subsequent revival under different names; change in order of preference shown by the commission, etc.

Some recommendations had been made by the administrative reforms commission (ARC) for improving the quality of membership of the commission.[17]

The commission recommended as follows:

1. In making appointments to a state public service commission, the governor should consult the chairman of the UPSC and the chairman of the state public service commission. (The latter may be consulted also with regard to the appointment of his own successor.)

2. In making appointments to the Union public service commission, the chairman of the UPSC should be consulted (even with regard to the appointment of his own successor).
3. Not less than two-thirds of the membership of the UPSC should be drawn from among the chairmen and members of the state public service commissions.
4. At least one of the members of a state public service commission should belong to a different state.
5. The minimum academic qualification for membership of a commission should be a university degree.
6. A member selected from among government offices should have held office under a state government or the central government for at least ten years, and should have occupied the position of a head of department or secretary to government in a state, or a post of equivalent rank under the central government, or a comparable position in an institution of higher education.
7. Members selected from non-officials should have practiced at least for 10 years in any of the recognized professions like teaching, law, medicine, engineering, science, technology, accountancy or administration.

Present Position of the UPSC

The commission is making all out efforts to recruit best candidates for the civil services but there have been difficulties over the last few years. In particular, since 1990 there have been allegations of prior leakage of the question papers. People have raised doubts about the genuineness of those who pass civil services examination because they question the reliability of their examination. It appears that the UPSC has become such a factory which causes more pollution than quality production. In many cases now courts have been approached including the high courts and Supreme Court. The problem of standardization of marks in any examination is not an easy task. The evaluation standards differ from one examiner to other examiner. The optional papers are not of equal standard, some subjects are more scoring than others. In spite of all these problems, the UPSC is doing very good work and selections are made on the basis of merit alone. Till now not a single finger has been raised against its honesty and fairness.

NOTES

1. Constituent Assembly Debates, Vol. IX, pp. 592–93.
2. K. V. Rao, *Parliamentary Democracy of India*, 2nd edition (Calcutta: The World Press, 1965), p. 335.
3. *Constituent Assembly Debates,* Vol. IX, p. 592.
4. *The Tribune*, Chandigarh, dated 28 August 1992, Editorial: Although the Constituent Assembly debate on the UPSC had envisaged that only half of the UPSC members should be from the bureaucracy, retired officers of the Government of India have virtually taken over the board. T. A. Kalyanakrishnan, S. K. Mishra, J. M. Quareshi, A. S. Padmanabhan, Otima Bordia, H. J. S. Chhatwal and Harish Chandra are all retired officials. So close-knit is the club of civil servants that even retired UPSC members are accommodated as head of ad-hoc selection boards. The practice has been continuing for the last two decades, though it is debatable whether the chairman can legally nominate outsiders without a single member of the UPSC being present; pointed out a rare non-bureaucrat on the board, Jagdish Rajan.

   The hold of the civil servants is such that even the specialists brought in for evaluating the performance of candidates for various government services are not allowed to give their assessments of candidates in writing; they can merely convey their ratings verbally to the chairman.
5. A. D. Gorwala, *Report on the Public Administration* (New Delhi: Government of India, 1951), p. 6.
6. Paul H. Appleby, *Report of a Survey* (New Delhi: Government of India, 1953), p. 11.

7. A. D. Gorwala, op. cit.
8. *Hindustan Times*, 20 April 1975.
9. Ibid.
10. R. K. Trivedi and D. N. Rao conducted a study in 1961 on 1291 IAS officers. Their findings prove that only 12 per cent were from agriculturist background. 'Higher civil service in India, a sample survey', *Journal of National Academic of Administration*, Mussoorie, 1961.
11. V. Subramanian, *Social Background of India's Administrators* (New Delhi: Government of India Publication Division, 1971).
12. C. P. Bhambri, *Administrators in a Changing Society* (New Delhi: National, 1972), p. 68.
13. See G. P. Pilania and Hoshiar Singh, *Administration and Social Change* (Jaipur: Printwell, 1985), Chap. 5.
14. *Hindustan Times*, New Delhi, 9 January 1992.
15. *Hindustan Times*, New Delhi, 8 January 1992.
16. *Report of the Study Team on Centre–State Relationship (ARC)*, Vol. I (New Delhi: Government of India, September 1967), p. 190.
17. *The ARC, Report on Personnel Administration, April 1969* (New Delhi: Government of India, 1969), pp. 55–58.

Public Services

Public administration concerns with policy formulation and implementation and management of public affairs by competent civil servants who constitute public services or civil services. The term 'civil service' has been defined by Herman Finer as a 'professional body of officials, permanent, paid and skilled'. The civil service is the backbone of the administrative system. 'It is this great body of men and women that translates law into action from one end of the country to the other and brings the national government into its daily contacts with the rank and file in the country—less in the public eyes than the ministry, this army of functionaries is not a whit less necessary to the realisation of the purposes for which government exists.'[1] Thus, the civil service performs vital administrative functions for the smooth conduct of state business.

In our country we have three classes of civil services, viz., the all-India services, the central services and the state services. We will discuss all these three kinds in this chapter.

Historical Background

The term civil servant was used to designate those servants of the East India Company who used to carry on the trade of the company. These civil servants became administrators when the company acquired political power and territorial empire and later the British government took over administration from the East India Company, The administrators then came to be known as civil servants. The term 'civil servants' was used to make a distinction between those engaged in trade overseas and others performing duties in naval or military spheres. In the beginning, the civil service of India had a limited functional area, confined to revenue collections but gradually the range of its activities widened with the introduction of services, such as public health, education, agriculture, irrigation, and so on. The civil servants were not well paid by the company, which was the cause of abuse of their position.

In 1715, Lord Robert Clive came to India and he undertook the task of purifying the services. He forced the servants of the company to sign 'covenants' with the company binding them not to accept presents or engage in private trade. It was for this reason that the services were classified as 'covenanted' and 'uncovenanted'. The 'covenanted', which were considered superior, were created by a law of the company while the 'uncovenanted' that were considered inferior were created otherwise. These services were manned by Europeans.

The foundation of the civil service in the modern sense was to tone up the morale laid down by Lord Warren Hastings. Lord Cornwallis made far-reaching changes in administration by reserving all the superior services for the European servants and also raised their salaries. This policy of Cornwallis was criticized by some enlightened Englishmen like Sir Thomas Munro. He said, 'there is perhaps no example of a conquest in which the natives have been so completely excluded from all shares of the government of their country as in British India.' The Charter Act of 1793 confirmed the principle of giving all the posts of responsibility and authority to the Europeans. As a result, during the first quarter of the 19th century, Indians occupied practically no post in public service. Later on Indians were given only lower posts like *munsif* and *sadar amin*.

In 1831–1832, a select committee of the British parliament sat to investigate into the East India Company affairs and the Indian administration. The committee said that it was not wise to exclude Indians from higher posts in the name of incapacity for business and lack of trustworthiness. Their association would have proved better for administration of justice and saving in expenses of the government.

The Indians resented their non-inclusion in running the administration of their country, therefore, to pacify them the Charter Act of 1833 included a clause which stated, 'No native of the said territories shall be, by reason only of his religion, place of birth, descent, colour or any of them be disabled from holding any place, office or employment under the Company.' In 1837, an amendment bill allowed the company board to adopt limited competition as the basis for selection. The board of directors used their patronage till 1853. The Macaulay committee was appointed in 1853, which strongly recommended the open competition system for recruitment to the civil services and listed the subjects to be offered in the competitive examination. It also recommended the age of 18–23 years for admission to the tests. The examinations were to be held in London. Consequently, the first examination under the new system for recruitment to the Indian civil service was held in 1855.

The East India Company's rule came to an end in 1858 and the British Crown assumed direct responsibility for the Government of India. The Crown issued a proclamation in 1858 empowering the secretary of the state-in-council to regulate appointments to the Indian civil service; he was to act with the aid and advice of Her Majesty's civil service commissioners. In 1860, the maximum age for admission to the open competition was lowered to 22 years from 23 years; it was again reduced to 21 years in 1864 and in 1878 it was further reduced to 19 years; making it practically difficult for Indians to appear in the said examination at such a lower age at London. In the same year (1878), the secretary of the state ordered that each member of the Covenanted Civil Service would be bound to serve anywhere in India. In this way, these services became all-India services.

The lowering of the age to appear for these examinations at London led to the demand for Indianization of the civil services. As a result in 1886, a commission under the chairmanship of Sir Charles Aitchison, the then lieutenant-governor of Punjab was appointed to suggest ways and means to associate natives in administration. The commission submitted its report in 1888, and recommended that the services should be divided into three categories—imperial services, provincial services and the subordinate services. The recruitment to the first category was to continue, as before, in England; however, recruitment to the other two categories was to be made by the provincial governments, partly on a competitive basis and partly through promotion from the subordinate services. About one-sixth of the posts which were reserved for the members of the covenanted civil services were thrown open to the members of the provincial civil services. It recommended that the age limit be raised to 23 years. The commission did not favour the idea of holding the competitive examination simultaneously in London and India. Further, a detailed review of the civil services in India was made by the Islington Commission (1912–1915), which recommended the amalgamation of the imperial and provincial sections in central departments into a single service divided into two classes, a higher and a lower one. The report was not given any serious consideration and was drastically changed. But, on 20 August 1917 the secretary of state announced in the House of Commons that Her Majesty's government had adopted the policy of 'the increasing association of Indians in every branch of the administration.' The nationalist Indians continuously demanded for greater representation in the civil services and Indianization of administration. Therefore, another commission was appointed under the chairmanship of Montford, which submitted its report in 1918. The report too recommended that the association of Indians in the administration should be increased and the examination should be held simultaneously in England and India. It also laid down that 33 per cent of the higher Indian civil services be filled by the Indians and this should follow an annual increase of one and a half per cent. As regard other services, the same procedure was to be adopted. The report also suggested fair salary, allowances and pension benefits.

The Government of India Act, 1919 decentralized administration by transferring certain subjects to the provinces, placed under popular control, generally known as 'dyarchy'. According to the rules framed under Section 96(B)-2 of the Act of 1919, the all-India services were mixed. These included the Indian Civil Service, the Indian Police Service, the Indian Forest Service, the Indian Educational Service, the Indian Agriculture Service, the Indian Civil Veterinary Service, the Indian Forest Engineering Service, the Indian Medical Service (Civil) and the Indian Service of Engineers.[2] The appointments to these services were made by the secretary of state. The Act provided for the establishment of the public service commission to conduct examinations in India for recruitment to the all-India and central services. The all-India services were ultimately responsible to the Government of India and to the secretary of state. Section 96(B)(1) of the Act had provided that no officer could be 'dismissed from the service by any authority subordinate to that by which he was appointed.' Further, Sections 67A and 72D of the Act laid down that these officers were not be dismissed by any authority in India, their pay, pensions and other emoluments were subject to vote in the legislature. During this period the nationalism movement had picked up momentum and Gandhiji had started the Non-Cooperation Movement in 1920–1922. This movement affected the officers, particularly the Europeans, therefore, they preferred premature retirement and by 1924 about 345 officers of the all-India services had retired. Further, with the transfer of power to the provinces, the propriety of all-India services was questioned. Therefore, the government appointed the Royal Commission on the superior services in India under the chairmanship of Viscount Lee in 1923 to examine the issue of all-India services and other matters such as Indianization of services.

The Lee Commission submitted its report in 1924 and made the following main recommendations:

(1) The commission recommended for the retention of the all-India services, viz., Indian Civil Service, Indian Police Service, irrigation branch of the Indian Service of Engineers, Indian Medical Services, Indian Forest Service (except Mumbai) to which appointments were being made and controlled by the secretary of state.

(2) No further recruitment should be made for provincial governments, particularly in transferred fields, namely, the Indian Education Service, the Indian Agriculture Service (Civil), the Indian Veterinary Service, the Roads and Building Branch of the Indian Service of Engineers and Forest Service in Bombay. The personnel for these services were, further, to be recruited by the provincial governments.

(3) Twenty per cent of the superior posts should be filled by promotion from the provincial services. Direct recruitment should provide equal share to Indians and Europeans so that 50:50 cadre should be created in about 15 years. For the Indian Police Service, direct recruitment was to be made on the basis of 5:3 among Europeans and Indians, respectively, and the remaining 20 per cent to be obtained by promotion from the provincial service. For the Indian Forest Service, it was to be in the ratio of 75 and 25 per cent, respectively, and for irrigation it was to be in an equal ratio of 40 per cent each, with the remaining 20 per cent to be filled by promotion from the provincial service.

(4) The British officers should have the freedom of retirement on proportionate pensions if at any time the department in which they had been employed should be placed under the control of the concerned ministers.

The recommendations of the Lee Commission were accepted by His Majesty's government although the commission did not fully operate in its recommendations the principle that responsibility should be matched by authority. The retention of Indian Medical Service and the Indian Service of Engineers as all-India was clearly in violation of this principle since medical and PWD were provincial subjects. Therefore, a section of Indian public opinion was opposed to the retention of the all-India services. In 1928, the all parties' conference set up a committee under the chairmanship of Motilal Nehru to determine the principles for the Constitution of India. This committee recommended that all-India services should be abolished and separate civil services for the central government and the provinces should be established. Similarly, in 1929, the nationalist members of the Indian central committee constituted by the central government to liaise with the Indian Statutory Commission pressed for provincialization of the services. The retention of all-India services was also opposed by some Indian members of the subcommittee constituted by the first Indian Round Table Conference (1930–1931) to consider the desirability of having all-India services. Dr Ambedkar, along with other two members opposed the further recruitment on all-India basis for Indian civil services and police services as all-India service. He said, 'we are framing a constitution in which we propose to give as large a degree of provincial autonomy to the provinces as possible, and it seems to me that no province can be deemed to have provincial autonomy if it has not the right to regulate the service that is going to work in its area.' Thus during the period of dyarchy, the Indian sentiment was continuously expressing itself against the continuance of all-India services.

With the growing demand by Indians for more responsible government, the British government constituted the joint committee on Indian Constitutional Reform (1933–1934) to frame a new constitution for India. However, this committee did not accept the view of the Indian nationalists that the all-India services were incompatible with the concept of provincial autonomy and, therefore, should be abolished. The committee felt that it was necessary to ensure the supply of British and Indian officers of high quality for running the administration of the central as well as the provincial governments. The all-India services recruited and controlled by the secretary of state were precisely performing this function. The committee thought that especially during the initial period of the operation of the new Constitution, it is necessary to continue the Indian civil service and the Indian police, the two 'scanty' services. The committee also recommended the continuance of the Indian Medical Service (civil) in deference to the British officers in that service and to provide the services of European doctors to the European members of other services. These recommendations of the committee were accepted and incorporated in the new Constitution of India. Therefore, Section 244 of the Government of India Act, 1935 listed only three all-India services. These were: (i) the Indian Civil Service; (ii) the Indian Police Service; and (iii) the Indian Medical Service (civil). The Act also provided for the establishment of a federal public service commission, provincial commissions and a common commission for two or more provinces. The protection given earlier to the civil servants was also continued by the Act.

The political opinion in India was against the continuation of all-India services. However, the Muslims were divided. The Muslims of the provinces, where they were in minority, favoured the existence of all-India services because it had a British element with which they felt safe. But in the Muslim majority provinces of Punjab, Sindh and Bengal the general opinion was against the all-India services which were not under complete control of the provincial governments. The Muslims there felt that an all-India service means domination by Hindus, therefore, they were against the provincial autonomy granted to them under the Government of India Act, 1935.

The question of having all-India services again came to the forefront when in 1946, independence of the country appeared to be in sight, as the interim government was formed in 1946 under the prime ministership of Jawaharlal Nehru and Sardar Vallabh Bhai Patel became the home minister. The question became urgent because the secretary of states for India had stopped recruitment to the ICS and IPS during war time. Even after the end of the war, the recruitment could not be resumed due to the changes taking place at that time. To choose the administrative system the then home minister, Sardar Vallabh Bhai Patel convened a conference of provincial premiers on 20 and 21 October 1946, in which all the provincial premiers were invited to attend the conference, but the non-Congress-ruled states sent ministers and civil servants only. The Congress-ruled states were represented by their premiers like Govind Ballabh Pant of UP, B. G. Kher of Mumbai and Ravi Shankar Shukla of Central Provinces. Sardar Patel expressed favour of setting up of all-India services. He pleaded that all-India services would facilitate liaison between the centre and the provinces, ensure uniform standards of administration and keep the central administration in touch with realities. He further said that the provincial administration would also be benefited by the wider outlook and the experience of the officers of all-India services. The reaction of the provinces was mixed. The Central Provinces, Bombay and Orissa supported the proposal, to set up all-India services, while Assam wanted adequate control of the provinces and a large intake of the local people in the all-India services. Uttar Pradesh agreed with the proposal with some reservations and Pant suggested that the provincial governments should have full control over these services and the centre should be restricted up to recruitment and training only. Bengal, Punjab and Sindh were Muslim majority provinces; they feared that all-India services will perpetuate the control by the Hindu majority central government over the Muslim majority provinces. Therefore, they opposed the creation of all-India services and preferred full provincialization of the civil services. But the persuasive power of Patel, the 'Iron Man of India', prevailed and he summed up by expressing a general feeling in favour of the formation of all-India services. The conference also discussed the method of recruitment and training. It recommended a combined competitive examination for the proposed all-India services and the Indian Foreign Service. The states were to be free to work out the number of posts for which the all-India services officers were required and to fix the cadre strength. The quota for promotion from the provincial civil service was proposed to be 25 per cent of the superior posts. The states were also to be free to select and devise rules for selection against the provincial services quota in consultation with the Union public service commission. The allotment of officers from the all-India services to different provinces was to be made in consultation with the concerned provincial governments. The states were free to award minor punishment to all-India service officers in consultation with the UPSC. In the end a 'consensus' of provincial premiers conference was reached for having the services for the first five years. But with the partition of the country, the way was cleared for the acceptance of all-India services by all the states. The recommendations of this conference were incorporated in the Constitution prepared by the constituent assembly.

Constitutional Base

The drafting committee of the Indian constituent assembly did not originally provide a constitutional base to the setting up of all-India services. It was felt that instead of constitutional provisions they should be regulated by Acts of the appropriate legislatures. However, Sardar Patel insisted for a constitutional provision to give civil services a strong and lasting basis. While the Acts of legislature can easily be amended, the Constitution may not be easily altered. Accordingly, the draft was amended and a new Article 282(C) was inserted providing for all-India services. The Constitution contained a provision for the setting up of all-India services under Article 312.

The public services in India are presently classified as follows:

1. The all-India services
2. The central services, classes I and II, III and IV
3. The central secretariat services classes I, II, III and IV
4. The state services

All-India Services

After Independence, a new Constitution was prepared for the country, which contains provisions for the creation of new all-India services. Articles 309–314 of the Constitution of India deal with the services under the Union and the states. Article 312 needs special mention which reads:

(1) Notwithstanding anything contained in Part XI, if the council of states has declared by resolution supported by not less than two-thirds of the members present and voting that it is necessary or expedient in the national interest to do so, Parliament may, by law provide for the creation of one or more all-India services common to the Union and the states, and subject to the other provisions of this chapter, regulate the recruitment, and the conditions of service of persons appointed to any service.

(2) The services known at the commencement of this Constitution as the All-India Administrative Service and the Indian Police Service shall be deemed to be services created by Parliament under this Article.

The Need for All-India Services

In a federation, the central and constituent state governments have usually separate services for the administration of subjects falling in their respective spheres of jurisdiction. The creation of all-India services in our country is something peculiar. The arguments given in favour of all-India services are:

(1) They help in attaining minimum standards throughout the country.

(2) The members of all-India services have an all-India outlook which helps in promoting national integration and unity of India by combating the parochial attitude of the state. Normally, the officers belonging to these services are posted outside the states they hail from, hence, are less susceptible to local and regional pressures than officers from within the state.

(3) These services attract better qualified and brilliant persons because of higher remuneration, status and prestige as compared to the state services.

(4) They being common to both the Union and state governments facilitate liaison and work as a link between the two.

(5) The members of all-India services hold key positions in the states and render independent advice to the ministers, which the officers from state services would, to a large extent, hesitate to do.

(6) When a state is under president's rule due to failure of constitutional machinery, the officers would carry out the president's policies more effectively and efficiently because they are under the direct control of the centre.

A close examination of the above arguments shows that in practice they do not stand as correct. The arguments that the members of the all-India service have an all-India outlook are neither based on facts nor on logic. The broad outlook is a cultural trait which not only the members of all-India services but many good citizens of the country are also having. Experience shows that the members of Indian administrative service are very conscious of their separate identity and mostly write IAS after their name to show their distinct class. They are very conscious of their status and privileges and resist sharing their privileged position with the members of other services which has caused the generalist versus specialist controversy in our administrative system.

The argument that all-India services promote the unity and integrity of the country by combating parochial attitude because the officers of these services are posted in different states than their own and they will be above local and regional influences does not hold true because in many cases, most of the officers are posted to their own states because they opted for it. A few officers hailing from other states do not meet the objective of the national unity and integration. Moreover, the 33 per cent of officers who are promoted from the state services to all-India services have to serve in their own state. There is no sufficient evidence to prove that officers of state civil service are more susceptible to the political pressures and influence of the political leaders of their state. The officers hailing from other states can as well be susceptible to this kind of political influences. In practice a large number of members of all-India services have aligned themselves with different political parties and pressure groups. It is a fact that cliques, caste, community, provincialism and parochialism play a considerable role in the actual administration run by the bureaucrats of the all-India service. Otherwise, how do we explain large-scale mass transfers of members of these services whenever political power changed hands. The recent mass transfers by Mayawati government in UP can be cited to prove this point.

The argument that officers of all-India services are talented because they are recruited on an all-India basis, they enjoy high remuneration, status and prestige is not valid. It is too much to presume that the best produce of the universities get into the all-India services only, the intellectual calibre of those competing for state services cannot *ipso facto* be taken as 'inferior'. Lastly, the argument that by virtue of holding the key posts in the states the members of all-India services can give independent advice to the state ministers, which the officers of state services would hesitate to do, is again not based on any factual data but is only an impression. The quality of officers to be able to give honest and objective opinion without hesitation to a political master cannot be said to be the monopoly of a particular service.[3]

The other criticism of all-India services are that services are legacies of British rule and ought to have no place after Independence, violates the spirit of federation and curtails the autonomy of states. Lack of knowledge of the language of the state makes the officer an ineffective administrator. The IAS officers' loyalty is to the centre and not to the state of their cadre and higher pay scale of the all-India services breeds discontentment in state services.

From the above analysis it is clear that the all-India services have lost their esteem in public eyes. The politicization of these services and politician-bureaucrat nexus and the idea of 'committed bureaucracy' have put a question mark on the vitality and utility of these services. With the rise of regional political parties in power in many states, the issue of centre-state relations is getting hotter day by day and now that the country is faced wih the problem of national integration for which these services were mainly retained, it may be useful to have a national debate to review the institution of all-India services. It may be mentioned that the Sarkaria commission which examined the problem of centre-state relations has favoured the retention of the all-India services and emphasized the need for creation of more all-India services.[4]

Legal Framework

Article 312 of the Constitution provides for setting up of all-India services, but the details of their recruitment, condition of service, etc. were to be laid down by a parliamentary legislation. So, the All-India Services Act, 1951 was passed by the Parliament on 15 October 1951. This Act, as amended from time to time, regulates the recruitment and service conditions for the personnel in all-India services. This empowers the central government to make rules in consultation with the state governments, to achieve the purposes of the Act. In practice, most of the state governments do not even respond to the communications of the central government on the issue. Legally speaking, the Government of India may make rules even if opposed by all the state governments.

At the time of Independence, there were only two all-India services. These were the Indian Administrative Service and the Indian Police Service. Later, the Indian Forest Service was also constituted in July 1966. There were proposals to constitute other all-India services also, but the state governments opposed their implementation. The rules relating to these services are of four types. There are some rules which are common to all the all-India services, whereas there are separate rules for the IAS; the Indian Police Service and the Indian Forest Service. Some of the important rules are as follows:

(i) The All India Services (Conduct) Rules, 1968

(ii) The All India Services (Discipline and Appeal) Rules, 1969

(iii) The All India Services (Confidential Rolls) Rules, 1970

These three are very important rules to govern the conduct and discipline of the All India Services. Then there are a large number of rules to regulate various other service conditions of the personnel of these services; namely, All India Services (Leave) Rules, 1955, the All India Services (Medical Attendance) Rules, 1954; the All India Service (Travel Allowance) Rules, 1954, etc.

Recruitment

The basic policy of recruitment to civil services was laid down in the 'Report on the Indian Civil Services' by Thomas Babington Macaulay in the year 1854. The spirit of this report dominated the system of public services recruitment in India. The only amendment in the policy was brought out in 1970 on the basis of Kothari committee report. This committee, it seems, has revised and updated the Macaulay report.

The direct recruitment to the Indian Administrative Service and the Indian Police Service is made through a competitive examination held annually by the Union Public Service Commission. Any citizen of India holding a graduate degree of any of the universities established by law in India or other educational institutions established by an Act of Parliament or a deemed university declared under Section 3 of the University Grants Commission Act of 1956 possess an equivalent qualification can appear in the examination. The age limit to appear in the examination is 21 to 28 years, and four attempts are allowed to each candidate to sit in the examination. In the case of candidates belonging to scheduled castes and scheduled tribes the age relaxation is up to a maximum of five years and there is no limit of attempts for examination for SC and ST candidates while other backward class candidates have been given seven chances to appear in the examination.

The recruitment prior to June 1979 examination was made through a single competitive examination which was at that time called the IAS and Allied Services Examination. At that time, the candidates for the IPS had a lower minimum age limit and had to appear in a less number of subjects. The number of candidates appearing in the exam was very large, which was proving to be unmanageable.

There had been lot of dissatisfaction with the above method of recruitment. Therefore, the Union Public Service Commission set up a committee under the chairmanship of D. S. Kothari in 1975 to suggest changes in the method of recruitment. The committee submitted its report in 1976 and made the following important recommendations.

(i) There should be a preliminary test to weed out the, non-serious and unsuitable candidates. It should consist of two papers of objective questions, namely, general studies and an optional subject.

(ii) There should be a common competitive examination for the all-India services as well as the central services examination. All candidates should appear in the same number of subjects and same marks allotted in the written examination as well as personality test.

(iii) After the preliminary examination, in the main examination, there should be two compulsory but qualifying papers of English and one Indian language. In addition there should be two papers of general studies and two papers each for two optional subjects. The list of optional subjects was to be broad based to give equal opportunity to students of humanities, science and technology.

The recommendations of the Kothari committee have been implemented with minor modifications since 1979.

Again in 1988, a committee under the chairmanship of Satish Chandra was appointed by the UPSC to recommend possible changes in the civil services examination. The committee submitted its report in August 1989. The following recommendations were accepted:

(i) The present system of holding a common competitive examination for civil services should be continued.

(ii) An essay paper carrying 200 marks to be re-introduced in the scheme (which was deleted due to Kothari committee recommendations) of the examination from 1993 and the candidates to be allowed to answer this paper in English or in any one of the languages included in the Eighth Schedule of the Constitution.

(iii) The marks of the personality test to be increased from 250 to 300 from 1993 examination. Thus with the introduction of an essay paper, the total marks for the written examination and personality test would be raised up to 2300, in the civil service (main) examination.

(iv) Medical services to be included as an optional subject from 1994 both for the preliminary and the main examination.

(v) The syllabi of the optional subjects for the examination has to be spelt out comprehensively and steps taken to periodically revise the syllabi of various subjects included for the optional papers.

Some other less important recommendations of the committee were not accepted such as group discussion, negative marking for objective type test, exception to the candidates from preliminary examination who once qualified for interview, age limit up to 26 years and introduction of education and electronics and communications as optional subjects, etc.

The medical science was included as a subject from the year 1994 examination. The enhancement of marks for personality test and introduction of essay paper are likely to make a better judgement of a candidate's level of articulation and leadership qualities essential for good administration.

The Scheme of Competitive Examination

The recruitment to the Indian Administrative Service, IFS, Indian Police Service and Central Services Group A is through a common examination conducted in two stages: (i) preliminary examination and (ii) main examination.

The preliminary examination consists of two papers of objective type (multiple choice questions) of maximum 450 marks. The question papers are set both in English and Hindi. Each paper will be of two hours' duration. Its standard would be of degree level. The two papers are (i) general studies of 150 marks and, (ii) one subject of 300 marks to be selected from the list of optional papers. The optional subjects are: agriculture, animal husbandry and veterinary science, botany, chemistry, civil engineering, commerce, economics, electrical engineering, geography, geology, Indian history, law, mathematics, mechanical engineering, medical science, philosophy, physics, political science, psychology, public administration, sociology, statistics and zoology.

The purpose of preliminary examination is to weed out candidates who are not serious and are incompetent for the main examination. It is a device to make the main examination manageable and meaningful. Now more than two lakh candidates apply for the civil services. In the year 1991, 3,32,343 candidates applied; in 1993, 2,15,034 candidates applied and in the year 1994, 2,56,651 candidates[5] applied for the civil services examination. Therefore, it is good to weed out the undeserving from the main examination. The screening test is only of an objective type to easily identify those who have the talent for the main examination.

The main examination consists of two parts: a written examination and an interview. The written examination consists of the nine papers of 300 marks each, except one essay paper which is of 200 marks. The papers are shown as follows in Table 16.1:

Table 16.1 *Papers of the written examination for civil services*

Paper I	One of the Indian languages to be selected from the languages included in the Eighth Schedule of the Constitution	300 marks
Paper II	English	300 marks
Paper III	Essay	200 marks
Paper IV and V	General studies	300 marks for each paper
Papers VI, VII, VIII	Any two subjects to be selected from the list of optional subjects. Each subject will have two papers	300 marks for each paper
Finally	Interview test will be of 300 marks	

The papers on Indian languages and English are of matriculation or equivalent standard and are of qualifying nature; the marks obtained 'in these papers are not counted for ranking'. Thus, the examination and interview together would consist of 2300 marks in total.

The papers on general studies and optional subjects of only such candidates are evaluated who attain such minimum standard as may be fixed by the commission in their discretion for the qualifying papers on Indian languages and English.

The optional subjects for the main examination include three more papers in addition to the optional papers mentioned for preliminary examination above. These three additional subjects are: anthropology, management and literature of one of the following languages—Arabic, Assamese, Bengali, Chinese, English, French, German, Gujarati, Hindi, Kannada, Kashmiri, Marathi, Malayalam, Oriya, Pali, Persian, Punjabi, Russian, Sanskrit, Sindhi, Tamil, Telugu and Urdu. Public administration as a separate subject was included as a full subject at the preliminary test and the main examination in 1987 only. The candidates are not allowed to offer the following combination of subjects:

(a) Political science and international relation and public administration
(b) Commerce and accountancy and management
(c) Anthropology and sociology
(d) Mathematics and animal husbandry and veterinary science
(e) Agriculture and animal husbandry and veterinary science
(f) Management and public administration
(g) Of the engineering subjects, viz., civil, electrical and mechanical not more than one subject
(h) Animal husbandry and veterinary science and medical science

The question papers for the examination are of conventional (essay) type. Each paper is of three hours' duration. Candidates have the option to answer all the questions except, the language papers in any of the languages included in the Eighth Schedule of the Constitution or in English. The question papers are set both in English and Hindi and the Commission has the discretion to fix the qualifying marks in any or all the subjects of the examination.

The number of candidates to be admitted for the main examination is about 10 times more than the total number of posts to be filled. Those candidates who obtain the minimum marks as are fixed by the UPSC in the preliminary examination are allowed to appear at the main examination.

The candidate who obtains such minimum qualifying marks in the main examination as may be fixed by the commission at their discretion are called for an interview and for a personal test. The number of candidates to be summoned for interview will be about thrice the number of vacancies to be filled. The interview carries 300 marks (with no minimum qualifying marks). The candidates are interviewed by a board which will have before it a record of his career. He will be asked questions on matters of general interest. The object of the interview is to assess the personal suitability of the candidate for a career in public service by a board of competent and unbiased observers. The test is intended to judge the mental calibre of a candidate. In broad terms this is really an assessment of not only his intellectual qualities but also social traits and his interest in current affairs. Some of the qualities to be judged are mental alertness, critical powers of assimilation, clear and logical exposition, balance of judgment, variety and depth of interest, ability for social cohesion and leadership, intellectual and moral integrity. The technique of the interview is not that of a strict cross-examination but of a natural though directed and purposive conversation which is intended to reveal the mental qualities of the candidate. Candidates are expected to have an intelligent interest not only in their special subjects or academic study but also in the events which are happening around them both within and outside their own state or country as well as in modern current of thought and in new discoveries which should rouse the curiosity of well-educated youth.

After the interviews are over, the rank-order list is prepared on the basis of total marks obtained by the candidates in the main examination and the interview. The allocation of candidates to different services is made on the basis of their rank in the examination and the preference expressed by them for various services and posts. The list is submitted by the UPSC to the Government of India, Department of Personnel, for further necessary action.

Under the present system of examination some trends are emerging now. The first is the domination of candidates of arts or social sciences subjects, particularly those who opted for history and law has diminished and the present system gives equal emphasis to science, technology and medical subjects. As a result, a large number of candidates from science, medical and engineering subjects are entering the service. For example, in 1993 out of the total number of 790 candidates who entered into the services, 219 were engineering graduates and 42 were medical graduates,[6] in addition to a large number of science graduates. Second, the representation of many states is very negligible, rather almost nil. The 10 universities which took the lion's share in providing candidates to these services in 1993 were Delhi, Allahabad, Patna, Jaipur, Lucknow, JNU, New Delhi and Chandigarh.[7] It appears that persons from Gujarat and Maharashtra prefer other professions or services as not many of them are represented in the services. Likewise, representation of states like Himachal Pradesh, Jammu and Kashmir and the north eastern states is also limited. Thus, the backward states as well as developed states appear to remain out of the services for different reasons. Third, a large number of universities are not sending any candidate. The concerned states need to improve their educational institutions. Lastly, the IAS is still a most wanted service and every year a large number of candidates selected for other services compete for Indian Administrative Service. A separate open competitive examination is organized by the UPSC for the Indian Forest Service (IFS) due to the requirement of knowledge of specialized subjects.

Recruitment Through Promotion

The all-India services including the IAS have a quota of promotion from state services. In the beginning this quota was 25 per cent but on the persistent demands of the states the quota has been increased up to 33.13 per cent. The UPSC is consulted by the Government of India in addition to the state governments for filling up the promotion posts. The state officers still feel that the promotion opportunities for them are very limited and they have to wait for a very long period near about 25 years for getting promoted to the all-India services. As regards recruitment from the state service, the ARC Report on Personnel Administration (1969), recommended that 'there should be a provision for recruitment of state government personnel for posts in the central government. The all-India services, the members of which are interchangeable between the two levels of government, should provide for a larger measure of intake by way of promotion from the ranks of the state level civil services, thus, broadening the area of interchangeability.' Further, the commission suggested that the quota for promotion from class II services to class I be increased to 40 percent.[8] However, those who favour direct recruitment say that the promotees do not have the same calibre and initiative as the direct recruits in spite of a very long experience in the state service before their promotion.

Central Civil Services

The central civil services are under the exclusive control of the central government and are recruited to administer the subjects allocated to the Union government under the Constitution of India. The central civil service is organized into four classes or groups, according to the difference in the responsibility of the work performed and qualifications required. Generally, such classification is done on the basis of pay scales attached to these posts. These four groups are as follows:

Class I—This group comprises posts carrying high responsibility and pay above a certain range as determined by the pay commissions.

Class II—This group comprises posts of middle level supervisory officers who are often required to perform various functions directly. Their pay is also determined by pay commissions.

Class III—This group comprises generally clerical posts. This classification is also based on pay scales determined by the pay commission.

Class IV—This class includes the persons who perform lesser functions such as messengers, peons, *daftaries*, *jamadars*, cyclostyling, etc. The lower category staff objected to the classification of class III and class IV due to psychological reasons. The various categories of services have, therefore, been renamed as Group A, Group B, Group C, and Group D services which, respectively, correspond to Class I, Class II, Class III and Class IV.

However, when we refer to the term central services, we generally include Group A and B cadres only. This is due to the fact that most of the responsible functions are performed by Group A and B officers while Group C and D personnel perform routine and lesser functions. Recruitment to the central services in Group A and B would be discussed here.

The central civil services Class I includes services such as Archaeological Science, Botanical Survey of India; Central Engineering Service; Central Electrical Engineering Service; Central Health Service; Central Water Engineering Service; Central Revenues Chemical Service; Central Secretariat Service; General Central Service; Geological Survey of India; Indian Audit and Accounts Service; Indian Defence Accounts Service; Indian Foreign Service; Indian Meteorological Service; Indian Postal Service; Indian Posts and Telegraphs Traffic Service; Indian Revenue Service; Indian State Service; Mercantile Marine Training Ship Service; Mines Department; Overseas Communication Service; Survey of India; Telegraph Engineering Service; Zoological Survey of India; Central Legal Service; Railway Inspectorate Service; Indian Foreign Service Branch B; Indian Inspection Service; Indian Supply Service; Central Information Service; Indian Statistical Service; Indian Economic Service; Telegraph Traffic Service and Railway Personnel Service.

The central civil service Class II are the Botanical Survey of India, Class II; Central Electrical Engineering Service, Class II; Central Secretariat Service, section officers grade; Central Secretariat Service, Grade IV; Central Secretariat Stenographer's Service, Grade I; Central Secretariat Stenographer's Service (combined), Central Engineering Service Central Health Service, Class II; Indian Meteorological Service, Labour Officers Service, Class II; Postal Superintendents Service, Class II; Post Master's Service; Central Excise Service, Class II; Customs Appraisees Service, Customs Preventive Service, Class II, Chief Inspectors; Customs Appraisees Service, Class II, Customs Preventive Service, Class II Inspectors; Income Tax Service, Class II, Telegraph Engineering and Wireless Service, Class II; Telegraph Traffic Service, Class II; General Central Service, Class II; Indian Salt Service, Class II; Survey of India, Class II; Geological Survey of India, Class II; Zoological Survey of India, Class II. Thus, there are 34 Class I and 25 Class II central civil services.

Recruitment

The recruitment to the central services Class I and II (Grade A and B) is made by the Union public service commission. Recruitment to Group C (Class III) is made by the staff selection commission. The UPSC holds common examination for the following first three all-India services and 17 central civil services Class A and nine central services Class 'B':

1. Indian Administrative Service
2. Indian Police Service
3. Indian Forest Service
4. Indian Foreign Service (though it belongs to the Central Services, this comes next to the IAS in ranking and is superior to the IPS as regards scale of pay)
5. Indian P and T Accounts and Finance Service, Group A
6. Indian Audit and Central Excise Service, Group A
7. Indian Customs and Central Excise Service, Group A
8. Indian Defence Accounts Service, Group A
9. Indian Revenue Service, Group A
10. Indian Ordnance Factories Service, Group A (assistant manager non technical)
11. Indian Postal Service, Group A
12. Indian Civil Accounts Service, Group A
13. Indian Railway Traffic Service, Group A
14. Indian Railway Accounts Service, Group A
15. Indian Railway Personnel Service, Group A
16. Posts of assistant security officer, Group A in Railway Protection Force
17. Indian Defence Estates Service, Group A
18. Indian Information Service (junior grade), Group A
19. Indian Trade Service, Group-A (Grade-III)
20. Posts of assistant commandant, Group A in Central Industrial Security Force
21. Central Secretariat Service, Group B (section officer grade)
22. Railway Board Secretariat Service, Group B (section officer grade)
23. Armed Forces Headquarters Civil Service, Group B (assistant civilian staff officer grade)
24. Customs Appraisers' Service, Group B
25. Delhi and Andaman and Nicobar Islands, Lakshadweep, Daman and Diu and Dadra and Nagar Haveli civil service, Group B
26. Delhi and Andaman and Nicobar Islands, Lakshadweep Daman and Diu and Dadra and Nagar Haveli police service, Group B
27. Posts of deputy superintendent of police in the Central Bureau of Investigation, Group B
28. Pondicherry civil service, Group B
29. Pondicherry police service, Group B

For the other central civil services like Archaeological Service, Central Health Service, Central Engineering Service, Indian Meteorological Service, Survey of India Service, etc. the UPSC conducts separate written examination or interview or both.

Besides the above examination, the UPSC also conducts several other examinations for individual services like Indian Forest Service, Indian Economic Service, Indian Statistical Service, Special Class Railway Apprentices, National Defence Academy examination, etc. The UPSC decides which method of examination is most suitable for the type of services for which the number of candidates is large. Usually a written examination is held, but where there are only a few qualified candidates available, only an interview is held.

On the basis of the merit list prepared by the UPSC and on the basis of the preference given by individual candidates, the successful candidates are allotted to different services. Before giving them an appointment the central government conducts a medical examination as well as the police verification. If a successful candidate is medically found fit and does not have a criminal or adverse political record he is appointed to the particular service to which he has been allotted.

Central Secretariat Service

The old name Imperial Secretariat was changed in 1948 and the service was named Central Secretariat Service. The service is organized on the following lines:

1. Selection grade — Joint secretary/Director/Deputy secretary
2. Grade I — Under secretary or equivalent
3. Section officer's grade
4. Assistant grade

The appointment to the selection grade is made by promotion on the basis of merit from amongst the permanent officers of Grade I having five years' service. A merit list is prepared for the purpose of promotion from which appointments are made as and when vacancies arise. Likewise, appointments to Grade I are made by promotion from amongst the section officers having at least 10 years' experience in that grade on the basis of merit. The appointments to the section officer's grade are usually made on the basis of one-third of the vacant posts by direct recruitment and the remaining by promoting the assistants already serving in the central secretariat on the basis of eight years' service and the departmental competitive examination. Assistants are appointed through direct recruitment, by an examination conducted by the staff selection commission and partly by/through promotion in the ratio of 3:1. The examination for recruitment of section officers is conducted by the UPSC.

Management of Central Services

The central services are performing some functions required in different ministries and departments. Therefore, management of these services is also vested in these ministries and departments. Thus, the Indian Foreign Service is managed by the Ministry of External Affairs, the Indian Revenue Service by the Ministry of Finance, the Indian Defence Accounts Service by the Ministry of Defence, and so on. The Class III and IV services are managed departmentally. The ministries maintain these cadres on the basis of departmental recruitment and promotion rules framed by them in consultation with the department of personnel. The departments are free to frame the departmental rules; they have to work under the guidance of the department of personnel which tries to maintain an overall uniformity in them. Generally, the recruitment rules provide for the method of recruitment as well as of promotion. For every promotion, a departmental promotion committee is constituted which for higher levels is presided over by a member of the UPSC. Promotions to senior posts are made on the basis of merit-cum-seniority.

Discipline and Control

The officers in any ministry work under the discipline and control of the minister. They are subject to the Central Government Servants (Conduct) Rules. These rules have prescribed a code of conduct for all the central Government employees. Any breach of conduct of these rules is liable to disciplinary action under the Central Government Servants (Discipline and Appeal) Rules. These rules have been framed in accordance with Article 311 of the Constitution. As per Article 311, no government servant can be removed or dismissed from the service by an authority subordinate to the appointing authority. Thus, Group A officers can be dismissed only by the president by whom they have been appointed (details are given in Chapter 17, Constitutional Protection to Civil Servants in India). However, powers have been delegated to award minor penalties to the central government servants. The Union public service commission is also consulted for all matters connected with disciplinary proceedings.

Some Important Issues

The rules in respect of recruitment to services such as Indian Income Tax, Indian Audit and Accounts, Indian Railway Traffic, etc. are well defined, but there are many services for which seniority and gradation list rules are not maintained and seniority of officers promoted from lower grades to B and Grade A often remains undecided particularly in the departments where officers are divided into a number of functional areas.

The promotion in any service is essential to determine morale of service. But the promotion prospects of central services are having large difference from service to service. In some services, the newly recruited ones do not get promotion for 10–15 years. This has a very adverse effect on their morale. Therefore, a satisfactory solution of the problem is required.

The other important complaint of the central services officers is that they have not been given secretariat posts in sufficient number. Generally, a large number of these posts are manned by officers of the central secretariat service or the Indian Administrative Service. The officers of central secretariat services complain that they should be given equal opportunity along with IAS and other services to compete for manning the secretariat posts/jobs. The arguments in favour of all-India service officers have already been discussed. They bring state level and district level field experience to the central secretariat, and take back the central secretariat experience to the state. The ARC has recommended the functional posts in the central secretariat should be manned by the officers belonging to the functional services. Therefore, to solve this problem, some balance has to be maintained between the central services and the all-India services in the matter of manning the secretariat posts.

Cadre Management

The cadre of the Indian Administrative Service is managed by the Department of Personnel and Training, the cadre of Indian Police Service is managed by the Ministry of Home Affairs and that of Indian Forest Service is managed by the Ministry of Environment and Forest. Usually the basis for fixing the cadre strength is the need for senior duty posts to which are added the central deputation reserves, leave reserves, state promotion quota, etc. The cadre strength is fixed by the central government in consultation with the state government and revised every three years. There are also a number of non-cadre posts which are also occupied by the officers of all-India services. In the states, general administration department or department of personnel control the state cadres of the all-India service.

State Services

The state services include those services and posts which are concerned with the administration of state subjects such as agriculture, education, forest, health, planning, police, etc. The recruitment to and service conditions of these services are regulated by rules under the Act which may be adopted by the state legislature. In the absence of legislation, the governor has been empowered to issue rules and regulations for the said purposes. The total services are manned by the local authorities.

The Indian Administrative Service and Indian Police Service as well as the state services occupy the higher posts in the state administration. Commissioners, secretaries, chief secretary, etc., are generally held by IAS officers, while in the police administration, the posts of superintendents of police, senior superintendents of police, DIGs and inspectors-general of police are occupied by IPS officers. The IAS and other officers work under the administrative control of the state in which they serve. The central government, in consultation with the concerned state, frames rules to regulate the service conditions of these personnel.

In the words of U. C. Agarwal, 'Generally, higher level appointments are becoming coterminous with a political party or persons in power who make such appointments. Nearly every change of political guard leads to a large reshuffle of top officials in most states. In fact, the political identification of officials is becoming so marked that even the bureaucracy itself is able to predict as to who among the officials in different services will occupy which top posts if 'X', 'Y' or 'Z' political party or individuals come to power. Although in the states most such reshuffles concern senior IAS and IPS officers, sometimes even technical officers heading the PWD or electricity boards or organizations like irrigation, forest, excise and mining are also not spared. Generally, the more honest, straightforward and rule-abiding officers figure in the hit lists unless any of them is able to muster support for survival.'[9] To correct it, we must keep civil services above politics. In the State of Haryana, a former deputy commissioner who was to retire on 30 September 1991 had sought voluntary retirement on 10 July in protest against mass transfer orders by the chief minister. On showing his inability to take up his new assignment, the state government suspended him on the charge of indiscipline. In a strongly worded letter, he said that politicians asserted their authority, sometimes extra-constitutional and quite often illegal, to bully the services into submission by harassing those who had been independent and fearless in their approach and win over those who collaborated by conferring favours on them. The present chief minister excelled in this game. Even senior officers failed to protect their subordinates from politicians given to intrigue and manipulation. He observed that the mass transfers by the Haryana government had defied all logic and the number of transfers was unprecedented.[10]

The state services have been classified into Class I, Class II, Class III and Class IV, based on work and qualifications. Members of Class I and Class II services are gazetted officers. Class III consists of clerical staff and Class IV comprises peons, *daftaries*, messengers, etc. The services are declared in official gazette notification. The appointments, leaves and transfers of the gazetted officers are notified in the gazette. The state normally has the following services:

1. State civil (for administrative) service—the former Provincial Civil Service (PCS)
2. Police service
3. Judicial service
4. Cooperative service
5. Educational service
6. Forest service
7. Medical service
8. Public health service
9. Agriculture service
10. Veterinary service
11. Service of engineers

As regard greater prestige and prospects, the administrative service or executive service like the IAS is considered to be the dominating one. The position is the same in the case of state police service. Both provide sufficient scope for promotion as the officers of the PCS and the state police service, under a certain quota to get promotion to the IAS and IPS cadres, respectively. Usually, each departmental service is a Class I cadre but it is not necessary that there should be uniformity in the pay scales. These posts are filled by both promotion and direct recruitment. So far as promotion is concerned, officers of Class I are promoted to Class I on the basis of their seniority. The state public service commission conducts open competitive examinations, followed by interviews for direct recruitment purposes.

Class II posts have lower status and responsibility than those of Class I services. Such posts exist in all the departments of a specialized nature. Again, as in the Class I service, there is no uniformity in the pay scales. Better pay scales are provided for some services, viz., medical, engineering, health, etc., than for those of education, development, etc. Recruitment to Class II posts is made through direct recruitment and by promotion amongst the Class III employees. The state public service commission holds open competitive examinations for filling up Class II posts of the general administration, judicial and police services. For other posts of a specialized nature, the commission makes selections on the basis of interviews. In the states of Maharashtra, Karnataka, Gujarat and West Bengal, the ratio of 50:50 for promotion and direct recruitment has been prescribed while it is 65:35 in Orissa.

Each department has Class HI services. For instance in the education department, there are the headmasters of high schools, masters, language teachers and JBT teachers, who have been placed in Class III, this category also includes the clerical staff. Recruitment to the posts is made either by departmental recruitment committees or by the state subordinate services selection board. In Haryana, recruitment to Class III posts is made through competitive examinations, interviews and temporary appointments made at local level. The ministerial services consist of clerks, cashiers, accountants, accounts clerks, store clerks, junior auditors, head clerks, head assistants, deputy superintendents, superintendents, private secretaries, etc. The posts are filled by promoting government servants holding ministerial posts and through direct recruitment, the Haryana subordinate services selection board conducts competitive examinations. Recruitment to the posts of *patwaris* is made from amongst those who qualify in the *patwar* examination, after having completed one year's *patwari* training. The candidates also undergo six months' field training and are then appointed as *patwaris*. As regard the posts of *naib tehsildars*, 50 per cent of the posts are filled through direct recruitment and 50 per cent by promoting the *kanungos*. The posts of *tehsildars* are filled both from within and from outside. Direct recruitment is made for 40 per cent of the posts by the public service commission, while 40 per cent of the posts are filled by promotion. Promotion is given to those *naib tehsildars*, who have completed two years' service. The remaining 20 per cent of the posts are for those eligible officials who have a revenue background. Generally, the clerical staff is recruited by the heads of departments. Some of the posts are also filled through promotion from Class TV to Class III in the clerical cadre. Class IV services are at the lowest rung and recruitment to these is in the hands of district as well as local officers. So, class IV employees such as peons, sweepers, *chowkidars*, carpenters, cooks, *daftaries*, binders, laboratory attendants, etc., are directly appointed on either regular or ad hoc basis through the state employment exchanges.

Management of State Services

The state civil services are formed in different departments having their own hierarchies of promotion. These services are managed by ministers assisted by the concerned department of their secretariat. Ministries frame rules for the recruitment and promotion of various cadres and classes of service serving in their department. The general administration department or department of personnel maintains uniformity in the service conditions and pay scales of different departments. The general administration department in the state performs the same functions which the department of personnel performs in Government of India. All the rules such as recruitment, promotion, deputation, etc., framed by any department have to receive the concurrence of general administration department (GAD). Thus, the general principles for the management of the state services are laid down and supervized by the GADs. The details are worked out by the concerned departments according to their needs. Each department of the government maintains several cadres of services depending upon the functions performed by the department. The strength of each category of officers is fixed in consultation with the GAD and the finance department. The other conditions of service and pay scales are laid down by the general rules framed by the GAD and the finance department.

Some Issues for Attention

After discussion of recruitment procedure, promotions, cadre management, etc. we would like to discuss some of the issues which concern these services and create tensions in the minds of the personnel of these services. These issues concern recruitment.

In the states for many services recruitment rules are not framed and appointment for these services as well as promotions is done on ad-hoc basis. This results in poor cadre management and ultimately a low morale in state government services. Sometimes, ad-hoc appointments are made because the state public service commission could not make recruitment in time. But when these ad-hoc appointees face the public service commission, some of them are not selected and the seniority of others is changed. Such a situation creates lot of problems in the management of services. Therefore, proper rules of all services should be made keeping in view the promotion opportunities of the employees.

Inter-Services Tensions

The technical services personnel in the state feel that they have not been given access to the higher echelons of service. Most of the senior posts in the secretariat and even at the level of heads of departments are occupied by the all-India services officers. Even technical departments like education, agriculture, veterinary services, etc., are drawn from the Indian Administrative Service. This causes a lot of heart-burning among the various technical services of the states. To solve this problem, a number of state governments have started giving secretariat posts to a number of technical officers at different levels. For example, in a number of technical departments such as public works and irrigation departments, technical officers have been appointed as secretaries to the government and in some like conservators of forests and superintending engineers are appointed as deputy or special secretaries to the government.

The Problem of Domicile or Residence Requirement

The system of providing entry in the state services to only choose those who belong to the state is a British legacy. It was probably sought to be justified on the grounds that it was the duty of the state to provide employment to the 'sons of the soil'. But short of arrangement was severely criticized and Parliament enacted Public Employment (Requirement as to Residence) Act, 1957 to prohibit this kind of discrimination. In spite of this Act the situation has not changed and states continue to practise discrimination on grounds of domicile. Two factors are mainly responsible for such situation, one is politicization due to democratic process based on adult franchise and the other is the prescription of regional language as a medium of examination.

The system of domicile requirement is against the spirit of national integration. It can only be countered by creating public opinion in favour of national unity and integration.

Reservation System

In all the states there is reservation for scheduled castes and scheduled tribes and backward communities. Articles 16(4) and 335 of the Constitution require that the government should discriminate in favour of the socially and economically backward classes of citizens including scheduled castes and scheduled tribes. The ways of such discrimination is reservation of posts for them in public employment.

Reservation for scheduled castes (SCs) and scheduled tribes (STs) is accepted by the people of the country but reservation for other communities up to the limit of 70 to 90 per cent, is ridiculous. Even the Supreme Court decision on not to exceed reservation above more than 50 per cent have not deterred populist politicians from going ahead with reservations. Reservation in promotion has created situations where juniors have been promoted over their seniors and in some cases subordinates have become bosses. This creates lots of tension among employees. Solution to these problems has to be found so as to create a congenial atmosphere for smooth working in the services.

LOCAL SERVICES

The local services comprise both urban and rural personnel. In this section, we will discuss local government services. These high ability and calibre services are needed to play prominent roles in the achievement of desired results in the management of local affairs. First, we take up the municipal service. The urban sector, consisting of towns and cities, is governed by municipal corporations in cities having a population of more than 5,00,000; by municipalities in large and medium size towns; and small towns have town panchayats. A municipal corporation has a commissioner as its chief executive officer. He is assisted by an assistant commissioner. Both are appointed by the state government from amongst its Class I officers. Normally, the commissioner is a senior civil servant and his appointment is made for a period of five years in Kolkata, Delhi, Patna and MP. His tenure is for a three-year period in Mumbai, Chennai, Karnataka and UP. For other services of a municipal corporation, the Punjab government had issued a notification on 21 June 1978, for constituting 21 municipal corporation services.[11] These include executive officers, secretaries, assistant secretaries, superintendents, assistant superintendents, accounts officers, accountants, engineers, assistant engineers, sectional officers, town planners, assistant town planners, head draftsman, planning assistant, medical health officers. Recruitment to these posts is made by the state government on the recommendation of a selection committee comprising three government representatives and two non-official members with sufficient experience in the field of working of the urban local government. It also has two specialists and among the members of the selection committee, there should be one member belonging to the scheduled caste. The methods of recruitment differ from state to state. For making appointments to the posts of clerks, overseers (JEs), mechanics, teachers, sanitary inspectors and other cadres, different methods are adopted. The personnel are appointed by an appointment committee or by the departmental heads, or by the commissioners, or by mayors as in the case of UP. The municipal personnel are categorized into the following three services:

Separate system: In this type of service the local body is the appointing authority for recruiting personnel who are not transferred from one municipality to another. The local body has full control over this category of personnel.

Unified local service: Personnel belonging to this type are the personnel of local authorities and make up career service for the whole state. They are transferred from one local authority to another. For instance, a secretary of a municipality falls in this category. The control of service conditions including discipline is in the hands of the state governments although day to day control is exercised by the local bodies under which the personnel are posted.

Integrated service: Personnel of this category remain interchangeable between the state government and the local government. These personnel, viz., superintendent engineers, executive engineers, assistant engineers, mechanical experts, etc., are the appointed by the state government. In fact it means that the executive personnel of the state governments in different cadres are sent on deputation to the municipal bodies for a fixed tenure. They come back to the state government after the completion of their tenure or even earlier. As they are responsible to the state government, they consider themselves independent of the local bodies, but their day to day control lies in municipal bodies.

Comparison of All Three Systems

We have discussed the integrated, unified and separate municipal personnel systems. Now an attempt would be made to compare the relative merits and demerits of these three systems.

Separate personnel system: Local self-government requires autonomy and authority to recruit and control the service conditions of its employees is essential for autonomy. A separate personnel system fulfils the need for autonomy of local government. However, the separate personnel system suffers from the following demerits.

First, the local governments are very small in size. They do not have the necessary resources to employ really competent staff. Second, the number of the employees in a municipality is small, therefore, it is not possible to provide necessary opportunities of promotion and good career. Third, the elected councils and chairman did not take interest with regard to the recruitment and control of these services and nepotism and favouritism was rampant. Therefore, it was difficult for competent people to serve in the municipalities.

Unified personnel system: Under unified personnel system, for all the municipal bodies of the state there is one common personnel system. The different categories of employees in all the state municipal bodies are categorized into common state-wide cadres. A state-wide separate service is created for each cadre and the municipal bodies have to draw their personnel from these cadres. The disadvantages of this system are: First, this system undermines the autonomy of the municipal bodies, because these cadres are created and managed by the state governments and municipal bodies are deprived of the powers of recruitment and control over their employees. Second, this system puts financial burden on the municipal bodies because the employees of state-wide cadres are given higher salary. Third, the employees under this system may not develop loyalty and commitment to the municipal bodies. They serve under the dual control of the municipal body as well as state government. Fourth, the system provides better sense of security of services to the employees. Fifth, this system reduces the chances of favouritism and nepotism in the recruitment of municipal bodies. Finally, the loyalty of the employees will be to municipal institutions because they know that they belong to state-wide municipal cadre and not to the state civil service. Therefore, they will be more devoted to their duty.

Integrated personnel system: Under this system the personnel of the local bodies are drawn from the state civil services. This solves the problem of their career development. The advantages of the system are: First, it curtails the autonomy of the local bodies. Second, because of the higher pay scale of the employees it creates financial problems. Third, the loyalty of the officers is divided. They always prefer the state government in comparison to municipal bodies. They belong to state cadre and municipal service is just like a sojourn for them. Finally, in this system the state governments send their unwanted and problematic officers to the municipalities on deputation. This affects the quality of municipal administration.

The advantages of the system are that talented youth join state civil services for better career opportunities. Therefore, there is a possibility for getting better talent for the service of municipal bodies in this system.

After discussing the merits and demerits of the three different systems, the question arises, which of these systems should be adopted. There is no clear-cut answer. A mix of these systems may have to be adopted according to the circumstances.

The first and second conferences of local self-government ministers in 1948 and 1954 recommended the creation of unified personnel system. Their argument was that the state-wide cadres facilitate recruitment from a wide field and provide a more efficient and contended service. The central council of local-self government also agreed with this proposal in 1956, 1959, 1960 and 1963. The Fourth Conference of Ministers of Town and Country Planning (1963) and Rural-Urban Relationship Committee (1966) recommended the creation of provincial cadres for certain important categories such as administration, health, engineering and town planning services. The committee on the service conditions of the municipal employees set in 1965 also recommended for setting up of state-wide cadres of state employees. The Taxation Enquiry Commission (1953–1954) suggested that the local bodies should be given some autonomy to control their affairs. The state control should not be too meticulous or minute.

Taking into account all these viewpoints, it seems that an integrated personnel system is not a good solution to the problem. It completely takes away the autonomy of the local bodies. Therefore, the following solution may prove more suitable:

(i) The posts in the local government should be grouped into usual four categories, Class-I, Class-II, Class-III and Class-IV, Class I and II posts should be covered by a unified state-wide cadre of municipal services. Class III and Class IV employees should be recruited and should be under the control of the municipal bodies.

(ii) The recruitment to these unified cadres should be made by a local civil service commission. The commission should be autonomous and independent organization.

(iii) Some representation should be given to the local bodies in the local service commission.

This arrangement will reduce the stronghold of the state governments from the local administrative service and also have the advantages of the unified cadres.

In the states of Punjab and Haryana, the municipal staff consists of: (a) superior staff such as executive officer, secretary, taxation superintendent, engineer, etc. and (b) subordinate officials, viz., clerks, librarians, fire-fighters, drivers, etc. Recruitment to higher posts is made on the recommendations of the state public service commission. The subordinate staff in Haryana is appointed by the director, local bodies, on the recommendation of the state subordinate services selection board. Class IV posts are filled by the deputy commissioner concerned.

In Haryana, the municipal services have been divided into two categories, i.e., state level services and the district level services. The former cadre consists of the following posts:

1. Executive officer
2. Secretary
3. Medical officer of health
4. Municipal engineer
5. Sectional officers
6. Superintendent (office, tax and octroi)
7. Accountant
8. Chief sanitary inspector
9. Fire station officer

The district level services are transferable within the district. These are as follows:

1. Assistant surgeon
2. Superintendent, water works
3. *Vaidyas*
4. Agriculture development officer
5. *Naib tehsildar*
6. Sanitary superintendent
7. Inspectors
8. Project officer
9. Sub-fire officer
10. Draftsman
11. Revenue officer
12. Senior and junior scale stenographers
13. Assistants
14. Assistant accountant
15. Head cashier
16. Head clerk
17. Foreman
18. Lady health visitor
19. Social education worker
20. Class IV employees

Rural Services

These services comprise officials of the *zila parishad*, the *panchayat samiti* and the *panchayat*. The official in charge of a *zila parishad* is the secretary or executive officer. In Maharashtra, the chief executive officer has been made the overall in charge of the *zila parishad*, and has the rank of a collector. He is assisted by a deputy chief executive officer having a deputy collector's rank. These officers have the district development officer and different heads of departments under them in the *zila parishad*. There are also other officials such as taxation officer, accountant, assistant, steno, clerk and Class IV employees, etc. The *panchayat samiti* works under the administrative control of the block development and *panchayat* officer. He is the ex-officio executive officer of the *samiti* and to assist him in the implementation of various development schemes, he has a team of extension officers from agriculture, industries, cooperation, animal husbandry, education, works, social, education, *panchayats*, etc. But in Punjab and Haryana most of these functionaries have been shifted to their own respective departments and presently they have under their control the social education and *panchayat* officer, *mukhya sevika*, *gram sevaks*, accountant, head clerk, stenographer, *panchayat* secretaries,* craft teachers, statistical assistant, Class IV employees, etc. At the *panchayat* level there is a *panchayat* secretary or *gram sachiv* who has been made in charge of some *panchayats*. According to the load of work, there may be one *panchayat* secretary for one *panchayat* only. In Kerala, each *panchayat* has an executive officer who belongs to the state cadre of service, a *panchayat* assistant and a bill collector to assist him. In some states, *panchayat* secretaries, head clerks, accountants, stenographers, clerks, tax collectors, peons, etc., are the personnel of the *panchayati raj* institutions and the related bodies which recruit them. While states such as Maharashtra, Gujarat, Rajasthan and Andhra Pradesh have created *panchayati raj* services, Gujarat has constituted a state *panchayat* service and some gazetted and non-gazetted officers of the state are allocated to the state *panchayati raj* service. The state government also sends its officers of the IAS cadre as well as other Class I, Class II and Class III personnel on deputation to the *panchayati raj* institutions. Andhra Pradesh has classified the *zila parishad* and *panchayat samiti* posts in state, district and block cadres.[12]

Recruitment to the state government staff for the *panchayati raj* bodies is made either by the state public service commission or the subordinate services selection board. For instance, half of the posts of the BD and POs in Punjab and Haryana are filled through promotion and the other half by direct recruitment by the state public service commission. As regards promotion, this is from amongst the social education and *panchayat* officers. In UP, the state public service commission conducts competitive examinations to fill all the posts. In Rajasthan, these posts are filled either through deputationists or by promoting extension staff. The extension staff has been on deputation or are recruited by the subordinate services selection board. Appointments to the subordinate staff in the *panchayati raj* institutions are made through the Rajasthan *panchayat samiti* and *zila parishad* service commission. Normally, the subordinate staff includes village level workers, *gram sevikas*, field men, stock men, sheep and wool supervisors, village panchayat secretary, UDCs, LDCs (including typists), etc. In Maharashtra, the government has constituted the divisional and district selection boards. The divisional board is headed by the divisional commissioner and has to recruit personnel for Class III technical services of the district. For recruitment to the district services (Class III) and district services (Class IV), there is a set-up known as the district selection board. The board consists of the district collector, a government officer and citizen member of the divisional selection board. The appointing authority is the chief executive officer of the *zila parishad*, who issues appointment letters to persons figuring in the list of candidates selected by the selection board.

Training of Civil Services

The importance of training was felt by the East India Company. The company set up a college at Fort William at Calcutta (1800–1806) and later the East India College (1809–1857) to train the company's employees, who came from abroad, mostly from Britain. The name and contributions of the Halsbury College, England are well known. World War II (1939–1945) changed the nature and functions of the state and as a result the need was felt for trained public servants to perform new functions.

In India after Independence in 1947, the IAS training school in Metcalfe House was set up at Delhi, where all the probationers were imparted training for one year. The Appleby Report of 1953 led for the establishment of the Indian Institute of Public Administration at New Delhi in 1954. This was followed by the establishment of the National Academy of Administration at Mussoorie in 1959 with the merger of the Training School, Delhi and IAS Staff College, Simla. Fresh impetus came after the creation in 1965 of a separate training division in the home ministry.

In subsequent years, a number of schools and institutes/academies were established in the states. In 1970, a separate department of personnel was created and finally in March 1985, a new ministry of personnel, public grievances and pension was created with the department of personnel and training as one of its three departments.

Types of Training

The training given to the officers is of two types, the in-service training and the mid-career training.

In-service training: After recruitment, the probationers of the Indian Administrative Service, IFS, IPS and the probationers of all the Class I central services selected on the basis of the combined civil services examination, are given foundational training for 16 weeks in the LBS National Academy of Administration, Mussoorie. The common foundational course has broad-based subjects like Indian history and culture, Constitution of India, public administration, Indian economy, law, science and technology in India, etc. The course is designed to give a broad idea of Indian history and culture and tradition as well as the present socio-economic conditions of the country. This is to broaden the outlook of the civil services and not to impart, any specific skills for the purpose of any departmental job.

After four months foundational course the IAS probationers continue to stay in the academy for continuing their professional training programme. The probationers of other services are sent to the specialized training institutions set up by their respective ministries for imparting specific knowledge relating to their particular jobs.

IAS Probationers Course (Phase I)

The IAS probationers training course in academy is divided into two phases. Phase I of a 24-week professional course and 52 weeks of field training in the states of their allotment as per approved scheme, and a 10-week professional course in Phase II in the academy on their return from field training. The objectives of the Phase I course are as follows:

1. To understand the all-India perspective of the administrative duties of the higher civil services and to develop a deep commitment to values of national integrity, unity and diversity
2. To develop skills for public management, including proficiency in computers
3. To understand the constitutional and legal framework of the public services in general and all-India services in particular
4. To develop good writing skills
5. To understand the working of the district administration
6. To appreciate the changed policy thrusts in the light of economic reforms
7. To understand poverty alleviation programmes and its impact on the poor in rural and urban areas
8. To became proficient in the language of the allotted state, the history, geography and culture of the state and its administrative ethos

To achieve the above objective the following subjects being taught are: (i) basic political concepts and the Indian Constitution, (ii) law, (iii) basic economic principles, (iv) public administration, (v) management in government, (vi) language and (vii) computers. The course is covered by lectures, panel discussions, tutorials, case studies, management games, guest lectures, video films, languages practice and computer by practical applications. Each probationer has to prepare a term paper which has to be based on independent study. The length of the 'term paper' has not to exceed 3,000 words. Hindi has been made a compulsory language for all the probationers but facilities to learn other languages are also provided at the academy.

After the completion of common foundational course, the training programme of IAS probationers is divided into two phases, Phase I and II. During Phase I after the inauguration of the course the next day, the officer trainees leave for their winter-study-tour-cum-*Bharat darshan*. On completion of the tour they are allowed station leave for a short duration and are asked to report back to Delhi for attachment with the bureau of parliamentary studies and training for a week. For example, the IAS probationers of the 1996 batch, after the inauguration of the professional course Phase I on Saturday, 21 December 1996 went on study-tour-cum-*Bharat darshan* on 22 December 1996 for 57 days and were allowed station leave for a week. They were asked to report back on 24 February 1997 for attachment with the Bureau of Parliamentary Studies and Training, Delhi for a week. The academic inputs at Mussoorrie started from 3 March 1997 till 6 June 1997.

After completion of the Phase I training the probationers further undergo on-the-job training or field training of a practical nature in the states of their allotment. There he calls on the chief secretary and other higher officials and if there is a training institute in the state, he is attached to it for the purpose of institutional training for a specific period. Then he is sent to a district where he has to work in certain administrative positions. This assignment enables him to grasp all the facets of district administration and to study policies, programmes, and institutions. Enough care is taken about the selection of district collector under whom the probationer is to receive on-the-job training. After district training, he returns to the secretariat and gets adequate knowledge of it. The probationer, during his district-level training, remains in constant touch with his counsellor at the academy. He communicates from time to time with the counsellor about his working experience, problems, observations and impressions, etc. He has to make a list of the subjects allotted to him before he leaves for district training. On completion of district training, he prepares reports which are evaluated at the academy and are taken into account for his final evaluation. The reports presented by the probationers are discussed at the academy during the second phase of training.

Thus, after a year of training in the district, the IAS probationers again return to their academy for further training, which is in the nature of experience sharing. This is the 'sandwich training' course which has been developed for the IAS.

At the completion of the training, the probationer appears at an examination conducted by the UPSC. Every probationer is required to secure at least 50 per cent marks in each subject to pass the examination. After the passing of examination the probationer becomes an officer and is sent to a state, where he is given charge of a sub-division and after six or seven years he becomes a district collector or a district commissioner.

Besides this, there is a great emphasis now on in-service training. The in-service training programme for an IAS officer has been chalked out keeping in view the pertinent training needs at the four stages, viz. six to nine years of service; 10–16 years service, 17–20 years of service and above 21 years of service. The course designed for the group of six to nine years of service is for a period of three weeks. It aims to equip the participants by upgrading their knowledge, skills and behavioural understanding to handle the existing job better. For the second stage, comprising 10–16 years of service, the main thrust is on the aspects of modern management concepts and decision analysis. So far the training for the 17–20 years of service group is concerned, it is for a period of three weeks and relates to policy planning and analysis. Apart from this, there is a programme of compulsory training of one week for each IAS officer every year.

Indian Foreign Service (IFS)

The IFS recruit to go through a three-year training programme. He is attached to a district for some time to enable him to understand practical work. After completion of foundational course at Lal Bahadur Shastri National Academy of Administration, Mussoorie, he has to undergo secretariat training. He has to take training in subjects related to diplomatic techniques and procedures as well as international affairs and learn a foreign language. For this purpose he is sent to an institute of foreign languages abroad.

Indian Police Service

The Central Police Academy, Hyderabad, imparts training to the new entrants to the Indian Police Service. The training of IPS is on similar lines as of IAS but the syllabus contents are different. It includes criminal law and procedure, criminal psychology, scientific aids in detection of crime, physical training, methods of combating corruption, riding and shooting, etc. After one year training, the recruit has to appear for the examination held by the UPSC. He also gets practical training for one year more and is required to work in various posts of the police hierarchy, like head constable, sub-inspector, inspector of police, etc. After completion of the training he is posted as assistant superintendent of police.

Training for the Indian Audit and Accounts Service

To provide training to the recruits of the IA and AS, there is a Departmental Training School at Simla. The training imparted has a direct relation with the job of the trainees. The recruits undergo the foundational course at the LBS National Academy of Administration, Mussoorie. After the completion of the course, the recruits have to pass the departmental examination in the subjects having a direct bearing on their work. For practical training, they are attached to the accountant-general's office, the divisional accounts of the PWD and the district treasury. At the end, the recruit passes the departmental examination and is appointed to the post of assistant accounts officer.

The probationers of service gets training at the Income Tax Training School, Nagpur, after completing foundational course at Mussoorie.

The Railway Staff College, Baroda, imparts training to the recruits in the railway, traffic, personnel and accounts services.

The Customs and Central Excise Training School, New Delhi, provides training to the recruits of customs and central excise service.

The Institute of Secretariat Training and Management, New Delhi, imparts training to the central secretariat services—section officer grade, assistant grade and lower division grade. It provides four weeks' training to directly recruited section officers in the field of public administration, office management and procedure, typing, the Constitution of India, organizational behaviour, basic economics and statistics, anti-corruption law, etc. This would be followed by a week's study tour to a voluntary agency/village in a remote backward area. Another four weeks' of training in the field of microcomputers, security institutions, organizational behaviour, purchase procedures for stationery and furniture, management of printing and publication, housekeeping functions, etc. At the end of four weeks, the group shall undergo two weeks' tour to visit a state capital and the secretariat, a nearby public undertaking and a rural development project.

In the third month, training is given concerning the various rules such as conduct rules, leave rules, pension rules, records management, personnel management, noting and drafting, etc. After finishing it, the group goes for two months' on-the-job training. The training imparted is closely connected with the officer's work. On the completion of the training, the official has to work for a short-period as an assistant, before he becomes a section officer.

The institute also organizes refresher courses for section officers and assistants. Such courses are organized to update their knowledge and skills. The assistants and UDCs employed in the central ministries are imparted training related to cash and accounts matters.

The various institutes/colleges/academies have been set up by the Government of India to provide training to public administrators.

These institutions are the following:

1. Administrative Staff College, Hyderabad
2. Indian Institute of Public Administration, New Delhi
3. Lal Bahadur Shastri National Academy of Administration, Mussoorie

4. National Police Academy, Hyderabad
5. Customs and Central Excise Training School, New Delhi
6. Indian Audit and Accounts Staff Training College, Simla
7. Indian Revenue Service Staff College, Nagpur
8. Railway Staff College, Baroda
9. National Institute for Educational Planning and Administration
10. National Institute of Rural Development, Hyderabad
11. Central Emergency Relief Training Institute, Nagpur
12. Institute of Secretariat Training and Management, New Delhi
13. National Institute of Health Administration and Education, Delhi
14. Small Industries Extension Training Institute, Hyderabad
15. Management Development Institute, Gurgaon

Out of above institutions, special mention may be made of the Indian Institute of Public Administration, New Delhi, and Administrative Staff College, Hyderabad.

Indian Institute of Public Administration, New Delhi

The institute was established in 1954 and it is in the forefront of providing in-service training to the civil servants in India. The institute conducts in-service training courses for the all-India services and central services. Some of these courses are techniques of administrative management, administrative leadership, development administration, modern aids to management, materials planning, performance, budgeting, project formulation, social policy and administration, etc. The institute also organizes seminars, conferences, and workshops for different categories of government employees. A very important programme conducted by the Indian Institute of Public Administration (IIPA) is advance professional programme in public administration of nine months' duration. The programme covers a wide range of subjects connected with public administration.

The Administrative Staff College, Hyderabad

The college was established in 1957 on the recommendation of the All-India Council for Technical Education and is patterned on the Administrative Staff College at Henley in Britain. The college aims at bringing together senior administrators from the administration, the private sector and public sector for a get-together to exchange ideas and experiences in order to enable them to assume higher responsibilities.

Training of State Services

At the state level most of the state governments have set up their own academy/institute/college/school to impart training to their employees. One of the very best institutions of such type is Harish Chandra Mathur State Institute of Public Administration at Jaipur. The aim of the institute is to contribute to a continuing improvement in Rajasthan administration so that it is also able to fulfil people's aspirations for development at an accelerated pace. To this end the institute strives to:

(a) design and conduct training courses appropriate to the specific identified needs of the administrators and the organizations they serve;

(b) assist the departments and agencies in finding solutions to several of their baffling organizational problems;

(c) serve as a forum for the interchange of ideas and experience among scholars and practitioners of public administration; and

(d) undertake research on problems of direct relevance to government agencies and disseminate widely through its publications knowledge of current developments in the vast field of public administration training programmes conducted at the institute, consisting of foundational courses; professional courses refresher courses; programmes in management, techniques and programmes in development administration.

The institute has its own teaching and training faculty which is a mix of academicians and administrators. The institute pays particular attention to the staff development administration. In addition to training, the institute also conducts research in the areas of direct relevance to government work. It has also taken up publication work.

For training of the state administrative services the training programmes are fixed according to rules of the state governments concerned. In some of the states there are training institutions to train up the different services. To name some of them, the Gopabandhu Institute of Administration, Bhubaneshwar, Orissa; Administrative College, Bombay, Maharashtra; Administrative Staff College, Gauhati, Assam; Administrative Training Institute, Mysore, Karnataka; Administrative Training Institute, Ranchi, Bihar; Directorate of Training, Union Territory Civil Services, New Delhi; Gujarat Institute of Training in Administration, Ahmedabad, Gujarat; Lal Bahadur Shastri Institute of Public Administration, Bhopal, Madhya Pradesh; Police Training College, Sagar, Madhya Pradesh; Officers' Training School, Naini Tal, Uttar Pradesh; Secretariat Training School, Trivandrum, Kerala. All the states do not have their own training institutions. They take advantage of training in the institutions maintained by other states. Some states take advantage of the central training institutions or autonomous/private training institutions partly or fully. There are as many as 16 central training institutions and as many as 25 autonomous/private training institutions in India.

The training for the state services is largely modelled according to the training programmes for IAS and IPS probationers. But training of the state services was not emphasised when the state administrative services were created in the early 1930s. The deputy collectors in the early years of the creation of that service were provided with on-the-job training, after Independence when central training institutions were established. It was also felt to have separate training institutions for the state services. Therefore, the different states established training institutions to train up their services on the model of central training institutions.

For the state services at present there are provisions for institutional training and field training. But there are differences relating to details of rules made by different states. The different states also prescribed different periods of training for their respective services. However, in order to maintain some uniformity and an average standard of training of the state personnel, all the training institutions have restructured their training programmes into sandwich pattern which is adopted by the centre academy.

There are secretariat training centres and institutes that provide working knowledge of the secretariat to enable the state civil servants to perform their duties efficiently. This training covers secretariat rules, regulations and procedures. In Haryana, new entrants and assistants undergo training of eight to ten weeks' duration. For imparting in-service training in accountancy, there is the Accounts Training Institute in Haryana. Those who get in-service training include the DDOs, junior auditors of the local audit department, clerks handling accounts, assistants of the finance department, non-gazetted staff of the treasury, class of SAA trainees, etc. The training of the subordinate staff of the state (Class III and Class IV) employees, who comprise the lower echelons of the hierarchy of the administration, however, remains substantially neglected. It has been found that about 75 per cent of the Class III and 90 per cent of Class IV employees are presently untrained. The training of civil servant's at junior levels is stressed, particularly of those who come in contact with the public or those who are generally referred to as the cutting edge of the administration. A study has revealed that most of the departments send for training only those employees who are likely to receive only minimal benefits because they are the ones whose absence causes the least inconvenience to development work. On the other hand, in many cases, departments have declined to send nominations for various training and development courses on the ground that their limited manpower did not permit them to do so. The working group on 'Training Challenges at the Grassroots Level' was of the view that training at the grassroots level should be a part of the total training strategy and it should carry intrinsic and extrinsic reward in respect of career promotion prospects. It was also of the view that training should lead to development of employees and effectiveness in their performance of the service. Moreover, it should be a continuous process, more particularly imparted at the induction level and later also at various stages of career progression.[13]

Training for Local Civil Services

Urban Local Services

To meet the training needs of higher level personnel in the municipal administration, training courses are organized by the Indian Institute of Public Administration, New Delhi and the All-India Institute of Local-Self Government, Mumbai. Training is imparted through short and long-term courses. The Government of India constituted a committee in 1963 under the chairmanship of Nur-ud-din Ahmed to study the problem of training for the municipal staff. On the recommendation of the committee, the National Centre for Training and Research in Municipal Administration, New Delhi, was established by the Government of India and later, four regional centres were started at Mumbai, Kolkata (Kolkata Centre has been closed), Hyderabad and Lucknow. The municipal executives in upper as well as middle classes undergo orientation courses of six weeks' duration in these centres. However, the training imparted at these centres is insufficient to cope with the country's requirements. To keep pace with the changing values, the training arrangements should be strengthened. Each state should establish a permanent training institute and every municipal official should be given in-service training at regular intervals.

Rural Local Services

The higher officials are trained at the National Institute of Rural Development, Hyderabad, Tata Training Institute of Social Sciences, Mumbai, and other training centres situated at Wardha, Allahabad, Lucknow, Anand, etc. These institutions strive to imbibe skills in the personnel to enhance development. For other officials, there are state-level training institutions. In Punjab, the BD and POs, extensions officers, accountants, *mukhya gram sevaks*, etc., undergo training organized by the Sardar Vallabhbhai Patel Community Development Training Centre, Batala. There is also another training centre at Nabha, where training is imparted to the *gram sevaks*. Pre-entry training as well as in-service training is given at these centres.

In Haryana, there is a training centre at Nilokheri to meet the training needs of the rural local personnel in the state. But the training being imparted to the rural personnel is not adequate and there are still some untrained personnel in service. The Vyas Committee in Rajasthan (1973), stressing the need for training, has recommended that training should be made compulsory for the *panchayati raj* personnel and increments may be withheld in respect of those who have failed to undergo the training. The state level committee in Haryana has noted that 'the training which is being imparted at present is of a general type and is inadequate. Not many officials have been sent to the national institute for training and much of the training imparted does not directly relate to conditions, systems, problems and requirements of the state. The state government has only one training centre at Nilokheri. For training of non-officials, the *panchayati raj* training centres were established at Ambala, Hisar and Rohtak but were on abolished later. Training is an important input of all development plans, therefore, detailed training programmes of various types can be drawn up. In the light of the additional responsibilities and new thrusts, it may be useful to revitalize the Nilokheri centre. The faculty should be strengthened and upgraded. More provisions should be made to cover the training of the non-officials. All the universities of the state should also be associated with these programmes. Special importance has to be attached to the programmes for adult education to develop the latent civic consciousness.[14]

Conclusion

After Independence, India established many institutions to impart training to various categories of civil servants. But our training arrangements including in-service training are inadequate to provide relevant training to our civil servants. The shortcomings in our training programmes are as follows.

First, present training arrangements are in favour of middle and senior levels and juniors, and lower level bureaucracy parts namely, inspectors, clerks, assistants, etc. stands neglected whereas they are in direct touch with the people. Second, refresher courses are neither properly structured nor well-defined content-wise. Training courses should be socially relevant and effectively communicated to make them useful for the functionaries. Third, most of the departments send for training only such employees to whom they consider trouble makers or to whom they do not want to involve in the departmental working. In many cases, departments even do not nominate persons for training on the ground that they have limited manpower. Therefore, it is necessary that the departmental heads develop a positive attitude towards training and development of their manpower. Fourth, in the absence of follow-up action we do not know about the impact of training. After the course is over, the organizers feel relieved. Finally, the success of any training programme depends upon the attitudes and interest of the trainees. Therefore, instead of college-type lectures by management academicians, a value- and emotion-rich curriculum-based activities and quasi-live interactions should be evolved. Training has to be suitably reoriented, emphasis being not on traditional management skills and techniques but on creating a tough, ethical, committed psyche.

Recent Developments

The need for a separate cell in the Government of India to look after the training requirements of the civil service was felt. The officers' shortage committee recommended for the establishment of a directorate to look after the training of various services. After some time the planning commission also made a similar recommendation and the directorate was set up in the department of personnel and administrative reforms. Now there is a whole wing under the charge of a joint secretary who is assisted by a number of directors, deputy secretaries/under-secretaries. The late Prime Minister Rajiv Gandhi gave lot of importance to training of civil services. As a result, a number of in-service training programmes of four weeks and one week were started for very senior persons.

Foreign Training Programmes

In addition to the training programmes organized in the Indian institutions, a large number of programmes are also being organized in foreign institutions. The funds for such programmes are made available by the host country governments under the Colombo Plan. Several programmes are organized with the assistance of UN institutions like Food and Agriculture Organization, United Nations Educational, Scientific and Cultural Organization, United Nations Development Programme, World Health Organization, International Labour Organization, etc. However, there has been a lot of discussion about training but so far not much systematization of these programmes has been attempted. In fact our country has sent teams to the UK and USA to study the various training courses in the field of public administration. It is hoped that in due course of time our training programmes will become more meaningful.

NOTES

1. F. A. Ogg, *English Government and Politics* (New York: Macmillan, 1947), p. 202.
2. *Report of the Royal Commission on the Superior Civil Services in India* (Simla: Government of India Press, 1924), p. 4.
3. S. P. Verma, 'Concept of All India Service in a Federal Polity', a paper presented in a National Seminar on Some Aspects of Indian Administration, Department of Public Administration, Punjabi University, Patiala, 21–22 October 1994.
4. *Report of the Commission on Centre State Relations, Part I*, Government of India, 1988, p. 229.
5. *45th Report of the U.P.S.C.* (New Delhi: Government of India Press, 1994–1995), p. 3.
6. Ibid., para 2.2.6, p. 4
7. Ibid., Table VI, p. 60.
8. *Report of the A.R.C. on Personnel Administration* (New Delhi: Government of India, Manager of Publications, 1969), p. 9.
9. *Tribune*, Chandigarh, 8 April 1991.
10. See, for details, *Tribune*, 7 September 1991.
11. Punjab Government Notification No. GSR 66/P.A. 42/76/S/71/78 dated 21-6-1978.
12. M. Shiviah et al., *Panchayati Raj—An Analytical Survey* (Hyderabad: National Institute of Community Development, 1976), p. 235.
13. A. P. Saxena (ed.), *Training in Government: Objective and Opportunities* (New Delhi: Indian Institute of Public Administration, 1985), p. 316.
14. *Note on Reorganization of Panchayati Raj in Haryana in the light of Asoka Mehta Committee Report* (Chandigarh: Directorate of Panchayats, Haryana, 1979), pp. 31–32.

Constitutional Protection to Civil Servants

In this chapter, an attempt has been made to discuss the role of civil servants in running the government, constitutional provisions and their importance to safeguard the services, implications of doctrine of pleasure in removal of civil servants and principle of natural justice along with judicial judgements in this respect.

The Role of Civil Service

The makers of our Constitution were fully aware of the role of civil service in a democracy. H. V. Kamath said in the constituent assembly that 'a country without an efficient civil service cannot make progress in spite of the earnestness of those people at the helm of affairs in the country. Wherever democratic institutions exist, experience has shown that it is essential to protect the public service as far as possible from political or personal influence and to give it that position, stability and security which is vital to its successful working as an impartial and efficient instrument by which government of whatever political complexion may give effect to their policies'.[1] Likewise, Anantasayanam Ayyanger concluded that 'a healthy, efficient and honest public service is the very backbone of a government or its administration'.[2] Further, H. N. Kunzru stated that provision should be made with the object to 'secure for the state efficient public servants who will serve all people equally well and will always watch over the interests of all communities and the state as a whole'.[3] This was found to be all the more important because ours is a federation having a concurrent list, due to which administration became complicated. To manage such administrative apparatus was a difficult task. Provisions in Constitution for civil servants need elaboration. One view is that administration is not a constitutional issue, it is a legal matter, therefore, it should not figure in the Constitution. It is a document containing principles and political philosophy. The other view is that the Constitution should have been specific about the civil service and they should not be left to the vagaries of a power coterie. H. V. Kamath, a former civil servant, expressed his fears and observed that 'the civil service will apprehend that amenability to ministerial pressure and a correct attitude towards questions in which a little coterie or the group for the time being in power is interested will secure them promotions rather than merit or efficiency.'[4] In view of this, our Constitution should have detailed provisions, but it does not contain any detailed provisions regarding the methods of recruitment, conditions of service of civil servants, etc. and left them to be decided by the acts of appropriate legislatures.[5] However, the law has not yet been enacted by the legislature. As a result, the civil servants continue to be governed by the rules framed by the executive which can be changed at any time in arbitrary manner. The Supreme Court commented on the frequent changes in the rules in the *B. S. Yadav v. State of Haryana*[6] case said 'there was a change in the government which evidently led to a change in the rules, as if service rules are a plaything in the hands of the government.'[7]

THE DOCTRINE OF PLEASURE

The tenure of our civil servants including defence and all-India services depends upon the 'pleasure of the president or the governor'[8] in case of state officers. It means they can hold office as long as the executive head is pleased to retain them. We borrowed this provision from the British system where the officers hold their offices during the pleasure of the Crown. Their appointments can be terminated at any time without assigning any cause. The exercise of pleasure by the Crown, can, however, be restricted by legislation enacted by Parliament. It is now well established in British constitutional theory, at any rate as it has developed since the eighteenth century, that any appointment as a Crown servant, however, subordinate, is terminable at will unless it is expressly otherwise provided by legislation. However, in practice, a dismissal takes place only as the result of well established disciplinary processes.

Though the Crown still retains the right of dismissal at pleasure, the legal position of civil servants has radically changed in recent years as a result of legislation and legally binding collective agreements can be entered into between the Crown and representatives of the staff and those representatives can sue for breach of any condition of service covered by these agreements. Even a civil servant can bring an action for unfair dismissal or sue on his conditions of service. But just as an ordinary employee cannot insist on continuing in employment, so also a civil servant cannot insist on continuing in employment. The remedy in both cases is to recover damages for wrongful dismissal.[9]

These consequences follow not because the pleasure doctrine is a special prerogative of the British Crown which has been inherited by India and transposed into our Constitution, adapted to suit the constitutional set up of our republic, but because public policy requires public interest needs and public good demands that there should be such a doctrine. The pleasure doctrine is not relevant in Indian conditions, it should not be applied here, because first, the pleasure of the president or the governor ultimately becomes the pleasure of the prime minister or the chief minister. Therefore, it is liable for political use. Second, in our country politics of patronage or 'patron-client politics',[10] has emerged and in such situation civil servants will be forced to fulfil the desire of politically powerful leaders at the cost of politically unorganized, socially weak and deprived people at the grassroots level. Third, ours is an independent nation and we need not borrow each and every principle from Britain. Rather, we should develop our own according to the need, requirement and ecology of our administration.

THE IMPORTANCE OF CONSTITUTIONAL SAFEGUARDS

Civil servants implemented the policies, programmes and decisions of the government faithfully. Nowhere in the world does the administrative system like to have a civil servant who is undisciplined, inefficient, dishonest or corrupt and has become a security risk. The power of the government to terminate the services of the civil servants on the above grounds cannot be denied. But it has to be ensured that the government does not follow the policy of harassment and victimization of honest and efficient civil servants on extraneous considerations. To ensure, against such type of actions, constitutional safeguards are required to check abuse and misuse, arbitrary and discriminatory exercise of powers by the government. In a democratic society governed by the rule of law, disregard of it would set aside the constitutional promise of justice, equality, liberty and freedom. Thus, constitutional safeguards are essential for liberty and its spirit.

CONSTITUTIONAL SAFEGUARDS

The Indian Constitution provides certain safeguards to the civil services so that they can discharge their duties freely and conscientiously, without any feeling of insecurity of tenure, under Article 311. These safeguards are as follows:

(1) That no civil servant would be dismissed or removed by an authority subordinate to that by which he was appointed. It means that an officer can be dismissed or removed or reduced in rank by an authority superior to the appointing authority.

(2) Before dismissal or removal or demotion in rank a reasonable opportunity will be given to the officer. What does reasonable opportunity mean? Does it mean giving a hearing to the officer before framing charges or does it mean hearing him before taking the final action? This was not discussed in detail in the constituent assembly, and as per the 16th Amendment of the Constitution, only one opportunity is essential to be given.

There are three exceptions to the procedural protection given by Clause (2) of Article 311.

(a) Where an officer is dismissed or removed or reduced in rank on the ground of conduct which has led to his conviction on a criminal charge. Here the question arises, what type of criminal charge? A charge of a grave nature or an ordinary type has not been specified.

(b) When the legitimate authority is satisfied that it is not reasonably practicable to hold an enquiry, it may dispense with it after indicating the reasons in writing.

(c) Where the president or the governor, as the case may be, is satisfied that in the interest of the security of the state it is not expedient to give to that person such an opportunity.

These are the safeguards as 'far as Article 311 is concerned'. But, in our Constitution, Article 320(3)(c) says that 'the Union public service commission or the state public service commission, as the case may be, shall be consulted on all disciplinary matters affecting a person serving under the Government of India or the government of a state in a civil capacity, including memorials or petitions relating to such matters.' It is implied in this clause that the charge sheet with the explanation of the officer concerned shall pass through the public service commission. Thus, our Constitution makers tried to give procedural protection to our civil servants against possible arbitrary use of executive powers by involving public service commission. However, the protection amounts to very little because opinion tendered by the public service commission is not binding on the government.

The second way is to go to the court and seek protection from judiciary, but judicial protection will also not be very effective because the courts will only examine whether the prescribed procedure is followed or not. The case of *Union of India v. Tulsi Ram Patel* is illustrative of this point.[11] It shows the ineffectiveness of judicial protection. In this case, Patel was dismissed under Article 311(2) and he went to the Supreme Court.

A five-judge bench including the chief justice of India decided the case in favour of the Government of India. The judges argued that the express language of the second provision to Article 311(2) is inevitable and there is no escape from it. The learned judges opined that although it may appear harsh, the second Proviso has been inserted in the Constitution as a matter of public policy and public interest and for public good. It is in the public interest and for the public good that a government servant who has been convicted of a grave and serious offence or on rendering him unfit to continue in office should be summarily dismissed or removed from service instead of being allowed to continue in it at public expense and to public detriment. Further, the Court pointed out that 'it is, however, as much in public interest and for public good that government servants who are inefficient, dishonest or corrupt or have become a security risk should not continue in service and that the protection afforded to them by the Acts and Rules made under Article 309 and by Article 311 be not abused by them to the detriment of public interest and public good.'

When a situation as envisaged in one of the three clauses of the second Proviso to Clause (2) of Article 311 arises, and the relevant clause is properly applied and the disciplinary inquiry dispensed with, the concerned Government servant cannot be heard to complain that he is deprived of his livelihood. The livelihood of an individual is a matter of great concern to him and his family, but his livelihood is a matter of his private interest and where such livelihood is contrary to public interest and for public good, the former must yield to the latter.

Principles of Natural Justice

The Court held the view that the principle of natural justice contained in Article 14 can be modified and in exceptional cases can be excluded. In this case, the principle of natural justice has been excluded by a constitutional provision, namely, the second proviso to Clause (2) of Article 311. The opportunity of hearing is wholly ruled out under second proviso and it cannot be reintroduced by recourse to Article 14. The second proviso is based on public policy and is in public interest and for public good. The Constitution makers who inserted it in Article 311(2) were the best persons to decide whether such an exclusive provision should be there and the situation in which this provision should apply. A government servant is not wholly without any opportunity where the second provision applies, though there is no prior opportunity to a civil servant to defend himself against the charges made, he has the opportunity to go for an appeal arguing that the charges made against him are not true and this would be a sufficient compliance with the requirements of natural justice. Thus, this case is an eye opener and judicial protection is no protection at all.

Soon after the judgement, many trade unions and even members of Parliament expressed their reservation and concern about the judgement. In Delhi, many trade unions organized a massive rally in protest against this judgement. On the other hand, some state governments, taking advantage of this judgement, removed several government employees.[12] Thus, the judgement has been misunderstood by the government as well as by employees associations.

The decision in the case of *Union of India v. Tulsi Ram Patel* needs to be reviewed first, because it appears that this decision has been given in haste because the then chief justice of India, Y. V. Chandrachud, was about to retire. Second, it is based on the doctrine of pleasure which is a legacy of colonial government and against social interest. To give a fresh lease of life to such a principle is unjust and unreasonable. Though the judgement is based on facts, it will lead to misuse of principles and theories of law inherent in it. If the points of the judgement are not understood properly and the limits of the case are not well taken, it will impose a permanent emergency on the government servants. Therefore, it is submitted that the *Tulsi Ram Patel*'s case should not be treated as a general law for disciplinary actions under Article 311(2) but its application should be rare, only if national security demands. The intention of our Constitution makers in providing safeguards to civil servants was to protect them from arbitrary victimization, discriminatory and fanciful actions of the government.

The question is where is the protection against the wrongful punishment of an officer by a determined political leader who holds the reins of power. The answer is in the negative. In our Constitution, the president/governor is a nominal head and he always acts on the advice of the ministry, meaning thereby that if a prime minister/chief minister is determined to dismiss an officer, reduce him in rank or not to promote him, there is nothing to protect the civil servant. H. V. Kamath pointed out in the constituent assembly that if a chief minister informs an officer that 'in the interests and security of the state, I hereby take action against you. You are removed from service.'[13] That is the end of it. This provision will always hang like Damocles' sword over the neck of a civil servant. Even if this step is not taken by the political bosses, in practice, it will be sufficient for an officer to do 'the needful' for the politicians who are in power and for their party.[14] This shows that services do not have even that amount of protection which an ordinary citizen has got the right to be heard before being condemned, that, 'to refuse to give opportunity is to refuse justice', and that the expression 'security of the state' which is so dear to the heart of everyone is a much exploited expression and has been needlessly over-emphasized in Proviso (C).[15]

The fact is that our services have not been put on a firm foundation. The constitutional provisions should be amended in such a way so that efficient, honest and hard-working civil servants should feel encouraged on one hand and on the other such servants should be punished who disregard their basic duties and set bad examples in society. Law implementers should not be law breakers. Civil servants who involve themselves in heinous social crimes, like rape, smuggling, criminally assaulting others; are involved in cases of moral turpitude; or do not implement policies meant for the poor segment of population should be severely punished.

NOTES

1. *Constituent Assemby Debates Vol. IX*, p. 586.
2. Ibid., p. 624.
3. Ibid., p. 627.
4. Ibid., p. 586.
5. Article 309, Constitution of India.
6. All India Reporter 1981 SC 562.
7. *Ibid.*, p. 569.
8. Article 310, Constitution of India.
9. See, *Halsbury's Laws of England*, 4th edition, Vol. 8, paras 1106 and 1303.
10. See, for details, G. P. Pilania and Hoshiar Singh, *Administration and Social Change* (Jaipur: Printwell Publishers, 1985), p. 71.
11. *Union of India v. Tulsi Ram Patel*, All India Reporter 1985 SSC 1416.
12. The Chief Minister of UP terminated the services of three senior officials. *Hindustan Times*, Delhi, city edition, 11 October 1985.
13. Quoted in K. V. Rao, *Parliamentary Democracy of India* (Calcutta: World Press, 1965), p. 332.
14. Ibid., p. 332.
15. Ibid., p. 332.

18

Machinery for Planning

Planning in India

Although the era of economic planning started in India on 11 April 1951 with the launching of the First Five-Year Plan, the concept of planning was well known to Indian leaders. Even before Independence our leaders had stressed the need of planning for the eradication of the poverty of the masses. In 1931, M. Visvesvarayya, emphasized the need of planning in his book, *Planned Economy of India*. He suggested 10-year plans for doubling the income of the country. In 1937, Congress ministers of the provinces tried to put these ideas into practice. In 1938, the national planning committee was set up under the chairmanship of Jawaharlal Nehru. This committee prepared a plan for the economic development of the country. Three other plans for the economic development of the country were prepared. These were Bombay plan (prepared by eight noted businessmen of the country), people's plan (prepared by M. N. Roy) and Gandhian plan (prepared by Shriman Narayan) but these plans were not paid adequate attention by the foreign rulers. In 1944, a department of planning and development was set up in the Government of India but it could not accomplish anything.

In 1946, interim government was appointed under the premiership of Nehru. He set up an advisory planning board under the chairmanship of K. C. Neogy. The board recommended for the appointment of a planning commission, which should continuously pay attention to the economic development of the country. It was in pursuance of the recommendations of the board that the planning commission was set up in March 1950 by a resolution of the Government of India, with the prime minister as its chairman.

Planning was concerned as a major instrument for realizing the objectives of removal of poverty and attainment of socio-economic justice. 'The entire plan aimed at mobilizing the material and human resources of the nation to bring about an accelerated growth, both of the infrastructural inputs as well as of consumer goods so as to improve the living conditions of the entire people of India. The basic concept was to bring about a balanced growth that would not only remove regional imbalance but also the imbalance between the rural and urban sectors.'[1] To achieve this ambitious goal, the planning commission started the formulation and execution of Five-Year Plans. So far 12 plans have been put into operation and 13th Plan is in the process of preparation.

In 1991, a new economic policy was adopted with the trend of towards privatization, de-nationalization, disinvestment and deregulation. The prime minister explained in national development council (NDC) the relevance of the planning process in the emerging situation of globalization and market economy. He said, 'There was thus no question of choice between the market mechanism on the one hand and planning on the other on an either or basis, both have to be deviated to realize our objective of reducing poverty among the masses.'

Planning Commission

Composition, Organization and Functions

Composition

The prime minister has been its chairman since its inception. Its members are both part-time ex-officio members and full-time members. Some cabinet ministers such as defence, finance and planning are its members. The chairmanship of the prime minister has added to the prestige and effectiveness of the planning commission. The prime minister being too busy, it was necessary to provide for a deputy chairman to look after the work of planning commission. Sometimes the planning minister also used to act as its deputy chairman. But generally the post is occupied by an eminent non-official who is not a minister but the office is equivalent in rank to a cabinet minister. He understands political realities and how to carry on with a team of experts. Now Montek Singh Ahluwalia is the deputy chairman of the planning commission. The members enjoy the status of a minister of state in the Government of India. There are four or five full-time members of the commission. Members are appointed by the prime minister. Persons of eminence in economic matters, administration, etc., are appointed full-time members of the commission. There are no prescribed qualifications for the members of the commission.

The question is whether cabinet ministers be appointed as members of the commission. It is further alleged that the association of the ministers with the planning commission has made it a 'super cabinet', a body to be reckoned with. Some people believe that the planning commission should be an independent expert organization and this detracts from the expert nature of the planning commission and brings in the influence of politicians. But others believe that the presence of ministers helps in the implementation of the plans as a number of important ministers get committed to the plan at its formation stage itself. The number of members of planning commission has been changing from time to time. It started with five members and the chairman. In March 1964 there were six full-time members. In 1975 there were four full-time members along with the prime minister and finance minister; while in February 1987, there were six full-time members along with the prime minister and five ministers, totalling 12 members. There is no hard and fast rule for the number of its members.

Functions

The commission performs the following functions:

1. To make an assessment of the material, capital and human resources of the country, including technical personnel and to investigate the possibilities of augmenting such of these resources as are found to be deficient in relation to the nation's requirements
2. To formulate plans for the most effective and balanced utilization of the country's resources

3. To define the stages in which the plan should be carried out and propose the allocation of resources for the due completion of each stage on determination of priorities
4. To determine the nature of the machinery required for the implementation of the plan in all its aspects
5. To conduct periodic appraisal of the progress achieved in the execution of each stage of the plan
6. To prepare the perspective of planning
7. To recommend for facilitating the discharge of its duties or for a consideration of the prevailing economic conditions, current policies and development programmes; or for an examination of problems referred to it for advice by central and state governments

In brief, the planning commission aims at promoting a rapid rise in the standard of living of the people by efficient planning of the resources of the nation. It aims to provide opportunities to all for employment by increasing production. The implementation of the plans is the work of the various state governments and central government and not of planning commission.

Working of the Commission

All the members of the commission work as a body, but for convenience, each member has the charge of one or more subject and directs the study of problems in these fields. The deputy chairman is concerned with matters of general coordination and administration. The minister of planning is responsible for the commission as a whole to the central cabinet and Parliament.

As far as the procedure and methods of work of planning commission are concerned, it works as a body. Policy matters are referred to the commission as a whole. The cases to be considered by the commission as a whole include recommendations in regard to the formulation and progress of the Five-Year Plans and annual plans, adjustment in the plan, matters involving departure from the plan policies. Important cases involving disagreement with a central ministry or a state government, or difference of opinion between two members of the commission, and any matters relating to the internal organization and methods of work, are cases which are referred to the whole commission.[2]

Organization

The planning commission has three major divisions, namely, programme advisors, general secretariat and technical divisions. It has three advisory bodies; these are the committee on irrigation and power projects, coordination committee and research programmes committee.

There are four senior officers designated as advisors. They assist the members of the commission in matters of concerning field study and observations of various schemes or projects and the progress of their implementation. The general secretariat and technical divisions are concerned with internal sections of the planning commission. The research programmes committee organizes research on problems of socio-economic growth. The programme evolution organization evaluates the work of rural development and anti-poverty programmes. The committee on plan projects organizes investigation of the working of important plan projects in order to secure, economy and efficiency.

Plan Formulation

The planning commission formulates the plan, lays down the priorities, targets, financial resources, main projects, etc. The procedure of plan formulation is such that the planning commission prepares a short memorandum of the Five-Year Plan and places it before the central government and the national development council. After their approval of the memorandum a 'draft' outline, narrating objectives main targets of the plan, is prepared. The draft is discussed in the press by the public and in Parliament. The planning commission manages detailed discussions with the states. The states prepare their own plan keeping in mind the broad targets, but the final shape is given by the planning commission. As a result, the work of plan formulation is centralized with the planning commission.

Planning Commission—An Evaluation

The composition and working of the planning commission ever since its inception, has been subject of great criticism for several reasons:

(i) The inclusion of the prime minister and a number of ministers in the commission is said to have made it an extension of the cabinet. The prime minister appoints its members in the way he appoints ministers according to his individual judgment. There is no mention of their qualifications and term is also not fixed. The strength of the commission also depends on the prime minister. The prime minister being its chairman, the commission has become a powerful body and is described by its critics as 'super cabinet'. This is against the spirit of parliamentary democracy in which cabinet is supposed to be the supreme executive body.

(ii) The estimates of the Five-Year Plans are mostly unrealistic. It is usually found that the targets fixed are too high for achievement by the administration. It does not consider what is practicable or workable. It is due to this reason that achievements have always far lagged behind the targets. The most cherished goals of full employment, eradication of illiteracy and poverty and creation of an egalitarian society are a distant reality.

(iii) It is losing its character as a 'staff agency' of the Government of India insofar as it is getting on an authoritarian pattern. It was created to suggest, advise and plan and not to dictate and or acquire lordship over the administration.

(iv) The planning commission has eroded the autonomy of states and reduced them to the status of grant-receiving agencies. This is against the principles of federalism. The state governments depend on the commission for economic advice and financial assistance. The planning commission not only formulates the plan of the central government but also approves state plans. The state governments are called one by one to justify their plan outlays. The commission may cut its outlays and, in most of the cases, it did and the central government provides finances for plan projects on the recommendations of the planning commission.

(v) The planning commission tends to take over the functions of the ministry of finance and finance commission. There is a good deal of overlapping between their functions. Conflicts arise with the role of the finance commission, a constitutional body, unlike the planning commission. Overlapping recommendations of the two commissions leads to problems.[3]

(vi) The planning commission has expanded itself too much. It has become victim of Parkinson's law. Its staff strength has been continuously increasing without proportionate in the volume of work. The overstaffing has caused unnecessary burden.

Once touted as a body of experts, the planning commission now has fewer technocrats or experts. The body has now turned into a waiting office for IAS officers, who are looking at plum postings in the central government. In the 1970s, these used to be only one IAS officer in the commission said a top advisor in the commission. Now their member is huge and they have turned the commission into another bureaucratic body.

The commission was constituted by Jawaharlal Nehru to provide expert views on different governance issues outside the preview of bureaucrats.[4]

(vii) The monitoring and evaluation is the weakest part of the commission's function. Partly, the central ministries and the state governments are also responsible for not providing data to the commission in time.

National Development Council

India is a federation having 25 states and Union territories. Therefore, links between planning commission and state government was essential. The national development council is one of such link which is important in achieving coordination between the planning commission and the state governments. The draft outlines of the First Five-Year Plan had expressed the need for such a body. The Government of India accepted this proposal and the NDC was created on 6 August 1952 by a resolution of the Government of India.

Objectives and Functions

The main objective of the NDC is to ensure uniformity of approach in the planning process to promote common economic policies in all vital spheres and to ensure the balanced and rapid development of all parts of the country, securing coordination between the states and central government and the planning commission in the formulation and implementation of the plan. The NDC has been allotted to following functions by the very resolution which set up the council.

1. Review the working of the national plan from time to time
2. Consider important questions of social and economic policy affecting national development
3. Recommend measures for the achievement of the aims and targets set out in the national plan including measures to secure active participation and coordination of the people, improve the efficiency of the administrative services, ensure the fullest development of the less-developed regions and sections of the community, and, through sacrifice borne by all citizens, build up resources for national development

In October 1967, on the recommendations of the administrative reforms commission, the council was reconstituted and its functions were refined to include: (i) prescription of guidelines for the formulation of the national plan, including the assessment of resources for the plan; (ii) consideration of the national plan as formulated by the commission. These functions are in addition to that mentioned in resolution setting up the council.

Composition of National Development Council

The NDC is a very high-powered body comprising the prime minister as chairman of the council, all the Union cabinet ministers, the chief ministers of all the states, the members of the planning commission and the representatives of all the Union territories. The state ministers may also be invited to participate in the deliberations of the council. The usual practice is to invite those ministers whose subjects are likely to be discussed during the meeting.

Committees

The NDC is a large body. To function effectively, therefore, standing committee was created in November 1954, comprising the members of the commission and chief ministers of nine states only. The council has been appointing committees from time to time for a detailed examination of certain problems. The secretary of the commission acts as the secretary of the council and the commission provides the council with administrative and other assistance. The council generally meets twice a year. Normally, it does not pass any formal resolution. The decisions are usually unanimous. The issues considered by the council have been quite varied in nature. It meets to undertake a review of the plan, thus securing its coordinated implementation. At times it considered important issues like the decentralization of industrial production, balanced development of the country, setting up of suitable indicators of general development, establishment of *Panchayati Raj*, etc.

The chief ministers of opposition party–ruled states demand greater say and autonomy for the constituent states of the federation.

Evaluation

The national development council has successfully linked the Union government, the planning commission and the various state governments. It has provided a good forum for discussion and free exchange of ideas and created a sense of high responsibility on the part of the state governments for making the plans a success. The council considers socio-economic policies from national point of view to secure uniformity. Thus, it provides directions to the country on local issues of policies, promotes collective thinking and joint action on the issues of national importance.

However, there are persons who view the increasing powers of the council as a danger to the privileges of the central and state cabinets. They charge the NDC for usurping authority and functioning as a 'super cabinet'. Brecher writes in the biography of Jawaharlal Nehru, 'The NDC was established as a supreme administrative and advisory body on planning. . . . It lays down policy directives invariably approved by the cabinet. Since their inception the NDC and its standing committee have virtually relegated the planning commission to the status of a research arm.'[5] A similar view has been expressed by H. M. Patel, a former ICS officer. He said, 'Among the advisory bodies to the planning commission is included the NDC. This is surely inaccurate, as is clear from its composition. The NDC is a body obviously superior to the planning commission. It is, indeed, a policy-making body and its recommendations cannot but be regarded as policy decisions and not merely as advisory suggestions.'

Further, K. Santhanam went to the extent of saying, 'the position of the NDC has come to approximate that of a super cabinet of the entire Indian federation, a cabinet functioning for the Government of India as well as for the governments of all states.'[6]

The effectiveness of the NDC as against the planning commission is not easy to determine. Some people say that the NDC is too unwieldy a body to take any effective decisions. Moreover, it has no independent secretariat and depends upon the planning commission to provide it with the necessary expert advice and planning commissions' expertise is formidable. Thus, it is unclear as to what extent the national development council is effective in influencing the working of the planning commission.

The NDC concerns with broad policy matters and meets only twice or thrice a year. On the other hand, the planning commission is a continuously functioning body. It has a good deal of expertise and due to this reason acquired a great deal of powers vis-à-vis the central government as well as state governments. The NDC therefore, can hardly match the planning commission in effectiveness. The chief ministers take little interest in NDC meetings, and are very preoccupied with their political mechanizations and have no time to give any serious thought to the planning process. The NDC is more a debating shop than a deliberative body. Therefore, the NDC is no match to the planning commission, which due to its compact size and expertise, is in a far better position to understand the problems of development and prepare suitable programmes. Therefore, it is not correct to say that the NDC has relegated the planning commission.

In spite of the above criticism of the NDC it is working successfully. It is a creation of the Union Cabinet. Therefore, its role is only advisory. It is only a high-ranking policy-making body and it is for the cabinet to decide to what extent its suggestions are to be followed. The nature of its composition allows the council to gain more power and influence but this should not be taken as an alarm to the powers of the Union and state cabinets. It has promoted partnership and cooperation between the Union and the states.

Planning Machinery at the State Level

The state plans account for about one half of the total outlay of the government under the Five-Year Plans. But the states do not have separate planning commissions but they have state planning departments. The department keeps touch with the planning commission, various ministries and departments of the state government for the preparation of the development plans for the whole state and for coordinating their developmental programmes while formulating the plans. The guidelines of the planning commission are usually followed.

The ARC recommended the setting up of state planning boards for the formulation of Five-Year Plans and evaluation of the plan performance. These planning boards 'should have their own secretariat to help them in the adequate discharge of these functions. The state plans largely concern investment in the field of agriculture, irrigation, power and social services. The plan formulation wing of the state planning board should, therefore, generally comprise three sectoral units—one for development of agriculture and allied areas including irrigation; the second to deal with power and also with industry and transport to the extent to which each state is concerned with these two latter subjects; and the third for social services. In addition, it would be necessary to have a strong evaluation unit. This should be the normal organizational pattern of the state planning boards.'[7]

Almost all the state governments have now set up state planning boards. The position of the board and its effectiveness in the planning process varies from state to state. The boards of Gujarat, Maharashtra, Tamil Nadu, Karnataka, West Bengal, etc. are effective while others are not so effective. Sikkim perhaps is the only state where the apex body has not been set up. In most of the states, chief minister is the chairman of the board. In Meghalaya and Tamil Nadu, non-official chairmen are nominated by the government.

In Maharasthra, Gujarat, Rajasthan, UP, Bihar and Nagaland, the minister of planning is either vice-chairman or deputy chairman. In Haryana, HP, Tripura the Meghalaya an MLA is nominated as full-time deputy chairman with the status of a minister. In the remaining states, either some officer or a prominent non-official is made the deputy chairman.

The number of members on the planning board varies widely from state to state. For example, in Assam there are only two members while in UP there are 24 members. Most of the members are part timers, and very few boards have full-time members.

The secretary of the planning department usually works as the secretary of the planning board. In Kerala and Tamil Nadu, there is whole-time member-secretary. In some states, joint secretary, special secretary or deputy secretary planning is made the secretary of the planning board.

The Functions of the Planning Board

The ARC prescribed the following functions:

(i) To make an assessment of the state's resources and formulate plans for the most effective and balanced utilization of these resources

(ii) To determine plan priorities of the state within the framework of the priorities of the national plan

(iii) To assist the district authorities in formulating their development plans within the spheres in which such planning is considered to be useful and feasible and to coordinate these plans with state plans

(iv) To identify factors which tend to retard the economic and social development of the state and determine the set of conditions for successful execution of the plans

(v) To review the progress of implementation of the plan programmes and recommend such adjustments in policies and measures as the review may indicate

Planning Machinery

There is no study on the planning machinery in the states and very little is known about the existing planning in the state. The usual pattern appears to be to have the planning secretary at the top with special secretary, deputy secretaries, under secretaries, etc. to help him. In some states, a few experts are also associated while some states are also using eminent persons from outside the government to help them in the planning process. The problems in formulation of state plans include inadequate consultation with the state governments in formulation of plans, detailed scrutiny of plan schemes by the planning commission and earmarking of outlays, which leaves little discretion with the state governments to decide their own priorities.[8]

The states, by and large, have not taken planning seriously. Their plans are mostly a collection of requirements prepared by different departments. These are mostly prepared in financial terms and do not indicate physical targets. The state planning boards have been set up due to the continuous pressure of Government of India. These are generally used to accommodate either, the defeated politician or the retired and unwanted government servant, etc.

Planning Machinery at the District Level

The Government of India had been exhorting the state governments to introduce district planning. The efforts were intensified during the Fifth and Sixth Plans periods due to the introduction of integrated rural development programmes (IRDP). As a result of the persistent efforts, many states have taken steps to set up district planning machineries. The machinery operates at two levels. As the apex level, there is a district planning board/committee to guide the planning process in the district. The planning machinery actually undertakes the necessary data collection and analysis for the formulation of the plan.

District Planning Boards/Committees

In the composition of the district planning boards in various states, four patterns had emerged.

(i) The minister chairman model, where a minister of the state government is the chairman of the body as is the case in Maharasthra, Gujarat, UP and Bihar.

(ii) The deputy commissioner/district collector chairman model. This pattern is prevalent in Assam, HP, J and K, Punjab, Haryana, Rajasthan, Karnataka and Nagaland.

(iii) The non-official chairman model. This is found in MP and Meghalaya.

(iv) The MLA chairman model is prevalent only in Sikkim.

The first model provides effective coordination at the district level and establishes linkages with the secretariat, but he may not find sufficient time to devote to district planning. The second model is advantageous because he is a senior officer in the district, having high prestige. He is a natural coordinator of district activities, but he is also an overburdened man.

The position in regard to the office of the member secretaries also differ from state to state. The collector, assistant development commissioner, chief development officer or ADM or district development officer has often been nominated member-secretary. In some states, the district planning officer happens to be the member-secretary.

Evaluation of District Planning

The shortcomings generally noticed in the district plans are that: (i) the objectives of the district plans are not formulated according to the national objectives; (ii) lack of detailed data on resources, demography, position of infrastructure, etc. (iii) lack of analytical machinery to analyse existing programmes and suggest modification; (iv) lack of integration of resources of centre, state, local bodies, credit institutions and voluntary agencies; (v) in preparation of employment programmes, manpower planning is not kept in mind; (vi) planning organization is very weak in almost all the states and full-time qualified staff is hardly available.

The reasons for the slow progress of district planning in India are many. The important ones among them are the following:

(i) Monitoring of progress of schemes at district and lower levels is not done on the quality or impact of the scheme but only on the amount spent on the programme.

(ii) The role of planning is not given sufficient attention by bureaucrats and politicians. They consider implementation more important than planning any effort concerning planning wasteful.

(iii) Centrally sponsored schemes carrying subsidies are taken by the states for getting subsidy money regardless of their suitability to the area.

(iv) Planning reduces the scope of discretion and arbitrary action, therefore, local level authorities avoid it as far as possible to exercise discretionary powers.

(v) State governments do not want to delegate adequate powers to lower levels.

(vi) The planners are used to centralized planning. Therefore, they have a natural bias towards centralization because it gives them power and authority.

The slow progress of district planning led the Government of India to give serious thought to improve district planning. Therefore, for the first time in the history of planning, district planning has been given constitutional position by creating a district planning committee through the 74th Constitutional Amendment Act, 1992.

District Planning Committee

The Constitution (Seventy-Fourth Amendment) Act, 1992 243-D, provides for the creation of a 'district planning committee' to consolidate the plans prepared by the *panchayat*s and the municipalities in the district and to prepare a draft development plan for the whole district.

Composition

The composition of the district planning committee will be according to the law passed by the state legislature, which will also mention the way to fill up the committee seats; but four-fifths members of the committee shall be elected from amongst the elected members of the *Panchayats* at the district level and of the municipalities in the district in proportion to the ratio of rural-urban population. The state law will determine the function of the committee relating to the district planning and the manner of choosing its chairperson.

The committee while preparing the draft development plan keeps in mind the matters of common interest between the *panchayats* and the municipalities including spatial planning; sharing of water and other physical and natural resources; the integrated development of infrastructure and environmental conservation; the extent and type of available financial and other resources; and consult such institution and organization, which the governor might specify by its order. After the preparation of the draft development plan and its passage by the committee, the chairperson of the district planning committee will forward it to the state government for incorporation in the state plan.

Thus, for the first time a constitutional planning body has been created and that too at the district level. The critics may argue that while there is no such constitutional planning body at national level, what useful purpose this district planning committee will serve, is to be seen. Second, the question may arise: Can decisions of a constitutional body be changed by non-constitutional body like the planning commission? The answer is that there are no conflicts between both these institutions. The district planning committee will send its draft development plan to the state government, and the state plan will be prepared incorporating plans of all the districts, and ultimately the planning commission, in consultation with the state concerned, will finalize the plan. Finally, it can be said, that is an appropriation step in the direction of planning from below, a suggestion put forth by almost all important planning bodies and economists for better development of all areas.

The situation of planning, by and large, appears that most of the state governments have not taken the planning task seriously. The state level planning boards have been set up under the pressure of the centre and are generally used to accommodate the defeated politicians, the retired and unwanted civil servants, etc. The district planning committees have yet to be set up by the states by passing laws for the composition and functions.

NOTES

1. Vasant Sathe, *National Government—Agenda for a New India* (New Delhi, UBS Publishers Distributors Ltd., 1991), p. 19.
2. C. P. Bhambhari, *Public Administration: Theory and Practice,* 12th edition (Meerut: Jai Prakash Nath & Co., 1992–1993), p. 236.
3. S. Venkatramanan, *The Economic Times,* New Delhi, 8 August 1996.
4. *Hindustan Times,* 14 August 2008.
5. M. Brecher, *Nehru—A Political Biography* (London: Oxford University Press, 1959), p. 521.
6. K. Santhanam, *Union-State Relations in India* (Bombay: Asia Publishing House, 1960), p. 47.
7. Administrative Reform Commission (ARC).
8. *Approach Paper to the Ninth Five-Year Plan (1997–2002)* (New Delhi: Government of India, Planning Commission, 1997), p. 105.

Public Undertakings

The old *laissez faire* theory of state activity has given way to the socialist and welfare theory of state. The trend is towards increasing government intervention in the economic field. We find examples of state enterprises in almost all the countries of the world; both developing and developed. Even in a country like America, where public undertakings are looked as curtailment of individual liberty, we find the Tennessee Valley Authority as a very good example of public enterprise. In France, public enterprises cover a large sector of the French economy. So is the case in Britain. In the developing countries like Sri Lanka, Pakistan, Turkey and Burma we find a number of public enterprises.

After Independence the public sector has emerged as a major factor in the country's economic growth and it has occupied 'commanding heights' in the Indian economy, according to a survey of economic growth in public sector during the successive plans. By the end of 1991, the number stood at 244 with a public involvement of Rs 99,315 crores. As many as 26,146 companies limited by shares were registered during 1991–1992 under the Companies Act, 1956. The Eighth Plan (1992–1997) envisaged a total investment of Rs 7,98,000 crores of which the amount in the public sector would be Rs 4,34,100 crores, having an investment component will be Rs 3,61,000 crores.

The need of public undertaking arises because there are many such activities in which private enterprises were not interested due to lack of resources. There are also such undertakings which the state has to keep under its direct control for reasons of security or strategic importance. The defence undertakings get first preference and basic industries fall under the second. Therefore, a number of government companies and public corporations have been formed in addition to the departmental undertakings, to undertake the economic and business activity on behalf of the government.

Organization of Public Undertakings

There are three principal forms into which our public enterprises have been organized. First, the departmental undertakings, government companies registered as joint-stock companies and statutory public corporations. A new fourth type is also worth mentioning, that is, control boards in the case of multi-purpose river valley projects. Recently, a new form has been increasingly used, which is 'operating contract', under which government contracts exist with private concerns for the operation and management of a public enterprise. We study here these three forms of organization, discuss their main features and then pass on to discuss their comparative merits and demerits.

Forms of Public Undertakings

Departmental Undertakings

Government participation in manufacturing and other organized business was rather limited. Whatever little business happened, it was conducted by the departmental undertakings. These were part of government departments and were run by them. Many of them are still run as departmental undertakings, such as the railways, posts and telegraphs, defence production units, various government workshops, All India Radio, Doordarshan, etc. The characteristics of this type of organization are:

(1) The enterprise is financed by annual appropriations from the treasury and all, or a major share of its revenues, are paid into the treasury.

(2) The enterprise is subject to budget accounting and controls applicable to other government departments.

(3) The staff of the enterprise consists of civil servants. Their service rules are guided by civil service rules.

(4) The enterprise is subject to the direct control of the head of the department. He is accountable through his minister for the activities of the enterprise.

(5) It is created by an executive resolution and its creation does not require prior approval of the Parliament.

(6) The enterprise can be sued only through the state, it has no legal personal standing.

Advantages

The advantage of the departmental type of public enterprise is that it is a well-known form of organization with set standard patterns and fixed procedures. The main advantages are as follows:

(i) It is a general form of governmental organization with set standard patterns and fixed procedures and does not require much innovation.

(ii) In this form the staffing pattern does not pose much problem as there are clear-cut rules and regulations for recruitment and control of public servants.

(iii) It is a well-controlled form of organization and assures maximum degree of control by the government.

(iv) It is most suitable form for sensitive type of industries like the defence production and ordnance factories, etc.

(v) In this form government money is secure and better ensured because every type of expenditure requires sanction from the competent authority.

Disadvantages

This form suffers from certain basic weaknesses such as too much centralization and insufficient delegation of authority; red tape and rigid procedures and rules and too much control. A. D. Gorewala observed,

'In many ways it is the direct negation of the requirements of autonomy. It militates against initiatives, flexibility . . . . For departmental management means management by one or more administrative departments as part of larger routine, inevitably in conjunction with the finance department as part of its own routine . . . against the background of the rules, regulations and procedures inseparable from ordinary administration and of the plenary control of the minister and Parliament, also inseparable from that administration.'[1]

Its main disadvantages are:

(i) The rules and procedures are very rigid and do not leave any scope for flexibility which a commercial or trade organization needs.

(ii) The financial arrangements are unsatisfactory as the money comes from the annual budget and lapses at the end of the financial year. This leads to discontinuity in business and trading operations which is harmful for the efficient working of the undertaking.

(iii) The civil servants taken on deputation to run the undertaking retain the usual bureaucratic attitude. They do not have the vision and are not enterprising enough to run such enterprises.

(iv) Departmental methods of purchase and sale are also slow and time consuming.

(v) Complicated system of accounting and audit.

(vi) The cash receipts have to be put into government account and cannot be taken out without special sanction.

(vii) The profits of the enterprise cannot be used for strengthening or enlarging its own business as they go to the government funds.

Government Company or Joint Stock Company

Most of the big private business is carried out by private limited companies or public limited companies. They are in the form of joint stock companies in which a number of participants pool their resources to provide the share capital. India has made extensive use of joint stock companies, registered under the Indian company law, for the management of commercial enterprises like the Fertilizer Corporation of India Limited, Heavy Electricals (Private) Ltd., Hindustan Machine Tools (Private) Ltd., etc. The formation of the private limited company needs only two share holders at the minimum, while to form a public limited company at least seven share holders are required. There is no restriction on the maximum number of share holders in case of public limited company while the private limited company has a maximum limit of 50 shareholders. The shares of a public limited company can be freely transferred but in case of private limited companies such a transfer is restricted. This is a joint form of ownership in which the government can also participate. The Companies Act, 1956 provides for a distinct category for government companies in which the controlling shares (more than 50 percent) belongs to the government. When the government is intended to invite subscriptions from the public, a public limited company may be floated by the government.

The main characteristics of the government companies are:

(i) The company form has most of the features of a private limited company in which whole or more than 50 percent of the stock is held by the government.

(ii) It is a corporate body created under the law of the Companies Act, 1956. It can sue and be sued, enter into contract and acquire property in its own name.

(iii) The majority of the directors are appointed by the government depending upon the extent of the share of the government in the capital stock.

(iv) Its articles and memorandum of association, although conforming to the Companies Act, are drawn up and are revisable by the government.

(v) Companies are generally exempted from the personnel, budgeting, accounting and audit laws, rules and procedures applicable to government departments.

(vi) All its employees are not civil servants except a few who are on deputation to these companies.

(vii) The majority of its share capital is obtained from the government In case of private limited government company, the entire capital is contributed by the government, the additional income comes through from sales of goods and services as well as from the financial institutions. Neither does it depend upon the government for its revenues nor does it have to draw its money from the treasury.

Advantages

The advantages of the company form of organizations are many. S. S. Khera a former cabinet secretary claims the following:

(i) A company provides a great deal of flexibility and freedom of action in management.

(ii) It is a good thing for a public undertaking doing business to constitute itself into, and be seen to be, a separate commercial entity.

(iii) The company being a separate commercial entity, the management is stimulated to adopt and adhere to sound commercial practices.

(iv) The company form provides for the association of non-officials.

(v) The company form enables legally very large formal delegation of functions and assignment of resources.

(vi) The discipline of the company law is a good thing for management.

The other advantages are that it provides autonomy in administration and financial matters. In this form the government can associate private enterprises, national or foreign to bring additional capital for investment and lastly, it provides adequate control by the government. This form, however, has its own limitations. The Economic and Social Council for Asia and the Pacific (ESCAP) in its seminar on organization and administration of public enterprises held in Rangoon called it 'a vague and extremely difficult form of organization and control.' A retired accountant-general, P. K. Wattal, remarked that 'such industrial undertakings whittle away parliamentary control over public money'. A former comptroller and auditor-general of India has gone to the length of calling it 'a fraud on the Companies Act and the Constitution'. Its main disadvantages are as follows:

(i) In the company form all or most of the functions normally vested in the share holders and in the management revert back to the government. It has full freedom to appoint or dismiss or change the management.

(ii) The undefined and unrestricted powers exercised by the government department of public enterprises gives it a lot of control over these companies.

(iii) This form weakens the control of the Parliament over the public enterprises.

(iv) The flexibility and autonomy of this type of organization is often abused by the government.

Public Corporations

A new form of organized public enterprises that has evolved during the last four or five decades is public corporation. It evolved because of defects in departmental and company system. The public corporation system is favoured because it provides just the right combination of commercial freedom and government control. According to the former US President, Franklin D. Roosevelt, 'A corporation is clothed with the power of government but possessed of the initiative and flexibility of private enterprise.' The reason for the creation of the modern type of public corporation is the need for a higher degree of freedom, boldness and enterprise in the management of undertaking of an industrial or commercial character and the desire to escape from the caution and circumspection which is considered typical of government department. Public corporation may be defined as a legal entity created by the government, but external to the government organization, and financially independent for the purpose of carrying on the specific activities in manner prescribed in the law made for its creation. The principal characteristics of a public corporation according to United Nations study are as follows:

(i) It is wholly owned by the state.

(ii) It is generally created by, or pursuant to a special law defining its powers, duties and immunities and prescribing the form of management and its relationship to established departments and ministries.

(iii) As a body corporate, it is a separate entity for legal purposes and can sue and be sued, enter into contracts and acquire property in its own name. The corporations contract and do business in their own name. They have been generally given greater freedom than ordinary government departments in making contracts and acquiring and disposing of property.

(iv) Except for appropriation to provide capital or to cover losses, a public corporation is usually independently financed. It obtains its funds either by borrowing from the treasury or the public and from revenue derived from the sale of goods and services. It is authorized to use and re-use its revenues.

(v) It is generally exempt from most regulatory and prohibitory statutes applicable to expenditure of public funds.

(vi) It is ordinarily not subject to the budget, accounting and audit laws and procedures applicable to non-corporate agencies.

(vii) In the majority of cases, employees of public corporations are not civil servants, and are recruited and remunerated under terms and conditions which the corporation itself determines.

Advantages

The main advantages of the public corporation form of organizations are as follows:

(i) The public corporation has proved to be a valuable instrument for social control of economic life. It provides flexibility required in the business and economic operations of the government.

(ii) The public corporation being an autonomous body is shielded from political influence, treasury control and governmental procedures. The statute by which the corporations are set up can be adjusted to suit the type of function it is supposed to perform and is not pliable so that the government cannot misuse it easily.

(iii) The corporation can hire the necessary expert personnel from the market without undergoing the rigid procedures of the government. This can utilize all the technical knowledge available to private concerns.

Disadvantages

However, the public corporation form of organization has also some weaknesses. The main disadvantages are the following:

(i) The so-called autonomy of the public corporation is a myth. It cannot be made immune from ministerial control and direction. The statute is helpless as the control of the ministry is informal.

(ii) It protects the corporation from parliamentary control, but it places political power in the hands of a small unrepresentative group with every possible danger of perpetuating itself in power.

(iii) The complaints are that the government departments are interfering in the working of the corporation. The Chagla commission, which was appointed in 1958 to enquire into Mundhara episode, said, 'The evidence before me clearly shows that there was a clear tendency on the part of the finance ministry to look upon the corporation (Life Insurance Corporation) as a wing or branch of that ministry and to issue orders to it in the belief that the corporation was bound to carry out these orders.'

Comparison

After discussing the strong and weak points of all the three forms of public enterprises, we may discuss the question as to which of the three forms of governmental undertakings is the more suitable for running the business, manufacturing and trading operations or the government. This question has been considered by various committees and commissions.

The first Industrial Policy Resolution of 6 April 1948 had envisaged that the management of the state enterprise will as a rule be through the medium of public corporations under the statutory control of the central government. The Second Industrial Policy Resolution of 20 April 1956 did not alter or modify the policy of government concerning public enterprises; and it has not been modified by any subsequent declarations. Its use has been confined to the organization of enterprises in certain fields like insurance, transport and electricity only. In practice, the central as well as state governments have shown preference for the company form.

The matter was also considered in detail by A. D. Gorwala in his report on the efficient conduct of state enterprises in 1951. He felt that a department form may be used in exceptional cases where the need of national security, strategic importance, etc. arose if it so demands. However, such cases must be defined, isolated and kept down to the minimum. He favoured the company form for substantial commercial functions because of its flexibility. He said that corporations should be used where the undertaking was to discharge what in fact were the extension of government functions, e.g., irrigation, hydro-electric projects and broadcasting. The First Five-Year Plan, 1952, under the influence of Gorwala recommendations, also suggested the adoption of the company form.

The Krishna Menon Committee Report on State Undertakings in India, 1959, had recommended the adoption of the corporation form. This question was also examined by the Estimates Committee (Second Lok Sabha) in its 18th Report, April 1960. The committee observed that no well-defined principles had been followed in determining the form of organization of public undertakings and haphazard decisions had been taken and proposed the setting up of an expert committee to advise the government in this matter. The committee favoured statutory corporations for wholly owned government enterprises and departmental form was justified only for special reasons like defence strategic or security needs. The committee wanted company form to be used for certain specific types of business only.

The government, however, decided to keep the question open while favouring the company form. The government's decision in the matter taken in 1961 stated, 'Government considers that the form of management of the undertakings should be determined by the requirements of each case. Accordingly, from the point of view of flexibility of operations, the company form of management would be preferable. In some instances, it would be necessary to form statutory corporations while in a few others, for various reasons, it would be desirable to run the undertakings as departmental organizations.'

The Administrative Reforms Commission

The Administrative Reforms Commission (ARC) considered this question in detail. The commission's preference was first for the corporation form and second for the company form. The commission said, 'We believe that there is an important advantage in adopting the form of a statutory corporation as compared to company form. Statutory corporations are set up after full public debate and with the approval and sanction of Parliament. This leads to a clear and precise definition of their objectives and obligations. It also results in a clear demarcation of powers between the government and the public undertaking. Further, having vested autonomy in the undertaking through an enactment, Parliament will itself take care to ensure that such autonomy is fully recognised by the executive agencies of the government.'[2]

The commission further observed that, 'in certain cases, however, the company form is preferable. For instance, the company form is more appropriate for undertaking, which have an element of private participation. It is also desirable those undertakings which are predominantly trading concerns or which have been set up to improve or stabilize a particular area or business, as in the case of the construction undertakings, the trading corporations and hotels.'[3] Finally, the commission recommended that:

(1) The form of a statutory corporation should in general be adopted for public sector projects in the industrial and manufacturing field.
(2) For projects in which there is an element of private participation, the government company form may be adopted.
(3) Promotional and developmental agencies should, as far as possible, be run as statutory corporations or departmental concerns.
(4) Undertakings which are predominantly trading concerns or which are set up to improve and stabilize particular areas of business may have the company form.[4]

Conclusions

The above discussion shows that no particular form of organization can be said to be suitable for every form of government activity. The Government of India's decision keeping in view the recommendations of ARC was 'for certain enterprises providing public utilities which are primarily intended to develop the basic infrastructure facilities, the statutory corporation form management may be preferable. For other enterprises, including those operation in the monopolistic field but where the commercial aspect is predominant, the present form of a company may allow more flexibility. The government, therefore, does not consider that the form of statutory corporation should, in general, be adopted for public enterprises.' The departmental form of enterprise may be suitable only for security and strategic purposes. The government has, thus, continued its earlier policy of preference for public company form of organization for public undertakings.

A discussion on public undertaking would be incomplete if we do not mention the shift in the ideological approach of socialist pattern of society towards the trend of privatisation. In July 1991, the then Prime Minister, P. V. Narasimha Rao, made a public statement on public sector policy. He said a policy of disinvestment will be followed and share-holding in the public sector would be offered to financial institutions and general public, the boards of these companies would be made more professional, through the system of memorandum of understanding (MOU) performance would be improved. In 1991, 71 public enterprises signed MOUs with their controlling ministries and since then number of public enterprises signing MOUs has been increasing day by day. The new economic policy's thrust is towards privatization. It has two components: deregulation and partial denationalization.[5]

Management of Public Undertakings

The management of public undertakings depends upon the type of its organization. In case of departmental undertakings, the management forms the general structure of the government departments. All its functionaries from top to bottom are government servants recruited according to the government recruitment rules. The situation in the case of corporation form and companies is different. Although these are owned by the government and their management is also appointed by the government, their procedure of appointment and terms and conditions are different than those of the departmental undertakings. These terms and conditions are decided by the statute meant for the corporation or by the memorandum and articles of association of the company.

The management of public corporations and the companies consists of two parts: (1) top management and (ii) operational management. The board of directors of public enterprises constitute the top management of the companies. They perform policy-making and executive functions. The boards have full power to frame policies and have a fair measure of managerial autonomy. The government do not interfere in the day-to-day operational matters of enterprises. The exact working depends upon the chief executive, the directors, the top officials in the administrative ministry and the minister concerned.

The board of directors may have full- and part-time members. There are many enterprises where only the chief executive is a full-time director (chairman-cum-managing director or managing director). All other directors are part-time. These part-time directors are expected to be professionals and represent interests such as labour and consumer, etc.

Accepting the ARC recommendation, the government decided that as a rule the larger corporations should have full-time functional directors and now most of the big corporations are having a number of full-time functional directors.

The part-time directors are mostly professional and public men, and they play a useful coordinating role between the enterprise and the ministry of finance and administrative ministry. The size of the board as recommended by ARC should be limited between 10 and 12. In rare cases it may go up to 15 but not more. The Government of India has, by and large, followed this policy.

Operational Management

The managing director provides a link between the board and operation management which is supposed to carry out the policy decided by the board. He sits on the board of directors as well as heads the operational management. The actual organization of the operational management depends upon the type of activities performed by the particular undertaking. The set-up is usually decided by the board of directors subject to some limitations, whereas sanction of the government is required for creation of certain levels of posts.

Policies of Appointment

In the beginning up to the 1960s, the top management of public sector was drawn from government services, both civil and defence, comprising generalists and specialists. The appointment to the top post was made by the administrative ministries. The administrative services, technical services like railways, PWD, etc. and army engineering services provided the bulk of personnel for these appointments. In 1965, a major policy for recruitment was adopted in the selection method. A screening committee of secretaries was constituted to assess the suitability of persons who wished to join the public enterprises. Interviews were held for those applying from the private sector. The committee made employment of suitable persons for appointment to the top management posts in the public enterprises. The panel was maintained by the Bureau of Public Enterprises which served as the secretariat of the committee. In 1970, some changes were made in the system and an empanel board was set up and it was decided that all persons, whether public or private, have to face interview before they were empanelled.

Public Enterprises Selection Board

In 1974, a public enterprises board was set up for advising the government for appointments on top posts. The top posts were those of the chairman, managing director and full-time executive directors where the government was the appointing authority. All appointments below the board level were brought under the purview of companies. The empanelment system was stopped. The public enterprises board was to make selections for specific vacancies. Its secretariat was located in the PEB. Recently, the Government of India decided that a government servant has to resign from his job if he joins a public undertaking. Thus, the system of deputation of government's servants to the public enterprises has been completely stopped.

Operational Management

The recruitment and selection for middle and junior level posts are now completely left to the board of directors of the concerned public undertaking. Some of them such as the public sector banks have set up recruitment boards while others set up their own selection committees and boards depending upon the circumstances prevailing in the organization.

The public enterprise for efficient functioning should make a clear-cut objective and obligation of the undertaking, they should have their corporate plans linked to the national plans, clear-cut choice of technology, inventory management, market planning and proper personnel management so that workers feel motivated. Training arrangements of employees have to be made for increase in productivity.

These are some of the important functions which the management of public enterprises has to perform for its good productivity and efficiency.

Control over Public Undertakings

Public undertakings in India enjoy autonomy except departmental undertakings. They are not answerable to the Parliament in the way departmental enterprises are. However, these enterprises cannot be made entirely free from responsibility to the people. The government has, therefore, devised various methods for exercising necessary control over the activities of the government undertakings. The main objectives of control over public enterprises are to promote efficiency to attain national objectives, to attain fixed targets and to regulate power concentration in the hands of ministers, civil servants or directors.

Instruments of Control

Public control over public enterprises is exercised through three main agencies—the minister, the Parliament and other special agencies. The methods of control exercised by these agencies are discussed below.

Ministerial Control

The general principles of ministerial control are as follows:

(i) To reserve such powers of the government as are required by them to determine the question of policy.

(ii) To see that the programmes of public enterprises is in conformity with the national plans.

(iii) To ensure that the enterprise is working on the commercial lines as per the general policies of the government.

The ministerial control is exercised through the following measures in the administrative field.

1. The government is empowered to appoint the chairman and members of the board of management and the managing director. The government can remove the members for reasons specified in the Act. This power of appointment and removal gives to the government sufficient authority to exercise effective and strict control, formally and informally, over the public enterprises.

2. The government is authorized to frame rules and regulations to facilitate the working of these enterprises. Besides, it has the power to issue policy directions. It is the duty of the board to implement the government policy as communicated to it. Such power is given to the government by the articles of association in the case of government companies and by the enabling Acts of public corporations.

3. The government can institute enquiries into the working of a corporation. Such an enquiry was made by Chagla in the investments made by the Life Insurance Corporation in Mundhra firms. Enquiries can be held in the case of government companies.

4. Every public enterprise submits to the government its annual report of working. The government can ask for any information or reports on any matter.

Minister exercises control over the working of public undertakings in the financial field also.

1. Ministers are authorized to appoint a financial advisor on the board of a corporation. Such an advisor exercises a kind of veto affecting the expenditure and financial policy of the government.

2. The sanction of the government is necessary to (i) sanction capital expenditure above a certain amount; (ii) for approving variation in estimates of over 10 per cent and (iii) for matters connected with borrowings, investments, securities, distribution of profits, etc. For instance, in the case of the Hindustan Steel (Private) Limited, approval of the central government is necessary for increase of capital, issue of new shares, reduction of capital, borrowing of money, issue of bonds, debentures and securities. Likewise, the Air Corporation Act, 1953 required the two air corporations to take the previous approval of the government for undertaking any expenditure for the purchase of any immovable property at a cost exceeding a particular limit.

3. The audit of the accounts of public enterprises is done by the auditors appointed by the government. The audit of the departmentally managed undertakings like any other department is done by the comptroller and auditor-general. In the case of government companies, the statutory auditors of the company audit

the company's accounts according to the principles of commercial audit and the comptroller and accountant-general conducts the audit of the same accounts more or less on the principles of financial, audit applicable to government departments. Under the Indian Companies Act, the company auditors are appointed by the Union government. A copy of the audit report of the company auditor is sent to the comptroller and accountant-general who has the right to comment upon the audit report. The audit of statutory corporations is conducted by an independent authority but these corporations are required to submit their annual reports and accounts to the parliament.

Department of Public Enterprises

Governmental control over the department of public enterprises (formerly known as the bureau of public enterprise) is dispersed among various ministries according to their functional areas. In order to provide an effective centralized coordinating unit for providing policy and overall guidance to public enterprises and for undertaking a continuous appraisal of the organizational set up, personnel requirement, performance, etc. of the public enterprises, a bureau of public enterprises, located in the ministry of finance, was set up in 1969 and assigned five specific functions: to provide a central point of reference and consultation and to deal with matters of general interests; to explore avenues of economy in capital costs of projects; to devise steps for improving productivity and profitability; to undertake appraisal and evaluation of selected areas in the performance of public enterprises; and to prepare an annual report on the working of industrial and commercial undertakings of the central government for presentation to Parliament. As a result of the recommendations of the administrative reforms commission, the bureau was assigned more functions, viz., assist the ministries in making an expert scrutiny of feasibility studies and project reports; act as a data bank and a clearing house of information in respect of important matters of common interest including information about organizational structure and pricing policies in public enterprises in other countries. It functions as the secretariat of public enterprises selection board and assists the enterprises in making other selection, arranges training programmes and advises public enterprises on management development. The ARC was of the view that the bureau should become the main if not the sole central agency. It will act as a staff agency but will not undertake any critical evaluation of performance of public enterprises.

The bureau in September 1985 became the department of public enterprises under the ministry of industry.

In practice, the relationship between the minister and the public enterprises has not always been smooth. The experience is that the ministers are exercising undue influence over the public undertakings without issuing directives. They want to exercise control without assuming responsibility. In the appointment of board of directors, they are not taking merit into account, but appoint such persons who are reliable and carry out their wishes without questioning them. Thus, it has been remarked that such a practice leads neither to autonomy nor to proper control.

Parliamentary Control

Public undertakings are created by investment of public money. The Parliament, being the people's representative, has a right to know how the investment made in these undertakings is being used for the benefit of the people in efficient manner. Therefore, like the minister, Parliament also exercises control over public undertakings. The methods of parliamentary control are the following:

1. Parliamentary questions
2. Raising half an hour discussion on any enterprise
3. Moving a motion for adjournment on matters of public importance
4. Raising discussion on matters of urgent public importance for short duration
5. 'Calling attention' of the house to matters of urgent public importance
6. Moving resolutions, and discussing any matter
7. Discussion on the president's address
8. Discussing the report of the enquiry committee, if any
9. Budget debates
10. Discussion on annual reports of the corporation
11. Parliamentary committees

Parliamentary Committees

There are several parliamentary committees through which the Parliament can exercise control over public enterprises. The committees which exercise control over the public enterprises are: (a) the public accounts committee; (b) the estimates committee and (c) the committee on public undertakings.

The committee on public undertakings was set up on 1st May, 1961, before that the other two committees were exercising the necessary control on behalf of the Parliament.

Committee on Public Undertakings

The committee consists of 15 members, 10 from the Lok Sabha and 5 from the Rajya Sabha, elected by the concerned house every year from amongst its members according to the principle of proportional representation by means of a single transferable vote. A minister cannot be a member and in case a member of the committee becomes the minister, he ceases to be the member of the committee with immediate effect. The term of office of members is one year, but members can be re-elected. One of the members is elected as the chairman of the committee. The functions of the committee are as follows:

(i) To examine the reports and accounts of the assigned public undertakings

(ii) To examine the reports, if any of the comptroller and auditor-general on public undertakings

(iii) To examine, in the context of the autonomy and efficiency of the public undertaking, whether the affairs of the public undertakings are being managed in accordance with sound business principles and prudent commercial practices

(iv) To undertake such other functions vested in the public accounts committee and the estimates committee relating to public undertakings as may be allotted to the committee by the speaker from time to time

Jurisdiction of the Committee

The committee on public undertakings has been assigned/allotted the work of Damodar Valley Corporation (DVC); Industrial Finance Corporation of India (IFCI); Indian Airlines Corporation (IAC); Air India (AI); Central Warehousing Corporation (CWC); Life Insurance Corporation of India (LIC); Oil and Natural Gas Commission (ONGC); Hindustan Aeronautics Limited (HAL); Bharat Electronics Limited (BEL); Mazagaon Docks Bombay; Garden Reach Workshop, Calcutta and all government companies. Presently, all the public undertakings except departmentally organized ones and nationalized banking institutions have been placed under the purview of the committee.

Limitations of Committee on Public Undertakings

The committee cannot discuss matters of government policy as well as matters of day-to-day administration. The committee has also no jurisdiction over matters for the consideration of which machinery is established by any special statute under which a particular public undertaking is set up.

Working of the Committee

The committee from the very beginning decided to select a few undertakings for detailed study each year. In addition it takes up one subject on the working of undertakings for horizontal study, for example, materials management. According to the convention the report of the committee is not discussed in the house. Only the action taken report is submitted to the Parliament. The main achievements of the committee are as follows: First, now Parliament gets more reliable information about the working of public enterprises. Second, the committees control is effective over public enterprises. Third, the public enterprises come to know their defects, weaknesses and shortcomings and may try to remove them. Finally, the committee provides an opportunity to the public enterprises to put their problems before the Parliament. The committee has also contributed towards greater efficiency and economy in the management of public undertakings by constructive and valuable recommendations made from time to time in its reports.

The other agency which exercises control over public undertakings is the comptroller and auditor-general of India, who conducts audit of these bodies and the planning commission which advises government on their compatibility.

The comptroller and auditor-general of India is responsible for conducting the audit of public undertakings. Two sets of auditors conduct the audit of government companies. First, statutory auditors of the companies audit the accounts of companies on the principles of commercial audit. Second, the comptroller and auditor-general of India also conducts the audit of the same accounts. The report of comptroller and auditor-general is finally placed before the Parliament.

The report of the comptroller and auditor-general is an important document which provides a very effective instrument of parliamentary control over public undertakings. In practice, this report is considered by the committee on public undertakings, which examines the concerned officers of the undertaking and prepares its own reports and suggestions to be considered by the Parliament.

Planning Commission

The investment in the projects of public undertakings needs governmental approval. The government, prior to according approvals, seeks the advice of the planning commission from the point of view of its utility and compatibility with the national plan objective. This scrutiny of the enterprise provides opportunity for the control of planning commission.

Conclusion

The control over public enterprises by the government is necessary as the owner of these undertakings. The government has a responsibility to the people to ensure proper use of public funds. Sometimes, this control is excessive and exercised informally without taking responsibility. The public undertakings consider it as an attack on their autonomy. Therefore, the government has to maintain a balance between legitimate control for the use of public funds and the autonomy of the public enterprises.

Problems of Public Enterprises

Public enterprises in India have now been functioning near about 50 years. They have come to occupy an important role in the socio-economic development of the country. In every Five Year Plan investments in these undertakings has been increased. In spite of huge investments, the performance of public sector has been unsatisfactory. The government has taken serious note of this situation and decided to follow the policy of liberalization and is considering closing down the sick public sector units. The poor performance of public sector has drawn attention towards the problems faced by them. The main problems are (i) problem of objective; (ii) problem of autonomy; (iii) organizational problems including personnel problems, (iv) problem of profitability.

The Problem of Objective

The objectives of the public enterprises are not clearly defined. Sometimes it is said that they have been established to achieve the socio-economic objective of the government. At another time, it is said that they have to earn reasonable profit on their investments. They are also expected to solve the problem of unemployment. These enterprises are also expected to bring new technologies for improving the technological base for industries. They have to enter into the areas where private enterprises are not willing to come forward. They are not allowed to change the market prices for the services they render or the goods they supply. When the objectives are not clear it is very difficult to lay down the criteria according to which the performance of the enterprise has to be judged.

The Problem of Autonomy

The important problem faced by the public enterprises is the question of autonomy. How much autonomy an enterprise should be given and to what extent it should be controlled posed a great problem. The tenure of the chief executive of the public undertakings has not been fixed. Sometimes extensions are given for six months or for a year. The minister concerned has the full authority to terminate the tenure of the chief executive of a public undertaking.

The public undertakings for taking up new projects have to go through an expenditure finance committee and project investment board depending upon the amount of investment involved. This is a very cumbersome procedure and the limits of investment over which this procedure has to be followed are rather low.

Ministers have tried to exercise control more through informal methods rather than formal channels. The ministers do not give written directives. His advice is taken as directive. This kind of informal control has destroyed the autonomy of the public undertakings. As a result there is neither autonomy nor complete control. The attitude of a minister towards public enterprises should be that of a friend, philosopher and guide, and not of unnecessary interventionist.

Organizational Problems Including Personnel

The form of organizations has an important bearing on the success of an enterprise. In the case of public undertakings no well-defined principles had been followed in determining their organizational forms. In the field of personnel, no scientific manpower planning has been developed for public enterprises. In the case of departmental forms, manpower is in far excess than the actual need. The reduction in strength is next to impossible.

The recruitment on top management posts is based on political grounds of acceptability rather than on merit. No all-India public sector service has been constituted, which would have been a right step.

Therefore, lack of proper recruitment, promotion and training has caused many problems in practice for efficient working of public enterprises.

There are a number of operational problems. Some of them are lack of corporate planning, paucity of resources, delay in project implementation, etc. Delayed implementation of the projects increase their cost to a great extent and adds to the inflation in the economy. The financial losses are due to poor operational performance, low capacity utilization, poor technology and defective pricing policy. The public sector for better performance should put its own house in order rather than blaming the government for its control and for all their failures. Still, there is a lot of scope for improving the operational efficiency within their organization.

NOTES

1. A. D. Gorwala, *Report on the Efficient Conduct of State Enterprises* (New Delhi: Government of India, 1951), pp. 13–14.
2. *ARC Report on Public Sector Undertakings* (New Delhi: Government of India, October 1967), p. 13.
3. Ibid., p. 13.
4. Ibid., p. 14.
5. Hoshiar Singh, 'Public Enterprises and Privatisation: Rationale and Problems.' Paper presented at the XVI World Congress of the International Political Science Association, 21–25 August 1994, Berlin (Germany), p. 5.

Control over Public Expenditure

In a parliamentary democracy, the political executive is responsible to the Parliament. The control exercised by the Parliament over the executive is its control on financial expenditure. This is exercised in two ways.

Control Through Budget

The executive cannot spend money without Parliament's approval. The second is post expenditure control by audit. The office of the Comptroller and Auditor-General of India (CAG) conducts a detailed audit of all the Government departments. He sends his report to the president, who lays it before the houses of the Parliament. He also submits report about the commercial and industrial undertakings of the Government of India. The Parliament is an unwieldy body for a serious technical discussion on the CAG's reports. It sends them to the parliamentary committees on public accounts committee (pac), estimates committee and committee on public undertakings for detailed examination. The committee on public undertaking has already been discussed in the chapter on public undertakings.

Public Accounts Committee

The Webly commission of 1896 felt the need for the establishment of an accounts committee to find out irregularities in financial administration. It was followed by the Montford Reforms of 1921, suggesting the creation of such a committee. 'The question of arming the legislature with a semblance of expenditure control came to be considered. Dealing with "Control by Legislature", the Government of India, in a despatch to the secretary of state, suggested that it should be the constitutional duty of the legislature to appoint a committee on public accounts, to receive reports from it and to deal with them, insofar as might be necessary, by resolutions. An important reservation was that these resolutions should not be mandatory. Thus, the function of this committee was defined as that of mere scrutiny and recommendations. The evolution of a definite authority to sanction or disallow expenditure was a much later development.'[1]

The public accounts committee was first constituted at the centre in 1923, its members were partly elected and partly nominated. The committee had twelve members: eight non-officials elected by assembly members and the remaining four officials nominated by the governor-general. The finance member was its chairman. The auditor-general having statutory recognition under the Government of India Act of 1919, used to assist the committee. The auditor-general performed two major functions, namely, that of keeping the accounts of the government and of auditing them. Since the accounts were too complex, he had to simplify them with a view to make them intelligible to the legislature and its committees. Accuracy, completeness and consistency of classification were some of his important concerns. He had to be vigilant about illegalities, irregularities, extravagance and waste. His reports were the principal source of information for the investigations of the public accounts committee.[2] Since its inception, the central public accounts committee became a major force in the legislative control of public expenditure. Despite the limitations on its constitution and restrictions on its authority it exercised enormous influence in bringing pressure to bear upon the government to enforce economy in the expenditure of public moneys.[3]

Before independence, the Indian public accounts committee was, only in a very qualified sense, a committee of the legislature.[4] However, during the pre-Independence days, the committee had performed useful service.

Since the inception of the Constitution, the public accounts committee has become a real parliamentary committee. Initially, it consisted of 15 members, all belonging to the house of the people but the strength was raised to 22 in 1953, to give representation to the council of states. Presently, 15 and seven members are elected by the Lok Sabha and the Rajya Sabha, respectively. The committee is an annually elected body and the election is held in accordance with the principle of the proportional representation followed by single transferable vote system. There is a convention that there should be a two-year tenure of membership to ensure continuity of the committee. The committee has a good number of its members duly re-elected with a view to providing it a core of well-experienced members. The committee is headed by a chairman, who is nominated by the speaker from amongst its members. Although in the majority of cases, the chairman of the committees have been from the ruling party, on two occasions, members belonging to the opposition parties have headed the committee.

The functions of the committee, as embodied in the rules of procedure and conduct of business, is to satisfy itself that:

(i) The moneys shown in the accounts as having been disbursed were legally available for, and applicable to, the service or purpose for which they have been applied or charged.

(ii) The expenditure conforms to the authority which governs.

(iii) Every re-appropriation has been made in accordance with provisions made in this behalf under rules framed by the competent authority.

It should also be the duty of the public accounts committee:

(i) To examine, in the light of the report of the CAG, the statement of accounts showing the income and expenditure of state corporations, trading and manufacturing, schemes and projects, together with the balance-sheets and statements of profit and loss accounts, which the president may have required to be prepared or are prepared, under the provisions of the statutory rules regulating the financing of a particular corporation, trading concern, or project.

(ii) To examine also the statement of accounts showing the income and expenditure of autonomous and semi-autonomous bodies, the audit of which may be conducted by the CAG of India either under the directions of the president or by a statute of Parliament.

(iii) To consider the report of the CAG in cases where the president may have required him to conduct an audit of any receipt or to examine the accounts of stores and stocks.

The report of the CAG is made the base of the functioning of the committee, and to perform its functions it makes use of sub-committees and study groups. The report is considered ministry-wise and the committee is empowered to send for persons, papers and records. The secretaries of the ministries concerned have to appear before the committee to clarify the points raised in the audit report. The CAG attends the meetings of the committee and he acts as its 'guide, philosopher and friend'. He also explains and acquaints the members with the technicalities of the matters being dealt with. Generally, questions are suggested by him, which the members of the committee may ask the concerned officials. To quote Ashok Chanda, 'the effectiveness of the committee is largely determined by the thoroughness with which the audit-examination has been conducted: Likewise, the value of audit criticism depends on the support it receives from the committee. Not only are the functions of these two authorities interrelated, but there is a measure even of inter-dependence in their relations.'[5]

The committee examines the report of the CAG with a view to find out whether the money voted by Parliament has been utilized by the authority concerned 'within the scope of the demand.' This means that:

(i) Public expenditure must not exceed the appropriations granted by Parliament without its prior approval

(ii) Grant is utilized for the purpose for which it was sanctioned by Parliament

(iii) The nature of items of expenditure compiled against a demand should justify their being so compiled

The committee also undertakes a review of the form and details in which the estimates are composed, in order to arrest any tendency to reduce the number of votes or to include large lump sum provisions, since these are regarded as diminishing the control of Parliament over the estimates.[6]

The committee finalizes its recommendations after examining witnesses and the report of the CAG. A convention has evolved that the recommendations of the committee are invariably accepted by the government after being discussed in Parliament. In case of any difference, the government has to place such reasons for non-acceptance and ask the committee to modify or reconsider. The committee may either reconsider the matter in the light of the government's views or adhere to its own. The differences are, usually, resolved by reaching an agreement.

Although it is open to the house of the people to discuss the reports of the committee, this is seldom done in practice. While addressing the conference of the chairman of the public accounts committee in 1959, the speaker said:

> Although it is open to the legislature to discuss the reports of the committee, a rambling discussion of the whole report leads us nowhere and tends to destroy the effectiveness of the recommendations of the committee. I am, therefore, of the opinion that special points should be raised for discussion, more particularly those points where there is an unresolved difference of opinion between the committee and the government.

The 55th report of the committee dealt with a specific issue (which arose out of the 50th report of the committee) on which there was disagreement between the committee and the government, and the speaker permitted discussion thereon with the direction that the discussion should be confined to the remarks, observation and comments of the committee.

With regard to substitute motions which some members had tabled to the motion for consideration of the report, the speaker observed that if he allowed substitute motions to be moved, there would be voting and the members would be in an embarrassing position because of a possible conflict between loyalty to the committee and to the respective parties. Such a situation was not desirable, he felt, as it would hamper the efficient and effective working of the committee. The consensus in the house was against any substitute motion on the report of a financial committee being moved or voted upon.[7]

The committee is quite often referred to as a post-mortem committee. It is, generally, argued that once money has been wrongly spent, it cannot be recalled and nothing can be done. However, it would not be absolutely correct to say that a post-mortem examination has no significance. The committee's job of scrutinizing accounts is a continuous process and it enjoys the prerogative of looking at the present as well as the future.

The very fact that there is someone who will scrutinize what has been done, is a great check on the slackness, or negligence of the executive. The examination, if it is properly carried out, thus leads to general efficiency of the administration. The examination by the committee may also be useful as guide for both future estimates and future policies.[8]

The role of the public accounts committee is quite significant in the context of the country's financial administration because it has kept the executive accountable to Parliament, and, thereby, considerably improved and lent a new dimension to the nation's fiscal policies and programmes. The committee has earned the reputation of being non-party in character, and it has pointed out many irregularities of expenditure with regard to various departments of the Government of India.[9] The chances of waste and misuse of the funds had increased with the increase in expenditure, and it was necessary to check the rise in such waste and misuse. The committee was able to bring to light certain cases where parliamentary authority on the administration of tax laws had been diluted by the executive fiat, and other cases of the government not carrying out the intentions of Parliament as expressed in laws. It had also drawn attention to differing interpretations given by officers to tax provisions which had led to citizens being taxed differently under the same statute. The government has been very cooperative with the committee and its reports have carried great weight with the government. It may be claimed that the traditions established and the conventions developed by the public accounts committee conform to the highest traditions of a parliamentary democracy.[10]

The control exercised by the public accounts committee is quite significant. The control relates to financial matters. The nature of control is quasi-judicial by an expert body. As a watchdog activity performed by an all-party committee, it acts as a deterrent on excesses committed by the executive.[11] However, the regular recurrence that is brought to light, year after year, does suggest that the value of the committee is limited.

If the public accounts committee has been reduced to a toothless watchdog, the fault lies at the door of the government. The politician in power and the acquiescent bureaucrat have together developed a vested interest for secrecy, shying away from accountability to Parliament and the people. Governments have perfected the art of treating parliamentary committees as sinecures and their reports as documents to be consigned to the dust-gathering morgue of secretarial shelves. Ministers and bureaucrats are not inhibited by the thought that the public accounts committee would be calling them in question for any profligacy on their part. Late Prime Minister Rajiv Gandhi, in his address to the chairman of public accounts committees in Delhi on 10 September 1986, rightly observed that the public accounts committees have been able to take the result of their labour to its logical conclusion. Unless Parliament asserts itself and tells the government to mend its ways in the light of suggestions and proposals from expert panels, the estimates committees and public accounts committees will be reduced to the status of powerless bodies composed of back-benchers in quest of minor perks of office. He wants 'the system' to be changed.[12]

ESTIMATES COMMITTEE

During the British rule there used to be a standing finance committee, which was constituted in 1921. The committee comprised 14 elected members of the legislative assembly and the finance minister. The finance minister was to be the nominated chairman and an officer of the finance department was to be appointed by him to act as the secretary of the committee. The committee was to scrutinize the voting expenditure of the Government of India. This committee was attached to the finance department of the Government of India and depended on the will of the executive; without having a statutory status, it had to function under severe limitations. The selected representatives of the legislative assembly were not satisfied with its functions, deliberations and constitution because it was not in any sense a committee of the legislature.

The desirability of setting up an estimates committee began to be mooted with fresh vigour after independence. The estimates committee, first constituted in April 1950, had 25 members and the membership was raised to 30 in 1956. The members are annually elected by the Lok Sabha from its members according to the principle of proportional representation based on the single transferable vote system. According to the established convention, since 1956, two-thirds of the members have been re-elected for another year. So the term of office of members is one year. The ministers are barred from the membership of the committee. The chairman of the committee is nominated by the speaker from amongst the members of the committee and if the deputy speaker is a member of the committee, he will act as the chairman.

The main function of the committee is to suggest 'economies in expenditure', hence, it has been described as a 'continuous economy committee'. It is not concerned with 'policy matters'. Its business is to ensure that within the framework of the policy of the government laid down by the house, only the minimum expenditure needed for the purpose of fulfilling the objectives of the government are incurred. The real business of the committee is to suggest, while accepting the policy and objectives of the government with which it is supposedly not concerned, how this policy and its objectives could be carried out with the least expenditure of public resources.[13]

The exact scope of the committee was clarified by the speaker in the following words, at the time of the committee's inaugural sitting: 'Your function is not to lay down policy; whatever policy is laid down by Parliament, your business is to see that the policy is carried out not divorced from its financial implications. You must bear in mind constantly that you are a financial committee and you are concerned with all matters in which the finances are involved. It is only where a policy involves expenditure and you find that policy has not worked properly, you are entitled and competent to go into it; where the policy is leading to waste, you are entitled to comment on it in a suitable way.'[14]

The committee examines the estimates referred to it by the Lok Sabha or the speaker and the estimates which it may deem fit with a view to:

(i) report what economies, improvements in organizations, efficiency and administrative reforms, consistent with the policy underlying the estimates may be effected;

(ii) suggest alternative policies in order to bring about efficiency and economy in administration;

(iii) examine whether the money is well laid out within the limits of the policy implied in the estimates; and

(iv) suggest the form in which estimates can be presented to Parliament.[15]

The committee does not confine itself to the examination of estimates but also makes use of estimates as sources of information in order to prevent waste and extravagance in spending public moneys. The expenditure reflects the use of men and material. It is, therefore, essential that, besides estimates, the committee pays close attention to those aspects of governmental activity where men and material are often wasted or not fully utilized. In actual practice, the committee examines current governmental activity in the light of what it costs the public.

Initially, the objective of the committee was to suggest economies consistent with the policy underlying the estimates which was further enlarged to include in its scope 'alternative policies'. There are a few possible explanations as to why the power to suggest alternative policies has been specifically conferred on the committee. First, before 1947, the government was not responsible and most of the policies were settled by the executive, and some of those policies continue to be followed. Second, some ministers are new to the task and have to be guided by the services in policy matters. Third, Parliament is still somewhat suspicious of the services as a result of historical reasons.[16]

The speaker, while inaugurating the estimates committee in May 1959, described its function as follows; 'The fundamental objectives of the estimates committees are economy, efficiency in administration and ensuring that money is well laid out; but, if on close examination it is revealed that large sums are going to waste because a certain policy is followed, the committee may point out the defects and give reasons for the change in policy for the consideration of the House.'

When the committee is constituted, it prepares its programme duly based on the decided estimates which are to be examined. It collects and collates the requisite materials for necessary examination. The committee issues questionnaires and interviews the officials of the concerned ministries/departments. It may also summon any official to produce relevant papers, records and files for evidence and witness purposes. If disclosure of any document is not in the public interest, such a matter is referred to the speaker for seeking guidance. The committee appoints study groups to conduct on-the-spot study of the selected projects. On the basis of its findings, the committee finally formulates its recommendations. Nothing finds a place in the report unless it is discussed with the ministry concerned. A copy of the report is sent to it in advance for verification of facts contained therein. The report, which is in the form of recommendations, is then submitted to the Lok Sabha. There is no regular debate on the report. The members refer to the report at the time of discussion on the budget and the demand for grants.

The recommendations of the committee usually relate to improving the organization and working of the department or ministry; securing economy; and providing guidance to general aspects of estimates presentation. Its recommendations are far-reaching in respect of functional and economic classification on budgets and introduction of performance budgeting, etc. The committee has also evolved the practice of presenting action taken reports to the Lok Sabha, showing how far the government has actually implemented the recommendations contained in its earlier reports. In the opinion of Ashok Chanda, 'as the committee usually concerns itself with policy matters, the government may have perforce to reject some of these recommendations. This creates a most undesirable situation, detracting as it does from the prestige and authority both of the government and of a parliamentary committee.'[17] However, this view is regarded by some as 'erroneous.'[18] In a seminar held at New Delhi, one of the participants while expressing his views said, 'In fact, sometimes one gets the feeling that the estimates committee merely gives a big list of advices.' The use of the word 'merely' is not right as, undoubtedly, some of the recommendations of the committee are really wise and useful. It was indicated by the speaker of the third Lok Sabha that 97 per cent of the committee's recommendations had been accepted by the government.

The Role of the Finance Ministry

Apart from the parliamentary control over public expenditure, the government exercises some internal control also. The internal control is usually exercised by the finance ministry operating through its budget division and expenditure department. In each ministry/department its representative is there by the name of integrated financial advisor. The control of finance ministry is exercised in two ways: (i) pre-budget scrutiny (ii) post-budget scrutiny.

The expenditure proposals of all the ministries/departments are scrutinized by the finance ministry before inclusion in the budget. The scrutiny includes economy and efficiency, availability of funds, allocation of funds. Post-budget scrutiny is conducted because the budget proposals are sometimes not fully scrutinized before inclusion in the annual budget. Therefore, a second scrutiny is needed.

The finance ministry control is criticized on the ground that too light a control of finance ministry causes delay and encourages departments to inflate their demands and breeds irresponsibility in the departments.

On the other hand, the control of finance ministry is justified by saying that it is an offshoot of the parliamentary control. The finance ministry, not being a spending ministry, is best suited to exercise this control. This ministry, to raise resources, proposes taxes, therefore, control of expenditure is also passed on to this ministry. The organization and working of finance ministry has already been discussed earlier in the book, therefore, for further details see Chapter 11.

Comptroller and Auditor-General of India

The Constitution of India has created the office of the Comptroller and Auditor-General of India[19], which is a very important constitutional appointment. He is the head of the Indian audit and accounts department and is the guardian of public funds. We shall discuss evolution of this office, appointment and conditions of service, functions and duties, role and evaluation.

History

In 1857, independent accounting offices of three presidencies were merged together to form an imperial establishment under one accountant general under the Government of India. In 1858, an independent auditor was appointed by the Queen Empress. In 1860, the audit and accounting functions were amalgamated and placed in charge of auditor-general in India. However, independent audit emerged after the constitutional reforms of 1919. The Act of 1919 made him independent of the Government of India, was appointed by the secretary of state for India and held office during His Majesty's pleasure. The Act of 1935 further enhanced his status and importance and his appointment began to be made by the King Emperor. He could be removed from office only in the same manner and on the same grounds as a judge of a federal court. The Constitution of India in 1950 re-designated the auditor-general as CAG of India. In 1976, accounts were separated from the functions of the CAG; and a new unit was set up in the ministry of finance, department of expenditure, to administer matters relating to departmentalization of accounts of the Union. The state governments were advised to pass similar laws with the permission of the president.

Appointment and Conditions of Service

He is appointed by the president of India. The Parliament enacted in 1953 the Comptroller and Auditor-General's (Conditions of Service) Act which was amended in 1971. This Act governs the conditions of his service. He holds office for six years up to the age of 65 years, whichever is earlier. In status, he has been equated with a judge of the Supreme Court and draws an equivalent salary of Rs 90,000 a month. To maintain his independence, after appointment he cannot be removed easily. He can be removed only on an address from both houses of Parliament on grounds of: (a) proven misbehaviour, and (b) incapacity. His salary and conditions of service cannot be altered to his disadvantage during his term of office. He cannot hold any further government appointment after his retirement so that he can perform his duties without any expectation from the executive, independently. There was a lot of criticism when retired CAG Ashok Chanda was appointed chairman of the third finance commission in 1960, although this office could not be called as an office of profit or an appointment under the government. His salary, allowances and pension are not subject to the vote of Parliament; these are charged from the consolidated fund of India and cannot be varied to his disadvantage during his term of office. He does hold office till the pleasure of the president.

Powers and Duties of CAG

The Constitution envisages duties, powers and conditions of service of the CAG to be prescribed by law made by Parliament. Such a law, called the Comptroller and Auditor-General's (Duties, Power and Conditions of Service) Act, was passed in 1971. The provisions of this Act provide for audit by the CAG:

- All receipts and expenditure from the consolidated fund of India and of the states and Union territories
- All transactions relating to the contingency funds and public accounts
- All trading, manufacturing, P&L accounts and balance sheets and other subsidiary accounts kept in any department
- All stores and stock of all government offices or departments
- All government companies set up under the Indian Companies Act, 1956
- All central government corporations whose Acts provide for audit by the CAG
- All authorities and bodies substantially funded from the consolidated funds
- Any body or authority even though not substantially funded from the consolidated fund at either the request of the governor/president or at his (the CAG's) own initiative

To enable him to discharge his duties effectively, the Act arms him with:

- The right to inspect any office of the entities which are subject to his audit
- The authority to call for any books of accounts or papers that he regards as necessary during audit
- The freedom to ask any question and order the collection of any information from any office of any government, company, corporation, etc

The jurisdiction of CAG covers all India missions abroad and any offices of the government, companies and corporations, autonomous bodies, etc., shall decide the manner in which their accounts shall be maintained in consultation with the CAG, so that he is satisfied that accounts are maintained in such a manner as to be easily and scientifically auditable.[20]

The Act also provides that the CAG shall keep and compile the accounts of the Union and the states, prepare and submit accounts periodically and, on the basis of these, provide information to the central and state governments which will help them in planning and carrying out their plans for development and growth of the country and improvement in the living standards of the people. However, through an enabling provision in the Act, the accounts of the Union have already become the responsibility of the ministry of finance.

The CAG also plays a judicial role in Union-state financial relations. He certifies the share assignable to the states out of due taxes collected by the Union. He also certifies the expenditure incurred by the states on programmes initiated and funded by the Union.

The salient features of Indian audit are:

(a) The audit of the Government of India as well as of the state governments is a Union subject. Audit work of these governments is entrusted to the CAG of India.

(b) The Indian audit is primarily concerned with expenditure. Like Britain all the receipts are not given for examination to our CAG, only limited items of receipts are covered by the audit system. Gradually, the scope is widening and items of railways, post offices and customs and part of income tax are now covered.

(c) It is an arm of the legislature, though technically the CAG submits his report to the executive, i.e., the president or the governor at the state level, and they in turn get the report placed before the legislature. The CAG acts as an aid to the legislature in exercising control over the public finance.

(d) It is primarily a legality audit. The audit is mainly concerned with the legal and technical aspect of the expenditure.

Audit Report

Audit means the certification of accounts by the CAG as correct subject to such comments and remarks as he may choose to make. The CAG report contains his comments and remarks which he submits to each of the governments whose accounts he audits. The audit report for Government of India is submitted to the president while for the states to their governors. The president makes arrangement to lay down the report in both houses of Parliament for discussion and the governor to the state legislature. The legislatures refer the reports to their respective public accounts committees (PACs). The report contains: (i) financial irregularities; (ii) excess of expenditure over the grants sanctioned by the Parliament; (iii) over and under budgeting; (iv) failure to obtain proper sanctions; (v) cases of non-compliance with the rules and regulations; (vi) cases of misappropriation and embezzlement; (vii) cases of improper expenditure.

Audit Against Rules and Orders

The CAG has to see that expenditure conforms to the constitutional provisions, laws and rules made under it as well as the rules, regulations framed and orders given by the competent authority.

Audit Against Propriety

A propriety audit is conducted to detect cases involving extravagance and waste although the expenditure has formally been conformed to regularity and legality. Such audits are discretionary and require to be conducted tactfully.

The CAG was earlier performing both the auditing and accounting duties in respect of all financial transactions of the central and all state governments in 1976, with the separation of accounts from audit, the CAG was relieved of the functions related to the compilation and maintenance of accounts. Since then, he has been entrusted with audit responsibility only.

So far as the audit of public enterprises is concerned, this is in more or less the same manner as applicable to the government departments and the results of the audit related to the public enterprises are also included in the CAG's report. The auditor-general's office conducts audit of the Employees State Insurance Corporation and National Cooperative Development Corporation as well as test audit of government companies. In this regard, the former CAG of India, V. Narhari Rao, opined 'that formation of companies under the Companies Act for the management of government industrial enterprises tended to whittle away parliamentary control. While the funds were provided from the consolidated fund of India for these companies, the Company Law did not give the CAG any automatic right to audit the enterprises. The CAG might be requested to undertake the audit of those enterprises by including the suitable provision in the articles of association. But this was neither proper nor binding, as the CAG's duties and functions were to be prescribed by Parliament and could not be regulated solely by the articles of association of a company. Furthermore, as the CAG was appointed as an auditor by the company, he would have to submit his report to the company and not to Parliament through the president. Parliament, therefore, could not watch the regularity of operational financial results through the public accounts committee.'

Section 619(2) of the Companies Act, 1956, lays down: 'The auditor of the government company shall be appointed or reappointed by the central government on the advice of the CAG of India'. The CAG has power to direct and prescribe the procedure through which the company's accounts would be audited by the auditors appointed by the government. He can comment upon or supplement the audit reports of the professional auditors. The audit conducted by the CAG is confined to the field which has not already been covered either by the internal auditor or by the professional auditors. He also conducts efficiency-cum-performance audit to see whether the public enterprises are fulfilling the objectives for which they were set up, whether adequate results have been achieved or obtained with the money spent, whether there has been any extravagance in the expenditure incurred and to locate weaknesses in management of affairs pertaining to unavoidable delays which hampered the progress.

On the recommendations of the ARC, an audit board has been established. It consists of a chairman and two members appointed by the CAG. The report of the board is included in the audit report (commercial) which is presented to Parliament.

Criticism

There are several critics of the role played by the CAG of India. In this regard, Paul H. Appleby has said, 'The function of the C & A G in India is, in large measure, an inheritance from colonial rule. The function did not impede British rule; it upheld that rule and was an integral part of it. It greatly restricted the Indians who served the Government. These restrictions were sought by the Governments in a situation of administration largely concerned with police and taxation functions and not engaged in rapid pursuit of Welfare State objectives.

'In the first flush of Independence, Indian ministries were disposed to disregard the Comptroller and Auditor-General, and abuses became vivid. This situation has been fully corrected, but in the process the old restrictive effects have been restored and strengthened at the very time that new policies were calling for more flexibility and more use of responsible direction. The net result of this un-corrected situation is that the Comptroller and Auditor-General is today a primary cause of widespread and paralysing unwillingness to decide and act.

'This repressive and negative influence is in considerable part indirectly impinging on the bureaucracy by way of Parliament because of the exaggerated and unselective attention given by Parliament to the petty exceptions and the inflated pretensions built around the pedestrian function of auditing.

'Parliament is surely at fault in this. It has a greatly exaggerated notion of the importance of auditing to 'Parliamentary responsibility' and so has failed to define the functions of the Comptroller and Auditor-General as the Constitution contemplated it would do. Into the vacuum, thus left, the Auditor has moved.

'The Comptroller and Auditor-General's function is not really a very important one. Auditors do not know, and cannot be expected to know, very much about good administration; their prestige is higher with others who do not know auditing—which is not administration; it is a necessary but highly pedestrian function with a narrow perspective and very limited usefulness.'[21]

To a larger extent these observations made by Appleby are misleading, unsound and incorrect. According to Ashok Chanda, in all recognized democracies, audit is not just tolerated as a necessary evil, but is looked upon as a valued task which brings to notice procedural and technical irregularities and lapses on the part of individuals, whether they be errors of judgement, negligence, or acts and intents of dishonesty. The contemporary roles of audit and administration are accepted as axiomatic, being essential for toning up the machinery of government. Unfortunately, in India, this conception of complementary relationship has yet to be evolved. Audit continues to be considered as something alien, something extraneous, and something of the nature of an impediment. A natural resistance has thus developed in the administrative system to the absorption of the suggestion of audit. This trend has become more and more pronounced in recent years. With the advent of Independence and the acceptance of the concept of a welfare state, there should be the development of a commonness of purpose, of endeavour and achievement. The need between audit and administration has, thus, assumed paramount importance.[22]

The audit board works as another 'audit agency' of the accountant general and its way of working is like the 'routine government audit'. A joint financial advisor has expressed his views in this regard as follows: 'If we go through the reports of the audit board on various organizations, it will be seen that in most of the cases, the scanty examination conducted by the small team is made on the basis of the examination and counter-examination of the views executive, and the audit board and the parliamentary committee of the public sector undertakings are busy on the examination of small objections thrown by the audit party during routine audits.' Further, he writes, 'Similarly, the audit has become duplication, sometimes creating irritation and unnecessary and avoidable work. The balance-sheet audit once conducted by qualified chartered accountants under the provisions of the Companies Act is further examined by an unqualified audit team from the audit board.'[23]

Position of the CAG

The position of CAG is a constitutional one. In the words of D. D. Basu, 'Though the designation of his office indicates that he is to function both as comptroller and auditor, our comptroller and auditor-general is so far exercising the functions only of an auditor . . . He has no such control over the issue of money from the consolidated fund and many departments are authorized to draw money by issuing cheques without specific authority from the comptroller and auditor-general, who is concerned only at the audit stage when the expenditure has taken place.'[24]

In the words of former CAG and now Rajya Sabha MP T. N. Chaturvedi, 'Surprisingly, still one gets the impression quite often in administrative functioning, the significance of this constitutional office and the support it ought to have in the discharge of its function, is not either known or adequately appreciated in the context of public accountability of the executive in democracy'. Thus, the role of CAG is limited but his position is eminent being constitutional authority.

The separation of audit from accounts in March 1976, had improved the financial management to some extent which needs more attention as the present financial scams like fodder, urea and fertilizers, etc.

had revived. Therefore, to safeguard country's economy it should be kept under the control of the minister, the parliamentary committees and the CAG.

The committees have been assigned more important functions for effective vigil and supervision. In April 1993, 17 committees of Parliament were formed, each consisting of 30 members from Lok Sabha and 15 from Rajya Sabha (ministers are kept out). Thus, it is clear that 'from now on the house will not only have the opportunity to discuss the details of every grant of every ministry or department but also have the committee's report to guide them.'[25] These committees were formed to scrutinize the proposals and send the report to the house. On the basis of their reports many demands for grants are likely to be quashed without further discussion to save the time of the house. Such committee system will provide opportunity to each party for discussion in the meetings for better results.

Separation of Accounts from Audit

In India both audit and accounts functions were performed by the CAG till 1976, except in the case of railways and defence. The system of both types of functions being performed by one officer was criticized by various committees. Muddinan committee in 1924 and Simon Commission in 1929 recommended the separation of audit and accounts. As a result, steps were taken to separate these functions in North-West Frontier Province, UP, and some central departments in 1931 but later these attempts were given up in the name of economy. After Independence, again the pressure was built up to separate both. Mr Narhari Rao, the first CAG of India in his report to the public accounts committee favoured separation of both these functions and agreed to give some staff for accounting system from his organization in the beginning. The public accounts committee in its third report (1952–1953) suggested to the Government of India for the separation of these functions. The Government of India was seriously considering for the separation of these functions for quite some time and ultimately separated them in 1976.

Arguments for the Separation of Audit and Accounts

First, the accounting function is an executive function while audit is quasi-parliamentary function. Accounting is meant to help the executive in performing its own functions while audit helps the legislature in exercising control over finances. Thus, both functions are separate. Second, the CAG office sends the accounts very late to the departments and by that time their expenditure exceeds the departmental grants given to them by the legislature. Thus, they are not in a position to control their expenditure. Third, due to the combination of both functions in one office, they both are not properly handled. The audit which requires detailed scrutiny and attention is the biggest casualty. Fourth, the CAG audits the accounts which he also compiles. Thus it is an embarrassing situation for him and theory of separation of powers should also be applied in this case. Fifth, the accounting functions should be with the departments so that they can get the financial information in time to prepare their budgets and revised estimates. Sixth, for better maintenance of the accounts, it is essential that the pay and accounts officers should remain in the departments to acquire the specialized knowledge of the accounts of the particular department, seventh, as a matter of principle the executive authority which is responsible for expenditure should also be responsible for maintenance of accounts. Eighth, the heads of departments get better control over the expenditure by knowing how much expenditure is being incurred under which head. In case of excess expenditure they can take proper steps for correction in time. In case of slow progress of any scheme they can take appropriate measures to speed up the work.

Lastly, some implied advantages such as maintenance of personal accounts like GPF, leave, etc. of employees to avoid their hardships.

Arguments Against the Separation of Audit and Accounts

First, the argument against the separation of audit and accounts is economic, and the critics say it involves extra cost because of performance of both functions by the CAG. But if both these functions are separated then extra staff will be required in each ministry. Thus, a lot of extra cost is involved and because of this reason the separation was delayed for a long period. Second, it is suggested that by increasing the staff and their efficiency in CAG's office the work of accounts can be expedited. Third, in the ministries of defence and railways, where the accounts were separated long ago, the position is not much better. On the contrary, excess expenditures are incurred and there are delays in preparation of accounts. Fourth, the system of accounts presently in operation is good because two accounts are maintained one by the head of the department and the other by the accountant general. Thus mistakes can be cross-checked. Fifth, the separation of accounts will involve payments to be made by different ministries through their own agency. Thus centralized payment like this will cause a lot of difficulty to the clients. Lastly, even in Britain where separation is operating since long time, the excess expenditure over the grants sanctioned by the legislature has become a common phenomenon; therefore, separation of both is no guarantee against excess expenditure.

Thus, after weighing the arguments of both sides the case for separation was found to be weighty and the Government of India separated them in 1976. Now the secretary of the ministry has been made the chief accounting authority. There is a financial advisor to assist him, who in turn is assisted by controller of accounts and by circle and pay officer. They have been also made responsible for keeping the accounts. In each circle there are one or more pay officers who pre-check all claims and make payments through cheques or demand drafts. After compilation of monthly accounts they send them to the internal financial advisor of the ministry.

The system has improved the position of accounts system and now it is felt that the accounts are available much earlier than the earlier combined system. Now the ministries know the position of the expenditure well in advance to take the corrective steps.

NOTES

1. Ashok Chanda, *Indian Administration* (London: George Allen Unwin, 1958), p. 172.
2. M. J. K. Thavaraj, *Financial Administration of India,* 2nd edition (New Delhi: Sultan Chand and Sons, 1987), p. 681.
3. Ibid.
4. Morris Jones, *Parliament in India* (London: Longman, 1957), p. 279.
5. Ashok Chanda, op. cit., p. 176.
6. Ibid., p. 177.
7. Lok Sabha Debates: 22 August 1966, CC. 6076–236.
8. G. V. Mavlankar, 'Speeches and Writings', speech to PAC, April 1950, p. 97.
9. C. P. Bhambhari, *Public Administration in India* (Delhi: Vikas Publishing House, 1973), p. 214.
10. Ashok Chanda, op. cit., pp. 170–80.
11. M. J. K. Thavaraj, op. cit., p. 685.
12. *The Tribune*, Chandigarh, 11 September 1986, p. 4.
13. C. P. Bhambhari, op. cit., p. 215.

14. M. N. Kaul and S. L. Shakdhar, *Practice and Procedure of Parliament* (Delhi: Metropolitan Book Co., 1968), p. 7.
15. *Rules of Procedures and Conduct of Business in Lok Sabha*, 9th edition (New Delhi: Lok Sabha Secretariat, 1957), p. 310.
16. R. N. Aggarwala, 'Financial committees of the Indian Parliament', in A. Avasthi and S. N. Verma, *Aspects of Administration* (New Delhi: Allied Publishers, 1964), p. 184.
17. Ashok Chanda, op. cit., p. 188.
18. Kaul and Shakdhar, op. cit., p. 33.
19. Article 148, Constitution of India.
20. Ashok Chanda, op. cit., p. 247.
21. Public Administration in India: Report of a Survey, pp. 28–29, Paul H. Appleby, *Re-examination of India's Administrative System with Special Reference to Government's Industrial and Commercial Enterprises* (New Delhi: Government of India, 1953), pp. 27–28, 42–43.
22. Ashok Chanda, op. cit., p. 258.
23. Paper titled, 'Financial Management and Control in Public Enterprises', by M. B. B. Jindal, submitted to the Sixth All-India Management Conference held at Nasik on 30–31 December 1974 and 1 January 1975.
24. D. D. Basu, *Introduction to the Constitution of India*, 1991 edition (New Delhi: Prentice Hall of India, 1991), p. 190.
25. *The Tribune*, Editorial, Chandigarh, 31 March 1993.

Administration of Law and Order

The police is the chief enforcement authority at the disposal of the executive for implementation of its orders. In order to effectively maintain law and order, the police is a strong arm of the government administration, which is responsible for the proper enforcement of the laws of the land. The police is required to act as a custodian of law to preserve the internal order of the society. It is only the police force which can check crimes in the country.

Law and order or policing according to our Constitution is a state subject. Therefore, it is the responsibility of state governments to maintain law and order and to perform this function they have their own police organizations. As per Union list, item 2 the Union government can raise naval, military and air forces as also other armed forces. The Union government has organized police forces under the category of 'other armed forces of the Union' and the word 'police' for CRPF and the ITBP is a misnomer. These 'other armed forces of the Union' are legally paramilitary forces. The police administration of the Union territories completely falls under the Central Government sphere and the 42nd Constitutional Amendment in 1976 has authorized the Union government at its own initiative to 'deploy any armed force of the Union or any other force subject to the control of the Union for dealing with any grave situation of law and order in any state'. Thus, the Union government has also its own police forces to deploy in disturbed areas of the country to maintain law and order.

Central Police Organizations

Central police organization could be broadly categorized into three groups:

(i) Organizations connected with national security

(ii) Organizations for political intelligence

(iii) Organizations of investigation and maintaining vigilance[1]

The organizations connected with national security are: (i) Central Reserve Police Force (CRPF); (ii) Border Security Force (BSF); (iii) Central Industrial Security Force (CISF); (iv) Assam Rifles (AR); (v) Indo-Tibetan Border Police (ITBP); (vi) Railway Protection Force (RPF); (vii) National Security Guard (NSG); (viii) Special Protection Group (SPG); and (ix) Rapid Action Force (RAF).

The organizations of intelligence network are: (i) the Intelligence Bureau (IB); (ii) Research and Analysis Wing (RAW); (iii) Joint Intelligence Committee (JIC).

The organizations for investigation and vigilance are: The Central Bureau of Investigation (CBI) and the chief vigilance officers in the ministries/departments and public undertakings, who are expected to investigate and maintain vigilance on public employees and employers of public sector undertakings.

Besides these organizations, there are other special services organizations such as: National Crime Records Bureau (NCRB); Bureau of Police Research and Development (BPRD), Directorate of Telecommunication; Central Forensic Science Laboratory (CFSL); Institute of Criminology and Forensic Service (NICFS); Sardar Vallabh Bhai Patel National Police Academy and Central Detective Training Schools, etc. under the Union ministry of home affairs.[2] The assistance is also sought by various police organizations from the national laboratories of the Council of Scientific and Industrial Research (CSIR); Indian Council of Agricultural Research (ICAR); Indian Council of Medical Research (ICMR), etc.

Central Reserve Police Force

The Central Reserve Police Force (CRPF) was organized after Independence and now consists of 123 battalions including a women's battalion.[3] These are headed by a director-general who is assisted by inspectors-general and deputy inspectors-general including range deputy inspectors-general (DIG) each having charge of a range/sector. The force is deployed by the central government in troubled spots for maintenance of law and order, fight insurgency and help and arrange relief at the time of natural calamities in any part of the country. States in times of crisis requisition its services. Recently, the Punjab government requested for CRPF services for conducting free and fair elections in the state. As its name shows it is a reserve force for emergencies.

Border Security Force

The Border Security Force (BSF) was raised in 1963[4] to check criminal activities on the borders. Its functions are to police and patrol the Indo-Pak and Indo-Bangladesh borders and provide protection to people and their property against depredations from across the border. It deals with incidents of intrusions, illegal infiltrations and trans-border smuggling, and coordinates the activities of the various law and order agencies involved in the detection and prevention of crime in the border areas. The ministry of home affairs, Government of India in its annual report of 1991–1992 states that 'BSF was also engaged in internal security duties especially in the North-East, Punjab, Rajasthan and Jammu and Kashmir to combat insurgency and terrorist violence.'

Central Industrial Security Force

The Central Industrial Security Force (CISF) was created in 1969 by Central Industrial Security Force Act, 1968; to provide security and ensure protection in the major public undertakings. It is headed by a director-general and its strength in 1991–1992 was 79,620. Its functions are: security of vital installations, buildings, offices, machinery and equipment, control of movement of personnel vehicles and material, security arrangements at times of strike, labour unrest, *dharnas*, *gheraos*, etc. and to prevent any encroachment/trespass on the property of the protected undertaking.

Assam Rifles

The Assam Rifles is the oldest police force which was raised for the maintenance of law and order in the hills of Assam; later it was reorganized under the Assam Rifles Act. The force is responsible for security at the international border, law and order in tribal areas and internal security of other areas of Assam in any emergency.

Indo-Tibetan Border Police

The Indo-Tibetan Border Police (ITBP) is headed by a director-general and its functions are similar to those of BSF. It checks crime on the Indo-Tibetan border and illegal infiltration from across the border. It also provides security to the people living in the border areas.

Railway Protection Force (RPF)

The railway police has two wings, one is the Government Railway Police (GRP) and other is the Railway Protection Force (RPF). The first is a special branch of the state police, generally headed by a deputy inspector-general of police or inspector-general of police. This force is responsible for preventing and investigating crimes committed on the railways. The second is a central government force meant to guard and protect railway property. It is headed by an independent director-general in the Railway Board.

Central police force such as the CRPF, BSF, CISF, ITBP, NSG, NCRD, RPF and security are headed by directors-general while the IB, CBI, SVPNPA, RAW, ICFS, Police Telecommunications and SPG have directors as their heads and joint intelligence committee is headed by a chairman. Generally, the top posts of these organizations are manned by IPS officers coming on deputation from various states.

Evaluation of Working of Various Central Agencies

Generally, the working of all central police organizations is considered good in the interests of the country. But sometimes, due to the federal form of our government some states have sometimes criticized the role of the CRPF not on ground of its performance but on the basis of its deployment by the centre in the states without their consent. This problem was resolved by the 42nd Constitutional Amendment in 1976 by giving power to the centre for deployment of its paramilitary forces in any part of the country. Presently, even states ruled by parties opposed to the Union government are demanding the CRPF for smooth conduct of election in their states, which shows the utility of this force. Recently, the leftist West Bengal government requested the central government to send more CRPF forces to control the Maoist menace in the state. Secondly, now the CBI is being criticized for its alleged partiality, susceptibility to pressure and selective persecution. The observation of N. K. Singh, who worked in the CBI in various capacities for a very long period, shows its importance. He says, 'the organization lived up to its motto of the three 'I's', 'industry', 'integrity' and 'impartiality'.[5] But he accepts that during Emergency period from 1975 to 1976 'the prestige of CBI also suffered.'[6] He further revealed that on 30 July 1996, the outgoing CBI director, Vijay Rama Rao, told New Delhi Television that undeniably there was 'political pressure'[7] on the CBI as a result of which some of the important cases remained pending investigation for five to six years and the organization could act only under the direction of the courts. In some of these cases such as hawala transactions, JMM bribery case, Lakhu Bhai Pathak cheating case, Bihar's animal fodder scam, fertilizer urea scam, etc. the CBI had been asked to report directly to the Supreme Court or the high courts and not to the government.[8] In a damning self-indictment, the CBI has admitted before the Supreme Court that it takes direction from the Union government, at least in politically sensitive cases. In an application filed in the court in connection with the disproportionate assets probe against Samajwadi Party chief Mulayam Singh Yadav and his family members, the agency said it wanted to withdraw a particular application 'in view of the legal advice and directions of the Union of India . . .' The CBI seems to have changed its earlier stand of request to the court to decide the matter, after the SP got cosy with the Congress. If the CBI's application is allowed, the centre, and not the Supreme Court, will decide the fate of Mulayam Singh Yadav and his family members.[9] Thus, the growing political pressure on CBI has to be checked by devising institutional safeguards.

The Estimates Committee of Parliament (1991–92) in its 13th report has made some major recommendations including giving statutory status and well defined legal powers to the CBI. Further, due to tremendous increase in its work load, some expansion and modernization of the organization with proper facilities is essential. The public has trust and faith in the CBI, this is proved by the fact that in large number of murder cases or criminal cases people demand CBI inquiry and they have no faith in local police.

The Union public service commission (UPSC), the central police organizations recruitment board (CPORB) and staff selection commission (SSC) are the recruiting agencies for the central police organizations. The UPSC conducts a combined civil service examination followed by interviews for recruitment to all India services, which includes Indian Police Service. The authorized strength of IPS on 1st January, 1992 was 3,380. The staff selection commission recruits the officers for various central police organizations. The central police organizations recruitment board selects officers for paramilitary and other forces of the country. The officers of various ranks are also drawn on deputation from the state governments.

The each central police organization has its independent training organizations such as internal security academy of CRPF, training institution of the intelligence bureau; the central detective training schools, central weapons training schools, central motor training school of BSF, the national institute of criminology and forensic science imparts training to senior officers from the police, judiciary, prosecution and correctional services, etc.

The police training in India has some weaknesses: 'Formal and informal training are rarely integrated and commented by experienced police officers for what goes on in the training academy is well known. Although police officers want to be considered as professionals, and their responsibilities would support such pretensions, they are trained much as one would have trained a bus conductor or a taxi driver. They are left to make sense of what they see and what they do entirely depends on the education they had before they made their entry into the organization.'[10]

Police Administration in States

Organizational Set-Up at the State Level

The real head of the state administration is chief minister. Generally in states, the home ministers holds the charge of the police portfolio and concerns with policy decisions regarding police administration. To assist the home minister, there is an IAS home secretary/commissioner. He exercises general control and supervision over the department for which he is answerable to the legislature. The home secretary aids and advises the minister in performance of his duties. He is generally a senior IAS officer who is a generalist and coordinates and supervises the activities of the police administration into the directive of the central government and the activities of the district level officials below him.

The actual power of supervision and control over police administration, vests in the director general of police in all states except five states/Union territories of Arunachal Pradesh, Goa, Chandigarh, Pondicherry and Andaman and Nicobar Islands, having inspectors-general as the heads of their police force. The director-general is assisted by a number of inspectors-general of police, the deputy inspectors-general and the assistant inspectors-generals, superintendents of police, deputy superintendents of police, inspectors of police, sub-inspectors/assistant sub-inspectors of police, head constables and constables.

Generally, states are divided into various police ranges mostly at the commissionerate headquarters for the purposes of field administration and each range is headed by deputy inspector general of police (DIG). The senior superintendent of police/superintendent of police is the head of the district police force, assisted by deputy superintendent of police at subdivision/*taluka* level and other subordinate office of the police force at various levels.

In the police headquarters at the state level there are officers to assist the director-general. There are also officers-in-charge of the armed battalions of the state, crime branch, special branch armed police training, anti corruption, home guards, traffic police, women police, finger print bureau, forensic laboratories, training and other wings as per requirements of the state or districts. Some districts in the state for operational purpose are divided into various units like superintendent of police (city) and superintendent (rural) and they are further divided into well-knit hierarchies. For example, the police organization at the state level in Rajasthan consists of director-general of police, RSBI, home guards; jails, inspectors general of police headquarters, administrations, intelligence, crime branch, police welfare, re-organization, training and RPA; deputy inspectors-general of police, ranges seven, RAC one, HQ one, CID (IB) one, CID (B) one, CID (security) one, CID (vigilance) one, railways one, RSBI two and forest one.

It has been noticed that frequently with the change of political leadership directors-general of police are also changed, which creates lack of credibility in police leadership. Thus, the selection of the DGP has become political and the officer chosen, without his own fault, is dubbed as a political man of particular party or chief minister, which erodes his stature and leadership and raises doubt to the political neutrality of the police. This gives an impression that the top man of police can be influenced to circumvent the rule of law. It is unfortunate that the well-established principle of seniority-cum-merit has been more or less completely discarded for transient political goals.[11]

The metropolitan cities such as Ahmedabad, Bangalore, Baroda, Bombay, Calcutta, Delhi, Hyderabad, Madras, Nagpur, Solapur, Pune, Trivandrum; etc. have a commissioner of police with a number of additional/joint commissioners (DIG), deputy commissioners (SPs), and assistant commissioners (DySPs) and other ranks to assist the commissioner.

The chief feature of the metropolitan police system is that the responsibility for law and order and prevention of crime vests in one single authority, the commissioner of police. Such unified control is essential when dealing with problems of large areas and expanding population in big cities, where firmness of action, speed of decision and singleness of purpose, have to be synonymous with the effective maintenance of law and order and control of crime.[12]

The commissioner of police system is conducive to promptness and efficiency in the police administration. The system of single control with full powers enables the commissioner of police to take quick decisions with full responsibility doing away with the deal control and evasive responsibility. But in spite of all these good points the system could not succeed in solving the law and order and rising crime problems in the national capital, Delhi.

Police Set-Up at the District Level

In India, the district is the pivot of field administration. The senior superintendent of police/superintendent is the head of the district police and wields enormous powers and prestige in the district. He works under the district collector/deputy commissioner for general control and direction. He is assisted by additional superintendent/deputy superintendent of police in areas of crime control, personnel matters and some other specific matters. As the chief intelligence officer of the district, he collects information from the lower levels and communicates to his superiors along with his assessment. In districts which have big cities, superintendent of police has to make arrangements to regulate and control traffic and handle political and communal conflicts.

Powers and Functions of the Superintendent of Police (SP)

The superintendent of police (SP) at district level performs the following functions:

(a) Takes steps to maintain law and order and ensures peace in the district
(b) Prevents crimes, investigates crimes of serious nature and maintains up-to-date records of criminals
(c) Supervises operations of special branches such as CID, CBI and CIB
(d) Maintains supply of vehicles, arms and ammunition and equipment to the police force in the district
(e) Inspects the police stations so as to activate their functioning
(f) Handles recruitment, training, promotion and disciplinary matters
(g) Evaluates the performance of his subordinates and takes appropriate actions
(h) Looks after police welfare activities and provides incentives to those who show outstanding performance
(i) Maintains and develops friendly and cordial police-public relations at the district level
(j) Makes arrangements of effective patrolling by his fleet
(k) Keeps a close watch over the movements and activities of bad characters and foreigners by his fleet

At the district level the SP is assisted by the deputy superintendents of police (DySP) in charge of police subs-divisions in the district. To assist DySP there are circle inspectors in charge of police circles. Below him are the sub-inspectors, head constables and constables. The numbers of posts of SP, DySP, inspectors, sub-inspectors, assistant sub-inspectors, head constables and constables vary from place to place and police station/post to station depending upon the requirements of an area.

The recruitment in the police is invariably done at the levels of constable, sub-inspector, DySPs by the state government. Other ranks are filled through promotion. However, states may also give direct rank of head constables, ASI, SI and inspector to a few meritorious candidates. The IPS officers are allotted to the states after recruitment and training. A fixed percentage of nearly one-third officers in the IPS are taken through promotion from the rank of DySPs of the state.

Training at the State Level

Almost all the states have their own training institutions namely, police training academies, and police training schools located in different parts of the state. The training is imparted in both the indoor and outdoor subjects. The indoor subjects are Indian Penal Code/Criminal Procedure Code/Police Act, police regulations and service rules, police duties, organization and administration of police duties and human behaviour, etc. The outdoor subjects cover physical training, drill, infantry training, police training, route march, etc. After the training the recruits are required to pass the written examination conducted by concerned institutions. They are also given on-the-job training at the police lines.

Generally, states also have a forensic science laboratory with or without branches in the whole state. In some states mobile forensic science laboratories are also in operation. The states have institutions for training in weaponry, motor vehicles, dog squad, etc. according to the requirements.

Training facilities in the states are unsatisfactory and inadequate, therefore, proper steps are required to modernize police training.

Police Reforms

The present atmosphere of terrorism in the country has draw attention of the government and society as a whole towards the police system in India. The present police structure is a colonial legacy. The present Indian Police Act governing the police in India was enacted in 1861 to protect and stabilize the British *Raj*. The broad framework regarding the police force clearly mentions that the police will work directly under the control of the state governments, as they have the power to transfer, promote, appoint and lay down service conditions for the police. Even after Independence, with some amendments the basic structure remains the same.

In our Constitution, police is a state subject and every state government controls the police force and no mechanism have been created to make the police accountable to the communities. Thus, police in the country is subordinate to the state government executive and is not an autonomous or independent institution; therefore, the police invariably succumb to the whims of political masters, more so in sensitive situations. The general impression is that the police is ineffective and partial in its working because of its subordination to the political class. This is one side of the story the problem of police force is much bigger than political interference. The police have the power to detain, arrest, even ensure and cause the death of citizens. To use these powers the police force can lawfully keep arms and curtail the liberty of citizens. This power has potential of abuse and there is no structural device to fix responsibility.

A recent study by a people's watch group in 48 districts of nine states, reveals that 'in the name of investigating crime, frequent police practices include absolute physical abuse, custodial death, rape, threats, psychological humiliation deprivation of food, water, sleep and medical attention. Torture is also inflicted on women and girls in the form of custodial rape, molestation and other forms of severe harassment.'

Corruption is so rampant in the police force that without greasing the palm it is difficult to get even an FIR recorded at police stations; therefore, people generally do not report crimes. A three-year intensive study, completed in January 2008 by the Rajasthan Police and conducted by the Massachusetts Institute of Technology in collaboration with Rajasthan Police, revealed that 71 per cent of the people did not report crimes because they believed that the police could not or would not do anything about it and instead would ask for a bribe to register a first information report (FIR). Further, 82 per cent said that no beat police man ever visits their village. It is more or less the same position in other states and this has nothing to do with the police subordination to the state executive. There are many reasons for the ills that plague the police force.

Police Reforms: Attempts and Outcome

The negative image of the police forced the government to take some corrective measures. The Janata Party which came to power shouting about police excesses during the Emergency, appointed a national police commission to go into various aspects of policing including conditions of work, accountability, transparency and interference from political executive. The commission submitted eight reports, making various recommendations, but none of these were implemented.

In May 1998, the central government appointed the Julio Ribeiro committee to go into various aspects of policing. It submitted two reports, one in October 1998 and the second in March 1999.

In January 2000, the central government appointed the Padamanabhaiah committee to look at various aspects of policing. This committee has also submitted its report.

The central government again appointed the Justice Mali Math committee in 2002. The committee has submitted its report and made several recommendation concerning police reforms.

The Supreme Court in the case of *Vineet Narain v. Union of India* (1998) pointed to the urgent need for police reforms and asked the central government to pursue the matter with the state governments particularly on the issues concerning selection, tenure, transfer and posting of police officers. The court observed that whimsical transfers not only had a demoralizing effect on the police force but also had the effect of politicizing police personnel.

All these committees broadly made the following common recommendation. First, that the Police Act of 1861 be repealed and replaced with a new law. Second, that various measures be undertaken to make the police force independent of executive interference including the method of recruitment, transfers, promotions, discipline, etc. Third, that the investigative wing of the police should be separated from the law enforcement wing. Fourth, mechanisms (by and large internal to the police force) be set up to deal with complaints against the police.[13]

Supreme Court and Police Reforms

In 1996 two retired police officers and a non-governmental organization (NGO) filed a case in the Supreme Court demanding implementation of the national police commission reports. After ten years, in 2006 the Supreme Court passed the order that is now famous as *'Prakash Singh* judgement'. This judgement deals with three aspects of the police—autonomy, accountability and efficiency. The Supreme Court has given detailed directions. Let us briefly discuss these directions.

The court, taking note of the police reports, directed that the director-general of police (DGP) in every state must be appointed by the state government from amongst the three senior-most meritorious police officers empanelled for promotion by the Union public service commission. The minimum term of the director must be two years. Similarly, other senior officers on operational duties in the field such as police station officers and above must be posted at a place for minimum of two years.

The Supreme Court directed every state to set up a 'police establishment board' to decide the cases of transfers, postings, promotions and other service-related matters of officers below the rank of DySP. The members of this board will be the director-general of police and four other senior members of the department. The state government can interfere with board's decision only in exceptional cases by giving reasons in writing. The board will also recommend to the state government about postings and transfer of officers above the rank of SP.

The central government was also directed to set up a national security commission at the central level to prepare a panel to be placed before the appointing authorities for selection of heads of central police organizations. The minimum term of appointment will be of two years. The commission will be headed by the central home minister and other member will be heads of the central police forces and some security experts as its members.

To make the police accountable, the Supreme Court directed that every state government will set up two authorities for police complaint, one at the district level, headed by a retired district court judge and other at the state level headed by a retired high court judge. These heads will be assisted by a panel of persons appointed by the state government to be selected from list of security experts, retired police officers and civil society submitted by the state human rights commission/*Lok Ayukt*/public service commissions. Complaints below the rank of superintendent of police will be tried by the district committee and others by the state committee. Recommendation of these committees will be binding on state authorities.

In the end the Supreme Court also directed that the investigating police should be separated from the law and order wing to ensure speedier investigation. The court suggested that the separation should first be effected in big cities having a population of 10 lakh or more and gradually extended to smaller ones.

In 2005, the central government appointed the Soli Sorabjee committee to draft a new model police act. Soon after the Supreme Court's *Prakash Singh* judgement on 30 October 2006, the Soli Sorabjee committee submitted the model Central Police Act to the government, which broadly covers the points raised/directions given by the Supreme Court in *Prakash Singh* judgement. The Supreme Court had ordered that its directions be complied with by 31 December 2006 by all states as well as the Union government. Some of the parties requested the court to review its judgment but their plea was rejected and the implementation time was extended up to 31 March 2007.

More than two years have passed since then. Some of the smaller states like those of the North-East, Uttarakhand and Goa have complied with the direction. But the big states have refused to do so at one pretext or the other. On 16 May 2008, the Supreme Court appointed a committee headed by retired justice K. T. Thomas to oversee the implementation of its directions.

Drawbacks in Reform Attempts

In our country police officers have been given protection under sections 132 and 197 of the Code of Criminal Procedure, which provide protection to the various categories of civil servants from prosecution for the acts they commit in the course of performance their duties. Sections 132 and 187 provide that a public servant cannot be prosecuted without the prior sanction of the state for an offence he is alleged to have committed. This provides immunity to the police from being prosecuted as hardly such sanction is granted. These sections are the biggest legal stumbling blocks to holding the police accountable. Neither the *Prakash Singh* judgement nor the draft bill, have taken note of this major problem.

Second, the idea of democratic policing has gathered momentum throughout the world. The police is expected to work with civil society rather than over it. The police under law and in practice are required to control rather than provide security to the community. Police must protect human rights, especially those that are required for the sort of unfettered political activity that is the hallmark of a democracy. Police should be transparent in their activities.

The third issue concerns with the dealings of the police with specific groups such as women, downtrodden, *dalits*, *adivasis* and religious minorities. Almost all the radical commissions that have been set up to enquire into major communal riots have deplored and condemned the biased role of the police force. This may be due to political interference but it is widely recognized that police is biased against *dalits*, women and religious minorities. No direction has been given in the *Prakash Singh* judgement concerning this bias of the police and the method to tackle it.[14]

It is a fact that political interference is a hurdle in the independent working of the police, and should be dealt with, but there are other important issues concerning police functioning, which also need proper attention. The reforms need to look at the conditions of work of lower level police functionaries and constabulary, who under go tremendous drudgery. They are underpaid and work in terrible conditions, and they are forbidden to pursue their demands through unions because they are not allowed to forms organizations.

In the end, it must be realized that in an unequal society, the police, whether autonomous or not, will lean towards power and powerful ones and no reform measure will be able to deal with this aspect. The important issues such as police accountability to communities, involvement of larger society in policing and the police bias against women, *dalits* and minorities in their dealing, require attention to be included in reform measures.

The Role of District Magistrate in Law and Order

At the district level, the collector/deputy commissioner represents the state administration and heads it in all aspects. The district magistrate or the DM is the head of the criminal administration in the district. He can inspect police stations and ask for any information, statement or record dealing with crime. The police officers are duty bound to obey his orders. As an executive magistrate, he has power to disperse unlawful assemblage of people, remove public nuisance and unite people to keep peace.

The question of relationship between the SP and DM has been discussed by several committees/ commissions in the past and they supported the system of DM's control and direction over the police at district level, but the national police commission has proposed that the police should be made solely responsible for the maintenance of law and order to the exclusion of the DM.

Conclusion

Maintenance of law and order and peace is the main function of any government. The role played by the central as well as state governments in this field is inadequate and unmatched to present situation in the country. The law and order being a state subject centre is not allowed to intervene in this sphere effectively by the state governments. The state police apparatus is stagnant and status quo, its methods of investigations are old and crude. Complaints of use of third degree methods, physical torture and harassment by police pile day by day The police officials know very little of modern methods to deal with communal riots, students agitation and violent social disorders. The criminalization of politics and politicization of criminals, politician criminal and business nexus has made the situation very complex. The degradation of moral values and passivity of integrative forces have contributed for such a sorry state of law and order in the country. The everyday murders by criminals in Delhi, the capital of our nation, demands some firm steps to improve the situation. The law and order machinery should be equipped with modern gadgets to face the challenge in future.

NOTES

1. K. S. Shukla, 'Police Administration in India', *Employment News*, 26 February–1 March, 1991, p. 1.
2. See, for details, Chapter 11 on Ministry of Home Affairs.
3. Report (1991–1992), Ministry of Home Affairs, New Delhi, Government of India.
4. N. K. Singh, *Hindustan Times*, Sunday Magazine, New Delhi, 18 August 1996.
5. Ibid.
6. Ibid.
7. Ibid.
8. Ibid.
9. *Hindustan Times*, 12 December 2008.
10. T. G. L. Iyer, 'Personnel Management in the Police', *Indian Journal of Public Administration*, Vol. XXIV, No. 1, January–March 1978, p. 89.
11. S. Venugopal Rao, 'Law and Order Administration: Some Emerging Trends', *Indian Journal of Public Administration*, Vol. XXXI, No. 31, July–September, 1985, pp. 767–68.
12. Maxwell Pereira, *Hindustan Times*, New Delhi, 21 October 1996.
13. Mihir Desai, 'Red Herring in Police Reforms', *Economic and Political Weekly*, Vol. XLIV No. 10, 7 March 2009, p. 9.
14. Ibid, p. 11.

Accountability and Control over Public Administration

Governmental accountability in a democratic country like ours is very important as it inevitably acquires a much larger dimension for the fundamental reason that it derives its legitimacy from the people at large. Governmental accountability has to be understood in relation to making of public policies and their implementation. Accountability in a democracy is believed to be a contributing factor to efficiency. 'Public officials have been found to be guilty of nonfeasance, malfeasance, and overfeasance. By "nonfeasance" is meant that they have not done what law or customs requires them to do owing to laziness, ignorance or want of care or corrupt influence; "malfeasance" means that a duty is carried out with waste and damage because of ignorance, negligence and technical incompetence, and "overfeasance" occurs when a duty is undertaken beyond what law and custom oblige or empower . . . it may occur out of dictatorial temper, vanity and ambition of an official or his genuine, sincere public-spirited goal. The public official must be held accountable for any of these three activities.'[1] Thus, the governmental accountability lies in the actual performance of roles by the governmental functionaries in their respective areas of work. This chapter examines the concept, major instruments of public accountability and extent of governmental accountability to the people.

THE CONCEPT

The concept of accountability is an offshoot of the concept of administrative responsibility. Governmental accountability comprises both political executive and administrative executive. Under the parliamentary democracy the administrative executive is accountable to the political executive and the latter is accountable to the Parliament. The executive's responsibility is to the representative body; it may be the Parliament or the legislature, regarding the proper implementation of laws, rules and regulations and if they have not been followed, then how and to what extent and why will the questions be answered? This accountability is the direct and genuine exercise of the supremacy vested in the legislature which is a representative body of the people.

At the outset it is necessary to distinguish between accountability as they are often used interchangeably. Administrative responsibility is 'the sum total of the constitutional, statutory, administrative and judicial rules and precedents and the established practices by means of which public officials may be held accountable for their official action.'[2] Further, the meaning of accountability is objective responsibility that connotes the responsibility of a person or an organization about some kind of performance to someone else means outside of self. It is considered to be closely akin to answerability or accountability. The second meaning of responsibility, which is subjective or psychological, focuses not upon to whom and for what 'one is responsible (according to the law and the organization chart) but to whom and for what one feels responsible and behaves responsibly. This meaning is more nearly synonymous with identification, loyalty and conscience than it is with accountability and answerability'.[3] The distinction lies between the two terms, 'accountability refers to the formal and specific location of responsibility' while the responsibility, 'has a highly personal, moral quality and is not necessarily related to formal status or power'.[4]

In a parliamentary form of government, intrinsically, accountability connotes the government's obligation to elucidate and justify its policies and their implementation to the legislature, which oversees and scrutinizes governmental activities so as to satisfy itself that public policies so framed are in accordance with the needs and aspirations of the people and are being executed efficiently in the best interest of the public. Thus, accountability mainly aims at increasing efficiency and effectiveness of administrative processes. The multifarious and technological functions of the government cannot be performed effectively without giving adequate powers and authority to the administrative agencies. But power, as the popular saying goes, corrupts and absolute power corrupts absolutely. Thus, power has a close relationship with corruption. Therefore, if democracy is to be made strong administration must exercise power with restraint. Power in a democratic society requires control, for its judicious exercise, and the greater the power the more need for control. Without proper check administration may abuse or misuse its authority by circumventing law; violating rules, regulations and established norms and procedures, using unfair practices for personal benefits, by favouritism or nepotism and encroaching on rights and freedom of people.

Our country is at the developing stage, therefore, with the expansion of developmental activities, the power vested in public administration is spontaneously growing and there are many chances of its abuse. To check it and make it accountable, certain safeguards are needed to make the administration accountable to the people through specific devices. In this chapter we shall discuss those devices and instruments of administrative control under the heads of legislative or of parliamentary control, executive control and judicial control.

Legislative or Parliamentary Control

The legislature or Parliament plays an important role in making administration accountable. There are several means through which Parliament exercises control over public administration. Some of the important means are: questions, discussions and debates, motions and resolutions on specific administrative actions and matter of grave concern. Members, through financial control by the budget and parliamentary committees, can call attention motions to draw the attention of the minister concerned to a matter of urgent public importance. Such matters concern national security and unity of the nation; drought or flood problems, maintenance of essential services; law and order problems; improper functioning of the administrative machinery; scarcity of essential commodities; foreign actions adversely affecting country's interest, border incidents; and serious incidents involving Indians abroad, for example, during Gulf War due to pressure of public opinion administration made arrangements through Air India for special flights to safely evacuate Indians from Iraq. Parliamentarians also get opportunity to hold administration accountable through budgetary process at the time of general discussion on the budget, discussion and voting of demands for grants and consideration and passing of both the appropriation bill and the finance bill. In this way, legislature, through its power over the public purse, seeks to ensure administrative accountability. Besides the standing committees such as public accounts' committee on subordinate legislation, committee on government assurances and so on, of the Parliament facilitate the exercise of the power of administrative accountability. There are consultative committees attached to the ministries and parliamentary committees of investigation such as the joint parliamentary committees (JPC) for the Investigation of Security Scam under the chairmanship of R. N. Mirdha, MP and a former minister. The committees are empowered to ask for files, information and other documents from government officials. Not only this, the officials may be called for evidence. It is interesting to note that in the proceedings of the committees, public servants are hard put to defend their policies and actions on grounds of laws, rules and their perception of public interest, and in such situations administrative accountability becomes more meaningful. It has been noted that scant attention is paid to the results and findings of the committees by the legislatures and their reports are hardly considered on the floor of the house. Thus, the results of their labour are shelved. Although the reports of all the parliamentary committees are not normally debated in Parliament yet they have great informative value because they enable the members of Parliament who sit on the committees to study in detail the working of the administrative machinery and suggest improvements, whenever necessary. Moreover, the public and the press can also find information on various aspects of administration which might not otherwise come to light. Thus, parliamentary committees contribute to a considerable extent to the efficient working of parliamentary democracy. After having consideration, action on such reports must take place. Further, the power of administrative accountability would be actively operationalized only with the active participation in its exercise by them. Ultimately, the success of the legislative devices for ensuring administrative accountability largely depends upon intelligence and enlightenment of legislators.

The system of post-audit of the governmental accounts is also among the important means of control and insuring accountability as it seeks to ensure that the funds sanctioned by the legislature are spent by the approved authorities for the same purpose for which they are appropriated. It means that actual spending is compared with authorized expenditure in order to detect the extent of administrative accountability for public spending. It is thought that this system of control loses some of its effectiveness when government finance becomes more complex in terms of variety of items purchased and complexity of financial arrangements, it is because of multiplicity of economic activities and almost every nation has found it advisable to allow sufficient latitude to the government in planning public spending, shifting the head of accounts and even aggregates of government expenditure. However, administrative accountability has acquired meaning only in the context of democratic political system having existence of some one to whom account has to be given and performance of actions which have to be accounted for.[5]

Limitation of Legislative Control

The exercise of parliamentary control over administration shows that it can be direct or indirect and positive or negative. Examples of direct control are creation of administrative agencies appointing commissions/committees of enquiry, etc. Indirect control can be exercised by asking questions, moving motions, and resolutions through consultative committees etc. Examples of positive control are sanction of new taxes and new expenditure items, approving policy, examination of administrative agencies through various committees, approving appointment, ratifying treaties, etc. Negative control can be exercised through refusal of demands for grants; refusing pass government bills, resolutions, passing adjournment motions, etc. But there is a general feeling that parliamentary control is not very effective. The reasons they cite are: First, that the work and complexity of administration has increased manifold and legislatures have neither time nor knowledge or competence to control administration. Second, Parliament meets twice in a year and in its sessions a lot of business has to be passed and transacted. Therefore, due to lack of time parliamentary control cannot prove to be effective, even for its legislative business, it leaves so many heads of work which are mostly performed under delegated legislative provisions. Strict party discipline and increasing executive powers have also limited the role of parliamentary control over administration in our country.

Executive Control over Administration

Executive control is an internal control over administration exercised either by the superior over the subordinate within the chain of administrative hierarchy or by other parallel agencies in the executive branch of the government. Administrative structure is hierarchical in nature. One level controls the other and none is outside the chain of command.

Types of Executive Control

The executive control is exercised in many ways. Most of the means of control are formal provided by the laws of the country but some of them are informal depending upon the good sense of the public servants. The system of internal control may be studied under the following heads:

(i) Political or ministerial control

(ii) Administrative control within the hierarchy

(iii) Personnel management control

(iv) Budgetary control

(v) Control by staff agencies

(vi) Professional or administrative ethics

Political or Ministerial Control

Ministerial responsibility is the cardinal principle of parliamentary democracy. The executive branch of the government consists of ministers as members of the cabinet. Each minister is individually in charge of a portfolio consisting of one or more department and thus, he is the chief executive so far as that portfolio is concerned and is responsible for the official working of the subjects under his charge. In running the administration of concerned department(s) he has to control the actions of civil servants under him so that they may help in implementation of the policies. This leads to the sensitive, complex issue of relationship between the minister and the civil servant.

Administrative Control Within the Hierarchy

In the above point we have discussed the political command structure but there is a hierarchical command structure in the permanent executive. The administrative head of the department is secretary. The department is divided into wings, under the charge of joint or additional secretary; a wing is sub-divided into divisions headed by deputy secretaries; each division is further divided into branches, under the charge of under secretaries; and then comes the section, presided over by section officer. The principle of secretariat procedure is that each paper must pass through the proper authorized channel both in its outwards and inward journey. The secretariat is the 'headquarter' which has hundreds and thousands of field offices located throughout the country. These field offices work under the direction and control of the secretariat. There are a number of techniques and devices through which the administration of the headquarter controls the field agencies. The devices include prior approval of individual project, promulgation of service standards; budgetary limitations upon the operations; and approval of the appointment of key subordinate personnel; audit, inspection, reporting and investigation, etc. Luther Gulick discussed and distinguished between three types of headquarters-field relationship. For example, All Fingers; Short Arms, Long Fingers, and Long Arms, Short fingers. Under the first, the headquarters office deals directly with the field units without any regional units, under the second type regional units are there but these are located in the central office and not in the field; and under the third type, territorial units are located in the entire area away from the central office.

Personnel Management Control

An important means of control is the centralization of establishment or personnel functions. The chief executive has a centralized personnel office. This office controls the methods of recruitment, salaries, promotions, conditions of service, etc. Uniformity in personnel matters throughout the administrative organization of the government is maintained. This is advantageous in preparation of projects, and estimates, etc. The system of giving rewards like increments, rise in salary, promotion, etc. are very powerful instrument of control in the hands of the executive. Likewise, public servants can be reprimanded, censured, removed and dismissed from the service if they do not behave in a desired way. These examples persuade the public servants to avoid undesirable behaviour and improving their performance on desirable lines.

Budgetary Control

To carry out the functions of the government the budget provides necessary finances. The activities of the public servants can be controlled by controlling the finances made available to them through budget. If budgetary system is effective, no official can escape its control. The budgetary control is exercised by the ministry of finance, through a system of hierarchy of financial powers. The other parts of this control are the expenditure reports sent by the operating units, the internal audit conducted by the Department and the central audit conducted by the comptroller and auditor-general. Appleby said that India has a faulty system of budgetary control. Expenditure control is exercised to an oppressive degree and converts the budgetary system into a fault finding system.

Control by Staff Agencies

There are two important staff agencies which also exercise control over various ministries, departments and other administrative agencies. The important agencies are: the planning commission and the department of administrative reforms, which is now part of a full-fledged ministry named ministry of personnel, public grievances and pensions. The administrative wing of the new ministry functions as the top agency for improving administrative capability on a continuing basis. The planning commission suggests new policies or programmes, coordinates policies and programmes started by other agencies of the government and maintains effective liaisons with the central ministries and state governments.

Professional or Administrative Ethics

In due course of time, every profession develops a code of conduct and behaviour for its members. Medical and legal professions have organized so well that they have shaped formal means of enforcing their ethics on members. However, the legal and medical professions have formal and legal methods of enforcement of their code of conduct for the sake of pride in their profession. Public services have also become a professional career and in many countries it has evolved its own code of ethics. In India there is a very voluminous code of conduct for civil servants. It lays down in great details what a civil servant should do and should not do. It even goes to the extent of specifying the need for reporting to the government even bona fide transactions with the members of the family and close friends. However, these tight controls have not inculcated the necessary sense of duty and discipline in the civil servants. At present, it is a very serious matter that our civil servants have also involved in numerous scams along with the politicians. Thus, they are not observing the conduct rules which often suffer from numerous loopholes.

JUDICIAL CONTROL OVER ADMINISTRATION

In a democratic country, the judiciary restricts the discretion and arbitrariness of both the executive and administrative agencies; safeguards the rights and liberty of the citizens; it helps in redress of the grievances of the citizens; curbs corruption in government and administration and can declare the acts of the government and administration *ultra vires* in case they exceed their jurisdiction.[6] Thus, if some administrative action causes loss to the citizen, he may knock at the door of the judiciary for redress of his grievances. It has been rightly pointed out that 'increased safeguards against their abuses, and as long as there is the possibility of official error, partiality or excess of zeal, the protection of private rights is an important object as the effectuation of some government policy'.[7]

Forms of Judicial Control

Judicial control can be exercised in the following forms: (i) judicial review of administrative acts and decisions; (ii) statutory appeals to the courts against the administrative acts and decisions; (iii) suits against the central or state governments by a private party for enforcing contract or torts; (iv) criminal suits against public servants by private parties; (v) extraordinary remedies such as: (a) *habeas corpus*; (b) *mandamus*; (c) injunction; (d) *certiorari*; (e) prohibition; (f) *quo warranto*.

Judicial Review

In India the subject of judicial review has not been properly explored. Normally courts do not interfere with purely administrative action unless it is *ultra vires* in regard to the scope and form or failure to follow proper procedure.

Statutory Appeals

Appeals to the courts of law or higher administrative tribunals are to be provided by statutes. Usually the appellate authority has wide discretion. It can accept the decision *in toto*, modify it or set aside by ordering the action *de novo*.

Suits Against Government

Article 300 of our Constitution provides for suability to the Union and the States. It reads as follows:

'(1) The Government of India may sue or be sued by the name of the Union of India; and the Government of a State may sue or be sued by the name of the State and may, subject to any provisions which may be made by Act of Parliament or of the legislature of such State enacted by virtue of powers conferred by this Constitution, sue or be sued in relation to their respective affairs in the like cases as the Dominion of India and the corresponding Provinces or the corresponding Indian States might have sued or been sued "if this Constitution had not been enacted".

(2) If at the commencement of this Constitution—

(i) any legal proceedings are pending to which the Dominion of India is a party, the Union of India shall be deemed to be substituted for the Dominion in those proceedings; and
(ii) any legal proceedings are pending to which a Province or an Indian State is a party the corresponding State shall be deemed to be substituted for the Province or the Indian State in those proceedings.'

Thus, it provides only for suability of the Union and the States and not for their respective liabilities. The real implication of this Article has not been perceived which has led to the unwanted perpetuation of errors of a colonial law. The contractual liabilities of both the Union and the State Governments, subject to any statutory conditions of limits, are the same as of an individual under the ordinary law of contract. As regards the liability of the State in sovereign functions for which the East India Company would have been liable and not to sovereign functions which include commandeering goods during war, construction or repair of a military road. But the State is liable for similar acts in course of constructing or repairing of non-military roads. The judges and the jurists are of the opinion that the present state of law on the matter is highly unsatisfactory and out of accord with the republican and democratic set-up of Indian polity.

Suits Against Public Officials

In fact liability is the legal accountability of a wrong-doer to the wronged. According to the Indian Civil Procedure Code, 1908, Section 80-2, an official, in exercise of his statutory power, would be liable in his acts if they were proved to be malicious and civil proceedings against a public officer for anything done in his official capacity can be only instituted according to a prescribed procedure requiring two months' written notice, etc. But no such notice is required when the action is to be brought against him for some action taken by him outside the scope of his duties and commits an assault. So far as criminal liabilities under the Indian Penal Code are concerned, 'nothing is an offence which is done by a person (this includes an official too) who is, or way by reason of a mistake of fact and not by reason of a mistake of law, in good faith believes himself to be bound by law to do it.' Further, under Section 197 of the IPC there is a provision of previous sanction of the president or governor as the case may be for starting criminal proceedings in respect of acts done in their official capacity against those officials whose removal from the office is subjected to the sanction of the state governments or some other higher authority thereof. The courts are forbidden to take cognizance of the official's offence until the requisite sanction is available. Some of the Indian jurists opine that this provision of the Indian Criminal Procedure Code is inconsistent with the right of equality before the law guaranteed by the Constitution and, therefore, it is unconstitutional.[8]

Extraordinary Remedies

The extraordinary remedies consist of five writs: (a) *habeas corpus*, (b) *mandamus*, (c) prohibition, (d) *certiorari* and (e) *quo warranto*.

The term writ has been defined in the dictionary as 'a formal order under seal, issued in the name of a sovereign, government, court or other competent authority, informing the officer or other person to whom it is issued or addressed to do or refrain from some specified act'. The main feature of a writ is that it protects the liberty of the citizen by speedy and summary interpretation.

Habeas Corpus

Habeas corpus literally means, 'you shall produce the body'. It is a court order directing an official who has a person in custody to bring the prisoner to show cause for his detention and to set him free if there is no legal justification for his confinement. It is a very important writ as it safeguards the liberty of the citizens.

The purpose of this writ is to determine whether the person seeking remedy is detained legally or illegally. It may be directed to a private person as well as a public officer. The writ is granted as a matter of right and not on the discretion of the court.

Mandamus

It literally means 'we command'. It is an order issued by a superior court to a lower court or to an officer, corporation, etc. to compel performance of an act. Through this writ a public officer and public bodies can be compelled to perform their legal duties.

Prohibition

It is an 'extraordinary judicial writ', issued by a superior court to an inferior court for the purpose of preventing it from usurping jurisdiction with which it is not legally vested. This writ can be claimed as a right. Its purpose is to determine the legality of proceedings in the lower court. It plays some part in the control of administrative tribunals which have quasi-judicial functions.

Certiorari

It literally means, 'to be certified' and to be made certain. It has been defined as 'a writ issued by the superior court to an inferior court of record, or other tribunal or office exercising a judicial function, requiring the certification and return to the former of some proceedings then pending, or the record and proceedings in some cause already terminated, in cases where the procedure is not according to the course of the common law.' It is an important instrument of control in respect of quasi-judicial functions of administrative officers and tribunals.

Quo Warranto

It literally means, 'by what authority'. It has been defined as 'the remedy or proceedings whereby the court enquires into the legality of the claims which a person asserts to an office or franchise and to oust him from its enjoyment if the claim is not well founded'.

In addition to the above writs, the superior courts have the power to issue injunctions. It has been defined as 'a judicial process operating in person and requiring the person to whom it is directed to do or refrain from doing a particular thing'.

In our country, the Supreme Court and high courts have the jurisdiction to issue writs. It may be noted that the powers of our courts are much wider than merely to issue writs: they can issue other directives and orders also. The Supreme Court can issue writs only for the enforcement of fundamental rights. But the high courts can issue writs for any other purpose. Thus, it is a very wide discretion and the courts can issue writs in any matter in which it feels that the interference of the court is necessary.

Limitations of Judicial Control

(i) The courts have no authority to stall proceedings *suo motu.* They take notice only when some person or party complains that their rights have been infringed by the actions of the government servants.

(ii) Thus, all administrative actions do not come under the purview of the judiciary. The Constitution exempts certain types of acts, regulations and orders from judicial purview. For example, Article 31A and B concerning *zamindari* abolition cases had been barred from the jurisdiction of courts in 1951.

(iii) The judicial control is a device of control after the event. One can approach the courts for judicial remedy only after the damage has been done.

(iv) The process of seeking judicial remedy is too costly to be accessible to the poor and needy.

(v) The judicial process is very slow, cumbersome and a lot of delay takes place in the final disposal of cases. Justice delayed is justice denied. There are still thousands of cases pending in various law courts. This is a serious matter and needs immediate solution.

Other Means of Control

Lok Pal

A good system of governance must provide a citizen an opportunity of seeking redress from arbitrary actions of civil servants, to look into the problems of individual citizens who feel aggrieved by the decisions of civil servants.

India has made attempts to institute the office of ombudsman to give the citizen an independent hearing about his grief; and to remove inefficiency and malpractices pervading in the administration. On the recommendation of the Administrative Reforms Commission, 1966, a Bill providing for an ombudsman was introduced in the house of people on 9 May 1968 but it lapsed due to dissolution of the Lok Sabha. Again in 1971, the Bill named *Lok Pal* and *Lok Ayukta* Bill 1971 was re-introduced and met with the same fate in 1977. Furthermore, another fresh Bill called the *Lok Pal* Bill 1977 was introduced in the Lok Sabha on 28 July 1977 and was referred to the joint committee but when it was under consideration the Lok Sabha was dissolved. A fresh *Lok Pal* Bill, 1985 was introduced in the Parliament with great enthusiasm and was referred to the joint committee whose report was placed in Parliament on 6 December 1988 but the Government withdrew the Bill. This move was vehemently criticized by the opposition. The Janata Dal Government[9] had introduced a comprehensive Bill in the Lok Sabha on 29 December 1989. The proposed *Lok Pal* had jurisdiction over the council of ministers including the prime minister and can go into a complaint of corruption within the meaning of the Prevention of Corruption Act, 1988. But again the Bill lapsed due to the fall of the National Front Government and dissolution of the Lok Sabha in 1989. Again a *Lok Pal* Bill was introduced in the Lok Sabha by United Front Government which was to be passed by Parliament in the session starting from 23 July 1997. (This aspect has been discussed in detail in Chapter 28 on 'Issues Areas in Indian Administration'.)

Lok Ayukta

Some states like Maharashtra, Madhya Pradesh, Karnataka, Bihar, Orissa,[10] Himachal Pradesh, Rajasthan have appointed *Lok Ayuktas*. With certain exceptions they have been empowered to look into complaints against ministers in their states and other senior officers. In the words of the *Lok Ayukta* of Rajasthan, the basic object of the institution is to work as a safety valve to protect violent eruption as a result of frustration, or persisting feelings of dissatisfaction, with what may sometimes appear to be blatant and continued maladministration.[11] Although ministers are included in the jurisdiction of the *Lok Ayukta,* the chief minister is totally excluded from the scope of the Maharashtra *Lok Ayukta* Act. To ensure government accountability the chief minister should be within the jurisdiction of the *Lok Ayukta*. The institution of *Lok Ayukta* is considered to be very useful and can effectively ameliorate the plight of the downtrodden people. However, it requires moral strength and material tools. It is said that the provision which empowers him to avail of the services of government investigating agencies is impracticable, ineffective and frustrating; therefore, it should have its own investigating agency.

People's Participation

To enforce administrative accountability, people's participation in the planning process, decision making and control over funds and expenditure is necessary. In developmental process, it is necessary to provide information to the progress of the project so as to find out problems and constraints in implementation. People's involvement in monitoring and evaluation reduces mismanagement of resources. When they are empowered to evaluate the performance of officials in the schemes being executed, it makes the government machinery accountable to them.

Political Parties, Press and People

In parliamentary democracy, political parties too play an important role in expressing public opinion and they check the arbitrary use of powers and actions of the executive. They try to bring the government on the right track, if it acts against public interests. But the prohibitive costs of electioneering and consequent control of money power over political parties and public media are not considered to be conducive to making legislature really representative. Not only this, even distortions in the electoral system and process can undermine government accountability to the people.[12]

People may pressurize public officials to be accountable through pressure groups and voluntary organizations in which they work constructively. The press also plays an important role in enforcing administrative accountability through editorials and providing news regarding administrative irregularities, mismanagement, inefficiency and corrupt practices of the officials. Citizens get their grievances ventilated through columns of magazines and newspapers and editorials. Government takes necessary steps to enquire into the business issues on the basis of news and views of the citizens. People become powerful instruments when they act as voters and show resentment against government actions by changing the government.

To conclude, government and administrative accountability in a democratic country like ours is of great importance. It brings efficiency and effectiveness in the administration and checks wrong and arbitrary actions. Administrative accountability has to be ensured through the dynamic role of the legislature, judiciary, political parties, press and the people. For making government honest, accountable and responsive, people should not only be aware of policy, programmes and their implementation but should also be active, vigilant, cooperative, intelligent and enthusiastic.

NOTES

1. Asok Mukhopadhyay, 'Administrative Accountability: A Conceptual Analysis', *Indian Journal of Public Administration*, July–September, 1983, p. 474.
2. L. D. White, 'Introduction to the Study of Public Administration', quoted in A. R. Tyagi, *Public Administration Principles and Practices*, (Delhi: Atma Ram and Sons, 1989), p. 747.
3. 'Editorial', *Indian Journal of Public Administration*, July–September, 1983, p. viii.
4. J. M. Piffner and R. V. Presthus, *Public Administration* (New York: Ronald Press, 1960), p. 522.
5. Asok Mukhopadhyay, op. cit., pp. 474–87.
6. A. Awasthi, *Central Administration* (New Delhi: Tata McGraw-Hill, 1980), p. 289.
7. Quoted by L. D. White, *Introduction to the Study of Public Administration, 4th edition* (New York: Macmillan, 1951), p. 510.
8. See, D. D. Basu, *Commentary on the Constitution of India* (Calcutta: S. C. Sarkar & Sons, 1962), pp. 818–19.
9. *The Tribune*, Chandigarh, 30 December 1989, p. 11.
10. Orissa has recently abolished the office of *Lok Ayukta*.
11. See, *Annual Report of the Lokayukta of Rajasthan*, Jaipur, 1975–1976, p. 10.
12. M. J. K. Thavraj, 'Financial Accountability in Government', *Indian Journal of Public Administration*, op. cit., p. 558.

State Administration

The pattern of state governance in India is on the lines of the Union. The head of the state, like his counterpart at the centre, is a mere nominal head who acts on the advice of the council of ministers having majority support in the state legislature.

The Governor

The governor is the executive head of the state. Article 154 of the Constitution vests all the executive powers of the state in the governor, which are exercised by him either directly or through officers subordinate to him in accordance with the Constitution. The governor is a nominal head and actual powers are exercised by the council of ministers headed by the chief minister.

Appointment of the Governor

The governor of a state is appointed by the president by warrant under his hand and seal and holds office during his pleasure. Anybody who is a citizen of India and above 35 years of age can be appointed as governor of a state. The person who is appointed a governor cannot remain member of either house of Parliament or of a house of the legislature of any state. If any such person is appointed as a governor, he shall be deemed to have vacated the seat in Parliament or state legislature. He must not hold any other office of profit, but the membership of the council of ministers, presidentship, vice-presidentship, etc. are not considered as offices of profit for this purpose. The manner of appointment of a governor has, however, raised a lot of controversy. The question was discussed at length in the Constituent Assembly. Initially an elected governor was proposed for every state, but the proposal was not accepted. The Constituent Assembly discussed various alternative methods of selecting a governor, and finally adopted 'appointment by the president'.

Arguments Against an Elected Governor

First, the governor was to be nominal head and no substantial powers were to be given to him, therefore, it was not thought proper to have an elected governor. Dr B. R. Ambedkar made the position clear by stating that 'we feel that the powers of the governor were so limited, so nominal, his position so ornamental that probably very few would come forward to stand for election.'[1] Second, it was felt that the elected governor might get into a clash with the chief minister, thinking that he is an elected representative of the people and thus might start exercising his powers as actual head. Third, an elected governor is, in all probability, a nominee/representative of the political party in power at the state. Such a situation did not fit into the parliamentary system of government. Fourth, election of the governor may include a lot of expenditure and time which will be unnecessary for a nominal post. Finally, an elected governor will not be amenable to the directions from the centre. This may create difficulties for the centre to deal with emergencies arising due to the failure of constitutional machinery in the state.

Arguments Against Nominated Governor

A nominated governor may also be a cause of tension between the centre and state particularly when different parties happen to be in power. States ruled by parties in opposition to that at the centre always oppose a central nominee as a governor. Second, when the elected president has not created problems for the central government and remained a nominal head, elected governor like president should be able to remain politically neutral. Third, a nominated governor being an outsider and not elected by them may not be sensitive to the needs of the local people. The question of appointment of governor out of a panel of four names suggested by the members of state legislature on the basis of proportional representation was also discussed and discarded on the grounds that it would create a lot of resentment in the state legislature if the person at number one in the panel is not appointed as the governor. Fourth, in most of the cases he would be a party man and a nominee of the chief minister. The Constituent Assembly, therefore, opted for a nominated governor, who would be able to ensure better control of the Union government over the state governments whenever the need arose. Alladi Krishnaswami Aiyyar said in the constituent Assembly: 'on the whole in the interest of harmony, in the interest of good working, in the interest of sound relations between the provincial cabinet and the governor, it will be much better if we accept the Canadian model of nominated governors.' The approach of the Constituent Assembly was for a strong centre and a nominated governor was a part of this strategy. The majority of our governors are former politicians who had resorted to every conceivable stratagem in fighting their rivals. The second largest category comprises retired civil servants who have been rewarded for their 'loyalty', the third category, which is the smallest, consists of retired military top brass, good to take the salute at a march-past.

Intellectuals, social workers, educationists and eminent people in other non-political spheres are seldom appointed as governors. Why is it that the choice invariably falls on disgruntled or crestfallen or inactive politicians? The answer is obviously for political purposes.

Selection of Type of Persons as Governor

Apart from the nominated governor another point of controversy was of selection of persons as governors. It has been said that the quality and standard of some of the persons, appointed as governors has not been befitting the dignity of the august office. Many state governments complained to the popular Sarkaria commission, appointed to look into the problems of centre–state relations, that ministers resigning on court strictures have been appointed as governors. Some of the governors have returned to active politics. Politicians defeated in elections, who could not be accommodated elsewhere, were appointed governors. Such persons cannot be expected to display the qualities of integrity, impartiality and statesmanship required of a person holding the high office of the governor. The Sarkaria Commission has suggested that a person to be appointed as governor should satisfy the following criteria:[2]

(i) He should be eminent in some walk of life.

(ii) He should be a person from outside the state.

(iii) He should be a detached figure and not too intimately connected with the local politics of the state.

(iv) He should be a person who has not taken too great a part in politics generally and particularly in the recent past.

In selecting a governor in accordance with the above criteria, persons belonging to the minority groups should continue to be given a chance as was earlier.

The governor is appointed by the president by a warrant under his hand and seal. In actual practice, the governors are appointed by the president on the recommendation of the prime minister. Although in the beginning up to 1967, there was a practice to consult the chief minister of the state before appointing a governor when the Congress party was ruling at the centre and in the states. But, when non-Congress parties came to power in the states after 1967, this practice was stopped. Since then many governors were appointed against the wishes of chief ministers. For example, Dharam Vir in West Bengal, Nitya Nand Kanungo in Bihar, B. N. Chakravarty in Haryana, and Ram Lal in Andhra Pradesh were all appointed governors in spite of opposition by the respective chief ministers. Dr Chenna Reddy was shifted to Tamil Nadu as governor from Rajasthan, even against the wishes of Tamil Nadu chief minister.

Term

The governor is appointed for five years, he can be given another term also. Even after the completion of his term, he continues in office till his successor joins the office. There are many examples where governors have continued after expiry of their five year term till further orders. The former governor of Andhra Pradesh Krishan Kant is an example in addition to many earlier ones. The term of office of the governor is five years, but he can resign at any time. Moreover, he holds his office during the pleasure of the president and the pleasure can be withdrawn at any time. Prabhu Das Patwari, former governor of Tamil Nadu in 1980, Raghukul Tilak, the governor of Rajasthan in 1981 and T. N. Singh, governor of West Bengal were forced to resign in 1982 under the same threats of withdrawal of pleasure.

Transfer of the Governor

The Constitution has no provision for the transfer of the governors but they are transferred like government servants from one state to another. The former Rajasthan governor, Dr Chenna Reddy was transferred to Tamil Nadu, Bali Ram Bhagat, former governor of Himachal Pradesh was transferred to Rajasthan, Ramesh Bhandari, former governor of Goa was transferred to UP, etc. In fact, transfer of governors from one state to another is a violation of the Constitution because they have to take fresh oath of office meaning thereby the start of a fresh term of five years. Therefore, this implies that he/she should not be transferred.

Emoluments

He is entitled to such emoluments, allowances and privileges as may be determined by Parliament. He draws the salary of Rs 75,000 per month along with free residence and other perks. His emoluments are not to be changed to his disadvantage, during his tenure of office.

Immunities

The Constitution has provided certain immunities and privileges to the governor under Article 361 which are as follows:

(a) He is not answerable to any court for the exercise of duties of his office.
(b) No civil or criminal proceedings can be instituted or continued against him in any court so long as he is in office.
(c) No process for his arrest or imprisonment can be issued by any court against him.

Power of the Governor

The governor is the head of the state; therefore, he has been given powers like our president except in the field of diplomatic, military or emergency powers. In certain cases, the governor can also act on his own discretion. His powers can be placed in four categories, namely, legislative, executive, financial and judicial.

Legislative Powers

The governor, though not a member of state legislature, is an integral part of the state legislature and has been bestowed with many legislative powers. Some of the important legislative powers are as follows:

(i) He can summon or prorogue either house of the state legislature and has the power to dissolve the legislative assembly.

(ii) He can address the legislative assembly (or both houses where the state legislature is bicameral) at the commencement of the new session after each general election and the first session every year.

(iii) He can send messages to the state legislature on a bill pending before it or otherwise.

(iv) If the offices of both the speaker and the deputy speaker of the legislative assembly fall vacant, the governor can appoint any member of the state legislative assembly to preside over the house. Such a member shall discharge all the duties of a presiding officer till the assembly elects its own speaker. Similarly, if the offices of the chairman and the deputy chairman of the legislative council fall vacant he can make ad-hoc arrangements in like manner.

(v) In those states where the legislative councils exist the governor appoints one-sixth of its members from amongst persons who have special knowledge of art, literature, science, co-operative movement and social service. He can also nominate some members to the legislative assembly from the Anglo-Indian community, if he feels that the community has not received adequate representation otherwise.

(vi) On the advice of the Election Commission, the governor can decide the case regarding disqualification of any member of the state legislature.

(vii) All the bills passed by the state legislature must receive the assent of the governor before they can reach the statute book. The governor reserves the right to withhold his assent or return the bill (other than money bill) for the reconsideration of the house. However, if the legislature again passes the bill with or without amendments, the governor has to append his signatures to the bill. The governor also enjoys the power to reserve certain types of bills passed by the state legislature for the assent of the president.

(viii) During the recess of the state legislature the governor can issue ordinances which have the same force as a law enacted by the state legislature. However, these ordinances cease to operate at the expiry of six weeks from the date of reassembly of the legislature or earlier if it passes resolution disapproving of such an ordinance.

Executive Power

The Constitution vests the entire executive powers of the state in the governor, which have to be exercised by him either directly or through officers subordinate to him in accordance with the Constitution. In other words, all the executive actions of the state are taken in the name of the governor. The executive authority of the governor extends to all those matters with respect to which the legislature of the state has power to make laws. It is the responsibility of the governor to ensure that the laws passed by the state legislature and the laws passed by the Parliament in relation to his state are faithfully executed in the state.

All major appointments of the state are made by the governor. Thus, he appoints the chief minister of the state and on his recommendations the other members of the council of ministers. He also administers the oath of office and secrecy to the members of the council of ministers. The allocation of portfolios among the various members is also done by the governor on the recommendation of the chief minister. The ministers hold office during his pleasure. However, in reality the governor cannot remove the ministers so long as they enjoy the support of the majority of the members of the state legislature.

The governor makes rules for the convenient transaction of the business of the state and allocation of business among the various ministers. The other important appointments made by the governor of the state include the advocate general, members and chairman of the state public service commission, etc.

The governor has a right to be kept informed about all the decisions taken by the council of ministers as well as the proposals for legislation. He can also call for any other information relating to the administration of the state and ask the chief minister about any matter on which a decision has been taken by a minister but which has not been considered by the council of ministers as a whole.

But probably the most significant executive power enjoyed by the governor of a state relates to his right to report to the president that a situation has arisen or is likely to arise under which the government of the state cannot be carried on in accordance with the provisions of the Constitution. It is on the basis of this report from the governor that the president can make a proclamation of emergency and assume the responsibility for the administration of the state. When a proclamation of emergency is made, the governor acts as the representative of the president and comes to wield very effective powers.

Financial Powers

In the financial sphere, it is the duty of the governor to put before the house or houses of the state legislature a statement of estimated receipt and expenditure of the state for the ensuing year. It means that no demands for grant can be presented before the state legislature without the recommendation of the governor. The responsibility for the submission of supplementary or additional grants, if any, also rests with the governor. In actual practice this power of the governor is exercised by the party in power.

The contingency fund of the state has also been placed at the disposal of the governor, who is empowered to take an advance out of it to meet unforeseen expenditure. However, all such advances must be subsequently approved by the state legislature and regularized.

Judicial Powers

The governor is consulted by the president while making appointment of the judges of the state high court. He enjoys full powers with regard to the appointments, postings and promotions of the district judges and other judicial officers of the state. As head of the state he enjoys the power to grant pardon, reprieve, respite or remission of punishment or to suspend, remit or commute the sentence of any person convicted of any offence against any law relating to a matter to which the executive power of the state extends.

Miscellaneous Powers

The miscellaneous powers of the governor include the following:

(i) The right to receive the reports of the auditor general regarding the income and expenditure of the state and to place the same before the state legislature.

(ii) The right to receive the annual report of the state public service commission and to transmit the same to the council of ministers for its comments. After these comments are received, the report along with the comments is placed before the state legislature.

(iii) He is the chancellor of all the universities within the state and appoints the vice-chancellors of these universities. However, in making these appointments he is chiefly guided by the chief minister of the state and the Union and state education ministers. In fact, the governor has hardly any discretion in making these appointments.

Position of the Governor

It is evident from the above survey of the powers of the governor that he has been assigned an important position in the state government machinery. Although he is expected to behave like a constitutional head and act on the advice of the council of ministers, his position fundamentally differs from that of the president of India vis-à-vis his council of ministers, Article 163(1) of the Constitution clearly lays down that 'There shall be a council of ministers with the chief minister at the head to aid and advise the governor in the exercise of his functions, except insofar as he is by or under this Constitution required to exercise his functions.' In Article 74(1), dealing with the relationship of the president with the council of ministers, we will find that while the president is expected to exercise his functions in accordance with the advice of the Central council of ministers, there is no such stipulation of the binding nature of the advice of the council of ministers so far as the state governor is concerned. It only suggests that the governor is normally expected to act as a constitutional head of the states, but under certain circumstances he can also exercise his discretion. However, the Constitution does not specify the subjects and the field in which the governor may exercise his discretion, although it can easily be implied that in the following cases the governor can act without the advice of the council of ministers: (i) selection of the chief minister—if no political party has a clear-cut majority in the house, or the majority party does not have any acknowledged leader; (ii) dismissal of the ministry; (iii) dissolution of the legislative assembly; (iv) seeking of information regarding legislative and administrative matters from the chief minister; (v) appending or refusing signatures to a non-money bill passed by the state legislature; (vi) reservation of a bill passed by the state legislature for the assent of the president; (vii) recommendation to the president regarding the failure of the constitutional machinery in the state, etc.

On the issue of selection of the chief minister in a situation when no party has majority in the state legislature, the governor's discretion to appoint a person as chief minister becomes very important. For example, in 1967 when no party was in majority in the Rajasthan Vidhan Sabha, the governor refused to invite the leader of majority support on the grounds that he did not count independents. In 1982, when no party was in absolute majority and the combination of the Lok Dal and BJP was in majority, the Haryana governor appointed Congress legislature party leader Bhajan Lal as chief minister and gave him one month's time to prove his majority. During this long one month's time, Bhajan Lal was able to manipulate majority through defections.

Dismissal of a ministry is another important discretionary power of the governor. In 1967, the governor of West Bengal, Dharam Vir, dismissed the ministry of Ajay Mukherjee on the ground that only such ministry had the right to be in office which enjoyed the majority support in the state legislature. The dismissal of Charan Singh ministry in 1970 in UP and on 2 July 1984, the Jammu and Kashmir governor, Jagmohan, dismissed Farooq Abdullah's ministry; Andhra Pradesh governor Ram Lal dismissed N. T. Rama Rao's ministry in 1984, although he was ready to prove his majority no action was taken by the governor; Punjab governor, S. S. Ray dismissed Surjeet Singh Barnala's ministry in 1987 and in Karnataka, the Janata Dal government led by S. R. Bommai was dismissed in April 1989. The DMK government led by Karunanidhi was dismissed in 1991 and the BJP led governments in UP, MP and Rajasthan were dismissed in 1993, not because they lost majority but on the other grounds. Thus, the governors have used their discretion in dismissing the ministries in various states.

Regarding the dissolution of assemblies, sometimes the governors dissolved the assemblies on the advice of outgoing chief ministers; sometimes they have not dissolved and appointed others as chief ministers, for example in Orissa and Jammu and Kashmir. The most controversial discretionary power of governor is the report to the president for imposition of president's rule under Article 356. An analysis of over 105 cases in which the centre took over the administration of the state governments under Article 356 clearly brings out the inglorious role of the governors.[3] The governors on several occasions allowed themselves to become the tool of New Delhi (centre) so as to serve the narrow partisan objective of the party in power at the centre, at times even the functional interests of the rulers.

A specific issue which has reappeared in recent times is the involvement of former Bihar chief minister, Laloo Prasad Yadav, in the fodder scam as investigated by CBI and its request to the governor of Bihar, A. R. Kidwai, to grant sanction for prosecution of the chief minister. There are judicial pronouncements on the issue. In the well-known Antulay case, the Supreme Court held that in taking a decision to sanction or withhold prosecution on charges of corruption of any minister from the council of ministers, the governor is required to exercise his judgement independently. The decision seems to be based more on the 'propriety' rather than 'legality'[4]. The Supreme Court in the case went by the provisions of Article 163(2) which says that when the governor acts in his discretion that decision cannot be questioned by the courts.

The governor of Kerala, exercising his discretion, gave his sanction to the CBI to prosecute CPI(M) state secretary Pinarayi Vijayan for his role in a major power scam when he was the state power minister in the late 1990s. Although the state cabinet passed a resolution urging the governor R. S. Gavai not to sanction prosecution, the action of the governor was contrary to the state government's advice.[5]

It may be further noted that the Constitution specifically provides that if any question arises regarding whether any matter is or is not a matter in respect of which the governor is by or under the Constitution required to act in his discretion, the decision of the governor in exercising his discretion shall be final, and the validity of anything done by the governor shall not be called in question on the ground that he ought or ought not to have acted in his discretion. However, the governor is not expected to act in his discretion in a matter prejudicial to the norms of parliamentary democracy.

But the question whether sanction to prosecute the chief minister is the exclusive function of the governor exercised by him in his discretion or not, is not yet settled in law because an appeal on this issue by the former Tamil Nadu chief minister, J. Jayalalitha, for her prosecution in a corruption case is pending before a five-judge constitutional bench of the Supreme Court against the judgement of the Madras High Court dismissing a petition moved by the state of Tamil Nadu challenging the sanction accorded by the then governor, M. Chenna Reddy.[6]

Although the discretionary powers of the governor have been made non-challengeable in courts of law but discretionary powers are not to be confused with arbitrariness. They should not be used without any norms or fixed criteria or unjustly. They should be exercised fairly and honestly on judicial grounds giving clear-cut reasons. In recent judgements, Supreme Court has declared all the discretionary quotas of central ministries *ultra vires* on the grounds of misuse. For example, the allotment of petrol pumps, cooking gas agencies and DDA houses by ministries on the basis of discretionary quota has been declared illegal by Supreme Court.

The Role of the Governor

The Constituent Assembly debates highlighted the governor's role as a friend, philosopher and the guide of the cabinet and the state government. The Supreme Court[7] held that the governor is not subordinate or subservient even to the Government of India, although he is appointed by the president. It is only a mode of appointment and does not make the governor a servant of the Government of India or of the state government or any other authority whatever. But the fact remains that the governor acts as an agent of the Central government. The method of the appointment and dismissal of the governor and the way the governors have been transferred, forced to resign or dismissed provide further proof that the governor has to carry out the wishes of the central government and can hardly act with an open mind and according to his best judgement based on his good conscience.

The working of the governor's office during last 50 years is good proof of his partisan role based on not facts and judicious considerations but on politically coloured decisions. The following trends emerge in practice about the role of the governor after Independence.

Some Examples

Some recent cases of governors' actions highlighted the controversial role played by them in the state *Raj Bhawans*. In 1998, UP governor Romesh Bhandari installed a government headed by Jagadamika Pal, dismissing the Kalyan Singh government. This happened on the evening before polling in one of the phases during 1998 Lok Sabha elections. One of the ministers in the Kalyan Singh government went to the high court against this decision and the court stayed the governor's order of dismissal of the government. After one and half days, Kalyan Singh was re-instated by the High Court order but Jagdambika Pal, the newly appointed chief minister by the governor went to the Supreme Court. The Supreme Court ordered convening of the state assembly for testing majority on the floor of the house on 26 February 1998. Kalyan Singh got 12 votes more than the majority support and became chief minister again within a week. The political drama in UP proved the unconstitutional role played by the governor into the open. The president asked the prime minister to 'advise' him on the conduct of Uttar Pradesh governor. The governor thereafter resigned. Thus politicization of the governor's office is one of the major problems in UP.

In September 1998, S. S. Bhandhari the governor of Bihar recommended the imposition of the president's rule in Bihar on the ground that 'The Bihar-government symbolises the most malignant and uncouth levels of function in Indian politics.' The then President, R. K. Narayanan, declined the Union cabinet's advice to impose president's rule and suspension of the state assembly and asked the government to reconsider its decision. The president saw no evidence of a constitutional breakdown in Bihar. The government withheld its recommendation on reconsideration.

In 2000, Bihar governor Vinod Pandey swore in JD(U) leader Nitish Kumar in Bihar as chief minister after the elections when he did not have the necessary members to prove his majority in the Assembly. Nitish was given sufficient time to prove his majority in the house but he failed to garner majority and had to quit.

On 30 June 2001, Tamil Nadu government of Jayalalitha, in an unprecedent move, arrested the former chief minister, M. Karunanidhi whose DMK party was supporting the NDA government at the centre. Hearing the news of arrest of Karunanidhi, central ministers, Murasoli Maran and T. R. Balu, who were in Madras on that day, went to his residence for his support and prevented the police from taking away the former chief minister. The police also arrested both the ministers. The NDA government asserted centre's authority against the Tamil Nadu government. On 1 July 2001, the Union cabinet recommended to the president to withdraw his pleasure from the Tamil Nadu governor Fathima Bibi as the Union cabinet felt that the governor had failed to fulfil her constitutional obligations of office. The governor's failure to send a report earlier was considered as 'a clear affiance' of the centre's authority. The governor's report came only after the strong letter words of the central government. The centre found the report totally unacceptable and noted that the governor's report was silent on 'the constitutional impropriety' of the state police in arresting the Union minister's without any case against them. The centre was expecting an independent report by the governor as per its liking but the governor sent a copy of the state government's report to submitted her. The governor sent her resignation to the president who forwarded it to the prime minister for acceptance.

In an another case on 2 February 2005, the Goa governor dismissed the 32-month-old government of Manohar Parrikar-led BJP coalition, even when the government had won a rather controversial vote of confidence, and the speaker was yet to send the confidence vote report of the governor. The dismissed chief minister termed the action as a 'violation of the Constitution'. He said that the governor himself asked the speaker to conduct the special assembly session and send a report immediately, but he did not wait for the speaker's report. 'He has not only disrespected the house, but also his own words.'

In Jharkhand, the assembly elections took place in February–March 2005. In the 81-member house, the ruling BJP emerged as the single largest party with 300 seats and its NDA partner JD(U) got six. On the other hand, the JMM got 17, Congress nine and RJD seven while the smaller parties and independents got 12 seats. Some independents supported the BJP. The NDA was closer to majority and with the support letters of the independents formed a majority. The Congress party, ruling at the centre, decided to support Shibu Soren; thereupon the governor rejected the BJP's claim to form the government. The BJP physically paraded the majority of MLAs before the governor but he was not convinced and swore in JMM leader Shibu Soren on 9 March 2005 as chief minister, giving him 20 days to prove his majority. *India Today* commented, 'The governor's decision to swear in Soren despite dubious claim of majority makes a mockery of the democratic process.'

BJP party leader Munda went to the Supreme Court and challenged Soren's appointment. Later, a three-member bench of apex court, headed by Justice R. C. Lohati, delivered judgement against Soren's government formation calling it a 'total fraud on the Constitution'. Further the court asked Soren to seek a vote of confidence on 11 March instead of 15 March fixed by the governor. Many termed it the crossing of limit by the judiciary to set the agenda for the legislature.

Soren failed to seek the trust vote on 11 March due to chaos in the house by UPA MLAs. Soren resigned on the directives of Prime Minister Manmohan Singh.

In the Bihar assembly election in 2005, no party got majority and president's rule was imposed on 7 March 2005 and Assembly was kept in suspended animation. But in May the governor sent the report for the dissolution of the assembly. The Union cabinet advised the president on 22 May 2005 to dissolve the assembly immediately. The president was on a state visit to Moscow, and acting on telephonic advice, gave his assent for dissolution of the assembly without proper consideration. The Supreme Court declared the presidential proclamation unconstitutional by its order of 7 October 2005.

The Bihar governor at that time was Buta Singh. He took this decision to forestall the formation of a new government by NDA partners, which was partisan and unfair. The Supreme Court in the final detailed judgement in this case on 24 January 2006 gave its reasons why earlier proclamation of president's rule was declared unconstitutional. The majority decision held the governor responsible for misleading the Union cabinet and considered his action mala fide and 'destructive of the democratic system.' The governor later resigned due to the harsh words used in the Supreme Court judgement.

Position of the Governor After 1967

The position and role of the governor of a state underwent a great change after the fourth general elections of 1967. So far the Congress party had enjoyed a position of dominance at the centre as well as in most of the states, which did not permit the governor to act on his own and he played the role of a constitutional head. After the elections of 1967, in a number of states the Congress was relegated to the position of a minority and governments were formed by a combination of different political parties without any coherent policies. This provided the right type of atmosphere to the governors to exercise their discretion and powers. In a number of states like Rajasthan, Madhya Pradesh, West Bengal, etc., differences cropped up between the governor and the chief minister. While the chief minister asserted that the governor was only a constitutional head and was bound by the advice of the council of ministers, the governors took the stand that they were very much within their rights to use their discretion. This situation persisted till 1971 when the Congress again succeeded in capturing power at the centre as well as in most of those states where it had been pushed out of power in 1967.

During this intervening period, efforts were made to define the role of governor in the state administration. V. V. Giri, the then President of India, appointed a committee under the Kashmir governor Bhagwan Sahay and four other governors to study the provisions of the Constitution relating to the power of appointment of council of ministers, summoning and dissolving of legislative assemblies and reporting failure of constitutional machinery in the state. The committee submitted its report in October 1971. However, it desisted from laying down rigid guidelines for state governors and asserted that erosion of democracy can be prevented only by greater discipline among legislators and parties rather than by laying down a set of rules for the governor. However, the committee admitted that the governor was bound to accept the advice of the chief minister, although he could record his objections regarding the actions of the council. The recommendation of the committee were discussed at the annual conference of governors in November 1971, but the idea of laying down the guidelines for the governor did not find favour with them.

Once again, with the victory of Janata Party in 1977 at the centre as well as in a number of states, the role of the governor evoked controversy. They tried to act at the behest of central party leaders and tried to act in a partisan manner. With the fall of the Janata government and formation of Congress (I) government at the centre once again the governors of states were involved in narrow party politics and being used as tools for the furtherance of party interests. Thus, the governor of the state has ceased to be a mere constitutional head of the state and more often than not acts as a tool of the party in power at the centre.

The recent developments in Andhra Pradesh, Gujarat and UP showed peculiar twists in the working of the parties inside the legislatures and outside. It became hard for the governors concerned to cope with them within the existing constitutional framework. The anti-defection law complicated the situation and it is the speaker and not the governor who became the arbitrator on matters arising from objections and rival claims. Several governors at the governors' conference in 1995 drew attention to the problem to be faced after coming elections.

Dr Shankar Dayal Sharma, our former president, called a meeting/conference of governors and political leaders in New Delhi on 2 June 1997 to discuss 'The role of the constitutional head, when, following an election, no party or combination of parties appears to have secured majority.'

Dr Shankar Dayal Sharma stressed on the need to safeguard and ensure smooth working of the Constitution with the help of institutions and systems 'which can efficiently and confidently deal with the phenomenon of hung legislatures.' Dr Sharma felt it was of utmost importance that in the given situation, the constitutional head functions with due impartiality, independence, constitutional propriety and transparency, and upholds the national interest. 'Some complexities cannot simply be wished away or left unattended and neglected.' Dr Sharma asked the governors and leaders of political parties as to what steps should be taken to safeguard and ensure that the institution of constitutional head is able to function as an important and independent constitutional authority.[8]

The current President, Pratibha Patil, in a two-day conference of governors on 17–18 August 2008 emphasized a proactive role for holders of gubernatorial offices. She asked the governors to share their assessments and analyses in their monthly reports to the centre. The president, quoting Mahatma Gandhi, said 'They (governors) should have enough power, enabling them to influence ministerial policy for the better. . . . Theirs must be an all-pervasive moral influence in their provinces.'[9]

The governor's position is very embarrassing. He is appointed by the centre but is obedient to the state cabinet. He is a pathetic functionary who is sometimes asked by the centre to take pathetic measures. He has to be an independent authority, his allegiance being wholly to the constitutional obligations to act on the advice of the council of ministers. But he has power to ask for information, explanation and reconsideration. These functions and the power to refer Bills to the president for consideration and assent may make him a factor to be reckoned with. Thus, he is more than a glorified cipher. He resigns, but does not rule. He advises, but is bound by the advice of his ministers. He is an elderly statesman but not an authority as the executive head of the state.

The *Hindustan Times* editorial 'Governors overboard', dated 3 July 2004, mentioned, 'The governor is no longer seen as a constitutional link between the centre and the state, but as a means of controlling opposition-ruled states. Politics, especially in the age of coalitions, has taken a life-and-death edge where no party is willing to forego any position of gain.'

To conclude, the role of the constitutional head should be impartial and without any pre-conceived notion, independent to protect the Constitution, dignity and prestige of the office.

The Chief Minister

While the governor is the constitutional head of the state, the actual executive powers vests in the council of ministers headed by the chief minister. He symbolizes the ruling power structure and wields more authority than anybody else in the state. He is the actual executive head of the state government. In the following pages we will discuss the methods of his appointment, his powers, functions and position in state administration.

Appointment of the Chief Minister

The chief minister is appointed by the governor of the state. Article 164 provides that the chief minister is to be appointed by the governor and other ministers are appointed on the advice of the chief minister. The leader of the majority party in the state assembly has to be invited to form the government and so long as the party enjoys an absolute majority in the assembly, the governor does not have much of a choice.

But when no political party holds an absolute majority in the assembly, the situation becomes fluid. No clear convention has been established in this regard and the governors have used their discretion in appointing the chief minister as already discussed under the discretionary powers of the governor.

Powers and Functions

The chief minister has been described like the prime minister as the 'key stone of the cabinet arch', or like the sun around which planets revolve. He exercises numerous powers and enormous authority at the state level.

The chief minister is appointed by the governor and other ministers are appointed by the governor on his recommendation. It is the privilege of the chief minister to choose a team of his liking but he has to take into consideration the political standings of various other leaders in the party. He cannot ignore senior leaders as well as leaders of various groups while forming the council of ministers. He can recommend the governor to dismiss the entire council of ministers. In fact, the chief minister's resignation means resignation of the entire ministry. Thus, he is creator, and destroyer of the entire council of ministers.

Allocation of Portfolios

The chief minister after formation of his ministry allocates portfolios to the other ministers. He can reallocate portfolios whenever he feels like. In allocation of portfolios like home and finance, he keeps in mind the usefulness of the person and seniority in the party and loyalty to himself.

Presides over Cabinet

He calls and presides over the meetings of the cabinet. These meetings are generally attended by all the cabinet ministers. The ministers of state holding independent charge of the department are also invited to attend the cabinet meetings.

As a Coordinator

He coordinates the policies and working of all the ministries. He resolves the disputes between two or more ministries. He maintains harmony between various groups in the ministry.

Link Between the Governor and Council of Ministers

The chief minister is a channel of communication between the governor and the council of ministers. The governor can seek any information from the council of ministers through the chief minister.

Leader of the House

The chief minister is the leader of the house and chief spokesman. He helps in maintaining discipline in the house. He comes to the rescue of any minister who feels shaky in the house while defending his department. The speaker of the assembly consults the chief minister before fixing agenda of the house. He can advise the governor to dissolve the house, though such advice can be rejected by the governor, and in many cases the governors have not dissolved the house on such advice. This point has been discussed under powers of the governor.

Vast Patronage

The chief minister has vast patronage in the matters of appointment on important posts in the state. Although such appointments are made by the governor but in actual practice they are the nominees of the chief minister. These appointments include the advocate-general of the state, chairman and members of state public service commission, vice-chancellors of state universities, etc.

Chief Minister and the Party

The chief minister belongs to a political party. He has to retain the support of his party in the assembly, as well as outside it. To stay in power, the chief minister has to maintain balance between his duties to the party and to the state. He is the leader of the party before elections and after the victory of the party.

Chief Minister as Head of the Administration

The chief minister controls the entire administration of the state. He controls the bureaucracy through the secretariat headed by the chief secretary who is his main instrument to perform this function. As head of administration he has to take care of the interests of state employees and keep them working. He has to keep direct touch with the senior civil servants and inspire them to perform their function to the best of their capacities. He also keeps a watch on their performance, through administrative channels or he may observe their work during his extensive tours of the state or through party workers or by some aggrieved persons who come to him for redress of their grievances, etc.

Chief Minister as a Public Relations Man

In a democracy, government depends upon the support of the people. The government has to project its good image before the people. The people have to be kept informed about the various government welfare programmes and the steps taken by the government to improve the conditions of the people. The chief minister daily meets large number of people including members of various interest groups and the press with whom he has to maintain good relations and supply them the information necessary for projecting proper image of the government. The chief minister is in an important position, hence he gets a good media coverage if he organizes this work properly. Therefore, his public relations department and his political advisors help in building his image.

Other Functions

In addition to above functions, the chief minister has to keep the governor informed about all the important decisions of the government and furnish him with all information relating to the administrative affairs of the state as he may call for. If the governor desires some matter to be considered by the council of ministers, which has not been considered by him, the chief minister has to submit that for the consideration of the council of ministers.

Further, he has to maintain a good rapport with prime minister and other Union ministers, so that problems of his state are promptly attended to at central level. For this purpose he takes the help of MPs from his state and has to maintain a good relationship with the MPs from the state, even with those belonging to opposition parties.

The powers, and functions discussed above proves that chief minister has vast powers but these powers depend upon the trend of politics and political circumstances. The powerful influence of the party high command at the central level does not allow the chief ministers to enjoy independent powers, and even sometimes high command nominees from Delhi were sent as chief ministers. Therefore, the chief ministers look to the party high command rather than the legislators and the people of the state. This has weakened the leadership of the chief minister. Even chief ministers are not given free hand in the selection of his team of ministers. He has to obtain the sanction of the high command for the formation and expansion and constitution of the ministry. In a coalition government chief minister's position is weak because he depends upon several parties.

Council of Ministers

The Constitution of India under Article 183 provides that there has to be a council of ministers with the chief minister as its head to aid and advise the governor. The governor is a nominal head and actual powers of the state government vests in the council of ministers. Though the governor has discretionary powers also but he exercises them rarely.

As already discussed the governor appoints the chief minister and on his recommendation other ministers are appointed. The governor has no say in the appointment of ministers. There is no fixed term of office prescribed for the ministers. He holds office during the pleasure of the governor. As a member of council of ministers, a ministry is collectively and individually responsible to the state assembly. The governor can at any time dismiss a minister on the advice of the chief minister. There have been many such examples in the states.

The council of ministers comprises various categories of ministers, cabinet ministers, ministers of state, deputy ministers and parliamentary secretaries. Like the Union government some state governments have also appointed cabinet committees for efficient transaction of government business. But these committees are not standing committees but most of them are formed for specific purposes and like central government, they are not popular in states. Most of the important matters are placed before the cabinet whose meetings are held regularly.

The size of the council of ministers is not uniform in all the states. Moreover, in a democratic government there is a great deal of pressure on the chief minister to increase the number of ministers. Therefore, the size of the council of ministers has been increasing, particularly in a coalition cabinet, the number is large. In Haryana, out of a total strength of 44 members, 39 members are from the Haryana Vikas Party and Bharatiya Janata Party along with some independents. The Haryana assembly has a strength of 90 MLAs in which the ruling Haryana Vikas Party and the BJP combined have a ministry of about 30 members having nine ministers from 11 BJP MLAs. Thus, in a coalition government the number of ministers is always large. The ARC suggested regarding the size of the ministry that it should be 10 per cent of its assembly strength. This suggestion was not accepted and council of ministers has been generally unwieldy.

The Functions

The functions of the state council of ministers are as follows:

1. To maintain law and order and ensure security of life and property of the people in the state
2. To formulate and decide the policies of the state and implement them effectively
3. To control the financial policy and decide the tax structure for public welfare of the state
4. To make important appointments of heads of departments
5. To decide the legislative programme of the legislative assembly and sponsor all important bills
6. To discuss disputes with other states
7. To chalk out programmes, schemes for the socio-economic changes so that the state makes headway in various inter-related fields
8. To consider state's share of work in the Five-Yearly Plans and determine obligations
9. To advise the governor on the appointment of judges of the high court
10. To frame proposals for incurring expenditure out of state reserves
11. Proposals of re-appropriation of funds to which the finance ministry has withheld his assent
12. Proposals for withdrawal of prosecution against the advice of law and justice department
13. Proposals involving important changes in the policy of practices in the administrative system
14. Action to be taken on the report of the state public service commission

This list is only illustrative; there are many more items which can be seen in the allocation of business rules of the concerned state government.

The powers of council of ministers are vast. Ministers formulate the policy of the state and implement it. But they are responsible to the state legislature. They are subject to criticism during question hour in the state legislature. The party high command and party discipline are the major check on them.

The State Secretariat

The executive functions of the government are performed by various departments. Each department or a number of departments are placed under the charge of a minister. The minister is the political head of the department while the secretary to the department is the administrative head. The secretary is a senior IAS man. He is secretary to the government as a whole and not to the concerned minister. It is intended to make it clear to the secretaries that they are not to be bogged down by the narrow considerations of a particular department. The secretary is the principal advisor to the minister. He is responsible for implementing the policies and decisions taken by the political chief. The secretaries have to take care of the interests of the officers and the clientele of their departments and the general policies of the government. The expression 'secretariat' is used to refer to the complex of departments whose administrative heads are secretaries and political heads the ministers. The place where the ministers have their offices is known as the secretariat, which is located in the capital of the state. The secretariat is the highest office and principal executive instrument of the government in state. The Secretariat is such an organization of the state government which ensures 'objectivity, continuity and consistency' in the administration. It is the chief authority to frame rules and procedure of the working of the government. Thus, the secretariat is the government.

The three essential components of the state government are the minister, the secretary, and the executive head. The most important function of the minister is to frame policy, of the secretary to provide the data on which the policy is based and to oversee the implementation of policy, and of the executive head to give practical shape to the decisions. The minister and secretary are served by the secretariat organization, which is a conglomeration of a number of administrative departments.

Organization of the Secretariat

The secretariat is divided into a number of departments. A secretariat department consists of officers and office staff, among which are secretary, additional/special secretary, joint secretary, deputy secretary, under secretary, officer on special duty (if any).

The office component of the secretariat officials includes personnel below the rank of the under-secretary. They are secretariat officials because they work in the secretariat for life long. The office staff consists of the superintendent (or section officer), assistants, upper division clerks (UDCs), lower division clerks (LDCs), steno-typists and typists. Below them are Class-IV employees, who are mostly engaged in manual and inferior work. The secretariat department is divided into divisions, divisions into branches and branches into sections.

The number of secretariat departments differs from state to state. Their number varies from 11 to 35. The most of the states have the following departments: general administration, home, revenue, agriculture, finance, law, public works, irrigation, power, education, industries, transport, cooperatives, food and civil supplies, jails, labour and employment, excise and taxation, local government, *panchayati raj*, forests, commerce, natural resources, public health, health and medical, tribal and social welfare, economics and statistics, housing, power, rehabilitation, complaints and science and technology.

Manning of the Secretariat Positions

Officers

The senior officers of the secretariat belong to the Indian Administrative Service. The secretary, the special secretaries, additional secretaries, the joint secretaries and often the deputy secretaries belong to this service. In some states, the position of deputy secretaries is manned by officers of state civil services on deputation. The operation of the tenure rule in the state is much more flexible. In the state governments, the officers are frequently transferred without any reference to any fixed tenure.

Officers from Other Services

Generally, the secretariat positions are manned by the officers of the civil services. Some officers are brought to the secretariat from technical services. In many states posts of deputy secretaries/joint secretaries/special secretaries/in technical departments like public works, irrigation and electricity, etc. are occupied by the members of the respective technical services. In many states, even posts of the secretaries of the technical departments like PWD, irrigation, power, etc., are manned by the officers of these departments.

Office

Office functionaries in the secretariat belong to the services recruited for the secretariat or secretariat service. There is a junior/subordinate service public service commission in many states to conduct the examination for their recruitment. Their service conditions, recruitment and promotion are governed by the relevant rules. These services are managed by the general administration department of the state government which functions directly under the chief secretary.

Functions of the Secretariat

The secretariat is at the apex of organization of state administration, therefore, it performs several functions. Its important functions are as follows:

First, it has to advise and assist the minister in the formulation of policies and programmes of the government. Second, it has to collect necessary data from field agencies and other sources that are required for the formulation of policies. Third, the secretariat gives general direction and guidance to the directorate and other field agencies for the efficient implementation of government policies and decisions. Fourth, the secretariat monitors the implementation of various programmes and evaluates the performance of different field agencies. After evaluation it suggests corrective action, if necessary. Finally, the secretariat acts as the spokesman of the government. It maintains contacts with the central government, with other state governments and outside agencies.

The functions of the secretariat are different from the executive departments. The question of functions of secretariat has been looked into by several committees. The Rajasthan Administrative Reforms Committee 1963 under the chairmanship of Harish Chandra Mathur has, for instance, prescribed the following functions which should be performed by a policy-making body like the secretariat.

General

1. All matters of general policy
2. Interdepartmental coordination
3. Matters involving the framing of new legal enactments or rules or amendments in the existing ones, cases involving interpretation or relaxation of existing rules or government orders
4. Correspondence with the Government of India and other governments
5. All matters relating to the preparations or adoption of new plan schemes and important modifications in the existing schemes

6. Review of the progress of plan schemes, both physical and financial
7. Inspection reports and tour notes, recorded by the heads of departments
8. All-India conferences and important conferences of state level
9. Public accounts committee, estimates committee, assembly and parliamentary questions
10. Delegation of powers
11. Territorial changes and changes at headquarters
12. Litigation notices under Section 80, Civil Procedure Code
13. Appeals, revisions, etc. within the powers of the state government

Financial Matters

1. Scrutiny and approval of development budget estimates, major appropriation of accounts, surrender of funds, and supplementary grants
2. All proposals involving new items of expenditure
3. Financial sanctions not within the competence of the heads of departments
4. Sanction of expenditure from the contingency fund
5. Writing off of cases beyond powers of heads of departments and audit objections regarding the offices of heads of department, etc

Service Matters

1. Approval of service rules and amendments thereto
2. Matters relating to senior appointments, promotions, transfers and cases of disciplinary proceedings against gazetted officers
3. Initial appointment of officers belonging to the state service and infliction of major punishments upon them
4. Creation of posts, their extension and continuance, reemployment, resignation, special pay, allowances and pensions not within the powers of the head of the department

Criticism of the Secretariat

The general complaint against the secretariat is that it has been concentrating most of the powers. The executive heads of departments generally complain that even for a small matter they have to approach the secretary for getting sanction. The reason for this tendency is inherent in the parliamentary form of government. The minister is responsible to the Parliament for omissions and commissions of the department under his charge. Hence, he has to keep himself informed of all the developments of his department. This leads to the concentration of functions in the secretariat. Certain human and psychological factors are also responsible for this monopolization of power. But this type of concentration leads to inefficiency in the working of the government. Second, since the secretariat is far away it is not aware of the problems in the field. Therefore, their examination of proposal put forth by field staff is not only superficial, but also leads to too many queries. This slow and tardy processing of the cases impairs the efficiency of the field agencies. Third, the posting in the secretariat these days are important and attractive and the condition in the field is difficult. The field officers have to face political pressures and have greater chance of coming into conflict with the political matters. While the secretariat officers have a very good existence, they work close to the centre of power and are able to develop better equation with them. Moreover, the secretariat posts carry additional remuneration which make them more attractive to the officers; have better educational and medical facilities and other amenities.

Therefore, most of the officers wish to remain in the secretariat. By staying for a long period in the secretariat these officers lose touch with the field and do not realise the field problems. It is, therefore, essential to have a balance between the field level and secretariat level experience of the officers.

Chief Secretary

The office of the chief secretary was first started in 1799 when Lord Wellesley, the then governor-general of India, appointed a chief secretary for the first time. G. H. Barlow was the first person to occupy this office. It is interesting to note that this office started functioning in the central government. In due course of time, the office disappeared from the central government. Now there is no office in Government of India which is equivalent to that of chief secretary in the state. To some extent, the cabinet secretary performs the functions which a chief secretary performs in the state. Moreover, several functions of the chief secretary are performed by the home minister, the ministry of personnel and finance ministry in the Government of India.

The chief secretary is the head of secretariat in every state. He always keeps the charge of general administration department, which forms part of the portfolio of the chief minister. But his control also extends to other departments of the secretariat. He is in reality the chief of the secretariat. Therefore, he is rightly called 'the kingpin of the secretariat'. He heads the civil services in the state. He works as an inter-departmental coordinator and gives general guidance to other officers. He also acts as the chief communication link between his state government on the one hand and the Union government and other state governments on the other. He is the mentor and the conscience keeper of the civil servants of the state. The civil servants look to him to deal with all their problems concerning their service and work. He provides administrative leadership. The office of the chief secretary is considered very important, that is why it has been excluded from the operation of tenure system. He is supposed to retire as a chief secretary or moves to Union government for better assignment.

Various committees appointed from time to time have recognized the important role of the chief secretary in the state administration. The Bengal Administrative Enquiry Committee (Rawland's Committee, 1945) pointed out that the chief secretary occupies a pivotal position in the administrative system and recommended that he should be the head of the civil service, secretary to the cabinet and chairman of the development board, etc. The Rajasthan Administrative Reforms Committee (1963) also recognized the importance of the office of the chief secretary. The committee observed, 'by virtue of his unique position as head of the official machinery and advisor to the council of ministers, the chief secretary has an extremely important role to play in the state administration. Apart from attending to the work of the departments which are directly under him. He should be in a position to effectively coordinate the work of different secretariat departments and ensure that there is a certain degree of uniformity in the policies adopted by the state government with respect to different departments.'[10]

Functions

The chief secretary performs the following functions:

(i) As the principal advisor to the chief minister. The chief secretary is the principal advisor of the chief minister in all administrative matters. It is customary for the chief minister to consult him in the matters of appointments to the senior posts of secretaries, special secretaries, deputy secretaries and heads of the departments.

(ii) As secretary of the cabinet. He is secretary to the cabinet. He gets the agenda prepared for the cabinet meetings by the departmental secretaries. He obtains the approval of the chief minister for the inclusion of items in the agenda of the cabinet meetings. With the approval of chief minister he makes arrangements for the cabinet meetings. It is he who records the minutes and the decisions of the cabinet.

(iii) As the head of the civil service. The chief secretary is the head of the entire civil service in the state. He is in charge of the general administration department (GAD) which controls the transfers and postings of all the Indian Administrative Service and state civil service officers. All the recruitments, rules and disciplinary matters are decided in consultation with the GAD only. The GAD also controls the secretariat service and arranges the maintenance and upkeep of the secretariat. Thus, the entire staff of all the departments is under his control.

(iv) As the coordinator. He is the chief of all the secretaries. He is to resolve the differences between various secretaries to the state government. He is the chairman of a number of committees of the secretaries. Thus, he coordinates the activities of the entire secretariat.

(v) As channel of communication. The chief secretary is a main channel of communication between his state government, Union government and Governments of other states. All correspondence with the Central government and with other state governments is made by him.

(vi) As the secretary of the zonal council. The States Reorganisation Act, 1956, provides setting up of a number of zonal councils in the country. The Union home minister presides over the meetings of the zonal council and other members are the chief ministers and a couple of other ministers from each state in the zone. The chief secretaries of different states act as secretaries to this council by rotation.

(vii) Residuary functions. As per the rules of business, the chief secretary has to look after all such matters which are not falling within the jurisdiction of any secretary. In crisis situations, he has to take immediate steps and coordinate the activities of various government departments. During president's rule, if no advisors are appointed he becomes very powerful and becomes advisor to the governor, and performs all the functions of the ministry. In short, his functions can be summarized as follows:

(a) He is the principal advisor to the chief minister.
(b) He exercises general supervision and control over the entire secretariat.
(c) He looks after all other matters not falling within the responsibility of other secretaries.
(d) As chief of all secretaries, he presides over a large number of committees and is a member of many others.
(e) He is the secretary by rotation of the zonal council of which the state is a member.
(f) He has control over the staff attached to the ministers.
(g) He is the main channel of communication between his government, and the central or other state governments.
(h) He receives all important and confidential communications from the Government of India and submits them to the chief minister.
(i) As head of the official machinery, advisor to the council of ministers and chief of the civil service, he is their mentor and conscience keeper. The chief, thus, has an important role to play in the state administration.

The Rajasthan Administrative Reforms committee report, commenting about the chief secretary, said, 'The chief secretary should be in a position to effectively coordinate the work of different secretariat departments and ensure that there is a certain degree of uniformity in the policies adopted by the state government with respect to different departments. To a certain extent, powers have already been vested in him under the 'rules of business' to enable him to discharge this role.'[11] In view of this, the committee recommended that all important cases involving adoption of new principles or new schemes, all cases of appointments, promotion, confirmation, postings and transfer of officers of the states of 'deputy heads of departments and above; all proposals suggesting deviation from existing rules and practices should be circulated by the secretaries of the department concerned to the minister-in-charge only through the chief secretary. The Administrative Reforms Commission has also highlighted the role of the chief secretary. It said, 'but the secretariat organization itself needs coordination and discipline. This can be achieved by strengthening the position of the chief secretary. Being the captain of the team of secretaries to government, the chief secretary should be senior person of outstanding ability. He should not only command respect and confidence of all the services in the state. The chief secretary by his tact, experience, ability and seniority, has to manage things so that the political leadership keeps to its essential task of laying down policies and programmes and of coordinating the work amongst the ministers themselves. This requires a person of high calibre and tact. We, therefore, recommend that the selection of the chief secretary should be made with great care. He should usually be the seniormost and fit person who by virtue of his ability, experience, integrity and impartiality commands the respect and confidence of all officers.'[12]

The post of chief secretary is of high significance; therefore, following the ARC recommendation, since 1973 the senior-most IAS officer is elevated as the chief secretary and the post in all the states has been brought at par with the rank of the secretary to the Union government.

In general, political process has worked in such a way that the position of the chief secretary has been significantly undermined. The chief minister has so many political advisors that he very often does not seek the advice of chief secretary on many administrative matters. Even some times the post of chief secretary is offered to a political favourite. For example, M. L. Mehta was appointed chief secretary of Rajasthan by the chief minister, Bhairon Singh Shekhawat, although he was junior to seven IAS personnel; as a result they were also given the same salary and equal status. Not only this, political favourites are given extension in their term just as Bihar chief secretary, Basak, and Rajasthan chief secretary, M. L. Mehta. Both the chief secretaries were given extension on reaching the age of superannuation. This practice adversely affects morale in the civil service. The chief secretary now does not enjoy any security of tenure, as soon as the political power changes hands in the state, chief secretary is also removed from his position, not on administrative grounds but on political considerations; Punjab and UP at present are examples of this practice. This also undermines the position of the chief secretary, with adverse effect on the morale of administration. The tenure of the chief secretary should be sufficiently long, so that he could have an impact on state administration.

Executive Departments/Directorates

The secretariat is concerned with the policy-making functions while the execution of policies is the functions of executive departments and their field agencies. The Simon commission defined the executive department as 'an administrative unit, separate from the secretariat which reaches its apex usually in a single officer like the inspector-general of police or the chief conservator of forest outside the secretariat altogether. Such a head of department will usually be concerned principally with a single secretary to government and a single minister for his orders and the funds which he has to spent.'[13] All secretariat departments are not having executive departments attached to them. The secretariat departments of finance and law which are, therefore, advisory and controlling functions do not have executive departments. Generally, there is a separate department for every activity of the state. These departments give the executive direction needed in the implementation of the policies laid down by the secretariat. The heads of the departments and their officers draw their powers either from any statute or by delegation from government or both. For example, the registrar of the cooperative societies derives his powers from the Cooperative Societies Act, while the director of agriculture and director, public health derive their powers mainly by delegation from the state government. Thus, a head of department enjoys specified financial and administrative powers delegated to him.

It would be worthwhile to know the distinction between the departments in the secretariat and the executive departments. First, the secretariat department works under a generalist secretary and performs the functions of laying down the policies. The executive departments are organized for the performance of field functions. Second, the executive departments are headed by a technical officer called by different names such, as the registrar of cooperative societies, director-general of police, chief engineer irrigation, PWD and public health engineering, etc. Third, the secretaries are the administrative advisors and assistants of the ministers while heads of departments are their executive instruments. Fourth, the secretaries are the 'ears and eyes' of the ministers and the heads of departments are their 'hands'.

The relationship between the secretary to government and head of department is based on two principles. First, policy making is the primary responsibility of the secretariat, implementation of policy is that of the department. Second, the head of the department is given fullest control over the personnel under him subject to the rules governing the conditions of service.

Organization

The number and size of the heads of departments depends upon the number of important subjects administered by the state. The heads of the departments are generally called directors or commissioners. For their assistance there are additional directors, joint directors, deputy directors and assistant directors.

For smooth working of the department they have been divided into headquarters, divisions and districts. The divisions are under the charge of a commissioner for supervision of departmental activities in a specific number of districts. At the district level, there is a regional officer but overall supervision of departmental activities vests in the head of department. The collector/deputy commissioner of a district is kept in touch with the activities by the departmental district representatives. The departments like *panchayat*, agriculture and revenue have their organizations up to the village levels. The departments are generally headed by technical officers but members of IAS also hold the charge of technical departments like agriculture, education, forests, health, sales tax, etc. This has become a point of controversy between the 'generalist and specialist' in state administration. Other office staff is also there which works in graded hierarchy from top to bottom. The head of the department uses the powers through a vast network of officials spread over the entire state.

After Independence, the number of departments has increased enormously due to creation of new departments. Table 23.1 shows the name of departments (almost in all the states) along with the designation of Head of Departments.

The above table clearly shows that there is no common nomenclature for all the executive agencies nor is there a common designation for their heads. Moreover, differences, sometimes marked, exist between the emoluments, position and roles of the heads of departments. Thus, there exists no uniformity in the relationship between the secretariat and the executive departments. It is true that in theory the departments are free in their internal working and for this purpose adequate administrative and financial authority is vested in them, but as subordinate agencies they have to submit periodic or/and ad-hoc reports on their activities to their superiors. There is also a provision for visits to or/and inspections of these offices by the secretariat officers. Another aspect that should be noted in this connection is that in the existing system disparities exist in the status, rank and remuneration of the heads of executive departments and the secretaries. The secretary's position is looked upon as one of higher status than that of the heads of field agencies who are

Table 23.1 *Names of departments and designation of heads*

Name of the executive agency	*Designation of the head*
1. Accounts of Treasuries Directorate	Director of Accounts and Treasuries
2. Agriculture Department	Director of Agriculture
3. Animal Husbandry Department	Director of Animal Husbandry
4. Archives of Historical Documents Department	Director of Archives and Historical Documents
5. *Ayurved* Directorate	Director of *Ayurved*
6. Buildings and Communications Department (Executive)	Chief Engineer (Buildings and Communications)
7. Charity Organization	Charity Commissioner
8. Cooperative Department	Registrar of Cooperative Societies.
9. Dairy Development Department	Dairy Development Commissioner
10. Education/Public Instruction Directorate/Department	Director of Education/Public Instruction
11. Employment Directorate	Director of Employment
12. Excise Department	Director of Excise/Excise Commissioner
13. Fisheries Department	Director of Fisheries
14. Food and Civil Supplies Department	Director of Food and Civil Supplies/Supply Commissioner
15. Forest Department	Chief Conservator of Forests
16. Geology and Mining Directorate	Director of Geology and Mining
17. Government Printing and Stationery Directorate	Director of Government Printing and Stationery
18. Housing Department	Housing Commissioner
19. Industries Directorate	Director of Industries/Industries Commissioner
20. Information and Publicity	Director of Information and Publicity
21. Irrigation and Power Department (Executive)	Chief Engineer (Irrigation)
22. Jail Department	Inspector-General of Prisons
23. Judicial Department	Advocate General, Registrar of High Court
24. Land Record Office	Director of Land Records
25. Language Directorate	Director of Languages
26. Labour Department	Labour Commissioner
27. Medical Service Department	Director of Medical Services—Surgeon-General
28. Motor Vehicles and Transport Department	Director of Transport
29. Planning and Development Department	Development Commissioner
30. Police Department	Inspector-General of Police or Director-General
31. Registration Department	Registrar/Registrar-General
32. Public Health Department	Director of Public Health
33. Sales Tax Department	Sales Tax Commissioner
34. Settlement Office	Settlement Commissioner
35. Social and Harijan Welfare Directorate	Director of Social and Harijan Welfare
36. Technical Education Department	Director of Technical Education
37. Tourism Directorate	Director of Tourism
38. Town Planning Department	Director of Town Planning

considered as subordinate to the secretaries. The service pattern has worked out in the present system that the general administrator is placed at a higher level than the professional and technical officers. This is at the root of all inter-service rivalries, tensions and conflicts and the inadequacy of the present system. One more aspect of the problem that deserves mention is that after the reorganization of the states in 1956, a trend has set in to disperse government offices all over the state instead of locating them at the capital. This has been done in deference to the regional and local demands. Thus, in states like Maharashtra, Rajasthan and Uttar Pradesh the headquarters of many executive departments are located outside the capital.

Functions of the Department

Generally, the head of the department is responsible for the following functions:

1. Formulation of departmental budget
2. Acting as technical advisor to the minister
3. Inspection of the execution of work of departmental district staff
4. Allocation of grants according to rules, making budget re-appropriation within prescribed limits
5. Making within approved rules all appointments, confirmations, postings, transfers, promotions of all subordinate officers including sanctioning of leave and making officiating arrangements
6. Exercising disciplinary power over all subordinate officers according to rules
7. Advising public service commission concerning promotions and disciplinary actions
8. Sanctioning the attendance of officers at conferences other than inter-state or Government of India conferences

Relationship Between the Secretariat and Field Departments

Any form of government organization must be based on three essential components—the minister or the political head, the secretary or the administrative head and the head of the executive agency called by various names such as department, directorate, inspectorate, etc. In the interest of good administration, it is essential that the respective functions of the three components should be broadly distinguished and defined and all must obviously work in the closest touch with each other. This describes the ideal relationship which should be maintained during normal times. However, in times of emergency and crisis, the relationship is naturally disturbed and with the centralization of authority the secretariat tends to become powerful.

The relationship between the secretariat and the field agencies is a problem in state administration that has led to much discussion, debate and controversy, and all committees/commissions appointed in recent years to recommend reforms in state governments have given due attention to this problem and made necessary recommendations. These suggestions vary all the way from a radical organizational overhaul to minor procedural changes. The need today is for a clear-cut demarcation of functions between the secretariat and the executive departments. The secretariat should concern itself mainly with issues of policy, leaving its implementation to the field agencies and exercising only a supervisory and coordinating role.

Flowing from the above suggestions is the need for liberal delegation of authority from the secretariat to the executive agencies. Since the responsibility of the examination of government policies rests with the heads of departments, it is essential that they should be given adequate powers and discretion to act effectively and exercise initiative. All reports on administrative reforms have agreed on the need for it. But, while some increased delegations have been made in some states in recent years, the overall approach has been one of hesitancy and caution. Delegations are often made piecemeal and with reservations and are hedged in by restrictions of various kinds.'[14]

Two suggestions have been given to improve delegation. First, it has been noticed that the powers delegated to various heads of departments are not uniform. It is desirable that there should be uniformity in the powers delegated to all the heads of departments, exceptions should be rare. Second, that secretariat should take steps to make delegation effective at all levels so that the powers are fully exercised. The heads of departments resent 'interference from above', but they do not allow their subordinates to exercise the delegated powers. The main reason for this seems to be failure to define the proper role of the head of department concerning the field agencies. Third, the suggestion is to confer an ex-officio secretariat status on the heads of the departments. This arrangement has been freely used in the past as well as at present, on the ground that it would save a lot of time in processing of the proposal at the secretariat. The arguments against this suggestion are, first, it mixes the role of secretariat and department while role of both are different. Second, the government loses the advantage of a second look at the proposal by the secretariat from the point of view of general policy of the government. Third, the head of departments have a lot of work in the field, therefore, they cannot give much time to policy-making functions. Finally, the appointment of the technical officers to the secretariat is a wasteful use of the expert. But most of the state administrative enquiry committees set up in recent times have favoured this suggestion. Lastly, the ARC study team on the machinery of the Government of India has recommended that the distinction between the secretariat as the policy-making body and the non secretariat organizations as executive agencies be abolished and the heads of all important non-secretariat organizations should be integrated with the administrative departments in the secretariat.

NOTES

1. Constituent Assembly Debates, Vol. VIII, p. 468.
2. *Commission on Centre–State Relations Report*, Part-1 Government of India Publications, 1987, p. 122.
3. K. K. Katyal, *Hindustan Times*, 1 January 1996.
4. Bisham Narain Singh, *Hindustan Times*, 25 May 1997.
5. *Hindustan Times*, 8 June 2009.
6. Balkrishna, *Hindustan Times*, 11 May 1997.
7. *Hargobind Pant v. Raghukul Tilak*, *All India Reporter* 1979 SC 1109–13.
8. *Hindustan Times*, New Delhi, 3 June 1997.
9. *Hindustan Times*, 18 August 2008.
10. *Report of the Rajasthan Administrative Reforms Committee, Jaipur*, Government of Rajasthan, 1963, p. 46.
11. *Report of the Administrative Reforms Committee, Rajasthan, Jaipur*, Government of Rajasthan, 1963, p. 46.
12. *Report of the Study Team (Administrative Reforms Commission) on the State Level Administration*, New Delhi, October 1968, p. 33.
13. *Report of the Indian Statutory Commission*, Government of India, Vol. I, 1930, p. 312.
14. Administrative Reforms Commission, *Report on State Administration*, November 1969, p. 30.

District Administration

District has been the basic unit of administration in India since ancient times. *The Oxford Dictionary* defines district as a 'territory marked off for special administrative purposes'. Further, the same dictionary defines administration as the management of public affairs. Thus, district administration combines both, thereby meaning the management of public affairs within a territory marked off for that purpose. Public affairs is a very wide term and it covers almost all the activities associated with the life of man. The scope of administration depends upon the nature of the state. A democratic welfare state has a wide scope for activities for the development of the people and the nation as a whole. The simple definition of district administration, therefore, is that it is the portion of public administration which functions in the territorial limits of the district. According to S. S. Khera, 'District administration is the total functioning of government in a district, that total and complex organization of the management of public affairs at work, dynamic and not static, in the territory of a geographically demarcated district.'[1]

The Evolution of District Administration

The pattern of district administration in India goes back to the times of Manu. In Manu's time, about a thousand villages formed a district, which were in the charge of a separate official. Even today the number of villages in a district is almost the same. During the periods of Hindu rulers of northern India such as Mauryans, Guptas and others, the kingdoms were divided into provinces which were divided into districts. The provinces were under the charge at governors and districts were under *Sthanika*s or *Rajjuka*s during the Mauryan period and under *Vishvapati*s during the Guptas.[2] They were assisted by other subordinate officers in charge of small parts/divisions of a district.

In the Mughal period, the head of the district was *faujdar*, a military officer, who was under the control of *subedar* (governor). The *'amil'* or *'amulguzar'* named officer collected the revenue, who was also having certain police and judicial powers. To balance him there were *zamindar*s who were also exercising similar powers.

The East India Company after acquiring the '*diwani*' rights from the Mughal emperors, appointed its own officials to collect revenue. The office of collector was created in 1872 by Warren Hastings for the purpose of collecting revenue and dispensing justice.

Lord Cornwallis disapproved the system of concentrating executive, revenue and judicial powers in the hands of one individual and as a result collector ceased to be a judge of the civil and revenue courts and became the magistrate/collector as the district head. This system continued till India became independent in 1947.

After Independence, the district administration still continues to be the hub of Indian administration. The activities which are essential for the welfare of the people are performed at the district level. With the introduction of planning and development functions the district administration has become overburdened and trying to build the country from below.

THE ROLE AND IMPORTANCE OF DISTRICT ADMINISTRATION

Every inch of land in India forms part of a 'district' and in the eyes of the inhabitants the district collector is the government. The activities of the district administration cover a wide range and affect the lives of millions of people. The introduction of democratic decentralization and *panchayati raj* has fundamentally changed the aims of the district administration.

The government at the centre and state levels cannot implement its policies directly from the headquarters; therefore, the state is divided into territorial divisions and districts. The actual work of the government is carried out at the district level. Here the various plans and programmes of the state take operational shape. People tend to judge the government by the way the programmes are actually administered in the district and not by the ministers and secretaries or the head of the department who might have prepared the programme. Thus, district administration comes into direct contact with the people more than any other higher level of administration. The role of district administration in the life of the people is, therefore, very crucial. To know the role of district administration we have to note some of the points of contact between the district administration and the people.

The major concern of the district administration is to ensure public safety, the protection of the citizen and all his rights. It includes the maintenance of law and order and the administration of criminal and civil justice. In an atmosphere and people can work without any fear but if public peace is disturbed, they expect help from the district administration. Thus, most important role of district administration is public safety. Second, the next important role is in the field of revenue administration carried on in a just and equitable manner. It includes land revenue, irrigation charges, agricultural income, tax levies, excise duties, entertainment tax, etc. It would also include the administration of treasury, land reforms, land acquisition, land management, land records and consolidation of landholdings, etc. People want to know their rights and obligation. Therefore, there must be proper land records to delimit the rights of people in the land. The farmers like to know how much land revenue they have to pay so that they can plan accordingly. To maintain proper land records and to make people aware about their obligations and liabilities towards the state, are some important roles of district administration.

The activities of the state have grown fast due to developmental functions and public welfare policies. The government has introduced a number of developmental functions in the field of agriculture, cooperation and industry. Special programmes have been launched by the government to develop the weakest sections of the society. All these programmes are implemented by the district administration vigorously according to the intention of the government and to the satisfaction of the people. A number of welfare programmes such as public health, education, social welfare including the welfare of children, women and handicapped, etc. To implement these programmes and to ensure people's participation is another important role of district administration. The district administration ensures the supplies of essential commodities to the people. A large section of our population lives in remote villages. They feel the shortage of most essential commodities such as salt and oil due to problems of transportation. To maintain civil supplies even in remote areas for the benefit of most neglected people is another important role of administration.

In times of natural calamities like floods, earthquakes, outbreak of locusts, occasional fires, etc. the district administration is supposed to play an important role. What is more, the district administration as a whole has to project itself as the friend, philosopher and guide of the people in normal times as well as in times of difficulties and disasters.

The role of district administration has also been stressed by the Planning Commission in the First Five Year Plan. 'In brief, from now, the primary emphasis in district administration has to be on the implementation of development programmes in cooperation with the active support of the people. The reorganization of district administration has to provide for: (a) strengthening and improving the machinery of general administration; (b) integration of activities of various development departments in the district and the provision of a common extension organization; (c) living up, in relation to all development works, of local self-governing institutions with the administrative agencies of the state government institutions with the administrative agencies of the state government; and (d) regional coordination and supervision of district development programmes.' It may be defined 'as the total functions of government in the district, and it may be armoured by saying that the form and contents of the district administration constitute a convenient method of performing the functions of government in a district.'

Thus, district administration is important since ancient times. Its importance increased during the time of British when people started looking to the district collector as 'mai-bap' or mini king. Therefore, the importance of district in the lives of the people can be easily realised.

The District Collector

The district is the basic unit of administration below state level in India. A district is placed under the charge of a district officer called the district collector or deputy commissioner, the kingpin of our administration. The district is also the unit of administration for the various other government departments like the police, industries, agriculture, education, medical and health, public-health, electricity, etc. However, the position of the collector is different from that of the officers of other departments functioning in the district. He is supposed to be the chief representative of the government in the district. His office corresponds directly with the government. He performs numerous functions which we will discuss further.

The Evolution of the Office of Collector

The present institution of the collector may be directly derived from the East India Company. It got the *diwani* rights and decided to take upon itself the administration of revenue. At the same time, the company decided that the collector has to supervise revenue collection and preside over the courts. At that time revenue collection was a major and very important function, hence, the collector came to occupy a very important position. In 1872, Sir George Campbell, at that time the lieutenant governor of Bengal said that the collector is the general controlling authority over all the departments in the district. He declared that the DM/collector should be supreme in his area, except in matters of courts of justice.

After Independence, the circumstances changed and the functions and powers and position of the collector also changed. Democracy and specialization in post-Independence pėriod had affected the powers and prestige of the district officer. The separation of judiciary from executive and advent of *panchayati raj* and growing resentment of technical departments and their officers towards the collector's dominant position in the district have some of the potent factors which have adversely affected the position of the collector. But he is still a chief coordinator of all the functionaries in the district and representative of the government as a whole at the district level.

The district officer is known as collector in Rajasthan, Gujarat, MP, Maharashtra and Andhra Pradesh, etc. In Punjab, Haryana, Assam, Jammu and Kashmir and Karnataka, the deputy commissioner and district magistrate (DM) in UP and West Bengal, is the head of district administration. He is a generalist IAS officer directly recruited or promoted from state civil service. He performs more undefined than defined functions. Thus, due to the multifarious nature of his functions he is called the pivot of the district administration.

Functions of the District Collector

The district collector is the ultimate boss of the district, responsible for every single event which happens in his jurisdictional area. In spite of the size of the districts, attendant lethargy and complexity and corruption, the institution of the district collector is one of the most powerful ones in the country. Even today, despite *panchayati raj* and the *mandal*, the collector is still perceived as being above petty politics, and truly for the people. First we will discuss his most important functions, namely, land revenue, law and order and developmental functions and others.

Land Revenue

The office of collector was created to collect revenue. The first governor-general of India, Warren Hastings, had created the office for the dual purpose of collecting revenue and dispensing justice. He is the head of the revenue department of the district. In this capacity he exercises the power of general supervision and control of the land records and their staff. He functions concerning land revenue are of several types such as collection of land revenue, canal dues and other government dues; distribution of *taccavi* loans and recovery of these dues; distribution distress *taccavi* due to losses to crops caused by natural calamites/disasters, relief to fire sufferers; payment of *zamindari* abolition compensation and rehabilitation grant; relief to the fire sufferers, assessment of loss of crops due to floods, drought or locusts in the harvest season for recommendation of relief given to the affected farmers, control over land records, land acquisition and all matters relating to land records; inspection of mutation work, hearing of appeals against the orders of the lower consolidation authorities, relief measures in cases of scarcity conditions caused by natural calamities like fire, drought, flood, water-logging and excessive rains, etc; assessment and realization of agricultural tax; collecting and furnishing multifarious agrarian statistics concerning rainfall, crops, etc.; supervision of the treasury and sub-treasuries; enforcement of Stamp Act; ensuring proper administration of land and proper sale and mortgages of land; submission of periodical reports to higher authorities and seeing that the rights in land are held and enjoyed and passed from one party to another according to law in a peaceful manner. For the proper performance of revenue functions the collector is assisted by other revenue officers. The district is divided into sub-divisions, *tehsils*, *kanungo* circle and *patwari* circles; and the officer in-charge of these are SDO, *tehsildar*, *kanungo*, *patwari* and village headman, *patel* or *chowkidar* to assist the collector.

After Independence and particularly after 1967 when the opposition parties captured power in many states, they announced the abolition of land revenue[3] because now it forms a very small part of the total revenue of the state. This has lessened the importance of revenue collection work of the collector. But the importance of land records has not reduced at all; rather it became a necessity to solve ownership problems.

The Maintenance of Law and Order

At the district level, according to the Police Act, 1860, and the police regulations of different states, police functions are under the overall supervision and control of the DM. He is responsible for maintenance of law and order. The district police under the superintendent of police (SP) is his main instrument to maintain law and order. As a DM he promulgates orders if there is any danger of breach of peace and public order. He can inspect police station and ask for any information, record, statement and register dealing with crime. He grants licenses for explosives and fire arms. He can order enquiry into an accident caused by explosion; can also issue warrants for the arrest of a suspected offender on apprehension of breach of peace, a person may be detained by him. In 1993, thousands of workers of the BJP were arrested to prevent them from participating in the rally at Boat Club, New Delhi by the district administration.

In serious cases of breach of peace, the DM can seek the assistance of special armed forces or the provincial armed constabulary (PAC) maintains peace. The home guards can also be called at a short notice in case of need. In case of widespread disturbances CRPF battalions may be requisitioned by him. The central government can ask the other state governments to send their armed forces. He may impose curfew in a particular area if situation demands. He has power to disperse unlawful assemblies and issue prohibitory orders under Section 144 of CrPC.

In case the civil police is not able to control the law and order situation the DM can seek the assistance of the army. The Criminal Procedure Code provides power to the DM to order the military officers to assist in the maintenance of law and order. There are liaison officers in the army, from whom assistance can be sought in times of need. The DM has to hand over the situation to the army, which then tackles it on its own under its own command and commanders. It means that army can open fire on its own without seeking the approval of the magistrate in each case. If at any time DM feels that the situation is under control, he can ask the army to withdraw.

The general consensus is that the army should be called only in extreme situations to assist civil authorities in the maintenance of law and order and as far as possible state police and the central paramilitary forces should control the situation.

The collector conducts inspection of jails, disposes the cases of undertrial prisoners, grants superior class to prisoners, orders premature release of prisoners, release of prisoners on parole, deals with mercy petitions of prisoners, submits annual criminal report to the government, appoints village *chowkidars*, deals with labour problems, strikes, etc. He takes necessary action for eviction under Public Premises (Eviction) Act and Rent Control Act. He hears general complaints of the people against any matter relating to the district administration. He makes necessary arrangements for the holding of fairs and exhibition in order to ensure peace.

Maintenance of law and order is impossible without proper intelligence system. The area which is known for mischief mongering needs special attention on the basis of intelligence gathered. In the district activities of student organizations, particularly of bigger ones; activities of communal organizations, of political organizations, they might be planning political agitations, and activities of such persons who are known for creating law and order problems needs constant watch and intelligence.

The intelligence system is organized by the special branch of the state government. It has a small unit at the district level which supplies information to the state and keeps informed of these developments to the SP and DM at district level. But the SP and DM do not solely depend on this official information, they also develop their own sources and check and cross-check the intelligence gathered by the official unit. Timely information is a great help in maintaining law and order. The police acts on the orders of the magistrate.

The relationship between the DM and SP is full of tension. The SP feels that his position has unnecessarily been subordinated to that of the DM, but the control of law and order by DM has stood the test of times since its inception. He being the head of district administration has wider resources to gather information and much broader view of administration compared to the SP. Many arguments have been given on both sides but the controversy is continuing.

Developmental Function

Since Independence, the nature and scope of governmental functions have increased. The government is striving to achieve socio-economic justice. The realization of these two-fold objectives has led the government to perform developmental functions. With the increasing activities undertaken by the government, this function of the collector has been gaining more and more importance.

To perform developmental functions, two types of patterns have emerged in different states. One is the Maharashtra and Gujarat pattern in which all the developmental functions have been brought under the control of the *zila parishad* and all district level officers of development department have been placed under the administrative control of *zila parishad*. A separate IAS officer has been appointed as chief executive officer of the *zila parishad*, who exercises control on all its officials.

The second pattern is found in Tamil Nadu and other states. The collector looks after both the regulatory as well as developmental functions. Both the patterns have worked satisfactorily. Prior to the introduction of *panchayati raj* in 1959 on the recommendations of Balwant Rai Mehta Committee, 1957, the collector was connected with all the developmental activities in the district, including community development. After the introduction of *panchayati raj*, developmental activities have been handed over to the elected bodies and the role of collector in this respect differs from state to state. Balwant Rai Mehta Committee had suggested that 'at the district level, the collector or the deputy commissioner should be the captain of the team of officers of all development departments and should be made fully responsible for securing the necessary coordination and cooperation in the preparation and execution of the district plans for community development. Where he is not already empowered to make the annual assessment of the work of the departmental officers in regard to their cooperation with other departments, their speed of work, their dealings with the people and their reputation for integrity, he should be invested with such powers.' He is responsible for the successful implementation of developmental schemes of the *panchayati raj*.

The prevailing practice in many states at present is to make the district collector the coordinator of developmental functions and appoint an officer as the additional district collector and chief executive officer of the *zila parishad*. The collector being the final authority in the district, is in a better position to get the cooperation of all district functionaries, therefore, look after the developmental functions in the district. In agriculture development programmes and even in other development programmes a large number of agencies were required to supply inputs wisely. Therefore, coordination is required to make sure that the necessary inputs are available to the farmers at proper time. Moreover, there are number of special programmes like integrated rural development programme (IRDP), drought-prone areas programme (DPAP), desert development programme (DDP), rural landless employment guarantee programme, national rural employment programme, training and visit system, JRY, prime minister's employment programme, etc. There is hardly any programme which does not involve the land acquisition, land management, regularization of sale and purchase of land, etc. A number of coordination committees are functioning for implementation of various programmes under the district collector to ensure successful implementation of different development programmes.

Other Functions

In addition to these above-discussed functions, he performs many other functions of various nature:

1. The collector is the returning officer for elections to Parliament and Vidhan Sabha constituencies and has responsibility for coordination of election work at the district level.

2. He conducts census operations every 10 years.
3. He grants old age pension and house-building loans.
4. He is concerned with preparation of district gazetteers and protection of ancient monuments.
5. He is concerned with supervision and control over municipalities in the district.
6. He is concerned with controlling, drawing and disbursing offices of the district staff.
7. He acts as the protocol officer in the district and issues tour programmes of ministers and VIPs and makes arrangement for stay of VIPs at circuit houses.
8. He is the responsible for national savings or the state loans floated from time to time and contributions to the national defence fund.
9. He is the chairman of several committees such as the soldiers and sailors welfare fund, staff committee, public grievances committee, family planning committee, etc.
10. He is concerned with management of government estates.
11. He is concerned with attending to character verification, issuance of certificates for domicile, scheduled castes and backward classes, political sufferers, etc.
12. He is concerned with training junior officers in official procedures and administrative work.
13. He is concerned with superintendence over all other branches of district administration.
14. He is concerned with enforcement of Press Act.
15. He is concerned with postings, transfer and leave of the land revenue officers working under his control.

In short, the duties and functions of the collector leave many things on him without formal mention, and he has to be very vigilant to face any eventuality.

The Position and Role of the Collector

The role of the collector is changing at a fast pace due to various welfare schemes. The collector as the head of the district administration is closely connected with the development programmes and has acquired a key position working as a guide and philosopher.

The district officer, as chief agent and the representative of the state, serves as a channel of communication between the government and the residents of the increase in developmental activities.

Other District Level Officers

The other district level officers are the district and sessions judge, civil surgeon or chief medical officer, superintendent of police, executive engineer, PWD, and PHEd (Public Health Engineering Department), district education officer, district food and supply officer, district social welfare officers and district development officer, etc. They are important officers of their concerned departments.

The district collector supervises and coordinates the work of these officers who have technical control and supervision over their own departments. These officers keep him informed of their activities and report to him any serious issue likely to disturb law and order.

Administration Below District Level

For administrative purposes, the district is divided into sub-divisions, *tehsils*, *parganas* or circle or *ferka* and village at the lowest level. The sub-division is headed by SDO/SDM/assistant collector. He performs revenue as well as law and order functions in his sub-division. He is a link between the district collector and the *tehsildar* in revenue matters and DM and the station police officers in law and order matters.

Tehsil—Each sub-division is divided into two or more *tehsils* under the charge of *tehsildar* to help the SDO in revenue collection. The *tehsil* is the basic unit for purposes of general administration, treasury, land revenue, land records, etc.

Pargana—The next unit to *tehsil* for revenue administration is *pargana* Circle *furka*, under the charge of *kanungo*. He compiles lands record and supervizes *patwaris* under him.

Village—The *tehsil* comprises more than 100 villages. The village is the lowest unit of administration and for all other purposes and its main functionary is *patwari/lekhpal* in UP, Rajasthan, Haryana, Punjab, HP, MP, etc., *patel* in Maharashtra, Karnataka and Tamil Nadu. He prepares all the records of land in the village. He performs multifarious activities including maintenance of land records and statistical data, land measurement, etc.

The Administrative Reforms Commission (ARC) also made some recommendations on district administration. The main recommendations are as follows:

(a) In the state where the judicial work of the collector has not yet been transferred to the judiciary, steps may be taken to have it so transferred. In those states in which only a partial transfer of judicial work has taken place, steps may be taken to make the transfer complete.

(b) The district administration should be divided into two sectors—one concerned with 'regulatory' functions and the other with 'developmental' functions. The district collector should be the head of the former and the *panchayati raj* administration should have the responsibility for the latter. The district collector and president of the *zila parishad* should meet at periodic intervals to resolve matters calling for coordination between the regulatory and developmental administration. This procedure should be given official recognition in the legislation dealing with the *panchayati raj*.

(c) The collector and DM as the head of the regulatory administration in the district should exercise general supervisory control over the police organizations in the district. Except in an emergency, he should not interfere with the internal working of the police administration. In the day to day work of the police organization and with regard to routine matters like postings and transfers, the district superintendent of police should have full control. The collector should annually record his views on the performance of the district superintendent of police after receipt from the officer concerned, in a note written by him on his performance during the period under review.

(d) It should not normally be necessary for the collector or any other district officer to wait upon a visiting dignitary unless his officers should spend a prescribed minimum number of days on tour with night halts in the camp. The tour should be utilized, among other things, for the redress of public grievances on the spot wherever possible.

(e) There should be only two administrative units whose heads are invested with powers of decision-making in the district administration—one in the *tehsil*, *talukas* or group of *tehsils/talukas* of a sub-division (in the states where there are no *tehsils/talukas*) and the other at the headquarters of the district. The intermediary levels where they exist may be abolished. Powers should be delegated to the maximum extent to the officer in charge of the sub-division district administrative unit.

(f) When conditions are more propitious for considering the question of readjusting the boundaries of district, the state governments may appoint committees for the purpose of examining the size and boundaries of districts in the light of administrative requirements.

The recommendations of the ARC are still relevant and we have to further strengthen district administration. The district administration from the collector downwards should meet the people in focal villages/

rural centres in rotation so that genuine rapport is established between the administration and the citizen and maximum participation is achieved. At district level if we want to give social and economic justice then there has to be a rapid change in the district official's mode of functioning/working. The districts should be rationally reorganized on the basis of area, population, productivity of land, means of communication, history and resources to remove the difficulties of the people. In the end, the revival of the authority of the district administration should be our prime national concern. At the same time, the district administration should be made responsible to the people.

District Rural Development Agency (DRDA)

Since 1978–1979, when the IRDP was launched, at district level there is District Rural Development Agency (DRDA) headed by the collector/DC or chief executive officer, and *zila parishad* in those states where he is of the same status. The DRDA is set up as a society registered under the Registration of Societies Act. The agency has a governing body chaired by the president/chairman/*pramukh* of the *zila parishad* and he will preside over the meetings of the governing body of DRDA. The executive and financial powers should, however, vest in the district collector/DM/deputy commissioner who may be designated as the chief executive officer or executive director.

To provide for close linkages and to ensure effective coordination between *panchayati raj* institutions and DRDAs, the organizational structure of DRDAs was revamped and they were placed under the supervision and control of *zila parishads*. Instructions were issued to state governments to reconstitute the governing body of DRDAs under the chairmanship of chief executive of *zila parishads*. Chairpersons of the various standing committees of *zila parishads* and a new chairperson of *panchayat samitis* (by rotation), as also representatives of local NGOs have been made members of the governing bodies. The technical wings of the DRDAs have also been augmented by inducting officers at appropriate levels to equip the DRDAs to handle the increased number of schemes and quantum of funds. It was decided that DRDAs should function under the overall supervision, control and guidance of the *zila parishad*, and provide executive and technical support to the *zila parishad* in discharging its functions. The chairman/president/*pramukh* of the *zila parishad* would be the ex-offlcio chairman of the governing body of DRDA. In this capacity, the chairman of *zila parishad* shall preside over meetings of the governing body of DRDA. The executive and financial powers should, however, vest in the district collector/DM/deputy commissioner who may be designated as the chief executive officer or executive director.

With a view to bringing about greater integration between the two institutions, the CEO of *zila parishad*, where the posts are not held by DMs/collectors/DCs in an ex-officio capacity, shall be a member-secretary of the governing body of the DRDA. However, the CEO of *zila parishad* should not be an officer below the rank of DM.

Organization of DRDA

Governing Body

The governing body of the DRDA consists of all MPs and MLAs of the district and district level officers of various development departments. Two ex-MPs and ex-MLAs, each from the district, in an alphabetical order will also be notified by rotation as members of the governing body of DRDA for a tenure of one year. It should also include at least one-third of the *panchayati samiti* chairmen as members to be nominated by rotation in alphabetical order for a tenure of one year, one of whom must belong to SC/ST and the other a woman. It should also include chairmen of standing committees of the *zila parishad*; collector/DM/DC/chief executive officer/executive director; head of the central cooperative bank of the district; chairman, regional rural bank;

district lead bank officer; NABARD representative at district level; general manager, DIC; representative of KVIB; district officer in charge of family welfare programme; district agriculture officer; district veterinary officer; district fisheries officer; district employment officer; project officer, IRDP; district forest officer; regional/district officer, scheduled caste/scheduled tribe finance corporation; district rural water supply and sanitation officer; APO, women's development; one woman worker/organizer with actual experience of organizing rural poor (to be nominated by the chairman, DRDA); district level chairman of the land mortgage bank; representative of district milk union (to be nominated by the chairman, DRDA); two representatives of the weaker sections, one of whom may be drawn from SCs and STs. These representatives may be the beneficiaries of the programme (to be nominated by the chairman, DRDA); one representative of rural women, preferably a beneficiary (to be nominated by the chairman, DRDA); a member belonging to the minority community (to be nominated by the chairman, DRDA); chief executive officer, *zila parishad*; member-secretary, *zila parishad*; project director, DRDA and one nominee of ministry of rural areas and employment.[4]

An executive committee can be formed by the chairman of the DRDA to assist the agency. The committee may consist of all the district level officers and any other officer deemed necessary for the planning and implementation of rural development programmes. The meetings of the governing body and the executive committee are held once a quarter and once a month, respectively. Despite all this, we find a multiplicity of agencies at the district level which makes effective co-ordination difficult. To solve the problem of coordination, the DRDA should be made a nucleus agency for rural development at the district level.

The DRDA has been made the overall in-charge of the planning, implementation, monitoring and evaluation of the rural development programmes in the district.

Functions of the DRDA

The functions of the DRDA are as follows:

1. To keep the district level and block level agencies informed of the basic parameters, the requirements of the programme and the tasks assigned to them
2. To coordinate and oversee the surveys conducted, preparation of perspective plans, annual plans of the blocks and finally prepare a district plan
3. To evaluate and monitor the programme so as to ensure its effectiveness
4. To secure inter-sectoral and inter-departmental coordination and cooperation
5. To give publicity to the achievements made under the programme, disseminate knowledge and build awareness about the programme undertaken
6. To send returns to the state governments periodically in the prescribed manner

The DRDA

The staffing pattern for the DRDAs is as follows:

The DRDA is headed by a full-time executive officer, preferably a senior-scale IAS officer or an equivalent officer of the state services. The post of APO (women) is created to look after the woman components of the IRDP and also DWCRA work. The APO, Industries, looks after TRYSEM and the district industries centre acts as the technical arm of the DRDA. Identification of investment opportunities, preparation of bankable projects, provision of experts service to the beneficiaries, designing of training programmes, identification of training centres, etc., are the functions being performed by the DIG. A scheme of the organizational hierarchy of DRDA is shown in Figure 24.1.

Figure 24.1 *Organizational hierarchy of district rural development agency (DRDA) officials*

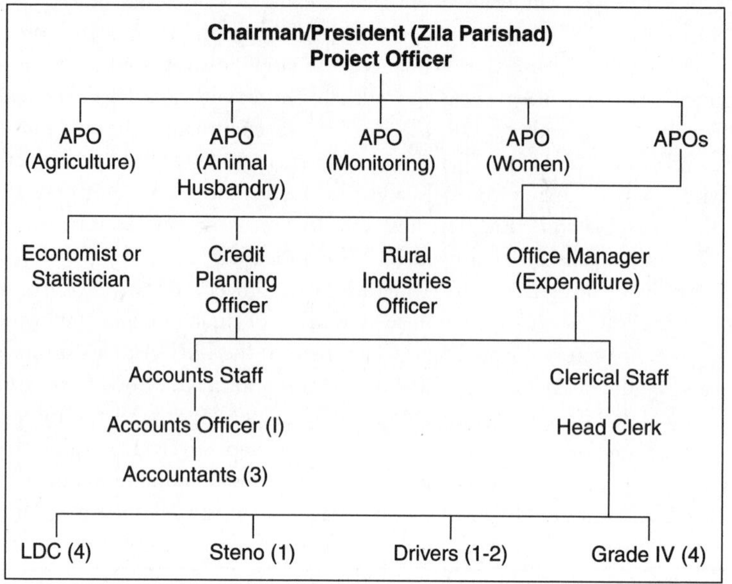

Evaluation studies have found that the officials who have been entrusted with the job of project formulation have not been able to muster sufficient expertise in formulating viable projects. Since it is a crucial area, in the absence of an effective implementing agency, the entire programme is likely to run aground. Another area of importance is the monitoring of the programme which is not possible without strengthening the DRDAs with more technical and specialized personnel. Thus, there is an immediate need to strengthen the technical wings properly along with the accounts wings. The committee set up by the ministry to suggest revised norms of administrative support has suggested and recommended a sample set up for both the engineering and accounting wings of DRDAs in consultation with the secretaries (RD) of various states and the states have been asked to implement these recommendations.

Nobody would mind the great concentration of powers in the hands of collector/deputy commissioner if the system runs efficiently, but this is far from actual reality so far as the function of law and order is concerned. Even with regard to other functions, i.e., land revenue and general administration services represented by the *patwari, kanungo, naib tehsildar, tehsildar,* deputy collector and collector hold all the powers and prestige. The courts of sub-divisional magistrates and collectors are full of litigants and decisions in cases take not months but years. Thus, the implementation of development programmes continues to lag behind. The DM nowadays is busy with law and order from morning to evening and is unable even to pay proper attention to revenue. The most eloquent proof of the collector being overloaded with regulatory functions is that land reform laws have not been implemented. He has to look after student unrest which is epidemic in most of the northern states and caste and communal tensions also demand his immediate attention. He has to carry out orders of almost all departments at secretariat level, orders from food, agriculture, local self-government, development and even collection. He has to prepare, amend and get correct voters list printed at very short notice and is also fully responsible for conducting elections peacefully. He has to make arrangements in case of shortage of essential commodities like diesel, kerosene, sugar, foodgrains, fodder and cement. Whenever any natural calamity occurs, he has to rush to the aid of the people.[5] Thus there are strong reasons that the collector should have nothing to do with development work. If he is spared from such activities he will have time to maintain law and order and root out corruption from the lower-level field officers involved in rural development and this will be a greater contribution to development than direct involvement.

Main Weaknesses

The weaknesses brought out by the evaluation studies are as follows:

(i) The Programme Evaluation Organization (PEO) of 1985 has pointed out that in most of the DRDAs, the requisite planning teams have not been organized and efforts did not seem to have been made to develop the capability for planning and formulation of viable schemes. Some of the posts of project officers and assistant project officers were lying vacant. The state-wise review showed that full sanctioned loan was not in position in many areas. There was general reluctance on the part of deputationists to take up assignments in the DRDA as they were not entitled to the normal perquisites enjoyed by them in their own department. Moreover, there is a tendency on the part of the sectoral departments to lay off their less competent personnel by sending them to DRDAs. In the absence of any deputation allowance such personnel lacked the keenness and motivation to work in the DRDAs.

(ii) Frequent changes in the incumbents of posts of project officers and assistant project officers greatly impaired the efficiency and effectiveness of the DRDAs.

(iii) The PEO study also indicates that the extent of trained personnel available with DRDAs was most inadequate. It was observed that only one-third of the project officers in the selected districts had undergone training in the IRDP. As regards assistant project officers, only 19 per cent of them were trained. None of the staff members in almost half of the selected districts had attended any training workshop or camps. In the preparation of plans, the officials were not sufficiently trained. Not to talk of this only, in some cases, the functionaries were not even clear about the basic concepts.

(iv) Another weakness pertains to the problem of coordination. There has been lack of coordination between the DRDA, block level officials and various government and quasi-government organizations, like department of agriculture, animal husbandry, state electricity boards, etc., because the DRDAs do not have formal authority and direct control over these organizations. The G. V. K. Rao committee observed, 'The important institution that could provide staff and line support and DRDA in functions directly related to rural development programmes, viz., the DIC, the DMPEGC, etc., continue to function under their own separate departments and have at best marginal coordination with DRDAs.'

(v) The Reserve Bank of India in its study conducted on IRDP in 16 districts covering 16 states, indicated inadequacies of field level staff both at the block and district levels.

(vi) Effective supervision on various schemes by the chairman of the DRDAs, project officers and other officials is not maintained. As a result, tangible benefits do not reach deserving people, and there is manipulation and mis-utilization of assistance made available to the beneficiaries.

(vii) For the monitoring of income of the beneficiaries and assets provided to them, *Vikas Patrikà* has been devised. The concurrent evaluation of IRDP, 3rd round, shows that *Vikas Patrika*s were provided to the beneficiaries in about 39 per cent cases at the national level and in about 24 per cent cases, these documents were updated. This shows poor performance of the DRDAs in ensuring qualitative monitoring on regular basis.

(viii) Lastly, the DRDAs pay little attention towards after-care services and government support on regular basis.

Suggestions

For improving the working of DRDAs, the following suggestions are made:

(i) The governing body of the DRDA should provide due representation to weaker sections and women.
(ii) DRDAs should have professionally competent, experienced and well-trained staff.
(iii) There should be a general policy regarding transfers of the project officers and assistant project officers. These functionaries should not be transferred before the completion of a minimum period of three years.
(iv) Identification and selection of beneficiaries should be done at the *gram sabha* meeting. The lists should be revised on a year-to-year basis after getting the approval of the *gram sabhas*.
(v) The chairman and project officer of the DRDA should be given proper powers for effective coordination.
(vi) The work of investigators responsible for monitoring must be checked regularly by the higher authorities.
(vii) For better service conditions of the DRDA it should be merged with the staff of rural development department.
(viii) Perspective plans and annual plans should be prepared with ensured people participation and full involvement of the block development personnel. The DRDA personnel should take the BDO into confidence and in turn, the BDO should consult the field functionaries, before taking final decisions relating to these plans.
(ix) Attitudinal changes of the functionaries is essential to seek people's participation and cooperation.
(x) The DRDAs should have integrated programme for each family to cross the poverty line. It should start scheme which can provide more employment and higher income to the beneficiaries.
(xi) The government should release sufficient funds to the DRDAs in time to meet the minimum staff requirements.

The DRDAs can find solution to the problems of the rural poor, if they have well-trained and dedicated staff for effective formulation, implementation, monitoring and evaluation of programmes.

Special Development Programmes

The rural development programmes up to the Fourth Five-Year Plan, it was found, had not benefited the poorest of the poor in rural society and they remained in the same poverty. The 'green revolution' increased the inequality in the rural areas because those who were landlords got maximum benefit of green revolution leaving aside the poor population of the villages. The *panchayati raj* institutions also did not help much the weaker sections of the society due to the domination and control of higher castes in these bodies. The cornered most of the benefits for themselves and only a very few/marginal weaker sections who aligned themselves with these castes at village level got some benefits. Therefore, after the evaluation of earlier programmes, a number of special programmes were taken up for poverty alleviation, in the hope that benefits of these programmes may reach to the people living below poverty line. The monetary limit and definition of the poverty line has been changing. At present the people earning less than Rs 7,500 per annum for a family of five are considered to be living below poverty line.

SPECIAL DEVELOPMENT PROGRAMMES

Numerous special development programmes were started after Independence to increase the income of those who were living below the poverty line. Table 24.1 gives details of the various programmes:

Table 24.1 *Rural development programmes*

Five-year plan	Programme	Year of introduction
I	1. Community development programme	1952
	2. National extension service	1953
II	3. Khadi and village industries programme	1957
	4. Village housing project scheme	1957
	5. Multipurpose tribal development blocks programme	1959
	6. Package programme	1960
	7. Intensive agricultural district programme	1960
III	8. Applied nutrition programme	1962
	9. Rural industries projects	1962
	10. Intensive agriculture area programme	1966
	11. High yielding variety programme	1966
1967	12. Farmers' training and education programme	1966
	13. Well construction programme	1966
1968	14. Rural Work Programme (RWP)	1967
	15. Tribal development block	1968
1968	16. Rural manpower programme	1969
	17. Composite programme for women and pre-school children	1969
IV	18. Drought prone area programme	1970
	19. Crash scheme for rural employment	1971
	20. Small Farmer Development Agency (SFDA)	1971
	21. Tribal area development programme	1972
	22. Pilot projects for tribal development	1972
	23. Pilot intensive rural employment programme	1972
	24. Minimum needs programme	1972
	25. Command area development programme	1974
V	26. Hill area development programme	1975
	27. Special livestock production programme	1975
	28. Food for work programme	1977
	29. Desert development programme	1977
	30. Whole village development programme	1979
	31. Training rural youth for self-employment	1979
	32. Integrated rural development programme	1979
VI	33. National rural employment programme	1980
	34. Prime minister's new 20-point programme	1980
	35. Rural landless employment guarantee programme (IREGE)	1983
	36. Development of women and children in rural areas	1983

(continued)

Table 24.2 *Rural development programmes (continued)*

Five-year plan	*Programme*	*Year of introduction*
VII	37. Integrated rural energy planning programme	1985
	38. Special Livestock Breeding Programme (SLBP)	1986
VIII	39. Jawahar *Rozgar Yojana*	1989
	40. Prime Minister's Rozgar Yojana (PMRY)	1993
	41. Employment Assurance Scheme (EAS)	1993
	42. National Social Assistance Programme (NSAP)	1995
IX	43. Swarnajayanti Gram Swarozgar Yojana (SGSY)	1999
	44. Jawahar Gram Samriddhi Yojana (JGSY)	1999
	45. Annapurna Scheme	2000
	46. Pradhan Mantri Gramodaya Yojana (PMGY)	2000

Source: Compiled from various five-year plan documents and schemes of rural development, Ministry of Development, Government of India.

Broadly, these programmes fall under the following three categories:

1. Area-based programmes to counter endemic poverty due to hostile agro climatic conditions and degeneration of ecosystems, such as drought-prone areas programme (DPAP), desert development programme (DDP) and hill area development programme comes under this category.
2. Targeted group or individual household and poverty group-oriented programmes of income generation through assets and skills endowment. The integrated rural development programme (IRDP), the national rural employment programme (NREP), rural landless employment guarantee programme (RLEGP) and *Jawahar Rozgar Yojana* (JRY) being run by the ministry of rural areas and employment belong to this category.
3. The minimum needs programme was started to support the poverty groups by providing sufficient consumption and social services to improve the quality of life and to provide infrastructural support to the programme of poverty alleviation.

Here, we discuss some important programmes briefly.

Area Development Programme

These programmes were started in areas chronically affected by drought and adverse weather conditions. The main programmes under this category are the DPAP (Drought-prone Area Programme), DDP (Desert Development Programme) and HADP (Hill Area Development Programme).

Drought-prone Area Programme

Drought-prone areas are characterized by soil erosion, water scarcity and environmental degradation. The DPAP was started in 1973–1974 as an integrated area development programme. The programme is being implemented in 627 blocks in 96 districts in 13 states. Out of these 627 blocks, nine blocks in Jammu and

Kashmir and three in Tamil Nadu have been created by bifurcating the existing DPAP blocks. Its coverage is about 553 lakh hectares or 5.54 lakh square kilometres comprising a total population of about 70.75 million as per the 1991 census.[6] The objectives of DPAP are the following:

1. To promote more productive dry land agriculture on the basis of the soil and water resources and agro-climatic conditions of the areas with suitable cropping pattern
2. To develop productive use of the water resources of the area, soil and moisture conservation including water harvesting and promotion of proper land use practices
3. Afforestation including farm forestry
4. Livestock development including development of pasture and fodder resources
5. Other diversified activities such as horticulture, sericulture, fisheries, etc

The components: The core components of the programme are soil and land development, water resources, moisture conservation, afforestation and pasture development.

There are some shortcomings in the component of the DPAP. For example, in the areas where the programme is in operation there is an acute shortage of drinking water for human beings as well as for cattle, and providing drinking water has not been included in DPAP. Likewise, the construction of roads has not been included in DPAP to link the villages in the areas with market centres on the plea that the funds for creation of such infrastructural facilities is the job of state government.[7]

Funding Pattern

This programme is a centrally sponsored scheme, the funds for which are shared equally by the centre and states on 50:50 basis. The amount given to each block in 1995–1996 was Rs 15 lakh, to a block of up to 400 sq. kms in area, Rs 25 lakh, to blocks of up to 800 sq. kms in area and Rs 30 lakh to blocks of over 800 sq. kms in area.[8]

The system of funding on the basis of area alone is not sufficient. It should also include geographical conditions and the requirements of the area for development.

Evaluation

It was found that the schemes under the programme fail to reduce the water stress. They have not given adequate emphasis on dry land farming, fodder and pasture development and absence of inter-school coordination.

The participation of the people in the schemes have not been properly mustered and lack of minimum facilities for staying are not available to the staff members involved in the implementation of the programme.

Integrated Rural Development

The integrated rural development programme was launched in all the blocks of the country on 2 October 1980 as a major credit-linked self-employment programme for alleviation of poverty. The objective of IRDP is to enable identified rural poor families to augment their income and cross the poverty line through acquisition of credit-based productive assets which would provide self-employment on a sustained basis.

Objectives of the IRDP

The main objectives are the following:

1. To help the families living below the poverty line to come up and cross it
2. To create substantial additional opportunities of employment in the rural sector

3. To reduce rural poverty
4. To make the family economically viable and self-sufficient
5. To assist the rural population to derive economic benefits from the developmental assets of each area

Thus, the overall objective of IRDP has been the reduction of unemployment and the provision of assets coupled with the inputs necessary to the rural poor for enabling them to rise above the poverty line on a lasting basis.

Financial Assistance Pattern

Under the IRDP income generation assets are provided to families who are below poverty line through a mix of subsidy credit. Credit is made available to the IRDP beneficiaries by financial institutions, i.e., commercial banks, cooperative banks and regional rural banks.

Coverage Under the IRDP

The selection of the beneficiaries under the IRDP has to be made carefully. Income is the main criterion of selection. The assistance is provided to a target group which comprises small and marginal farmers, agricultural labourers and rural artisans. This reflects its focus on the poorest of the poor. Although the poverty line is drawn at an annual income level of Rs 11,000, the assistance is targeted primarily at families whose annual income is up to Rs 6,000. In order to ensure that benefits reach the more vulnerable sections of the society, it is stipulated under the programme that in the identified target group at least 50 per cent should be from SC and ST with corresponding flow of resources to them. Further, to ensure better participation of women in the development process, it has been decided that at least 40 per cent of those assisted should be men and three per cent from amongst the physically handicapped. Priority in assistance is also given to the green card holders of family welfare programme, and freed bonded labourers.

The Pattern of Subsidy

The pattern of subsidy is 25 per cent for small farmers, 33 and one-third per cent for marginal farmers, agricultural labourers and rural artisans and 50 per cent for SC/ST beneficiaries and physically handicapped persons. The ceiling on subsidy is Rs 4,000 in non-DPAP and DDP areas, Rs 5,000 in DPAP and DDP areas and Rs 6,000 for SC and ST and physically handicapped persons.

Evaluation

To review the performance of the IRDP in the Sixth Plan, the programme evaluation organization of the Planning Commission, RBI, NABARD, the Institute of Financial and Management Research (Madras) and a number of other institutions have conducted studies. These reflected both the negative aspects as well as strong positive features. In this context it is not wrong to say that the Sixth Plan period was a trial period in which the programme gradually came to be known, understood and even stabilized. The gaps and weaknesses were delineated in the process. They were sought to be remedied in the Seventh Plan so as to make the IRDP an effective instrument of poverty alleviation in India. The performance of the IRDP in terms of the physical and financial targets and achievements has remained more than satisfactory. The basic thrust of the Eighth Plan has continued to be on the existing special employment programmes like the IRDP. The programmes need careful selection of beneficiaries, timely health adequate help in terms of finances, and insurance cover to meet unforeseen situations in assets such as milch cattle and poultry birds in case of their deaths, streamlining of bank credit, etc., will make the programme more successful.

Jawahar Rozgar Yojana

The experience gained in the implementation of various employment-oriented rural development programmes and the weaknesses in their implementation enabled the government to come up with another programme by merging the two programmes of the NREP and RLEGP. Both these programmes were employment generating where no other source of funding was available. The JRY, a massive all-comprehensive plan for providing jobs to the rural unemployed has been named after the first Prime Minister, Jawaharlal Nehru.

Objectives of the JRY

The twin objectives of the JRY are as follows:

(a) *Primary objective*—Generation of additional gainful employment for the unemployed and underemployed in rural areas

(b) *Secondary objective*—Creation of sustained employment by strengthening the rural economic infrastructure and also assets in favour of the rural poor for their direct and continuing benefits. It also aims at improvements in the overall quality of life in the rural areas.

The main components of JRY are as follows:

(i) Creation of physical assets

(ii) Creation of additional employment

(iii) Indira *Awas Yojana*

(iv) Digging of a million wells scheme

(v) Wages under JRY

(vi) Foodgrain distribution

(vii) Operational blackboard

All these components get financial support.

Evaluation

The JRY has been implemented throughout the country. It gave free hand to the bodies in both planning and execution of the work. Thus, decision making has been decentralized and the DRDAs/*zila parishads* decide on the works to be taken up in their respective areas. Some micro-level studies were conducted and they revealed certain problems and constraints, such as lack of awareness among the villagers about the JRY, low coverage, low women participation, poor quality and maintenance of the assets created paucity and leakages of funds, lack of proper monitoring, absence of inter-departmental coordination, absence of mechanism for determining local priorities and preparing projects, etc. all these limit the effectiveness of JRY.[9]

Thus, it is clear that the JRY does not indicate a perceptible improvement in the designing and implementation of various wage and employment generation schemes. The placing of huge amounts at the disposal of the *panchayats*, no doubt, gives the much needed political and financial strength, but may not lead to the alleviation of poverty.

Restructuring of the JRY

In the light of the experience gained, and the suggestions of state governments and the project directors, the modalities of implementing the JRY have been decided to continue the JRY first and third stream on the existing line. However, the Indira *awas yojana* (IAY) and million wells scheme (MWS) will henceforth be implemented as separate schemes in there own right and will not form part of JRY first stream. Further, in the second stream of JRY, i.e., the intensified JRY stands merged with the employment assurance scheme, w.e.f. 1 January 1996.[10]

Swarn Jayanti Gram Swarozgar Yojana

A new holistic self-employment programme, namely, *Swarn Jayanti Gram Swarozgar Yojana* (SGSY) was launched on 1 April 1999. With this, the erstwhile programmes, viz., integrated rural development programme (IRDP), development of women and children in rural areas (DWCRA), training of rural youth for self-employment (TRYSEM), supply of improved tool-kits to rural artisans (SITRA), *Ganga Kalyan Yojana* (GKY) and million wells scheme (MWS) ceased to be in operation. SGSY has been devised keeping in view the positive aspects as well as deficiencies of the earlier programmes.

SGSY is a credit-cum-subsidy programme. Credit is the critical component in SGSY, subsidy being only an enabling element. Accordingly, SGSY envisages greater involvement of the banks in the planning and preparation of projects, identification of activity clusters, choice of activity of the SHGs, selection of individual *swarozgaris*, pre-credit activities and post-credit monitoring including loan recovery, etc. It seeks to lay emphasis on skill development through well-designed training courses. Those who have been sanctioned loans are assessed and given necessary training. SGSY ensures upgradation of the technology in the identified activity clusters. The technology intervention seeks to add value to the local resources. SGSY provides for promotion of marketing of the goods produced by the SGSY *swarozgaris*. Subsidy under SGSY is uniform at 30 per cent of the project cost, subject to a maximum of Rs 7,500. In respect of SCs and STs, however, these are 50 per cent and Rs 10,000, respectively. For groups of *swarozgaris* (SHGs), the subsidy is at 50 per cent of the cost of the scheme, subject to a ceiling of Rs 1.25 lakh. There is no monetary limit on subsidy for irrigation projects. SGSY has a special focus on the vulnerable groups among the rural poor. Accordingly, SCs/STs would account for at least 50 per cent of the *swarozgaris*, women 40 per cent and the disabled 3 per cent. SGSY is implemented by the DRDAs through the *panchayat samitis*.

Jawahar Gram Samridhi Yojana

Jawahar Gram Samridhi Yojana (JGSY) is the restructured and comprehensive version of the erstwhile *Jawahar Rozgar Yojana* (JRY). Launched on 1 April 1999, it has been designed to improve the quality of life of the rural poor. The JGSY is implemented throughout the country in all the village *panchayats* except in Delhi and Chandigarh. The main objective of the JGSY is to create demand-driven village infrastructure including durable assets for increasing the opportunities for sustained employment and generation of supplementary employment for the under-employed poor in the rural areas. The unemployed/under-employed people living in villages constitute the target group of the JGSY. Special safeguards are provided under the scheme to the weaker sections of the community.

Annapurna Scheme

The *Annapurna* Scheme has been launched with effect from 1 April 2000 to provide food security to those senior citizens (65 years or above) who, although eligible, have not remained covered under the national old age pension scheme. Under the scheme, each beneficiary is provided 10 kg of foodgrains per month free of cost. A budgetary provision of Rs 100 crore has been made for the scheme during 2000–2001.

Pradhan Mantri Gramodaya Yojana

A new initiative in the form of *Pradhan Mantri Gramodaya Yojana* (PMGY) has been introduced during the current year to achieve the objective of sustainable human development at the village level. The PMGY envisages allocation of additional central assistance to states and Union territories for the selected basic minimum services in order to focus on certain priority areas of the government. Total allocation for the scheme is Rs 5,000 crore in the annual plan 2000–2001. It has two components, viz., rural roads, having an allocation Rs 2,500 crore, and the other component covering five programmes for primary health, primary education, rural shelter, rural drinking water and nutrition, having a total allocation of Rs 2,500 crore. The ministry of rural development is the administrative ministry responsible for the implementation of the rural roads scheme and the two components of rural drinking water supply and rural shelter. The ministry will manage and implement the rural drinking water component of the PMGY. The Government of India has issued guidelines for the implementation of PMGY-run rural drinking water scheme. The agencies which are implementing accelerated rural water supply programme (ARWSP), are also implementing the PMGY rural drinking water scheme. Under the scheme it is envisaged to make provision of potable drinking water in rural areas not covered (NC) and partially covered (PC) habitations, tackle quality-related problems like fluoride, arsenic and iron contamination, brackishness and sustainability of drinking water sources.

National Rural Employment Guarantee Programme

The Parliament passed a landmark legislation in August 2005 called the National Rural Employment Guarantee Act 2005 (NREGA). This was brought into force by the Union government in February 2006. It guaranteed 100 days of unskilled jobs per rural household. The NREGA was started in 200 most backwards districts of 27 states in the country in the first phase during the year 2006–2007. In the second phase 130 more districts were added in 2007–2008 and in the third phase in 2008 it was extended to the whole country. The Act aims at eradication of poverty and at making villages self-sustaining through productive assets creation.

National rural employment programme implementers include the following works in their order of priority: (a) water conservation and water supply, (b) drought proofing (including afforestation), (c) irrigation canals including micro and minor irrigation words; (d) provision of irrigation facility to land owned by households belonging to the SCs and STs, beneficiaries of land reforms or beneficiaries of Indira *Awas Yojana*, (e) renovation of traditional water bodies, including desilting of tanks, (f) land development (g) flood control and protection works including drainage in water-logged areas, (h) rural connectivity to provide all-weather access, and (i) any other work notified by the central government in consultation with the state government.

Main Features of the Programme

(i) It provides legal guarantee to work.

(ii) *Panchayati raj* institutions (PRIs) have a principal role in planning and implementation.

(iii) The *gram sabha* (village council) is to monitor all works and applications.

(iv) Contractors are not allowed in any manner.

(v) Transparency, accountability, social audit and people's participation are ensured through institutional mechanisms.

(vi) Grievance redress mechanism is present.

(vii) One-third of the beneficiaries are women.

(viii) Any adult person in the notified area willing to do unskilled manual work can apply for registration with *gram panchayat*. He/She will then be issued a job card.

(ix) The job card is the legal instrument that entitles the registered person to apply for employment under the Act.

(x) Registration is on throughout the year.

(xi) Employment given within five km of the applicants' residence; otherwise additional wages will be paid.

(xii) Workplace facilities include free medical care and compensation for death or permanent disability.

The Act provides for certain rights to the labourers.

As per the Act, local administration is legally bound to provide work on demand to any worker or group of workers who apply, within 15 days of receipt of work application on public works operated under NREGA. In case the local administration fails to provide work, an unemployment allowance is to be paid to the worker. The wages are equal for both men and women; and minimum wages as fixed by the state government has to be given. It also provides the right to worksite facilities like drinking water, sheds for children and first aid.

The ministry of rural development after two years of the implementation of NREGA, requested the CAG to conduct the audit of its performance. The records of offices between February 2006 and March 2007 were audited. The CAG's report pointed out three types of weaknesses. First, the national level average of beneficiaries, availing 100 days of employment is only 3.2 per cent; second, violation of operational guidelines; and third, rampant corruption. Other weaknesses mentioned in the programme were financial irregularities in payment of wages to fictitious labourers, tampering of muster rolls by using white fluid and marking absent as present and also overwriting the number of days worked was noticed in general during examination of muster rolls pertaining to the works selected in certain selected *gram panchayat*s in Andhra Pradesh shows the weaknesses of the programme.

Further, if the states failed to pay NREGA mandatory unemployment allowance to those who failed to get employment under the scheme. The NREGA stipulates that if a job seeker does not get work within 15 days of registering with the local authorities, he/she must be paid an unemployment allowance. The state governments' unwillingness to pay has led to agitations in many parts of the country. Barwani district in MP, Raichur district in Karnataka, Bolangir, Navrangpur and Kalahandi districts in Orissa and Sitapur district in UP.

However, three states, Andhra Pradesh, Sikkim and Goa, have no dues at all as they were able to provide work to all those who sought it. Most of the Union territories were also similarly placed.[11]

The NREG Act is unique as compared to any other schemes so far implemented in our country, in spite of some weaknesses. Under this scheme, landless and poor labourers got opportunity for earning for 100 days. The scheme has become very popular in the villages within a short span of time. Almost every adult in the villages is aware about this employment scheme. It has become a powerful 'vote bank' in rural India for the political party in power at the state level. The recent assembly elections of some states have amply proved that NREGA labourers have voted in favour of the parties which have given them the opportunity to earn under the scheme.

In the era of economic liberalization, privatization and globalization, adequate attention is given to the social sector schemes and for those sections of population which are vulnerable to exploitation by market forces. The various programmes supplement the social sector schemes launched by the government to tackle rural poverty and the NREG programme is the most important one of them all.

NOTES

1. S. S. Khera, *District Administration*, 2nd edition (New Delhi: National Public House, 1979), p. 79.
2. D. C. Patter, *Government in Rural India* (London: G. Bell and Sons Ltd., 1964), p. 8.
3. The Punjab government of the Akali Dal and BJP coalition had announced the abolition of land revenue on as declared by its chief minister, P. S. Badal.
4. *Gramin Vikas*, a monthly journal of the ministry of rural areas and employment, July, 1996, Vol. 12, No. 1, p. 19.
5. See, the 'collector in the Nineteen Sixties', *Indian Journal of Public Administration* (Special Number), Vol. 9, No. 3, July–September, 1965.
6. Hoshiar Singh, *Administration of Rural Development in India* (New Delhi: Sterling Publishers, 1995), p. 139.
7. Ibid., p. 141.
8. Annual Report, Government of India, Ministry of Rural Areas and Employment, New Delhi, 1995–1996, p. 41.
9. See, for details, Hoshiar Singh, *Administration of Rural Development in India*–(New Delhi: Sterling Publishers, 1995), Chapter 12.
10. Annual Report, Ministry of Rural Areas and Employment, Government of India, 1995–1996, p. 7.
11. *Hindustan Times*, 10 November 2009.

Panchayati Raj

The panchayats were established by most of the state governments in India after Independence, but a major step in this direction was taken on the basis of Balwantrai Mehta Committee's report in 1957 which recommended three-tier panchayati raj system in India. During this period several steps were taken to strengthen panchayati raj by central as well as state governments in the country. Keeping in view many past attempts, the central government found the solution in the form of the 73rd Constitution Amendment Act, to remove the weaknesses of panchayati raj. It is argued that 'this Act seeks to enshrine democracy at grassroots,' as it intends 'to give power to the people', and it will end corruption and fight and finish power brokers and middlemen in politics. This chapter will focus on the conceptual aspects of panchayati raj, working of panchayati raj till now and its shortcomings. It will also discuss the features of the 73rd Constitution Amendment Act, 1993, its strengths and weaknesses.

The Concept of Panchayati Raj

Mahatma Gandhi was well aware about the Indian society and wanted village self-sufficiency (*Gram Swaraj*) to be the aim of independent India, but the chairman of the Constitution Drafting Committee, B. R. Ambedkar, was against village panchayats[1] and only lip service was paid to the concept in the draft Constitution. When Gandhi came to know about this, he insisted for its inclusion in the Constitution. As a result the provision of village panchayats was included in the Directive Principles of State Policy in Article 40 which mentioned that 'the state shall take steps to organise village panchayats and endow them with such powers and authority as may be necessary to enable them to function as units of self-government.'

To operationalize this provision into action, the Balwantrai Mehta Committee was appointed in 1957 to suggest the introduction of panchayati raj. As a result of the recommendations of this committee a three-tier panchayati raj system: the *gram panchayat* at the village level, the panchayati samiti at the block or intermediate level, and *zila parishad* at the district level, was introduced. All the three units were organically linked together, as the chairmen of lower level bodies were ex-officio members of higher level bodies. These bodies were given all the planning and development work. The committee remarked about the philosophy of panchayati raj that 'panchayati raj system establishes a linkage between local leadership enjoying confidence of local people and the government, and translate the policies of the government into action.'[2] Thus, village panchayats were made subordinate units of the government at lowest level to implement its programmes and not the agencies of self-government or *gram swaraj* as Gandhi thought. Slowly the panchayati raj lost its glamour and people's participation was weakened, because regular elections of the panchayati raj bodies were not conducted.

In 1977, the Janata Party government came to power after the defeat of Congress (I). The leaders of Janata Party were interested in assigning meaningful role to panchayati raj, therefore, they tried to revitalize these institutions and appointed a committee under the chairmanship of Ashok Mehta in December 1977 to suggest a viable organization for grassroot institutions to mobilize people's participation and their active support. In its report in 1978 (a landmark in the history of panchayati raj) the Mehta Committee suggested structures with development orientation at two levels; the district and the Mandal panchayats (covering about 15,000 to 20,000 population) for grassroots level. The other recommendations were open participation of political parties in panchayati raj elections, constitutional protection to further the decentralization of power. The committee wanted panchayati raj institutions to participate in development activities, in the areas of agriculture, forestry, cottage industries, welfare activities, etc.

In the 1980s, due to expansion of anti-poverty programmes and creation of district rural development agency (DRDA) and other organizations for rural development purposes at lower levels, it was required to integrate panchayati raj system with development programmes. As a result, the C. H. Hanumantha Rao Working Group on District Planning was set up (1983)[3] and the G. V. K. Rao Committee was set up to review the existing administrative arrangements for rural development and poverty alleviation programmes (1985).[4] The G. V. K. Rao Committee had recommended strengthening of *zila parishad* and endorsed the recommendations of Rao's working group for district level planning as well as better integration of block and lower level planning with lower level panchayati raj institutions. Another committee headed by L. M. Singhvi (1986) has prepared the concept paper on panchayati raj[5], which states that panchayati raj institutions should be closely involved in planning and implementation of rural development programmes at lower levels. The committee has also recommended that the panchayats should be made financially viable by combining 2–3 villages in one panchayat. It has supported the recommendations of the G. V. K. Rao Committee for integration of administrative structures with panchayati raj institutions.

Thus, the concept of panchayati raj has undergone some changes since its inception; from its narrow span it has expanded to and covered areas of rural development and economic planning but it still suffers from a number of shortcomings. First, it does consider panchayati raj bodies as only agencies which can play an important role in the overall development of our rural areas. In other words, the present concept does not consider panchayati raj bodies as planning and implementation agencies for various rural development programmes. Second, there is no clarity about the relationship between panchayati raj bodies and development administration; because there is no separate cadre of administration for panchayati raj bodies, the dual responsibility of the administration towards state departments and towards (panchayati raj bodies) creates lot of confusion and complications. Third, there is no systematic method to involve the weaker sections in the functioning of panchayati raj bodies. On one hand, there is a feeling that panchayati raj leaders do not involve the poor in these bodies and, therefore, the administration has to intervene to provide the benefits of growth to the poor, while on the other hand, the involvement and control of panchayati raj office bearers in rural development activities is increasing continuously. Finally, there is no clear trend emerging in the context of decentralization of power. On one hand, there is a lot of talk about decentralization of power to district and lower level bodies, on the other central schemes are increasing both in number and in size. One cannot make out what kind of decentralization we are heading to.[6]

In spite of all these shortcomings, the concept of panchayati raj has great potential, capacity and role in a big country like ours. Panchayati raj has to play an important role in the overall development of economy and polity of the country.

Working of Panchayati Raj

The working of panchayati raj institutions during these three decades has developed two streams of thoughts. One view is that the panchayati raj functionaries, both political as well as administrative, were interested in power politics and distribution of patronage, created tensions in village communities and disturbed the village harmony. Panchayati raj bodies have failed to protect the interests of the poor in the villages. They even failed to protect and strengthen the planning process at micro level and these bodies have not played significant role in the development of agriculture, minor irrigation, social welfare, etc. The other point of view attributes the limited success of panchayati raj to lack of finances, cooperation from the government departments, half-hearted policies, too much penetration by the state authorities from above and defective structure of panchayati raj institutions.

In the beginning panchayati raj system worked successfully in some states like Rajasthan, Maharashtra, Gujarat, Andhra Pradesh, etc. but within 10 years of its working, it became apparent that their performance is not glorious as it was being painted and studies showed that the benefits of development are being cornered by organized vested interest groups in these bodies at the cost of rural poor. Several studies conducted by scholars in various states and also by some state level and all-India committees[7], made it clear that panchayati raj bodies could not fulfil the expectations of the rural people. The recent experiment of Karnataka and West Bengal on panchayati raj system is cited as a success story.[8] It is said that the *zila panchayati*s in Karnataka are really emerging as a power centre below the state. But studies by George Mathew[9] and Gurumurthy[10] have shown that the power in the districts is enjoyed mainly by dominant castes belonging to the top power groups, and the interests of the poor are sacrificed for strengthening the vested interests of the district leadership.[11]

The West Bengal study also shows that panchayati raj bodies do not allow their benefits to percolate down to the poor in the villages.[12] The study by Hirway clearly shows that the socioeconomic power structure in rural areas does not allow the benefits of panchayati raj system to flow towards the weaker sections.[13] Most of the benefits are being taken away by dominant castes in the panchayats.[14] It is very clear that panchayati raj is working for elite groups or for groups of big farmers and rich businessmen. The masses and the poor do not get much benefit out of the system but they are being exploited by the panchayati raj leaders. On the whole, the performance of these institutions has not been satisfactory. Slowly the panchayati raj institutions lost their glamour and people's participation declined.

Reasons for the Decline of Panchayati Raj

On the basis of the literature available on the operational aspects of panchayati raj, the reasons for its decline are many. Important among them are the political repercussions of electoral competition between state and panchayati raj representatives which were largely responsible for the eclipse of panchayati raj institutions. The state level leaders began to see their rivals in these institutions and out of fear they started withdrawing important functions from these bodies making them only dumping grounds for discarded state cadre administrative officers. Most of the extension and development functions were taken away by several amendments in the relevant acts. For example, development of land, water, forests, grazing lands, animal husbandry, rural health, etc. should be in the hands of panchayati raj bodies, but these are being controlled by state level departments. Such an irrational approach in functional distribution has diminished panchayati raj system. Thus, these bodies remained only panchayats and not institutions of *raj*. Moreover, to add to the woes, panchayati raj elections were repeatedly postponed on one or the other flimsy ground. The result was lack of people's faith in these institutions because of their functional inability.

Political considerations played a major role in patronage distribution in these institutions and panchayati raj bureaucracy, and BDOs were not allowed to take free and objective decisions in running and distributing annual grants to various panchayats. The state wheel did not stop here and went even further almost to ruin these institutions by creating parallel alternative structures for rural development functions, i.e., district rural development agency (DRDA) (a recent Sixth Plan creation) made responsible for the IRDP, TRYSEM, NREP, RLEGP, and other programmes. A number of overlapping committees at district level comprising of MPs and MLAs are functioning and various lead banks provide finance for different schemes (outside the panchayati raj structure) and a multiplicity of departmental organizations also exist side by side. In practice, the plethora of rural development programmes and schemes implemented under the control of central/state governments had minimized the scope for the functioning of panchayati raj bodies.

The capacity of panchayati raj institutions was further hampered due to inadequate finances. Most of the finances come from the state government. Even the central government is keen to spend its own resources through its own organizations, which have been created at every level. To add to the miseries of panchayati raj bodies, people have developed apathy and lost faith in their capacity to fulfil their needs. The problem of panchayati raj has further been compounded by the penetration of state authority by using of stringent controls like dissolution and supercession of panchayati raj institutions. Even *sarpanch*es were suspended or removed by government on flimsy grounds. The bureaucrats serving in these institutions do not want to be subordinated by panchayati raj leaders and created obstacles in smooth working of these bodies. The worst part of the whole politicization was that panchayati raj became the dumping ground for discarded state cadre officials. Those who are inefficient or non-functional were transferred to manage these units and no expert staff, which is required for planning, implementation and monitoring of various schemes and programmes, was given to these institutions to manage them efficiently. The result was administrative chaos and politics without any morals. The bureaucrats who were forcefully sent to panchayati raj bodies were always opposed to the system and created several obstacles in the smooth working of these institutions. The most dangerous trend was to undermine the authority and importance of panchayati raj in the form of power relations. The state level higher organizations not only curb and mar the development of panchayati raj bodies but at the same time try to show that they have more powers, and as compared to them panchayati raj institutions are very small. The MLAs and MPs of the area belonging to the party in power pose as if in power hierarchy they are above panchayati raj institutions. Their proximity and linkages with the concerned minister and chief minister provide them ample power to create psychological environment in their favour to increase their following at the cost of panchayati raj. This nature of our political elite certainly requires immediate rectification otherwise panchayati raj will not be able to regain people's faith which is an essential requirement at present. Moreover, the elected *panch*es, *sarpanch*es, *pradhan*s and *zila pramukh*s who have not received any training do not know what to do for the welfare of the people.

How to make panchayati raj effective or successful is a million dollar question. The answer to this question needs deep analysis. For the success of panchayati raj a comprehensive concept is needed. It is a political as well as development and planning concept. Panchayati raj has to work as an agency of decentralization for political as well as administrative powers to encourage for mass participation and self-governance in practice. Further, the panchayati raj concept has to strengthen the planning process at the grassroot level (micro level) for overall rural development. The concept has to provide opportunities to the poor masses for decision making in these bodies. Such a concept will require many steps such as multilevel planning along with micro level planning and integration of panchayati raj institutions in planning and administration of local areas. It also needs organizing the poor to protect them from exploitation by the rich in rural areas. The present rural power structure exploits the poor, therefore, some steps are required to check the position. The following measures can improve the situation:

(a) Arrangements for social security, loan facilities from banks, effective public distribution system of foodgrains, clothes and other necessary items for rural poor for daily use are important factors in reducing their dependency on money lenders and exploiters

(b) Continuous employment for rural poor in development work programmes, such as JRY, IRDP, etc. and provision of minimum employment and sources of income to live on

(c) Distribution of diesel pumps, gas agencies, fertilizer and pesticide agencies in rural areas to the weaker section people and access to common property resources for the poor

(d) Encouragement to organizations of the rural poor so that they can demand their rights

(e) Panchayati raj bodies should be provided unified administrative set up,[15] created exclusively for rural development. This cadre should be protected from unwanted political pressures with suitable transfer and promotion policy rules. Training of panchayati raj members about their roles is also essential for its success.

Seventy-Third Constitution Amendment Act and Its Main Characteristics

The 73rd Constitution Amendment Act has a chequered history. It struggled for nearly three years to see the light of day as an Act. The Rajiv Gandhi government introduced a Panchayati raj Bill in 1989, and it was passed by Lok Sabha but failed to gain requisite majority in the Rajya Sabha. The V. P. Singh government also tried to push a Bill on the panchayati raj in 1990, but it lapsed with the dissolution of the Lok Sabha. In 1991, the present Congress government again introduced the Bill on panchayati raj with some modified provisions. The Bill was referred to a select committee by the Parliament. The Bill was first discussed by a joint parliamentary committee and then by Parliament. It was passed by the Lok Sabha on 22 December 1992 and by the Rajya Sabha on the following day. After ratification by 17 state assemblies, including West Bengal and Bihar, both opposition-ruled states, the president gave his assent to the Bill on 20 April 1993 and it became an Act. Through a gazette notification, the Act was brought into force with effect from 24 April 1993.

The constitutional base for panchayati raj was required because state governments were not enthusiastic about the creation of panchayati raj bodies and sharing power with them in their states. In fact some states have taken back powers from the panchayati raj bodies. Status and dignity under constitutional support if given to panchayati raj bodies shall make them essentially viable and responsive institutions. In our Constitution, local self-government and panchayati raj are state subjects and the central government cannot pass any legislation unless the Constitution is amended. Hence, the 73rd Constitution Amendment Act, 1993 was enacted.

The main characteristics of the 73rd Constitution Amendment Act are that the Act proposed to establish *gram sabhas* consisting of all the voters in the panchayat area. It established a three-tier system of panchayati raj, in an ascending order, except in those states whose population was less than 20,00,000, the panchayat at the village level, intermediate level and district level at the top. The members of all these panchayats will be directly elected by the people. Members of the Lok Sabha/Rajya Sabha (MPs) and the legislative assemblies (MLAs) from the area would continue to be members of these bodies with the right to vote in the meetings of the panchayats but having no right to vote in the election of chairpersons of intermediate and district level panchayats. They are also debarred to be chairperson of these panchayats. The term of each panchayat would be five years and elections will be held every five year under the supervision, direction and control of the state election commission/commissioner. If superseded in mid-term, a mid-term election will be held within six months. The reconstituted panchayat will serve for the remaining period of a five-year term only.

The Act also provided for reservation of seats, for the scheduled castes and scheduled tribes (SC and ST) in proportion to their percentage against the total population of a panchayat. It has further reserved seats of chairpersons for the SC and ST candidates in all the three tiers of the new panchayati raj system in direct proportion to their percentage of the total population of the state. Out of these reserved seats one-third will be reserved for SC and ST women. The 1993 Act also provides that one-third of the seats in the panchayats at all levels will be reserved for women including SC and ST women. The Act directed the states that reservation be carried out by rotation in each and every panchayat at each level. Another feature of the Act is that it has left to the states to decide the question of reserving seats for backward classes.

Financial paucity has been one of the main causes of failure of panchayati rajs in the past. To remove this hurdle, the panchayats have been empowered to levy and collect appropriate taxes, duties, tolls and fees and they would be entitled grants-in-aid from the consolidated fund of the state. Every five years the state governor would appoint a finance commission to review and advise the state government on the principles governing the distribution of funds to the panchayats. The manner of audit of panchayat accounts would be decided by the state governments. The state governments also would devolve power to the panchayats to prepare plans for economic development and social justice. Significantly, a whole new schedule called the 11th Schedule was drawn up to ensure better utilization of central and state funds. The Schedule contains entire agriculture and allied activities, minor irrigation schemes, land reforms and improvement, small industries including food processing, cottage industries, rural housing, drinking water, rural electrification, non-conventional energy programmes, poverty alleviation programmes, primary and secondary education, vocational education, health and family welfare schemes, public distribution system, welfare schemes for weaker and handicapped sections, etc.

Some of the provisions of the 73rd Amendment Act are good, such as the insistence on regular elections for panchayats after expiry of their term, making them financially viable and involving them into micro level planning. The time limit allowed to enforce the 73rd Constitution Amendment Act throughout the country was one year, which seems to be sufficient. The 73rd Amendment Act protects the autonomy of the states, for example, supervision and control of panchayati raj elections has been given to the state election commission, framing of laws relating to audit and accounts has been left in the hands of state legislatures and power of appointment of finance commission to review the financial position of panchayats and to recommend principles governing distribution of taxes and grants-in-aid between states and panchayati raj bodies has been given to the states. Even composition of these panchayats has been left to the states. Thus, the states have not been undermined by this Amendment. These are all welcome provisions.

But there are some lacunae in the Act, such as it has little to offer to the panchayats by way of functions, powers and resources to shape them as 'units' of self-government. This task has been left to each state legislature to determine and past experience has shown that the states are always reluctant to part with their powers. The reservation scheme for the office of chairpersons of panchayats in rotation would affect the smooth working of these bodies and this provision is likely to be misused by the party in power at the state level to weaken the stronghold of other opposition parties in regions and panchayats of the state by reserving their chairperson's office for ST, SC and women. This will ensure that even in the upper caste-dominated panchayats, SC and ST candidates would come to acquire the posts of chairpersons. Similarly, women will also come to chair in each and every panchayat by rotation. This will create social tensions in a caste-ridden and male-dominated Indian society. It would be wise to let conventions secure a share in chairpersonship for the disadvantaged groups rather than rely on a legislative stick.[16] Further, the Act has given voting rights to the ex-officio members, i.e., MPs and MLAs in these bodies which would lead to the over riding domination of these institutions by the legislators and this would go against the intent of decentralization.[17] The 73rd Amendment Act dispenses with the flexibility of structure of panchayati raj. The question such as three-tier or two-tier system, the extent of mode of reservation for women and SC and ST are decided in a uniform pattern for the entire country. This inflexibility will cause great harm, for example, in Kerala, where after protracted discussion for nearly two decades, it was decided to have two-tier system. Likewise, West Bengal, Karnataka and Andhra Pradesh adopted two-tier panchayati raj system which has shown good results. But the 73rd Constitution Amendment Act makes it obligatory for Kerala as also for every other state whose population is above 20 lakh to have a three-tier system.[18] All the functions assigned to panchayati raj institutions in the 11th Schedule, will not be devolved to these bodies in practice by the state governments. The organizations of teachers are opposing transfer of primary and secondary education management to panchayati raj bodies. Similarly, items 14 and 23 of the 11th Schedule, distribution of electricity including rural electrification and health and sanitation, including hospitals, primary health centres and dispensaries, respectively, are functions which involve substantial technical know-how that is hardly available at the village panchayat level. The one-year period given for the implementation of the Act may be misused by states to delay its implementation.[19] As per the provisions of the 73rd Amendment Act, if state governments hold the panchayati raj elections prior to the enactment of the new legislation the term of the newly elected panchayats will be delayed by more than one year, even up to four years till the term of the newly elected panchayats expires.

Further, the Act has failed to mention the role of political parties. Neither does the Act specify their role nor does it mention about the working of political parties. Likewise, it is completely silent on the relationship between panchayati raj bodies and local bureaucracy. The local level bureaucracy was instrumental in creating and spreading the anti-panchayati raj climate which led to their failure. If the control of bureaucracy in panchayati raj institutions is not given to the local leaders and kept in the hands of state governments then panchayati raj is bound to fail. The Act is also silent on the exclusive jurisdiction of panchayats, while the states have areas of exclusive jurisdiction carrying legislative, executive and judicial authority as given in the Constitution. The 11th Schedule mentioned in the 73rd Amendment is not mandatory but only advisory in nature. It does not specify the division of sphere, it only gives the number of developmental activities considered suitable for panchayats.

Finally, although this is not the intention of the Act but by implication, in some cases, it appears that this will undermine the powers of the states. For example, the Act has placed panchayati raj (local government) in the concurrent list and out of the state list so that the central government can legislate in this area. This amounts to increase in power of the centre at the cost of the states. Further, the unilateral decision of the centre on one-third reservation of seats for women in general membership as well as for chairperson's office and prescription of direct method of election for village panchayats and intermediate level panchayats, creation of the finance commission to provide finances to panchayati raj institutions in place of state governments and flow of Jawahar Rozgar Yojana funds directly from centre to panchayats, also undermines the powers of the states. The important questions are the following:

(a) To what extent does the 73rd Amendment Act support and encourage decentralization of power or decentralization of decision making at all the levels in the country?
(b) To what extent is the Act capable of removing the weaknesses of the present panchayati raj system? Does the Act ensure healthy growth of panchayati raj in the country?
(c) Does the Act fulfil the requirements of Article 40 of the Directive Principles of State Policy of the Constitution? The government has mentioned this Article as the main source for this amendment.

The reply to all these questions is not an easy task, but an attempt has been made to analyse these questions in the following pages.

Decentralization

The 73rd Constitution Amendment Act tends to provide meaningful panchayati raj bodies in the country. This amendment is certainly a step forward in the direction of decentralization of powers to the people at grassroots level by creating responsive village panchayats to the *gram sabha*, regular elections and sufficient representation in these bodies to the weaker sections of society such as SC and ST and women. The one-third reservation for the chairperson's office for women and SC and ST persons provides a handle to the party in power at the state level for manoeuvrability and political use, but this will certainly check the control of these bodies by powerful vested interests in the villages. This provision will also provide opportunities to the weaker sections of communities for decision making in these institutions at the highest level.

Although the act is a step forward in the direction of decentralization, it is far short of what can be termed as desirable degree of decentralization of powers. Under the Act, the panchayati raj institutions have not been conferred with vital administrative powers, whose decentralization would make the lives of the people somewhat tolerable. For example, the powers relating to the cases of transfer of family pension in the name of widows of the soldiers of defence forces, who mostly belong to the village, are in the hands of BDO or the treasury or the gazetted officer. These only add to their woes and instead power should be transferred to panchayati raj institutions for actual decentralization.

The provisions of the 73rd Amendment Act, if implemented sincerely, are capable of strengthening panchayati raj bodies in the country. Timely elections by the state election commission, distribution of finances by the finance commission and greater representation of weaker sections are all such provisions which will enhance the status, credibility and dignity of these institutions.

The 73rd Amendment Act emanates from Article 40 of the Constitution, which says that 'the state shall take steps to organise village panchayats and endow them with such powers and authority as may be necessary to enable them to function as units of self-government. The plain meaning of this provision is that the self-government for panchayats is the central objective of this amendment. The only point to be seen is while endowing powers to the panchayati raj bodies what meaning is given by the state legislatures to the expression "self-government".' But after this Act, the states now have no choice but to implement the provisions of the Constitution or face the wrath of the Union government.

Thus, the approach of this amendment is the creation of meaningful and viable panchayati raj bodies to serve the purpose of promoting the cause of local self-government institutions in rural India.

Conclusion

It is a fact that panchayati raj system in the country was not functioning in the right direction, hence the need was felt to revitalize them. The basic need is to evoke a comprehensive concept of panchayati raj which should clearly mention the role expected from them. The theory that representative participation leads to mass participation is not relevant in the context of the Indian socio-economic power structure. Therefore, there is a need to either change this structure, which seems to be a difficult task, or strengthen the position of weaker sections/poor in rural areas so that they can rise above their exploitation. The 73rd Constitution Amendment Act is certainly an attempt in that direction and will revitalize panchayati raj for decentralization and rural development.

NOTES

1. B. R. Ambedkar said: 'that they [the villages] have survived through all vicissitudes may be a fact. But mere survival has no value. The question is on what plane they have survived. Surely, on a low, selfish level. I hold that these village republics have been the ruination of India. I am therefore, surprised that those who condemn provincialism and communalism should come forward as champions of the village. What is the village but a stink of localism, a den of ignorance, narrow-mindedness and communalism? I am glad that the Draft Constitution has discarded the village and adopted the individual as its Unit', *Debates of the Constituent Assembly*, Vol. 7, Issue 1, p. 39.
2. *Report of the Committee on Plan Projects*, Vol. I (New Delhi: Planning Commission, 1959), p. 5.
3. *Report of the Working Group on District Planning*, Vols 1 and 2 (New Delhi: Planning Commission, Government of India, 1983), Chairman C. H. Hanumantha Rao.
4. *Report of the Committee to Review the Existing Administrative Arrangements for Rural Development and Poverty Alleviation Programmes (CAARD)* (New Delhi: Department of Rural Development, Ministry of Agriculture, Government of India, 1985), Chairman G. V. K. Rao.
5. Concept paper on Panchayati Raj, Ministry of Agriculture, New Delhi, Government of India, 1987.
6. Indira Hirway, 'Panchayati Raj at Crossroad', *Economic and Political Weekly*, 22 July1989: 1663–64.
7. Some of the studies are as follows:
   (a) L. C. Jain, panchayati raj and Decentralisation, Kurukshetra, February, 1989.
   (b) B. P. S. Bhadouria (ed.), *Panchayati Raj and Rural Development* (New Delhi: Commonwealth Publishers, 1989).
   (c) P. C. Mathur, *Political Dynamics of* Panchayati Raj (Delhi: Konark Publishers, 1991).

   Some of the state committees are as follows:
   (a) *Report of the Study Team on* Panchayati Raj, (Jaipur: Panchayat and Development Department, Government of Rajasthan, 1964), Chairman Sadiq Ali.
   (b) *Report of the High Power Committee on* Panchayati Raj *Community Development and* Panchayats *Department* (Jaipur: Government of Rajasthan, 1973), Chairman Girdhari Lal Vyas.
   (c) *Report of the Evaluation Committee on* Panchayati Raj (Mumbai: Government of Maharashtra, 1971), Chairman Bongirwar.
   (d) *Report of the High Level Committee on* Panchayati Raj (Gandhi Nagar: Government of Gujarat, 1972), Chairman Zinabhai Darji.
   (e) *Report of the* Panchayati Raj *High Power Committee* (Gandhi Nagar: Government of Gujarat, 1978), Chairman Rikhavdas Shah.

8. Prabhat Kumar Datta, 'Democratising Rural Administration: The West Bengal Experience', *Indian Journal of Administrative Science*, Vol. 1, Issue 1 (January–June 1990); 144–64.
9. George Mathew (ed.) Panchayati Raj *in Karnatai Today* (New Delhi: Concept Publishing House, 1985).
10. V. Gurumurthy, Panchayati Raj *and the Weaker Sections* (New Delhi: Ashish Publishing House, 1987).
11. See Amal Ray, 'New Panchayat System in Karnataka: Elections and After', *Economic and Political Weekly*, 14 February 1987.
12. G. K. Lieten, 'Caste, Gender, and Class in Panchayats—Case of Barddhaman, West Bengal', *Economic and Political Weekly*, 18 July 1992.
13. Indira Hirway, *Abolition of Poverty in India with Special Reference to Target Group Approach in Gujarat* (New Delhi: Vikas Publishing House, 1986).
14. A. Inbanathan, *The New* Panchayati Raj *in Karnataka: An Evaluation* (New Delhi: Institute of Social Sciences, 1992), p. 32.
15. Hoshiar Singh, 'Rural Development: Need for Unified Set Up', *Hindustan Times*, 6 December 1980.
16. L. C. Jain, 'Future of Panchayats', *Hindustan Times*, New Delhi, 10 April 1991.
17. Rakesh Aggarwal, 'Panchayati Raj: Still a Far Cry', *The Economic Times*, New Delhi, 14 August 1992.
18. E. M. S. Namboodiripad, 'Panchayati Raj Bill, A Deceptive Measure', *The Tribune*, Chandigarh, 31 December 1989.
19. For example, West Bengal government has just completed its panchayat elections under its old Act. Since the term of Bengal panchayats is five years, a new legislation even after enactment within a year, would not be implemented for the next four years, till the term of the state panchayats expires. This device can be adopted by other states to delay the implementation of this Act.

26

Urban Local Government

In its present form municipal government in India is a colonial legacy which underwent hardly any structural changes even after Independence in 1947. The issue of municipal reforms—institutional change for efficient management and development has assumed importance due to several reasons. The tremendous urban population growth has led to many problems and it was realized that one of the primary obstacles to meet the challenges of urbanization has been the absence of capacity and managerial skills at the urban government level. The problems of municipal governments are many such as its outdated administrative structures, multiplicity of urban development authorities, tension between deliberative and executive wings, unwanted interventions of state governments, inadequate finances and lack of proper planning and development.[1] Further, the growth of densely populated metropolitan cities with a large number of persons living in slums and single rooms have caused social tensions. The solution and appropriate management of tensions and conflicts requires viable local institutional framework.

With the advent of liberalization and privatization culture in the 1980s, attempts were made to reform municipal government in India. As a result, the 74th Constitution Amendment Act, 1992 was passed to accord constitutional status to municipal government. The basic characteristics of the 74th Amendment are 'three types of municipal bodies—*nagar panchayats*, municipal councils and corporations as per the population of cities; reservation of electoral wards for the weaker sections (SC and ST) and women; a suggestive municipal functional list, creation of planning committees in the districts and metropolitan areas, appointment of state election commission and state finance commission (SFC), etc.[2] Thus, an attempt has been made to ensure some degree of institutional uniformity of municipal government by the 74th Amendment. Almost all the state governments have passed the conformity legislations as a step to enforce and implement the Amendment.

The present chapter discusses the structural changes and management processes of municipal government after the 74th Amendment Act, the extent of decentralization and deficiencies in the Act and suggests the future lines of reforms for municipal institutions and management.

Structure of Urban Local Governance

The 74th Constitutional Amendment provides for three categories of structures for urban local bodies: (a) *Nagar panchayats* (town councils) for a transitional urban area which is turning from a rural to an urban area, (b) municipal councils for smaller urban areas, and (c) municipal corporations for larger urban areas. In addition to the census definition of an urban area, the *nagar panchayats* in Haryana would be created with a population of 10,000–50,000, a municipal council with a population of 50,000–5,00,000 and a municipal corporation over 5,00,000 along with consideration of other factors such as density of population, internal revenue prospects, the percentage of employment in non-agricultural activities and other significant factors may be considered for creation of municipal institutions, except where municipal services are provided by the industries in an industrial township. The size and population criterion of municipal classification is not uniform in all the states and the Act empowers the state to determine the population and other factors for the creation of an urban governance institutional framework. The criterion for creation of municipal bodies is not uniform in all the states.

The implication of categorization of 'municipal institutions' into three classes, barring self-sufficient industrial areas, would have to be totally elected and the different municipal classes could be differentiated in terms of their population and council, size, functions, tax powers, degree of state control, executive and personnel system.

Municipal Council

In every urban body the composition of municipal councils would comprise elected members and some additional members as mentioned in the 74th Amendment. The additional members could be: (a) members of state legislatures (MLAs) and members of Parliament (MPs) whose constituencies fall in the municipal area; (b) chairpersons of the ward committees of municipal corporations with a population of 3,00,000 and more and (c) nominated experts without voting rights. The mention of ward and zonal committees in the 74th Amendment in big cities is considered an innovation because this provides opportunities for decentralization of municipal services and greater involvement of the people in municipal affairs.

The 74th Amendment provides reservation of council seats and the post of the chairperson for scheduled castes, scheduled tribes and women and entirely left it on states to reserve seats for backward classes. No time limit has been prescribed for reservations. In the case of SC and ST, it mentions that it is limited to the period specified in the Constitution for all other purposes but the Act has provision for reservation of wards as well as posts of chairperson in rotation to provide opportunity to other caste people to get themselves democratically elected from these wards and thus remove the apathy of voters in electoral process. In almost all the states except UP and Andhra Pradesh, the municipal chairpersons are indirectly elected. Since the municipal elections are fought on party basis, the chairperson is chosen from the majority party. In municipalities he is called president or chairman, while in municipal corporations he is called the 'mayor' who presides over the council meetings, but in municipal corporations of West Bengal the chairperson of the council acts as the speaker, while the mayor heads a cabinet-type executive called the 'mayor-in-council'.

The 74th Amendment mentions the state election commission for the superintendence, direction, control and preparation of electoral rolls for the conduct of municipal elections. The election commissioner will be appointed by the governor of the state but he could be removed only through an impeachment motion moved in Parliament and not by the governor under the state law. This is repugnant to the 'spirit of the federation.'

The requirement of separate set of electoral roll for municipal elections and voting rights for the MPs and MLAs on the local bodies and provision for reservation of the post of chairpersons for members of SC and ST or women also found to be 'inconsistent with the doctrine of party-based election and democratic principle'.

Planning and Finance

For planning purposes, the 74th Amendment has provided for the establishment of two planning committees, one for district and the other for metropolitan areas for the preparation of municipal plans for matters of common interest between the '*panchayats*' and the 'municipalities', mainly planning of physical and natural resources, infrastructure development and environmental conservation. The state governments are supposed to identify and assign district planning functions to these committees. If these planning functions are more than the municipal revenue functions, then there would be fiscal imbalance by way of maintenance gap with which the state finance commission (SFCs) would have to contend. The existing separation of urban development from municipal maintenance tasks may have to be removed either by integrating the urban development and maintenance tasks within the municipalities or through their municipalization of urban planning and contracting of the development tasks to other agencies, both public and private.[3]

The constitution of the district and metropolitan planning committees are heavily dominated by members of the '*panchayats*' and 'municipalities' to the extent of four-fifths (80 per cent) for the former and two-thirds (67 per cent) for the latter to be shared in proportion to their population. This has many implications. First, the district planning committee will have more members from *panchayats* while metropolitan planning committee will have more from urban areas, and will thus create tension between rural and urban people. Second, the manner of composition of these committees will reduce the weight of the states (and the central) representatives in these committees. Third, the plans prepared by these committees will be submitted to the state governments, that is, mostly to the planning departments of the state governments. Thus, a feeling may arise that both the constitutional bodies are being subjected to an agency which lacks constitutional backing. The integration of urban development plans into the states' Five-Year Plans, will be subjected to the discipline of state plans and like Union–state relations, planning is thus expected to take its toll of 'self-government' in state municipal relations also. Finally, there will be tension, conflicts and overlapping in the functions of these committees because the operational field of both will be the same.

The present liberalization and deregulation of economic policy of the government compels the municipal institutions to find out alternative resources for municipal development from market and for this purpose they should be creditworthy, otherwise markets will not finance their plans. But at present they are not creditworthy. Therefore, finances for their developmental functions/plans have to be met by grants from the states, which seem to be a difficult task in coming years.

The 74th Amendment did not provide a municipal tax list along with the functional list in the 12th Schedule, it only mentions about the state finance commission (common for municipalities and *panchayats*) to be constituted within a year of the commencement of the 73rd Amendment Act for *panchayats* (i.e. by 23 April 1994). The state finance commission is supposed to decide the principles, after reviewing the financial position of 'municipalities', on which the net proceeds of the taxes, duties, tolls and fees levied by state government will be shared, and allocated between state and municipalities. But the vagueness of 12th Schedule for municipal functional domain makes it difficult for SFC to suggest an appropriate municipal tax list. The composition of SFC has been left on the states. As a result many of these either consists of serving civil servants or politicians as their chairpersons (i.e. Rajasthan, Haryana). Thus, the very organization of SFC will have partisan considerations in their recommendations in place of independent ones. The recent trend of octroi abolition by states will put municipalities in financial difficulties and will lead to their dependence on states for getting their share in lieu of octroi tax. Thus, municipal finance will be a major cause of tensions between state governments and municipal institutions.

Municipal Functions

The 74th Amendment has not specified the functions of municipal bodies but the Amendment vaguely mentioned that the state by law may endow the municipalities with such powers and authority which is required to enable them to function as institutions of self-government and attached the 12th Schedule of 18 functional areas for devolution by the state governments. No time limit has been fixed for devolution of these functions listed in the 12th Schedule. Further, these functions do not correspond with the Union, state and concurrent list subjects mentioned in the Constitution, i.e., protection of environment at No. 8 in 12th Schedule, slum improvement at No. 10, urban poverty alleviation at No. 11 and promotion of cultural aspects at No. 13, etc. There are certain omissions also in the 12th Schedule functions concerning human development, e.g., basic health care facilities, while under the 73rd Amendment Act for *panchayat*s these functions have been suggested for devolution to rural *panchayat*s in the 11th Schedule. Although it has been left to the state governments to devolve more functions beyond those listed in the 12th Schedule, MPs area development scheme of the central government has also encroached upon the functions of 'municipalities'. It is imperative to examine and analyse what implications the allocation of functions like slum improvement and upgradation, urban poverty alleviation and town planning will have on state and district level machinery set up to perform the functions of centrally sponsored schemes like NRY and UBSP, JRY, slum boards and city improvement trusts/urban authorities.

Municipal Management and Personnel

The location of executive authority for municipal management is the most controversial issue. In municipal corporations, the executive powers are being exercised by the city council, the state-appointed municipal commissioner and the standing committee, but in West Bengal the executive is known as mayor-in-council and the executive powers are exercised by the council, the mayor-in-council and the mayor. The number of statutory authorities has been increased in some instances to give autonomy within the general framework of the corporations to the administration of specific public utility services, such as water supply and sewerage, transport and electricity, etc. The corporations of Delhi, Mumbai and a few others fall in this category.[4]

The municipalities in southern states Tamil Nadu, Andhra Pradesh, Kerala and Karnataka follow the corporation type of municipal executive model. It this model municipal powers have been fragmented in a number of authorities, such as the council, a standing committee, the chairman and the executive officer, who heads administration. In other states, the executive officer functions under the general guidance and direction of the municipal chairman, except in West Bengal and Assam where the municipal chairman is the designated executive and in all the municipal councils, the whole council and the statutory standing committees along with the designated executive exercise executive powers. In the newly created *nagar panchayat*s the situation is not clear, but it is likely to follow the pattern of municipal councils or in some states the chairman may emerge the sole executive authority as in the case of *panchayat*s in Rajasthan and West Bengal. The 74th Amendment ensures elective existence of the municipalities and the nature of political executive will be plural executive in both the municipal corporation and the municipal councils. The *nagar panchayat*s may develop a single political executive.

Municipal personnel system combines mostly three types: separate, unified and integrated personnel systems. The separate personnel system which was almost universal throughout India has gradually given way to unified or integrated cadres of municipal services controlled by the state governments except in Gujarat. The demand of municipal staff for better pay scales and security and services benefits, general inability of the municipalities to evolve progressive personnel policies and attract qualified staff and eagerness of state governments to extend the radius of state control are primarily responsible for the provincialization of municipal services. The unified or integrated cadres for key municipal personnel has been accepted by the municipalities, but the subordinate positions in the 'municipalities' are not covered by any centralized personnel system. The state governments have internalized their control over the municipal bodies by controlling the key officers of municipalities.

The municipal personnel would have to be made accountable to its political executive, and in the process municipal staffing arrangements have to be recast for accountability and better staff. For this purpose a separate municipal service commission for selection of municipal staff and for removal of their grievances would be imperative.

State and Municipal Governments

The 74th Amendment led to constitutionalization of 'municipal bodies' and provided a continuous organizational skeleton which cannot be dismantled and extinguished by the states as earlier. This has fundamentally changed the nature of state municipal relations. The punitive powers of state governments which included removal of elected members, rescinding municipal resolutions, issuing directions, approving budgets, deciding on expenditures and contracts, emergency and default powers of dissolution,[5] etc. have been scrapped or limited. But even now the role of state governments is of crucial importance in promoting healthy growth of the urban local bodies.

The state machinery for municipal supervision and control in almost all the states is located in the department of urban development. The municipal corporations are directly dealt with this department and other municipalities are supervised by its municipal directorate and the field administration at district and divisional levels in their areas. The officers of the directorate and field administration interface with the municipalities not through the minister-in-charge but directly. In future the municipal political executive would certainly dislike this practice.

For strengthening of local government one department of local government at state level for municipalities and *panchayats* would be more appropriate for the emergence of unified system of local government. Separate functional departments have assumed competing functional responsibilities for municipalities and *panchayats*, rather than promoting the cause of local self-government as a whole.

The 74th Amendment for control of municipal finance prescribes that the state governments would make rules for maintenance and audit of municipal accounts. This control in most of the states is exercised by the state examiner of local fund accounts and in all probability state governments will continue their past practice for municipal audit but it would be better if state governments introduce policy audit for municipal finances by an independent local audit commission on the lines of Britain.

People's Participation

In order to make municipal administration accountable, greater people's participation and resolution of competing local interests do not occur at the local level, as public interest would tilt towards more articulate and affluent sections of population. Public services would tend to be inequitably distributed and low access of urban basic services to low income areas would endanger public health and safety of the whole city. Keeping this in view, the 74th Amendment, through the creation of ward committees in the larger 'municipalities' having population of 3,00,000 or more, would provide opportunities for people's involvement and access in municipal services in their wards. Thus, citizen's participation in decision making in their neighbourhood services would certainly increase in coming years and lead to the greater degree of decentralization.

Future Trends

The past experience of fragmentation of municipal governments will continue to serve the ends of state-level politicians. The unclear functional span of municipalities and dependence on state government for devolution will not promote the cause of local self-government in spite of their constitutional existence. For finance, technical know-how, planning and intelligence the municipal bodies will have to lean towards the state governments and in this process a new concept of state municipal functional co-operation is expected to emerge which will take away the idea of local 'autonomy' or the new trend of privatization and economic liberalization may enter into municipal arena along with some environmental control machinery devices. The reform process at municipal level will be a continuous process and will include state municipal political bargaining. The French local government system of dual membership, i.e., membership of Parliament or council of state along with municipal leadership can be considered to strengthen and make municipal governments strong and which may require future constitutional amendments.

NOTES

1. Hoshiar Singh, 'Municipal Government and Administration: Need for Reforms and Restructuring', *Quarterly Journal of Local Self Government Institute*, Bombay, April–June, 1985: 107.
2. See, for details, Hoshiar Singh, *Aspects of Indian Administration*, (Jaipur: RBSA Publishers, 1994), Chapter 15, p. 181.
3. Abhijit Datt, 'Municipal Reform in India: Comparative Models and Processes' *Economic and Political Weekly*, 23 September 1995: 2396–97.
4. Mohit Bhattacharya, *Management of Urban Government in India* (New Delhi: Uppal Book Stores, 1976), p. 10.
5. See Hoshiar Singh, *State Supervision over Municipal Administration* (New Delhi: Associated Publishing House, 1979).

Administration for Welfare

India is a vast country inhabited by people of several religions and castes. In this country, caste is the basic institution of the social system. The concept of divine origin of the caste system has the authority of the holiest Hindu scriptures. *Rig veda* describes the creation of four *varnas*. *Taithiya Samhita* ascribes the origin of *chaturvarna* from the limbs of the creator and gives divine justification of their functions and status. In *Gita,* Lord Krishna says: 'the four-fold order was created by me, on the basis of quality and action.' Thus, 'all the Hindu *dharma shastras* take caste for granted. All *Puranas* assume the existence of caste and look upon it as a permanent order of society.'[1] Further, the *dharma shastras* mention that 'if a men does good deeds he will be born in a high caste and be well endowed, while if he does evil acts he will be born in a low caste, or even as an animal, a pig or a donkey.'[2] Thus, it is very clear that this section of our society has tolerated injustice since very long. But in independent India several welfare steps have been taken to develop this section of our society, so that they can also lead a respectable life in our country.

At the national level the systematic attempts for the welfare of 'depressed classes' was made by the Montague–Chelmsford Reforms in 1919 through separate representation on a number of public bodies to the members of these classes. The term 'depressed classes' at that time included 'scheduled castes', 'scheduled tribes' and 'other backward classes'. In the census of India, 1931, the term 'depressed classes' was changed to 'exterior castes' which covered only the untouchable castes. Aboriginal and hill tribes were enumerated under the term primitive tribes.'[3] Under the Government of India Act, 1935, the term scheduled caste was used in place of 'depressed class', and a separate list of scheduled castes were notified for various provinces in 1936, likewise the term 'primitive tribes' was replaced by 'backward tribes' and their lists notified in respect of provinces where there was substantial representation of these castes. It was only after Independence that the term 'scheduled tribes' was used for 'backward tribes' in the Constitution.[4]

The term, 'backward class' is difficult to define. Backwardness is expressed as lack of adequate opportunity for groups and individuals for self-development, especially in economic life and in matters of health, housing and education. It is measured in term of low levels of income, the extent of illiteracy and the low standard of life demonstrated by living conditions.[5] The backward classes constitute, three broad categories: (1) scheduled castes (SCs), (2) scheduled tribes (STs), other backward classes (OBCs).

Scheduled Castes

The concept of Scheduled Caste (SCs) is hardly half a century old. The SCs are those deprived castes as are listed in the Constitution so that they can get benefits from various provisions of the constitutional protection meant for them. According to Indian Independence Act, 1947, 'the "Scheduled Castes" means such castes, races or Tribes or parts or groups which appear to the Governor-General to correspond to the classes of persons formerly known as the "Depressed Classes" as the Governor-General may by order specify.' We do not find any definition of SCs and STs in the Constitution of India. However, the president draws up a list in consultation with the governor of each state. In this context, Article 341 empowers him to specify 'the castes, races, or tribes or part or groups within castes, races or tribes which shall for the purpose of the constitution be deemed to be Scheduled Castes.' This is the fact that the SCs are socio-economically most deprived sections of Indian society. Historically, our social structure is responsible for their pathetic conditions as in ancient India, Hindu society was divided into four *varna*s: The *Kshatriya*s as rulers and warriors; the *Brahmin*s as priest, the *Vaishya*s as traders and *Shudra*s or the low class SCs, STs and backward castes. They were subject to disabilities and humiliation and condemned to a life of degradation for centuries.[6] This system, in time gave prominence to the idea of purity of blood and division of labour among the castes. The *Shudra*s engaged in menial jobs like sweeping, scavenging and removal of dead animals and were relegated to the lowest status in the caste hierarchy. The performance of menial jobs made them untouchables—characterized by discrimination in social relations and occupational activities denied the opportunity for achieving the status of the higher castes. In this way, the social system resulted in deep-rooted oppression and discriminatory practices in social and economic relations against the SCs for centuries and they were deprived of a chance to share equally with the higher castes the opportunities for social and economic mobility.[7] Further, these *shudra*s were not given equal rights like other three castes. They were not allowed to live with other people of the so-called upper castes. They could not use public places. They could not even touch the people of upper castes. They were only to serve the upper castes. This discrimination was carried to such an extent that even the shadow of an untouchable was considered polluting to a caste Hindu.[8]

Scheduled Tribes

Tribes have been given different names such as *vanyajati*, *vanvasi*, *pahariya*, *adimjati*, *janjati* and *anusuchit janjati*, etc. The most popular term used is *anusuchit janjati*. The term 'Scheduled Tribes' (STs) as mentioned in Article 366(25) of the Constitution of India means 'such tribes or tribal communities or parts of or groups within such tribes or tribal communities as are deemed under the Article 342 to be scheduled tribes for the purpose of the Constitution'.

The Parliament has the right to amend such notification; it can add and delete the names of tribes from the list. For example, the president issued a notification in 1950 mentioning the names of STs and the Parliament amended it through Scheduled Castes and Scheduled Tribes Order (Amended) Act, 1956.

Tribes also have many categories such as Denotified Tribes which include such people who are not permanently settled at one place. They keep on moving from one place to another for their livelihood. The Criminal Tribes Act, 1924, which categorized about 137 groups of these tribes as diehard criminals, but this Act has been abolished after Independence on 31 August 1952 and arrangements have been made to educate, train and provide employment to these people.

OTHER BACKWARD CLASSES (OBCs)

The basic concept of the Constitution of India was to build up a polity in which there would be justice—social, economic and political for all sections of society. Any plan or programme for promoting social justice will require measures to check exploitation of the vulnerable sections of our population, improve the economic condition of the masses and to ensure equality of opportunity for development. The backward classes, the Constitution makers felt, require special treatment because they were socially, economically and educationally backward at the time of Independence. The backwardness of this section of the population was not based on their religious and ritual condition but on their socio-economic position. After Independence, the central government tried to define other backward classes in order to make special provisions for their advancement as Articles 15(4) and 16(4) refer to the making of such provisions for the advancement of socially and educationally backward classes. To achieve this objective, Article 340 of the Constitution empowers the state to investigate the conditions of backward classes and help them by providing grants. The Constitution has taken illiteracy, lack of education, poverty, exploitation, non-representation in service and untouchability as the criteria for backwardness. After making attempts at the national level through two backward classes commissions popularly known as Kaka Saheb Kalelkar Commission and Mandal Commission, the job of identification of backward classes has been assigned to the states.

The first backward classes commission, popularly known by the name of its chairman Kaka Saheb Kalelkar, formulated the following criteria for identifying socially and educationally backward classes:

(a) Low social position in the traditional caste hierarchy of Hindu society
(b) Lack of general educational advancement among the major section of a caste or community
(c) Inadequate or no representation in government service
(d) Inadequate representation in the field of trade, commerce and industry[9]

The second backward classes commission, headed by B. P. Mandal, gave 11 indicators for determining social and educational backwardness under three broad heads, i.e., social, educational and economic reasons.[10]

CONSTITUTIONAL PROVISIONS TO SAFEGUARD THE INTERESTS AND WELFARE OF THE SCs, STs AND OTHER BACKWARD CLASSES

Our Constitution makers were well aware of the problems of SCs and STs and other backward classes, therefore, they thought it proper to provide constitutional safeguards to these castes. As a result our Constitution contains provisions for this purpose, which are as follows:

Article 15 of the Constitution provides that 'the State shall not discriminate against any citizen on grounds only of religion, race, caste, sex, place of birth or any of them. Further, no citizen shall on these grounds be subject to any disability, liability or condition with regard to: access to shops, public restaurants, hotels and places of public entertainment; or the use of wells, tanks, bathing ghats, roads and places of public resort maintained wholly or partly out of state funds or dedicated to the use of general public. It also provides that nothing in this article or in Clause (2) of Article 29 shall prevent the State from making any special provision for the advancement of any socially and educationally backward classes or for the SCs and the STs.'

Article 17 says, 'Untouchability is abolished and its practice in any form is forbidden. The enforcement of any disability arising out of "untouchability" shall be an offence punishable in accordance with law.'

Under Article 16(4) the state can reserve any post or appointment in favour of any backward class of citizens who in the opinion of the state are not adequately represented in the services under it. Further,

Article 46 protects the educational and economic interests of weaker sections and the SCs and STs. It reads as: 'The state shall promote with special care all the educational and economic interests of the weaker sections of the people and in particular, of the SCs and the STs and shall protect them from social injustice and all forms of exploitation.' Article 29(2) provides that there shall be no discrimination in admission to any educational institution maintained by the state or state funds on the grounds of religion, race, caste, language or any of them. Provision for reservation of seats for the SCs and STs in the house of the people and the legislative assembly has been made in Articles 330, 332 and 334. Articles 164 and 338 and the Fifth Schedule make provision for the setting up of advisory councils and separate department in the states and appointing of a special officer at the centre to promote the welfare and safeguard the interests of the SCs and STs. Moreover, under Article 244 and the Fifth and Sixth Schedules, there is a special provision for the administration and control of the scheduled and tribal areas.

Untouchability

Untouchability being a corollary of the institution of caste system has given rise to several social disabilities and inequalities. It has thrown a big chunk of our population into the dark abyss of gloom and despair, shame and disgrace. Gandhiji expressed his views on this evil and pinpointed that 'untouchability as it is practised in Hinduism today, is in my opinion, a sin against God and man and is, therefore, like a poison slowly eating into the very vitals of Hinduism. In my opinion, it has no sanction whatsoever in the Hindu *Shastra*s as a whole. . . . It has degraded both the untouchables and touchables. It has stunted the growth of nearly 30 million human beings. They are denied even the ordinary amenities of life. The sooner, therefore, it is ended, the better for Hinduism, the better for India and perhaps the better for the mankind in general.'[11] Adequate safeguards against this social evil have been provided in the Constitution. This historic measure to abolish the age-old practice of untouchability was welcomed.[12] The Parliament under Article 35, enacted Untouchability (Offences) Act, 1955, which came into force from 1 June 1955. In 1976, this Act was amended and renamed as Protection of Civil Rights Act. It outlaws the enforcement of disabilities on the ground of untouchability, in regard to *inter alia* entrance to places of worship at temples, access to shops and restaurants, use of water sources, places of public resort and accommodation, public conveyance, hospitals, educational institutions, construction and occupation of residential premises, holding of religious ceremonies and processions, etc. For this offence, there is a provision of six months' imprisonment or fine up to Rs 500 or both. No doubt, legal measures are available but untouchability has not disappeared to a larger extent, particularly in the countryside. The commission for SCs and STs in its Twenty-seventh Report in 1979–1981 pointed out that the *Harijan Sevak Sangh* and other organizations have given detailed description about the prevalence of untouchability in various parts of the country. Unfortunately, the reports submitted earlier have not attracted sufficient attention of either the central or the state government concerned. But such surveys should not be allowed to remain on the shelf. They require that sustained efforts must be made by the state governments to ensure that the evil of untouchability is eliminated from the places indicated in the various survey reports.

Reservations

The Constitution of India does not provide any time limit for reservations. However, the reservation of seats in the Lok Sabha and state assemblies initially were for 10 years and subsequently, the time limit was extended. Under Articles 335 and 16(4) of the Constitution, reservation in services is permitted to SCs, STs and backward classes for not being adequately represented. For SCs, reservation is 15 percent of the vacancies for which recruitment is made by open competition on all-India basis and 16 times two-thirds per cent of the vacancies to which recruitment is made on all-India basis other than by open competition. For STs, the reservation is seven and a half percent in both cases. Reservation in direct recruitment to Groups C and D posts, which normally attract candidates from one locality or region, is fixed in proportion to the population of SCs and STs in the respective states/UTs.

'Reservation is also made at 15 per cent of the vacancies for SCs and seven and a half per cent of STs in promotions on the result of competitive examinations limited to departmental candidates in Groups B, C and D, in promotion by selection in Groups B, C and D and to the lowest rung of Group A in grades or services to which direct recruitment if any, does not exceed seven and a half per cent. Reservation has been provided for STs in promotion on the basis of seniority subject to fitness in Groups A, B, C and D posts in grades or services to which direct recruitment if any, does not exceed seven and a half per cent. '[13] The scheme of reservation is also in operation in the public sector undertakings. But there is no scheme of reservation in vast area of private sector industry and business. An overall assessment shows that in the working class, the lower castes are largely confined to the hard labour and 'menial' jobs and in Class III employees, clerical, staff, reservation have been partially implemented. Similar situation is in the case of skilled workers. As regards Classes I and II, the surface of upper caste domination has barely been scratched. Not only this, the situation is even worse in the professions.[14] Figures pertaining to filling up vacancies reserved for SCs and STs to Class I posts, viz., IAS, IFS and IPS show that during 1985–1988, more than 13 percent and 11 percent of the vacancies could not be filled up for SCs and STs, respectively. Even the reserved quotas for SCs and STs in Groups C and D of the services have not been fulfilled. The percentage of their representation in central government services and public sector undertakings has increased over the years as can be seen from Table 27.1 given as follows:

Table 27.1 *(A) Percentage of scheduled castes/scheduled tribes: Representation in central government services*

Category	Scheduled castes 1.1.1971	Scheduled castes 1.1.1991	Scheduled tribes 1.1.1971	Scheduled tribes 1.1.1991
Class I	2.68	9.09	0.41	2.53
Class II	4.06	11.82	0.43	2.35
Class III	9.59	15.65	1.70	4.98
Class IV	18.37 (excluding sweepers)	21.24	3.65	6.82

(B) Percentage of SC/ST representation in public sector undertakings

	1971	1989	1971	1989
Class I	0.52	5.76	0.17	1.29
Class II	1.54	8.41	0.16	2.31
All categories	8.17	20.36	2.24	9.68

Source: Eighth Five-Year Plan, Planning Commission, Government of India, New Delhi, 1992–1997, Vol. II, p. 419.

The table clearly shows that the representation of SCs/STs in government services is increasing every year but the number of unemployed is very large. At the end of 1990, there were 44.53 lakh SC and 11.48 lakh ST job seekers on the live register of employment exchanges.[15]

From the figures it is clear that various provisions of reservation and the government efforts to implement them have had some positive impact in relative terms, on the socio-economic development of SCs and STs, but it is very meagre in absolute terms. This being the reality while ignoring the social justification, so much hue and cry has been raised from time to time against the continuance of the policy of reservation.[16] Some of the critics are of the view that reservation is the factor causing inefficiency in the effective functioning of administration. But it is not true, as Justice Krishna Iyer in *A. B. S. K. Singh's* (Railway) case (*All India Reporter* 1981 Supreme Court) rightly observed, 'The preponderant majority coming from the unreserved communities are presumably efficient and the dilution of efficiency caused by the minimal induction of a small percentage of 'reserved' candidates, cannot affect the overall administrative efficiency significantly. Indeed, it will be gross exaggeration to visualize a collapse of the administration because 5 to 10 per cent of the total number of officials in the various classes happen to be sub-standard. Moreover, care has been taken to give in-service training and coaching to correct the deficiency.'

In the context of reservation leading to inefficiency, Justice Chinnappa Reddy in *Vasanth Kumar's* case (1985) said, 'There is neither statistical basis nor expert evidence to support the assumptions that efficiency will necessarily be impaired if reservation exceeds 50 percent, if reservation is carried forward or if reservation is extended to promotional posts.' A. Ramaiah had also aptly questioned the issue of inefficiency due to reservation. In his words, 'most officers involved in assisting the planners and policy makers in various ways and carrying out the programmes suggested by them fall in the category of Group A posts. If there is inefficiency it is the responsibility of the Group A category of officers who have control over B, C and D category employees. Of the total number of employees belonging to different castes employed in Group A posts, the SCs (8.23 per cent) and STs (2.07 per cent) together share only 8.62 per cent. Certainly, the 8.62 per cent of employees cannot be blamed for inefficiency. So it can be asked, what about the 91.38 per cent employees selected purely on merit?[17]

The Mandal Commission[18] had also noted that it is generally argued that looking to the large population of OBCs (52 percent), recruitment of a few thousand OBCs every year against reserved vacancies was not going to produce any perceptible impact on their general condition. On the other hand, the induction of a large proportion of employees against reserved vacancies will considerably impair the quality and efficiency of the government services. It is also stated that the benefit of such reservations will be skimmed off by those sections of OBCs who are already well off and the really backward sections will be left out. Another argument advanced against this approach is that the policy of large-scale reservations will cause great disappointment to those meritorious candidates whose entry into service will be barred as a result. However, the apprehensions regarding drop in the quality of government services owing to large-scale induction of SC/ST and OBC candidates against reserved posts may be justified only up to a point. The commission also questioned, whether it is possible to maintain that all candidates selected on merit turn out to be honest, efficient, hard working and dedicated? Highlighting this issue, the commission pointed out that, at present, top echelons of all the government services are manned predominantly by open competition candidates and if the performance of our bureaucracy is any indication, it has not exactly covered itself with glory. Of course, this does not imply that candidates selected against reserved posts will do better. Chances are that owing to their social handicaps, they may be generally less competent. But, they will have the great advantage of possessing first-hand knowledge of the sufferings and problems of the backward sections of society and this is not a small asset for field workers and policy makers.

As the SCs and STs comprise 22.5 per cent of the country's population, they were already enjoying 22.5 per cent reservation in all the services of Union and public undertakings, therefore, the commission has recommended 27 per cent reservation to the OBC population, which is about 52 per cent of the total population of our country. The commission proposed the overall scheme of reservation for OBCs as follows:

1. Candidates belonging to OBCs recruited on the basis of merit in an open competition should not be adjusted against their reservation quota of 27 per cent.
2. The above reservation should also be made applicable to promotion quota at all levels.
3. Reserved quota remaining unfilled should be carried forward for a period of three years and de-reserved thereafter.
4. Relaxation for the upper age limit for direct recruitment should be extended to the candidates of OBCs in the same manner as has been done in the case of SCs and STs.
5. A roster system for each category of posts should be adopted by the concerned in the same manner as is presently done in respect of SC and ST candidates.

This proposed scheme of reservation should be made applicable to all recruitments of public sector undertakings of union and states; government-aided undertakings; nationalized banks; and universities and affiliated colleges. The government has accepted Mandal Commission's recommendation concerning reservation.

Educational Development

The weaker sections of society have been given various kinds of preferences. First, they have been given special facilities for education. In the Seventh Five-Year Plan emphasis was laid on the educational development of SCs and STs. Pre-matric stipends and scholarships were given by the state governments to 190 lakh SC/ST students/backward class students. Even the central government gives national overseas scholarships to SC and ST students. Other educational incentives included free supply of uniforms, stationery and text books to about 100 lakh students. Post-matric scholarships were given to about 15 lakh students of these castes in 1991–1992. The book bank facility benefited about 21,000 students of SC/ST studying in medical and engineering colleges. Hostel facilities for the students of these castes have been considerably expanded.[19] In technical educational institutions, seats are reserved for SC/ST students. To prepare them for civil services coaching facilities have been created for them in 103 pre-examination training centres throughout the country. The coaching facilities and reservation both have increased their representation in central government as well as state government services.

The state governments have also launched many schemes to improve the educational standards of SCs. Most of the schemes at pre-matric stage are with the respective state governments. These schemes are pre-matric scholarships, boarding grants, hostel facilities, free supply of books, stationery and uniforms, mid-day meals and attendance scholarships etc. These schemes vary from state to state.

Economic Development

Economic backwardness of SC and ST has been given special preference by the government. For their economic development, two national level institutions were set up. These are: (i) Tribal Cooperative Marketing Development Federation in 1987 as an apex body for state tribal development cooperative corporations; and (ii) National Scheduled Castes and Scheduled Tribes Finance and Development Corporation primarily to act as a catalytic agent in developing schemes. To deal with this problem a new strategy of special component plan was adopted in the Sixth Five-Year Plan. This strategy was a combination of these important instruments, namely (i) The special component plans (SCP) of the states and central ministries; (ii) The special central assistance to special component plans of states; and (iii) scheduled castes development corporations (SCDCs). Besides these there are centrally sponsored schemes being implemented by the ministry of welfare. The special component plan is designed to channel the flow of benefits and outlays from the general sectors in the plans of states and central ministries for development of SCs, both in physical and financial terms. It aims at identification of schemes in the general sector of development which would be of benefit and SCs, quantification of funds from all devisable programmes under each sector and determination of specific targets in terms of number of families which were to be benefited from those programmes under each sector besides ensuring adequate flow of benefits from other sectors/programmes for SCs. These plans were envisaged to help the poor SC families belonging to all major occupational groups among them such as agricultural labour, small and marginal farmers and share-croppers.[20] For employment generation and financing pilot projects, the scheduled castes and scheduled tribes development corporation in the states continue to provide economic assistance for self-employment projects such as leather works and other subsidiary occupations like dairy farming, piggery and sheep rearing. Economic assistance was given to 118.82 lakh SC families and 52.26 lakh ST families under various programmes including the IRDP. Margin money loan was disbursed to 22.56 lakh SC families through 21 state SC development corporations.[21]

At present the most important antipoverty programme, the integrated rural development programme (IRDP), has accorded special consideration for SC and ST families. The target of coverage of SC/ST beneficiaries in the Seventh Plan was 30 per cent of the total number of beneficiaries. However, the actual coverage was 32.05 per cent in the case of SCs and 13.04 per cent in the case of ST beneficiaries; both SC and ST beneficiaries are getting 50 per cent subsidy subject to the ceiling of Rs 5,000 per SC and ST families, and freed bonded labourers are given preference under the *Jawahar Rozgar Yojana*, at the village level. Fifteen per cent of the annual allocation is expected to be spent on items of works which directly benefit SCs/STs. Diversion of funds meant for SCs and STs is not permitted.[22] Further, for the development of SC and ST, special central assistance was given to states under special component plans envisage identification of schemes under general sector of development which would be of benefit to the SCs, quantification of funds from all divisible programmes under each sector and determination of specific targets as to the number of families which are to be benefited from these programmes under each sector. The overall objective is to assist the SC families to substantively improve their income. Provision of basic services and facilities and access to opportunities for social and educational development are also to be brought into special component plans. These plan outlays are shown in Table 27.2.

Table 27.2 shows that the amount increased constantly from 1979–1980 to 1990–1991 although the percentage decreased slightly during 1982–1983 to 1987–1988. The Union government also directed the state governments to take corresponding measures including allocation of funds, setting up separate departments, passing necessary laws and formulating plans at their level from time to time for the welfare and uplift of the SCs, STs and backward classes and also to give due attention and importance to the reports and recommendations of the commissioner for SCs and STs. The ultimate responsibility of ensuring the implementation of policies and direction naturally lay with the Union and the state executives.

In spite of extensive development efforts, a very large number of SCs and STs continue to be socially and educationally backward and are languishing at the bottom of the social and economic pyramid. In rural areas, in 1987–88,ST population 52.6 as compared to the all-India percentage 33.4,[23] while in 1983–1984 all-India figure was 40.4 per cent, SC 53.1 per cent and ST 58.4 per cent, likewise in the year 1977–1978, all-India percentage was 51.2, SC 64.6 and ST 72.4 per cent. This proves that there has been reduction in the percentage of population below the poverty line in case of both SCs and STs, but the incidence of poverty is still very high. The reasons for their backwardness are many, important among them are that

Table 27.2 *Special component plan outlays*

Year	*State plan outlay Rs in crores*	*Special component programme out-lay Rs in crores*	*Percentage*	*Special component assistance*
1979–1980	5967.03	240.54	4.03	50
1980–1981	7140.31	547.84	7.67	100
1981–1982	8229.31	632.76	7.69	110
1982–1983	9445.49	675.76	7.15	120
1983–1984	11120.80	754.86	6.79	130
1984–1985	12504.38	924.15	7.39	140
1985–1986	13303.56	1001.03	7.52	165
1986–1987	16222.53	1201.62	7.41	175
1987–1988	19039.84	1450.24	7.62	175
1988–1989	20412.50	1644.56	8.19	180
1989–1990	22343.90	2066.01	9.19	180
1990–1991	—	2245.50	—	—

Source: India 1991 (New Delhi: Publications Division, Ministry of Information and Broadcasting, February 1992), pp. 261–62.

most of the SC and ST families do not own land or other productive assets. They constitute bulk of agricultural landless workers, construction workers and workers in the unorganized sector. They suffer from long periods of unemployment and under-employment. They are also handicapped due to non-enforcement of productive laws such as the Minimum Wages Act and Prevention of Land Alienation Acts. Inequality and exploitation of SCs and STs, particularly in rural areas whether in the form of bonded labour or in other forms, both latent and manifest still continue. Poverty, ignorance, lack of options in employment opportunities and non-existence of organizations which can fight for their rights, facilitate the continuance of age-old exploitation. SCs and STs families have often not been able to derive the full benefit of development programmes. Wrong identification of beneficiaries, poor selection of projects, unrealistic and simplistic assumptions in regard to their viability, administrative costs and leakages have been other problems which have been further compounded by a largely unresponsive administrative structure.[24]

Administrative Set Up for the Development of SCs and STs and Backward Classes at the Central Level

The administrative set-up for the development of SC and ST and backward classes is not well knit at the central level. There is no single agency responsible for the development of these classes. Therefore, at the central and state levels, there are many organizations which are performing these functions. At central level two posts of secretaries have been created in the cabinet secretariat to look after development of SCs and STs. The ministry of home affairs, education ministry and two commissioners, one for SCs and other for STs, are mainly responsible for their development. At the state level, social welfare departments and their directorates deal with the development of these castes. At the district, tehsil/block level government officers are engaged in the welfare and development activities for these sections of the society.

At the central level, a ministry of welfare was created in 1985, and the development functions of SCs and STs performed by the home ministry and other ministries were transferred to this ministry. Now the ministry of welfare is the nodal ministry for the overall policy planning and coordination of special programmes for the development of SCs, STs and other backward classes.

Institutional Arrangements for SCs, STs Development: Commissioner for SCs and STs : The President of India has been empowered by Article 338 of the Constitution to appoint a special officer to look after the interest of SCs and STs. The president appointed a commissioner for SCs and STs. In 1951, for the first time and since then, several important officers have held this post. The major functions of the commissioner for SCs and STs were to investigate all matters relating to the safeguards provided for the SCs and STs under the Constitution. He submits his report to the president who places the report before each house of Parliament. In 1978, the Government of India by a resolution constituted a commission for SCs and STs. In September 1987, the National Commission for Scheduled Castes and Scheduled Tribes was constituted with a chairman and four members in place of the commission for SCs and STs. In 1990, by a Constitutional Amendment (65th Act) Act, the powers of the National Commission for SCs and STs were enhanced and functions of the commissioner for SCs and STs were given to this commission. Therefore, the office of the commissioner for SCs and STs ceased to function from 12 March 1992. At the central level the national SCs and STs finance and development corporation was created in 1989 to support the state SC's development corporations (NSFDCs). Its broad role is to take up supportive activities with the state SC's development corporations by mobilizing enough resources associating the national level organizations including banks and international bodies. This corporation is expected to play the role of a catalyst, promoter and guarantor. The corporation has been planning to get suitable projects prepared[25] for the benefits of SCs and STs. In addition, the federation would organize training courses to provide skills. At the state level, the SCs development corporations and the tribal finance development corporations were established from 1978 onwards in addition to tribal development corporations (TDC), which were already working since long in the states where there was tribal population.

Parliamentary Committee for the Welfare of SCs, STs and Backward Classes

A parliamentary committee for the welfare of SCs and STs was constituted in 1968. The committee become a standing committee having a term of one year as a consequence of the incorporation of the rules regarding its constitution and functions in the Rules of Procedure and Conduct of Business in Lok Sabha in December 1973. The committee looks after the safeguards for SCs and STs and ensures the implementation of recommendations made by the commissioners/commission in his reports. The committee comprises 30 members in all, 20 from the Lok Sabha and 10 from Rajya Sabha.

To sum up, SCs and STs are downtrodden people of our society. They suffer from economic exploitation and are the worst victims of social discrimination. In spite of development efforts during the last four decades, SCs and STs need a great boost to emancipate their socio-economic life. Herculean efforts by state and central governments are required to enable the SCs and STs to cross the poverty line. To achieve this objective, besides governmental efforts, motivation and orientation of these groups to lead a honourable life is also essential. Concentrated efforts by administration through adequate and efficient administrative machinery will help the SCs and STs to enhance economic and social status in society.

Women Welfare Programmes

Census 1991 figures show that the number of women in India was 407.1 million (406,332,932) or 48.14 per cent of the total population of the country while the male population was 437,597,929. The sex ratio per 1,000 men was 929 women. The literacy ratio for women in 1991 was 39.42 percent compared to 63.86 per cent of men and 52.11 per cent for the nation as a whole. The above figures show that the women in all spheres, social, economic or political enjoy an inferior status than men. But no special attention was given for their development, perhaps in the hope that general development programmes would benefit the women also.

The principle of gender equality has been basic to Indian thinking for over a century. It was fully realized that the progress of the nation was integrally linked with the status of women and for that the advancement of women was placed at the centre-stage of Indian planning and polity. In the 1970s, there was a shift in paradigm from viewing women as targets of welfare policies in the social sector to regarding them as critical groups for development. The Sixth Five-Year Plan (1980–1985), realizing the problems of 'women's development', advocated a multi-pronged strategy for holistic women's development with interventions in the sectors of (a) employment and economic independence; (b) education; (c) access to health care and family planning; (d) support services to meet the immediate gender needs of women; (e) the creation of enabling policy, institutional and legal environment.[26]

The Seventh Five-Year Plan continued the efforts. A core group of the department of women and child development has prepared a national perspective plan for women for the period 1988–2000. It aims at outlining a long-term overall policy for Indian women, guided by principles and directives relevant to the development process. It is linked to the national targets determined concerning health, education and employment. In the Eighth Five-Year Plan special emphasis has been given on employment and income-generation activities for women. The objective of all these efforts is to make women economically independent and self-reliant. But the most vital question is the creation of a proper administrative framework for the purpose. We propose to study in this chapter, the administrative machinery and various development programmes for women.

Administrative Machinery at the Central Level

At the central level the programmes of women welfare are looked after by the ministry of human resource development. The department of women and child development was set up in the year 1985 to give the required impetus to the holistic development of women and children. The activities of the department are performed by the following bureaus, each headed by a joint secretary.

(i) Bureau of Nutrition and Child Development (NCD)

(ii) Bureau of Women's Welfare and Development (WWD)

(iii) Bureau for women's programmes of *Mahila Samriddhi Yojana*, *Indira Mahila Yojana* and *Rashtriya Mahila Kosh*[27]

The department has three organizations, viz., National Institute of Public Cooperation and Child Development (NIPCCD), *Rashtriya Mahila Kosh* (RMK) and the Central Social Welfare Board (CSWB). The first two, NIPCCD and RMK, are societies registered under the Societies Registration Act, 1860, while CSWB is a charitable company registered under the Indian Companies Act, 1956. These organizations are funded by the Government of India, and they assist the department in its functions including implementation of some programmes/schemes. The last organization deals with the women's development programmes, therefore, we are discussing them in this chapter.

The secretary is in charge of the department of women and child development. There are three joint secretaries who look after the bureaus and one financial advisor. They are assisted by directors/deputy secretaries and under-secretaries besides the office staff.

The department formulates plans, policies and programmes, enacts or amends legislation and guides and coordinates the efforts of both governmental organizations working in the field of women and child development. The department implements certain innovative programmes in the areas of welfare and support services, employment and income generation, awareness generation and gender sensitization for women in particular. All these efforts are directed to ensure that women are empowered both economically and socially and thus become equal partners in national development along with the men.

Central Social Welfare Board

In addition to the department, there is a Central Social Welfare Board (CSWB) set up by the government in 1953, with the object of promoting social welfare activities and implementing welfare programmes for women, children and the handicapped through voluntary organization. It has a 'general body' which comprises all chairpersons of state and Union territories boards, five professionals, one each from the field of law, medicine, nutrition, social work, education and social development, three eminent persons with extensive experience in social work, one representative each of ministries of welfare, rural development, health, education, labour, finance and the planning commission, two MPs of Lok Sabha and one of Rajya Sabha, chairman of the board and executive director of the board as member secretary all nominated by the minister of welfare.

The administration of the board is carried out by the executive committee which comprises 15 members including the chairman and the executive director. The chairman of the board is its chief executive. The executive director works under him. He is responsible for all aspects of the working of the board and performs numerous functions. Some of them relating to women's development are: awareness generation among rural and poor women, condensed courses of education for adult women, vocational courses and socio-economic programmes. General grants-in-aid programme, hostels for working women, welfare extension projects, *mahila mandals*, voluntary action bureaus and family counselling centres, creches for working and ailing mothers, etc., are arranged by the board.

Administrative Set Up at the State Level

Generally in states, the department of social welfare looks after the women development programmes. The secretary of the social welfare in addition to his other welfare functions also looks after the welfare of women. In a combined department the work of women welfare is handled by a deputy secretary or a special secretary.

Directorate

At the directorate level, work is looked after by the director of social welfare who is director of social welfare programmes in general. Only two states—Andhra Pradesh and Tamil Nadu—have separate departments for women and child welfare. In other states the work of women welfare is looked after by the functionaries of the department of social welfare. Although states like Punjab, Haryana, Rajasthan and MP, etc. have set up separate directorates of women and child welfare, but these are not adequately staffed.

The major programmes and schemes for the welfare and development of women are as follows.

Social Legislation

The Constitution of India grants equality to women with men and also empowers the state to adopt measures of positive discrimination in favour of women for neutralizing the cumulative socio-economic, educational and political disadvantages faced by them. Article 14 of the Constitution confers equal rights and opportunities on men and women in the political, economic and social spheres. Article 15 prohibits discrimination on the grounds of religion, race, caste, sex, etc. and enables the state to allow affirmative discrimination in favour of women. Article 16 guarantees equality of opportunity in public employment. The state also imposes a fundamental duty on every citizen to renounce practices derogatory to the dignity of women.

To uphold the constitutional provisions, the state has enacted various laws to ensure equal rights, to counter social discrimination and various forms of violence and atrocities and to provide support services especially to working women. Although all laws are not gender-specific, the major provisions affect women significantly. These include the following:

(i) The Hindu Marriage Act, 1955; (ii) the Hindu Succession Act, 1956; (iii) the Hindu Adoption and Maintenance Act, 1956; (iv) the Maternity Benefits Act, 1961; (v) the Dowry Prohibition Act, 1961; (vi) the Medical Termination of Pregnancy Act, 1971; (vii) the Equal Remuneration Act, 1976; (viii) the Child Marriage Restraint (Amendment) Act, 1976; (ix) the Immoral Traffic (Prevention) Act, 1986; (x) Indecent Representation of Women (Prohibition) Act, 1986; (xi) the Commission of '*Sati*' (Prevention) Act, 1987; (xii) National Commission for Women Act, 1992; (xiii) the Prenatal Diagnostic Techniques (Regulation of Prevention and Misuse) Act, 1994. The new laws concerning the rape of minor girls, compulsory registration of marriages and domestic violence against women have been proposed by the department to cover loopholes. The other laws which have protected and given equality to women are: The Factories Act, 1948; Mines Act, 1952; Plantation Labour Act, 1951; the Employees State Insurance Act, 1948; Factories (Amendment) Act, 1976; Contract Labour (Regulation and Abolition) Act, 1978, etc. The 73rd and 74th Constitutional (Amendment) Act dealing with *panchayti raj* and urban local bodies, respectively, have provided one third reservation of seats in these elected bodies for women. A bill is pending to give one-third reservation to women for representation in Parliament and state legislatures. All these legislative measures effectively affirm and promote the principles of equity and equality of women and to take care of their special needs.

The programmes of the department for the development of women include those of employment and income generation; welfare and support services and gender sensitization and awareness generation programmes.

Major Women Welfare Programmes

The major development programmes for the development and social welfare of women are the following:

(i) Assistance given to NGOs/voluntary agencies and local bodies for construction of working women's hostels for working women with children up to eight years of age

(ii) A scheme for the rehabilitation of women in distress and other children through training and employment programme so that these women could become economically independent

(iii) A scheme for integrated child development services (ICDS) for providing a package of nutritional health and pre-school services to children below six years of age and expectant mothers

(iv) A scheme of financing literacy for adults for providing non-formal education within the format of ICDS

(v) A scheme of short stay homes for women and children who are in social and moral danger

(vi) A scheme for crèches for children of working women. The popular programmes in most of the states are as follows:

(a) Working women's hostels
(b) Homes for destitutes
(c) Providing funds to NGOs for promoting women's welfare

(vii) *Mahila Samriddhi Yojana* was launched on 2 October 1993. Under this scheme, rural adult women are encouraged to open MSY accounts in post offices into which they may deposit whatever amount of money they can save. For an amount of up to Rs 300 with a one year lock-in-period, the government contributes an incentive of 25 percent, i.e. Rs 75. The account holder can withdraw money from the account twice in a year.

(viii) *Indira Mahila Yojana* (IMY). This scheme was launched on 20 August 1995 in 200 blocks throughout the country. The IMY has three basic constituents namely: convergence of inter-sectoral services; income generation activities; and a sustained process of awareness generation/education.

In this scheme women groups would be organized under *Indira Mahila Kendra*s (IMK) to be set up at village/*anganwadi* levels in the blocks comprising 100 to 250 members in every IMK. A block will consist 120 *anganwadi*s, each *Indira Mahila block Samiti* (IMBS) at block level will thus cover 12,000 to 30,000 women. The Government of India provides funds at the rate of Rs 5,000 per IMK as a one-time grant.

Thus, earnest efforts are being made for the development of women. The following three institutions: women's development corporations, national commission for women and *Rashtriya Mahila Kosh* need detailed mention here.

Women's Development Corporations

The women's development corporations established by states are playing important role in the development of women. The central government provides 49 percent of the share capital of the corporation while the remaining 51 percent is contributed by the state government. The functions of the corporations include identification of potential areas of employment, assistance for project formulation and raising required finances, identification of women entrepreneurs, encouragement of entrepreneurial talent among them, arrangement of raw material for working women and providing training facilities and infrastructure for marketing the products.

The corporations provide loans at highly subsidized rates of interest to promote entrepreneurship among women. They arrange loans from banks and allow the benefit of interest subsidy.

National Commission for Women

The report of the committee on the status of women in India (1974) recommended the establishment of a commission at the centre. The Janata Dal government passed the National Commission for Women Act on 30 August 1990. However, it became effective from 31 January 1992 by a notification published in the *Gazette* the same day. The composition of the commission as per the Act provides for a chairperson committed to the cause of women and five members nominated by the government from amongst social scientists, experts in legislation, trade union movement, industrial management, administration, socio-economic development, etc., and a member secretary. The commission has been strengthened by setting up a counselling cell which provides family counselling services as well as legal guidance to aggrieved women who approach the commission. The commission has five members and one chairperson. Its first chairperson was Mrs Mohini Giri, the widow of former President of India, V. V. Giri. The term of office of the chairperson and members of the commission is three years. The members, including the chairperson, were nominated by the government for three years on 21 July 1995.

Functions of the Commission

The functions of the National Commission for Women are mainly as follows:

(i) To investigate and examine the legal safeguards provided for women under the Constitution and other laws and to recommend measures to the government for their effective implementation

(ii) To review the existing provisions of the Constitution and other laws affecting women and recommend amendments to meet any lacuna, inadequacy or shortcoming in these laws

(iii) To look into complaints and to take *suo motu* notice of matters relating to deprivation of women's rights and take up the issues with appropriate authorities

(iv) To take up studies/research, etc. on socio-economic issues

(v) To participate and advise on the planning process of socio-economic development of women and evaluate the progress made

(vi) To inspect jails, remand homes, etc., where women are kept under custody and seek remedial action wherever necessary

(vii) To find litigation involving issues affecting a large body of women

(viii) To send to the central government annually and at such other times as the commission may deem fit report on the making of safeguards for women

(ix) To make periodical reports to the government on any matter pertaining to women

(x) Any other matter that may be referred to the commission by the central government

Procedure of Working

In cases of violation of safeguards and complaints relating to women's rights, the commission has the power of a civil court trying a suit. The commission can summon any person and examine the person on oath. It can requisition documents and receive evidence on affidavits. It is obligatory on the part of the central government as per Section 16 of the Act to consult the commission on all major policy matters affecting women.

To assist the commission in performing his functions, a number of expert committees have been set up to advise on various subjects dealt by the commission. These committees were on the issues of social security, prostitution, environment, *panchayti raj*, women development, women and media, tribal women, custodial justice for women and problems of SC women.

The report submitted by the commission to the central government is placed before each house of Parliament by the government along with a memorandum of action taken on the recommendations and the reasons for non-acceptance, if any.

Evaluation

Several women's organizations have pointed out that the Act is not comprehensive and the commission has been given large number of functions without commensurate powers to perform them. Some women's organizations want that the commission should be given constitutional status and its recommendations should be mandatory, while some others want that it should function on a decentralized basis. A commission at the national level is hardly accessible to the common women. As a result eight states have formed such state commissions during 1995. These states are Maharashtra, Tripura, West Bengal, Orissa, Assam, Tamil Nadu, Punjab and Delhi.[28]

The commission is successfully doing its work. During the year 1995, the commission received 318 complaints regarding various kinds of injustice and atrocities suffered by women and more than 167 cases suitably disposed of. The commission members visited jails in Bihar and Gujarat where women were kept in detention, the commission also held meetings with police officers including those working in crimes against women cell and held meetings with experts, NGOs and women activists in different fields of women development to identify priority areas for their development. The commission's chairperson attended the Fourth World Conference on Women at Beijing from 4 to 15 September 1995. The other members and secretary of the commission also participated in seminars concerning gender issues and women's welfare and development. Thus, it is obvious that the commission is performing its functions dutifully.

Rashtriya Mahila Kosh

The *Rashtriya Mahila Kosh* (RMK), a national credit fund for women was set up in March 1993. It aims to provide a resource base to reach credit to poor women. It delivers credit to the beneficiaries through non-governmental organizations, women development corporations, cooperative societies, etc.

The RMK has a governing board of 16 members including the chairperson for its management. The minister/state minister for women and child development is the ex-officio chairman, secretaries to the Government of India of seven related departments as ex-officio members and seven members selected for their significant service to society from various fields of social development. The executive director, responsible for the day-to-day administration is also a member of the board.

The RMK was established with an initial fund of Rs 31 crore and by the end of March 1996, the funds had increased to Rs 43 crore. It has sanctioned loans to the tune of Rs 18.13 crore to 99,627 women through 103 NGOs. Short-term loans repayable in six to 15 months are limited to Rs 2,500 per borrower and medium-term loans repayable in three to five years are limited to Rs 5,000.

Thus, it is a good step in right direction for the development of women, but the loan amount is meagre and hardly any worthwhile self-employment work can be started with such a low amount. It should not be less than Rs 20,000.

NOTES

1. K. M. Pannikar, *Hindu Society at Cross-roads* (Bombay: Asia Publishing House, 1971).
2. M. N. Srinivas, *Caste in Modern India* (Bombay: Asia Publishing House, 1964).
3. *Report of the Backward Classes Commission* (New Delhi: Government of India, 1980), First Para, Vol. 1, p. 5.
4. Ibid.
5. *First Five Year Plan* (New Delhi: Planning Commission, Government of India ,) p. 634.
6. S. K. Ghosh, *Protection of Minorities* and SC*s* (New Delhi: Ashish Publishing House, 1986), p. 1.

7. Ratna Murdia, 'Issues in Positive Discrimination Policies for Disadvantaged Groups,' *Indian Journal of Social Work*, Vol. XLIII, No. 4, January 1983: 432.
8. Vagiswari Alladi, *Income-Earning Trend* and *Social Status of the Harijan Community in Tamil Nadu* (Madras: Sangam Publishers, 1972), p. 1.
9. *Report of the Backward Class Commission* (New Delhi: Government of India, 1980), First Part, Vol. 1, p. 1.
10. See, for details, *Report of Backward Classes Commission* (New Delhi: Government of India, 1980), First Part, Vol. 1, p. 52.
11. *The Harijan*, 2 February 1993.
12. *Constituent Assembly Debates*, Vol. VIII, p. 665.
13. See *India 1990* (New Delhi: Government of India, Publications Division, Ministry of Information and Broadcasting) pp. 236–37.
14. D. N., 'Reservation and Class Structure of Castes,' *Economic* and *Political Weekly*, Vol. XXV, No. 2, 13 January 1990: 83.
15. *Eighth Five Year Plan* (New Delhi: Government of India, Planning Commission, 1992–1997), Vol. II, p. 421.
16. A. Ramaiah, 'Reserved, but Restricted.' *Mainstream*, 20 January 1990, p. 15.
17. Ibid.
18. See, Report of the Backward Classes Commission, op. cit., p. 57.
19. *Eighth Five Year Plan, 1992–1997* (New Delhi: Government of India, Planning Commission) Vol. II, p. 418.
20. *Report of the Working Group on Development* and *Welfare of* SC*s during Eighth Five Year Plan* (New Delhi: Ministry of Welfare, Government of India, 1990–1995), p. 4.
21. *Eighth Five Year Plan* (New Delhi: Planning Commission, Government of India, 1992–1997), Vol. II, p. 418.
22. Ibid.
23. Ibid., p. 419.
24. Ibid., p. 420.
25. *Report of the Working Group on Development* and *Welfare of* SC*s During Eighth Five Year Plan, 1990–1995* (New Delhi: Ministry of Welfare, Government of India, August 1990), p. 30.
26. *Annual Report Part IV*, Department of Women and Child Development, Ministry of Human Resource Development (New Delhi: Government of India, 1995–1996), p. 48.
27. Ibid., p. 8.
28. Ibid., p. 94.

28

Issues in Indian Administration

Political and Permanent Executive

India opted for parliamentary democracy after Independence on the lines of the British parliamentary system. In parliamentary democracy, the relationship between political and permanent executive is very important and crucial for its smooth working. Therefore, it is essential to know the pattern of relationship between political and permanent executive emerging in our democratic working. In this chapter, this relationship will be discussed mainly under three heads namely, (i) relation between the minister and the secretary, (ii) political interference in administration, and (iii) neutrality of the civil service.

The Relationship Between Minister and Secretary

It is the duty of the secretary to introduce the minister to the department's senior officials on the first day when he assumes charge of the ministry/department. The secretary briefs the minister about the working of the department, gives a detailed account of all offices under the ministry. It is the responsibility of a civil servant to ensure that the lawful orders of political executive are carried out and properly followed. The functions of the secretary are not only confined to the policy execution but also to policy formulation. As no watertight compartmentalization is possible between policy and administration, in such a situation, the relations between minister and civil servants becomes more complex in practice. It demands that civil servants shall do their work without personal public blame or praise for policy and that they shall act with impartial, but enterprising and unrelated helpfulness to governments of any party or complexion. This demand involves certain rules and standards of conduct to be obeyed by both ministers and civil servants.[1] However, whenever there are some policy matters, both discuss and on the basis of their discussion, a note incorporating the decision taken is prepared by the secretary. This is put before the minister. If it is approved by him the decision is final. It is an important point to note here that the secretary, keeping in mind the overall policy of the department, interprets the mind and thinking of his political boss and then carries out the work of administration. So far as delegation of authority to the secretary by the minister is concerned, its extent depends on his rapport and personal equation with the minister. Hence, personal equation plays a significant role in determining their relationship. Moreover, if they work with cooperation and harmony, the administration can work efficiently and smoothly.

As the relationship between the minister and the secretary is one of mutual confidence and trust, therefore, the former is expected to provide the overall leadership and direction. A. D. Gorwala, in his report on administrative reforms, discussed the relationship between the minister and the secretary. He pointed out that the secretary should not be an amicable yes-man to carry out the whims of the minister but should be able to provide free and frank advice on policy formulation based on an objective examination of the administrative issues involved. The secretary and his senior officers have a right to express their views fully and frankly. If the minister interferes in the day-to-day work like deciding the appointment of juniors, etc., he may be encroaching on the legitimate work of the secretary and his subordinates and may not find enough time and energy to concentrate on his essential work as minister, namely, enunciation of objectives, establishment of priorities and policy formulations. This is the main work of every minister and this should be properly performed. Further, A. D. Gorwala remarked: 'The relationship between the ministers and the officials of whatever rank and between officials of various ranks is not that of master and servant but rather that of junior colleagues engaged on the same beneficial tasks.'

The political executive must acquire a deep understanding and knowledge of the subject placed under his charge. In the words of V. N. Gadgil: 'Vallabhbhai (i.e., Sardar Patel) was watchful regarding the state of affairs in the government. He used to invite the secretaries of the various departments to tea or dinner almost every week by turns, listen to their problems and difficulties, and advise and guide them. The civil servants were greatly encouraged by this and worked with greater self-confidence. The cabinet had introduced the innovation of referring difficult problems to committees of secretaries of the ministries. This too has encouraged the civil servants who considered the problem with enthusiasm and offered their suggestions. This innovation was entirely by Vallabhbhai Patel.'[2]

Friction and Conflict

Soon after Independence, the ministers had to face problems as the civil servants particularly at the higher rungs wanted to manage the governmental affairs according to their own guidelines and directives. Even the prime minister faced difficulties in checking this trend and getting his policies implemented.[3] There is no denying the fact that the ICS officers tried to continue independent outlook in the beginning but gradually they found it advantageous to change their attitude and a majority of them began to give reports and notes on files as their ministers would have wanted them to do.

Some Episodes

After Independence, the conflict in the relationship between the minister and the civil servant came to public knowledge first in 1957, when funds amounting to more than rupees one crore of the Life Insurance Corporation were invested in a private enterprise. In this case, T. T. Krishnamachari, the then finance minister levelled changes against H. M. Patel, the then principal finance secretary that he had 'casually' mentioned to him about the purchase of the shares of a private concern. On the other hand, H. M. Patel maintained that he had been acting all along with the knowledge and approval of the minister. Thus, both blamed each other. The government appointed the Vivian Bose Board of Inquiry to examine the mode of consultation with the minister. The board observed: 'all we can say is that if that is Mr Patel's way of briefing his minister on a grave issue that requires a high level decision of policy, he is very much to blame; and from the minister's point of view, we cannot blame him if he thought, as he says he did that this was just casual information about the Life Insurance Corporation which did not require any decision from him.' This rift ended when the minister resigned on the grounds of constitutional responsibility and the secretary preferred retirement from the government service.

Another episode took place during the anti-cow slaughter demonstration by Bharat Sadhus Samaj in New Delhi in 1966, when Gulzari Lal Nanda, the then home minister, complained about non-cooperation on the part of L. P. Singh, the then home secretary and wanted his replacement. In his resignation letter submitted to the prime minister, he charged that his senior civil servants were not cooperating with him in the proper implementation of policies. In his resignation he wrote to the prime minister that 'on a number of occasions I brought to your notice that I was not getting adequate secretarial assistance. I wanted the set up to be suitably strengthened. All these appeals were ignored. Devoid of adequate political support at the level of my ministry, and denied the kind of assistance and cooperation I needed from a civil service set-up not in tune with my ideas I was made to feel that I had no say in the making of decisions at policy making level.'[4] The home secretary was retained by the prime minister and it was the minister who had to resign.

The third incident which was interesting took place in 1971 when the then Railway minister, K. Hanumanthaiya, did not appreciate certain steps taken for streamlining of railway administration by B. C. Ganguli, the then chairman of the railway board. As a result, the state of affairs worsened to such an extent that the minister abruptly cancelled the chairman's tour to certain places of Rajasthan and his saloon was detached at a suburban station in Delhi just a couple of minutes before the departure of the train. The chairman resented this and ordered that the bogie be locked there. As a result rail traffic was blocked. This controversy naturally became the subject of public discussion. The government terminated the services of the chairman and the dispute came to an end. It marked the triumph of a minister over a civil servant whose rank was equal to that of a principal secretary.[5] The fourth was on 4th June 1979 when Madhu Dandavate, the then railway minister, under the plea of toning up and improving the efficiency of railway administration removed K. S. Rajan, the chairman of the railway board. The main reason of dispute between them was that the latter wanted to import locomotives from some developed countries, while the former had opposed it, but the chairman took exception to minister's interference and this led to his removal from the post. The fifth incident took place in 1982 when A. B. A. Ghani Khan Chaudhary, the then railway minister sacked the chairman of the railway board while reconstituting the railway board. The sixth was the announcement by the then Prime Minister Rajiv Gandhi at a press conference in 1987 for replacement of the then foreign secretary, A. P. Venkateshwaran. At the state level there are several cases of this type, about which we read everyday in newspapers/magazines.

Causes of Rift

The causes of rift between ministers and secretaries at the central level are many but some of them are listed as follows:

(a) The frequent changes in the portfolios of the ministers do not provide adequate time to both the minister and the secretary to develop proper trust and understanding for happy relationship between the two.[6]

(b) Ministers do not often appreciate the value of independent advice when the same has been unpalatable to them; they rather think that civil servants are putting hurdles.[7] Some of them have irrational attitudes, for instance when some case is put before them for decision they would write, 'I do not agree', without stating any reason for disagreement. In such circumstances mutual co-operation and understanding cannot be inculcated.

(c) Some of the officers are in the habit of criticizing individual ministers or their respective policies in private and in social circles.[8] When the ministers come to know about those officers they also react and it is the officers who are the sufferers.

(d) Both the minister and the secretary lack proper understanding of their respective roles.[9] It has been noted that the ministers sometimes interfere even in petty matters of day-to-day administration of the department while the secretaries on their part put through 'half-baked' proposals before the ministers, such letters or correspondence which have important nature are not brought to the notice of the ministers. Such tendencies can never provide sound backing to the growth of better relations. The secretary must present full facts before the minister and the minister must have the last word.[10] Moreover, the minister's interference in the day-to-day administration of the department in matters like licences, permits, promotions and transfers, etc., is also considered to be harmful.

(e) Ministers are in the habit of giving an impression to the politicians, legislators and others that they are prepared to do something but are helpless because the officers of their departments are putting unfavourable notes. Not only that, the ministers are known to have sometimes shown the files to the politicians to prove that they are innocent and that only the officers are to blame for a particular thing.

(f) It is also complained that in some states, group politics of the Congress party has filtered down to the civil services. As a result of this, certain officials have come to be identified with some ministers and become instruments in their hands for the retention of political power. Such tendency is harmful for administration as such officials cannot be loyal to their successors.[11]

Political Interference in Administration

Political interference in administration has become very common nowadays. It has taken two forms, first, tampering with rules and regulations, and second, distribution of patronage, appointments on key and important positions, transfers and plump postings. Politicians do not like to observe rules and regulations if they come in the way of their interest. Every day politicians telephone directly to the lower level officials to get some work done, without going through the proper channel, the secretary of the department, and officials who develop access to the ministry do not care for superiors in the hierarchy. Thus, in every ministry/department a coterie of convenient officials have been formed by the ministers to safeguard and watch their interests. Such collusion of politicians with administration is harmful for the public as well as for the administration. The civil servants who insist on rules and regulations have to face remote transfers on unimportant positions and several other kinds of harassment. Accounts in writing by some retired civil servants proved how they were forced to resign or were harassed beyond imagination. Dr Nabagopal Das, who had resigned from the ICS, said of his Bengal experience: '. . . (there) functioned an administration in which decisions were taken by only one man (Dr B. C. Roy, chief minister), who would often impatiently brush aside advice given by senior officers. I do not deny that, in a problem state like West Bengal, a certain degree of firmness was both necessary and desirable, but I have always held that even the most well-meaning dictator cannot rise above his predilections and prejudices and these latter need not necessarily be always for the common good. It was not, therefore, to be wondered that the chief minister and I often clashed. The climax came in 1958 when, as special secretary, home department, in charge of anti-corruption and the enforcement of special laws, I started submitting reports on corruption and other malpractices in high places and desired that action be taken against certain individuals. A gentle hint was given to me that I should "go slow" with these enquiries. I was even promised a better assignment if only I would be a little more accommodating. Unfortunately, I was far too pig-headed to listen to such counsel. The result was a virtual deadlock causing considerable mental agony and worry to me.'[12]

N. Bakshi, in his paper 'In Bihar—The state of My Adoption', narrated how he was pressurized and harassed by the minister in the Bihar government headed by Dr Krishna Sinha. The harassment was so acute that he had resigned on 16 March 1959, stating that 'my spirit was not in harmony with the official environment of my life'.[13]

Similarly, N. B. Banarjee, the former chief secretary of UP, resigned because he found himself unable to fit smugly into the altered administrative ethic. About his own experience as chief secretary, he said: 'the question of appointments has become the subject of personal likes and dislikes and the sources of canvassing the administrative merits of officials ceased to be criterion; one minister even went so far as to pass orders to me that no postings should be made to his home district without his specific consent. Even when it was explained to him that if all ministers were to pass similar orders, no postings could ever be made, it was doubtful whether he understood the position. The postings of key men to the districts thus became shuttle-cocks between a number of politicians motivated solely by their own personal idiosyncrasies. So much so that in some cases it became impossible to make appointment at all without considerable delay, and important and heavy duties were left in the hands of junior and inexperienced staff at a critical time.'[14]

Recently in Bihar, an IAS secretary in the health ministry was maltreated and beaten up by a member of Parliament for not nominating his son for admission to MBBS in the state's discretionary quota, which is a gross violation of all decency and norms. Many IAS officers have resigned from their services during the last 10 years due to political interference.

Political interference leads to frustration and demoralization of civil servants. Some important causes responsible for the demoralization of civil services identified and reported by the Punjab Administrative Reforms Committee in 1966 are: constant interference with delegated authority; victimization of otherwise good officials for political and personal reasons; special pay and posts for favourite officials; protecting corrupt officials to enjoy political favour or influence; indifference to the essential needs of officials such as proper houses, wages and recreational facilities; unhealthy conditions in which officials have to work because of inadequate office accommodation, frequent and irrational transfers, etc. Sometimes, the civil servants succumb to the political pressure and do wrong things to please their political boss. For instance, the Das commission's inquiry into the conduct of Pratap Singh Kairon, the then chief minister of Punjab has highlighted how highly placed officials indulge in nepotism to curry favour with the political head of the state. The Das Commission revealed that the official's conduct was influenced by a desire to please the chief minister, hence they did illegal acts without hesitation.[15] Recently, many civil servants were suspended, or frequently transferred in Bihar and Haryana for not fulfilling the illegal telephonic requests of politicians.

Neutrality and Civil Servants

The issue of neutrality is one of the important challenges faced by the civil servants in India. The notion of neutrality implies the absence of any political activity or bias on the part of individual civil servant in the performance of his duties. Neutrality means 'acceptance of the discipline of working without reservation—indeed with devotion—for the success of every government lawfully in power.'[16] If any administrator shows his inclination towards a particular party or adherence to a particular ideology, he would experience difficulty in working when another party with a different ideology comes into office.[17] Indian civil service is not neutral but deeply enmeshed in politics. A number of civil servants from the 1950 itself, like Dr John Mathai, C. D. Deshmukh, Barve, L. K. Jha, H. M. Patel, K. Natwar Singh, K. R. Narayanan, Krishna Kumar, Yeshwant Sinha, M. G. K. Menon, Dr Raja Ramanna, Mani Shankar Iyer, T. N. Chaturvedi and Manmohan Singh have joined different political parties. Indian civil service has been working in collusion with the politicians of party in power at centre or at state level. Bureaucrats have projected and defended their group interests with the help of politicians by supplying secret files to them whenever necessary.[18] Not only this, they have also got international posts after retirement.[19] During the 1970s, the concept of 'neutrality' was replaced by committed civil service. To quote D. P. Dhar, 'Commitment to a new social and economic order has to be consciously built and nurtured through the careers of our civil servants.[20] The late Mohan Kumaramangalam, a minister in the late Prime Minister Mrs Gandhi's cabinet, talked of committed bureaucracy and even to the duties and obligations of the civil service or the judiciary not to the country but solely to the government of the day. Mrs Indira Gandhi said that committed civil service means committed to a number of policies and to a popularly elected government without being committed to the politics of the party in power.' These views of Mrs Gandhi were vehemently criticized by all shades of people and it was said that the 'civil servants should be committed to their duties and the society which they are supposed to serve. Social commitment rather than political commitment is imperative in modern times.'[21]

Thus, it appears that the concept of 'neutrality', is irrelevant in the conditions prevailing in a developing nation like India. But for a parliamentary democracy, political neutrality is indispensable. It is all the more necessary for India because ministerial changes are frequent in Indian states; and after 1977, even at the centre. 'In the absence of neutrality, the civil service will develop cleavages, factionalism and percolate the belief that some would be promoted and some others would be penalized due to their political bias. Development of such a feeling in the civil service will be detrimental to their morale.'[22]

The civil servants must observe neutrality in the implementation of policies and programmes of the party in power. They should not be biased but should be ready to cooperate if some new party comes in power. They should not identify themselves with the political programme of a particular party.

The above recommendations are relevant even today and these should be followed properly. As the relationship between the political and permanent executive has grown in complexity, therefore, it is necessary that both the minister and secretary should try to know and understand their respective fields and must not try to dominate each other. If some controversy arises that should be solved through discussion, mutual trust and confidence. In a democratic set up like ours they should go hand in hand in the service of the country. They should work together while keeping in view their respective status and dignity. It is desired that they should be sincere, dedicated and committed towards their roles and should not evade responsibility.

Generalist and Specialist in Administration

The generalists and specialists are found in every administrative system. But generalists are at the 'top' and specialists are at the 'tap', which has caused heartburn in specialists. The controversy of generalist–specialist is one of the important problems of public administration in India. The problem has acquired new dimensions due to the increasing role being played by science and technology in all walks of life. In the 1940s or 1950s no one thought of about the department of space or ocean development or atomic energy or communication technology such as fax, Internet, computers, etc. Therefore, the role of the specialist in administration has acquired immense significance. The problem of law and order has also acquired new dimension due to the invention of several kinds of rifles, missiles and chemical weapons. Therefore, attempts had been made to define the roles of generalists and specialists in many countries. For example, Fulton Committee (1966–1968) of Britain has made important recommendations on the subject. The ARC (1960–1969) has also examined this problem in detail and made many recommendations concerning this problem. Here we propose to define the terms 'generalist' and 'specialist' and would examine the arguments advanced in favour and against both and in the end try to synthesize both the views.

Definition of Generalists and Specialists

There is no precise definition of generalist. A generalist may be defined as a public servant who does not have a specialized background and is easily transferable to any department or branch of government. He has also been defined as an administrator who belongs to the managerial class and who is well versed with rules, regulations and procedure of administration and generally performs POSDCORB functions. A generalist is said to be a jack of all trades and master of none.

The 'specialist' generally is a person who has special knowledge or skill in a specific field, for example, engineers, physicians, agriculturists, educationists, lawyers, etc. He can be easily distinguished on the basis of his education and training. He generally performs a job in which his specialist knowledge is required. However, expert or specialist is a relative term depending upon the contexts. For example, a general medical practitioner is an expert in relation to the patient but in comparison to a surgeon, dentist or gynaecology, etc. is only a generalist. Likewise there is equally a problem between the working engineer in the field and his counterpart in the laboratory. The ARC has called such specialized services 'functional services' and included even those services where officers have to specialize after joining the service. For example, the officers joining services like income-tax, audit and accounts, defence accounts, etc., do not require any specialized degree at the time of entry. However, over a period of time in their service they tend to specialize in their particular fields.

The civil service committee of Britain (1966–68), popularly known as the Fulton committee used the term 'specialist' for those whose career provides opportunities for the exercise of their qualifications and specialist skills. This category includes economists, accountants, architects, lawyers, scientists, doctors, engineers, draughtsmen, technicians and so on. Some of these, i.e., doctors and engineers have acquired their professionalism of speciality by recognized training outside the service. Others like technicians and draughtsmen may acquire and develop their skills after joining the service. The committee used the term administrators for those members of the administrative and executive classes who are now treated and regarded themselves as 'generalists'.

Thus, it is clear that a generalist is one who does not possess special knowledge at any field. On the other hand, specialists have special knowledge of his field of specialization.

The Controversy

In India, generalists have been given superior position in administration. The 'policy formulation' and the 'consideration' levels in the central as well as state secretariats are occupied by the generalists while positions in the field are filled by the specialists. Further, to make the 'humiliation' still more apparent, even the heads of executive agencies are appointed from amongst the generalists. For example, in Haryana, the director of higher education, director of health and director of agriculture are IAS civil servants. At district level, there is generalist collector/DC leading a team of technical district officers who are heads of technical departments at the district level. At block level, block development officer is the generalist who leads a team of technical extension officers in the field of agriculture, education, cooperative and veterinary service, etc.

The specialist demand parity with IAS generalists in matter of pay scales and service conditions, and access to administrative positions at the secretariat so that they can contribute in policy formulation of the government. They complain that during school days generalists were not brilliant students as compared to them but they enjoy more powers than specialists due to their position at secretariat level. The problem is that the specialists have to submit to the final decisions taken by the generalists on issues which have an important bearing on his field of specialization. This resulted in the conflict between the power of knowledge of experts and power of position of generalists. Thus, the problem is more of power sharing in administration. Let us now study the views expressed in favour of generalists and specialists.

Arguments in Favour of Generalists

(i) In India, the Macaulay Report on Indian Civil Service (1854) followed the British tradition of superior position of generalist administrator propounded by Northcote-Trevelyn Report (1853). The philosophy of these reports is that a person with liberal education and varied multifunctional experience is much better than the specialist who has deep knowledge of a very narrow field. Therefore, generalists occupied superior positions in Indian administration.

(ii) The important argument in favour of the generalist civil service is that it has established contact with top to the grassroots level administration. This is a peculiar system in which generalist administrative service is organized as an all-India service based on the permanent cadres of the state governments. Officers of this service serve at the district level and come in contact with the people at the lowest level. They are later transferred to the various positions in the state up to the secretariat and get experience of the working of the state governments. Some of these officers are deputed to the government of India to man senior positions. Such 'tenure' system was introduced by Lord Curzon in which these officers serve in the Government of India for a fixed tenure and go back to the state of their cadre. These officers serve at senior levels in the Government of India, having the advantage of vast experience of working at the state secretariat and in the field. This connects the entire system of administration from the top level to the grassroots level. The knowledge and vision provided by this kind of experience cannot be equalled by the limited technical experience of the specialist.

(iii) The administration in India has been based on the principle of 'area administration'. Thus, the village, the block, the tehsil, the district and the division continue to remain the units around which the administration at that level revolves. Each area requires a generalist administrator to perform the managerial functions of planning, directing, coordinating, etc. Such role can be performed by experienced generalist administrator successfully.

(iv) The generalist secretary is in a much better position to tender correct and proper advice to his minister because he usually has complete understanding of the total effect of various factors on a particular policy decision.

(v) The generalist charge the specialists of being parochial and narrow minded. They say specialists are prone to display bias because of a restricted view of matters. The specialist is one who knows more and more of less and less. In their favour they quote Paul Appleby 'the price of specialisation of every kind is parochialism.' The generalist possesses the broad vision and outlook and high thinking while a specialist does not possess all these qualities.

(vi) It has also been said that it is wrong to call these senior administrators as generalists. They are also professionals in their own field. To advise the political executive in their policy formulation functions are specialized tasks in themselves. Those who perform these tasks have to develop a professional expertise to become successful. These generalists can be called administrative professionals in that sense.

(vii) In any decision-making process, technical inputs form only a small part. Other matters like financial, administrative, legal and political issues are of equal importance. The generalist with a broad background of working in various departments is better suited to perform these jobs.

(viii) Experience shows when the specialists are required to do the job of a generalist they lost both words. Neither do they remain specialists nor do they prove to be good generalists.

Arguments in Favour of Specialists

The grievance of the specialist is the discrimination in pay and allowances as between the Indian Administrative Service and their services and quick chances of promotion for the IAS. The other grievances include that a large number of top posts both in central and state governments are manned by the members of IAS. Therefore, now a new trend is emerging in the composition of higher civil services that is a large number of professionals are now appearing for the civil services examinations. They are leaving medicine, engineering and chartered accountancy positions to enter the civil services. The specialists complain that they are excluded from the top policy-making positions. Therefore, it would be pertinent to examine the arguments given in favour of specialists.

(i) In colonial days prior to Independence, the main functions of administration were maintenance of law and order, collection of taxes and revenues. But now the tasks of administration have become very complex and cannot be properly performed by the generalists. Therefore, the specialists should be given due weightage in performing these jobs from the lowest to the highest levels.

(ii) Specialists feel that generalists are not required to intervene between them and the minister. They have better knowledge of their own field and can explain it better to the minister.

(iii) The generalists do not understand the implications of the technical proposals and cause inordinate delays in the clearance of the project proposals submitted to them. The generalists have to depend on the advice of the specialists and in the absence of their expert advice, knowledge are unable to take final decision soon.

(iv) It is further cited that our public enterprises headed by the generalists have become the centres of mismanagement and resulted in heavy financial losses. On the contrary, Dr Bhabha, a specialist, proved to be an administrator of great acumen. He built the atomic energy commission into a very good organization.

(v) In England, the Fulton Committee recommended greater role for the specialists in administration and observed that to meet the challenge of the scientific and technical developments the specialists have to be given due place in the administration. The same arguments run in the case of specialist in India.

(vi) The ARC recommended that the senior posts in functional areas should be held by the specialists in those cadres. The ARC further recommended that non-functional posts should be thrown open to all the cadres including the specialists and the generalists.

The Way Out

The Government of India is aware of the problem and a number of steps have been taken to solve the problem. The present controversy stems largely from the differences in scales of pay and in position and power between the generalist and specialist. The administrative system of Britain in which generalists have been given predominance on one hand and the USA administrative system on the other hand where specialists have been in predominant positions. In both the countries, governments have realized that such a situation is good for efficiency of administration. The Fulton Committee in England has suggested that now the generalist administrators should try to get more training and specialize in certain broad functional areas. At the same time it suggested that the specialists should be given training in broad general management principles. In the USA also, the Second Hoover Commission emphasized the need of greater coordination of the technical specialists and suggested for the creation of senior executive service comprising both the generalist and the specialist.

Thus, in our country, a middle way should be worked out to utilize the services of both generalists and specialists for national development. The good and well-meaning administrators could not deny the importance of technical considerations and expert services. Likewise no specialist who is good should assume that his administrative colleague is an important bigot. Where the attitude is one of mutual understanding, public service benefits greatly.

Some steps in this direction have been taken.These are as follows:

(i) Weakening of the tenure system: As already discussed, the tenure system was introduced by British. This system is now in no position to deliver the goods and has been weakened. It is felt that the senior civil servants should remain permanently in the central secretariat in violation of tenure system. In practice now very few officers of the rank of joint secretary go back to the states. The creation of the central secretariat services has also weakened this system.

(ii) Creation of new specialist all-India and central services: Our Constitution has a provision to create more all-India and central services. In 1961, two new central class I services were constituted, the Indian economic service for the economists and the Indian statistical service for the statisticians. All these services aim to provide better status and pay scales to specialists.

(iii) Appointment of specialists to positions of administrative responsibility: A new trend of appointing specialists to administrative positions is taking place. For example, some time ago the education secretary in the Union ministry of education was an educationist by profession and secretary to the scientific affairs department in the same ministry was an eminent scientist. In some ministries expert advisers have been appointed to take advantage of their expertise.

Another method of giving the specialist head of department ex-officio status of joint/additional/full secretary to government has been followed. The railway board is a good example of such arrangement. The members of the board operate as heads of departments and are also ex-officio secretaries in the railway ministry. So also is the case in the department of atomic energy where the specialist has reached the top instead of generalist. In the same way the Rajasthan government has appointed the chief engineer (PWD & BR) and the director of industries and supplies, ex-officio additional secretaries to the government.

In addition to these above steps several other solutions have been offered to solve the problem. The ARC in its report on personnel administration recommended functionalization of all services including Indian Administrative Service and recommended that senior management posts in functional areas should be filled by the members of respective functional services. Several other suggestions including unified civil service are given to solve this problem. In the words of R. G. S. Brown, a generalist is a facilitator, mediator, arbiter and coordinator, therefore, his role is very important in administration, but at the same time specialists should also be given rightful place which they deserve. Inter-service mobility and cooperation is essential for any good and effective administration.

Integrity in Public Administration

Nowadays we hear a lot about various kinds of scams and lack of integrity in public life. The public servants on the other hand complain that their emoluments have not kept pace with the rising prices. This forced them to collect money from other means at slightest opportunity while exercising their discretionary powers. Corruption has become a widespread phenomenon. Everyone appears to be concerned, but no one appears to be able to do anything about it. What are the causes of such widespread lack of integrity in public administration? What can be done and what has been done to check the problem of corruption?

What sort of institutional arrangements are necessary to contain this evil of corruption? Here an attempt will be made to find out answers to these questions.

The dictionary meaning of integrity is soundness of moral principles, character of uncorrupted virtue, uprightness, honesty, sincerity. 'The concept of integrity is an outcome of modern legal system of rule of law'. In earlier times government favours were given to the highest bidder or to those who were giving gifts. This system started changing with the advent of concepts of state sovereignty and citizenship. The government appointed civil servants and paid them a monthly salary, and they were forbidden to take gifts from people. The state started taking taxes from the citizens for their services and the taxes were imposed on the basis of laws. Slowly this developed into the concept of integrity in administration and civil servants' recruitment started on merit with determined salary and promotion till they perform their functions honestly according to the rules, regulations and laws. Those who deviate from the set procedure of work render themselves liable for action. Integrity as a concept includes honesty, courage and cleanliness in pecuniary matters. Lack of integrity is known as corruption which means using unfair means in taking pecuniary benefits.

Definition of Corruption

To define corruption, is not an easy task. The corruption is a general term covering misuse of authority for personal gains. The term corruption is full of malpractices and unlawful, unethical and unfair dealing. Thus, corruption is deliberate misuse of one's own position, directly of indirectly for personal gains, it may be material gains or enhancement of position or influence to determine to the interest of others. The Indian Penal Code and the Prevention of Corruption Act, 1947, provide scope and legal definition of corruption.

Section 161 of the Indian Penal Code defines corruption as, 'Whoever, being or expecting to be a public servant, accepts or obtains or agrees or accepts, or attempts to obtain from any person, for himself or for any other person, any gratification whatsoever, other than legal remuneration, as a motive or reward for doing any official act or to show or forebear to show, in the exercise of his official functions, favour or disfavour to any person, or for rendering or attempting to render any service or disservice to any person with the central or any state government or Parliament or the legislature of any state or with local authority, corporation or government company referred to in Section 21, or with any public servant, as such shall be punished with imprisonment of either description for a term which may extend to three years, or with fine, or with both.'

The Prevention of Corruption Act, 1947, calls it criminal misconduct and defines it in the following manner. According to this Act, five kinds of acts constitute criminal misconduct: (i) habitual acceptance of gratification; (ii) the obtaining of any valuable thing without consideration; (iii) misappropriation; (iv) the abuse of position for pecuniary advantage; and (v) the possession of pecuniary resources or property disproportionate to his known sources of income.

Any public servant who commits criminal misconduct shall be punishable with imprisonment for a term which shall not be less than one year but which may extend to seven years and shall be liable to fine. K. Santhanam, chairman of the committee on prevention of corruption declared, 'Any action or failure to take action in the performance of duty by a government servant for some advantage is corruption'. The word advantage refers to 'quick money'.

The Representation of the People's Act, 1950, includes within its definition political malpractices too. Section 23 of aforesaid Act includes the following as corrupt practices.

(i) Bribery; (ii) undue influence; (iii) appeal to vote or refrain from voting on the grounds of religion, races, caste, community or language or the use of appeal to religious or national symbols; (iv) promotion or attempt to promote enmity between classes; (v) publication of false statement on the personal character or conduct or candidature of candidates; (vi) hiring or procuring of vehicles for the conveyance of electors to or from polling stations; (vii) incurring or authorizing of expenditure in contravention of Section 77 of Representation of the People's Act; and (viii) obtaining or procuring the assistance of persons in government service.

Forms of Corruption

The modes of corruption are numerous. The report of the Santhanam committee on prevention of corruption states that securing some kind of pecuniary or other material advantage directly for oneself or family, relatives or friends constitute the most common form of corruption. With the advent of modern welfare state, a number of laws, rules and regulations have come into force. As a result getting any service from the government requires the fulfilment of procedures and formalities which take lot of time, sometimes officials also cause delay to charge some bribe or 'speed money'. Another form of corruption is in the form of liaison men who cultivate close relations with senior officers who are in a position to influence the government policies in their favour and in return get benefits in the form of cash or kind. Some other identified forms of corruption are as follows: donations in the form of cash or kind, sometimes private companies offer jobs to retired officials, contracts of construction, purchases, sales, etc. are well-known forms of providing benefits for consideration of money.

The Central Vigilance Commission has identified the following modes of corruption:

1. Acceptance of substandard stores/works
2. Misappropriation of public money and stores
3. Incurring pecuniary obligation of persons to whom the public servants have official obligations
4. Borrowing money from contractors and firms having official dealings with officers
5. Showing favours to contractors and firms
6. Claiming false travelling allowance, house rent, etc
7. Possessing assets disproportionate to income
8. Purchase of immoveable property, etc., without prior permission or intimation
9. Causing loss to the government by negligence or otherwise
10. Abuse of official position or power
11. Acceptance of illegal gratification in recruitment, postings, transfers, and promotions
12. Misuse of government employees for personal work
13. Production of forged certificates of date of birth or community
14. Irregularities in reservation of seats by rail and by air
15. Non-delivery of money orders, insured covers, value payable parcels, etc
16. Replacement of new postage stamps by used ones
17. Irregularity in grant of import and export licence
18. Misuse of imported and allotted quotas by various firms with the connivance of public servants
19. Irregularity in grant of telephone connections
20. Moral turpitude
21. Acceptance of gifts
22. Under-assessment of income-tax, estate duty, etc. for pecuniary considerations
23. Misuse of advances sanctioned for purchases of scooters and cars
24. Abnormal delay in settlement of compensation claims to displaced persons
25. Wrong assessment of claims of displaced persons
26. Cheating in connection with sale and purchase of plots for residential purposes
27. Unauthorized occupation and sub-letting of government quarters

The modus operandi of corruption is a major reason why it is difficult to identify and measure its intensity. There are three different ways in which corruption surfaces. First of all, there is collusive corruption, a form of corruption that involves the willing and planned cooperation of the giver and taker. Most cases of political corruption, scams involving large contracts and other favours, belong to this category. Second, there is extortion corruption that implies forced extraction of bribes or other favours from vulnerable victims by those in authority. This tends to work when people who seek certain services or decisions are in a tight corner, with very few options. Third, there is anticipatory corruption, the best example of which is the tendency among some people to pay a bribe or present a gift in anticipation of favourable actions or decisions from those in authority.[23] Collusive and anticipatory corruption are difficult to unearth. It is only extortion corruption that is easy to unearth.

The findings of the public affairs centre's recent studies provide evidence on the extent of the retail corruption in India. Although it covers only selected urban centres of Ahmedabad, Bangalore, Chennai, Pune and Calcutta, the extent of retail corruption in Chennai was that every fourth person in the general population ends up in paying a bribe in dealing with agencies such as the urban development authority, electricity board, municipal corporation and telephones. In Bangalore, it is one in eight persons while in Pune, it is only one in 17 who pays a bribe. Even the poor living in slums are not spared. In Bangalore, every third slum dweller claims to have paid a bribe for getting a service or solving a problem with a public agency. Pune and Calcutta have reported much lower incidence of this problem.[24] This proves that corruption is a pervasive phenomenon in India's public services.

Causes of Corruption or Decline of Integrity

Decline in integrity and public morality is a complex phenomenon which obviously has several causes. To talk about corruption is easy, but it is quite difficult to find out the causes of corruption in this technological world. Several factors such as historical, socio-economic and political are responsible for corruption. An attempt has been made to highlight these causes of corruption here.

Historical Causes

The colonial government paid their senior officers a very good salary but the local level functionaries were given paltry payments. Therefore, they leaned towards corruption. The Second World War created scarcity of food and clothing articles including those of other commonly used goods, and due to shortage of goods, ration cards were issued to control the supply. These controls had created opportunities for corruption. The inflation that followed was also created a climate of large-scale corruption. After independence a large number of British and Muslims officers left the country. Therefore, a large number of officers were promoted even without merit. Large-scale recruitment had also brought down the quality of the recruited staff. All this caused turmoil in the administrative system.

Social Causes

In our society material possession and economic power determines the status and prestige of a person in society. Therefore, the acquisition of wealth has become a necessary part of life, without caring the means they adopt for accumulating wealth. The present phenomenon of various kinds of scams, Bofors, hawala, urea, fertilizer, fodder, housing, etc. are examples of corruption for collecting and hoarding money. Even wives of the civil servants indulge and encourage them to lean towards corruption. Their various demands beyond their financial resources forced their husbands to adopt questionable methods to collect money to fulfil the desires of wives. The competition of status, drawing room show culture, has created a lot of strain on the integrity of the administrative officers.

Economic Causes

One of the important causes of corruption is inadequate salary of the employees. The increasing cost of living has brought down the real income of salaried persons and the standard of living has suffered. To maintain their standard of living, employees accept illegal gratification. Black money was poured to win over the discretionary favours from the government officials, and large-scale corruption became the order of the day.

Environmental Causes

The rapid urbanization and industrialization has changed the value system. The concept of simple living and high thinking has been taken over by luxurious living style and vulgar show of money power. The nexus between politicians and civil servants and clever businessmen has resulted in the form of large-scale corruption which we now call scams of unprecedented nature.

Cumbersome Procedure

The complicated procedures even for small things like getting a ration card or diesel permit have resulted in corrupt practices. The clientele's anxiety to obtain prompt services and benefits has encouraged the growth of dishonest practices such as 'speed money' and gifts to speed up the process of movement of files. In all such cases officials pay lip service to rules, regulations, methods and procedures. Thus, it will be most revealing to experience that the work procedure which are primarily intended to be available in the nature of instrumental values will turn out to be the terminal values.[25]

Inadequate Laws

The Indian Penal Code and Prevention of Corruption Act do not have adequate laws to punish the guilty officers. The administration of these laws is not proper and not many prosecutions are launched. If some are booked, prosecution is not pursued. As a result a large number of the guilty do not get punishment and feel encouraged to pursue corrupt practices.

Constitutional Protection to Civil Servants

Civil servants have been given protection in our Constitution under Article 311. The Constitutional provisions and disciplinary procedures make it impossible to take action against dishonest and corrupt employees. The Interpretation of Article 311 by the courts has made it very difficult to deal effectively with corrupt employees.

Evil Effect of Corruption on Administration

Corruption in high places causes decline of people's faith in government. People expect high moral standards from rulers. The decline in such standards raises question mark on the legitimacy of the government and people's cooperation declines. Second, corruption increases the cost of administration. The people start paying the officials though informally, instead of paying taxes to the government for its services. This causes lot of loss to the government. Third, the prevalence of corruption jeopardizes the feeling of sacrifice for the good of society and nation. Fourth, sometimes due to corruption, decisions are not taken on merit and national interests are compromised for the sake of economic benefits. The national interest may be overlooked in purchasing sub-standard arms which may not be effective during a war for monetary 'consideration'. Lastly, corruption adversely affects the efficiency and morale of the honest civil servants because in placement and promotion considerations other than merit dominate. Thus, it causes inefficiency in administration.

Anti-Corruption Measures and Machinery

After World War II corruption became rampant and to deal with this problem, the Government of India constituted the special police establishment (SPE) in 1941. In 1963, the Government of India set up the Central Bureau of Investigation (CBI) in the ministry of home affairs and SPE was made one of its divisions. We have already discussed the CBI and its functions. In spite of these measures corruption could not be controlled and the Government of India appointed a committee under the chairmanship of Santhanam in 1962 to suggest measures to check corruption. The committee submitted its report on 31 March 1964. Some of the main recommendations of the committee were:

(i) Article 311 of the Constitution should be amended in order to provide a simplified procedure for corruption cases related to government servants.

(ii) Government servants conduct rules should be amended restricting the employment of retired government servants by private or commercial concerns for two years after their retirement.

(iii) Recommendations with regard to disciplinary rules including withdrawal of pension in full or part compulsory retirement of a government servant on completion of 25 years of service or after attaining 50 years of age if his integrity is suspected to be doubtful and an appropriate machinery to review cases of doubtful integrity.

(iv) Laws, rules, procedures and practices for the purpose of deciding the level of discretionary powers, the manner of such exercises, the control of such exercise of power, etc. should be reviewed.

(v) The Defence of India Bill, 1962 should be amended.

(vi) Section 21 of the Indian Penal Code may be amended to define the term 'public servant' to include every person in the service or pay of the government, a local authority or a cooperation established by a central or state Act, or a government company as defined in Section 617 of the Companies Act, 1956, and/or who is remunerated by fee or commission for the performance of any public duty.

(vii) The committee suggested re-organization of the entire vigilance organization, improvement in the vigilance organization for railways, setting up of vigilance organizations in public sector undertakings and the judiciary.

(viii) The committee recommended for an independent central vigilance commission.

Legal and Institutional Devices to Check Corruption

The following enactments and institutional arrangements have been provided to investigate corruption cases and take legal action:

(i) The Indian Penal Code, Section 161

(ii) Prevention of Corruption Act, 1947

(iii) Government Servant Conduct Rules

(iv) Central vigilance commission (CVC)

(v) State vigilance commission

(vi) Central Bureau of Investigation (CBI)

(vii) *Lok Ayukta*s in many states

Vigilance Organizations in the Ministries

In the ministry of home affairs a vigilance division has been created and vigilance units in the respective Ministries, departments and public undertakings have been established. Each ministry has a vigilance officer and attached offices have a vigilance officer. They maintain close relations with the administrative vigilance division in the ministry of home affairs and central vigilance commission (CVC).

Central Vigilance Commission (CVC)

The commission is headed by a commissioner who is appointed by the president by 'warrant under his hand and seal'. He holds office for a term of six years or till the age of 65 years, whichever is earlier. He cannot be removed or suspended from office except in the manner provided for the removal or suspension of the chairman or member of Union public service commission.

Functions

The CVC is an advisory body which makes recommendations to the government for taking action against erring officials. The central vigilance commission has been entrusted with the following functions.

(i) The commission undertakes an inquiry into any transaction in which a public servant is suspected or alleged to have acted for an improper purpose or in a corrupt manner.

(ii) To investigate into any complaint against a civil servant who has exercised or refrained from exercising his powers against improper or corrupt purposes, and any complaint of corruption, misconduct, lack of integrity or other kind of malpractices on the part of a public servant.

(iii) To initiate a review of procedures and practices of administration relating to the maintenance of integrity in administration.

(iv) To ask for reports from other agencies to exercise check and supervision over the vigilance and anti-corruption work.

(v) The commission has been authorized to take over under its direct control complaints for further action. Such action can pertain to either (a) to ask the CBI to register a regular case and investigate it, or (b) to enlist it for enquiry by the CBI or the agency concerned.

In 2006, the central vigilance commission has instructed government departments to put all application forms that lead to interface with public and businesses on the Internet by December-end. The directive made 'first come first served' principle is applicable in cases of applications for driving license, approval of building plans, environmental clearances for industrial projects, allotments of petrol pumps, sanction of funds to NGOs and registration of contractors and suppliers and the states of their bill payments. These instructions were meant to prevent the possibilities of corruption. The instruction will eliminate a common strategy adopted by clerical staff to harass applicants and extract a bribe, raising one query after another to delay processing of requests on the pretext of incomplete forms. (*Hindustan Times*, 28 November 2008.)

The commission receives complaints from individual persons. It also collects information about corruption and malpractices or misconduct from other sources such as (i) press reports; (ii) information provided by the members of Parliament; (iii) comments appearing in the reports of parliamentary committees; (iv) audit reports; and (v) information reaching the commission through the CBI. At the same time, it welcomes the assistance in this regard by voluntary organizations like *Sadachar Samiti* and responsible citizens and press. The commission submits its annual report to the ministry of home affairs about its activities, drawing specific attention to its recommendations which have not been acted upon or accepted. The home ministry, in turn, submits the report to the Parliament.

State Vigilance Commission

At the state level, there is a state vigilance commission since 1964. Like the central vigilance commission, the state vigilance commission owes its existence to executive resolution. The vigilance commissions also have their own investigating agencies. Besides the vigilance commissioner, there is a commissioner for departmental inquiries who conducts departmental inquiries into charges of corruption.

The commission submits an annual report of its activities to the state government. The report is to be placed before the state legislature.

The central vigilance commissioner holds an annual meeting of all the vigilance commissioners of states. This forum provides opportunities for discussion of mutual problems and exchange of views. It gives publicity to vigilance efforts of the central as well as of state governments. Such efforts inspire public faith in government's sincerity to streamline integrity.

Lok Pal and *Lok Ayuktas*

The ARC in its report recommended for the setting up of the institution of *Lok Pal* and *Lok Ayukta*s at centre and state levels respectively on the lines of ombudsman of the Scandinavian countries. Accepting the recommendation of the ARC, the government introduced a bill in the Parliament to create the office of *Lok Pal*, which, of course, lapsed.

Some of the state governments have set up the institution of *Lok Ayukta*s on the pattern of the *Lok Pal*. They have their own investigating machinery and have jurisdiction over the actions of the ministers. The *Lok Ayukta*s are drawn from the senior judiciary. In some cases, person who has been chief justice of a state can hold this post. In spite of all the prestige of the organization the office has not proved up to the expectations to combat corruption.

Some Suggested Remedies

What should be done to control corruption? What kind of reforms are required and in what field? The Santhanam committee recommended the following important measures for prevention of corruption:

(i) Greater care should be taken in selecting officers for appointment to higher administrative posts.

(ii) Promotion to higher and more responsible positions should be guided by the consideration of integrity of the personnel.

(iii) Enquiry-cum-reception offices should be established to promptly identify the problems of corruption.

(iv) A clear distinction should be made as to what information should be treated secret and what should be made freely available to the public.

(v) The annual confidential reports should include a column for the comments of the superiors on the integrity of the officer.

(vi) Ban on government servants accepting private, commercial and industrial employment for a period of two years after retirement.

(vii) Discouragement of the existence of contract men and touts.

(viii) Widespread publicity of dismissals and removals and compulsory retirement of corrupt officers.

A study of the opinion of politicians, administrators, educators and businessmen on the problems of corruption, has suggested the following prerequisites for the eradication of corruption: (i) simple laws and administrative procedures; (ii) better paid but rigidly supervized officials; (iii) stricter and quicker punishment for the improper use of public authority; and (iv) a tax structure which could be effectively imposed. Above all, there is no substitute for a vigilant public.[26] A recent study has suggested four essential building blocks for a national agenda for corruption control:[27] (a) reform of the political process, (b) restructuring and re-orienting the government machinery, (c) empowerment of citizens, and (d) creating sustained public pressure for change. It is the awareness, resolve and demand for reform by the people that will determine the success of many legal, institutional and policy changes proposed for controlling corruption.

Looking to the present political and administrative environment of the country, it is difficult to believe that our political leaders will take initiative to clean the system. The reluctance to implement reform promises made in their party manifestos, dilution of goals and scope of the reforms, the recent move to exclude elected representatives from the purview of the Prevention of Corruption Act, etc. proves that our political leadership will not take initiative to cleanse the system because they are the beneficiaries of this system. Only people's initiatives can attempt for some reforms. Public interest litigation (PIL) is the most effective manifestation of such initiatives. Judicial response to PIL in the form of judicial activism is positive. In some states local movements against corrupt practices and seeking access to information as in Rajasthan, and demand for reform even from civil service associations as in UP and highlighting these developments by media generates the confidence of challenging the culture of corruption. All these are positive signs of checking cancerous growth of corruption in our country.

Redress of Citizens' Grievances

The goal of the government in a civil society, particularly in democracy, is the happiness and welfare of the people who formed it or over whom it governs. However, at cutting edge of administration, the common man is being harassed and deprived of the services for which he is entitled. The problem of public administration is how to make the official at the lowest rung of hierarchy, responsive, sympathetic sober and courteous in dealing with the citizens. The citizens generally feel agitated and want to ventilate their grievances against the officials and government agencies.

The *Chambers* dictionary defines grievance as 'a ground of complaint, a condition felt to be oppressive or wrongful.' A grievance may arise as a complaint against some action or decision taken by the government or any other agency. The causes of grievances are mostly corruption, indifference, incompetence and insensitiveness on the part of government servants. The grievances of citizens are of two types: general grievances and individual grievances. General grievances are 'against the government, its acts and policies and may be common to all or any section of the community, shortage of food, rise in prices, over-crowding in transport services, late running of train, etc. are instances of such grievances which do exist and find expression in widespread disturbances that occur from time to time.'[28] Individual grievances are those which the citizens face, as individuals, on account of any omission or act of the government. We are concerned in this chapter with individual grievances. The citizen today, due to rule of law and democracy, expects the public servant to be impartial, honest, responsive, fair and competent in the performance of his official duties.

Existing Arrangements for the Redress of Grievances

The redress of grievances of citizens is not an easy task. The traditional apparatus for their removal is legislative, judiciary and administrative authorities. But all these instruments of control have not proved effective. The legislative instrument is more suited for the consideration of matters of large public importance than for redressal of citizen's grievances arising due to day-to-day administration. Justice through judicial instrument is very expensive, dilatory and inconvenient, therefore, citizens in majority do not approach courts for action, they find it cheaper and less humiliating to suffer wrongs than approach the courts. Likewise, various administrative arrangements made in the departments of government have not satisfied the citizens. The ARC pointed out: 'Nor have the various administrative tiers and hierarchies proved adequate for the purpose. A tendency to uphold the man on the spot, a casual approach to one's own responsibilities, an assumption of unquestionable superiority of the administration, a feeling of sanctity of authority and neglect or indifference on the part of superior authority may prevent a citizen from obtaining justice even at the final stage of the administrative system.'[29]

After Independence, several steps have been taken to enhance integrity and capacity of administration. The Prevention of Corruption Act, 1947, was amended in 1955 to check corrupt practices in administration. A number of commissions/committees were also set up to enquire into the evil of corruption and suggest ways to eradicate it. For example, the Railway Corruption Inquiry Committee (popularly known as the Kriplani Committee) 1953, the Vivian Bose Commission (1956), the Justice Chagla Commission (1958) to enquire into the affairs of LIC, the establishment of vigilance division and vigilance units in ministries/departments in 1955, creation of O & M division in the home ministry in 1954. In 1962 Government of India appointed the Committee on Prevention of Corruption (popularly known as Santhanam Committee) and on its recommendation established the central vigilance commission in 1964. A number of ad hoc commissions of enquiry were appointed to inquire into the charges of corruption and abuse of power, the Das commission of enquiry, Punjab (1965) to enquire into the charges of corruption against the then chief minister of Punjab, Sardar Pratap Singh Kairon, the Mudhorkar Commission of Enquiry (1968) against ex-United Front ministry of Bihar. Jaswant Singh Commission to enquire into the charges of corruption against Bhajan Lal, the former chief minister of Haryana and a host of other such commissions were appointed to look into the charges of corruption against state chief ministers. Thus, about two hundred commissions were appointed but they could not solve these problems and an ordinary citizen cannot hope to get his grievance relating to small problems redressed through this method.

The states have also created agencies to deal with corruption, such as the anti-corruption department, district complaints committees, the commissioner for inquiry, O & M units in the secretariats along with some other agencies. The most important step was appointment of vigilance commission in most of the states in 1964 on the pattern of central vigilance commission.

Therefore, for effective solution of the problem the ombudsman type institution demand by eminent public men and jurists. This matter was considered by the ARC in detail and it pointed out in 1966 itself. 'We are of the view that the special circumstances relating to our country can be fully met by providing for two special institutions for the redressal of citizens' grievances. There should be one authority dealing with complaints against the administrative acts of ministers or secretaries to government at the centre and in the states. There should be another authority in each state and at the centre for dealing with complaints against the administrative acts of other officials. All these authorities should be independent of the executive as well as the legislature and judiciary.'[30] The first one was to be called the *Lok Pal* and the second one, *Lok Ayukta*.

The Government of India accepted the recommendations of the ARC and as a result *Lok Pal* and *Lok Ayukta* Bill for the first time was introduced in the Parliament on 9 May 1968.

Lok Pal

The Administrative Reforms Commission in its interim report on 'Problems of Redressal of Citizens' Grievances' in 1966, recommended the establishment of the *Lok Pal* and *Lok Ayukta* for India. *Lok Pal* and *Lok Ayukta*s are the Indian Hindi names of the office of ombudsman. Ombudsman is a Scandinavian institution first established in 1809 in Sweden to investigate into the cases of injustice, corruption and favouritism. In India, no less than five attempts have been made in 1968, 1971, 1977, 1985 and 1990 to have *Lok Pal* law adopted by Parliament. But it did not happen, either Parliament was dissolved or the Bill just lapsed. The 1985 bill did not die as the others but was killed through withdrawal. Lapses after lapses took place to fulfil the election promises to introduce it, and administrative tendencies to abort it.

The government did introduce the promised bill, the *Lok Pal* Bill 1996 in Parliament on 13 September 1996. This bill is also bogged down in controversy over a variety of contradictions.

Jurisdiction of *Lok Pal*

The *Lok Pal* Bill proposes to cover the prime minister and members of Parliament, present and past ministers and inquire into complaints against them. The MPs and ministers will have to periodically disclose their assets to the *Lok Pal*. The basic assumption of the bill is that persons in high places should be accountable to the people and there should be an independent machinery to investigate charges against them.

The *Lok Pal* will be a three member institution like the Election Commission. The chairman and the two members are to be appointed by the government in consultation with a seven member committee. The members of this committee would be prime minister, the speaker of the lok sabha, the home minister, the minister of personnel, the vice-president and the leader of opposition of both houses. The irony of such a committee is that it consists of the very persons that the *Lok Pal* is supposed to investigate, but also clearly controlled by the government and is hardly likely to proceed boldly against powerful politicians.[31]

Procedure of Working

The Bill mentions how the *Lok Pal* will work. The *Lok Pal* has been prohibited under Section 33(b) from acting *suo motu*, which says that the *Lok Pal* is not to make any inquiry upon its own knowledge or information. According to Section 11 of the 1996 Bill the *Lok Pal* can act only on the basis of complaint of a person, in a prescribed form, accompanied by an affidavit in support of the allegations and the complainant has also to pay the prescribed fee. All this has perhaps been made obligatory to discourage frivolous complaints or may be to have lesser complaints due to difficult process to be followed in such cases.

The *Lok Pal* has not been given its own independent investigating agency. He has to depend upon the official investigating agencies like CBI, whose services he can borrow with their 'concurrence' as mentioned in the Bill. This kind of arrangement will create hindrances in the satisfactory working of the *Lok Pal*, because it requires a good deal of power, authority to get work done by other investigating agencies. Even the Supreme Court's constant direction to CBI to expedite the investigation in sensitive cases has little impact. In such situation work of *Lok Pal* will be hampered, without its own investigating machinery.

Weaknesses of the Bill

There are many weaknesses in the present Bill. First, under Section 24(2) of the Bill, if the complainant fails to prove the allegations, he is liable to imprisonment for a term of 'not less than one year and which may extend to three years' and also to a fine up to Rs 50,000. Second, the *Lok Pal*'s enquiry has to be in camera and premature publicity or disclosing the identity of the person against whom the inquiry is in progress is punishable by the *Lok Pal*. The punishment may be up to six months imprisonment and a fine up to Rs 10,000. But the *Lok Pal* has no power to inflict punishment on the person against whom the complaint is made and charges against whom are *prima facie* proved. The *Lok Pal* can only 'communicate his findings and recommendations' to the 'competent authority' for necessary action. The prime minister is the competent authority for all ministers and the Lok Sabha for prime minister. He has not been given any powers to suggest or recommend punishment to be imposed. The only obligation placed on the competent authorities is to report to the *Lok Pal* what follow-up action has been taken, but he has not been given any power to direct punishment against the aberrant 'public functionary'. It is surprising that the Bill seems more directed at creating a scare among the complainants against the 'public functionaries', rather than providing them with a weapon to seek relief for them. Thus, the *Lok Pal* will prove to be a safety valve to the government in answering to the public criticism by saying that the accusers are free to approach the *Lok Pal* and 'he would be a crusader without a sword.'[33] Third, the *Lok Pal* has been conferred powers under Section 14 of the Bill to stay any criminal case 'till the completion of such inquiry . . . the investigation shall remain deferred.' Further, even if a complaint filed by a third person concerning the same matter and the *Lok Pal* holds that the allegations against the public functionary are not established, the findings will not only lead to the dismissal of the complaint before him, but also a bar on his conviction and trial on these facts by courts. The critics of this provision say that it has been incorporated to save the politicians who are involved in various scams. They say now that when someone will move to the *Lok Pal*, that will make possible for tainted politicians to secure a stay of criminal proceedings going against him/her in courts and if he succeeds in obtaining an opinion from the *Lok Pal* that allegations against him are unsustainable, the criminal case will get dissolved. The arrangement and the way it will work can be manoeuvred by legal craftsmanship to make anti-corruption law against political persons a farce. This bill will simply become yet another cover for politicians to do evil things and get away under the cover of the *Lok Pal*.

To make the institution of *Lok Pal* really effective for which it was conceived, the improvements of the *Lok Pal* Scheme may be on the following lines.

(a) The *Lok Pal* should be accorded constitutional status. Parliamentary law is liable to frequent changes, as it was done in Orissa when Biju Patnaik was chief minister. He got rid of an inconvenient *Lok Ayukta* by repealing the law.

(b) He should be empowered to cancel wrong orders and provide suitable relief to aggrieved parties subject to appeal to the Supreme Court only.

(c) He should be empowered to initiate enquiry *suo motu* against any person on getting information from any source.

(d) He should be empowered to get criminal complaints investigated by his own investigating agency, making only such supportive uses of official agencies like CBI as he may consider necessary.

(e) He should be empowered to impose damages, launch criminal prosecution through his own agency in designated special courts in case of persons held prima facie guilty.[34]

In addition to all these, all enquiries should be open unless the *Lok Pal* decides to have it in camera. A complaint neither should be in any prescribed form nor accompanied by any affidavit but may be on payment of a prescribe fee to discourage frivolous complaints. If a complaint is found false and malicious, the complainant should be suitably fined by the *Lok Pal* and punishment need not be awarded. The person falsely implicated could take defamatory legal action against the complainant. Unless such changes are made in the *Lok Pal* scheme, it may prove to be a failure under the prevailing political culture and low ethics.

Lok Ayukta

Though, at central level no institution of *Lok Pal* or *Lok Ayukta* has yet been established but at state level many states like Maharashtra, Rajasthan, MP, Karnataka, Bihar, HP, etc. have appointed *Lok Ayukta*s on the lines suggested by the ARC to deal with the problems of public grievances.

The problem of redressal of people's grievances cannot be solved by high-powered bodies like *Lok Pal* and *Lok Ayukta*s situated at capital headquarters away from the public. The citizens' grievances mostly concern the 'cutting edge of administration mostly at district level and below the point of contact between the citizen and the administration. The remedy lies in decentralization of administration to make it accountable to the people. The second remedy is the organization of various interests of consumers or of various functional groups to look after their own particular interests. The farmers' lobby, chambers of commerce, the labour organizations and consumes organizations are examples of such organizations. The organization of government servants, teachers, students, etc., compel the government to agree to their demands. As a result the unorganized people suffer and their grievances mostly remain unsolved.

Consumer Protection as the Removal of Public Grievances

Recently under the Consumer Protection Act, 1986, central consumer protection council, the state consumer protection councils and the district forum have been set up for redress of public grievances.

Consumer Protection Machinery in India

The Consumer Protection Act envisages the setting of the consumer protection council at the centre, namely the central consumer protection council and in all states the state consumer protection councils. The objects of the councils shall be to promote and protect the rights of the consumers.

Central Consumer Protection Council

The central government has made the Consumer Protection Rules, 1987, which came into force on 15 April 1987. The notification concerning the central council was issued on 1 June 1987. Composition of the Central council shall be as follows:

The Central council shall consist of the following 150 members:

(a) The minister-in-charge of consumer affairs in central government shall be the chairman of the council
(b) The minister of state (where he is not holding independent charge) or deputy minister in-charge of consumer affairs in the central government shall be the vice-chairman of the central council
(c) The minister of food and civil supplies or minister-in-charge of consumer affairs in states
(d) Eight members of Parliament, five from the Lok Sabha and three from the Rajya Sabha
(e) The secretary of the national commission for scheduled castes and scheduled tribes

(f) Representatives of the central government departments and autonomous organizations concerned with consumer interests not exceeding 20
(g) Representatives of the consumers or consumer organizations not less than 35
(h) Representatives of women not less than 10
(i) Representatives of farmers, trade and industry not more than 20
(j) Persons capable of representing consumer interests not specified above, not exceeding 15
(k) The secretary in the department of civil supplies shall be the member-secretary of the central council

The chairman of the central council shall be the minister-in-charge of consumer affairs in the central government; and the secretary in the department shall be the member-secretary of the central council.

The central council, which has a wide base and multi-sectional representation, has to play a vital role in creating consumer awareness and in the development of a widespread, responsive and responsible consumer movement in the country.

Working Group

The central government is empowered to constitute from amongst its members such working groups as it may deem necessary. Every working group so constituted shall perform such functions as assigned to it by the central council. It seems that such working groups may prove to be more useful and effective in dealing with the specific problems allocated to them. The findings of such groups are required to be placed before the council for its consideration.

Term of the Central Council

The term of the central council shall be three years. There is no provision either under the Act or the Consumer Protection Rules, 1987, as to the renewal of term of the council. Thus, for the continuous existence of the central council it is necessary that the central government must reconstitute the council before the expiry of the term of the existing council. In view of the past experience, however, it is doubtful whether central government will be able to fulfil its legislative obligation. It will be difficult to reconstitute the whole council consisting of 150 members after every three years.

In view of the utility of the council it is suggested that 'the term of the member other than ex-officio members of the council shall be three years and not the term of the council consequently, the members may keep on changing on the expiry of their terms but the council will always remain in existence to protect the interests of the consumers.'[35]

Meetings

(1) The central council shall meet as and when necessary, but at least one meeting of the council shall be held every year.

(2) The central council shall meet at such time and place as the chairman may think fit and shall observe such procedure in regard to the transaction of its business as may be prescribed.

Objectives of the Central Council

The objectives of the central council are as follows:
The central council shall be to promote and protect the rights of the consumers such as:

(a) The right to be protected against marketing of goods which are hazardous to life and property
(b) The right to be informed about the quality, quantity, potency, purity, standard and price of goods so as to protect the consumer against unfair trade practices

(c) The right to be assured wherever possible, of access to a variety of goods at competitive prices
(d) The right to be heard and to be assured that consumer interests will receive due consideration at appropriate forums
(e) The right to seek redress against unfair trade practices or unscrupulous exploitation of consumers
(f) The right to consumer education

The State Consumer Protection Councils

The state governments have been authorized to establish their respective state consumer protection councils. They have been given a free hand to have such members of the council as they may deem necessary. Various state governments have constituted such councils in their states.

Generally speaking, the state governments have followed the pattern similar to the central council. It is submitted that in the interest of the uniformity of working of such councils in the whole country, the state governments may adopt similar rules as are provided under the Consumer Protection Rules, 1987 by the central government.

Composition

Section 7(2) of the Act of 1987 provides that the state council shall consist of following members:

(a) The minister-in-charge of consumer affairs in the state government who shall be its chairman
(b) Such number of other officials or non-official members representing such interests as may be prescribed by the state government

The state councils have to play a vital role in creating consumer awareness and in the development of consumer movement in their states as well as in the country.

The objectives of every state council shall be to promote and protect within the state the rights of the consumer as laid down in the main Act.

District Forum

Each district of the state shall have a consumer disputes redressal forum known as district forum. Each district forum is to be established by the state government.

The state governments have laid down in their respective consumer protection rules that the district forum shall be located at the headquarters of the district.

Powers

The district forum shall have the same powers as are vested in a Civil Court under the Code of Civil Procedure, 1908, while trying a suit.

Composition

Each district forum shall consist of the following:

(a) A person who is, or has been, or is qualified to be a district judge, who shall be its president
(b) Two other members, who shall be persons of ability, integrity and standing and have adequate knowledge or experience of, or have shown capacity in dealing with problems relating to economics, administration and one of whom shall be a woman

These members are appointed by the state government on the recommendation of a selection committee consisting of the following:

(i) The president of the state commission—chairman

(ii) Secretary, law department of the state—member

(iii) Secretary-in-charge of the department dealing with consumer affairs in the state—member

Every member of the district forum shall hold office for a term of five years or up to the age of 65 years, whichever is earlier and shall not be eligible for re-appointment. The salary or honorarium and other allowances payable and the other terms and conditions of service of the members of the district forum shall be such as may be decided by the state government.

The Consumer Protection Act and relevant Rules made thereunder contain many provisions to secure the independence of the district forums. The terms and conditions of the services of the president and the members of the forum cannot be varied to their disadvantage during their tenure of office. In order to ensure the impartial working of the president and the members, each of them is required before appointment to make an undertaking that he does not or he shall not hold any office of profit.

It is also important to note that the procedure for the removal of the president or a member prevents the state government from acting on any extraneous ground or arbitrarily.

Jurisdiction of the District Forum

(1) Subject to the other provisions of this Act, the district forum shall have jurisdiction to entertain complaints where the value of the goods or services and the compensation, if any, claimed does not exceed rupees five lakh.

(2) A complaint shall be instituted in a district forum within the local limits of whose jurisdiction the opposite party or each of the opposite parties where there are more than one, at the time of the institution of the complaint actually or voluntarily resides or personally works for gain provided that in such case either the permission of the district forum is given.

The consumer protection institutions established to remove public grievances are doing good work and as compared to other arrangements, it is nearer to the people and provides cheap justice at the doorsteps.

NOTES

1. Herman Finer, *The Theory and Practice of Modern Government* (New York: Methuen, 1962), p. 719.
2. N. V. Gadgil, *Government from Inside* (Meerut: Meenakshi Prakashan, 1968), pp. 181–82.
3. Sri Prakasa, Early Days in Pakistan-II: 'Public Men and Permanent Officials', *Hindustan Times*, 17 March 1963, Sunday Magazine, p. 1.
4. *Indian Express*, New Delhi, 10 November, 1966.
5. See *The Statesman*, New Delhi, 11 October 1971.
6. R. Dwarkadas, *Role of Higher Civil Servants in India* (Bombay: Popular Book Depot, 1960), p. 61.
7. Ibid.
8. A. D. Gorwala, *Report on Public Administration* (New Delhi: Planning Commission, 1951), pp. 31–32.
9. Report of Vivian Bose Board of Enquiry, 1958, p. 167.
10. B. S. Narula, 'Ministers and Civil Servants in a Developing Society', *Management in Government*, October–December, 1969, p. 58.

11. O. P. Motival (ed.), *Changing Aspects of Public Administration in India* (Allahabad: Chugh Publications, 1976), p. 75.
12. Nabagopal Das, 'My Life in the ICS', in Kewal L. Panjabi (ed.), *The Civil Servant in India* (Bombay: Bhartiya Vidya Bhawan, 1969), pp. 263–64.
13. Kewal L. Panjabi (ed.), Ibid., p. 211.
14. N. B. Banarjee, *Under Two Ministers* (London: Oxford University Press, 1970), p. 233.
15. Quoted in C. P. Bhambhri, *Administrators in a Changing Society* (Delhi: National Publishing House, 1972), p. 146.
16. F. M. Marx, 'The Higher Services as Action Group in Western Political Developments' in Joseph La Palombara (ed.), *Bureaucracy and Political Development* (Princeton, New Jersey: Princeton University Press, 1963), p. 93.
17. G. P. Pilania and Hoshiar Singh, *Administration and Social Change* (Jaipur: Printwell Publishers, 1985), p. 57.
18. C. P. Bhambhari, *Bureaucracy and Politics in India* (New Delhi: Vikas Publishing, 1971), pp. 266–67.
19. Such examples are numerous, to name a few, B. K. Nehru, Dharam Vira, Bhagwan Sahay, B. D. Pandey, O. P. Mehra, I. H. Latif, S. L. Khurana, L. P. Singh, M. M. K. Wali, A. R. Kidwai; Nirmal Kumar Mukherjee, General K. V. Krishna Rao, Julio Rebeiro, P. C. Alexander, Lt Gen. B. N. K. Chhibber and Romesh Bhandari, etc.
20. D. P. Dhar, *New Perspective in Management* (New Delhi: Department of Personnel and Administrative Reforms, Cabinet Secretariat, 1973).
21. G. P. Pilania and Hoshiar Singh, op. cit., p. 47.
22. Ibid., p. 47.
23. Samuel Paul, 'Corruption: Who Will Bell the Cat?' *Economic and Political Weekly*, No. 23, 7–13 June 1997, Mumbai, p. 1351.
24. Ibid., pp. 1351–52.
25. M. A. Muttalib, 'Strengthening Work Procedures to Curb Corruption in India,' in Hoshiar Singh and D. P. Singh (eds), *Indian Administration* (Jaipur: Aalekh Publishers, 1990), p. 335.
26. A. H. Som, 'Social Perspectives on Corruption in India', *Political Science Review*, Vol. 13, Nos. 1-4, January–December, 1974, pp. 183–84.
27. S. Guhan and Samuel Paul (eds), *Corruption in India: Agenda for Action* (Delhi: Vision Books, 1997).
28. *Report of the Study Team of the ARC on Redress of Citizens' Grievances* (New Delhi: Government of India, 1966), p. 1.
29. Report of the Study Team on Citizens Grievances, op. cit., p. 7.
30. Ibid., p. 18.
31. Bindeshwar Pathak, '*Lok Pal* Dump the Bill, Change the System', *Hindustan Times*, New Delhi, 23 March 1997.
32. P. N. Duda. 'Many Steps Backward', *Hindustan Times*, New Delhi, 9 December 1996.
33. U. G. Agarwal, 'Crusader without Sword', *Hindustan Times*, New Delhi, 16 April 1997.
34. Ibid.
35. V. K. Agarwal, *Consumer Protection Law and Prospect*, 3rd edition (Bangalore: Bhart Law House, 1997), pp. 270–71.

Administrative Reforms

Administrative reform is concerned with the process and the specific devices, techniques, systems and procedures of national federal government which identify, prepare, support or put into effect improvements in administration or the machinery of government. The term 'administrative reform' applies to improvements in executive machinery ranging all the way from fundamental realignments in the structure or the government, to relatively minor changes in the methods of carrying on work within a department or ministry.

The term 'administrative reform' is used in common parlance interchangeably with 'administrative change' and 'administrative reorganization', but there is a slight difference between all these words. 'Reform' means eradication of abuses in the existing system, 'reorganization' means reconstructing the existing system in the light of needs and new demands. 'Change' stands for any type of renovation to suit the ideological or socio-economic environment.

To some modern advocates, administrative reform is synonymous with the rationalizing process that commenced with the bureaucratic revolution. Gerald E. Caiden has defined administrative reform as 'the artificial inducement of administrative transformation against resistance.'[1]

Whatever definition is adopted, there remains the question of delineating administrative reforms from other kinds of societal reform. Where does administration stop and politics or economics or sociology or psychology begin? Take, for instance, the links between administrative reform and political science, Administrative reform is 'power politics in action: it contains ideological rationalization, fights for control of areas, services, and people, political participants and institutions, power drives, campaign strategies and obstructive tactics, compromises and concessions.'[2]

Montgomery defines administrative reform as 'a political process designed to adjust the relationships between a bureaucracy and other elements in a society, or within the bureaucracy itself in order to change the behaviour of the public services.'[3] . . . both the purposes of reforms and the evils addressed vary with their political circumstances. Similarly, one could describe administrative reform as an economic process (redistribution of resources and the alteration of end products or a psychological process (the alteration of behaviour patterns, beliefs, attitudes, and individual actions). But what is there administration about it? What kinds of reforms are administrative reforms?

Before World War II, administration or the administrative aspects or social activities were identified functionally—administration was what administrators did that could not be identified under the rubric of any other discipline. After World War II, Herbert Simon added rational decision-making to the POSDCORB formula, and then the strict dichotomy between 'policy' and 'administration' collapsed. Attention turned from what administrators did to how they did it (processes), where they did it (institutions), and finally within what circumstances they did it (ecology). The general analysis of administrative reform is more applicable to public administration.

As defined above, the term 'administrative reform' applies to improvements in executive machinery ranging all the way from fundamental realignments in the structure of the government to relatively minor changes in the methods of carrying on work within a department or ministry. It must promote openness, accountability, decentralization, public ethics, citizen satisfaction in public administration, recognized administrative ideas.[4] Administrative reform itself is an evaluative concept and not all sorts of changes are administrative reforms.

Need of Administrative Reform

The incredible rate of technological progress, the rapid advances in industrialization, the changes in the status of countries previously subject in whole or in part to the control of other governments, and the associated growth in the number and complexity of governmental activities have imposed extraordinary strains on the traditional machinery of government in every part of the world. The result has been a rising concern with ways and means of modernizing public administration and raising its effectiveness to a level capable of meeting current and prospective demands.

The central objective of administrative reform is to develop and put into effect whatever changes are required to enable the administrative organs of a government to execute public policies in an effective and responsible manner. It is not sufficient to pass laws designed to meet the essential needs of the people, for those needs will not be met unless the system of administration can follow through with prompt and efficient execution. Improvements in administration, therefore, help assure that the intentions of a government are actually translated into action. They also help to produce maximum benefits for the money which a government is able to devote to a particular public purpose.

The great new responsibility of the change in the spheres of life, social, economic and political of the state in the developing society has to be implemented through its instrument, public administration. Thus, the objectives and possible role of public administration have, almost suddenly, expanded greatly, it is to be the instrument of 'total' transformation. However, before the administrative apparatus can hope to bring any transformation, it must get itself transformed to deal with the new tasks. This poses the problem of administrative reform. S. G. Barve wrote in 1966: 'I have two thoughts to suggest in this connection, the first is that some steps must be taken immediately to restore faith in the bona fides of the public administration and the integrity of public life; second that means must be devised whereby pressures of parliamentary opinion will be focussed constructively on the framing and execution of governmental policies so as to impart them the necessary drive, make performance match up to promise and pronouncement, and to promise a wider sense of participation by political elements not in office.'[5]

The most important weakness of our administrative system is its inability to carry out the social and economic policies of the government. Our most serious failures have undoubtedly been in economic administration. Our late Prime Minister, Indira Gandhi, in her very first broadcast to the nation observed: 'In economic development as in other fields of national activity, there is a disconcerting gap between intention and action. To bridge this gap we should adopt whatever far reaching changes in administration may be found necessary.' Naturally, therefore, the national tasks of reconstruction and development facing the administration in India are stupendous.

The nature and scope of reforms vary depending on the magnitude of the problem. Reforms can be conceived very narrowly as has been done in the past, both at the centre and in the states in the form of procedural improvements such as the single file system, the officer oriented pattern and increases in financial and administrative delegations, or they can take a wide perspective and be drastic to the extent of replacing them by something entirely new and better suited to meet new needs.

In another way, broadly speaking, there are two kinds of problems. First, the overall problems which affect the working of all government organizations, like personnel administration, the staffing pattern of ministries and departments, the need for reviewing financial administration in all its aspects, etc. Second, there are other problems of a local character which concern only particular areas of administration or particular ministries along with them are the problems of State government and local administration because of the essential unity of the administration of the country under a federal constitution.

Tools of Administrative Reforms

There are several tools of administrative improvement. The foremost among them is organization and methods (O & M), which include the study of the entire process of management namely, planning, organizing, coordinating, motivating, directing and controlling. The term when used in the restricted sense, means organization and methods and is concerned with the organization of public bodies or private firms, and of the office procedures they adopt. One of the important tasks of O & M work, undoubtedly, is to conduct reviews of an organization with a view to streamlining it. It is confined to improve only the internal structure of the unit concerned. The work of reorganizing the structure at a higher level is done by the highly placed committees like the Ayyangar committee and commissions like the Administrative Reform Commission. In brief, the usual functions of O & M are: the examination of the structure of the organization under review and the study of administrative and clerical procedures and methods, office and equipment mechanization, office layout and working conditions.'[6] This is too limited an interpretation of the term O & M. Many a time it is used as equivalent to management improvement. In this sense it is not only a technique but becomes a function, namely, that of improving administration. 'It exists not only as a management tool as an agent of top management but also as a service for managers, auditors, or others who need it because they themselves do not have the time or the necessary expertise. This dual purpose of agent and service makes the position difficult. In some companies it is all about agent, in others all about service, but somehow both roles need to be combined. There are widely differing views not only about the content of O & M but also concerning its relationship with other techniques concerned with improving effectiveness and efficiency.'[7]

Appleby envisaged a broad role for the O & M unit which he recommended to be set up in the Government of India: 'I recommend that the Government of India give consideration to the establishment of a central office charged with responsibility for giving both extensive and intensive leadership in respect to structure management and procedures. At one level of highly technical and scientific sort, it would give attention to work measurement, work flow, office management, filing systems, space arrangements and the like, at another level it would be charged with general governmental structural studies and proposals. I should hope that at this level also it would have a charter of responsibility for the enhancement of democratic manner and method, within the bureaucracy and between the bureaucracy and the public.'[8]

The main function of an O & M unit is to assist line officials to improve management. In brief, the chief functions of a central O & M unit may be enumerated as: 'Comprehensive reviews of departments; planning new activities; research in O & M techniques; training O & M officials and employees; coordinating the work of different O & M units in government; studying problems of common interest to different units of government; undertaking; ad hoc assignments to investigate and help to solve particular problems; analysing organization methods and procedures; developing management policies, handbooks and other guidelines to help supervizors to do a better job of managing; and acting as a sort of clearing house for all material and information relating to O & M work.'[9]

Another important tool related to the O & M is, work study. It is the application of detailed analysis of work to achieve higher output. It aims at discovering, through systematic methods and a scientific approach, simpler, easier, and more effective and economical ways of doing work. It includes the two different techniques of method study and work measurement. Whereas the former aims at improving methods of work resulting in more effective use of staff and equipment, etc.; the objectives of work measurement are (i) better internal control of work scheduling and individual assignments; (ii) more effective budgeting, forecasting and allocation of funds; and (iii) laying basis for method simplification, organizational changes, etc.

The Special Reorganization Unit (SRU) has developed a system of organization analysis and work study. Another important aspect of O & M work is work simplification. It aims at simplifying procedures and methods. Some of the important techniques for improving work methods are: (i) work distribution analysis; (ii) work content analysis a technique for analysing flow and sequence of operations; (iii) motion analysis a technique for making maximum use of physical motion; and (v) layout analysis—a procedure designed to lead to better utilization of space, personnel and equipment.

Operational research is, in essence, the organized application of the methods of scientific research to operating problems outside the conventional field of science. Its objective is to provide executive with quantitative basis of decisions regarding operations under their control. Its technique is to find new measures of effectiveness and to develop, where necessary, refined and powerful numerical methods specially adapted to the problems at hand. Finally, there is the automation, i.e., the use of mechanical devices or processes. The approach towards office automation is made through the system of punched cards, electronic data, processing and integrated processing. Automation is an important aid to efficiency in office work.

Administrative Reforms in India

The problem of administrative reforms in India is obviously a very difficult one, some of the most glaring defects of the existing administrative systems are: (1) faults in administrative organization and structure, (2) delay in the despatch of business, (3) inefficiency (4) corruption or lack of integrity. Other defects are diffusion of responsibility and the plethora of consultation before a decision is reached accompanied by a general lack of follow up and implementation. The last but not the least important issue faced by us today is that of the relationship between ministers and civil servants. It is certain that no administration can successfully discharge its duties unless it is left alone and allowed to implement the policies of the government. But experience shows that during the last 50 years there has been constant interference in the administration right from the top to the lowest level. Therefore, the civil servants are fast losing self-confidence and sense of responsibility and administrators do not want to do any original thinking at all. That is why administrative reform is needed urgently.

The question of administrative reforms has engaged the attention of the Government of India, state governments, statesmen and administrators. Therefore, various attempts at reforming the administrative system have been made after Independence. An impression has grown that the administration is immune to reforms and innovations and remains status-oriented rather than work-oriented. The abolition of the ICS privileges has not increased the responsiveness of the higher services to the need for change but only strengthened the bureaucratic hold of the IAS. The method of recruitment for the IAS has introduced a serious imbalance in the system and the UPSC examinations neither test intellectual attainments sufficiently nor qualities of initiative and leadership of the candidates and has made the service a preserve of the upper classes hailing from urban centres.

The central government was very much concerned with the matter and since 1947, appointed about 30 committees/commissions to suggest, administrative reforms, as listed below:

Reports on Indian Administration, 1946–1997

1. Reorganization of Central Government (Richard Tottenham), 1946 (This report is significant in understanding independent India's public administration; hence its enumeration here.)
2. Secretariat Reorganization Committee (Girija Shankar Bajpai), 1947
3. Central Pay Commission (Srinivas Varadachariar), 1947
4. Economy Committee (Kasturbai Lalbhai), 1948
5. Reorganization of the Machinery of Government (N. Gopalaswami Ayyangar), 1949
6. Report on Public Administration (A. D. Gorwala), 1951
7. Report on the Efficient Conduct of State Enterprise (A. D. Gorwala), 1951
8. The Machinery of Government—Improvement of Efficiency (R. A. Gopalaswami), 1952
9. Report on Indian and State Administrative Services and Problems of District Administration (V. T. Krishnamachari), 1952
10. Public Administration in India—Report of a Survey (Paul H. Appleby), 1953
11. Railway Corruption Enquiry Committee (J. B. Kriplani), 1955
12. Notes on Changes Necessary in System of Budgetary and Financial Control (Asoka Chanda), 1956
13. Re-examination of India's Administrative System with special reference to Administration of Government's Industrial and Commercial Enterprises (Paul H. Appleby), 1956
14. Public Service (Qualifications for Recruitment) Committee (A. Ramaswami Mudaliar), 1956
15. Balwant Rai Mehta Committee on Community Projects and National Extension Service, 1957
16. Commission of Enquiry of Emoluments and Conditions of Service of Central Government Employees (Jagannadha Das), 1959
17. Staff Welfare Review Committee (Fateh Singh), 1961
18. Committee on Prevention of Corruption (K. Santhanam), 1964
19. The Administrative Reforms Commission (Chairman, Morarji Desai and Late K. Hanumanthaiya), 1966–1970
20. Third Central Pay Commission (Raghubar Dayal), 1973
21. Committee on Recruitment Policy and Selection Methods (D. S. Kothari), 1976
22. Asok Mehta Committee on *Panchayati Raj* Institutions, 1977
23. National Police Commission, 1977
24. Economic Administration Reforms Commission (Chairman, L. K. Jha), 1981–1985
25. Fourth Central Pay Commission Report, 1983
26. Sarkaria Commission on Centre–State Relations, 1983
27. Committee to Review the Existing Administrative Arrangements for Rural Development and Poverty Alleviation Programmes (CAARD) (Chairman, G. V. K. Rao), 1985–1988
28. Committee to Review the Scheme of Civil Services Examinations (Satish Chandra), 1988–1990
29. Dr Raja J. Chelliah Committee on the Tax Reforms, 1991–1992

30. Fifth Pay Commission Report, 9 April 1994—30 January 1997
31. Second Administrative Reforms Commission Chairman (Veerappa Moily), 2005

Administrative reform is a continuous process, therefore, it is better to study it in the historical perspective. The attempts at administrative reforms in our country for the sake of study, can be divided into the following periods:

First Phase 1947–1964: A period of building historically till the death of Jawaharlal Nehru.

Second Phase 1964–1976: A period of comprehensive reforms and the era of Administrative Reforms Commission till the Congress ruled at the centre.

Third Phase 1977–1990: A period of new ideas and reforms.

Fourth Phase 1990 onwards: A period of privatization and decentralization.

First Phase (1947–1964)

In July 1947, a secretariat reorganization committee, which functioned like an officer's shortage committee, was appointed. The government set up in 1948 the economy committee to review the increase in the civil expenditure of the central government since 1938–1939 and to make recommendations for the promotion of true economy in the administration by the elimination of unnecessary wasteful or extravagant expenditure, under the chairmanship of Kasturbhai Lalbhai, a prominent industrialist. It was followed by the Government of India Reorganization of Machinery of Government Report in 1949 by N. Gopalaswamy Ayyangar. His major recommendations were on the grouping of central governmental ministries into four bureaux that was primarily designed to secure co-ordination of policy and planning, the establishment of a common financial advisory organization and a common central administrative office for the efficient performance of common services and administrative coordination. Administrative innovations devised by Ayyangar were perhaps far ahead of the time, however, the ministry of economic and defence coordination was a belated vindication of Ayyangar's rationalism and foresight. The O & M division originally suggested by Ayyangar was also set up in 1954.

The Planning Commission was set up in March 1950, in July 1951 asked A. D. Gorwala, a retired administrator, to assess how far the existing administrative machinery and methods were adequate to meet the requirements of planned development. Gorwala's report served as the basis for the formulation of certain important proposals for the reform of administration, which were later included in the First Five-Year Plan.

The two reports by Paul H. Appleby, submitted in 1953 and 1956 to the Government of India, had a significant influence on the thinking about administrative reforms in government circles as well as the educated public. His first report, 'Public Administration in India: Report of a Survey', dealt more with changes in the basic principles and concepts including the Indian administrative organization and practice and less with the details of the administrative machinery and methods. In his second report 'Re-examination of India's Administrative System' he made several suggestions for streamlining organization, work procedures, recruitment, training and relations between administration and Parliament, administration and planning commission, and administration and the comptroller and auditor-general.

In 1954, Asoka Chanda submitted his report titled 'Notes on Changes Necessary in the System of Budgetary and Financial Control and in Other Methods' to eliminate delays in execution of projects. Chanda recommended greater measure of delegation, creation of all-India services, adoption of office-oriented system of functioning, constitution of a common service divided vertically into departments to provide for specialized training in the different spheres of governmental activity.

In 1962, the government set up a committee under the chairmanship of K. Santhanam known as the Committee on Prevention of Corruption, to examine the problem of corruption in government. The committee submitted its report in 1964.

In 1963, while conducting the mid-term appraisal of the Third Plan it was found that the pace of economic growth was slow, therefore, central and state governments were directed to enhance the administrative efficiency for speedy implementation of development programmes. The review resulted in setting up a new department of administrative reforms in the home ministry in March 1964 and O & M division was transferred from cabinet secretariat to this department. In 1965, the bureau of public enterprises was set up in the ministry of finance for better management of public enterprises. In September 1985, it became the department of public enterprises under the ministry of industry. As already mentioned, the Government of India appointed a number of other committees and commissions to make suggestions for administrative improvement.

Apart from these committees, there have been five pay commissions, which the central government set up in 1946, 1958, 1971–1972, 1982–1983 and 1996. The Fifth Pay Commission's reform proposals are important and will be discussed in the end of the chapter.

The Planning Commission has also been recommending changes in the public administration of the country. Each Five Year Plan contains a chapter on public administration. The Planning Commission determines the nature of the administrative machinery to secure the successful implementation of the plan. The Estimates Committee of the Parliament also covers the reform of the machinery of government and its personnel within its ambit. Some of the reports are devoted entirely to questions of administrative reform. Mention in this connection must be made of its second report on reorganization of the secretariat and departments of the Government of India (1950–1951), ninth report on administrative, financial and other reforms (1953–1954) and 93rd report on public services (1965–1966).

The discussion may be summed up by saying that government took several steps as a result of the recommendations of these committees. The special reorganization unit was set up in 1958 to incorporate the use of work study techniques for determining work loads and staff complements and overhauling procedures. Two high-level institutions, the central O & M division and the Indian Institute of Public. Administration (IIPA), were set up in 1954. In August 1960, administrative vigilance division was set up in the ministry of home affairs to render assistance and to coordinate the activities of the central government in their campaign against corruption in the public services.

The Government of India set up the department of administrative reforms in the ministry of home affairs in March 1964. Now it is under a separate ministry known as the department of personnel and administrative reforms, pensions and public grievances to deal with problems of reform, reorganization and modernization of administration at all levels so as to make it an efficient and sensitive instrument for carrying out the task of economic development and social welfare, and for achieving the general social objectives which the country has set and the need for setting up of the agency for evolving a machinery for the redress of grievances of citizens arising from unsound procedures, delays, lack of courtesy and consideration in official dealings.

The first and the second pay commissions, which submitted their reports in 1947–1948 and 1956–1957 respectively, made several important observations concerning public administration. Many suggestions were made by the estimates committee and other committees of the Parliament. State governments also appointed number of committees which suggested administrative reforms.

The O & M division was basically meant to provide leadership for cooperative effort to improve the administration. It encourages civil servants to use the scientific method to find out what is wrong and what the remedies are.

The ministry of finance also set up a special reorganization unit in the department of expenditure to assess the requirement of staff in various ministries/departments through work measurement techniques. This unit also became a permanent agency for reviewing the organization and procedure of the Government of India and suggested improvement in the existing methods of works.

Indian Institute of Public Administration (IIPA)

The institute was set up as a result of Paul H. Appleby's recommendation. It runs a number of training courses for the public administrators and conducts researches on subject matters of public administration. It publishes the *Indian Journal of Public Administration* which provides very good material for the implementation of public administration. Several other developments took place during this period. On the recommendation of Santhanam committee in 1964, a central vigilance commission was established to inquire into the cases of corruption by higher civil servants. Likewise, on the recommendations of the second pay commission (1957), a Whitley-type machinery for redressal of grievances of civil servants was set up by the government. In November 1963, the Das commission was appointed to inquire into the corruption charges against Pratap Singh Kairon, chief minister of Punjab. In March 1964, the O & M division was converted into a full-fledged department of administrative reforms in the ministry of home affairs. The department provided impetus to the administrative reforms.

Main Features of First Phase

The first phase of administrative reforms is full of establishment of new institutions for efficient administration. Some of its main features are: First, the administrative reforms were based on the parallel lines, i.e., the O & M and through committees set up from time to time. Second was the erosion in the integrity of administration, which caused the establishment of central vigilance commission. Third, during this period, the Parliament asserted itself in matters of administrative reforms. Fourth, entrance of the government in business in the form of public enterprises provided opportunity to judge the effectiveness of bureaucracy in economic growth.

Second Phase (1965–1976)

Administrative reforms, until the setting up of the administrative reforms commission, have been carried out mostly in the spirit, style and shape of improvizations. Those several committees that have been set up to report on administrative reforms have been content to suggest some alterations here and some additions there. Few have gone deeper and examined the whole system of administration as such; almost all have been the prisoners of the existing framework and the system that underscores it.[10]

K. Hanumanthaiya while commenting on this period rightly pointed out, 'during the last 20 years, there were only adjustments and no reforms in the administration.'[11] Thus, this period is characterized by 'too ready a disposition on the part of the government to appoint committees but on equal measure of apathy or even indifference to profit from their labours.'[12] The government even delayed the implementation of the recommendations made by the committees.

Administrative Reforms Commission (1966–1970)

The resolution of setting up the administrative reforms commission, issued in 1964, said that 'it will give consideration to the need for ensuring the highest standards of efficiency and integrity in the public services, and for making public administration a fit instrument for carrying out the social and economic policies of the government and achieving social and economic goals of development as also one which is responsive to people.' The commission was asked to consider the following:

(i) The machinery of the Government of India and its procedures of work; (ii) the machinery for planning at all levels; (iii) centre–state relationships; (iv) financial administration; (v) personnel administration; (vi) economic administration; (vii) administration at the state level; (viii) district administration; (ix) agricultural administration; and (x) problems of redress of citizens' grievances.

Thus, the commission was asked to examine and report on such a vast array of subjects. It is an example of all-embracing attempt at reform. The commission submitted 20 reports for the reforms in various fields of administration in India. The commission has made, in all, 581 recommendations and suggestions. The government has accepted 80 per cent of recommendations made by the commission. As the commission also explored areas within the states' jurisdiction, the central government evidently lacks direct authority to take or compel action on them. It may bring such recommendations to the notice of the states and at best, use moral pressure in favour of them. The recommendations directly concerning the centre broadly fall into two categories from the angle of implementation. Some recommendations concern formal structure and procedures of work. The other category calls for restructuring of rules, behaviour and attitudes, which, in turn, ultimately rests on the inner urges and orientations of the elective and permanent administrators. A large number of structure- and procedure-based recommendations are rather mild, emphasizing as they do only minor re-adjustments, modifications and realignments. Even after taking into account all these factors, one cannot escape the painful conclusion that the record of acceptance of the commission's recommendations has been discouraging and disheartening.[13]

During the period 1979–1980, due to ARC recommendations and efforts of the central reform agency, enormous changes in administrative structure, system and procedures took place. On the recommendation of the ARC, the department of personnel was set up, department of administrative reforms was restructured for better performance, system of secretariat working was improved by introducing desk officer system, performance budgeting was introduced by all government ministries; maximum possible powers were delegated, and the working of bureau of public enterprises was improved after the recommendations of the ARC report on public sector.

The department of administrative reforms carried out many studies relating to management such as on organizational structure, methods and procedures, information system, records management, employees satisfaction, use of modern office machines, equipment and financial administration, etc. These studies improved the working of the offices and attention was paid for citizen's satisfaction. All the states set up the department of personnel and administrative reform at the state level along with state bureau of public enterprises, during the 1970s. In 1976 audit and accounts were separated for administrative improvements. However, the Emergency in 1975–1977 gave a rude shock to the image of public administration when the credibility of the policy-making and policy-executing levels suffered.[14]

Third Phase (1977–1990)

After the internal Emergency, elections were held in March 1977 and the Janata Party came in power at the centre. The Janata Party government appointed various commissions to point out the Emergency excesses and no tangible improvement took place in the administration. Again in 1980, Congress party came in power and reform process started.

The Fazal Committee (1980–1982) on public enterprises also felt the need of accountability in public sector. The Jha Commission (EARC 1981–1985) in its report on 'accountability' stressed the need of accountability and laid emphasis on performance and results rather than rules and procedures.[15] Both the Fazal committee and Jha commission suggested the changes in organizations relating to clear-cut definition of their goals and objectives, delegation of powers, system of performance appraisal, a system of reward and punishment, etc. As a follow-up action on the recommendations of these two committees the MPI and DPAR took concrete steps to institutionalize accountability in the government by introducing annual action plan (AAP). The AAP would mention the key activities/functions and the responsibility centres at the level of joint secretary by name.

In March 1985, a full-fledged ministry of personnel public grievances and pensions was set up with three departments, namely the department of personnel and training, department of administrative reforms and public grievances and department of pensions and pensioners' welfare. This ministry was placed directly under the prime minister assisted by a minister of state. During this period more emphasis was laid on work culture and highest priority was given to performance, results and outcomes. Prime Minister Rajiv Gandhi, addressing the nation on 5 January 1985, announced several measures to equip administration for social and economic transformation. These measures included decentralization, accountability, effective machinery for redress of public grievances and prompt courteous service to the citizens. In September 1985, a new ministry of programme implementation was created under the charge of the prime minister. The ministry mainly coordinated all poverty alleviation programmes and made administration more responsive. The ministry of programmes implementation (MPI) introduced the concept of management by objective (MBO). According to tills a task plan along with a time frame for each task has to be prepared and allocated to the individual officers and units to fix specific responsibility. Monitoring of the target achievements is done every month at the level of secretary and MPI. A new system of memorandum of understanding was adopted at the direction of the then Prime Minister, Rajiv Gandhi, for public enterprises. This is an annual action plan drawn up by public enterprises and agreed upon between the PEs and administration, ministries/departments.[16]

To match the responsibility, powers have been delegated by the ministries to the lower level functionaries by finance ministry to administrative ministries, so that responsibility for the performance can be pinpointed. Likewise inter-ministerial consultations took a long time to arrive at any decision. Hence, to improve the situation and avoid delay, improved procedures have been evolved for speedy decisions. In such cases, time has been fixed and within that period the ministry/department has to send his comments otherwise it will be presumed that the concerned ministry/department has nothing to comment.

The department of administrative reforms and public grievances has also taken several steps to improve administrative reforms. The department has prepared a scheme for modernization of government offices to make them model office through functional layouts, better services to the public and removal of public grievances and cost effective management. All the offices have been given separate budgets for purchase of modern equipments such as photocopiers, electronic typewriters and computers. To increase productivity, the concept of work improvement team has been introduced. The scheme seeks to generate higher employee morale, improved productivity and reduction in cost through participation at the grassroots level. This scheme has been introduced in the departments which come in contact with large number of people daily such as railways, posts, DDA, health, labour, banking, etc. Other measures include lump-sum payment of road tax for personal vehicles like cars, scooters and motorcycles, new telephone number through electronic exchanges which are easy to remember, computerized reservation facilities for rail reservations, reduced paper work and several other procedures have been simplified. Attention has also been paid for speedy removal of public grievances by setting and strengthening grievances removal machinery. A senior officer in each ministry/department is designated as director of grievance for speedy disposal of complaints.

Personnel reforms were also proposed during the 1980s and a major step in this field was introduction of compulsory training programme for IAS officers. These programmes were structured to meet the needs of officers with six to nine years' service, 10–16 years and 16–20 years in regard to programme implementation, management concepts, decision-making techniques, policy planning and analysis, respectively.[17] The 15 months national management education programme was also devised for young civil servants and managers of public and private sector organizations with the cooperation of all IITs, the Xavier Labour Relations Institute, Jamshedpur and Management Institute, Gurgaon (Haryana).

Main Characteristics of Third Phase

In this phase three steps were taken for comprehensive administrative reforms. In this period the Administrative Reforms Commission (ARC) was appointed, which examined our administrative system comprehensively and put forth 581 recommendations in all for the administrative reforms. Second, the government accepted the recommendation of creating 'ombudsman' institutions like the *Lok Pal* and *Lok Ayukta* in India to deal with public grievances and Bill is pending before the Parliament for the establishment of *Lok Pal*, while *Lok Ayukta*s have been appointed in many states. Third, during this phase, the government had created 'administrative tribunals' for expeditious disposal of the grievances of the public servants. Fourth, the central government have introduced performance budgeting since 1970–1971. Fifth, during this period administrative reforms were more management oriented. A greater emphasis was laid on management and administrative reforms began to be viewed as management-intensive exercise. During this period, behavioural approach also emerged, which insists on the human element in administration. The concept emanated from the business schools which remained highly influenced by the American thought. Sixth, for the improvement of civil servants, greater emphasis was laid on the institutional training. Of course, in India training of civil servants has a longer history, but a new emphasis was given in 1966 by creating a separate training division in the ministry of home affairs. Now this training division is a part of the department of the personnel administrative reforms and training of the ministry of personnel and administrative reforms, public grievances and pensions. The training programmes have been diversified and have grown in numbers. But the emphasis on training has been criticized on the grounds that the contribution of training to the overall efficiency of the organization is limited, civil servants have no sufficient motivation to take training seriously, trainers are not selected properly and training material sometimes is also not up to the mark.

Fourth Phase, 1990 Onwards

This period is marked by minority unstable governments at the centre with weak political leadership. The process of liberalization started during this period has paved the way for removal of controls and delicensing in industrial policy. The new economic policy since 1991 has simplified the process of industrialization in the country.[18] Moreover, in this period steps have been taken to decentralize the powers through the 73rd and 74th Constitution Amendments Acts, 1992, which have constitutionalized *panchayati raj* and municipal bodies. We have already discussed this aspect in detail in the relevant chapters.

The Government of India constituted a tax reforms committee on 29 August 1991 under the chairmanship of Dr Raja J. Chelliah to examine the structure of direct and indirect taxes. The committee, in its interim report submitted in December 1991, observed that 'certain important administrative and policy issues, however, deserve brief mention in this interim report because of the urgent need for initiating suitable action in regard to them. First and foremost among them is the need to tone up the administration. No amount of tax reform, rationalization or simplification can substantially improve tax compliance, unless there is a substantial improvement in public perception regarding the efficiency, technical competence, integrity and ability of tax authorities to relentlessly pursue and punish tax evaders, without political or other interference.' The committee suggested that 'for this, the morale of the work force should improve. The government should recognize the paramount importance of the revenue departments and should spare no efforts in improving their condition of service, technical skills and work environment.[19] The committee submitted its final report on 25 August 1992 to the finance minister and made wide-ranging recommendations.

In this period, the nexus between politicians, civil servants and business houses became clearly visible when scams of various kinds were unearthed. These include the Bofors case, security scam, urea and fertilizer, hawala and the much talked about fodder scam of Bihar in which the chief minister of the state has been charge sheeted by the CBI even then he had not resigned. He resigned after much dilly-dallying. He could not be easily arrested due to fear of large-scale violence by his political supporters in the state. Thus, the administration was unable to perform its legitimate functions leave alone administrative reforms.

Fifth Pay Commission and Administrative Reforms

The Fifth Central Pay Commission (FCPC), while recommending high salaries for the government employees, also pleaded for administrative reforms keeping in view that substantial pay hike unaccompanied by administrative reforms would amount to further pampering government employees. The FCPC, in its voluminous report consisting of 172 chapters and 1600 pages, devoted Chapter 33 to discussing administrative reforms. The reform package states that the government should do for less than now and it should be confined to the core functions that cannot be performed by the market and everything else should be left to private hands as the public choice theory propagates. The commission, therefore, recommends the dismantling of the permit-licence system, disinvestment in the public sector, corporatization of departmental undertakings and privatization and contracting out of services now performed directly by the government. Thus, the government has to perform the core function only. Only the FCPC proposed to cut manpower by 30 per cent amounting to about 3.5 lakh posts in 10 years, which seems to be a long-drawn-out period. The government has not accepted this recommendation.[20]

The other recommendations of the FCPC are the enactment of a Right to Information Act, all government services to be covered by the Consumer Protection Act, establishment of a national election fund as well as an anti-corruption agency having an independent constitutional status and introduction of a citizen's charter. These steps would address problems like lack of transparency, spread of corruption and absence of people-friendly administration. Further, the commission has recommended that no file should be required to move through more than three hierarchical levels for any decision to be taken. This step would certainly lessen file pushing, quicken decision making and promote accountability.

The commission rightly recommended that legitimacy should be accorded to contract employment, especially in situations like short-term vacancies up to five years, time-bound special projects and specialized jobs not generally required. Contract appointments are seen as opening the door to the lateral entry of experts. It may prove better if all government employments are made contractual because constitutional guarantee of security of service under Article 311 to government personnel had gone counter to accountability. The recommendations of the commission that the army should be withdrawn from its counter-insurgency role and that the Rashtriya Rifles should be disbanded to strengthen democracy because it restores responsibility for dealing with inter-security problems to civil governments were warmly welcomed. Moreover, the commission has recommended that the 'central public organizations' have grown at the cancerous rate of 5.6 per cent per annum, as against 1 per cent for the bureaucracy as a whole, therefore, their numbers should be pruned by one-third in 10 years is timely and good but 'the pruning should be far more and effected much quicker. A substantial reduction of the Union's paramilitary forces would help move its management out of the coercive trap.'[21] The commission's suggestion for a 'carefully funded scheme for improving the effectiveness of state police forces' seems to be meaningless because police reforms need decentralization of police administration under democratic cover.

The commission has given pre-eminence to the IAS, which has caused much resentment among other services. The commission's assertion that bureaucrats are catalytic agents of change, that they enforce socially beneficial regulations, that they act as watchdogs supporting good people and suppressing malefactors, and so on, is a retrograde and regressive proposition. Further, the commission has made the extraordinary assertion that only a network of 'all-India services' can ensure the country against disintegration as if without the all-India services, the country would not remain united. But experience proves it otherwise. In spite of all-India services, separatist movements like Gorkhaland in Bengal, Bodoland in Assam, and Vidharbha in Maharashtra have gained momentum. The unity of the country depends on emotional attachment, cultural bonding and feeling of nationalism rather than on administration. Not only this, the commission has suggested for the creation of more all-India services in the name of the country's larger interests, forgetting that the states have earlier objected to it. This is an anti-federal move and the country should be left to decide which way it wants to go. The suggestion of the commission to have civil service boards at the centre and in the states, headed by retired Supreme Court/high court judges, to control transfers of government servants. In case a particular state government overrules its board the matter should be placed before the concerned legislature. This suggestion of the commission is anti-democratic.[22] Let the people decide whether they want more bureaucracy or a strong and clean democracy.

The other suggestions of the commission to have only three national holidays—Republic Day, Independence Day and Gandhi Jayanti and 12 casual leaves is timely to promote work culture, but the question is will it be implemented? The suggestion that bonus should be linked to productivity and not to production is good. The suggestion for modernization through automation and computers needs to be supported.

The government has accepted the report of the commission with some modifications. The government has not accepted the commission's recommendation of increase in the retirement age from 58 years to 60 years and reduction of employees posts up to 30 per cent in 10 years, etc.

Second Administrative Reforms Commission (2005)

The resolution to set up second Administrative Reforms Commission was issued on 31 August 2005. It stated that the commission will suggest measures to achieve a proactive, responsive, accountable, sustainable and efficient administration for the country at all levels of government. The commission was asked to consider the following:

(i) Organizational structure of the Government of India

(ii) Ethics in governance

(iii) Refurnishing of personnel administration

(iv) Strengthening of financial management system

(v) Steps to ensure effective administration at state level

(vi) Steps to ensure effective district administration

(vii) Local self-government/*panchayati raj* institutions

(viii) Social capital, trust and participative public service delivery

(ix) Citizen-centric administration

(x) Promoting e-governance

(xi) Issues of federal polity

(xii) Crisis management

(xiii) Public order

Thus, the terms of reference of the commission were wide; almost covering all aspects of administration at all levels.

Administrative Reforms in the States

At the state level, many states have also appointed administrative reforms commissions/committees, for example, Kerala Administrative Reforms Commission, 1958; Administrative Enquiry Committee, Orissa, 1958; Andhra Pradesh Administrative Reforms Enquiry Committee, 1964; Punjab Administrative Reforms Committee, 1964; Rajasthan Administrative Reforms Committee, 1966; MP Administrative Reforms Commission, 1969; Tamil Nadu Administrative Reforms Commission, 1973; and West Bengal Administrative Reforms Committee, 1982.

As a result of the recommendations of these commissions/committees several states have introduced reforms in their administration.

Features of Administrative Reforms

The administrative reforms in India has passed through many stages and during the process acquired some important features. These are as follows:

(i) In India, the main sources of reforms are mainly three. First, some reforms have come from the political process such as re-organization of states or public enquiries against the chief ministers or a political scandal. Some reforms have been initiated by the reform committees/commissions; i.e., the ARC, whereas others have been initiated by the central agencies such as department of personnel and administrative reforms.

(ii) The Union government has played the leadership role in the field of administrative reforms in the country for all the three levels—central, state and local. This has happened mainly because of centralized planning. The Union government has set up several committees on state list subjects such as Balwant Rai Mehta Committee, 1957, to suggest ways for people's participation and *panchayati raj*, V. T. Krishnamachari Committee report on Indian and state administrative services and problems of district administration, Asok Mehta committee on *panchayati raj* institutions, etc. Even the ARC has reported on state administration.

(iii) Academic and research institutions in the country have not made any significant attempt to provide leadership in the field of administrative reforms. Even the IIPA has not contributed much in this field.

(iv) NGOs, voluntary organizations and citizen's forums, etc. have also not taken active interest in the field of administrative reforms.

Overall Impact and Shortcoming of Administrative Reforms

First, a number of committees and commissions examined and made recommendation for reform but the problems of field administration have not been examined in detail. Not only this, the reports containing recommendations of committees and commissions appointed from time to time were either not read or not considered for years. Second, the recommendations of committees and commissions were many but their implementation was very poor; this is because our bureaucratic culture frustrates implementation of reforms leading to any change. Third, administrative reform is a low priority subject for the political leadership. They take interest in short-term changes here and there, not in long-term administrative reforms. Fourth, lack of integrity and prevalence of quick money for any work in administration has also slowed down the process of administrative reform. Issues such as administrative morality, public accountability, democratization and decentralization of administration and openness of administrative actions, etc. are beyond the vocabulary of administrative reforms.[23] Fifth, neglect of democratic decentralization efforts during last four/five decades in spite of Balwant Rai Mehta Committee (1959), Ashok Mehta Committee (1978) and G. V. K. Rao Committee (1985) recommendations for democratic decentralization. In 1992, Parliament passed 73rd Constitution Amendment Act for the establishment of *panchayati raj* in the country for decentralization purposes. Sixth, the efforts for ministerial/departmental accountability through the system of annual action plans (AAP) that were launched with great zeal diluted as the time passed. The number and quality of AAPs deteriorated very fast with the passage of time. AAPs and performance budget have become only rituals. Thus, civil servants have evaded any accountability for their decisions and actions. MBO techniques and MOU extended to public enterprises have both not been taken in right earnest.

The success of administrative reforms depends on top politicians and bureaucratic support, but unfortunately both are usually busy in the furtherance of their mutual interests and hardly find time to pay attention to administrative reforms. The politics in the country has remained unstable after 1989 and bureaucrats hardly provide leadership for administrative reforms. What has been lacking in our administrative reform efforts in the last 50 years is congruence between strategy, structure and substance.

NOTES

1. Gerald E. Caiden, *Administrative Reform* (Chicago: Aldine Publishing House, 1969), p. 8.
2. Ibid., p. 9.
3. John Montgomery, 'Source of Bureaucratic Reform: A Topology of Purpose and Politics,' in Ralph Braibanti (ed.), *Political and Administrative Development,* (Durham: Duke University Press, 1969).
4. S. R. Maheshwari, *Theories and Concepts in Public Administration* (New Delhi: Allied Publishers Limited, 1991), p. 143.
5. S. G. Barve, 'The Larger Political Context of Administrative Reforms', *Indian Journal of Public Administration,* July–September 1966, p. 353.
6. G. E. Milward (ed.), *Organisation and Method* (London: Macmillan Co., 1959), p. 253.
7. Ibid., p. 252.
8. Paul H. Appleby, 'Public Administration in India', Report of a Survey, 1953, p. 59.
9. A. Avasthi and S. R. Maheshwari, *Public Administration,* 2nd edition (Agra: Lakshmi Narain Agrawal and Co., 1991), p. 553.
10. S. R. Maheshwari, *The Administrative Reforms Commission* (Agra: Lakshmi Narain Agrawal and Co., 1972), p. 15.
11. *Hindustan Times,* 28 April 1967.

12. S. R. Maheshwari, op. cit., p. 16.
13. See for details, S. R. Maheshwari, op. cit., pp. 143–151.
14. M. A. Muttalib, 'Trends in Administrative Reforms', in Kuldeep Mathur (ed.), *A Survey of Research in Public Administration, 1970–1979* (New Delhi: Concept Publishing Company, 1986), p. 120.
15. See for details, Prahlad K. Basu, 'Strategic Issues in Administrative Reorganisation, Developing Countries Perspective', *EPW*, 30 May 1992.
16. Ibid., p. 50.
17. Ibid., p. 53.
18. See, for details, Hoshiar Singh, *Aspects of Indian Administration* (Jaipur: R. B. S. A. Publishers), pp. 137–145.
19. *Interim Report of the Committee on Tax Reforms* (New Delhi: Government of India, December 1991), p. 299.
20. *Hindustan Times*, New Delhi, 19 July 1997.
21. Nirmal Kumar Mukerji, 'Pay Commission and All That', *EPW*, No. 15, Bombay, 12–18 April 1997, p. 753.
22. Ibid., p. 752.
23. Hoshiar Singh and Pankej Singh, 'Administrative Reforms in India: A Historical Perspective', *Journal of Constitutional and Parliamentary Studies*, Vol. 40, Nos. 3–4 July–December 2006.
24. S. R. Maheshwari, *Theories and Concepts in Public Administration* (New Delhi: Allied Publishers Limited, 1991), p. 138.

National Human Rights Commission

The concept of human rights is an ancient doctrine of natural right based on natural law. The concept of human right can be traced to natural law philosophers in modern era, who advocated for these rights to protect the individual from the excesses of the state. In the 18th and 19th centuries in Europe several philosophers proposed the concept of 'natural rights', rights belonging to a person by nature and because he is a human being. The term 'natural rights' eventually fell into disarray but the concept of 'universal rights' took root. Philosophers such as Thoman Paine, John Stuart Mill and Henry-David Thorean expounded the concept. Thorean was the first to use the term 'human rights' in his book, *Civil Disobedience*. John Stuart Mill, in his *Essay on Liberty*, and Thomas Paine, in his essay, *The Rights of Man*, were the other proponents of human rights. The concept of human rights represents an attempt to protect the individual from oppression and injustice by the state. They provide a human standard of achievement for all the people and all the nations.

Preamble to the Universal Declaration of Human Rights, 1948

The Charter of the United Nations, which was adopted after the Second World War on 25th June 1945, used the words 'human rights'. This is the first document in which the words 'human rights' were used. The Charter was not binding. This deficiency was removed by the UN General Assembly by adopting the following two covenants for the observance of human rights in December 1965: (i) The covenant on civil and political rights and (ii) the covenant on economic, social and cultural rights. The first one formulated loyalty enforceable right of the individual and the second one was addressed to the states to the implement them by legislation.

India was party to the above-mentioned covenants, therefore, for the protection of human rights a 'Human Rights' Bill was passed by both the Houses of Parliament, which received the assent of the president on 8 January 1994 and became the Protection of Human Rights Act, 1993 (Act 10 of 1994). Under the provisions of the Act, the National Human Rights Commission was constituted to perform the functions assigned to it concerning the human rights protection.

Constitution of National Human Rights Commission

1. The Commission shall consist of:
   (a) A chairperson who has been a chief justice of the Supreme Court
   (b) One member, who is, or has been, a judge of the Supreme Court
   (c) One member, who is, or has been, the chief justice of a high court
   (d) Two members to be appointed from amongst persons having knowledge of, or practical experience in, matters relating to human rights
2. The chairpersons of the National Commission for Minorities, the National Commission for the Scheduled Castes and Scheduled Tribes and the National Commission for Women shall be deemed to be members of the Commission for the discharge of functions specified in clauses (b) to (j) of Section 12. Thus, the Commission consists of one chairperson and six other members.
3. There shall be a secretary-general who shall be the chief executive officer of the Commission and shall exercise such powers and discharge such functions of the Commission as it may delegate him.

The headquarters of the Commission shall be in Delhi, and the Commission may, with the prior approval of the central government, establish offices at other places in India.

The chairperson and other members of the Commission are appointed by the president on the recommendation of a committee consisting of

(a) The prime minister—chairman
(b) Speaker of the House—member
(c) Minister in-charge of the Ministry of Home Affairs in the Government of India—member
(d) Leader of the Opposition in the House of the Peoples—member
(e) Leader of the Opposition in the Council of the States—member
(f) Deputy Chairman of the Council of the States—member

The sitting judge of the Supreme Court or sitting chief justice of a high court shall be appointed after consultation with the chief justice of the Supreme Court.

Removal of a Member of the Commission

The president can remove the chairperson or any member of the Commission from his office on the ground of proved misbehaviour or incapacity, subject to the inquiry report of the Supreme Court on the grounds of any disqualification such as being adjudged an insolvent, or engaged in any paid employment, or being of unsound mind, or involved in moral turpitude.

Term of Office of Members

The term of office of the chairperson of the Commission and members shall be five years or till the age of 70 years, whichever is earlier. They shall be eligible for re-appointment for another five years up to the age of 70 years. After retirement, a chairperson or a member is barred for further employment under Government of India or under the government of any state.

In the event of vacancy in the office of the chairperson by reason of death, resignation or otherwise, the president can appoint, by notification, one of the members of the Commission to act as the chairperson until the appointment of a new chairperson. Likewise, the president may authorize a member to discharge the functions of the chairperson until the date on which the chairperson resumes his duties after leave.

The salary and allowances and the other terms of conditions of service of a member shall not vary to his disadvantage after his appointment.

Officers and Staff of the Commission

The Central Government will provide an officer of the rank of secretary to the Government of India who shall be the secretary-general of the Commission and police and investigative staff under an officer not below the rank of a director-general of Police (DGP) and other investigative staff. The Commission appoint other administrative, technical and scientific staff as per central government rules.

Functions and Powers of the Commission

The Protection of Human Rights Act, 1993, Chapter III, Section 12, enumerates the following functions of the Commission:

(a) enquire, suo motu or on a petition presented to it by a victim or any person on his behalf, into a complaint of (i) violation of human rights or abetment thereof or (ii) negligence in the prevention of such violation, by a public servant;

(b) interview in any proceeding involving any allegation of violation of human rights pending before a court with the approval of such court;

(c) visit under intimation to the state government, any jail or any other institution under the control of the state government, where persons are detained or lodged for purposes of treatment, reformation or protection, to study the living conditions of the inmates and make recommendations thereon;

(d) review the safeguards provided by or under the Constitution or any law for the time being in force for the protection of human rights and recommend measures for their effective implementation;

(e) review the factors, including acts of terrorism, that inhibit the enjoyment of human rights and recommend appropriate remedial measures;

(f) study treaties and other international instruments on human rights and make recommendations for their effective implementation;

(g) undertake and promote research in the field of human rights;

(h) spread human rights literacy among various sections of society and promote awareness of the safeguards available for the protection of these rights through publications, media, seminars and other available means;

(i) encourage the efforts of non-governmental organizations and institutions working in the field of human rights;

(j) such other functions as it may consider necessary for the promotion of human rights.

Powers Relating to Enquiries

The Commission shall have the powers of a civil court in the case of enquiries. The Commission shall have power to summon and enforce the attendance of witnesses and examine them on oath, discover and produce any document, receive evidence on affidavits, requisition any public record or copy thereof from any court or office, and issue commissions for the examination of witnesses or documents, any other matter which may be prescribed.

The Commission has power to call any person to furnish information on such points which may be useful for, or relevant for the enquiry. The Commission can search any place or building for documents concerning the enquiry. The Commission has powers of a civil court and can deal with the cases as per the law.

The Commission shall, for the purposes of conducting any investigation pertaining to the enquiry, utilize the services of any officer or investigation agency of the central government or any state government with the concurrence of the respective governments. The investigating agency shall, after the enquiry, submit the report to the Commission with the prescribed period. After the completion of the enquiry, the Commission may take any action as per the Act.

The Commission can also deal with complaints of violation of human rights by members of the armed forces. The Commission can seek a report from the central government regarding violation of human rights by the armed forces. After receiving the report, the Commission shall make its recommendation to the government and the central government will revert back within three months. The Commission will publish its recommendation and action taken by the government on such recommendation in its report.

The Commission will submit its annual report or special report to the central government and to the state government concerned. The respective governments place these reports before each house of Parliament or state legislature, respectively, along with the action taken/or proposed to be taken on the recommendations of the Commission and the reasons for non-acceptance of the recommendations.

Much of the concern of human rights has been regarding the victims of police atrocities committed in the course of maintenance of law and order. The Supreme Court, in such cases, not only condemned police atrocities but has gone ahead and provided compensation to the victims of police atrocities while noting that incidents of harassment result in the violation of fundamental rights to life and personal liberty. The Supreme Court has taken such cases in all seriousness. In spite of all these efforts by the Supreme Court, the goal of human rights as a common standard of achievement for all people is still far off.

The Human Rights Commission and its working during these past years has shown little impact in protection of human rights of the common man. In rural India, human rights are an everyday casualty and carry little meaning for the weaker sections of society human rights. Police authorities are increasingly resorting to human rights violations and as a force have been casual about torture.

The Human Rights Commission is a low profile institution from the very start. It has been headless for a long time and, having no sufficient administrative machinery for proper investigation, is unable to fulfil its functions for the betterment of society.

Problems of Governance in India

Governance has always been a difficult task. Around 2,000 years ago, Confucius, the Chinese philosopher and patron saint of administrators, was asked 'What is government?' He replied, 'straightening'. Even today government means straightening—thinking straight, making straight policy, taking straight action, 'straight' meaning that which always serves the public regardless of any sectional group, party or personal interest. Nowadays, because of exposure of all sort of scams and Tehelka.com crusades, everyone talks of corruption-free, accountable and transparent governance. Recently, 'good governance' entered into the vocabulary of public administration via the World Bank. The chapter discusses the meaning of governance, instruments or actors in governance, dimensions and problems of governance and the ways to overcome these.

The dictionary meaning of governance is an 'act or manner of governing' and 'the 'office or function of governing'. 'To govern' is to 'rule or control (a state, subject, etc.) with authority; to conduct the policy and affairs of an organization, etc.' Thus, governance refers to a process or the act or function of exercising authority to regulate the affairs of people in a state. Governance is a wider term and is not confined to governments. Governance extends beyond governments and includes all institutions and organizations that serve citizens, whether in public, private, cooperative or voluntary organizations. The strengthening and capacity building of these institutions and organizations for collective decision-making and resolution of conflicts are an essential function of governance. Thus, governance is of the people and the government is only an instrument of governance.

The World Bank and Governance

A World Bank document entitled 'Governance and Development' (1992) states: 'governance is defined as the manner in which power is exercised in the management of a country's economic and social resources for development.' The document further pointed out that good governance is central to creating and sustaining an environment which fosters strong and equitable development, and it is an essential complement to sound economic policies.' Thus the concept of 'governance' includes the forms of political regime, the process of exercise of authority in the management of socio-economic resources of the country and the capacity to perform governmental functions.

The bank's document deals with the problems of 'governance' and points out that despite technical soundness, programmes and projects have failed to produce desired results. Laws are on paper only and they are not implemented properly or often delayed in implementation. Privatization and market-oriented growth fail to succeed due to lack of clear rules and institutions. In the absence of proper accounting systems, budgetary provisions are not implemented or monitored and the procurement system encourages corruption and distorts public investment priorities.

This kind of wrong governance has led the bank to focus on the main dimensions of governance such as public sector management, accountability, legal framework for development and information and transparency in governmental decision-making.

The Indian Context

Let us examine the Indian scenario against all these prescriptions of governance. The main actors in the game of governance are the politicians, bureaucrats and big business houses or the corporate world. Let us examine all the three combined to pinpoint the issue.

The root cause for the sorry state of governance is the fact that India has been made into a soft state with politicians compromising on every issue and our elite civil servants choosing to be mere file-pushing bureaucrats instead of dynamic administrators. The public associate bureaucracy with terms like inaccessibility, indifference, procedure oriented, poor quality, self-oriented, corruption provenance and unaccountable. The need of the hour is to convince people and improve the image of bureaucracy and to provide efficient, accountable, responsive, clear and transparent administration. Therefore, urgent steps are required to restore people's faith in the capacity and fairness of administration.

The Conference of Chief Secretaries

Realizing the need of people's confidence in administration, the conference of chief secretaries of all the states/UTs was held on 20 November 1996. The agenda was entitled, 'An Agenda for Effective and Responsive Administration in India.' It accepts that 'the public administration and the civil services at all levels are passing through difficult times in terms of eroded credibility and effectiveness of the civil service, growing public perception of an unholy nexus between certain elements among politicians and civil servants and criminals (as elaborated in the Vohra committee report), and increasing criticism of the low level of honesty, transparency and accessibility to the political and bureaucratic elements in charge of administration.'

The Chief Ministers' Conference

Subsequently, a chief ministers' conference, which was inaugurated by the then prime minister, was held on 24 May 1997 to discuss the action plan for effective and responsive administration and in his address the prime minister said that 'we are a modern state but mindsets are feudal, and this causes anxiety.' The cabinet secretary presented an action plan for responsive and efficient administration in the conference. The nine-point plan calls for: citizens' charter and accountable administration, effective and speedy public grievance redress system, empowering elected local bodies in rural and urban areas and decentralized delivery of services, review of laws and procedures, transparency, access to information from public offices, code of ethics for public services, tackling corruption and stability of tenure of civil servants. The document on action plan presented at the conference says that the adoption and implementation of the plan would require 'a strong political will and reiteration from both the central and state governments of their commitment to provide an accountable and responsible administration'. It was agreed that 'each state would work for the implementation of the Action Plan.'

The realization that the governments at all levels must re-invent themselves and define their roles, responsibilities and reform in all such areas which have an impact on the lives of the people proves that Indian administration has suddenly opened its eyes to the prescriptions of good governance given by donor organizations such as the World Bank and OECD countries.

PROBLEMS OF GOVERNANCE

After the fourth general elections, the country's political and administrative culture has radically changed. The Congress party's monopoly on the states and the centre was lost. Regional parties emerged mostly at state level and opposition coalitions started forming governments in the states. As a result, governance got politicized at the central and state levels and even development decisions got politically coloured. Hence, policy advice based on an apolitical and objective criteria became increasingly less welcome in the governments.

The state came to be ruled by caste coalitions from 1980s onwards and not by ideologically oriented parties. This was an inevitable stage in the progress of Indian democracy and societal consolidation. However, it made decisions in governance increasingly politicized. This has downgraded the role of the IAS as a neutral, apolitical all-India service. Now the grievances of the people are handled by the politicians and not by the administrators because people with grievances go to the MLA and MPs for redress. In fact the term 'Indian Administrative Service' has become a misnomer since there is hardly any administrative content in the way this service is functioning. With the advent of new technology and management practices, the 'jack of all trades and master of none' style of administration and the 'arrogance of ignorance' shown by several civil servants of the service, have made them irrelevant and has had a negative effect on governance. No serious steps have been taken to reform and restructure this service so as to tune it with the times. Bureaucracy, with the status quo and regulatory mindset, is considered to be a great stumbling block for governance.

THE WAY OUT

In a democracy like India, for open and good governance, a public–private popular partnership approach is appropriate and relevant rather than the over-burdened government machinery functioning alone and making people's life difficult.

The goal of governance in the Indian context is the socio-economic development and well-being of the masses. The imperative of such governance would be the 'enabling framework' for overall development to encourage and support a vast range of large, medium and small initiatives, investment and expenditure by individuals, households, communities, cooperatives, business and voluntary organizations; creation of capacity and capability to manage changes caused by technology and management, transparency or open decision-making system in citizen's related matters; encouraging initiative, innovation and creative thinking at all levels; change of the top-to-bottom reactive administrative machinery to bottom-up and proactive management system.

These imperatives of governance call for the adoption of reforms. Such an opportunity came when the Fifth Pay Commission recommendations were being implemented but at that time even vocal votaries of reform and excellence compromised for status quo and mediocrity. Without adequate reform, it is difficult to understand as to how a stagnant and inefficient administrative system, allergic to openness and transparency, will ever be able to give good and competent governance to such a vast country with so much of diversity and complexity.

The government of Manmohan Singh, realizing the weaknesses and shortcoming of the administrative system, appointed the 'Second Administrative Reforms Commission'[1] on 31 August 2005 under the chairmanship of Veerappa Moily, the present law minister, to propose a detailed blueprint for revamping the public administrative system. The terms of reference of the commission cover almost all aspects of administration including reforms in the present structure of administrative system. The details of the terms of reference of the commission have been incorporated in Chapter 2 which deals with administrative reforms.

Further, to promote transparency and accountability in the working of the government, Dr Manmohan Singh's government has passed the Right to Information Act, 2005. At the central level, the Central Information Commission and at the state level, the State Information Commission for each state have been constituted, to provide information of government decisions to citizens, on demand. The Act has made the government answerable for its acts of omission and commission, and bureaucracy, now, cannot take the shelter of 'official secrecy' in giving the details of their decisions. Within a short span of time, the Act has produced desired results and made bureaucracy responsive. This step of the government will empower the 'common man' of our country.

NOTE

1. Government of India, Ministry of Personnel, Public Grievances and Pensions, Department of Administrative Reforms and Public Grievances, Resolution No. K-11022/9/2004/RC New Delhi, 31 August 2005.

Bibliography

Avasthi, A., *Central Administration* (New Delhi: Tata McGraw-Hill, 1980).
Avasthi, A., and S. R. Maheshwari, *Public Administration* (Agra: Lakshmi Narain Agarwal, 1996).
Avasthi, A. and S. N. Varma (eds), *Aspects of Administration in India* (New Delhi: Allied, 1964).
Azgal, R., *Municipal Government in India* (Allahabad: Agrawal Press, 1967).
Agarwal, V. K., *Consumer Protection Law and Prospects* (Bangalore: Bharat Law House, 1997).
Arvind, S., *Indian Administration* (Bombay: Himalaya, 1992).
Bajpai, Ashok, and M. S. Verma, *Panchayati Raj in India: A New Thrust* (Delhi: Sahetya Prakashan, 1995).
Bhambri, C. P., *Bureaucracy and Politics in India* (New Delhi: Vikas, 1971).
———, *Administrators in a Changing Society* (New Delhi: National, 1972).
———, *Public Administration in India* (New Delhi: Vikas, 1973).
Bhattacharya, Mohit, *Management of Urban Government in India* (New Delhi: Uppal, 1976).
Brecher, M., *Nehru—A Political Biography* (London: Oxford University Press, 1959).
———, *Succession in India: A Study in Decision Making* (London: Oxford University Press, 1966).
Basu, D. D., *Introduction to the Constitution of India* (New Delhi: Prentice Hall of India, 1976).
Caiden, Gerald E., *Administrative Reforms* (Chicago: Aldime, 1989).
Chamber, Robert, *Rural Development* (London: Longman 1983).
Chanda, Ashok, *Indian Administration* (London: George Allen and Unwin, 1967).
Charles, J. C., *Governmental Administration* (New York: Harper and Bros, 1951).
Damoderan, K. M., *Accountability in Administration Case for Employees Charter* (New Delhi: 11PA, 1998).
Das, S. K., *Civil Service Reform and Structural Adjustment* (Delhi: Oxford University Press, 1998).
Dubey, K. N. (ed.), *Planning and Development in India* (New Delhi: Ashis, 1990).
Dubhasi, P. R., *Administrative Reforms* (New Delhi: B.R. Publishing, 1986).
Dwarkadas, R., *Role of Higher Civil Service in India* (Bombay: Popular Book Depot, 1960).
Finer, H., *Theory and Practice of Modern Government* (New York: Methuen, 1971).
Ghosh, S. K., *Protection of Minorities and Scheduled Castes* (New Delhi: Ashish, 1986).
Greenwood, John, and David Wilson, *Public Administration in Britain Today* (London: Unwin Hyman, 1989).
Gill, S. S., *The Pathology of Corruption* (New Delhi: Harper Collins, 1998).
Guhan, S., and Samuel Paul (ed.), *Corruption in India, Agenda for Action* (New Delhi: Vision Books, 1997).
Hirway, Indira, *Abolition of Poverty in India with Special Reference to Target Group Approach in Gujarat* (New Delhi: Vikas, 1986).
Jain, S. N., (ed.), *The Union and the States* (Delhi: National, 1972).
Jayaswal, K. P., *Hindu Polity* (Bangalore City: Bangalore Printing and Publishing Co., 1943).
Jones, Morris, *Parliament in India* (London: Longman, 1957).
———, *The Government and Politics of India* (London: Hutchinson, 1971).
Kaul, M. N., and S. L. Shakdhar, *Practice and Procedure of Parliament* (Delhi: Metropolitan, 1960).
Khandwalla, Pradib N., *Revitalizing the State: A Menu of Options* (New Delhi: Sage, 1999).
Khera, S. S., *District Administration in India* (New Delhi: IIPA, 1960).

———, *The Central Executive* (New Delhi: Orient Longman, 1975).
Maheshwari, S. R., *Evolution of Indian Administration* (Agra: Lakshmi Narayan Agarwal, 1970).
———, *Local Government in India* (New Delhi: Orient Longman, 1971).
———, *Administrative Reforms Commission* (Agra: Lakshmi Narayan Agarwal, 1972).
———, *Theories and Concepts in Public Administration* (New Delhi: Allied, 1991).
———, *Indian Administration* (New Delhi: Orient Longman, 2001).
Mathur, P. C., *Political Dynamics of Panchayati Raj* (Delhi: Konark, 1991).
Mathew, George (ed.), *Panchayati Raj in Karnataka Today* (New Delhi: Concept, 1985).
Mehta, Usha, *Kautilya and His Arthshastra* (New Delhi: S. Chand and Co., 1980).
Milward, G. E. (ed.), *Organization and Methods* (London: Macmillan, 1959).
Mishra, B. B., *The Central Administration of the East India Company (1773–1834)* (London: Manchester University Press, 1959).
———, *The Administrative History of India (1834–1947)* (London: Oxford University Press, 1970).
———, *The Bureaucracy in India* (Delhi: Oxford University Press, 1977).
Moraes, Frank, *Jawaharlal Nehru: A Biography* (New York: Macmillan, 1956).
Paranjape, H. K., *Planning Commission: A Descriptive Account* (New Delhi: IIPA, 1964).
Potter, D. C., *Government in Rural India* (London: G. Bell and Sons, 1964).
Puri, B. N., History of Indian Administration, Vols I and II (Bombay: Bhartiya Vidya Bhavan, 1968, 1975).
Pylee, M. V., *India's Constitution* (Bombay: Asia Publishing House, 1967).
Quaraishi, Z. M., *Struggle for Rashtrapathi Bhawan* (Delhi: Vikas, 1973).
Rao, K. V., *Parliamentary Democracy of India* (Calcutta: World Press, 1965).
Roy, N. C., *The Civil Service in India* (Calcutta: K.L. Mukhopadhyay, 1960).
Sachdeva, D. R., and B. D. Dua, *Studies in Indian Administration* (Allahabad: Kitab Mahal, 1969).
Santhanam, K., *Union–State Relations in India* (New Delhi: Asia Publishing House, 1960).
Sarkar, J. N., *Mughal Administration* (Calcutta: M.C. Sarkar and Sons, 1952).
Sathe, Vasant, *National Government—Agenda for New India* (New Delhi: UBS, 1991).
Saxena, A. P.(ed.), *Training in Government: Objective and Opportunities* (New Delhi: IIPA, 1976).
Sharma, Dasharatha, *Lectures on Rajput History and Culture* (Delhi: Motilal Banarsidass, 1970).
Sharma, S. K., *Deputy Commissioner in Punjab* (New Delhi: IIPA, 1971).
Shiviah, M., et al., *Panchayati Raj—An Analytical Survey* (Hyderabad: N.I.R.D., 1976).
Sriniwas, M. N., *Caste in Modern India* (Bombay: Asia Publishing House, 1971).
Sri Prakash, *State Governors in India* (Meerut, 1969).
Shukla. J. D., *State and District Administration in India* (New Delhi: IIPA, 1976).
Sinha, R. K., *Fiscal Federation in India* (New Delhi: Sterling, 1987).
Singh, Charan, *Economic Nightmare of India: Its Cause and Cure* (New Delhi: National, 1981).
Singh, Hoshiar, *Aspects of Indian Administration* (Jaipur: RBSA publishers, 1994).
———, *Administration of Rural Development in India* (New Delhi: Sterling, 1995).
———, *Indian Administration* (Allahabad: Kitab Mahal, 1998).
Singh, Hoshiar (ed.), *Higher Civil Services in India* (Kurukshetra: Nirmal Book Agency, 1995).
———, *Public Service Commissions in India* (Allahabad: Kitab Mahal 1999).
———, *Local Governance Concepts and Networks* (Jaipur: RBSA, 2000).
Singh, Katar, *Rural Development: Principles Policies and Management* (New Delhi: Sage, 1986).
Singh, Pankaj, *Administrative Reforms in India* (Allahabad: Kitab Mahal, 2008).
Subramanian, V., *Social Background of India's Administrators* (New Delhi: Government of India, 1971).
Thavaraj, M. J. K., *Financial Administration of India* (New Delhi: S. Chand, 1978).
Thummaiah, G., *A Critique of the Finance Commission* (Allahabad: Whealer, 1981).

Tummala, K. K., *Public Administration In India* (Singapore: Times Academic Press, 1994).

———, *The Ambiguity of Ideology and Administrative Reforms in India* (New Delhi: Uppal, 1997).

Yugandhar, B. N., and Amitava Mukherjee, *Decentralized Planning* (New Delhi: Concept, 1991).

Zaheer, M. and J. Gupta, *The Organization of the Government of Uttar Pradesh* (Delhi: S. Chand, 1970).

Reports

Report on the Efficient Conduct of State Enterprises (A. D. Gorwala Report) (New Delhi: Government of India, 1951).

Report on Public Administration, (A. D. Gorwala Report) (New Delhi: Government of India, 1951).

Report of a Survey on Public Administration in India (Paul Appleby) Report (New Delhi: Government of India, 1953).

B. R. Mehta, Ashok Mehta and M. L. Singhvi, Reports on Panchayat Raj Bodies (New Delhi: Government of India).

Report of Backward Classes Commission (New Delhi: Government of India, 1980).

Report of the Centre–State Relations Inquiry Committee (Raja Mannar Committee) (Madras: Government of Tamil Nadu, 1971).

Report of the Commission on Centre–State Relations, Parts 1 and 2 (Sarkaria Commission Report) (New Delhi: Government of India, 1988).

Reports of Central Vigilance Commission, New Delhi.

Relevant Reports of Finance Commissions, Government of India.

Report of the Indian Statutory Commission, Vol. 1 (Delhi: Government of India, 1930).

Report of the Committee on Plan Projects, Vol. I Planning Commission (New Delhi: Government of India, 1959).

Report of the Working Group on District Planning, Vols 1 and 2, Planning Commission (New Delhi: Government of India, 1983).

Report of the Committee to review the existing Administrative Arrangements of Rural Development and Poverty Alleviation programmes (CAARD): Department of Rural Development, Ministry of Agriculture (New Delhi: Government of India, 1985).

Reports of National Police Commission (New Delhi: Government of India 1985).

Reports on the Re-organization of Central Government (two reports) (R. Tollenham Committee Reports) (New Delhi: Government of India, 1945 and 1946).

Report on the Reorganization of the Machinery of Government of India (Gopalaswami Ayyanger Report) (New Delhi: Government of India, 1949).

Report of the Government of India Secretariat (Wheeler) Committee (New Delhi: Government of India, 1936).

Relevant Reports of Administrative Reforms Commission (ARC) (New Delhi: Government of India).

Report of the ARC on Public Sector Undertakings (New Delhi: Government of India, 1967).

Report of ARC on Accounting and Auditing (New Delhi: Government of India, 1968).

Report of the ARC on the Machinery of the Government of India and Procedures of Work (New Delhi: Government of India, 1968).

Report of the ARC on Personal Administration (New Delhi: Government of India, 1969).

Report of the Administrative Reforms Committee, Rajasthan (Jaipur: Government of Rajasthan, 1963).

Report of the Rajasthan Administrative Reforms Commission, Vol. 1 (Jaipur: Government of Rajasthan, 2000).

Report of the Rajasthan Administrative Reforms Commission, Vol. II (Jaipur: Government of Rajasthan, 2001).

Index

S

T

U